STUDENT WORKBOOK AND RESOURCE GUIDE

MEDICAL–SURGICAL NURSING

Preparation for Practice

STUDENT WORKBOOK
AND RESOURCE GUIDE

MEDICAL–SURGICAL NURSING

Preparation for Practice

KATHLEEN S. OSBORN, RN, MS, EdD
California State University
Sacramento, California

CHERYL E. WRAA, RN, MSN
University of California,
Davis Medical Center
California State University
Sacramento, California

ANNITA WATSON, RN, MS, DNSc
California State University
Sacramento, California

Pearson

Boston Columbus Indianapolis New York San Francisco Upper Saddle River
Amsterdam Cape Town Dubai London Madrid Milan Munich Paris Montreal Toronto
Delhi Mexico City Sao Paulo Sydney Hong Kong Seoul Singapore Taipei Tokyo

Publisher: Julie Levin Alexander
Publisher's Assistant: Regina Bruno
Editor-in-Chief: Maura Connor
Executive Acquisitions Editor: Pamela Fuller
Development Editor: Pamela Lappies
Editorial Assistant: Lisa Pierce
Managing Production Editor: Patrick Walsh
Production Liaison: Cathy O'Connell
Production Editor: Roxanne Klaas, S4Carlisle Publishing Services
Manufacturing Manager: Ilene Sanford
Art Director: Mary Siener
Director of Marketing: Karen Allman
Marketing Specialist: Michael Sirinides
Marketing Assistant: Crystal Gonzalez
Composition: S4 Carlisle Publishing Services
Printer/Binder: Bind-Rite Graphics/Robbinsville
Cover Printer: LeHigh-Phoenix Color/Hagerstown

Notice: Care has been taken to confirm the accuracy of information presented in this book. The authors, editors, and the publisher, however, cannot accept any responsibility for errors or omissions or for consequences from application of the information in this book and make no warranty, express or implied, with respect to its contents.

The authors and publisher have exerted every effort to ensure that drug selections and dosages set forth in this text are in accord with current recommendations and practice at time of publication. However, in view of ongoing research, changes in government regulations, and the constant flow of information relating to drug therapy and drug reactions, the reader is urged to check the package inserts of all drugs for any change in indications of dosage and for added warnings and precautions. This is particularly important when the recommended agent is a new and/or infrequently employed drug.

www.pearsonhighered.com

10 9 8 7 6 5 4 3 2 1
ISBN-10:   0-13-505201-7
ISBN-13: 978-0-13-505201-3

PREFACE

Students entering the field of nursing have a tremendous amount to learn in a very short time. This Study Guide that accompanies *Medical–Surgical Nursing,* first edition, is designed to reinforce the knowledge that you—the student—have gained in each chapter and to help you master the critical concepts.

At the beginning of each chapter in this Study Guide, you will find a MyNursingKit box. MyNursingKit offers you a rich resource for chapter-specific interactive exercises that will help you learn the chapter material and prepare for class, clinical, and for the NCLEX® exam. Chapter by chapter, MyNursingKit helps you hone your critical thinking skills and enables you to apply concepts from the book to practice.

Each chapter includes a variety of questions and activities to help you understand difficult concepts and reinforce basic knowledge gained from textbook reading assignments. The following features will enhance your learning experience:

- **Outcome-Based Learning Objectives** tell you what you will learn in the chapter.
- **Chapter Outlines** give you a tool for reviewing chapter content.
- **Key Term** exercises and activities test your knowledge of the core vocabulary for each chapter.
- **NCLEX-RN® Review Questions** help you practice for this crucial examination. These review questions correspond with the Outcome-Based Learning Objectives, and are numbered so students can identify which questions relate back to which Learning Objective.
- **Answers** to all questions are available in the Answer Key. These answers are numbered to correspond with the Learning Objectives and the review questions.

We hope that this **Study Guide** will serve as a valuable learning tool and will contribute to your success in your nursing program and in the nursing profession.

CONTENTS

CHAPTER 1

PREPARATION FOR PRACTICE

OUTCOME-BASED LEARNING OBJECTIVES

1-1. Distinguish the characteristics of nursing as defined in the roles of caregiver, advocate, educator, researcher, and leader.

1-2. Apply the six components of caring as defined by Roach to nursing practice.

1-3. Describe the roles of the professional nurse within the health care delivery system.

1-4. Compare and contrast the nursing role in the care delivery models for nursing practice.

1-5. Explain the importance of cultural competence as defined by Campinha-Bacote.

CHAPTER OUTLINE

I. Medical–Surgical Nursing
  A. Components of the Nursing Role
    1. Caregiver
    2. Advocate
    3. Educator
    4. Researcher
    5. Leader
  B. Framework for Nursing Practice
    1. Nursing Process
    2. Critical Thinking
      a. Development of Critical Thinking Skills
  C. Six Components of Caring
    1. Development of Caring Skills
  D. Health and Wellness Promotion
  E. Standards of Nursing Practice
  F. Code of Ethics for Nurses
  G. Guiding Ethical Principles
II. Roles of the Nurse
  A. Acute Care Nurses
    1. Staff Nurse
    2. Parish Nurse

   3. Long-Term Care Nurse
      a. Assisted Living Nurse
   4. Occupational Health and Industrial Nurse
   5. School Nurse
   6. Clinic Nurse
   7. Hospice Nurse
   8. Gerontologic Nurse
   9. Nurse-Midwife
   10. Certified Registered Nurse Anesthetist
   11. Academic Nurse Educator
III. Nursing Care Delivery Models
   A. Models of Organizing Patient Care
   B. New Types of Care Delivery Models
      1. Patient-Centered Care
         a. Case Management
      2. Community-Based Care
IV. Influences in Health Care Delivery
   A. Population Demographics
      1. Aging Population
      2. Informed Consumers
      3. Cultural Diversity
         a. Cultural Competence
   B. Changing Disease Patterns
   C. Complementary and Alternative Therapy
      1. Complementary or Alternative: What Is the Difference?
      2. Integration of Complementary and Alternative Systems into Traditional American Health Care
      3. Safety and Effectiveness of Alternative Therapies
   D. Advances in Technology and Genetics
      1. Technological Changes
         a. Biomedical Technology
         b. Information Technology
            i. Informatics
         c. Telecommunications
         d. Internet
         e. Future Projections
      2. Genetics
   E. Economics
   F. Demand for Quality Care
V. Summary

KEY TERMS MATCHING EXERCISE 1

Write the letter of the correct definition in the space next to each term.

Term

_____ 1. academic nurse educator
_____ 2. acute care nurse
_____ 3. advanced practice nursing
_____ 4. allopathic medicine
_____ 5. alternative therapy
_____ 6. assignment
_____ 7. assisted living
_____ 8. caring

Definition

a. Method of treating disease with remedies that produce effects different from those caused by the disease itself.

b. Type of nursing practice for registered nurses who work in various health district programs.

c. The core of nursing; constitutes the essence of nursing regardless of the level at which nursing is practiced.

d. A nurse who works with patients experiencing sudden illness or trauma, usually in the prehospital, hospital, or emergency department.

_____ 9. clinical judgment

_____ 10. code of ethics

_____ 11. community-based care

_____ 12. community health nursing

e. A complex skill involving several cognitive phases and integrative processes; clinical reasoning across time about a particular patient.

f. A nurse who is responsible for designing, implementing, evaluating, and revising academic and continuing education programs for nurses.

g. A residential setting in which patients are provided long-term assisted care.

h. Specialized type of nursing practice in which nurses diagnose and treat illnesses and provide health care.

i. The transfer of a task and the accountability for the outcome.

j. A setting for practice outside of acute care institutional walls.

k. A formal statement by a group that expresses the group's ideals, values, and ethical principles, which have been agreed on by the group's members to reflect their moral judgments and serve as a standard for their professional actions.

l. A therapy used instead of conventional or mainstream therapy.

KEY TERMS MATCHING EXERCISE 2

Write the letter of the correct definition in the space next to each term.

Term

_____ 13. complementary therapy

_____ 14. cultural competence

_____ 15. cultural diversity

_____ 16. culture

_____ 17. information technology

_____ 18. nursing process

_____ 19. Nursing's Agenda for the Future

_____ 20. patient-centered care

_____ 21. population-based care

_____ 22. standards of care

_____ 23. standards of nursing practice

_____ 24. standards of professional performance

_____ 25. values

Definition

a. The American Nurses Association statement outlining issues related to nursing practice.

b. Authoritative statements by which the nursing profession describes the common level of performance or care by which the quality of practice can be determined and responsibilities for which its practitioners are accountable.

c. General standards of care and guidelines for nursing practice formulated in 1991 by the American Nurses Association.

d. Learned patterns of behavior, beliefs, and values that can be attributed to a particular group of people.

e. A therapy used in addition to a conventional therapy.

f. Variety and differences in the customs and practices of defined social groups; refers to the variation among groups of people with respect to the habits, values, preferences, beliefs, taboos, and rules determined to be appropriative for individual and social interaction.

g. An innovative approach to the planning, delivery, and evaluation of health care that is based on mutually beneficial partnerships among health care patients, families, and providers.

h. Care focused on aggregates and communities. A population is a collection of individuals who have in common one or more personal or environmental characteristics.

i. Freely chosen beliefs or attitudes about the worth of an individual or object.

j. Standards that address the professional nursing role with regard to education, ethics, research, collegiality, and resource utilization.

k. The ongoing practice of knowing, respecting, and incorporating the values of others; being open to the cultural beliefs and behaviors of others.

l. A thinking/doing approach to patient care that provides the nurse with a systematic means of identifying, preventing, and treating actual and potential health problems .

m. Refers to those systems, including software programs and computer hardware, used to manage and process information.

SHORT ANSWER QUESTIONS

26. Explain the difference between complementary and alternative therapies.

_____

_____

27. What is the greatest danger of using complementary and alternative therapies?

_____

_____

28. What is the nurse's patient care responsibility in regard to complementary and alternative therapies?

_____

_____

29. Which of the following can be used as a complementary therapy? Explain your answer.

Reiki

Yoga

Herbal medicine

Acupuncture

Hypnosis

_____

_____

30. Dr. Campinha-Bacote includes cultural self-awareness as one of the components nurses need to develop in order to provide culturally competent health care. How would you rate yourself in terms of cultural self-awareness? Write a short essay in which you explore your own cultural/ethnic background and honestly assess your own prejudices and biases toward other cultures. Include your assessment of how that may impact your patient care, negatively or positively.

_____

_____

_____

_____

_____

_____

31. List five nursing roles that interest you. List the educational requirements for each.

_____

_____

_____

_____

_____

_____

_____

_____

_____

_____

NCLEX-RN® REVIEW QUESTIONS

1-1. The nursing process is the decision-producing model for the role of caregiver. The central concept in this model is which of the following?
 1. Assessment
 2. Caring
 3. Advocacy
 4. Education

1-2. Without the caring components of conscience, confidence, commitment, competence, and comportment, the nurse will not see what needs of the client?
 1. Physical and comfort
 2. Psychological and spiritual
 3. Physiological
 4. Ethics and moral

1-3. A nursing unit has a group of professional nurses whose experience ranges from expert to novice. A delivery model is selected that will utilize the skills of each staff member and is associated with democratic leadership. The nurse manager feels that recognizing the worth of each staff member will result in high job satisfaction. Which delivery model has been selected?
 1. Functional nursing
 2. Team nursing
 3. Primary care nursing
 4. Total patient care nursing

1-4. The nursing role that integrates the concepts of public health nursing, theory, holistic evaluation, primary prevention, surveillance, and compliance is which of the following?
 1. Industrial nurse
 2. School nurse
 3. Assisted living nurse
 4. Parish nurse

1-5. Campinha-Bacote defines four components of the cultural competence model. They are cultural awareness, cultural knowledge, cultural skills, and
 1. Cultural encounters.
 2. Cultural studies.
 3. Cultural diversity.
 4. Culture.

CHAPTER 2

EXPERIENTIAL LEARNING: SKILL ACQUISITION AND GAINING CLINICAL KNOWLEDGE

OUTCOME-BASED LEARNING OBJECTIVES

2-1. Recognize and describe their own clinical learning in the form of an experience–near-first-person narrative account.

2-2. Give at least three examples of practical and theoretical knowledge related to adult medical–surgical nursing.

2-3. Give two examples of clinical interventions that can be standardized and two examples of clinical interventions that cannot be standardized.

2-4. Give an example of phronesis or clinical judgment that illustrates adjusting to transitions in the patient's clinical condition, or the clinician's understanding of the patient's clinical condition.

2-5. Give two clinical examples of how the nurse's relationship with the patient may alter the nurse's clinical judgment.

2-6. Explain how and why the nurse's moral agency might change with experience, according to the Dreyfus model of skill acquisition.

2-7. Characterize three distinct differences between competent and expert clinical nursing practice.

CHAPTER OUTLINE

KEY TERMS MATCHING EXERCISE 1

Write the letter of the correct definition in the space next to each term.

Term

_____ 1. clinical judgment

_____ 2. clinical knowledge

_____ 3. Dreyfus model of skill acquisition

_____ 4. ethos

_____ 5. experience

_____ 6. experiential learning

_____ 7. limits of formalization

Definition

a. An active process of gaining knowledge and skill, not just a passage of time.

b. Knowledge necessary to perform proficiently in the clinical setting, including recognizing signs and symptoms, applying skilled know-how in titrating an intravenous rate, recognizing signs of physiological distress and changes in patient's vital signs, and using clinical judgment.

c. In philosophy, the inability to make explicit or formal all elements of a social practice.

d. A complex skill involving several cognitive phases and integrative processes; clinical reasoning across time about a particular patient.

e. Requires a turning around of preconceptions, or an adding of nuances to one's understanding.

f. Notions of what counts as good nursing or good scientific practice.

g. A learning model based on determining the level of practice evident in particular situations. It elucidates strengths as well as problems.

KEY TERMS MATCHING EXERCISE 2

Write the letter of the correct definition in the space next to each term.

Term

_____ 8. moral agency

_____ 9. phronesis

_____ 10. practical knowledge

_____ 11. rationality

_____ 12. salience

_____ 13. skills of involvement

_____ 14. techne

Definition

a. A form of rationality and skill-based character that is similar to clinical judgment.

b. Something that can be standardized and replicated.

c. The ability to affect and influence situations.

d. The ability to reason across time when changes in the patient's condition occurs. It includes noticing subtle changes not limited to explicit vital signs and that may not show up immediately in the vital sign trends.

e. Having some things stand out as more or less important in a practical situation, it is a form of practical knowledge that is learned from many concrete clinical experiences in which a range of relevant clinical issues stand out as high priority.

f. The skills of perceiving relevant changes or nuances in clinical situations; these skills are experientially learned and form part of a nurse's practical clinical knowledge.

g. Knowledge shaped by one's familiarity with the discipline and practice of the science and technology relevant to the situation at hand.

SHORT ANSWER QUESTIONS

15. Explain the difference between clinical knowledge and clinical judgment.

_____

_____

_____

_____

16. Contrast the use of techne with the use of phronesis in a clinical setting. How would an experienced nurse acquire and use each?

_____

_____

_____

_____

17. Why is the quality of learning in clinical situations different for advanced beginners and proficient-level nurses?

_____

_____

_____

_____

18. How does the knowledge and understanding of the Dreyfus model of skill acquisition impact the way you view your nursing preparation and career?

_____

_____

_____

_____

TRUE OR FALSE?

19. _____ T/F Practical knowledge cannot be acquired through diligent studying in nursing school.

20. _____ T/F Techne and the rational-technical model are examples of clinical judgment.

21. _____ T/F The skills of involvement are an example of clinical judgment.

22. _____ T/F Clinical judgment and the ability to act on it are phronesis.

23. _____ T/F Phronesis is not an aspect of practical knowledge.

24. _____ T/F Clinical judgment requires moral agency.

25. _____ T/F Experiential learning based on past patient care enables the nurse to develop a greater sense of salience.

NURSING STAGE OF DEVELOPMENT

For each description, name the appropriate stage of nursing:

Novice
Advanced beginner
Competent stage
Proficiency
Expertise

26. _____ Uses both techne and phronesis appropriately

27. _____ Clinical forethought and clinical grasp developing

28. _____ Knows the limits of formal knowledge and that not everything is in textbooks

29. _____ New clinical knowledge is developed from practice

30. _____ Matches actual cases with textbook descriptions

31. _____ Sees the "big" picture of the patient's world and clinical situation

32. _____ Situation speaks to practitioner. Practice is becoming more situated, patient-response based

33. _____ Requires rules and broad guidelines to organize task world

34. _____ Establishing boundaries of the role and expectations of the nurse

35. _____ Skill of involvement varied and suited to individual patient's need

NCLEX-RN® REVIEW QUESTIONS

2-1. A patient's condition deteriorates rapidly and the nurse questions previously assessed findings that could have predicted this patient's current status. Which of the following levels of experience is this nurse most likely to be?
   1. Novice
   2. Advanced beginner
   3. Competent
   4. Proficient

2-2. A patient is seen in the emergency department with a sudden onset of lower extremity weakness and elevated blood pressure. After all routine respiratory and cardiac interventions have been concluded, the patient is taken for a head CT scan. The reason for this test would be:
   1. To follow up on the findings from the serum laboratory tests.
   2. To follow up on the findings from the heart monitor tracing.
   3. To rule out a cerebral hemorrhage from the elevated blood pressure.
   4. To rule out a brain tumor.

2-3. A patient being treated for diabetic ketoacidosis has orders to receive regular insulin via continuous infusion for the next four hours. The latest laboratory findings show a significant reduction in blood glucose level. The nurse should:
   1. Maintain the insulin infusion and give the patient a sugary snack to eat.
   2. Maintain the insulin infusion and give the patient a bolus of intravenous dextrose and water.
   3. Stop the infusion and notify the physician.
   4. Stop the infusion and administer a bolus of intravenous dextrose and water.

2-4. Before administering a patient's morning cardiac medication, the nurse measures the blood pressure and pulse. Both measurements are outside of the parameters for administering the medication. Which of the following should the nurse do?
1. Do not give the patient the medication and call the physician.
2. Give the patient the medication and assess the vital signs again in 30 minutes.
3. Give the patient the medication and call the physician.
4. Give the patient the medication as prescribed.

2-5. An elderly patient with scoliosis is asking for medication for wrist pain yet is able to feed herself and complete normal self-care activities. The nurse should:
1. Delay giving the patient pain medication.
2. Ask the physician if the patient is really in pain considering the ability to use the wrists.
3. Administer a placebo.
4. Provide the prescribed pain medication.

2-6. One nurse observes another provide an incorrect medication dose to a patient. The observing nurse should:
1. Approach the nurse who provided the medication and encourage the error to be reported.
2. Ignore the situation but keep an eye on the patient.
3. Report the situation to the physician.
4. Tell another nurse what was witnessed and then focus on other patient care activities.

2-7. A nurse is providing care to a patient recovering from a total hip replacement. Which of the following activities demonstrates proficiency when providing care to this patient?
1. Giving the patient a sheet of exercises to read the first day after surgery
2. Telling the patient that pain is expected and should be ignored for several weeks after the surgery
3. Medicating the patient for pain 3 hours before attending physical therapy
4. Assessing the patient's pedal pulses, skin warmth, and color before helping the patient to ambulate to a chair

CHAPTER 3

HEALTH CARE TRENDS AND REGULATORY ASPECTS OF HEALTH CARE DELIVERY

OUTCOME-BASED LEARNING OBJECTIVES

3-1. Discuss how major trends in health care quality and patient safety are related to nursing practice.

3-2. Compare the differences between the types of managed care plans: health maintenance organizations, preferred provider organizations, Medicare, and Medicaid.

3-3. Describe the key components of the budget process for hospitals and health care systems.

3-4. Explain the nurse's role in assisting patients with insurance and financial issues.

3-5. Differentiate between the three types of standards used to measure quality in health care settings.

3-6. Compare and contrast the impact of licensure, regulation, and accreditation on health care delivery systems.

3-7. Differentiate between the types of advance directives for health care and describe the nurse's responsibility in advocating and documenting the patient's wishes related to an advance directive.

3-8. Explain the patient's rights with regard to his or her medical record according to the legal principles of documentation in the patient's medical record.

3-9. Identify the three main components of the Health Insurance Portability and Accountability Act.

3-10. Identify the components of case management in the hospital and the associated acute care nursing responsibilities.

CHAPTER OUTLINE

I. Health Care Delivery Systems
    A. Future Delivery Implications
    B. Hospital Organizations
II. Health Care Costs
    A. Historical Development of Health Care Economics
    B. Managed Care and the Current Status of Reimbursement Practices
    C. Forms of Managed Care
        1. Health Maintenance Organization
        2. Independent Practice Association
        3. Preferred Provider Organization
        4. Government Programs
    D. Future Economic Projection
III. Financial Aspects of Health Care Organizations
    A. Budgeting Process for Health Care Institutions
IV. Health Care Trends
    A. Evidence-Based Practice
    B. Hospital Report Cards
    C. Patient Safety Standards
    D. Emergency Preparedness
    E. Scientific and Technical Advancements
        1. Telemedicine
        2. Minimally Invasive Surgery
        3. Robotics
        4. Gene Therapy
        5. Inpatient to Outpatient Shift
    F. Health Care Worker Shortages
    G. Hospitalist Programs
    H. Information Technology
    I. Demand for Quality Care
        1. Quality Defined
            a. Regulatory Agency Impact
            b. Quality Measurement
            c. Quality Improvement and Research Studies
V. Licensure, Regulations, and Accreditation of Health Care Organizations
    A. Occupational Safety and Health Administration
    B. Fire and Life Safety Standards
    C. Infection and Disease Control
    D. Professional Practice Oversight
    E. Accreditation
VI. Legal Aspects of Health Care
    A. Advance Directives
        1. Patient and Caregiver Issues and Concerns
        2. Documentation and Legal Requirements
    B. Legal Aspects of Documentation
        1. Trends in Documentation
        2. The Medical Record
    C. Health Insurance Portability and Accountability Act
        1. Impact of HIPAA Standards
    D. Case Management
        1. Focus of Case Management in the Hospital
        2. Staff Nurse Case Management Responsibilities
        3. Case Management by Health Plans
VII. Summary

KEY TERMS MATCHING EXERCISE 1

Write the letter of the correct definition in the space next to each term.

Term

_____ 1. accreditation
_____ 2. evidence-based practice
_____ 3. health maintenance organization (HMO)
_____ 4. preferred provider organization (PPO)
_____ 5. independent practice association (IPA)
_____ 6. horizontal organizational model
_____ 7. vertically integrated models
_____ 8. hospitalist
_____ 9. for-profit (proprietary) organization
_____ 10. health care delivery system

Definition

a. Physician who concentrates her or his practice in the acute care environment.

b. Organization that provides coverage for medical care and controls costs through utilization review and management and by restricting access to a specific network of providers.

c. Organization that provides health care coverage through a coordinated plan for medical care that includes a network of contracted providers.

d. Process of evaluating an organization against performance standards.

e. Organization that contracts on the behalf of individuals or groups of physicians to provide health care to members of a health maintenance organization.

f. System that provides client-centered, comprehensive, interdisciplinary, integrated, and accessible health care that meets the needs of the clients.

g. Service structure of hospitals aligned to form a multihospital system; focuses on traditional acute care services.

h. Organization that focuses on making a profit from operations and distributing those profits to the owners or investors in the organization.

i. A problem-solving approach to clinical decision making that incorporates a search for the best and latest evidence, clinical expertise, and assessment, and a patient's preferences and values within a context of caring.

j. Organizational service structure of hospitals and related health care services aligned along a continuum of care.

KEY TERMS MATCHING EXERCISE 2

Write the letter of the correct definition in the space next to each term.

Term

_____ 11. risk management
_____ 12. repatriation
_____ 13. telemedicine
_____ 14. robotics
_____ 15. quality in fact
_____ 16. quality in perception
_____ 17. outcome standards
_____ 18. process standards
_____ 19. case management
_____ 20. sentinel event

Definition

a. Systems or programs that use video or computer-based equipment to link providers or monitor patients electronically.

b. A comprehensive program for identifying and evaluating potential risks to the health care organization.

c. An approach to coordinating care for patients in the hospital or in an outpatient setting.

d. Quality standards that focus on whether the activities within an organization are being conducted appropriately.

e. Quality standards that focus on whether the services provided by an organization make any difference to patients or to the health status of the patient population.

f. Meeting the customer's expectations.

g. Return of patients from one health care setting to another appropriate level of care or to a contracted institution.

h. Unexpected occurrence that has the potential to, or actually does, result in death or serious physical or psychological injury.

i. Conforming to standards and meeting one's own expectations.

j. Electromechanical devices that are computer controlled and used to perform surgical tasks.

SHORT ANSWER QUESTIONS

21. Explain why the advent of diagnosis-related groups (DRGs) has caused many Medicare patients to be discharged before they have recovered.

_____

_____

_____

_____

_____

22. As a nurse, what must you consider before making a decision based on evidence-based practice? What resources will you need to consult?

_____

_____

_____

_____

_____

23. Explain the differences between structure standards, process standards, and outcome standards.

_____

_____

_____

_____

_____

COMPLETE THE SENTENCE

For each description, insert the appropriate organization or legislation. (Acronyms are acceptable for answers with more than two words.)

24. The federal law called _____ was designed to improve the portability of health care coverage for people who lose or change employment, to simplify the administrative process through the use of electronic transactions, and to ensure the privacy of membership information.

25. The independent, private, not-for-profit organization called _____ _____ is the accrediting body for hospitals and health care organizations.

26. Consisting of Part A and Part B, the health insurance program called _____ administers its own managed care plan and is federally sponsored for people over 65 and for some younger people with disabilities and end-stage renal disease.

27. The _____ ensures that patients have access to emergency services regardless of their ability to pay.

28. By providing unbiased, evidence-based, authoritative information on medicine and health, the _____ serves policy makers, professionals, and the public at large in an effort to improve health.

29. The _____ _____ is a coalition that provides public information on medical errors, health care standards, and health care provider quality performance measures.

30. Low-income individuals can access medical care through the federally aided, state-operated, and -administered program called _____.

31. _____ is the agency under the U.S. Department of Labor responsible for inspecting and enforcing safety standards in the workplace.

TRUE OR FALSE?

32. _____ T/F   Licensure refers to the process of approving a health care organization to provide medical care and services.
33. _____ T/F   Improving organization performance and leadership are considered patient-focused functions by the Joint Commission's Hospital Standards.
34. _____ T/F   A living will is a legal document that establishes a surrogate decision maker to make medical treatment decisions for the individual should he or she become incapacitated.
35. _____ T/F   A do-not-resuscitate order can be implemented by the patient's family.
36. _____ T/F   Case management is an approach to coordinating care for patients in the hospital or in an outpatient setting.

NCLEX-RN® REVIEW QUESTIONS

3-1. A nurse is working on a committee to address the national patient safety standards. These standards will be analyzed when which of the following regulatory bodies visits the organization?
   1. Institute of Medicine
   2. The Leapfrog Group
   3. The Joint Commission
   4. Committee for Physician Order Entry

3-2. A patient tells the nurse that she has the kind of health insurance that allows her to go to any doctor she wants at any time and the health plan pays for it. She gets a check in the mail for any doctor fees. The nurse realizes this patient's health insurance is:
   1. Traditional indemnity insurance
   2. Medicare
   3. Through an HMO
   4. A self-funded plan

3-3. The nurse is preparing the annual budget for a care area. In which of the following categories would Training and Orientation be included?
1. Charges
2. Overhead
3. Salaries/Wages
4. Purchased Services

3-4. A patient tells the nurse that he can't have the MRI done because he can't afford it. Which of the following should the nurse do?
1. Cancel the MRI.
2. Confirm the patient's health insurance coverage and contact social services.
3. Instruct the patient on ways to improve his health.
4. Contact the physician and schedule the patient for a follow-up appointment.

3-5. Prior to being discharged, a patient tells the nurse that he "appreciates the care that he received" and wants the hospital administration to know they are fortunate to have such good nurses. This patient's feedback would be considered which type of quality standard?
1. Structure
2. Process
3. Outcome
4. Joint Commission

3-6. An acute care facility is completing several large remodeling projects. Which of the following should be done at the conclusion of these projects?
1. Have an inspection conducted by the fire marshal.
2. Call OSHA to conduct an inspection.
3. Call the CDC to schedule an inspection.
4. Ask the Joint Commission to come and inspect the new care areas.

3-7. The family of a terminally ill patient are requesting that everything "be done" to save their family member's life. The nurse is aware of the patient's advance directive, which is in conflict with the family's expectations. What should the nurse do?
1. Tell the family that what the patient wants is what the patient will receive.
2. Agree with the family and follow the family's wishes.
3. Tell the family to make a decision and for them to talk with the physician once they've done so.
4. Talk with the physician and a hospital administrator.

3-8. The nurse is documenting in a patient's medical record. Which of the following should the nurse do to ensure a legally correct entry?
1. Include personal opinions about the care the patient is receiving.
2. Document on every patient once per day to cut the time needed for documentation.
3. Sign the entry and include personal credentials.
4. Use as many abbreviations as possible to cut the time needed to document.

3-9. A patient tells the nurse that another, nonattending physician is a family member and the patient wants this physician to review his medical record. The nurse should:
1. Provide the medical record to the physician family member.
2. Phone the attending physician on the case and report the request.
3. Contact the nursing supervisor about the request.
4. Ask the physician family member to leave the care area.

3-10. On the morning of a same-day surgical procedure, a nurse talks with a patient about his home, his family, and how he expects to recover successfully when he's no longer in the hospital. This nurse was conducting:
1. An admission assessment.
2. A home care referral.
3. An analysis on potential length of stay in the hospital.
4. Discharge planning.

CHAPTER 4

ETHICAL AND LEGAL GUIDELINES FOR NURSING PRACTICE

OUTCOME-BASED LEARNING OBJECTIVES

4-1. Explain how ethical theories and principles influence nursing practice in a clinical setting.

4-2. Identify and apply the steps of the MORAL model in ethical decision making.

4-3. Compare and contrast the three distinct structures that ethics committees demonstrate in health care institutions.

4-4. Explain how the state nurse practice act governs and guides nursing practice.

4-5. Distinguish among the types of laws that typically affect nursing practice: common, civil, tort, contract, and criminal.

4-6. Identify the six elements of malpractice law as described in the chapter.

4-7. Discuss the importance of standards of care and how they are differentiated between internal and external standards.

4-8. Distinguish between regional and national norms.

4-9. Identify the three most common intentional torts and three most common quasi-intentional torts seen in health care settings and explain the defenses against them.

4-10. Explain the doctrine of informed consent as it relates to the use of implied consent in nursing settings.

4-11. Explain actions that the nurse may take to avoid or prevent possible liabilities.

CHAPTER OUTLINE

I. Ethics and Nursing
  A. Ethical Theories
    1. Deontological Theories
    2. Teleological Theories
    3. Principlism
  B. Ethical Principles
    1. Autonomy
    2. Beneficence

   3. Nonmaleficence
   4. Veracity
   5. Justice
   6. Paternalism
   7. Fidelity
   8. Respect for Others
C. Ethical Decision Making
   1. Ethical Dilemma
D. Ethics Committees
   1. Committee Structures
II. Legal Concepts in Nursing
A. Sources of Law
B. Nurse Practice Acts
C. Divisions or Types of Law
   1. Common and Civil Law
      a. Tort Law
      b. Contract Law
   2. Criminal Law
D. Sources of Civil and Criminal Litigation for Nurses
E. Negligence and Malpractice
   1. Elements of Malpractice
      a. Duty Owed the Patient
      b. Breach of the Duty Owed the Patient
      c. Foreseeability of Harm
      d. Causation
      e. Injury
      f. Damages
   2. Liability for Negligence by Students
F. Regional and National Norms for Standards of Care
G. Intentional Torts
   1. Assault, Battery, and False Imprisonment
H. Quasi-Intentional Torts
   1. Defamation of Character
   2. Invasion of Privacy
      a. Breach of Confidentiality
      b. Health Insurance Portability and Accountability Act (HIPAA)
I. Consent
   1. Informed Consent
   2. Implied Consent
   3. Revocation of Consent
   4. Signing of a Consent Form
III. Preventing Possible Liability
A. Nurse–Patient Relationship
B. Patient Rights
IV. Defenses Against Torts
A. Defenses Against Intentional Torts
B. Defenses Against Quasi-Intentional Torts
C. Defenses Against Nonintentional Torts
   1. Immunity
V. Critical Thinking, Decision Making, and Clinical Judgment

KEY TERMS MATCHING EXERCISE 1

Write the letter of the correct definition in the space next to each term.

Term

_____ 1. tort law

_____ 2. intentional torts

_____ 3. nonintentional torts

_____ 4. quasi-intentional torts

_____ 5. malpractice

_____ 6. negligence

_____ 7. civil law

_____ 8. regional (locality) rule

_____ 9. common law

_____ 10. defamation of character

Definition

a. Actions that result in harm to another, but intent is lacking; often synonymous with carelessness.

b. Professional misconduct; failure to meet the standards of care that a reasonably prudent member of the profession would employ.

c. Existence of a prevailing community standard.

d. Failure to exercise the degree of care that a person of ordinary prudence would exercise under the same or similar conditions.

e. Volitional actions that result in harm to another, but intent is lacking.

f. Rules and regulations that form the bases of legal actions; branch of law that pertains to contracts, torts, patents, and the like.

g. Wrongful conduct that is intentional in nature and designed to cause harm or damage to another.

h. System of law derived from principles rather than rules and regulations; consists of principles based on justice, reason, and common sense.

i. A brand of civil law concerning legal wrongs committed by one person against another or against another's property.

j. Publication of anything that is injurious to the good name or reputation of another or that tends to bring another's reputation into question.

KEY TERMS MATCHING EXERCISE 2

Write the letter of the correct definition in the space next to each term.

Term

_____ 11. breach of confidentiality

_____ 12. implied consent

_____ 13. informed consent

_____ 14. invasion of privacy

_____ 15. scope of practice

_____ 16. foreseeability of harm

_____ 17. deontological theories

_____ 18. teleological theories

_____ 19. principlism

_____ 20. substituted judgment

Definition

a. Refers to legally permissible boundaries of practice for a given health care profession.

b. In ethics, theories that derive norms and rules from the duties human beings owe one another by virtue of commitments that are made and roles that are assumed.

c. An emerging theory in ethics that incorporates the various ethical principles in attempting to resolve conflicts in clinical settings.

d. A subjective determination of what a person would have chosen to do had that person been capable of making his or her opinion known.

e. Failure to prevent the disclosure of all or parts of a patient's medical record without the proper authority to do so.

f. Doctrine that mandates that individuals must be fully appraised of the nature, risks, benefits, alternative therapies, and potential consequences of procedures and therapies in health care settings.

g. Violation of the right to protection against unreasonable and unwarranted interference with one's solitude.

h. Theories that derive norms or rules for conduct from the consequences of actions; looks merely at consequences to determine the rightness or wrongness of an action.

i. Concept that certain actions are known to cause or create specific outcomes.

j. Permission that is inferred by a person's conduct or by law.

SHORT ANSWER QUESTIONS

21. What are the eight ethical principles nurses encounter in clinical settings? Name each principle and provide an example of how it might be used.

_____

_____

_____

_____

_____

_____

_____

_____

22. As a nurse, you are caring for a family considering whether to allow their elderly parent to remain on life support. What questions would have to be answered in order for you to apply the MORAL model?

_____

_____

23. A state's nursing board is responsible for upholding the state's nurse practice act. Go to your state's board of nursing and notice what topics are currently being considered or discussed in regard to the practice act. List them below.

_____

_____

_____

_____

24. A breach of contract could result in what events?

_____

_____

_____

_____

25. Explain how a nurse would determine whether a 16-year-old girl can be treated for a sexually transmitted disease without a parent's consent.

_____

_____

_____

_____

TRUE OR FALSE?

26. _____   T/F   A nursing student practices under the instructor's license and therefore is not directly accountable for clinical actions.

27. _____   T/F   Malpractice is considered an intentional tort and negligence a nonintentional tort.

28. _____   T/F   Nurses cannot be charged with violation of criminal law while working in the clinical setting.

29. _____   T/F   The nurse having individual malpractice insurance is at greater risk of being sued.

30. _____   T/F   A malpractice suit is successful if four of the six elements considered are proved.

31. _____   T/F   Failing to provide patient education and discharge planning can be an element of a malpractice suit.

32. _____   T/F   The nurse who does not act as patient advocate is at risk of being charged with malpractice.

33. _____   T/F   Using medication to prevent a patient from leaving the health care setting can be considered false imprisonment.

34. _____   T/F   Restraining a patient in order to perform a procedure is not considered battery.

35. _____   T/F   When documenting a patient's condition, the nurse who unnecessarily describes the patient's demeanor in a derogatory manner can be accused of defamation of character.

NCLEX-RN® REVIEW QUESTIONS

4-1.   A nurse has promised a patient being discharged that she would make sure the home care nurse visit for the next day is coordinated; however, the physician is questioning the need for home care. Which ethical principle is this nurse most likely experiencing?
   1. Fidelity
   2. Justice
   3. Respect for others
   4. Nonmaleficence

4-2.   The staff nurse is reviewing the outcome of a meeting held to address an ethical dilemma that surfaced while providing care to a patient. This nurse is utilizing which step in the ethical decision-making model?
   1. Options
   2. Resolve
   3. Act
   4. Look back

4-3.   A patient has been in a coma for several weeks and has been given a poor prognosis for recovery. Decisions need to be made regarding continuation of care and to what degree. Which ethics committee structure would best benefit this patient?
   1. Nonmalficence
   2. Autonomy
   3. Patient benefit
   4. Social justice

4-4. A nurse is expected to remain competent to provide patient care. Which of the following can the nurse do to ensure this expectation is met?
1. Take college-level nursing courses.
2. Attend all staff meetings at the hospital.
3. Take the state board of nursing examination every 5 years.
4. Read professional journals and participate in continuing education.

4-5. The narcotics count on a patient care area is missing five injectable doses of morphine. Currently no patients on the care area are prescribed morphine for pain. The nurse realizes that the laws about this situation would be considered:
1. Contract.
2. Criminal.
3. Tort.
4. Civil.

4-6. A nurse is concerned that a patient is going to file malpractice charges because she did not receive a dose of medication at the correct time it was prescribed to be administered. What response should the nurse manager make to this nurse?
1. Do you have malpractice insurance?
2. You will be suspended until this matter has been investigated.
3. I wouldn't worry about it.
4. There are specific elements that have to be proven before a situation is seen as malpractice.

4-7. A nurse is planning the care for a patient recovering from a cerebral vascular accident. Which of the following external standards would be beneficial for the nurse to access when planning this care?
1. Organization policies and procedures
2. Scope and Standards of Neuroscience Nursing Practice
3. Registered nurse position description
4. The Joint Commission standards

4-8. A nurse does not understand the purpose of using national standards of care when planning and providing patient care. What would be an appropriate response to make to this nurse?
1. It costs less to use national standards.
2. All patients have the right to receive quality health care.
3. It takes less time to use national standards.
4. There aren't any other standards to use.

4-9. Two nurses are discussing a patient while waiting for an elevator. These nurses are violating a HIPAA regulation or the quasi-intentional tort of:
1. Defamation of character.
2. Invasion of privacy.
3. Breach of confidentiality.
4. Assault.

4-10. A patient had previously agreed to have a diagnostic procedure performed but tells the nurse that she has "changed her mind." Which of the following should the nurse do?
1. Tell the patient that she's already consented to the procedure and will have it done.
2. Take the patient to the procedure, claiming it is an emergency.
3. Cancel the procedure.
4. Inform the nursing supervisor and the physician of the patient's decision about the procedure.

4-11. A patient tells the nurse that he does not want to take cholesterol medication but feels pressured to do so by the physician. Which of the following can the nurse access to help preserve this patient's rights?
1. Values-based decision model
2. Respect for persons model
3. Rights protection model
4. Patient Bill of Rights

CHAPTER 5

NURSING CARE DELIVERY SYSTEMS

OUTCOME-BASED LEARNING OBJECTIVES

5-1. Identify the four types of nursing care delivery systems most commonly used in health care settings.

5-2. Analyze the influences of each nursing care delivery system on professional nurse satisfaction, patient satisfaction, and quality of care delivered.

5-3. Explain the delegation responsibilities of the registered nurse for each nursing care delivery system.

5-4. Distinguish among the economic variables influencing the selection of a nursing care delivery system.

5-5. Differentiate the roles of advanced practice nurses and case managers within the context of the four nursing care delivery systems identified in this chapter.

EXPLORE **mynursingkit**

MyNursingKit is your one stop for online chapter review materials and resources. Prepare for success with additional NCLEX®-style practice questions, interactive assignments and activities, web links, animations and videos, and more!

Register your access code from the front of your book at **www.mynursingkit.com**

CHAPTER OUTLINE

I. Nursing Care Delivery Systems: Past to Present
   A. Historical Influence
   B. Current Influence
   C. Evidenced-Based Management Practices
   D. Integration of RN Roles in Care Delivery Systems
II. Care Delivery Models
   A. Case Method
      1. Work Allocation
      2. Clinical Decision Making
      3. Communication
      4. Management
   B. Functional Nursing
      1. Work Allocation
      2. Clinical Decision Making
      3. Communication
      4. Management

    C. Team Nursing
       1. Work Allocation
       2. Clinical Decision Making
       3. Communication
       4. Management
    D. Primary Nursing
       1. Work Allocation
       2. Clinical Decision Making
       3. Communication
       4. Management
       5. Relationship-Based Care
III. Providing Safe Patient Care

KEY TERMS MATCHING EXERCISE

Write the letter of the correct definition in the space next to each term.

Term

_____ 1. certified nurse midwife (CNM)

_____ 2. certified registered nurse anesthetist (CRNA)

_____ 3. acuity

_____ 4. unlicensed assistive personnel

_____ 5. case manager

_____ 6. advanced practice nurse (APRN)

_____ 7. associate caregiver

_____ 8. clinical nurse specialist (CNS)

_____ 9. nurse practitioner (NP)

_____ 10. clinical nurse leader (CNL)

Definition

a. An advanced practice nurse with postgraduate training and state certification to administer anesthesia without direct supervision by a physician.

b. An advanced practice nurse with postgraduate training with the responsibility to integrate care among other disciplines and manage care at the bedside.

c. An advanced practice nurse with postgraduate training and state certification to deliver healthy babies without direct supervision by a physician.

d. An advanced practice nurse with postgraduate training in a clinical disease specialty.

e. An LVN/LPN or unlicensed assistive personnel assigned to provide care to patients according to the plan established by the primary nurse.

f. Health care personnel who are not licensed; they may be technicians or certified nurses' aides or nursing assistants.

g. An advanced practice nurse with postgraduate training who is licensed by the state to provide basic medical care under standardized procedures.

h. A nurse who has been trained to practice beyond the scope defined for a registered nurse by the state nurse practice act.

i. A person who collaboratively plans, coordinates, and evaluates services for cost effectiveness, but does not provide direct patient care.

j. The measurement of severity of illness in a patient and the amount of nursing care required to care for the patient.

SHORT ANSWER QUESTIONS

11. Describe the benefits and risks of delegation in a functional nursing delivery system.

_____

_____

_____

_____

_____

12. Which nursing care delivery system best allows for relationship-based care? Why is it more conducive to that end than the other nursing care delivery systems?

_____

_____

_____

_____

13. If evidence-based nursing care delivery systems are to be employed, which of the four nursing care delivery systems is best supported by research? Why does that system qualify?

_____

_____

_____

_____

TRUE OR FALSE?

14. _____ T/F A magnet hospital meets the requirements set forth by the American Nurses' Credentialing Center.

15. _____ T/F To retain its magnet status, a hospital must submit paperwork annually and reapply every five years.

16. _____ T/F Communication among members of the team nursing delivery system is often a greater challenge than with the other systems.

17. _____ T/F All four nursing care delivery systems involve a charge nurse.

18. _____ T/F Delegation is employed in team nursing more than in the other three nursing care delivery systems.

19. _____ T/F The physical design of the patient care area is of minimal importance when determining which nursing care delivery system to implement.

20. _____ T/F The Joint Commission is responsible for accrediting hospitals and health care systems.

NCLEX-RN® REVIEW QUESTIONS

5-1. An organization is implementing the care partner approach to patient care. This type of care delivery system is also considered:
1. Case method.
2. Functional.
3. Team.
4. Primary.

5-2. On a satisfaction survey, one patient wrote "how nice it was to know that I had one nurse who was responsible for my care." This patient's statement reflects which of the following care delivery systems?
1. Case method
2. Functional
3. Team
4. Primary

5-3. The nurse is delegating responsibilities to both registered nurses and unlicensed assistive personnel during a start of shift meeting. The care delivery system that uses this approach would be:
1. Case method.
2. Functional.
3. Team.
4. Primary.

5-4. Based upon the quality and type of caregivers, which of the following care delivery systems would be the highest cost to sustain?
1. Team
2. Case method
3. Functional
4. Primary

5-5. A clinical nurse specialist is helping a nurse work through an unfamiliar treatment plan prior to coordinating the ongoing care for this patient. The care delivery system most likely being used would be:
1. Case method.
2. Functional.
3. Team.
4. Primary.

CHAPTER 6

NURSING DOCUMENTATION

OUTCOME-BASED LEARNING OBJECTIVES

6-1. Explain regulatory and professional standards for patient care documentation.

6-2. List general principles that guide documentation.

6-3. Differentiate advantages and disadvantages of different documentation systems.

6-4. Apply the nursing process to the Preparation for Practice exercises.

CHAPTER OUTLINE

I. Documentation Standards
   A. Accreditation Standards
   B. State, Federal, and Professional Standards
   C. Health Insurance Portability and Accountability Act
II. Documentation Principles
   A. Complete, Concise, and Accurate
   B. Objectivity
   C. Timeliness
   D. Legibility
   E. Abbreviations
   F. Corrections
III. Legal Situations
   A. Consent Forms
   B. Advance Directives
   C. Using Restraints
   D. Leaving Against Medical Advice
   E. Incident Reports
IV. Nursing Process
   A. Assessment
   B. Nursing Diagnosis
   C. Outcome Identification
   D. Planning
   E. Implementation
   F. Evaluation

V. Documentation Systems
  A. Narrative System
  B. Problem-Oriented Medical Record
    1. Database
    2. Problem List
    3. Initial Plan
    4. Progress Notes
    5. Discharge Summary
  C. Problem, Intervention, Evaluation System
    1. Problem
    2. Intervention
    3. Evaluation
  D. Focus System
  E. Charting by Exception System
  F. FACT System
  G. Electronic Medical Record
    1. Nursing Care Documentation
VI. Preparation for Practice
VII. Summary

KEY TERMS MATCHING EXERCISE

Write the letter of the correct definition in the space next to each term.

Term

_____ 1. critical pathways
_____ 2. medical record
_____ 3. medication reconciliation
_____ 4. nurse practice act

Definition

a. State guidelines that define the practice of nursing and give guidance in terms of scope of practice issues; they are designed to ensure safe practice.

b. The legal document for all information regarding a patient's hospital course and evidence for the extent of care provided and the outcome of that care.

c. Comprehensive plans of care for specific patient situations or disease processes.

d. Process of identifying an accurate list of all medications the patient is taking, and using this list to provide correct medications for the patient anywhere in the health care system.

SHORT ANSWER QUESTIONS

5. Explain how the Focus system is centered on the nursing process.

_____

_____

6. What are the disadvantages of the electronic medical record?

_____

_____

_____

7. Rewrite the following medical record entry to be specific and accurate by adding new information: "Patient looked sleepy and didn't seem to want to eat."

_____

_____

8. Rewrite the following medical record entry to be specific and accurate by adding new information: "Patient appeared not to hear my questions."

_____

_____

9. Rewrite the following medical record entry to be specific and accurate by adding new information: "Patient seemed to have trouble swallowing."

_____

_____

10. Rewrite the following medical record entry to be specific and accurate by adding new information: "Patient did not drink much water and had stomach pains."

_____

_____

TRUE OR FALSE?

11. _____ T/F The possibility of needing information for legal proceedings is the primary reason for accurate documentation.
12. _____ T/F An incident report becomes a permanent part of the patient's medical record.
13. _____ T/F Nurses are licensed to diagnose and treat the patient's response to illness and need for education.
14. _____ T/F The nursing care plan becomes a permanent part of the patient's medical record.
15. _____ T/F The medical record is important to quality nursing care but is not considered a legal document.
16. _____ T/F Preventing adverse drug reactions by medication reconciliation is a primary reason for using electronic medical records.
17. _____ T/F The nurse must never make changes to a medical record without striking through the incorrect content, initialing the change, and noting the time and date of the change.
18. _____ T/F The narrative system consists of five components: baseline data, a problem list, a plan of care for each problem, multidisciplinary progress notes, and a discharge summary.
19. _____ T/F It is the nurse's responsibility to document that the patient received information about the patient's right to refuse treatment.
20. _____ T/F The Joint Commission's ruling on abbreviations not to be used applies only to nurses and unlicensed assistive personnel.

NCLEX-RN® REVIEW QUESTIONS

6-1. A nonauthorized person asks to see a patient's medical record. The regulatory body that created standards to protect patient information is:
1. The Joint Commission.
2. The state board of nursing.
3. Medicare.
4. The Department of Health and Human Services.

6-2. The nurse is preparing medications for assigned patients and sees that several are receiving doses every 2 hours in the morning. The nurse should:
1. Document all doses of medications that are being given now.
2. Document all doses of the medications for the morning.
3. Document all doses of medications for the first four hours of the shift.
4. Document all doses of medication for the entire day.

6-3. An organization follows the charting by exception (CBE) method of charting. This method of charting:
1. Saves time and decreases the amount of documentation needed.
2. Improves communication because of standardized terminology.
3. Allows the reader to easily find information about a problem.
4. Uses the SOAP method for documentation.

6-4. The nurse is analyzing assessment data collected prior to determining appropriate nursing diagnoses for a patient's care plan. Which of the following skills is the nurse most likely using to analyze this data?
1. Observation
2. Intuition
3. Listening
4. Critical thinking

CHAPTER 7

NURSING PROCESS

OUTCOME-BASED LEARNING OBJECTIVES

7-1. Differentiate between the roles in nursing as specified by the American Nurses Association.

7-2. Explain the five steps of the nursing process and their relationship to each other.

7-3. Describe the cognitive, affective, and psychomotor skills necessary to conduct a comprehensive nursing assessment.

7-4. Differentiate between nursing diagnoses and collaborative problems.

7-5. Explain the relationship between critical thinking and the nursing process.

EXPLORE **mynursingkit**™

MyNursingKit is your one stop for online chapter review materials and resources. Prepare for success with additional NCLEX®-style practice questions, interactive assignments and activities, web links, animations and videos, and more!

Register your access code from the front of your book at **www.mynursingkit.com**

CHAPTER OUTLINE

I. Nursing Process
II. Nurse–Patient Relationship
III. Steps of the Nursing Process
  A. Assessment
    1. Data Sources
    2. Data Types
    3. Data Collection Process
    4. Guidelines for Data Collection
      a. Data Collection and the Patient's Health Record
      b. Sequence of Components in the Health Record
      c. Frameworks for Data Collection
  B. Nursing Diagnosis and Outcome Identification
    1. Outcome Identification
  C. Planning
  D. Implementation
    1. Evidence-Based Practice
  E. Evaluation
    1. Patient Care Plan

KEY TERMS MATCHING EXERCISE

Write the letter of the correct definition in the space next to each term.

Term

_____ 1. assessment
_____ 2. evaluation
_____ 3. outcome
_____ 4. intervention
_____ 5. planning
_____ 6. nursing diagnosis
_____ 7. implementation
_____ 8. collaborative problems
_____ 9. patient care plan
_____ 10. critical thinking

Definition

a. Focuses on a patient's behavioral changes and compares them with criteria stated in predetermined patient outcomes. This action is ongoing through all phases of the nursing process.

b. An action designed to facilitate achievement of desired patient outcomes. It must be purposeful, must be supported by a rationale, and involve organization and actual delivery of nursing care, which ideally leads to achievement of stated patient goals and objectives.

c. The end product of the nursing assessment. Describes an actual or potential health problem, based on gathered data, that a nurse can legally manage.

d. A purposeful, two-dimensional, goal-directed process that is context bound. Two dimensions are necessary for the development of this process: the cognitive, which is reflective, reasoned thinking, and the affective, which is open-mindedness to divergent perspectives and an inquisitive spirit.

e. The "doing" or intervening phase of the nursing process.

f. Problems that are identified by other health care workers, such as physicians, in contrast to nursing problems, which are identified by nurses.

g. Individual, measurable patient objective; measurable criterion that indicates the patient's care objectives have been met; a change in patient behavior that results from nursing interventions.

h. The act of evaluating or appraising.

i. A documented record of the nursing process, a plan designed to incorporate the patient's identified problems, outcomes, and actions to be implemented by the nurse.

j. Determining how expected patient outcomes can be achieved through nursing interventions by establishing priorities of care.

OBJECTIVE OR SUBJECTIVE DATA?

Identify each observation as objective data or subjective data.

11. _____ Seemed eager to leave and was fidgety and edgy.

12. _____ Posture was slumped and gaze downcast.

13. _____ Face was flushed and damp with perspiration.

14. _____ Said she felt dizzy and slightly nauseated.

15. _____ Brow was furrowed; frowned throughout interview.

16. _____ Temperature increased from 99.0°F to 101.3°F within 2 hours.

17. _____ Reported that hands and feet were cold.

18. _____ Fingers and much of the hands were white.

19. _____ Said he felt sick all over and clammy.

20. _____ Reported a lump in the groin area that was more pronounced when standing.

TRUE OR FALSE?

21. _____ T/F Checking the patient's vital signs is an independent nursing activity.

22. _____ T/F Coordinating the patient's physical therapy session is an independent nursing activity.

23. _____ T/F Administering medicine is a dependent nursing activity.

24. _____ T/F Without honest self-evaluation and recognition of biases, beliefs, and assumptions, the nurse cannot fulfill the ideals of the nurse–patient relationship.

25. _____ T/F The nursing process must be employed only once for each patient.

COMPLETE THE SENTENCE

26. Interpreting and validating data takes place during the _____ phase of the nursing process.

27. Formulating goals and objectives occurs during the _____ phase of the nursing process.

28. During the assessment phase of the nursing process, the nurse must distinguish between data that is

_____ and _____.

29. Nursing diagnoses are _____ _____ about an individual, family, or community response to actual or potential health problems and life processes.

30. The two kinds of data sources the nurse uses are _____ and _____. The _____ data source is the patient. _____ data sources include family, friends, other health care professionals, the patient's current health care record, and the nurse's own knowledge base.

NCLEX-RN® REVIEW QUESTIONS

7-1. The nurse is discussing a patient's plan of care with the physical therapist. This nurse is engaging in which nursing role?
1. Independent
2. Interdependent
3. Dependent
4. Co-dependent

7-2. The nurse has just prioritized a patient's nursing diagnoses and is now setting goals. The nurse is functioning within which phase of the nursing process?
1. Assessment
2. Planning
3. Implementation
4. Evaluation

7-3. The nurse is asking a patient a variety of questions about the patient's current health status. This nurse is utilizing which skill for conducting this section of the assessment?
1. Psychomotor
2. Affective
3. Psychosocial
4. Cognitive

7-4. The nurse notes a change in a patient's status and provides a prescribed medication. This nurse is addressing which of the following aspects of patient care?
1. Intervening according to findings from a nursing diagnosis
2. Collecting data
3. Addressing a collaborative problem
4. Evaluating an aspect of care

7-5. The nurse uses a tool that improves decision making by identifying key events of patient care with expected time frames. This tool is considered a:
1. Standardized assessment form.
2. Care plan.
3. Form of evidenced-based practice.
4. Critical pathway.

CHAPTER 8

ROLE OF RESEARCH IN NURSING PRACTICE

OUTCOME-BASED LEARNING OBJECTIVES

8-1. Differentiate between basic and applied research.

8-2. Differentiate between quantitative and qualitative research.

8-3. Identify three types of quantitative and three types of qualitative research.

8-4. Describe the first step of the research process.

8-5. Determine how a research design is selected.

8-6. Differentiate between research utilization and evidence-based practice.

8-7. Describe the three ethical principles that guide research studies.

8-8. Describe the impact of HIPAA on nursing research studies.

8-9. Explain the four stages of completing a quantitative research critique.

CHAPTER OUTLINE

    I. Nursing Research
       A. Basic and Applied Research
   II. The Research Process
 III. Conducting Research
       A. Research Problem and Purpose
          1. Research Purpose
       B. Literature Review
       C. Research Design
          1. Types of Research Design: Quantitative and Qualitative
             a. Quantitative Research
             b. Qualitative Research
          2. Research Setting
             a. Sample Selection
                i. Convenience Sampling
               ii. Quota Sampling

iii. Purposive Sampling
iv. Network Sampling
v. Simple Random Sampling
vi. Stratified Random Sampling
  b. Sample Size
IV. Research Utilization and Evidence-Based Practice
  A. Research Utilization
  B. Evidence-Based Practice
    1. Development of Evidence-Based Practice
    2. Implementation of Evidence-Based Practice
      a. Barriers to Evidence-Based Practice
      b. Strategies to Promote Evidence-Based Practice
V. Research and Ethics in Health Care
  A. Ethical Frameworks
    1. Utilitarian Perspective
    2. Deontological Perspective
  B. Codes and Guidelines for Ethical Decision Making
  C. Principles of Ethical Research
    1. Respect for Persons
    2. Beneficence
    3. Justice
  D. Methods of Protecting Human Subjects
    1. Informed Consent
    2. Institutional Review Boards
  E. Rules for Conducting Ethical Research
  F. Rules for Socially Responsible Nursing Research
  G. Privacy and the Health Insurance Portability and Accountability Act
VI. Informatics
VII. The Research Critique
  A. Elements of a Research Critique
    1. Quantitative Research Critique
    2. Qualitative Research Critique
VIII. Future of Perspectives of Nursing Research
  A. Future Research Goals

KEY TERMS MATCHING EXERCISE 1

Write the letter of the correct definition in the space next to each term.

Term

_____ 1. research problem
_____ 2. theoretical connectedness
_____ 3. statistical significance
_____ 4. research critique
_____ 5. literature review
_____ 6. research utilization (RU)
_____ 7. analytical preciseness
_____ 8. qualitative research
_____ 9. research process
_____ 10. research purpose

Definition

a. A critical appraisal of a piece of completed research.

b. A concise, clear statement of the specific goal or aim of the study that is generated from the problem.

c. Measure of how findings emerge from the data, how the data collection process is made flexible, and how themes emerge from the data.

d. A systematic, subjective approach used to describe life experiences and give them meaning.

e. A term indicating that the results from an analysis of sample data are unlikely to have been caused by chance, at some specified level of probability.

f. Requires that the theoretical schema developed for the study be clearly expressed, logically consistent, reflective of the data, and compatible with the practice of nursing.

g. Process of undertaking discrete steps to conduct a research study. Includes identifying a researchable problem, completing a literature review, creating the theoretical/conceptual framework, selecting an appropriate design, and collecting, analyzing, and distributing data/findings.

h. The purposeful application of research findings to the clinical setting to improve patient care.

i. A search of the latest research articles and scholarly studies.

j. A situation or circumstance that requires a solution to be described, explained, or predicted.

KEY TERMS MATCHING EXERCISE 2

Write the letter of the correct definition in the space next to each term.

Term

_____ 11. convenience sampling

_____ 12. network sampling

_____ 13. nonprobability sampling

_____ 14. purposive sampling

_____ 15. simple random sampling

_____ 16. stratified random sampling

_____ 17. descriptive vividness

_____ 18. heuristic relevance

_____ 19. methodological congruence

_____ 20. research question

Definition

a. A research problem stated in an interrogative form.

b. Type of sampling in which elements and participants are selected by nonrandom methods.

c. In qualitative research, the practice of describing the site, participants, experience of collecting data, and the thinking of the research so clearly that the reader has a sense of personally experiencing the event.

d. Type of sampling that gives individuals within designated categories an equal chance of selection. The population is first divided into two or more strata or subpopulations. The goal is to enhance representation.

e. Type of sampling strategy in which each person in a population has an equal chance of being selected for a study.

f. Discovering or revealing a relationship that may lead to additional development along a particular line of research.

g. Type of sampling in which participants refer other participants to the study. Also referred to as *snowball sampling*.

h. Type of statistical sampling in which the most available persons or units are selected for inclusion in the study; the researcher has no control over the characteristics of the sample. Also referred to as *accidental sampling*.

i. Congruence among four dimensions of a research study: documentation rigor, procedural rigor, ethical rigor, and auditability.

j. Type of sampling that implies that certain people or elements are deliberately selected for the study.

WORD SEARCH

First identify the word from its definition. Then find and circle it in the puzzle on page 39.

21. _____ Type of sampling that involves random selection when choosing the elements and participants.

22. _____ Subjects are randomly assigned to treatment versus control groups.

23. _____ A formal, systematic, and organized method of answering a question, solving a problem, validating and redefining existing knowledge, and developing new knowledge.

24. _____ Attributes of a person or object that vary, that is, take on different values. Examples include body temperature, age, and blood pressure.

25. _____ Entire aggregation of cases in which a researcher is interested.

26. _____ The environment or place (locale) in which research is conducted; may be classified as natural, partially controlled, or highly controlled.

27. _____ The theory, science, and practice of the use of computer and informational technologies to store, retrieve, transmit, and manipulate data.

28. _____ A form of research that focuses on the sociology of meaning through field observation and description of a sociocultural phenomenon.

29. _____ A portion selected from a population and interpreted to represent that population; a subset of the population.

30. _____ Process of selecting a portion of the population to represent the entire population.

31. _____ A statement that predicts a certain relationship between two or more variables.

32. _____ A small preliminary study prior to conducting a larger study.

33. _____ Research undertaken to extend the knowledge base in a discipline or to formulate or refine a theory.

34. _____ Sampling to the point at which no new information is obtained and redundancy is achieved.

35. _____ Type of sampling in which participants are selected by a researcher in a nonrandom manner using prespecified characteristics of the sample to increase their representation.

36. _____ A qualitative research method that describes the meaning of a lived experience through the perspective of the participant.

37. _____ A research design's ability to detect relationships that exist among variables.

38. _____ Overall plan or blueprint for a study; guides an investigator in planning and implementing a study.

39. _____ The idea that the conclusion of a qualitative study should be grounded in the data, that is, based on direct and careful observations of everyday life within the group.

40. _____ Research that focuses on finding solutions to existing problems.

A	P	T	R	S	I	S	Y	L	A	N	A	R	E	W	O	P	I	R	T
Q	O	R	E	H	O	N	V	A	R	I	A	B	L	E	S	P	Y	E	R
U	N	O	O	W	E	G	F	C	F	G	I	O	E	L	O	I	E	S	T
O	T	I	R	B	R	A	M	O	W	G	A	S	W	P	Z	L	D	E	R
R	R	G	Q	U	A	R	P	Y	R	H	M	S	U	A	H	O	R	A	L
S	N	R	H	L	N	B	U	S	A	M	P	L	I	N	G	T	O	R	K
S	I	O	T	K	D	E	I	U	B	E	A	Y	W	H	Q	S	Q	C	I
B	L	U	U	P	O	A	Z	L	A	T	M	T	S	X	A	T	U	H	P
A	I	N	R	D	M	R	E	R	I	E	S	F	I	T	E	U	O	D	H
S	H	D	X	S	A	H	V	O	H	T	K	R	S	C	V	D	T	E	E
I	Y	E	T	R	S	B	N	A	U	O	Y	E	W	Y	S	Y	A	S	N
C	P	D	H	B	S	A	M	P	L	E	I	S	A	E	D	B	S	I	O
R	O	T	Z	T	I	E	S	E	O	F	R	E	A	L	I	Y	A	G	M
E	T	H	N	O	G	R	A	P	H	Y	L	A	J	M	A	I	M	N	E
S	H	E	B	Y	N	I	D	H	T	T	A	R	R	E	P	H	P	T	N
E	E	O	W	V	M	U	E	R	O	F	C	P	I	O	L	L	E	O	
A	S	R	S	S	E	T	T	I	N	G	S	H	L	R	E	U	I	B	L
R	I	Y	H	E	N	V	A	W	Y	U	O	D	F	O	U	I	N	N	O
C	S	N	O	I	T	A	R	U	T	A	S	A	T	A	D	B	G	D	G
H	I	R	A	P	P	L	I	E	D	R	E	S	E	A	R	C	H	E	Y

COMPLETE THE SENTENCE

Add the correct term(s) to complete each sentence.

41. A type of quantitative research, _____ most often occurs in a laboratory setting and is used to determine the effects of an intervention or of the manipulation of an independent variable.

42. A(n) _____ _____ _____, consists of studies in which the researcher collects data without introducing an intervention.

43. A(n) _____ _____ _____ is aimed at examining linear relationships between two or more variables.

44. The term _____ indicates a research design with an intervention, but one in which it is difficult to manipulate or control the setting, subjects, or variables as needed for a true experimental study.

45. A(n) _____ _____ _____ is used to determine the effects of an intervention, and it is highly controlled.

46. _____ _____ _____ often search for associations among certain variables.

47. Compared to _____ research, _____ research uses methods that are more subjective, a smaller sample size, and fewer research controls.

48. _____ research focuses on finding solutions to existing problems.

49. _____ research is important when little is known about a topic because it can identify factors of influence.

50. Research utilization is part of _____ _____ _____ and is a prescribed task of summarizing and using research findings to address a particular practice problem.

NCLEX-RN® REVIEW QUESTIONS

8-1. The nurse is planning a study using applied research. This nurse is most likely going to be studying:
   1. Maslow's hierarchy of needs.
   2. The application of Orem's theory to the nursing process.
   3. How certain conditions exist to substantiate a particular nursing theory.
   4. Patients' physiological response to a blood pressure medication.

8-2. The nurse researcher is conducting a qualitative research study. One characteristic that will be seen during this study will be:
   1. Collect numerical values.
   2. Use a small sample size and figure out how data will be collected as time goes on.
   3. Have specific subjects within certain groups for the study.
   4. Undertake efforts to control researcher bias.

8-3. The nurse researcher is following the emergent design of a qualitative research study. Which of the following is a characteristic of this design?
   1. The design changes according to findings learned.
   2. There is a search for associations between variables.
   3. There is a search to find associations between several variables.
   4. There is a search to find the effects of a particular intervention.

8-4. A nurse notes that a particular medication is not prescribed for some patients and believes it is because of the long-term cost needed to continue the medication. Studying this issue would be:
   1. Applicable to the discipline of nursing.
   2. Feasible because of the volume of patients affected.
   3. Inappropriate because it is a moral or ethical issue.
   4. Interesting to the other nurses on the care area.

8-5. The nurse researcher has a number of possible designs to use for a research project. The one that would be the best to use will:
   1. Maximize the possibility of having accurate information in the results.
   2. Be the easiest to use.
   3. Be the one that has the least cost.
   4. Ensure the research study is conducted without bias.

8-6. Educational sessions are being planned for the nursing staff to learn evidence-based practice. Which of the following should be included in this education?
    1. How to prepare and conduct research projects
    2. Where to access results of research projects
    3. How to apply research results in everyday clinical practice
    4. How to look at different pieces of evidence and rank their strength

8-7. A nurse researcher is preparing information for patients that addresses informed consent, privacy, and confidentiality. This information will ensure the study takes into consideration the ethical principle of:
    1. Respect for persons.
    2. Justice.
    3. Beneficence.
    4. Nonmaleficence.

8-8. The nurse researcher will be creating data from individual patient interviews. Which of the following must be done with this data to adhere to HIPAA regulations?
    1. The data have to be de-identified.
    2. Be sure the patient authorizes the use of the information.
    3. Share the data with the organization's research committee members.
    4. Review the information with the patient's physician for accuracy.

8-9. A nurse researcher is completing Stage 2 of a quantitative research critique. This researcher is currently:
    1. Reviewing the purpose of the study with the design and methodology.
    2. Determining if the research was conducted correctly.
    3. Studying the findings of the study.
    4. Evaluating the contributions of the study to nursing.

CHAPTER 9

HEALTH ASSESSMENT

OUTCOME-BASED LEARNING OBJECTIVES

9-1. Describe the components of the health assessment.

9-2. Explain the steps of the patient interview for the health history.

9-3. Compare and contrast verbal and nonverbal responses that enhance the collection of information.

9-4. Explain how the techniques of inspection, palpation, percussion, and auscultation can be applied to the physical assessment of the major body systems.

9-5. Differentiate between the steps of the critical thinking component as it relates to health assessment.

CHAPTER OUTLINE

I. National Guidelines: *Healthy People 2010*
   A. The *Healthy People 2010* Leading Health Indicators
      1. Physical Activity
      2. Overweight and Obesity
      3. Tobacco Use
      4. Substance Abuse
      5. Responsible Sexual Behavior
      6. Mental Health
      7. Injury and Violence
      8. Environmental Quality
      9. Immunization
      10. Access to Health Care
II. The Health History
   A. Conducting the Health Interview
      1. Biographical Data
      2. Present Health/Illness
         a. Health Patterns
         b. Health Beliefs and Practices

KEY TERMS MATCHING EXERCISE 1

Write the letter of the correct definition in the space next to each term

Term

_____ 1. inspection

_____ 2. palpation

_____ 3. subjective data

_____ 4. tympany

_____ 5. percussion

_____ 6. indirect percussion

_____ 7. blunt percussion

_____ 8. auscultation

_____ 9. direct percussion

_____ 10. hyperresonance

Definition

a. Data that consist of information the patient or caretaker tells the nurse; information that can be perceived only by the patient and not by the observer.

b. Technique of either pushing, tapping, or using a device to generate a sound vibration. The vibrations produced will help in determining the position of organ structures.

c. The deliberate, systematic examination of a patient using both sight and smell.

d. Technique of listening to the sounds produced by different body areas.

e. Technique of using gentle tapping to elicit the presence or absence of fluid, which results in a dull sound; used to examine such areas as the sinuses.

f. Technique that involves using the hyperextended middle finger of the nondominant hand (pleximeter) and then the finger tip of the middle finger of the dominant hand (plexor) to strike the pleximeter by using a wrist action that will elicit a sound.

g. Technique of placing the palm of the nondominant hand over a body area (such as the kidney) and striking the palm with the closed fist of the dominant hand.

h. Technique of using touch to collect data to determine specific characteristics of the body.

i. (1) A high-pitched, drum-like tone of medium duration. It is commonly heard over the air-filled intestines. (2) Abdominal distention with gas.

j. A loud, low tone of longer duration than resonance. It is heard when air is trapped in a space such as the lungs.

KEY TERMS MATCHING EXERCISE 2

Write the letter of the correct definition in the space next to each term.

Term

_____ 11. chief complaint
_____ 12. resonance
_____ 13. comprehensive exam
_____ 14. focused exam
_____ 15. objective data
_____ 16. metabolic equivalent level (MET)
_____ 17. leading health indicators
_____ 18. sequelae
_____ 19. vital signs
_____ 20. flatness

Definition

a. A measure of oxygen consumption. One is the energy requirement for a person at rest while sitting: around 3.5 mL of oxygen per kilogram of body weight per minute.

b. A soft, high-pitched tone of short duration. It is heard over muscle and bone.

c. An exam performed in emergent or urgent situations that focuses on a specific problem.

d. A head-to-toe assessment usually performed on new patients who will be seen on a routine basis by various clinicians.

e. Residual problems that result from an illness.

f. Ten indicators from *Healthy People 2010* that reflect major public health concerns: (1) physical activity, (2) overweight and obesity, (3) tobacco use, (4) substance abuse, (5) responsible sexual behavior, (6) mental health, (7) injury and violence, (8) environmental quality, (9) immunization, and (10) access to health care.

g. Temperature, pulse, respirations, blood pressure, and pain level. Used to monitor patients for infection and hemodynamic changes.

h. Behaviors, activities, and events that can be observed or measured by another person using the senses of observation, palpation, auscultation, percussion, and smell.

i. Information about what brought the patient to the health care provider in the patient's own words.

j. A low-pitched, clear, hollow tone of long duration. It is commonly heard over the lungs.

LABELING EXERCISE 1: APICAL, BILATERAL RADIAL, AND BILATERAL PEDAL PULSE LOCATIONS

Place the term in the correct location.

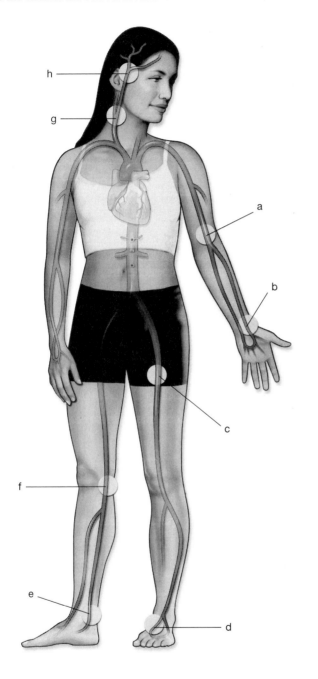

a. _____

b. _____

c. _____

d. _____

e. _____

f. _____

g. _____

h. _____

Brachial artery

Common carotid artery

Dorsalis pedis artery

Femoral artery

Popliteal artery

Posterior tibial artery

Radial artery

Temporal artery

LABELING EXERCISE 2: PALPATION

Place the term in the correct location.

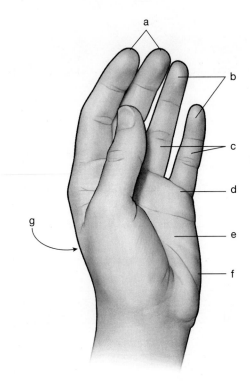

a. _____

b. _____

c. _____

d. _____

e. _____

f. _____

g. _____

Dorsal surface   Palmar surface
Finger pads   Palmar surface of fingers
Fingertips   Ulnar surface
Metacarpophalangeal joint

LABELING EXERCISE 3: PATIENT POSITIONING DURING PHYSICAL EXAMINATION

Place the term in the correct location.

a. _____

b. _____

c. _____

d. _____

e. _____

f. _____

g. _____

h. _____

Dorsal recumbent
Knee-chest
Lithotomy
Prone
Sims' (posterior view)
Sitting
Standing, bent over examining table
Supine

NCLEX-RN® REVIEW QUESTIONS

9-1. The nurse is preparing to conduct a health assessment of a Vietnamese patient. Which of the following should the nurse consider while conducting this assessment?
   1. Loud talking is a characteristic of this cultural group.
   2. Eye contact is a sign of respect within this cultural group.
   3. Avoid pointing because it is a sign of disrespect in this culture.
   4. Use one hand when providing something to the patient as a sign of respect.

9-2. While conducting a patient interview, the nurse nods her head while documenting the content of the patient's responses. This nurse is demonstrating which of the following interviewing techniques?
   1. Facilitation
   2. Explanation
   3. Clarification
   4. Empathy

9-3. The nurse notes that during an interview, the patient begins to yawn and glance out of the window. The nurse realizes this patient is demonstrating:
   1. Fatigue.
   2. Attentiveness.
   3. Negative nonverbal messaging.
   4. Hostility toward health care providers.

9-4. While conducting a physical examination with a patient, the nurse uses percussion over the patient's abdomen. Which of the following sounds is the nurse most likely to hear with this assessment technique?
   1. Resonance
   2. Tympany
   3. Flatness
   4. Hyperresonance

9-5. The nurse is creating a plan of care for a patient after completing a health assessment. In which of the following critical thinking steps is this nurse functioning?
   1. Evaluation
   2. Generation of alternatives
   3. Selection of alternatives
   4. Analysis of the situation

CHAPTER 10

THE AGING PATIENT

OUTCOME-BASED LEARNING OBJECTIVES

10-1. Identify normal age-related changes of the head, neck, respiratory, cardiovascular, gastrointestinal, genitourinary, musculoskeletal, integumentary, and neurological systems when completing a nursing assessment.

10-2. Explain the rationale for recommended immunizations and screening exams as proposed by the U.S. Preventive Services Task Force and as stated in the chapter for the patient over 65 years of age.

10-3. Discuss medications contraindicated in the aging patient as identified by the Beers criteria.

10-4. Recognize signs and symptoms of elder mistreatment to determine appropriate referrals.

10-5. Differentiate between residential, assisted living, and skilled nursing care in accordance with the type of patient care services provided.

10-6. Provide direction and advice to the elderly by describing available innovative housing options.

10-7. Explain the implications of technological advancements in providing care to the elderly.

PEARSON
EXPLORE mynursingkit™

MyNursingKit is your one stop for online chapter review materials and resources. Prepare for success with additional NCLEX®-style practice questions, interactive assignments and activities, web links, animations and videos, and more!

Register your access code from the front of your book at **www.mynursingkit.com**

CHAPTER OUTLINE

I. Theories of Aging
  A. Biological Aging Theories
  B. Psychosocial Theories of Aging
II. Demographics of the Aging Population
III. Health Assessment of the Aging Patient
  A. Interviewing the Older Patient to Obtain a Health History
    1. Cultural Considerations
      a. African American
      b. Asian
      c. Hispanic/Latino
      d. Native American
    2. Past Medical History
    3. Psychosocial History

IV. Physical Assessment of the Older Patient
    A. General Impression
    B. Assessment of the Head and Neck
        1. Age-Related Disorders of the Head, Neck, and Mouth
    C. Respiratory Assessment
        1. Age-Related Disorders of the Respiratory System
    D. Cardiovascular Assessment
        1. Age-Related Disorders of the Cardiovascular System
    E. Gastrointestinal Assessment
        1. Age-Related Disorders of the Gastrointestinal System
    F. Genitourinary Assessment
        1. Age-Related Disorders of the Genitourinary System
    G. Musculoskeletal Assessment
        1. Age-Related Disorders of the Musculoskeletal System
    H. Skin Assessment
        1. Age-Related Disorders of the Integumentary System
    I. Neurological Assessment
        1. Age-Related Disorders of the Neurological System
V. Health Care Promotion and Preventive Care
    A. Immunizations
        1. Pneumococcal Vaccine
        2. Influenza Vaccine
        3. Tetanus Vaccine
        4. Herpes Zoster Vaccine
    B. Screening Exams
        1. Vision
        2. Hearing
        3. Breast Exams/Breast Cancer Screening
        4. Pap Smears
        5. Prostate Exam/Prostate Cancer Screening
        6. Colon Cancer Screening
VI. Pharmacology and the Aging Patient
    A. Polypharmacy
    B. Medication Administration Principles for the Aging Patient
VII. Resources for Caring for an Aging Population
    A. Medicare and Medicaid
    B. Long-Term Care Insurance
VIII. Legal and Ethical Issues of Aging
    A. Elder Mistreatment (Abuse)
    B. Advance Directives
IX. Care Options for the Aging Patient
    A. Independent Living
    B. Adult Day Health Care and Adult Day Care
    C. Residential Care Facilities
    D. Assisted Living Facilities
    E. Intermediate/Skilled Nursing Care
    F. Home Care
    G. Hospice
    H. Palliative Care
X. Innovations in Caring for the Aging Patient
    A. Team-Based Primary Care in the Home
    B. Program of All-Inclusive Care for the Elderly
    C. Green House Project
XI. Elder Cohousing

KEY TERMS MATCHING EXERCISE 1

Write the letter of the correct definition in the space next to each term.

Term

_____ 1. activity theory of aging
_____ 2. wear-and-tear theory of aging
_____ 3. programmed theory of aging
_____ 4. disengagement theory of aging
_____ 5. rate of living theory of aging
_____ 6. continuity theory of aging
_____ 7. cross-linking theory of aging
_____ 8. error theories of aging
_____ 9. immunologic theory of aging
_____ 10. free radical theory of aging

Definition

a. Theory of aging based on the premise that successful aging is obtained by maintaining values, habits, and behaviors from adult life.

b. Theory of aging based on the premise that decreased activity later in life leads to meaninglessness and life dissatisfaction, and maintaining activity tends to increase life satisfaction.

c. Theory of aging based on the premise that aging follows a biological timetable.

d. Theory of aging based on the premise that the binding of glucose to protein causes various problems. Also referred to as the *glycosylation theory of aging*.

e. Theory of aging based on the premise that exposure to internal and external stressors results in the death of cells.

f. Theory of aging that postulates that aging changes are caused by free radical reactions that cause cells and organs to lose function and reserve energy.

g. Theory of aging based on the premise that the aging body is less able to distinguish its own cells from foreign cells.

h. Theory of aging based on the premise that environmental factors negatively impact the human body, causing destruction and damage.

i. Considered one of the oldest theories on aging, it is based on the belief that individuals possess a finite amount of some "vital substance." When that substance is exhausted, the person dies.

j. Theory of aging based on the premise that age-related changes bring about a mutual and reciprocal withdrawal of the individual from society.

KEY TERMS MATCHING EXERCISE 2

Write the letter of the correct definition in the space next to each term.

Term

_____ 11. adverse drug event (ADE) or adverse drug reaction (ADR)

_____ 12. delirium

_____ 13. dementia

_____ 14. insomnia

_____ 15. kyphosis

_____ 16. sleep apnea

_____ 17. polypharmacy

_____ 18. U.S. Preventive Services Task Force (USPSTF)

_____ 19. mandatory reporter

_____ 20. gerontological nurse practitioner (GNP)

Definition

a. Noxious and unintended patient event caused by a drug accompanied by various symptoms, signs, and laboratory abnormalities.

b. A group of health care experts that makes recommendations for appropriate preventive services and screening exams in adults ages 65 and over.

c. A general term for brain dysfunction characterized by a decline in cognition and memory that causes loss of ability to carry out activities of daily living and communicate with others, ultimately resulting in death.

d. A registered nurse with a master's degree from a nurse practitioner program specializing in the care of older adults.

e. A person required by law to report allegations and/or suspicions of abuse.

f. A disturbance in consciousness resulting in decreased attention and a change in cognition, or development of a perceptual disturbance that develops over a short period of time and tends to fluctuate throughout the day.

g. A disorder in which a person stops breathing for more than 10 seconds, typically more than 20 to 30 times in an hour. The three main types are central, obstructive, and a combination of central and obstructive.

h. Difficulty falling or remaining asleep.

i. The administration of many drugs together; also, the administration of excessive medications.

j. Curvature of the spine that creates a stooped-over "humpback" appearance.

AGE-RELATED OR DISORDER?

Identify the following conditions as an age-related change or as a sign of a disorder.

21. _____ Slower heart rate due to a decrease in the normal number of pacemaker cells

22. _____ Systolic hypertension and arrhythmias

23. _____ Reduced ciliary function of the lungs

24. _____ A thin grayish-white ring at the margins of the cornea called arcus senilis.

25. _____ Impacted cerumen

26. _____ Dry oral mucosa

27. _____ Decreased bladder capacity

28. _____ Enlarged prostrate

29. _____ Osteoarthritis and rheumatoid arthritis

30. _____ Slowed reaction time with poorer coordination and decreased muscle strength

31. _____ Seborrheic or senile keratoses

32. _____ Brain atrophy

33. _____ Herpes zoster

34. _____ Normal pressure hydrocephalus (NPH)

35. _____ Kyphosis

36. _____ Actinic keratoses

37. _____ Reduced ciliary function of the lungs

38. _____ Bunions

39. _____ Pulmonary emboli

40. _____ Cataracts

TRUE OR FALSE?

41. _____ T/F   A 78-year-old patient who scored 25 out of 30 on the Folstein Mini-Mental State Exam has no sign of dementia.
42. _____ T/F   Medicare does not contribute to long-term care insurance.
43. _____ T/F   All U.S. citizens over the age of 65 are automatically enrolled in Medicare Parts A and B.
44. _____ T/F   Nurses are required by law to report allegations and/or suspicions of abuse.
45. _____ T/F   The aging patient takes longer to metabolize and excrete medications due to decreased renal and hepatic function.
46. _____ T/F   Fecal occult blood testing (FOBT) is recommended every 5 years for persons age 65 or older.
47. _____ T/F   A woman who is at low risk for cervical cancer no longer needs screening after one negative Pap smear after the age of 65.
48. _____ T/F   Problems getting or staying asleep are normal for the aging patient.
49. _____ T/F   Health plans and Medicare cover the expense of life care communities.
50. _____ T/F   Most nursing homes have palliative care programs.

NCLEX-RN® REVIEW QUESTIONS

10-1. The student nurse has just completed a class on the expected age-related physical changes and assessment techniques of the geriatric patient. Which of the following statements made by the student nurse indicates the need for further instruction?
   1. "Oral assessments should include removal of dentures to check for cancerous lesion formation."
   2. "The exposed conjunctival tissue seen with ectropion might be mistaken for an eye infection."
   3. "The tympanic membrane must be readily visible in order to conduct an accurate hearing test."
   4. "Cheilosis causes the abdominal muscles to weaken and can result in prolonged constipation."

10-2. The nurse is educating an elderly patient regarding recommended immunizations and screening exams that may help optimize the patient's general health and well-being. Which of the following statements made by the patient indicates a clear understanding of these guidelines?
1. "I need a booster shot of the pneumococcal vaccine every 10 years."
2. "I should have my vision and hearing checked on a yearly basis."
3. "I can be proactive in my care by performing annual breast self-exams."
4. "I will require a colonoscopy every year since I'm over 65 years old."

10-3. The Beers criteria can aid the health care provider in making more appropriate prescribing choices for elderly patients. Based on this information, which of the following statements correctly identifies a medication that has potential adverse outcomes for an elderly patient?
1. Ketolorac may worsen asymptomatic pathologic gastrointestinal conditions.
2. Amiodarone causes increased risk of angioedema in African American clients.
3. Disopyramide can produce convulsions from by-products of its metabolism.
4. Ticlopidine is an ineffective antiemetic that may cause extrapyramidal symptoms.

10-4. An elderly patient and the patient's caregiver present to a health care provider's clinic with complaints of a recurrent perineal rash. During the client assessment the nurse notices multiple bruises in various stages of healing and an unkempt appearance. The nurse should:
1. Suspect possible physical abuse and neglect and notify the health care provider and Adult Protective Services immediately.
2. Suspect possible sexual abuse and financial exploitation and notify the health care provider and law enforcement immediately.
3. Suspect possible physical and psychological abuse and notify the health care provider and the local newspaper immediately.
4. Suspect possible self-neglect and financial exploitation and notify the health care provider and the office manager immediately.

10-5. Which of the following describe an intermediate care facility? Select all that apply.
1. Accepts bedbound clients.
2. Assists with gastrostomy tube feedings.
3. Performs complicated wound care.
4. Moderate help with ADLs.
5. May receive Medicare and Medicaid.
6. Can provide special diets.
7. Only available during the day.
8. Focus is fostering socialization.

10-6. An elderly patient is moving into a Green House Project facility. Which of the following instructions is most important for the nurse to include in the client's treatment plan?
1. "Remember to call the nurse's station when your intravenous fluids have finished infusing."
2. "Changes to your lunch menu choices need to be made before the aide brings your tray."
3. "Your costs may be higher for the opportunity to live in a home-like setting with other seniors."
4. "Since this option only focuses on fostering socialization it will not be covered by Medicare."

10-7. A student nurse is discussing the use of innovative technology for the aging client with a Geriatric Nurse Practitioner. Which of the following statements made by the student nurse would indicate the need for further instruction?
1. "Clients with complex medication regimens or problems with forgetfulness might benefit from some of the newer wireless medication administration devices and technologies."
2. "To alleviate communication challenges, many elderly patients are choosing the improved technology of text telephone (TTY) over older Voice over Internet Protocol."
3. "There are simple monitoring systems, such as those that offer video cameras and door sensors, that can have similar benefits to continuous body monitoring but that cost much less."
4. "Seniors involved in the Internet Health File project are able to submit and amend their health information online, while reserving the ability to share this data with family."

CHAPTER 11

GENETICS

OUTCOME-BASED LEARNING OBJECTIVES

11-1. Describe the role of genetics in health care and nursing.

11-2. Discuss events of cell division that result in chromosomal abnormalities.

11-3. Describe the organization of the human genome and the DNA sequence.

11-4. Describe the influence of the genome on differences among patients.

11-5. Identify patterns of inheritance and variables influencing interpretation of inheritance patterns.

11-6. Discuss the role of nurses in detection, management, and care of patients with genetic disorders.

11-7. Describe emerging genetic technologies and therapies.

CHAPTER OUTLINE

   I. Foundations for Genetics
      A. Cells and Chromosomes
      B. Cell Division
      C. The Human Genome
         1. DNA and RNA Structure
         2. Gene Expression
  II. Polymorphisms and Mutations
      A. Polymorphisms
      B. Mutations
         1. Types of Mutations
         2. Disease-Causing Mutations
      C. Genetic Variance and Phenotype
 III. Types of Genetic Disorders
      A. Single-Gene Inheritance Patterns
         1. Mendelian Inheritance
         2. Autosomal Recessive Inheritance
         3. Autosomal Dominant Inheritance
         4. X-Linked Inheritance
         5. Atypical Patterns of Inheritance

B. Chromosomal Genetic Disorders
  1. Nondisjunction
  2. Deletions
  3. Translocations
C. Complex or Multifactorial Disorders
  1. Alzheimer Disease
  2. Cancer
  3. Coronary Artery Disease
  4. Diabetes Mellitus
  5. Obesity
D. Hemoglobinopathies
  1. Sickle Cell Disease
  2. Thalassemias
IV. Nursing Role in Detection, Management, and Care of Individuals with Genetic Disorders
  A. Pedigrees
  B. Genetic Testing
    1. Prenatal Testing and Newborn Screening
    2. Carrier Genetic Tests
    3. Diagnostic Genetic Tests
    4. Predictive Genetic Tests
    5. Benefits and Limitations of Genetic Testing
  C. Ethical, Legal, and Social Issues of Genetic Information
V. Emerging Genetic Technologies and Therapies
  A. PCR and Microarrays
  B. Gene Therapy and Stem Cell Therapy
  C. Pharmacogenomics
           HEALTH PROMOTION
           NURSING MANAGEMENT
           ASSESSMENT
           NURSING DIAGNOSIS
           PLANNING
           INTERVENTIONS
           EVALUATION

KEY TERMS MATCHING EXERCISE 1

Write the letter of the correct definition in the space next to each term.

Term

_____ 1. aneuploidy

_____ 2. autosome

_____ 3. chromosome

_____ 4. diploid

_____ 5. deoxyribonucleic acid (DNA)

_____ 6. genotype

_____ 7. phenotype

_____ 8. messenger ribonucleic acid (mRNA)

_____ 9. trisomy

_____ 10. monosomy

Definition

a. Threadlike structures in the nucleus of a cell that contain the genes.

b. Having too many or too few chromosomes in a cell or any number other than 46 chromosomes in somatic or body cells or other than 23 chromosomes in germ cells or the eggs and sperm.

c. The genetic makeup of an individual that is not evident as outward or visible characteristics.

d. A single chromosome from any 1 of 22 pairs of the chromosomes that is not a sex chromosome (XX or XY).

e. A chromosomal constitution in which one member of the chromosome pair is missing.

f. The number of chromosomes in most cells except the gametes.

g. The state of having three representatives of a given chromosome instead of the usual pair.

h. RNA containing genetic information that is transcribed from DNA and translated to produce polypeptides.

i. Observable characteristics of an organism produced by the organism's genotype interacting with the environment.

j. A complex protein present in the chromosomes of the nuclei of cells that is the basis of heredity and the carrier of genetic information for all organisms except RNA viruses.

KEY TERMS MATCHING EXERCISE 2

Write the letter of the correct definition in the space next to each term.

Term

_____ 11. single-gene disorder
_____ 12. polymorphism
_____ 13. penetrance
_____ 14. point mutation
_____ 15. missense mutation
_____ 16. mosaicism
_____ 17. germ line cells
_____ 18. genomic imprinting
_____ 19. human genome
_____ 20. expressivity

Definition

a. Genetic inheritance process in which both maternal and paternal alleles are present, but one allele is expressed and the other remains silent.

b. The sex cell or gamete (egg or spermatozoan).

c. The complete DNA sequence that contains the entire genetic information for a human.

d. A mutation that changes a codon specific for one amino acid to specify a different amino acid.

e. A common variation in the sequence of DNA among individuals seen in more than 1% of the population.

f. The degree or amount of symptomology to which an individual with a genotype is affected.

g. A single nucleotide base-pair change in DNA.

h. A disorder due to one or a pair of mutant alleles at a single locus.

i. The proportion of individuals with a genotype known to cause a genetic disorder who have signs and symptoms of the disorder.

j. Nondisjunction of a pair of chromosomes that occurs in a mitotic division after formation of the zygote, and leads to an individual with at least two cell lines differing in genotype or karyotype, derived from a single zygote.

WORD SEARCH

First identify the word from its definition. Then find and circle it in the puzzle on page 59.

21. _____ One of the two chromosomes that determine an individual's genetic sex.

22. _____ A permanent structural change in DNA.

23. _____ The failure of two members of a chromosome pair to separate during meiosis or mitosis, resulting in daughter cells with either a missing or an extra chromosome.

24. _____ A set of photographed, banded chromosomes of an individual, arranged from largest to smallest.

25. _____ A diagram that shows the heredity of a particular trait or genetic disorder through many generations of a family.

26. _____ A specialization of genetics that involves the study of chromosomes.

27. _____ Disorder in which a trait is dominant if it is phenotypically expressed in heterozygotes due to one or more genes located on the X chromosome.

28. _____ Disorder in which a trait is recessive if the trait is expressive only in homozygotes due to one or more genes located on the X chromosome.

29. _____ The sequence of three nucleotides in mRNA that specifies a single amino acid.

30. _____ The portion of a gene that contains the code for producing the gene's protein.

31. _____ Reproductive cell, ovum or sperm, with the haploid chromosome number.

32. _____ A noncoding segment of DNA that is transcribed into nuclear RNA, but removed in the subsequent processing into mRNA.

33. _____ A single base substitution in DNA that results in a chain-termination codon.

34. _____ The number of chromosomes in an egg or sperm cell; it is half the diploid number.

35. _____ The application of genomic information or methods to pharmacogenetics problems.

36. _____ Fertilized egg.

37. _____ The field of genetics concerned with structural and functional studies of the genome.

38. _____ Having identical alleles at a given location.

39. _____ Having two different alleles for a given gene, one inherited from each parent.

40. _____ The tip or end of each chromosome arm.

41. _____ A normal allele of a gene or its normal phenotype.

42. _____ Variation in genotype that is associated with phenotype.

43. _____ The functional unit of heredity that occupies a certain position on a chromosome and is passed from parent to offspring.

44. _____ An alternate or variant form of a gene.

45. _____ All of the DNA in an organism or cell to include the 44 autosomes, 2 sex chromosomes, and the mitochondrial DNA.

X	N	O	N	S	E	N	S	E	M	U	T	A	T	I	O	N	D	W	Q	U
Z	P	A	I	E	O	H	I	R	P	L	Y	H	E	U	R	T	K	Y	U	P
W	L	S	R	X	L	I	N	K	E	D	R	E	C	E	S	S	I	V	E	H
I	H	C	E	C	L	H	S	A	D	C	S	T	A	E	Y	H	U	K	A	A
L	A	I	G	H	F	I	N	X	I	W	E	E	I	D	O	J	A	P	G	R
D	U	T	V	R	W	E	N	U	G	L	W	R	N	M	R	U	L	I	D	M
T	I	E	V	O	U	O	U	K	R	O	S	O	O	H	P	O	E	F	L	A
Y	X	N	P	M	S	Y	A	I	E	T	N	Z	R	T	I	A	R	N	T	C
P	O	E	A	O	U	R	Y	L	E	D	Y	Y	J	D	A	S	D	A	E	O
E	D	G	T	S	Y	F	J	C	I	G	D	G	E	N	O	M	I	C	S	G
S	C	O	D	O	N	Y	I	S	O	R	I	O	S	O	T	S	C	P	I	E
D	I	T	T	M	E	R	J	U	R	T	G	U	M	U	T	A	T	I	O	N
L	O	Y	K	E	A	U	S	A	O	H	A	S	L	I	E	A	S	A	E	O
U	P	C	Y	U	N	N	O	E	G	E	M	N	N	M	N	E	P	N	E	M
E	A	J	S	C	I	D	R	L	E	U	E	F	O	Y	M	A	J	O	T	I
O	G	E	T	O	G	Y	Z	E	N	A	T	N	X	U	I	K	N	R	R	C
R	H	I	A	C	K	F	O	L	O	C	E	R	E	M	O	L	E	T	U	S
U	O	H	J	K	L	F	A	L	A	G	P	L	H	U	A	D	S	N	S	H
N	E	E	C	N	A	I	R	A	V	C	I	T	E	N	E	G	A	I	G	L

TRUE OR FALSE?

46. _____ T/F Individuals who have autosomal dominant disorders have a 50–50 chance of passing the mutant allele and disorder to their children.

47. _____ T/F With autosomal recessive inheritance, the mutant gene is located on the X chromosome, rather than an autosome.

48. _____ T/F Genetic disorders are rarely caused by chromosome disorders.

49. _____   T/F   Gene therapy is the correction of a genetic mutation by the introduction of DNA into a cell as a treatment modality to improve the patient's health.

50. _____   T/F   The loss of the short arm of chromosome 5 or 5p– is the most common deletion in humans.

51. _____   T/F   The Human Genome Project (HGP) resulted in identification of the double-helix structure of DNA.

53. _____   T/F   When the mRNA uses DNA as a template to transfer the genetic information from the DNA to the protein-forming apparatus in the cytoplasm, the process of transcription is occurring.

55. _____   T/F   Transcription occurs when the mRNA is decoded to produce the protein that has been designated by the gene.

54. _____   T/F   Breaks in two or more chromosomes, with reattachments in new combinations, are known as translocations.

55. _____   T/F   Pharmacogenetics refers to the area of genetics that focuses on the variability of responses to medications due to genetic variation.

LABELING EXERCISE 1: THE CHROMOSOME

Place the term in the correct location.

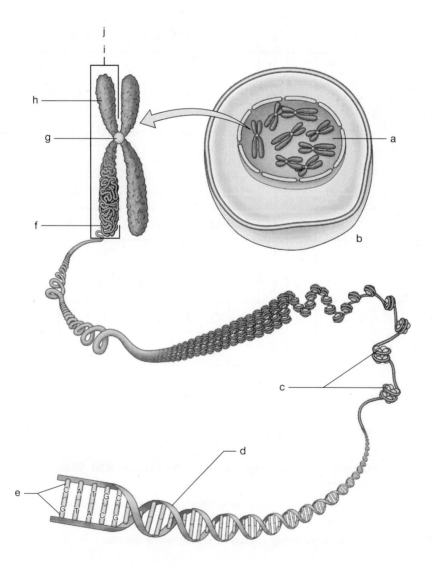

a. _____

b. _____

c. _____

d. _____

e. _____

f. _____

g. _____

h. _____

i. _____

j. _____

Base pairs
Cell
Centromere
Chromatid
Chromosome
DNA (double helix)
Histones
Nucleus
Telomere
Telomere

LABELING EXERCISE 2: STRUCTURE OF A CHROMOSOME

Place the term in the correct location.

a. _____

b. _____

c. _____

d. _____

e. _____

Centromere
P-arm
Q-arm
Sample-loci
Telomere

NCLEX-RN® REVIEW QUESTIONS

11-1. After attending a lecture on genetics, the nurse understands that:
1. Knowledge of the association between the client's karotype and phenotype is key for understanding the clinical presentation.
2. The recognition of inheritance patterns and disease clusters within a family is important in determining a genetic risk assessment.
3. A client who has tested positively for a gene associated with a specific disease will be predisposed to that particular disease.
4. Predictive genetic tests are performed on symptomatic individuals to identify and assist treatment of genetic disorders.

11-2. The nurse is providing genetic counseling for the parents of a child with Down syndrome. Which statement made by the parents would indicate the need for further teaching?
1. "One chromosome from each pair of chromosomes is inherited from each parent."
2. "A trisomy refers to an extra or a third chromosome instead of the normal pair."
3. "Down syndrome results from an abnormal individual gene within a chromosome."
4. "Heterozygous alleles are different forms of the same gene in a chromosome pair."

11-3. As it relates to the human genome, the nurse understands that:
1. The purines and pyrimidines bases in DNA always bind in a complementary nature to form a double helix.
2. Although each cell contains the entire genome, most cells only express about 10% of the genes within the genome.
3. Each nucleotide in RNA contains the deoxyribose sugar component instead of the ribose sugar component.
4. Adenine always binds to uracil and cytosine always binds to guanine to form the building blocks of DNA.

11-4. The nurse is educating other health care team members about single-gene disorders. Which statement made by one of the health care team members indicates a clear understanding of single-gene disorders?
1. "The fluorescence in situ hybridization method can detect the small chromosomal deletions that cause many single-gene disorders, like cri du chat syndrome."
2. "Because of its prevalence among the Amish community, thalassemia screenings are done routinely to identify carriers of this autosomal recessive disorder."
3. "Most of these Mendelian inheritance disorders are caused by a permanent structural change in the DNA of a gene on one or both chromosomes of a pair."
4. "Complex disorders are single-gene disorders that result in the adolescent client having an increased susceptibility to a disorder, illness, or disease process."

11-5. Which of the following statements made by the patient indicate the need for further teaching regarding inheritance patterns?
1. "The only important information to obtain on the pedigree is the age and ethnicity."
2. "Not everyone with the same genetic disorder will have the same signs and symptoms."
3. "A pedigree provides information that can help prevent some single-gene disorders."
4. "Some genetic disorders rely on gene location and whether it is dominant or recessive."

11-6. When planning care for the patient with an inherited susceptibility to cancer, the nurse recognizes it is essential to consider which factor in the patient's family history?
1. Monozygotic twin with a head injury as a child
2. LDL receptor disorder in one or both grandparents
3. Male smoker diagnosed with lung cancer at age 89
4. A recognizable Mendelian inheritance pattern

11-7. Therapies for a patient at risk for malignant hyperthermia can best be planned using the genetic technologies or therapies of:
1. Gene therapy and embryonic stem cell therapy.
2. Pharmacogenetics and cytochrome P450 enzymes.
3. Polymerase chain reaction and microarray analysis.
4. Serum cholinesterase sensitivity and karotype.

CHAPTER 12

STRESS AND ADAPTATION

OUTCOME-BASED LEARNING OBJECTIVES

12-1. Differentiate between internal and external stressors, and provide examples of each.

12-2. Differentiate between theories of stress as a response, a stimulus, and a transaction.

12-3. Explain the physiological components of the general adaptation syndrome (GAS).

12-4. Explain the relationship of oxidative stress to the disease process.

12-5. Explain ways in which a maladaptive response to stress can increase the risk of illness and cause disease.

12-6. Describe nursing assessment criteria for patients experiencing stress.

12-7. Explain the nursing management of patients with physiological stress.

CHAPTER OUTLINE

   I. Stress, Adaptation, and Coping
      A. Classifications of Stressors
         1. Internal and External Stressors
         2. Acute Versus Chronic Stressors
         3. Human Response Stressors: Developmental and Situational
      B. Coping
  II. Historical Development of Stress Theories
 III. Contemporary Interpretations of Stress
      A. Stress as a Response: The General Adaptation Syndrome
         1. Alarm Stage
            a. Physical Signs and Symptoms
         2. Resistance Stage
            a. Physical Signs and Symptoms
         3. Exhaustion Stage
            a. Physical Signs and Symptoms
         4. Interruption Theory as a Response Theory

B. Stress as a Stimulus
1. Hardiness and Sense of Coherence
C. Stress as a Transaction
1. Primary Appraisal
2. Secondary Appraisal
3. Cognitive Reappraisal
4. Hassles and Uplifts
5. Factors That Lead to Stressful Appraisals
6. Cognition, Emotions, and Stress
D. Theoretic Summary
IV. Stress Research
V. Nursing Theories Based on Systems and Adaptation
VI. Physiological Responses to Stress
A. Nervous System
1. Cerebral Cortex
2. Limbic System
3. Reticular Formation
4. Hypothalamus
a. Sympathetic Nervous System Response
B. Endocrine System
1. The Hypothalamic–Pituitary–Adrenal Response
C. Immune System
D. Physiological Responses of Acute Versus Chronic Stress
E. Stress at the Cellular Level
1. Cellular Injury
a. Hypoxia
b. Nutritional Imbalance
c. Physical Agents
d. Chemical Agents
e. Infectious Agents
2. Cellular Response to Injury
3. Cellular Healing
F. Oxidative Stress (OS)
1. Formation of ROS
VII. Negative (Maladaptive) Effects of Stress
A. Psychological Effects of Stress
B. Stress and Illness
1. Stress Circuit
a. Cardiovascular System
b. Cerebrovascular System
c. Gastrointestinal System
d. Immune System
i. Susceptibility to Infection
e. Endocrine System
i. Stress and Growth
f. Reproductive System
2. Cancer
3. Pain
4. Eating Problems
5. Sleep Disturbances
6. Memory, Concentration, and Learning
7. Other Disorders
a. Depression
C. Self-Medication with Unhealthy Lifestyles

KEY TERMS MATCHING EXERCISE 1

Write the letter of the correct definition in the space next to each term.

Term

_____ 1. stress perception

_____ 2. stress response

_____ 3. stressor

_____ 4. oxidative stress

_____ 5. internal stressor

_____ 6. acculturative stress

_____ 7. eustress

_____ 8. acute stress

_____ 9. chronic stress

_____ 10. developmental stressor

Definition

a. Recognition of a stressor by the brain.

b. Stress that occurs on a daily basis and is the result of an ongoing situation.

c. A stimulus that activates a stress response.

d. Stress associated with positive events.

e. Stressor that occurs during specific periods of the life span, for example, as a child, adolescent, young adult, middle adult, or older adult.

f. Activation of physiological fight-or-flight-or-fright systems within the body.

g. Stress to the cells caused by a decrease in the removal of or an overproduction of oxygen free radicals, common in physiological disorders of the critically ill; the imbalance between reactive oxygen species and the body's defense system.

h. A reaction to an immediate threat; commonly triggers the fight-or-flight response.

i. Job-related stress that is exacerbated by cultural differences such as diverse assumptions, values, and beliefs among the participants.

j. Stressor that originates within a person.

KEY TERMS MATCHING EXERCISE 2

Write the letter of the correct definition in the space next to each term.

Term

___d___ 11. atrophy
___f___ 12. cognitive reappraisal
___g___ 13. hypothalamic–pituitary–adrenal (HPA) axis
___i___ 14. homeostasis
___e___ 15. hyperplasia
___j___ 16. hypertrophy
___a___ 17. dysplasia
___h___ 18. metaplasia
___c___ 19. reticular activating system (RAS)
___b___ 20. reactive oxygen species (ROS)

Definition

a. Change in the appearance of cells after they have been subjected to chronic irritation.

b. Intermediary products, or species, that are produced in the metabolic production of energy; occur when oxygen is used to oxidize molecules and generate energy. A phenomenon that occurs during oxidative stress development and a major contributing factor in diseases in patients who are critically ill.

c. Network of neurons that is involved with arousal and consciousness.

d. A reduction in the size of a cell and tissues or in muscle size.

e. An increase in the number of new cells in an organ or tissue.

f. The process of allowing for changes in the person's evaluation of an event or a relabeling of the cognitive appraisal.

g. A feedback loop by which signals from the brain trigger the release of hormones needed to respond to stress.

h. Cell transformation in which a highly specialized cell changes into a less specialized cell.

i. The tendency toward stability within an organism; it is the first reaction toward that stability when a wound occurs.

j. An increase in the size of an organ caused by an increase in the size of the cells and tissues rather than the number of cells.

COMPLETE THE SENTENCE

Add the correct term(s) to complete each sentence.

21. The general adaptation syndrome is composed of three stages: _____, _____, and _____.

22. Noise, high temperatures, demanding deadlines at work, and the birth of a baby are all examples of _____.

23. Maintaining social status and standard of living, helping teenage children to become independent, and adjusting to aging parents are typical _____ stressors of the _____.

24. _____ stressors are unpredictable, may occur at any time of life, and may be positive or negative.

25. Recurrent responses to stress that are not effective and do not promote adaptation are known as _____

_____ _____.

26. Hardiness refers to a condition demonstrated by four qualities: _____, _____, _____, and

_____.

27. An individual with a strong _____ _____ _____ has an enduring tendency to see her or his life as ordered, predictable, and manageable.

28. According to transactional theories of stress, the first reaction to a stimulus, the _____ _____, is an evaluation of the significance of the transaction as it relates to the person's well-being.

29. The _____ _____ of a transaction between a person and his or her environment takes into account the available coping resources and options.

30. Daily experiences and conditions appraised as threatening or harmful and relevant are known as _____,

while daily experiences appraised as positive are known as _____.

TRUE OR FALSE?

31. ___F___ T/F Acute stressors often become a routine part of daily life and consequently may go unrecognized.
32. ___T___ T/F Adaptation to situational stressors can depend upon the developmental stage of the individual experiencing the stress.
33. ___F___ T/F Coping occurs whether an individual is experiencing stress from internal and external demands that exceed resources or not.
34. ___F___ T/F Stressful situations are considered unwanted or undesirable by the individual only when resources to cope are lacking.
35. ___T___ T/F Inflammation serves a protective function by neutralizing, controlling, or eliminating the offending agent to prepare the injured site for repair.
36. ___T___ T/F Depression and anxiety are associated with the inability to adapt to stress.
37. ___F___ T/F The gastrointestinal and cardiovascular systems are equally vulnerable to stress.
38. ___T___ T/F Stress from an antagonistic work relationship may put an individual at a greater risk to develop an infection than stress from a major change in living conditions.
39. ___F___ T/F Living in a rural area increases the likelihood of being stressed.
40. ___T___ T/F Following a stressful event, an elderly person has more difficulty achieving a relaxed state than a younger person.

LABELING EXERCISE: DISORDERS CAUSED OR AGGRAVATED BY STRESS

Place the term in the correct location.

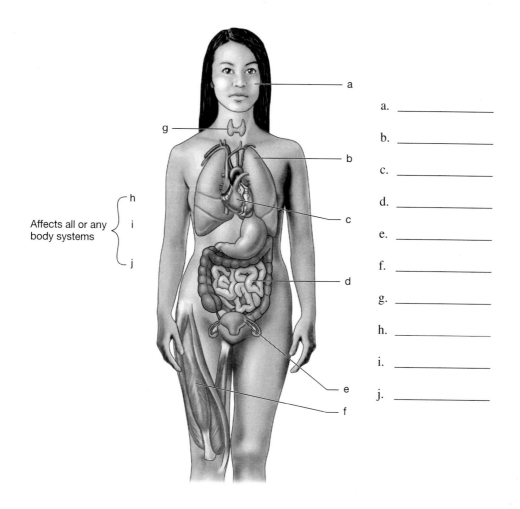

a. _____

b. _____

c. _____

d. _____

e. _____

f. _____

g. _____

h. _____

i. _____

j. _____

Accident proneness
Cancer
Cardiovascular disorders: coronary artery disease, essential hypertension, congestive heart failure
Decreased immune response
Gastrointestinal disorders: constipation, diarrhea, duodenal ulcer, anorexia nervosa, obesity, ulcerative colitis
Menstrual irregularities
Metabolic disorders: hyperthyroidism, hypothyroidism, diabetes
Musculoskeletal disorders: rheumatoid arthritis, low back pain, migraine headache, muscle tension
Respiratory disorders: asthma, hay fever, tuberculosis
Skin disorders: eczema, pruritus, urticaria, psoriasis

NCLEX-RN® REVIEW QUESTIONS

12-1. The nurse is concerned that a patient is experiencing several internal stressors. Which of the following would be considered an internal source of stress?
1. Noisy work environment
2. High caffeine intake each day
3. Home flooded during the recent heavy rains
4. Broken garage door opener

12-2. A patient tells the nurse that even though coming to the hospital was stressful, it turned out to be necessary. The nurse realizes this patient is demonstrating:
1. Primary appraisal.
2. Cognitive reappraisal.
3. Secondary appraisal.
4. Sense of coherence

12-3. A patient is receiving blood and intravenous medication in the intensive care unit. This patient is most likely being treated for which phase of the general adaptation syndrome?
1. Shock phase
2. Counter shock phase
3. Resistance phase
4. Exhaustion phase

12-4. A patient with a cardiac rhythm disturbance is arguing with her husband in the hospital room. Which of the following should the nurse do?
1. Encourage the patient to complete the conversation.
2. Suggest the conversation end.
3. Interrupt the conversation and find out what the argument is about.
4. Call Security to have the husband escorted out of the hospital.

12-5. A patient is being treated for malnutrition. The nurse realizes the body organ responsible for helping remove excessive free radicals is:
1. The spleen.
2. The liver.
3. The colon.
4. The kidney.

12-6. During an assessment, a patient tells the nurse of increasing forgetfulness, the inability to make decisions, and the daily desire to call off from work. A nursing diagnosis appropriate for these findings would be:
1. Anxiety.
2. Ineffective individual coping.
3. Caregiver role strain.
4. Decisional conflict.

12-7. A patient tells the nurse that she has no energy after working all day and having to take care of the house and her family. The nurse realizes that this patient would benefit from which of the following interventions to aid in stress reduction?
1. Mild to moderate physical activity
2. A support group
3. Increase ingestion of caffeinated drinks
4. Anger management techniques

CHAPTER 13

PSYCHOSOCIAL ISSUES IN NURSING

OUTCOME-BASED LEARNING OBJECTIVES

13-1. Discuss conceptual foundations that inform psychosocial nursing.

13-2. Define the characteristics of a therapeutic nurse–patient relationship.

13-3. Utilize culturally competent principles of therapeutic communication for the care of patients and significant others.

13-4. Apply the principles of teaching and learning to the care of patients and significant others.

13-5. Identify the dimensions of crisis and the nursing actions that promote adaptive coping.

13-6. Discuss the impact of illness and hospitalization on patients and significant others.

13-7. Compare and contrast the psychodynamics of anxiety, frustration, anger, depression, and loss and grief.

13-8. Utilize the nursing process for patients experiencing loss and grief, anxiety, depression, and anger.

EXPLORE mynursingkit™

PEARSON

MyNursingKit is your one stop for online chapter review materials and resources. Prepare for success with additional NCLEX®-style practice questions, interactive assignments and activities, web links, animations and videos, and more!

Register your access code from the front of your book at **www.mynursingkit.com**

CHAPTER OUTLINE

I. Theoretical Foundations
   A. Psychoanalytical Perspective
   B. Developmental Perspective
   C. Humanistic Perspective
   D. Cognitive Development
   E. Cognitive Theory
   F. Family Systems
   G. The Biopsychosocial Model
II. The Therapeutic Nurse–Patient Relationship
   A. Introductory (Orientation) Phase
   B. Working Phase
   C. Termination
   D. Self-Awareness in the Nurse–Patient Relationship
   E. Caring

KEY TERMS MATCHING EXERCISE 1

Write the letter of the correct definition in the space next to each term.

Term

_____ 1. ego
_____ 2. accommodation
_____ 3. affective learning
_____ 4. conscious
_____ 5. locus of control
_____ 6. ego defense mechanisms
_____ 7. psychomotor learning
_____ 8. unconscious
_____ 9. subconscious
_____ 10. superego

Definition

a. An extension of the ego that represents an individual's early moral training and ideal values imparted by societal norms.

b. The perception a person has about how much control he or she exerts over the events that happen in his or her life.

c. Involves changes in attitudes, values, and feelings.

d. Learning that occurs when a physical skill has been acquired.

e. Process a child goes through to modify existing schema because the incorporation of new knowledge does not fit into existing schema.

f. Mediates the drives of the id with a dose of reality.

g. Utilized to alleviate anxiety by denying, distorting, and misinterpreting reality

h. A mental state that encompasses all things that are easily remembered.

i. A mental state that encompasses all of those things that cannot be remembered or brought to conscious thought.

j. A mental state that encompasses things that have been forgotten but can easily be brought to consciousness.

KEY TERMS MATCHING EXERCISE 2

Write the letter of the correct definition in the space next to each term.

Term

_____ 11. assimilation
_____ 12. basic human needs
_____ 13. crisis
_____ 14. growth needs
_____ 15. holism
_____ 16. pleasure principle
_____ 17. sick role
_____ 18. id
_____ 19. schema
_____ 20. teaching

Definition

a. As defined by Abraham Maslow, needs on the first four rungs of Maslow's hierarchy.

b. The top levels of Maslow's hierarchy associated with psychological needs.

c. A set of expectations that people who are ill must meet and which society, including caregivers, expects of them.

d. Coordinated patterns of recurring actions that are created for the purpose of organizing and interpreting information.

e. Any deliberate act that involves the planning, implementation, and evaluation of instructional strategies that meet expected learner outcomes.

f. The occurrence of an event or series of events that creates a situation that is perceived as threatening.

g. The principle of tension reduction.

h. Incorporation of new concepts into existing schemas.

i. Represents all of a person's biological and psychological drives.

j. An idea based on the premise that the whole is more than the sum of its parts.

THERAPEUTIC OR NONTHERAPEUTIC?

Identify each response to the patient as either therapeutic or nontherapeutic by circling the correct word. After those that are nontherapeutic, provide an alternative that would be more appropriate to establishing a therapeutic relationship. Leave the blank line empty if you identify a response as therapeutic.

21. "I wouldn't worry about that."   *therapeutic   nontherapeutic*

_____

22. "I wouldn't do it like that."   *therapeutic   nontherapeutic*

_____

23. "Please help me understand that situation in more detail."   *therapeutic   nontherapeutic*

_____

24. "Hang in there!"   *therapeutic   nontherapeutic*

_____

25. "Most people are unhappy sometimes."   *therapeutic   nontherapeutic*

_____

26. "Please help me understand what you were feeling."   *therapeutic   nontherapeutic*

_____

27. "What seemed to lead up to this?"   *therapeutic   nontherapeutic*

_____

28. "How come you were drinking and driving?"   *therapeutic   nontherapeutic*

_____

29. "I'm sure your doctor has your best interests at heart."   *therapeutic   nontherapeutic*

_____

30. "Why did you feel that way?"   *therapeutic   nontherapeutic*

_____

SHORT ANSWER QUESTIONS

31. Explain the difference between therapeutic communication and therapeutic alliance.

_____

_____

_____

32. Explain the difference between an internal locus of control and an external locus of control.

_____

_____

_____

33. Describe the five stages of Kubler-Ross's stages of grief and mourning.

_____

_____

_____

_____

_____

34. What interventions are appropriate to help a patient with depression?

_____

_____

_____

_____

_____

_____

_____

_____

35. What are the three phases of a nurse–patient relationship conceptualized by Peplau?

_____

_____

_____

LABELING EXERCISE: MASLOW'S HIERARCHY OF NEEDS

Place the term in the correct location.

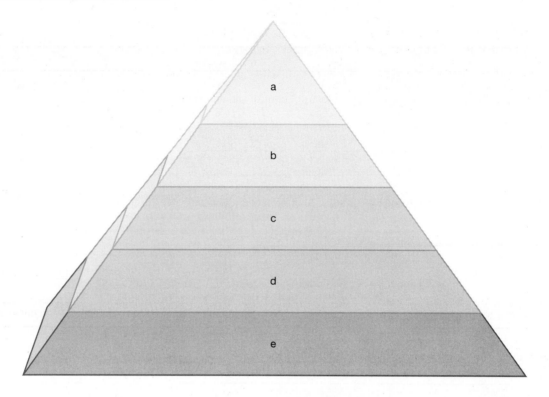

a. _____   Love and belonging
                                     Physiological needs
b. _____   Safety and security
                                     Self-actualization
c. _____   Self-esteem

d. _____

e. _____

NCLEX-RN® REVIEW QUESTIONS

13-1. A patient is diagnosed with a cognitive triad. This means the patient has:
    1. A positive schema.
    2. Embraced holism.
    3. Mastered assimilation.
    4. A negative schema.

13-2. The nurse is establishing a trusting relationship with a patient. The nurse is working within which phase of the nurse–patient relationship?
    1. Introductory
    2. Working
    3. Termination
    4. Both working and termination

13-3. The nurse is having difficulty communicating with a foreign-born patient. Which of the following should be done to support a culturally sensitive therapeutic relationship?
   1. Ask another nurse to try to understand the patient.
   2. Call the doctor.
   3. Ignore the patient's attempts to communicate and obtain objective data.
   4. Obtain an interpreter to help establish a communication method with the patient.

13-4. The nurse is assigned several patients all needing instruction on physical activity after experiencing a myocardial infarction. Which of the following approaches could the nurse use to maximize time while successfully instructing the patients?
   1. Teach each patient individually.
   2. Teach one patient and have that patient teach another.
   3. Conduct a group teaching session with all of the patients together.
   4. Teach one family member of each patient and then the family member can teach the patient.

13-5. A patient is having a postsurgical visit for an emergency colon resection. Which of the following should the nurse do to support this patient's needs?
   1. Assess vital signs.
   2. Ask the patient how he feels about having emergency surgery.
   3. Ask the patient to list his needs and concerns.
   4. Ask how the patient is working through everything since the surgery and if there are any problems that still need to be addressed.

13-6. A patient is not actively engaged in his health care treatment plan. Which of the following can the nurse do to increase this patient's autonomy and empowerment?
   1. Tell the patient that he doesn't have to make any decision.
   2. State that the patient doesn't have to worry about anything.
   3. Tell the patient that all he has to do is rest.
   4. Explain the treatment plan, including any plans for procedures.

13-7. A patient says, "I don't know where I am or what's going on and no one is helping me!" The nurse realizes this patient is demonstrating:
   1. Depression.
   2. Anger.
   3. Anxiety.
   4. Loss.

13-8. A patient, scheduled to begin chemotherapy for cancer, is demonstrating signs of panic. Which of the following should the nurse do?
   1. Leave the patient and go and phone the physician.
   2. Ask the patient, "What's wrong?"
   3. Begin the chemotherapy as soon as possible.
   4. Provide a rest period after the attack.

CHAPTER 14

NUTRITION

OUTCOME-BASED LEARNING OBJECTIVES

14-1. Explain components of a comprehensive nutrition assessment as part of the nursing care process.

14-2. Apply the nutritional component of national standards for disease prevention and treatment.

14-3. Discuss the metabolic effects of physiological stress and the potential impact on nutrition status.

14-4. Outline the nutrition therapy guidelines for patients with physiological stress, such as postoperative wound healing and burn injury.

14-5. Differentiate among the principles of medical nutrition therapy in treating general medical conditions.

14-6. Explain the indications and nursing interventions associated with enteral and parenteral nutrition support.

14-7. Defend the important role of nursing care in successful medical nutrition therapy.

CHAPTER OUTLINE

I. Nutrition Assessment
   A. Nutrition Assessment Parameters
      1. Physical Assessment
      2. Laboratory Measurements
      3. Nutrition History
   B. Nutrition Assessment Tools
      1. REAP and WAVE
      2. Mini Nutrition Assessment and Subjective Global Assessment
II. Special Considerations Affecting Nutrition Care
   A. Malnutrition
   B. Physiological Stress
III. Health Promotion
IV. Medical Nutrition Therapy for Medical–Surgical Patients
   A. Weight Management
      1. Overweight and Obesity
      2. Disordered Eating

    M. Cancer
    N. Chronic Obstructive Pulmonary Disease and Mechanical Ventilation
    O. Nutrition and Wound Healing
        1. Pressure Ulcers
    P. Burns
    Q. Nutrition and the Surgical Patient
        1. Bariatric Surgery for Morbid Obesity
        2. Transplant Surgery
        3. Trauma
  V. Nutrition Support
    A. Enteral Nutrition
        1. Types of Enteral Formulas
        2. Routes of Delivery
        3. Administration of Feedings
    B. Parenteral Nutrition
        1. Formula Composition
 VI. Research

KEY TERMS MATCHING EXERCISE 1

Write the letter of the correct definition in the space next to each term.

Term

_h_ 1. aerophagia
_e_ 2. anthropometric measurements
_b_ 3. binge-eating disorder (BED)
_i_ 4. cachexia
_j_ 5. celiac sprue
_f_ 6. dysphagia
_g_ 7. hypercatabolism
_a_ 8. hypermetabolism
_d_ 9. physiological stress
_c_ 10. respiratory quotient (RQ)

Definition

a. Metabolic state in which resting energy expenditure is elevated.

b. Disorder characterized by the same type of binge eating as bulimia nervosa, but without the compensatory purging.

c. Ratio between carbon dioxide produced and oxygen consumed per molecule of fat, carbohydrate, and protein.

d. Metabolic conditions characterized by hypermetabolism and hypercatabolism.

e. Any physical measurement of the body.

f. Difficulty swallowing.

g. Metabolic state in which degradation of protein stores is elevated.

h. The swallowing of air; may lead to intestinal bloating.

i. Wasting of skeletal muscle and adipose.

j. A lifelong condition affecting the small intestine in which the villi morphology is damaged because of the presence of gluten in the diet.

KEY TERMS MATCHING EXERCISE 2

Write the letter of the correct definition in the space next to each term.

Term

_G_ 11. enteral nutrition

_i_ 12. parenteral nutrition

_a_ 13. peripheral parenteral nutrition (PPN)

_c_ 14. hypertonic formula

_j_ 15. isotonic formula

_e_ 16. total parenteral nutrition (TPN)

_d_ 17. refeeding syndrome

_b_ 18. indirect calorimetry

_f_ 19. lipodystrophy

_h_ 20. steatorrhea

Definition

a. Provision of nutrition intravenously through a peripheral vein.

b. The measurement of energy expenditure by measuring oxygen intake and carbon dioxide output.

c. An enteral or parenteral nutrition formula with an osmolality, or concentration, that is greater than that of the body's plasma.

d. Syndrome consisting of metabolic disturbances that arise from reinstitution of nutrition to patients who are severely malnourished.

e. Provision of nutrition intravenously via a central vein.

f. Abnormal deposition of adipose on the body.

g. Use of the gastrointestinal tract for feeding.

h. Feces that have a high fat content. The stool is typically foul-smelling, greasy, and floats.

i. Provision of nutrients and energy by means of intravenous access, without use of the gastrointestinal tract.

j. An enteral or parenteral nutrition formula with an osmolality, or concentration, that is approximately equal that of the body's plasma.

COMPLETE THE SENTENCE

21. An unplanned weight loss of _____ in 1 month or _____ in 6 months is clinically significant and warrants attention.

22. According to the food pyramid, an individual should consume _____ servings of grains, _____ servings of fruit, _____ servings of vegetables, _____ servings of protein, and _____ servings of dairy daily.

23. A body mass index of _____ is considered normal, _____ is considered overweight, and _____ or more is considered obese.

24. Clinical eating disorders include _____, _____, and _____, which includes binge-eating disorder and disordered eating not meeting the strict criteria for anorexia or bulimia.

25. The NIH's Dietary Approaches to Stopping Hypertension (DASH) diet emphasizes _____, _____, _____, and _____ while also reducing _____ and _____ levels.

26. An individual meets the criteria for metabolic syndrome when three out of five cardiovascular risk factors are present. The five risk factors are (1) _____, (2) _____, (3) _____, (4) _____, and (5) _____.

27. A(n) _____ diet is prescribed as medical nutrition therapy for cardiac failure.

28. Diabetic patients are urged to include carbohydrates in the form of _____, _____, _____, and _____.

29. People with diabetes must be aware of the potential _____ and _____ effects of alcohol and consume it with food.

30. The diet of a patient with lactose intolerance should be assessed for adequate _____ and _____, especially for those who have broadly eliminated dairy foods from their diets.

TRUE OR FALSE?

31. _____ T/F Undernutrition is a form of malnutrition in which the needed nutrients are being ingested but at an inadequate level to support health.

32. _____ T/F Malnutrition and protein-calorie malnutrition are synonymous.

33. _____ T/F Consuming an excess of calories and fat results in overnutrition.

34. _____ T/F Taking multiple medications puts an individual at a lesser risk of poor health from inadequate nutrition.

35. _____ T/F Asking a patient "What did you have for breakfast?" is the appropriate start to a 24-hour nutrition history.

36. _____ T/F Examining the oral cavity of an elderly patient with dentures is unnecessary.

37. _____ T/F A hypermetabolic response because of physiological stress can lead to rapid protein catabolism even when it seems energy and protein intake are sufficient.

38. _____ T/F Unintentional weight loss and signs of malnutrition among the elderly should be considered a normal part of the aging process and usually require no further consideration.

39. _____ T/F Both hospitals and long-term care institutions are required by accrediting agencies to have a diet manual specific to their organization available in each medical unit that describes all therapeutic diets and texture-modified diets offered.

40. _____ T/F Patients receiving enteral nutrition support have a greater risk of bacterial translocation and sepsis compared to those on parenteral support.

THERAPEUTIC LIFESTYLE CHANGES FOR CARDIOVASCULAR DISEASE

Add the missing recommendations for lifestyle changes for an individual with cardiovascular disease.

Lifestyle Component	Recommendation
Diet	Saturated fat:
	Trans fatty acids:
	Monounsaturated fat:
	Polyunsaturated fat:
	Total fat:
	Cholesterol:
	Fiber:
	Carbohydrate:
	Protein:
Weight Management	
Physical Activity	

NCLEX-RN® REVIEW QUESTIONS

14-1. A patient's twenty-four-hour nutrition diary indicates a lack of dairy products. To best determine if the patient has a poor intake of calcium, the nurse should do the following:
1. Perform a food frequency questionnaire.
2. Determine if the patient is a vegetarian.
3. Offer the patient dairy products frequently.
4. Check the patient's albumin level.

14-2. The nurse is instructing a patient on the National Guidelines for nutrition to reduce the risk of disease. Which of the following should be included in these instructions?
1. Limit milk products.
2. Limit food choices.
3. Prepare foods with little salt.
4. Select foods according to preference and not caloric content.

14-3. When caring for a client with acute pancreatitis the nurse recognizes the following physiologic response impacts the client's nutritional needs.
1. In severe states the catabolic rate can increase to 80%.
2. The pancreas is no longer able to produce digestive enzymes.
3. All enteral feedings will stimulate exocrine function and increase metabolism.
4. Metabolism is reduced until the inflammation has subsided.

14-4. The nurse has identified a goal to maintain positive nitrogen balance in a patient with major burns. Which of the following assessment findings would be of most concern?
1. Patient demonstrates maintenance of admission weight.
2. Patient demonstrates a 10% loss of body weight from baseline.
3. Patient requires nocturnal feedings to maintain weight.
4. Patient refuses to eat between-meal nutritional supplements.

14-5. The nurse is reviewing a patient's history and identifies a need to instruct the patient on therapeutic lifestyle changes for cardiovascular disease, based on collection of which data?
1. Cholesterol intake is less than 100 mg/day.
2. Patient consumes a high-protein diet.
3. Patient eats 5–6 servings of high-fiber foods daily.
4. Intake of saturated fat is avoided totally.

14-6. Which of the following interventions should the nurse include in the plan of care of a client receiving total parenteral nutrition (TPN)?
1. Monitor for signs of hypoglycemia.
2. Check electrolytes levels daily.
3. Withhold all oral feedings.
4. Do not exceed infusion rate of 50 mL/hour.

14-7. The nurse observes a client with COPD has had a steady weight loss of 20 pounds over the past 6 months. In order to optimize medical nutrition therapy, the nurse makes the following recommendation.
1. Two-thirds of your dietary calories should come from protein.
2. Always try to consume more than the recommended amount of calories.
3. Eat most of your nutrient-dense foods early in the day.
4. Consume as many calories as possible, regardless of the nutrient content.

CHAPTER 15

PAIN ASSESSMENT AND MANAGEMENT

OUTCOME-BASED LEARNING OBJECTIVES

15-1. Recognize pain as a distinct and frequently encountered human problem in the health care field.

15-2. Compare and contrast the ethical and legal issues related to pain and pain management.

15-3. Distinguish the sensory, cognitive, affective, and behavioral components of pain.

15-4. Apply common pain assessment tools and strategies to elicit details of the multidimensional pain experience.

15-5. Differentiate between acute, chronic, and cancer-related pain.

15-6. Describe and give examples of basic pharmacodynamic and pharmacokinetic properties of commonly used pharmacologic therapies, including the role of balanced analgesia in pain management.

15-7. Examine the usefulness of nonmedication interventions to alleviate pain in clinical practice.

15-8. Apply nursing pain management techniques in relation to established theories and current research.

15-9. Specify the major patient-related barriers to adequate pain management and demonstrate effective collaboration as a nurse-member of a multidisciplinary team in the management of pain.

CHAPTER OUTLINE

I. Epidemiology
II. Definitions of Pain
   A. Pain Descriptors
   B. Evolution of Pain Theories
III. Pain as a Multidimensional Phenomenon
   A. Physiological Dimension
      1. Physiological and Pathological Consequences of Unrelieved Pain
   B. Sensory Dimension
   C. Affective Dimension

KEY TERMS MATCHING EXERCISE 1

Write the letter of the correct definition in the space next to each term.

Term

_____ 1. absorption
_____ 2. adjuvant medications
_____ 3. biotransformation
_____ 4. distribution
_____ 5. elimination
_____ 6. metabolism
_____ 7. pattern theory
_____ 8. specificity theory
_____ 9. neuromatrix theory
_____ 10. hepatic first-pass metabolism

Definition

a. A group of theories that asserts that pain receptors share nerve pathways with other sensory pathways and that the intensity of the stimulus determines the frequency of firing of the receptor.

b. Medications that are not primarily indicated for treatment of pain, but are used to augment pain relief medications.

c. All energy and material transformations that occur within a living cell.

d. The process of excretion from the body that is generally accomplished in the renal system.

e. Theory asserting that pain is directly related to the degree of injury.

f. The process of moving a medication into the bloodstream and the extracellular and intracellular compartments, as well as in the compartment that is the site of absorption.

g. Refers to the reduction of a medication's effect due to partial metabolism in the liver prior to distribution to the ultimate site of action.

h. The process of changing a medication's structure in preparation for elimination.

i. The process by which a medication leaves the site of administration to cross membranes as it journeys to the site of action.

j. Addresses the brain's role in pain perception as well as other multiple determinants.

KEY TERMS MATCHING EXERCISE 2

Write the letter of the correct definition in the space next to each term.

Term

_____ 11. Brief Pain Inventory (BPI)

_____ 12. McGill Pain Questionnaire (MPQ)

_____ 13. simple verbal descriptive scale (SVDS)

_____ 14. numeric rating scale (NRS)

_____ 15. visual analog scale (VAS)

_____ 16. endorphins

_____ 17. enkephalins

_____ 18. noxious stimuli

_____ 19. transduction

_____ 20. nociception

Definition

a. Scale that uses a horizontal line marked with the numbers 0 to 10 from left to right, but also includes interval descriptors of "no pain," "mild," "discomforting," "distressing," "horrible," or "excruciating pain."

b. Tissue damage that activates sensory neurons to send a pain message to the central nervous system, resulting in a nociceptive pain response.

c. The transmission of pain from the periphery to the central nervous system.

d. The process by which tissue damage (noxious stimuli) activates sensory neurons to send a pain message to the central nervous system, resulting in a nociceptive pain response; literally means "pain sense."

e. Questionnaire that asks multiple questions regarding pain and its impact on patient function and addresses the multidimensionality of the pain experience.

f. Does not have numeric intervals; rather it uses "no pain" and "pain as bad as it can possibly be" as descriptors at either end of a horizontal line measuring 10 cm in length.

g. A horizontal line marked with the numbers 0 to 10 from left to right with three interval descriptors of pain located along the scale: "no pain," "moderate pain," and "worst pain."

h. Assesses pain intensity, character, and location of pain using a body diagram, and also the duration of the pain experience.

i. Pentapeptides produced in the brain that act as an opiate.

j. Endogenous, morphine-like substances that reduce or inhibit pain perception in the descending pathways.

DIMENSIONS OF PAIN

For each description of pain, name the most appropriate dimension:

Physiological sensory
Affective
Cognitive
Behavioral

21. _____ Neuropathic pain resulting from injury

22. _____ Acceptance of pain

23. _____ Intensity of pain

24. _____ Locus of control

25. _____ Situational, developmental, or learned behaviors commonly associated with the expression of pain, both verbal and nonverbal

26. _____ Localized sharp pain conducted by A-delta fibers

27. _____ Temporal patterns of pain

28. _____ Dull, aching pain conducted by C-fibers

29. _____ Emotions related to pain

30. _____ Pain resulting from dysfunction in peripheral nervous system

TYPES OF PAIN

For each description of pain, name the appropriate type:

31. _____ Transitory exacerbation of pain that occurs on a background of otherwise stable pain in a patient receiving chronic opioid therapy.

32. _____ Pain that is a result of injury or dysfunction in the peripheral nervous system and can progress to the CNS, altering its function and resulting in a chronic painful disease.

33. _____ Pain felt in the amputated part of the body as a result of the brain misinterpreting the nerve signals as coming from the site of the amputation.

34. _____ Pain of relatively short duration that coincides with injury, surgery, or illness.

35. _____ Goals for managing this pain are (1) reducing the sympathetic stress response following surgeries or treatments; (2) safely optimizing comfort through appropriate use of analgesic treatments and complementary or alternative strategies; (3) facilitating participation in recovery and rehabilitation activities; (4) increasing active participation in ADLs, work, and relationships; and (5) preserving a sense of purpose despite a potentially lethal diagnosis.

36. _____ Pain associated with malignancy that is acute and chronic in nature.

37. _____ Pain associated with minor tissue damage that is brief and then resolves completely such as the pain associated with a needlestick for phlebotomy or an intramuscular injection.

38. _____ Pain episodes that are relatively short in duration, then completely resolve, leaving the patient pain free for a period of time, and then reoccur.

39. _____ Pain resulting from the process of nociception.

40. _____ Persistent pain lasting for more than 3 to 6 months that is associated with low or absent levels of pathology that can be linked to injury, surgery, or illness.

TRUE OR FALSE?

41. _____ T/F Agonists are opioids such morphine, codeine, meperidine, dihydromorphinone, and methadone that bind to the mu, kappa, and delta receptors of the cell.

42. _____ T/F The effects of agonist and agonist-antagonist drugs are irreversible and must be endured until the drug wears off.

43. _____ T/F Pruritus usually occurs when dosages of opioids exceed the patient's requirements for pain relief.

44. _____ T/F Unrelieved pain can impair healing.

45. _____ T/F Administering opioids for any reasons increases the patient's risk of addiction.

46. _____ T/F Pain relief is the primary reason for prescribing an adjuvant medication.

47. _____ T/F Intravenous (IV) administration of medications is usually preferred over other delivery methods.

48. _____ T/F Medications that are less lipid soluble, such as morphine, are not recommended for the oral transmucosal route.

49. _____ T/F When pain is consistently present, analgesic medications should be administered continuously.

50. _____ T/F It is the nurse's responsibility to assess the ongoing effects and intensity of pain, administer medications and nonmedication treatments, communicate changes in the patient's condition to the other members of the team, and advocate for change.

NCLEX-RN® REVIEW QUESTIONS

15-1. The nurse realizes that pain:
1. Is a minor health problem in this country with abounding knowledge and resources for treatment and pain relief.
2. May be associated with misconceptions regarding treatment, making pain relief more difficult for clients.
3. Has not been related as a contributor to delayed wound healing, pneumonia, or other postoperative complications.
4. Is usually covered fully by health coverage benefits, making finding and utilizing pain care specialists easier.

15-2. After attending a seminar on the legal and ethical issues related to pain, the nurse realizes:
1. Patients are becoming more educated health care consumers who have high expectations about their pain management.
2. The pain management standards set in place by the Joint Commission require that all patients receive opioid medications.
3. The fundamental responsibility of nurses to cure patient addiction sometimes requires nurses to withhold pain medications.
4. Patients are treated for chronic pain according to the nurse's assessment findings and goals, not client verbal reports.

15-3. A patient with spinal stenosis pain appears calm and relaxed; however, the patient begins to demonstrate signs of increasing pain when the nurse is present. This patient is exhibiting which component of pain?
1. Cognitive
2. Behavioral
3. Affective
4. Sensory

15-4. To best evaluate the patient's multidimensional pain experience, the nurse should expect to use which of the following assessment tools?
1. The numeric rating scale
2. The visual analog scale
3. The behavioral assessment
4. The patient interview

15-5. Which of the following statements made by a patient reflects an understanding of cancer-related pain?
1. "My pain is caused by the progression of a malignancy."
2. "My pain will not last long, but will return after a while."
3. "This pain I am having corresponds to a recent injury."
4. "This pain should be fleeting and go away, not to return."

15-6. The nurse prepares to implement the patient's prescribed pain regimen. It is imperative that the nurse be familiar with which of the following fundamentals related to pain management?
   1. If questions about the medication prescription arise, the pharmacy must immediately be contacted for clarification of the order.
   2. Whenever possible, a balance of opioid antagonist, nonopioid, nonsteroidal anti-inflammatory, and adjuvant medications is optimal.
   3. The absorption, distribution, metabolism, and elimination of each prescribed medication should be considered prior to administration.
   4. Administration of intramuscular injections of analgesic medication allows for rapid onset of effect and reliable absorption rates.

15-7. Which patient statement best exemplifies a clear comprehension of integrating nonpharmacologic therapies into the pain management regimen?
   1. "Most people who choose to start nonmedication strategies can stop taking their prescribed pain medicines."
   2. "The help and support of my friends and family has no bearing on how successfully my pain therapies will work."
   3. "Since the physical therapy I received in the hospital was helpful in reducing my pain, I should continue it at home."
   4. "The music I listen to at home often relaxes me, but I am afraid to tell my doctor because of the ridicule I might face."

15-8. Which of the following statements is consistent with an effective nursing plan of pain management?
   1. Data obtained from both the pain and physical assessments are used in the planning of nursing interventions.
   2. The education and emotional support for patients and their families affected by chronic pain should be identical.
   3. A client might feel a loss of control when allowed choices within his or her pain management regimen.
   4. Equianalgesic properties are important in determining the best medication for nociceptive versus neuropathic pain.

15-9. Which of the following accurately reflects the nurse's role within a collaborative care approach to pain management?
   1. Assisting the patient in meeting immediate financial needs, such as obtaining specialty pain management care.
   2. Providing counseling regarding the long-term needs of the client who is unable to be gainfully employed.
   3. Offering expert help in the management of technical pain treatment modalities, such as epidural opioid infusions.
   4. Coordinating care within the multidisciplinary team while continually assessing and treating the patient's pain.

CHAPTER 16

SUBSTANCE ABUSE

OUTCOME-BASED LEARNING OBJECTIVES

16-1. Explain the major theories about substance-related disorders.

16-2. List why some groups are at risk for substance-related disorders.

16-3. Discuss how the physical, psychological, and withdrawal effects of the major categories of substances manifest themselves.

16-4. Incorporate nursing assessment components to detect patients who have substance-related disorders.

16-5. Demonstrate knowledge of a variety of short-term and long-term nursing intervention strategies for clients who have substance-related disorders.

16-6. Develop outcome criteria for clients who have substance-related disorders.

16-7. Establish what impact your own feelings and attitudes about clients with substance-related disorders have in your nursing care.

CHAPTER OUTLINE

I. Definitions and Terminology
   A. Substance-Related Disorders
   B. Substance Dependence
   C. Substance Abuse
   D. Substance Intoxication
   E. Substance Withdrawal
   F. Postacute Withdrawal Syndrome
II. Etiology
   A. Biological Theories
   B. Psychological Theories
   C. Sociocultural Theories

III. Management of Patients Who Are Substance Abusers
   A. Alcohol
     1. The Effects of Alcohol
      a. Assessment Aides
     2. Alcohol Withdrawal Syndrome
      a. Hangover
     3. Delirium Tremens
     4. Medical Detoxification
      a. Minor Withdrawal
      b. Major Withdrawal
     5. Blackouts
     6. Fetal Alcohol Syndrome
   B. Amphetamines
     1. Methamphetamine
   C. Caffeine
   D. Cannabis
   E. Cocaine
     1. Crack
     2. Freebase
   F. Hallucinogens
   G. Inhalants
   H. Nicotine
   I. Opiates
   J. Phencyclidine
   K. Sedatives, Hypnotics, and Anxiolytics
IV. Gerontological Considerations
V. Impaired Health Care Professional

     NURSING MANAGEMENT
      ASSESSMENT
       LABORATORY TESTS
      NURSING DIAGNOSIS
      OUTCOMES AND EVALUATION PARAMETERS
      PLANNING AND INTERVENTIONS
       GENERAL HOSPITAL CARE
       OTHER TREATMENT SETTINGS
       SELF-HELP GROUPS
       TWELVE-STEP PROGRAMS
        WOMEN FOR SOBRIETY
        RATIONAL RECOVERY
      RELAPSE
      OTHER TREATMENT APPROACHES
       COMPLEMENTARY AND ALTERNATIVE THERAPIES
       USING CONFRONTATION STRATEGIES
       EDUCATION
       REFERRAL AND SELF-HELP GROUPS
       LIFESTYLE CHANGE
      HELPING THE FAMILY
      EVALUATION
     COLLABORATIVE MANAGEMENT
VI. Summary

KEY TERMS MATCHING EXERCISE

Write the letter of the correct definition in the space next to each term.

Term

_____ 1. blackouts

_____ 2. delirium tremens (DTs)

_____ 3. fetal alcohol syndrome (FAS)

_____ 4. postacute withdrawal syndrome (PAWS)

_____ 5. substance abuse

_____ 6. substance dependence

_____ 7. substance intoxication

_____ 8. substance withdrawal

_____ 9. substance withdrawal syndrome

_____ 10. tolerance

_____ 11. withdrawal

Definition

a. Physical and mental defects found in babies of women who consumed alcohol during pregnancy.

b. Repeated use of a substance despite significant and repeated negative substance-related consequences.

c. A substance-specific mental disorder that follows the cessation or reduced intake of a substance that has regularly been used to induce a state of intoxication.

d. Uncomfortable and maladaptive physiological, cognitive, emotional, and behavioral changes associated with lowered blood or tissue concentrations of a substance after an individual has established some tolerance toward it, usually through heavy recent use.

e. Reversible substance-specific changes in thinking, emotions, behavior, and/or physiological functions caused by recent substance ingestion.

f. A pattern of substance use that is continued despite significant consequences, usually with physiological tolerance effects and a withdrawal syndrome if the substance is withdrawn.

g. Tremor and clouding of consciousness that can accompany physiological withdrawal from alcohol.

h. Physiological habituation to a substance, resulting in the need for progressively greater amounts to achieve intoxication and/or a diminished effect from continued use of the same amount of the substance.

i. Amnesia for short-term events; can occur in patients with alcohol abuse problems.

j. The symptoms that occur when drug use is reduced or discontinued.

k. An enduring physical remnant of neurotransmitter production and/or receptor site damage. The mood is affected, as are interpersonal interactions and cognitive skills.

SHORT ANSWER QUESTIONS

12. Describe the difference between substance abuse and substance dependence.

_____

_____

_____

13. Discuss the genetic considerations that factor into substance abuse.

_____

_____

14. What characteristic features are associated with alcohol abuse?

_____

_____

15. What are the four CAGE questions most frequently used for the detection of alcoholism in clinical settings?

_____

_____

_____

_____

16. What are delirium tremens or DTs?

_____

_____

17. What are the five stages of the transtheoretical model of behavior change and their characteristics?

_____

_____

_____

_____

_____

18. Explain the risks associated with heroin addiction.

_____

_____

19. What self-help groups are available to recovering addicts?

_____

_____

20. What diagnostic tests are often indicated for individuals seeking help for substance abuse?

_____

_____

21. Explain why including relapse prevention in treatment for addictions is important.

_____

_____

TRUE OR FALSE?

22. _____ T/F Blacking out and passing out are not the same.

23. _____ T/F Minor withdrawal from alcohol occurs 18 hours after an alcoholic's last drink.

24. _____ T/F Major withdrawal from alcohol can be life threatening.

25. _____ T/F Disulfiram (Antabuse) can cause a powerful reaction if alcohol is consumed, with symptoms including nausea, vomiting, flushing, dizziness, and tachycardia that last for up to 2 weeks.

26. _____ T/F The most common psychological pitfalls in recovering from the use of amphetamines or speed are sleepiness and excessive hunger.

27. _____ T/F Symptoms of methamphetamine use include an inability to competently perform activities of daily living (brush teeth, wash face, etc.), difficulty remembering or problem solving, and delusional accusations or reactions.

28. _____ T/F Peak concentrations of caffeine are achieved 30 to 60 minutes after ingestion.

29. _____ T/F Marijuana, which has become more potent in the past few decades, can be detected in the body for up to 6 weeks.

30. _____ T/F Marijuana is an effective treatment for glaucoma and has been declared legal for that use in at least one state.

31. _____ T/F Euphoria from cocaine diminishes after approximately 1 to 1½ hours.

NCLEX-RN® REVIEW QUESTIONS

16-1. The nurse is assessing the genetic and biologic risk factors for alcohol and substance abuse in a patient who is planning on becoming pregnant. Which question should the nurse ask?
  1. "Do you have a history of alcoholism in your family?"
  2. "Have you been diagnosed with any personality disorder?"
  3. "Are you in a lower socioeconomic group?"
  4. "Does your partner display self-centered behaviors?"

16-2. The nurse is assisting a patient with identifying factors that will increase his risk to resume substance abuse. Which of the client's situations would pose the greatest risk?
  1. Family gatherings always involve excessive alcohol use.
  2. Two of his close friends are currently in drug abuse recovery programs.
  3. His parents are not willing to attend Narcotics Anonymous meetings.
  4. His sibling refuses to enable his drug and alcohol use.

16-3. The nurse determines the following behaviors are most related to a long history of methamphetamine abuse when they are observed in a patient hospitalized for pneumonia.
  1. Repetitive tapping of fingers
  2. Frequent episodes of crying
  3. Difficulty combing hair
  4. A ravenous appetite

16-4. The nurse is teaching a parent about the physiological effects of inhalants. The nurse should provide the following information.
1. Inhalants cause CNS depression within minutes of use.
2. Inhalants will often decrease the heart rate and respirations.
3. Continuous use of inhalants can lead to glaucoma.
4. Sudden death can occur with the use of inhalants.

16-5. A patient is admitted to the hospital following PCP intoxication. The nurse should plan to observe for effects of the drug for how long?
1. 3–4 hours
2. 6–12 hours
3. 24–48 hours
4. 72–96 hours

16-6. The nurse develops which outcome as most appropriate for a patient with a diagnosis of altered nutrition related to alcohol abuse?
1. Patient will eat 100% of all meals.
2. Patient chooses high-protein foods from the menu selection.
3. Patient requests between-meal snacks.
4. Family will provide patient with meals of favorite foods.

16-7. When conducting a drug and alcohol assessment, the nurse understands that which of the following techniques should be utilized?
1. Maintain a nonjudgmental attitude.
2. The CAGE instrument needs to be used when conducting all assessments.
3. Always have a witness present when conducting the assessment.
4. A signed consent is required before the nurse can ask questions related to drug use.

CHAPTER 17

NURSING MANAGEMENT AT END OF LIFE

OUTCOME-BASED LEARNING OBJECTIVES

17-1. Review ethical theories that influence decisions in end-of-life care.

17-2. Define advanced directives and their role in end-of-life care.

17-3. Compare and contrast pharmacological and nonpharmacological therapies used for relief of pain at end of life.

17-4. Discuss beliefs surrounding death held by various cultures and religions.

17-5. Identify the need for interdisciplinary collaboration in planning end-of-life care.

17-6. Identify the role of hospice during end-of-life care.

17-7. Review the principles of palliative care.

CHAPTER OUTLINE

I. End of Life in the Acute Care Setting
II. End of Life in the Intensive Care Unit
III. Ethical Issues
  A. Respect for Persons
  B. Privacy
  C. Autonomy
  D. Veracity
  E. Beneficence
  F. Nonmaleficence
  G. Justice
IV. Ethical Issues and Dilemmas at End of Life
  A. Advanced Care Planning
    1. Advance Directives
    2. Living Wills
    3. Durable Power of Attorney
  B. Communication During End-of Life Care

KEY TERMS MATCHING EXERCISE

Write the letter of the correct definition in the space next to each term.

Term

_____ 1. durable power of attorney for health care (DPAHC)

_____ 2. hospice

_____ 3. living will

_____ 4. medical durable power of attorney (MDPA)

_____ 5. palliative care

Definition

a. Palliative care and support services for patients with terminal illnesses and their families.

b. Comprehensive care focused on alleviating suffering and promoting the quality of remaining life of patients living with a chronic life-threatening or terminal illness; allows patients and families to guide treatment and set goals for care.

c. A document that allows a patient to appoint a decision maker in the case of future incapacity.

d. A document that sets out wishes for health care if an individual becomes too ill to make those decisions; a trusted person is designated to make health care decisions.

e. A form of an advanced directive that describes a patient's preferences in case he or she becomes incapacitated.

SHORT ANSWER QUESTIONS

6. Explain the difference between beneficence and nonmaleficence.

   _____

   _____

7. Describe the advanced directive documents typically used and the purposes they serve.

   _____

   _____

8. Explain why opioids are the standard treatment for relief of dyspnea in a patient who is near death.

   _____

   _____

9. Explain why the occurrence known as double effect may impact the level of comfort and pain for the dying patient.

   _____

   _____

10. Describe the four types of complicated grief and their characteristics.

   _____

   _____

   _____

   _____

TRUE OR FALSE?

11. _____ T/F As a caregiver you must abide by the principle of not inflicting harm on your patients, even if it means not being truthful with them about their condition.

12. _____ T/F The appointed person responsible for making medical decisions does not need consent from other family members or friends.

13. _____ T/F During end-of-life care, the withdrawal of food may actually assist the patient to be more comfortable.

14. _____ T/F Under no circumstances should opioids be administered in anticipation of pain.

15. _____ T/F The transition from curative care to comfort care can be inconsistent with some therapies aimed at comfort and some at cure.

16. _____ T/F Journaling has been proven to relieve the level and duration of pain and in some cases is used in place of pharmacologic pain management.

17. _____ T/F The primary purpose of hospice care is to provide treatment for the patient's disease or condition within the home.

18. _____ T/F Hospice care also encompasses bereavement services for families and caregivers for a minimum of 1 year after the death of the patient.

19. _____ T/F Palliative care integrates all aspects of patient care except for the spiritual domain.

20. _____ T/F One barrier to hospice care is the reluctance of many physicians to suggest that patients and families look into it.

NCLEX-RN® REVIEW QUESTIONS

17-1. Regarding ethical decision making in end-of-life care, the nurse understands that:
1. Decisions should be made with regard to stress relief for families and not necessarily to optimal patient care.
2. Use of moral and ethical principles to systematically appraise and determine justified choices is best.
3. The principle of beneficence helps ensure clients make informed decisions based on truthful information.
4. A key component of the palliative care plan is the shift in focus from comfort advances to curative processes.

17-2. When educating a patient about advance directives, it is most appropriate for the nurse to include which of the following instructions in the teaching plan?
1. The appointed health care proxy will continue to require consent from other family members prior to making medical decisions.
2. The advance directive will ensure the health care team will remain truthful when communicating with the client and family.
3. Advance directives direct the health care team regarding the types of treatments the client desires should he or she become incapacitated.
4. A living will is a form of the durable power of attorney for health care that allows the client to select a decision-making surrogate.

17-3. As it relates to pain control in the palliative care client, the nurse understands that:
1. Increasing the lighting in the hospital room may create a more peaceful and comfortable environment.
2. The opioid Duragesic (fentanyl) is not recommended because its metabolism produces potentially toxic effects.
3. Neuroleptic medications have synergistic sedative and anticonvulsant effects when administered with opioids.
4. Withdrawal or withholding oral intake and allowing hypoxia may assist the patient in being more comfortable.

17-4. The most appropriate nursing intervention when planning care for a terminally ill client of a different culture is to:
1. Ask about any personal preferences regarding end-of-life or postmortem care.
2. Maintain continuous direct eye contact during communication as a sign of respect.
3. Facilitate the patient's acceptance of hospital policy for preparation of the body after death.
4. Encourage the patient to have closure by always expressing feelings of grief openly.

17-5. When planning care for the terminally ill patient, the nurse understands that a collaborative approach to end-of-life issues:
1. Guarantees adequacy in continuing education experiences for the multidisciplinary team.
2. Helps the patient and family achieve a pain-free and meaningful death experience.
3. Decreases the possibility of civil or criminal liability in response to treatment changes.
4. Ensures that the newest palliative care technologies will guide the patient's care goals.

17-6. A cancer patient newly placed under hospice care asks, "Does this mean the doctor is going to stop trying to treat me?" The most appropriate response by the nurse would be:
1. "Your prognosis is less than six months, so there is no reason to keep treating you."
2. "Radiation therapy is never continued after hospice care has been initiated."
3. "The health care team will continue to treat you, but the goal of your care has changed."
4. "Death is inevitable for all people, and there is no way to prolong your life."

17-7. Which of the following choices is most closely associated with palliative care as it relates to the acute care setting?
1. The routine and frequent utilization of medications for the purposes of producing their double effect
2. Respite care and bereavement services provided for the client's family to help with the grieving process
3. Withholding sedatives and neuromuscular blocking agents for the client during terminal extubation
4. The greater obligation of nonmaleficence over beneficence regarding invasive procedures

CHAPTER 18

FLUID AND ELECTROLYTES

OUTCOME-BASED LEARNING OBJECTIVES

18-1. Explain the normal composition of fluids and electrolytes in the body.

18-2. Describe the normal osmolality of the blood and urine.

18-3. Define the normal ranges of electrolytes in the body.

18-4. Discuss various circumstances that place the patient at risk for fluid and electrolyte imbalances.

18-5. Evaluate fluid status of an adult according to normal fluid and electrolyte values.

18-6. Identify nursing interventions to restore fluid and electrolyte balance.

18-7. Explain discharge teaching implications to assist patients to maintain fluid and electrolyte balance.

CHAPTER OUTLINE

I. Body Fluid Composition and Function
   A. Osmolality
   B. Electrolytes
   C. Regulation of Body Fluid
   D. Tests for Evaluating Fluid Status
   E. Clinical Manifestations of Overhydration and Dehydration
      NURSING MANAGEMENT
      COLLABORATIVE MANAGEMENT
   F. Homeostatic Mechanisms
      1. Electrolyte Balance
II. Electrolyte Imbalances
   A. Sodium
      1. Hypernatremia (Sodium Excess)
         NURSING MANAGEMENT
      2. Hyponatremia (Low Serum Sodium)
         NURSING MANAGEMENT

B. Potassium
  1. Hyperkalemia
      NURSING MANAGEMENT
          ASSESSMENT
          OUTCOMES AND EVALUATION PARAMETERS
          PLANNING, INTERVENTIONS, AND RATIONALES
  2. Hypokalemia
      NURSING MANAGEMENT
          ASSESSMENT
          PLANNING, INTERVENTIONS, AND RATIONALES
          EVALUATION

C. Calcium
  1. Hypercalcemia
      NURSING MANAGEMENT
          ASSESSMENT
          PLANNING, INTERVENTIONS, AND RATIONALES
  2. Hypocalcemia
      NURSING MANAGEMENT
          PLANNING, INTERVENTIONS, AND RATIONALES

D. Magnesium
  1. Hypermagnesemia
      NURSING MANAGEMENT
          ASSESSMENT
          PLANNING, INTERVENTIONS, AND RATIONALES
  2. Hypomagnesemia
      NURSING MANAGEMENT
          PLANNING, INTERVENTIONS, AND RATIONALES
  3. Phosphorus
      a. Hyperphosphatemia
          NURSING MANAGEMENT
              PLANNING, INTERVENTIONS, AND RATIONALES
      b. Hypophosphatemia
          NURSING MANAGEMENT
              ASSESSMENT
              PLANNING, INTERVENTIONS, AND RATIONALES

E. Chloride
  1. Hyperchloremia
  2. Hypochloremia
      COLLABORATIVE MANAGEMENT

F. Research

III. Summary

KEY TERMS MATCHING EXERCISE 1

Write the letter of the correct definition in the space next to each term.

Term

___ 1. diffusion
_c_ 2. extracellular fluid (ECF)
_e_ 3. electrolytes
_b_ 4. filtration
_a_ 5. insensible fluid loss
_g_ 6. interstitial fluid

Definition

a. Water lost from the body carried as vapor in exhaled gases and evaporated from the body as sweat.

b. Number of molecules of solute per kilogram of water.

c. Having the same osmolality as blood (275 to 295 mOsm/kg of body weight).

_i_   7. intracellular fluid (ICF)

_c_   8. isotonic

_b_   9. osmolality

_d_   10. osmosis

d. The movement of water from one compartment of low solute concentration through a semipermeable membrane into a second compartment with high solute concentration.

e. Ionized minerals (calcium, chloride, magnesium, phosphorus, potassium, and sodium) serving as energy transfer mechanisms in combinations of positive charges (cations) or negative charges (anions).

f. Fluid between the cells (interstitial fluids) and in plasma (serum).

g. Fluid between cells, but not in serum.

h. The movement of molecules from an area of higher concentration through permeable membranes to an area of lower concentration as a result of hydrostatic pressure.

i. Fluid contained within the cells.

j. The movement of molecules from an area of high concentration to an area of low concentration in liquids, gases, and solids.

KEY TERMS MATCHING EXERCISE 2

Write the letter of the correct definition in the space next to each term.

Term

_____ 11. aldosterone

_____ 12. antidiuretic hormone (ADH)

_____ 13. atrial natriuretic peptide (ANP)

_____ 14. calciphylaxis

_____ 15. hydroxyapatite

_____ 16. hypertonic

_____ 17. hypotonic

_____ 18. oncotic pressure

_____ 19. specific gravity (SG)

_____ 20. sodium

Definition

a. A hormone secreted by the right atrium in response to fluid overload that causes the excretion of sodium, which results in loss of the excess fluid; however, most regulation of excess volume is through decreased aldosterone secretion.

b. A small peptide molecule released by the pituitary gland at the base of the brain. It has an antidiuretic action that prevents the production of dilute urine.

c. Most numerous cation in extracellular fluid (ECF); maintains ECF volume through osmotic pressure, assists acid–base balance, and conducts nerve impulses via sodium channels.

d. Inorganic hexagonal matrix of bone composed of calcium and phosphorus.

e. A condition during severe serum calcium excess, as in renal failure, in which calcium is deposited into the soft tissues of the body.

f. A hormone secreted by the adrenal cortex in response to the conversion of angiotensinogen to angiotensin II; causes sodium reabsorption from the renal tubules and thus causes the body to retain water.

g. Term used to identify a solution that contains a higher concentration of electrolytes than that found in body cells.

h. Term used to identify a solution in which the concentration of electrolyte is below that found in body cells.

i. An estimate of the solute concentration in a volume of liquid measured with a hydrometer which compares the liquid to an equal amount of distilled water.

j. In the circulatory system, the term refers to a form of osmotic pressure exerted by proteins in blood plasma that normally tends to pull water into the circulatory system.

SHORT ANSWER QUESTIONS

21. Explain the importance of sodium in extracellular fluid.

_____

_____

22. Describe the clinical signs of hyperkalemia.

_____

_____

23. Discuss the role vitamin D can play in hypocalcemia.

_____

_____

24. Explain why potassium is never administered as IV push.

_____

_____

25. Describe the clinical indications and risks of hypermagnesemia.

_____

_____

TRUE OR FALSE?

26. ___T___ T/F   Electrolyte intake is primarily oral, but may include the rectal route and intravenous fluids for hospitalized patients.

27. ___T___ T/F   Aldosterone, antidiuretic hormone, and atrial natriuretic peptide are hormones that regulate the sodium level in extracellular fluid.

28. ___T___ T/F   The most common cause of dehydration is the loss of water through urination.

29. ___F___ T/F   Stool consistency is an unreliable method of evaluating hydration status.

30. ___F___ T/F   Foods high in sodium (highly processed foods, such as chips) are contraindicated for patients with hyponatremia.

31. ___T___ T/F   The function of potassium is to maintain intracellular osmolality and participate in the sodium-potassium exchange that causes cellular depolarization and repolarization.

32. ___T___ T/F   Calcium serum levels depend on vitamin D, calcitonin from the thyroid gland, and parathyroid hormone (PTH) from the parathyroid glands.

33. ___F___ T/F   As serum phosphorus levels decrease, there is a simultaneous drop in calcium, resulting in symptoms of hypocalcemia.

34. ___T___ T/F   Chloride combines with hydrogen ion (H+) to form hydrochloric acid for digestion and hydrolyzing nutrients for absorption in the GI tract.

35. ___T___ T/F   Pathophysiologic symptoms of hypernatremia are most likely to occur with sudden onset, and brain symptoms include altered mental status, neuromuscular irritability, and occasionally coma or seizures.

FOOD SOURCES OF ELECTROLYTES

Match the electrolyte with the food sources that provide it.

Electrolyte

_b_ 36. Magnesium

_f_ 37. Potassium

_a_ 38. Sodium

_b_ 39. Phosphorus

_c_ 40. Chloride

_d_ 41. Calcium

Food Sources

a. Highly processed foods, such as chips

b. Glucose, insulin, or sugar-containing foods, milk, dried beans and peas, eggs, fish, organ meats (brain, liver, kidney), Brazil nuts, peanuts, poultry, seeds (pumpkin, sesame, sunflower), whole grains (oats, barley, bran)

c. Green leafy vegetables, nuts, legumes, seafood, whole grains, bananas, oranges, and chocolate

d. Milk, antacids, dairy products, spinach and other leafy green vegetables

e. Table salt or other dietary sources of sodium

f. Vegetables such as spinach, broccoli, carrots, green beans, tomato juice, acorn squash, and potatoes

NCLEX-RN® REVIEW QUESTIONS

18-1. A patient recovering from abdominal surgery has 750 cc of wound drainage. The nurse realizes that this fluid loss could lead to:
1. Interstitial fluid volume overload.
2. Intracellular fluid volume deficit.
3. Interstitial fluid volume deficit.
4. Extracellular fluid volume deficit.

18-2. A patient is actively hemorrhaging. The nurse would plan to administer which of the following types of intravenous fluids for this patient?
1. 0.45% sodium chloride
2. 0.9% sodium chloride
3. Dextrose 5% in 0.45% saline
4. Sodium bicarbonate solution

18-3. The nurse is instructing a patient about ways to prevent the onset of hypokalemia. Which of the following laboratory values would indicate that the instruction was effective for the patient?
1. K+ 6.5 mEq/L
2. K+ 4.1 mEq/L
3. K+ 2.9 mEq/L
4. K+ 2.5 mEq/L

18-4. The nurse is providing care to a patient with an elevated serum calcium level. The nurse realizes that which of the following are considered causes of this electrolyte level?
1. Long-term use of cardiac medications
2. Hyperthyroidism
3. Bone malignancy
4. Malnutrition

18-5. The serum sodium level for a newly admitted patient is 120 mEq/L. Which of the following questions should the nurse include when assessing this patient?
1. Are you having any difficulty thinking or remembering things?
2. Have you been able to drink water and keep it down?
3. Have you noticed numbness and tingling of the fingers?
4. How much alcohol do you regularly consume per day?

18-6. The nurse is planning care for a group of patients. Which of the following would benefit from having a tracheotomy tray at the bedside?
1. The patient with Cushing's syndrome
2. A patient with primary hyperparathyroidism
3. A patient admitted with acute alcohol intoxication
4. The patient undergoing hemodialysis

18-7. The nurse is planning discharge instructions for patient with a fluid volume deficit. Which of the following should the nurse include in these instructions to the patient?
1. Primarily drink fluids such as tomato juice, skim milk, and carbonated beverages.
2. Notify your health care provider if you gain five or more pounds in a week.
3. Having the sensation of being thirsty the majority of waking hours is normal.
4. Feeling dizzy upon standing should be reported to your physician.

CHAPTER 19

ACID–BASE IMBALANCE

OUTCOME-BASED LEARNING OBJECTIVES

19-1. Describe the role of hydrogen ions in the determination of plasma pH.

19-2. Compare and contrast the processes that produce respiratory and metabolic acids in the body and the processes by which they are eliminated.

19-3. Calculate minute ventilation and explain the effect of minute alveolar ventilation on acid–base balance.

19-4. Evaluate the process of respiratory compensation for a metabolic abnormality.

19-5. Discuss the renal handling of hydrogen ion and bicarbonate.

19-6. Discuss a systematic stepwise process for the interpretation of the arterial blood gas values related to acid–base balance.

19-7. Relate the major causes, pathophysiology, signs, symptoms, consequences, and medical management for respiratory acidosis and alkalosis and metabolic acidosis and alkalosis.

19-8. Describe the nursing assessment used in the assessment of acid–base abnormalities.

19-9. Describe nursing actions to alleviate the symptoms of acid–base abnormalities.

PEARSON
EXPLORE **mynursingkit**™

MyNursingKit is your one stop for online chapter review materials and resources. Prepare for success with additional NCLEX®-style practice questions, interactive assignments and activities, web links, animations and videos, and more!

Register your access code from the front of your book at **www.mynursingkit.com**

CHAPTER OUTLINE

   I. Acid–Base Homeostasis
  II. Buffer Systems
 III. The Role of the Lungs
     A. The Role of the Kidneys
 IV. Assessment of Acid–Base Balance
     A. Complex Acid–Base Disorders
  V. Acid–Base Imbalances
     A. Respiratory Acidosis
        1. Etiology and Pathophysiology
        2. Signs, Symptoms, and Consequences

3. Medical Management
   a. Bilevel Positive Airway Pressure
   b. Intubation
   c. Supplemental Oxygen
B. Respiratory Alkalosis
   1. Etiology and Pathophysiology
   2. Signs, Symptoms, and Consequences
   3. Medical Management
C. Metabolic Acidosis
   1. Etiology and Pathophysiology
   2. Signs, Symptoms, and Consequences
   3. Medical Management
D. Metabolic Alkalosis
   1. Etiology and Pathophysiology
   2. Signs, Symptoms, and Consequences
   3. Medical Management
           NURSING MANAGEMENT
           COLLABORATIVE CARE
           HEALTH PROMOTION
E. Research
F. Summary

KEY TERMS MATCHING EXERCISE 1

Write the letter of the correct definition in the space next to each term.

Term

_____ 1. hypercarbic drive

_____ 2. hypoxic drive

_____ 3. acids

_____ 4. bases

_____ 5. hydrogen ion

_____ 6. pH

_____ 7. buffer

_____ 8. alkalis

_____ 9. sodium bicarbonate

_____ 10. secretion

Definition

a. Compounds in solution that have a pH of greater than 7.40, which is caused by either an increase of base/alkali or a loss of acid.

b. A single, charged atomic proton that is not orbited by any electrons. It is the smallest ionic particle and is extremely reactive.

c. A base or alkali that removes hydrogen ion when added to the blood.

d. The stimulus for ventilation that occurs when elevated levels of carbon dioxide alter the pH of the blood and cerebrospinal fluid, making them more acid. Central chemoreceptors located in the brainstem react to this change in the pH and stimulate the body to breathe more deeply and more rapidly. It is the strongest stimulus of ventilation.

e. Compounds that combine with hydrogen ion in solution. A proton acceptor.

f. The stimulus to ventilation that occurs when peripheral chemoreceptors located in the carotid arteries and the aorta sense a decrease in the oxygen concentration in the blood.

g. A compound that minimizes the change in hydrogen ion concentration (and also the pH) when ions are added to or removed from solution.

h. Compounds in solution that have a pH of less than 7.40. They form hydrogen ion in solution and are proton donors.

i. The active process of moving substances, such as H+ ion, from the blood into the tubular fluid against the concentration gradient.

j. An indicator of hydrogen ion concentration; the negative logarithm of the hydrogen ion concentration expressed in nanomoles per liter.

KEY TERMS MATCHING EXERCISE 2

Write the letter of the correct definition in the space next to each term.

Term

_____ 11. anatomic dead space

_____ 12. dead space

_____ 13. pathologic dead space

_____ 14. anion gap

_____ 15. base excess

_____ 16. carbon dioxide

_____ 17. carbonic acid

_____ 18. compensation

_____ 19. electroneutrality

_____ 20. hyperventilation

_____ 21. hypoventilation

_____ 22. minute ventilation

_____ 23. minute alveolar ventilation

Definition

a. The principle that asserts that the sum of all positive or cationic charges in plasma must equal the sum of all negative or anionic charges.

b. Correction of the blood pH by the system that is *not* the cause of abnormal levels of carbon dioxide or bicarbonate.

c. The volume of alveolar air per minute that takes part in gas exchange, transferring oxygen to the blood and removing carbon dioxide from the blood.

d. A portion of the tidal volume that does reach the alveoli, but does not take place in gas exchange. Various lung pathologies and disease conditions can increase this dead space amount and affect the lungs' ability to oxygenate and ventilate.

e. An atmospheric gas composed of one carbon atom and two oxygen atoms.

f. Part of the blood gas report, this is a calculated value that is based on the bicarbonate and carbon dioxide levels and the hematocrit.

g. Area in the transporting airways or upper airways and bronchi that results when no gas exchange occurs.

h. Decreased ventilation, which causes an increased $PaCO_2$; exists when there is a higher than normal level of carbon dioxide in the blood. Also referred to as *hypercapnia.*

i. The portion of the tidal volume that does not reach the alveoli of the lungs or take part in the exchange of oxygen and carbon dioxide.

j. A state that exists when there is a lower than normal level of carbon dioxide in the blood. Also referred to as *hypocapnia.*

k. A measurement of how much air the lungs move in 1 minute; it is equal to respiratory rate times tidal volume.

l. A weak acid formed by water reacting with carbon dioxide.

m. Represents the concentration of all unmeasured anions in plasma. It is comprised of negatively charged proteins as well as the acid anions produced during metabolism such as lactate.

SHORT ANSWER QUESTIONS

24. What are the four basic categories into which abnormalities in acid and base balance can be grouped, and what are their characteristics?

_____

_____

_____

_____

25. What conditions can cause acute and chronic respiratory acidosis?

_____

_____

_____

_____

26. What conditions can cause respiratory alkalosis?

_____

_____

_____

_____

27. What conditions can cause metabolic acidosis?

_____

_____

_____

_____

28. What conditions can cause metabolic alkalosis?

_____

_____

_____

_____

29. Explain the importance of the hypercarbic drive.

_____

_____

_____

_____

30. Explain the process and purpose of the hypoxic drive.

_____

_____

_____

_____

31. Explain the role of the lungs in maintaining acid–base balance.

_____

_____

32. Explain the role of the kidneys in maintaining acid–base balance.

_____

_____

_____

_____

33. What are normal arterial blood gas values?

_____

_____

_____

_____

TRUE OR FALSE?

34. _____ T/F Disturbances in hydrogen ion concentration may result in improved functioning in many organs such as the pulmonary, renal, or cardiac systems and can also alter such processes as blood clotting and the metabolism of drugs.

35. _____ T/F Strong acids hold their hydrogen ion weakly, so the ion dissociates easily and can then act on other substances.

36. _____ T/F The intracellular buffer system, dihydrogen phosphate, and hydrogen phosphate remain in equilibrium in the cell unless there is an excess hydrogen ion or hydroxide in the blood plasma.

37. _____ T/F A high pH indicates an increase of base.

38. _____ T/F The tidal volume is made up of the alveolar volume and the anatomic dead space.

39. _____ T/F Arterial blood gas (ABG) values are most often used to assess acid–base balance.

40. _____ T/F A deficiency of hydrogen in the blood will lead to alkalosis; an excess to acidosis.

41. _____ T/F An excess of carbon dioxide in the blood will lead to acidosis; a deficiency will lead to alkalosis.

42. _____ T/F Intubation is indicated if the patient has a $PaCO_2$ in the 80- to 90-mmHg range and a pH of less than 7.10 to 7.25.

43. _____ T/F Imbalances between acids and bases rarely occur as a result of diseases, organ dysfunction, or other pathologic conditions.

ACID AND BASE TERMINOLOGY

Insert the terms or measurements into the correct columns.

Caused by increase of base/alkali
Blood pH > 7.40
Raises the 20:1 bicarbonate to carbonic acid ratio
Caused by loss of base/alkali
More base/less acid
Blood pH < 7.40
Caused by loss of acid
Lowers the 20:1 bicarbonate to carbonic acid ratio
Caused by increase of acid
Less base/more acid

Acidemia/Acidosis	Alkalemia/Alkalosis

NCLEX-RN® REVIEW QUESTIONS

19-1. A patient is demonstrating an increase in carbon dioxide levels. The nurse realizes that this patient's blood pH will most likely:
1. Increase.
2. Decrease.
3. Stabilize.
4. Increase, then stabilize at a higher level.

19-2. A patient with chronic kidney disease is admitted with a fractured hip. The nurse realizes that this patient's current problem could be because of:
1. Kidney reabsorption of hydrogen ions.
2. Insufficient calcium intake.
3. Poor hemoglobin transport of bicarbonate.
4. Bone absorption of hydrogen ions.

19-3. The nurse is going to calculate the minute alveolar ventilation for a patient. Which of the following is needed for this calculation?
1. Patient's weight in kilograms
2. Anatomic dead space
3. Current heart rate
4. Pulse oximetry reading

19-4. While caring for a patient with acidosis, the nurse notes that the patient's respiratory rate has changed from 24 per minute to 16 per minute. The nurse realizes that this respiratory rate change is due to:
1. Hypoventilation.
2. Kidney reabsorption of bicarbonate.
3. Hyperventilation.
4. Hemoglobin transport of bicarbonate.

19-5. A patient in metabolic acidosis has small amounts of bicarbonate in his urine. The nurse realizes this patient is most likely demonstrating:
   1. A worsening condition.
   2. Evidence of buffering by the blood system.
   3. Evidence of buffering by the bone.
   4. Evidence of a normal response by the kidneys.

19-6. The nurse is reviewing a patient's arterial blood gas results. After studying the patient's pH and $PaCO_2$, the nurse should then assess:
   1. Compensation.
   2. Bicarbonate.
   3. PaO_2.
   4. Minute ventilation.

19-7. The nurse is providing care to a patient who has had a nasogastric tube to low suction for five days. The nurse realizes that this patient is at risk for developing which acid–base imbalance?
   1. Respiratory acidosis
   2. Metabolic acidosis
   3. Respiratory alkalosis
   4. Metabolic alkalosis

19-8. A patient is admitted to the hospital in metabolic acidosis. Which of the following questions should the nurse ask to gain more information about this imbalance?
   1. "How much do you smoke?"
   2. "Do you have a history of emphysema?"
   3. "How long have you been vomiting?"
   4. "When was your last dose of insulin?"

19-9. The nurse is caring for a patient experiencing respiratory acidosis. For which of the following situations should the nurse be cautious when administering supplemental oxygen?
   1. Chronic emphysema
   2. Acute asthma
   3. Panic disorder
   4. Deviated septum

CHAPTER 20

INFECTIOUS DISEASE

OUTCOME-BASED LEARNING OBJECTIVES

20-1. Describe the infectious process and its effects on the body.

20-2. Identify risk factors for infection.

20-3. Describe the chain of infection.

20-4. Describe measures to prevent and control infection.

20-5. Identify common pathogens causing infection.

20-6. Differentiate between active and passive immunity.

20-7. Describe *Healthy People 2010* guidelines for prevention of infection.

20-8. Identify the assessment and interventions required by a patient with an infection.

CHAPTER OUTLINE

   I. Defense Mechanisms
     A. Inflammation
       1. Manifestations of Inflammation
     B. Immune Responses
       1. Humoral and Cellular Immunity
         a. Humoral Immunity
         b. Cellular Immunity
     C. Increased Susceptibility to Infection
   II. Infectious Process
     A. Chain of Infection
     B. Stages of the Infectious Process
  III. Infection Control and Prevention
     A. Hand Hygiene
     B. Patient Placement
     C. Protective Equipment
     D. Disposal of Soiled Equipment

IV. Pathogens Causing Infectious Disease
    A. Bacteria
    B. Viruses
    C. Mycoplasma
    D. Rickettsiae
    E. Fungi
    F. Parasites
 V. New or Reemerging Infection
    A. Biological Warfare
    B. Isolation Precautions
    C. Immunization Programs
    D. *Healthy People 2010* Guidelines
              NURSING MANAGEMENT
                 ASSESSMENT
                    FEVER
                  PATIENT HISTORY
              PHYSICAL EXAMINATION
                DIAGNOSTIC TESTS
             NURSING DIAGNOSIS
               HEALTH PROMOTION
                 DISCHARGE PRIORITIES
         COLLABORATIVE MANAGEMENT
VI. Research

KEY TERMS MATCHING EXERCISE 1

Write the letter of the correct definition in the space next to each term.

Term

_____ 1. nosocomial infection
_____ 2. community-acquired infection
_____ 3. mode of transmission
_____ 4. carrier
_____ 5. chain of infection
_____ 6. pathogenicity
_____ 7. portal of entry
_____ 8. portal of exit
_____ 9. antigenicity
_____ 10. reservoir

Definition

a. People or animals that do not have symptoms of infection but carry an active pathogenic microorganism.

b. Consists of a causative agent, reservoir, portal of exit, mode of transmission, portal of entry, and susceptible host.

c. An infection that occurs in a hospitalized patient.

d. The ability of a pathogen to elicit an immune defense in its host. It affects the ability of the host to develop a long-term immunity.

e. An infection acquired outside a health care facility.

f. The path by which an infective organism enters a susceptible host.

g. A place where an organism can survive and may or may not multiply.

h. Means by which an organism travels from a reservoir to a susceptible host.

i. Path in the chain of infection that allows a causative agent to escape from a reservoir.

j. Disease-causing potential of a microorganism, the number of invading microorganisms, and the host defenses.

KEY TERMS MATCHING EXERCISE 2

Write the letter of the correct definition in the space next to each term.

Term

_____ 11. invasiveness

_____ 12. viability

_____ 13. virulence

_____ 14. infectivity

_____ 15. endotoxins

_____ 16. exotoxins

_____ 17. active immunization

_____ 18. passive immunization

_____ 19. fever of unknown origin (FUO)

_____ 20. notifiable disease

_____ 21. empiric therapy

Definition

a. Immunization that involves the introduction of a live, killed, or attenuated toxin of a disease organism into the body. The immune system responds by producing antibodies.

b. Therapy that is begun before culture results are available; physicians determine if empiric therapy is necessary based on the severity of the infection.

c. Any of certain diseases or conditions that must be reported to local, county, or state public health departments.

d. Degree to which an organism can spread through the body.

e. The ability of a pathogen to enter a host and then live and grow within that host.

f. A fever that lasts 2 weeks or more without identification of the cause.

g. Immunization that provides immunity for a short period of time, usually around 6 to 12 weeks; involves the injection of already formed antibodies into the body.

h. Produced by live bacteria and released when the bacteria are killed.

i. The ability of a pathogen to survive outside its host.

j. Related to the severity of disease a pathogen is capable of causing; virulence can vary depending on the ability of the host to mount an immune response. It is expressed as the number of cases of infection that are serious or produce a disability in all those infected.

k. Proteins released by bacterial cells during growth; they have very specific actions.

TRUE OR FALSE?

22. _____ T/F   Hand washing done using the correct procedure and frequency has been shown to be the most important single action in preventing the spread of infection.

23. _____ T/F   The data show that surgical site infections are the leading type of infection in hospitalized patients.

24. _____ T/F   Proper hand washing requires vigorously rubbing soaped hands together for approximately 25 seconds.

25. _____ T/F   Some viruses, especially those causing hepatitis, can survive outside a host cell.

26. _____ T/F   Rickettsiae, a pathogen that can kill cells directly, is responsible for pelvic inflammatory disease.

27. _____ T/F   Clostridium difficile is a type of bacteria that can live in the environment for long periods and is able to withstand normal cleaning procedures.

28. _____ T/F   Parasites are transmitted through the bites of arthropods such as ticks, lice, fleas, or mites or through exposure to their waste products.

29. _____ T/F   Fungi can live in a wide variety of environments and do not necessarily need a host.

30. _____   T/F   A fever of 40.5°C (105°F) can cause or worsen cardiac and pulmonary problems and also cause febrile seizures.

31. _____   T/F   Patients who are immunocompromised may be at high risk of developing infections.

SHORT ANSWER QUESTIONS

32. What are the five local symptoms of inflammation?

_____

_____

_____

_____

_____

33. What are the two systemic systems of inflammation?

_____

_____

34. What are the two types of immune response to antigens?

_____

_____

35. Name the ten areas to be assessed for an infection during a physical exam.

_____

_____

_____

_____

_____

_____

_____

_____

_____

_____

36. What seven diagnostic tests are performed related to infection?

_____

_____

_____

_____

_____

_____

_____

LABELING EXERCISE: CHAIN OF INFECTION

Place the term in the correct location.

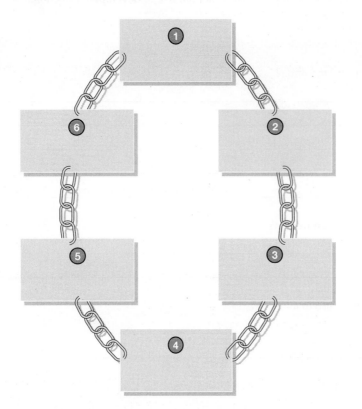

1. _____

2. _____

3. _____

4. _____

5. _____

6. _____

Etiologic agent (microorganism)
Method of transmission
Portal of entry to the susceptible host

Portal of exit from reservoir
Reservoir (source)
Susceptible host

NCLEX-RN® REVIEW QUESTIONS

20-1. A patient is exhibiting inflammation. Which of the following is the nurse least likely to assess in this patient?
    1. Redness
    2. Coolness
    3. Swelling
    4. Pain

20-2. The nurse is planning the care for a group of patients. Which of the following patients would have the greatest risk for developing an infection?
    1. A 50-year-old menopausal female
    2. A 15-year-old with acne
    3. A 28-year-old with job-related stress
    4. A 75-year-old with emphysema

20-3. A patient with hepatitis B asks the nurse how he acquired the infection. Which of the following modes of transmission should the nurse explain to this patient?
    1. Contact
    2. Airborne
    3. Vehicle
    4. Vector

20-4. The nurse is aware of an outbreak of infections among patients on one care area. Which of the following should the nurse do to prevent the ongoing spread of this infection?
1. Wearing personal protective equipment with all patient contact
2. Washing hands with the correct frequency and technique
3. Placing all patients in isolation precautions
4. Using biohazard bags to dispose of contaminated items

20-5. A patient is admitted with an infectious disease. The nurse realizes that this disease was once under control but is now becoming more common. This disease is most likely:
1. Smallpox.
2. Clostridium difficile.
3. Tuberculosis.
4. Anthrax.

20-6. The nurse is providing a patient with a booster vaccination to help the patient maintain immunity to a specific disease process. Which of the following types of immunizations requires a booster?
1. Flu vaccine
2. Measles
3. Mumps
4. Pertussis

20-7. The community health nurse is planning a community education offering to address infection control. Which of the following is a *Healthy People 2010* goal for preventive care of infections?
1. Reduce chronic hepatitis B virus infections in infants and young children.
2. Reduce bacterial meningitis in the elderly population.
3. Reduce nosocomial infections in outclient settings.
4. Reduce the need for drug prescriptions for peptic ulcer.

20-8. A patient is demonstrating signs of a urinary tract infection. Which of the following should the nurse do when collecting a urine specimen from this patient?
1. Ask the patient to urinate in the specimen cup and place it on the bedside table once filled.
2. Label the specimen with the patient's room number.
3. Place the specimen in the refrigerator for pickup the next day.
4. Make sure the specimen gets to the laboratory as soon as possible.

CHAPTER 21

HYPERTENSION

OUTCOME-BASED LEARNING OBJECTIVES

21-1. Compare and contrast the differences between the types of hypertension: prehypertension, stage 1 hypertension, and stage 2 hypertension.

21-2. Describe the pathophysiology of hypertension.

21-3. Discuss the risk factors associated with the development of hypertension.

21-4. Explain the therapeutic agents used to manage hypertension.

21-5. Compare and contrast how social and cultural influences affect the plan of care for the hypertensive patient.

21-6. Develop a nursing plan of care with the hypertensive client.

21-7. Discuss how multidisciplinary therapeutic interventions are associated with patient outcome.

CHAPTER OUTLINE

I. Regulation of Blood Pressure
   A. Neural Regulation
   B. Arterial Baroreceptors and Arterial Chemoreceptors
   C. Regulation of Fluid Volume
   D. Humoral Regulation
      1. Renin-Angiotensin-Aldosterone System
      2. Vasopressin
      3. Epinephrine and Norepinephrine
II. Epidemiology and Etiology of Hypertension
III. Pathophysiology of Hypertension
   A. Risk Factors
   B. Culture, Environment, Race, Genetics, and History
   C. Psychosocial Assessment
IV. Clinical Manifestations
   A. Assessment
   B. Blood Pressure Measurement

V. Diagnostic Tests
VI. Medical Management
   A. Diet
   B. Exercise
   C. Weight Control
   D. Stress Reduction
   E. Alcohol Consumption
   F. Pharmacologic Agents Used to Treat Hypertension
   G. Complementary and Alternative Therapies
       NURSING MANAGEMENT
       HEALTH PROMOTION
       DISCHARGE PRIORITIES
       COLLABORATIVE MANAGEMENT
VII. Complications of High Blood Pressure
   A. Hypertensive Emergencies
     1. Hypertensive Crisis
   B. Hypertensive Encephalopathy
   C. Dissecting Aortic Aneurysm
VIII. Research

KEY TERMS MATCHING EXERCISE 1

Write the letter of the correct definition in the space next to each term.

Term

_____ 1. blood pressure
_____ 2. systolic
_____ 3. diastolic
_____ 4. peripheral vascular resistance
_____ 5. pulse pressure
_____ 6. prehypertension
_____ 7. white coat phenomenon

Definition

a. A blood pressure reading of the maximum pressure in the aorta and major arteries, which occurs when the left ventricle contracts and ejects blood into the central vascular system.

b. The pressure created by blood circulating through the arteries and veins and the chambers of the heart.

c. A term used to describe those individuals who have a blood pressure finding on two or more office visits of 130 to 139/80 to 89 mmHg. These individuals are at twice the risk of developing hypertension as those with lower values.

d. A blood pressure reading of the minimum pressure in the arteries, which occurs just prior to the next cycle of ventricular ejection of blood; reflects cardiac relaxation.

e. The resistance in the pulmonary vasculature.

f. Phenomenon that occurs when a patient's blood pressure is susceptible to elevation as a result of apprehension and anxiety in a health care provider's office or during any other stressful situation.

g. The difference between the systolic and diastolic pressure, which is about 40 mmHg.

KEY TERMS MATCHING EXERCISE 2

Write the letter of the correct definition in the space next to each term.

Term

_____ 8. stage 1 hypertension

_____ 9. stage 2 hypertension

_____ 10. DASH diet

_____ 11. dissecting aortic aneurysm

_____ 12. hypertensive crisis

_____ 13. hypertensive encephalopathy

_____ 14. vasodilator

Definition

a. A localized dilation of the aorta that has a longitudinal dissection between the outer and middle layers of the vascular wall.

b. A blood pressure of greater than 160 mmHg systolic or greater than 100 mmHg diastolic measured during multiple office visits following the guidelines for obtaining accurate blood pressure measurements.

c. A very dangerous state of multifocal cerebral ischemia due to a severe acutely or subacutely elevated blood pressure.

d. A rare, sometimes fatal, occurrence that is characterized by the sudden onset of a diastolic blood pressure reading of 120 to 130; the clinical manifestation indicates target organ vascular damage and the presence of retinal exudates and hemorrhages.

e. A substance that causes the dilation of blood vessels.

f. A blood pressure of 140 to 159 mmHg systolic or 90 to 99 mmHg diastolic measured during multiple office visits following the guidelines for obtaining accurate blood pressure measurements.

g. A diet low in saturated fat, cholesterol, and total fat. There are two versions of the plan: Plan 1 limits the patient to 2,000 mg of sodium per day; plan 2 limits the patient to 1,500 mg of sodium per day.

BLOOD PRESSURE REGULATORS

Name each system that influences blood pressure change in the body and summarize how it works.

15. _____

_____

_____

16. _____

_____

_____

17. _____

_____

_____

18. _____

_____

_____

SHORT ANSWER QUESTIONS

19. What factors that contribute to hypertension can be modified?

_____

_____

20. What factors that contribute to hypertension cannot be modified?

_____

_____

21. What organs are most often damaged over an extended period of time as a result of uncontrolled high blood pressure?

_____

_____

22. What causes a hypertensive crisis?

_____

_____

23. How is blood pressure related to an individual's culture, environment, race, and genetics?

_____

_____

24. High blood pressure is asymptomatic initially, but some clinical signs and symptoms may be reported. What are these symptoms?

_____

_____

25. How does exercise help to lower blood pressure?

_____

_____

CLASSIFICATION OF BLOOD PRESSURE FOR ADULTS

Add the appropriate blood pressure readings for each category

BP Classification	SBP (mmHg)	DBP (mmHg)
Normal		
Prehypertension		
Stage 1 hypertension		
Stage 2 hypertension		

NCLEX-RN® REVIEW QUESTIONS

21-1. The nurse would plan teaching for a client with two consecutive blood pressure readings, a month apart, of 132/80 and 130/88 to be focused toward:
1. Understanding the adverse effects of propanolol (Inderal)
2. Increasing nutritional potassium intake daily
3. Understanding the warning signs of cerebral vascular accident
4. Therapeutic methods to manage daily stressors

21-2. The nurse recognizes that which of the following terms describes the difference between the systolic and diastolic values?
1. Pulse pressure
2. Ankle-brachial index
3. Normal blood pressure
4. Stroke volume

21-3. Place the following scenarios in order of highest to lowest risk factors for developing hypertension.
1. 46-year-old female, African American, recently fired from her job
2. 46-year-old female, Caucasian, 50 pounds over ideal body weight
3. 56-year-old male, African American, insulin-dependent diabetic
4. 56-year-old male, Caucasian, excessive alcohol consumption

21-4. The nurse realizes that the action of a drug such as Enalapril (Vasotec) is to:
1. Block the conversion of angiotensin I to vasoconstrictor angiotensin II.
2. Block the calcium ion from entering the cells of the smooth muscle and myocardium.
3. Stimulate the alpha adrenergic receptors in the central nervous system.
4. Relax smooth muscle tone of the blood vessel, thus reducing the peripheral resistance.

21-5. The nurse realizes that the area in the United States with the highest percentage of hypertension is:
1. Pacific coast
2. Midwest
3. Southeast
4. Great Lakes region

21-6. Which of the following diet menus chosen by a patient with prehypertension reflects understanding of health promotion education?
1. Turkey on wheat bread, carrot sticks, orange sherbet
2. Grilled cheese sandwich, dill pickle, apple, tomato juice
3. Fried fish on white bread with tartar sauce, green beans, whole milk
4. Two-egg omelet, strawberries with ice cream, water

21-7. A group of health care professionals are meeting with a patient who is nonadhering to prescribed methods to control hypertension. Which of the following should the patient be instructed as to the most common complication of high blood pressure?
1. Renal insufficiency
2. Diabetes
3. Ischemic heart disease
4. Aortic aneurysm

CHAPTER 22

INFUSION THERAPY

OUTCOME-BASED LEARNING OBJECTIVES

22-1. Compare and contrast the types and uses of catheters for parenteral administration of solutions and medications.

22-2. Describe the types and uses of parenteral administration equipment and infusion devices.

22-3. Evaluate the tenets of infusion nursing practice including competencies, skill validation, and patient assessment.

22-4. Describe components of infusion-specific documentation.

22-5. Discuss the recognition and management of infusion-related complications, and strategies to prevent complications for the patient receiving infusion therapy.

EXPLORE PEARSON **mynursingkit**™

MyNursingKit is your one stop for online chapter review materials and resources. Prepare for success with additional NCLEX®-style practice questions, interactive assignments and activities, web links, animations and videos, and more!

Register your access code from the front of your book at **www.mynursingkit.com**

CHAPTER OUTLINE

I. Vascular Access Devices
   A. Peripheral Vascular Access Devices
      1. Peripheral-Short Catheters
      2. Winged Steel Infusion Set
      3. Over-the-Needle Peripheral-Short Catheters
      4. Through-the-Needle Peripheral-Short Catheters
      5. Midline Catheters
   B. Central Vascular Access Devices
      1. Nontunneled and Noncuffed CVADs
      2. Tunneled and Cuffed CVADs
      3. Implanted Ports
   C. Specialized Infusion Catheters and Devices
      1. Dialysis and Pheresis Catheters
      2. Arterial-Venous Shunts
      3. Arterial Catheters
         a. Hepatic Artery Catheters

KEY TERMS MATCHING EXERCISE 1

Write the letter of the correct definition in the space next to each term.

Term

_____ 1. vascular access device (VAD)

_____ 2. flashback chamber

_____ 3. self-sheathing

_____ 4. winged steel infusion set

_____ 5. midline (ML) catheter

_____ 6. percutaneously

_____ 7. implanted port

_____ 8. hypodermoclysis

_____ 9. continuous subcutaneous infusion (CSI)

_____ 10. Ommaya reservoir

Definition

a. Small space located after the hub of the catheter and attached to the stylet; used to collect blood.

b. Passing through the skin.

c. A metal needle manufactured with flexible plastic attachments to facilitate insertion technique; used for phlebotomy procedures or for single-dose parenteral administrations and infusions of less than 4 hours duration.

d. The uninterrupted infusion of small-volume parenteral medication via the subcutaneous route.

e. A surgically placed central vascular access device; a chambered device comprised of a reservoir and an attached catheter; used for long-term or chronic infusion therapies.

f. A flexible catheter measuring not more than 8 inches with the distal tip dwelling in the basilica, cephalic, or brachial veins, level with the axilla and distal to the shoulder.

g. Continuous subcutaneous infusion of a large volume of isotonic parenteral fluids for purposes of rehydration.

h. A catheter, tube, or device inserted into the vascular system.

i. Nonvascular infusion device inserted with the catheter tip residing in the ventricles of the brain; used to deliver targeted therapies (i.e., pain and antineoplastic therapies) or to obtain cerebrospinal fluid.

j. Engineered safety mechanism in which a needle is encased in a protective chamber.

KEY TERMS MATCHING EXERCISE 2

Write the letter of the correct definition in the space next to each term.

Term

_____ 11. primary set
_____ 12. secondary set
_____ 13. add-on devices
_____ 14. administration set
_____ 15. drip factor
_____ 16. infiltration
_____ 17. chemical phlebitis
_____ 18. dialysis catheter
_____ 19. bacterial phlebitis
_____ 20. nontunneled and noncuffed device

Definition

a. Infusion set used to administer supplemental infusion therapies via the primary infusion system.

b. Inadvertent administration of a nonvesicant solution or medication into surrounding tissues.

c. Any extra equipment such as filters, stopcocks, extensions, connectors, and injection ports or caps added to the primary intravenous set.

d. Infusion set with a single fluid pathway from the fluid container to a vascular access device.

e. Type of central vascular access device; inserted by a puncture directly through the skin and to the intended location without passing through subcutaneous tissue.

f. A large-bore vascular access device used as a temporary means to facilitate dialysis procedures; its configuration is similar to that of a pheresis catheter.

g. Inflammation of a vein associated with infusates of varying ranges of pH or osmolarities.

h. Infusion-specific tubing that delivers parenteral fluid via a sterile pathway from its container to the patient via a vascular access device.

i. The number of drops equal to 1 mL of fluid.

j. Inflammation of a vein associated with an infectious process.

WORD SEARCH

First identify the word from its definition. Then find and circle it in the puzzle below.

21. _____ The time period during which an infusion catheter remains in place.

22. _____ The bore or internal opening of a catheter.

23. _____ A device that is introduced through the skin, into the vascular network, for the purpose of infusing parenteral solutions and medications.

24. _____ Portion of a catheter that is used to affix infusion equipment to a vascular access device. Also known as the *hub*.

25. _____ Type of access needle required to access an implanted port or reservoir; used to prevent accidental coring of the port's septum.

26. _____ Term used to describe fluids and medications that are administered via routes other than the alimentary canal.

27. _____ Material covering a portal; access point of an implanted port or reservoir, usually made of compressed silicon.

28. _____ The number of drops equal to 1 mL of fluid.

29. _____ Pole-mounted electronic infusion devices that have multiple channels for infusion within a single device.

30. _____ Electronic infusion device often used in critical care areas; used to administer multiple parenteral therapies simultaneously.

31. _____ Authoritative statements by which the nursing profession describes the common level of performance or care by which the quality of practice can be determined and responsibilities for which its practitioners are accountable.

32. _____ The slanted or angled part of a needle or stylet.

33. _____ Needle or catheter size.

34. _____ Add-on device used to screen particulate matter, bacteria, and toxins from the infusion system.

35. _____ Electronic infusion device that calculates the volume of solution delivered based on the amount displaced in the set's reservoir.

36. _____ Parenteral fluid or medication.

37. _____ Inadvertent administration of a vesicant solution or medication into surrounding tissues.

38. _____ Obstruction of a blood vessel by an air bubble.

39. _____ Inflammation of a vein associated with a catheter, its insertion, and the selected insertion site.

40. _____ Procedure performed to maintain device patency and prevent mixing of incompatible solutions or medications.

41. _____ Devices used for administration of two or more infusates simultaneously. Access to the multiflow adapter is usually via a cap that maintains sterility of the fluid pathway.

42. _____ Administration of parenteral fluids via the bone marrow; used in emergent situations when vascular access is not available.

43. _____ Manually operated add-on device used to direct the flow of an infusate.

44. _____ Tubing that adds length and/or access ports to an administration set.

45. _____ Screw-type locking mechanism used to prevent accidental separation of infusion equipment.

Y	P	A	R	E	H	T	S	U	O	E	S	S	O	A	R	T	N	I	A
M	S	I	L	O	B	M	E	R	I	A	C	C	P	T	A	R	R	Y	Y
A	U	E	R	A	F	E	D	T	E	S	N	O	I	S	N	E	T	X	E
F	I	L	T	E	R	S	A	D	T	P	A	R	E	N	T	E	R	A	L
E	C	I	T	C	A	R	P	F	O	S	D	R	A	D	N	A	T	S	D
R	D	A	E	I	T	W	Z	B	T	R	P	O	O	Y	T	R	E	Y	E
N	R	R	A	T	C	A	T	H	E	T	E	R	E	D	X	P	T	C	E
O	I	R	E	A	T	H	E	E	D	S	M	N	E	O	T	R	A	C	N
I	P	A	G	A	N	G	A	U	G	E	S	R	B	U	D	S	S	D	G
T	F	R	N	S	T	A	D	N	O	K	K	E	M	W	S	B	U	I	N
A	A	V	I	E	E	Y	A	P	N	T	V	C	E	R	L	T	F	O	I
S	C	R	H	A	Z	L	P	L	U	E	R	L	O	K	R	I	N	O	R
A	T	S	S	T	A	U	T	E	L	S	L	F	I	C	Q	U	I	P	O
V	O	L	U	M	E	M	E	T	R	I	C	P	U	M	P	T	Y	O	C
A	R	S	L	E	Y	E	R	R	A	R	E	H	U	T	U	O	Y	O	N
R	R	A	F	T	E	N	I	O	S	E	E	T	E	M	M	T	T	E	O
T	D	U	A	L	C	H	A	N	N	E	L	P	U	M	P	A	S	S	N
X	Y	G	E	U	R	E	N	I	L	L	O	U	T	L	O	Y	R	W	R
E	M	E	C	H	A	N	I	C	A	L	P	H	L	E	B	I	T	I	S

COMPLETE THE SENTENCE

Write the missing words in the blanks.

46. The winged steel infusion set is biocompatible; therefore, low rates of device-related _____ are documented with this infusion product.

47. _____ _____ _____ catheters are made of radiopaque materials that allow x-ray visualization. They cannot be used for long dwells.

48. A(n) _____ _____ _____ catheter allows passage of the catheter through the lumen of the steel introducer needle, which is the rigid device that allows passage into the vessel.

49. A(n) _____ _____ _____ _____ (_____) is a catheter inserted into a centrally located vein with the tip residing in the vena cava.

50. The three types of CVADs are the _____ _____ _____ _____, the _____ _____ _____ _____, and _____ _____.

51. Specialized infusion catheters and devices, such as the _____ _____, are used exclusively for cardiac monitoring and hemodynamic analyses in the critical care setting.

52. _____ and _____ catheters are used for procedures where large volumes of blood need to be treated for specific medical indications. They may be inserted at the bedside or in the radiology or operating suite.

53. One order conversion technique is to divide the milliliter rate per hour by a specific number associated with the _____ _____.

54. Necessary components of the assessment process for a patient undergoing infusion therapy include, but are not limited to, the patient's _____, _____ _____, _____ _____, and renal function tests.

55. Site selection should be routinely initiated in the _____ areas of the _____ extremities with subsequent cannulations made proximal to previous cannulated sites.

LABELING EXERCISE: COMMON VEINS USED FOR INTRAVENOUS THERAPY

Place the term in the correct location.

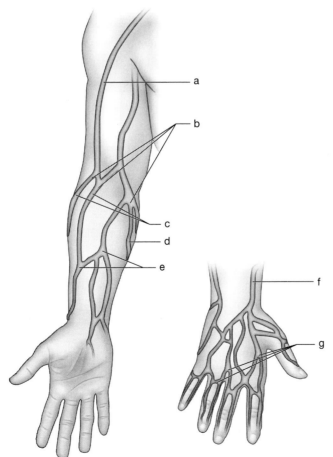

a. _____

b. _____

c. _____

d. _____

e. _____

f. _____

g. _____

Accessory cephalic veins
Basilic vein
Cephalic vein
Median veins
Median veins—cephalic, cubital, and basilic
Metacarpal and dorsal veins
Superior cephalic vein

NCLEX-RN® REVIEW QUESTIONS

22-1. The nurse is accessing a patient's implanted port. Which of the following should the nurse do when accessing this device?
1. Use sterile gloves.
2. Use nonlatex gloves.
3. Use a noncoring needle.
4. Be sure to puncture the septum.

22-2. A patient is receiving parenteral therapy through an infusion pump. The pump is alarming "other." Which of the following should the nurse do?
1. Turn the machine on and off until the alarm stops.
2. Turn off the alarm.
3. Check the machine for indications of a low battery.
4. Remove the fluids from the pump and administer using gravity.

22-3. A patient is prescribed parenteral fluids with the addition of potassium chloride. Which of the following should the nurse do prior to beginning the infusion?
1. Flush the access device with normal saline.
2. Flush the access device using the SASH technique.
3. Secure a volumetric pump.
4. Assess the patient's current electrolyte levels.

22-4. A nurse, trained in peripherally inserted central catheters, is removing the line from a patient. What should the nurse be sure to document once the line is removed?
1. The length of the catheter removed from the patient
2. The patient's pulse
3. The patient's blood pressure
4. The physician's order for removal of the catheter

22-5. A peripheral access device was placed in a patient's right hand. The patient was instructed not to bend the hand or make a fist; however, the patient was using the hand to write. The nurse realizes this patient is at risk for developing:
1. Bruising.
2. Thrombosis.
3. Infection.
4. Mechanical phlebitis.

CHAPTER 23

BLOOD ADMINISTRATION

OUTCOME-BASED LEARNING OBJECTIVES

23-1. Describe the rationale for blood donation requirements and restrictions.

23-2. Describe the advantages of blood component therapy and the therapeutic uses for each component.

23-3. Compare and contrast the hazards of transfusion therapy and the nursing measures used to assess and prevent them.

23-4. Using the nursing process, describe the administration procedure for blood administration.

23-5. Delineate the critical thinking and clinical judgment nursing skills necessary to appropriately treat adverse reactions to blood transfusions.

PEARSON
EXPLORE

MyNursingKit is your one stop for online chapter review materials and resources. Prepare for success with additional NCLEX®-style practice questions, interactive assignments and activities, web links, animations and videos, and more!

Register your access code from the front of your book at **www.mynursingkit.com**

CHAPTER OUTLINE

   I. Donor Considerations
      A. Donation Procedure
      B. Complications of Donation
  II. Blood Supply Safety
      A. ABO and Rh Factor Testing
      B. Disease Testing
 III. Therapeutic Uses of Blood Products
 IV. Types of Blood Products
      A. Homologous Transfusion
      B. Designated (Directed) Blood
      C. Autologous Transfusion
         1. Preoperative Donation
         2. Perioperative Blood Salvage
         3. Postoperative Blood Salvage
      D. Therapeutic Apheresis

V. Risks Associated with Transfusion Therapy
    A. Disease Transmission
    B. Bacterial Contamination
    C. Transfusion Reactions
        1. White Blood Cell Reproduction
    D. Noninfectious Serious Hazards of Transfusion Therapy
        1. Mistransfusion and ABO/Rh Incompatible Transfusion
        2. Circulatory Overload
        3. Transfusion-Related Graft Versus Host Disease
        4. Transfusion-Related Acute Lung Injury
    E. Less Common Noninfectious Transfusion-Related Hazards
        1. Iron Overload
        2. Multiple and Massive Transfusion Reactions
VI. Nursing Responsibilities Before, During, and After Transfusions
        NURSING MANAGEMENT
        ASSESSMENT
        NURSING DIAGNOSIS
        PLANNING
        EQUIPMENT PREPARATION
        OUTCOME AND EVALUATION PARAMETERS
        INTERVENTIONS AND RATIONALES
        EVALUATION
VII. Blood Alternatives
VIII. Research

KEY TERMS MATCHING EXERCISE

Write the letter of the correct definition in the space next to each term.

Term

_____ 1. autologous transfusion
_____ 2. fresh frozen plasma
_____ 3. homologous transfusion
_____ 4. perioperative blood salvage
_____ 5. postoperative blood salvage
_____ 6. transfusion-related acute lung injury (TRALI)

Definition

a. The process of collecting blood from a donor for transfusion into other individuals who are in need of blood.

b. The process of collecting and reinfusing a patient's own blood.

c. A serious, life-threatening clinical syndrome that is a complication of blood transfusions. It is thought to be caused by the presence of granulocyte antibodies and biologically active lipids in the donor plasma to which the recipient reacts.

d. The process of salvaging blood in which blood is obtained from mediastinal and chest tubes, and then reinfused.

e. The process of collecting and reinfusing blood lost during both the intraoperative and early postoperative periods.

f. A process in which the plasma portion of blood is separated from the cells and frozen until needed.

KEY TERM CROSSWORD

Complete the crossword puzzle below using key terms.

Across:

1. Blood type for an individual with A antigen.
4. A commercially prepared product that is derived from the plasma portion of blood.
6. Blood type for an individual with neither A nor B antigens.
7. Blood type for an individual with B antigen.
9. Red blood cells that have had the plasma portion of the blood removed by a centrifuge process.
10. Blood that is obtained from a donor, processed, and infused into a recipient.
12. A clotting factor that may be administered intravenously for the treatment of hemophilia A.
15. A protein substance made up of numerous complex antigens.

Down:

2. A unit of packed red blood cells that had most of the white blood cells removed as soon as the blood was taken from the donor (i.e., pior to storage).
3. Blood type for an individual with both A and B antigens.
5. Red blood cells coated in glycerol prior to freezing and then washed after thawing to remove the glycerol prior to administration. This is a method of storage.
8. A technology in which the blood of a donor or patient is passed through a machine that separates out one specific particle and returns the remainder of the blood to circulation.
11. Clotting factors used to treat bleeding associated with hemophilia and disorders that cause a depletion of the clotting factors.
13. The process of infusing blood products in order to restore circulating volume and therefore increase oxygen-carrying capacity.
14. Red blood cells that have undergone a washing process to remove immunoglobulins and proteins that cause reactions.

TRUE OR FALSE?

7. _____ T/F It is more economical to separate blood into its component parts and use only that portion needed by the patient for a specific condition or disease.

8. _____ T/F A person with hypertension is ineligible to be a blood donor regardless of whether or not the condition is being treated.

9. _____ T/F Excessive bleeding at the venipuncture site, angina chest pain, and migraine are complications of blood donation.

10. _____ T/F Most of the platelets and WBCs are removed or destroyed during the processing of donating blood.

11. _____ T/F Initial symptoms of bacterial contamination during or after a transfusion are often fever, chills, and hypotension.

12. _____ T/F Little progress has been made in reducing the risk of noninfectious serious hazards from transfusions.

13. _____ T/F The nurse must always obtain baseline vital sign, temperature, and lung sounds in order to monitor and assess significant changes during a transfusion.

14. _____ T/F To increase the rate of the transfusion and decrease the viscosity of the blood, dextrose solutions may run simultaneously to help thin the blood product.

15. _____ T/F Rapid, massive infusion of warmed blood may precipitate cardiac dysrhythmias and cardiac arrest.

16. _____ T/F A 12- to 16-gauge catheter is required for RBCs to pass through without being damaged.

BLOOD TYPES, ANTIGENS AND ANTIBODIES, AND TRANSFUSION TYPES

Add the missing information in the table below.

Blood Type with Antigen	Antibody Produced	Type for Transfusion
Blood type A, Antigen A		
Blood type B, Antigen B		
Blood type AB, Antigen AB		
Blood type O, No antigens		

NCLEX-RN® REVIEW QUESTIONS

23-1. A patient comes into the Blood Bank desiring to be a blood donor. This patient has frequently lived in foreign countries and is a recovering intravenous drug user. Which of the following should the nurse instruct this patient?
1. Nothing. Prepare for this patient to donate blood.
2. Blood can only be donated every 56 days.
3. Blood donation can occur only after having lived in the United States for 5 consecutive years.
4. Unfortunately, living in foreign countries and being a recovering intravenous drug user would cause the patient to be ineligible as a blood donor.

23-2. A patient who is hemorrhaging is prescribed a transfusion of fresh frozen plasma. The nurse realizes this transfusion:
1. Will increase platelets.
2. Will decrease transfusion reactions.
3. Is given through a filter and will cause rapid volume replacement.
4. Is the most common blood product given.

23-3. A patient who had had a unit of PRBCs several hours ago begins to complain of chills, is febrile, and has a drop in blood pressure. What should the nurse do to help this patient?

1. Provide an antipyretic.
2. Question bacterial contamination of the PRBCs and provide appropriate care.
3. Administer epinephrine.
4. Explain to the patient that this is a normal reaction for up to 12 hours after a transfusion.

23-4. The nurse is currently administering a unit of PRBCs to a patient. Which of the following should be included in this implementation?

1. Remain with the patient for the first 15 minutes and observe for transfusion reactions.
2. Assess for signs of increased tissue perfusion.
3. Check size and insertion date of the IV catheter.
4. Check for compatibility of blood product to patient's blood type.

23-5. A patient, receiving a unit of PRBCs, begins to complain of itching, hives, and chills. Which of the following should the nurse do to assist this patient?

1. Stop the transfusion, call for help and begin life-support measures.
2. Obtain a urine and blood sample.
3. Administer epinephrine.
4. Slow the transfusion, provide an antihistamine, and then resume the transfusion.

CHAPTER 24

HEMODYNAMIC MONITORING

OUTCOME-BASED LEARNING OBJECTIVES

24-1. Explain the concept of hemodynamic monitoring.

24-2. Identify components of a hemodynamic monitoring system.

24-3. Compare and contrast arterial, central venous, and pulmonary artery pressure monitoring.

24-4. Identify adequate central venous and pulmonary artery pressures.

24-5. Evaluate nursing management of arterial lines and central venous and pulmonary artery catheters.

24-6. Discuss how alterations in preload, afterload, and contractility affect cardiac output.

24-7. Compare and contrast how measurements obtained from a central venous catheter differ from the data obtained from a pulmonary artery catheter.

CHAPTER OUTLINE

I. Equipment
   A. Informed Consent
   B. Components of the Monitoring Equipment
      1. Heparin Versus No Heparin Flush Bags
   C. Leveling, Zero Referencing, and Performing the Dynamic Response Test
      1. Leveling the Transducer
      2. Zero Referencing the Transducer
      3. Dynamic Response Test/Square Wave Test
II. Hemodynamic Terminology
   A. Stroke Volume
   B. Cardiac Output
   C. Cardiac Index
   D. Ejection Fraction
   E. Contractility
   F. Preload
   G. Afterload

III. Normal Hemodynamic Pressures
    A. The Pump and the Circuit
    B. Waveforms and the Cardiac Cycle
IV. Invasive Pressure Monitoring
    A. Intra-Arterial Catheters
        1. Insertion of Arterial Catheters
        2. Arterial Pressure Waveforms
        3. Complications of Arterial Blood Pressure Monitoring
        4. Factors Influencing Arterial Pressure
            NURSING MANAGEMENT
                ASSESSMENT
                NURSING DIAGNOSIS
                PLANNING
                OUTCOMES AND EVALUATION PARAMETERS
                INTERVENTIONS AND RATIONALES
                EVALUATION
    B. Central Venous Catheters
        1. Insertion of Central Venous Catheters
        2. Central Venous Pressure Monitoring
        3. Central Venous Pressure Waveform
        4. Complications of Central Venous Pressure Monitoring
            NURSING MANAGEMENT
                ASSESSMENT
                 NURSING DIAGNOSIS
                PLANNING
                OUTCOMES AND EVALUATION PARAMETERS
                INTERVENTIONS AND RATIONALES
                EVALUATION
 V. Measuring Cardiac Output
VI. Invasive Methods with Pulmonary Artery Catheters
    A. Ports and Lumens on a Pulmonary Artery Catheter
    B. Insertion of the Pulmonary Artery Catheter
            NURSING MANAGEMENT
                ASSESSMENT
                NURSING DIAGNOSIS
                PLANNING
                OUTCOMES AND EVALUATION PARAMETERS
                INTERVENTIONS AND RATIONALES
                EVALUATION
    C. Complications of a Pulmonary Artery Catheter
    D. Pulmonary Artery Occlusion Pressure
        1. Correlating the PAOP Waveform with the Cardiac Cycle
    E. Thermodilution Cardiac Output
        1. Influence of Heart Rate on Cardiac Output
        2. Influence of Preload on Cardiac Output
        3. Influence of Afterload on Cardiac Output
    F. Specialized Pulmonary Artery Catheters
        1. Continuous Cardiac Output PAC
        2. Continuous Mixed Venous Oxygen Saturation
        3. Right Ventricular Ejection Fraction Volumetric Catheter
    G. Transpulmonary Thermodilution with Pulse Contour Analysis
            NURSING MANAGEMENT
                ASSESSMENT
                NURSING DIAGNOSIS
                PLANNING

KEY TERMS MATCHING EXERCISE 1

Write the letter of the correct definition in the space next to each term.

Term

_____ 1. hemodynamic monitoring

_____ 2. phlebostatic axis

_____ 3. transesophageal ultrasound

_____ 4. leveling

_____ 5. stroke volume (SV)

_____ 6. dynamic response test

_____ 7. cardiac index (CI)

_____ 8. cardiac output (CO)

_____ 9. preload

_____ 10. afterload

Definition

a. The amount of blood leaving the left ventricle per minute.

b. The monitoring of pressures and blood flow within the cardiovascular system.

c. A diagnostic test that uses an ultrasound device that is passed into the esophagus of a patient to create a clear image of the heart muscle and other parts of the heart.

d. The volume of blood in the ventricle at the end of diastole.

e. Reference point used to level transducers.

f. The amount of pressure or resistance the ventricles must overcome to eject blood during systole.

g. Positioning of a transducer system in line with the chamber being monitored.

h. A test to assess whether a transducer system is accurately transmitting pressures.

i. The amount of blood leaving a ventricle with each contraction.

j. Individualized measurement of cardiac output by taking into account the body surface area.

KEY TERMS MATCHING EXERCISE 2

Write the letter of the correct definition in the space next to each term.

Term

_____ 11. central venous pressure (CVP)

_____ 12. contractility

_____ 13. Frank-Starling law

_____ 14. arterial line

_____ 15. mean arterial pressure (MAP)

_____ 16. thermistor

_____ 17. pulmonary artery occlusion pressure (PAOP)

_____ 18. mixed venous oxygen saturation

_____ 19. pulmonary artery catheter (PAC)

_____ 20. thoracic impedance

_____ 21. ejection fraction (EF)

_____ 22. Allen's test

Definition

a. An indwelling catheter inserted into an artery in order to monitor blood pressure.

b. Measurement of venous oxygen content in the pulmonary artery; used to assess oxygen consumption and metabolic needs of the tissues.

c. A flow-directed, balloon-tipped catheter used to measure intracardiac pressures.

d. The ability of muscle fibers to stretch to accommodate filling during diastole.

e. An external, noninvasive method of hemodynamic monitoring.

f. The amount of blood ejected from the left or right ventricle; calculated by comparing end diastolic volume to stroke volume.

g. The average pressure in the arteries during one cardiac cycle.

h. Test performed prior to arterial line insertion to test the patency of the palmar arch.

i. Measurement of venous return to the right atrium after insertion of a central venous catheter.

j. Thermometer embedded in a pulmonary artery catheter that is used to detect core temperatures.

k. A mechanical function that enables the cardiac cells to shorten and cause the muscle to contract in response to an electrical stimulus. Also referred to as rhythmicity.

l. Pressure obtained by inflating the balloon on a pulmonary artery catheter at the end of expiration to reflect left ventricular end diastolic pressure.

TRUE OR FALSE?

23. _____ T/F   An arterial line is used for infusion of IV solutions or medications.

24. _____ T/F   For a healthy heart, the expected SV is 60 to 100 mL per beat.

25. _____ T/F   When atrial pressure exceeds ventricular pressure, the tricuspid and mitral valves open and blood passively flows into the ventricle.

26. _____ T/F   When a patient's arterial line monitor alarm sounds, the nurse's first task is to troubleshoot the equipment by systematically inspecting and, if necessary, tightening all connections and tubing from insertion site to pressure bag.

27. _____ T/F   Both IV solutions and medications are irritating to the vessel and may compromise tissue perfusion distal to the catheter.

28. _____ T/F   When inserting the pulmonary artery catheter, the nurse inflates the balloon when the catheter is in the right ventrical.

29. _____ T/F   Heart rates greater than 100 increase diastolic filling time.

30. _____ T/F   Replacing administration sets, including secondary sets and add-on devices, no more frequently than at 72-hour intervals is one way to prevent infection.

31. _____ T/F   By leveling and zero referencing the transducer and performing the dynamic response test, the nurse can help ensure that CVP values are accurate.

32. _____ T/F   Four factors affect mixed venous oxygen saturation: cardiac output, hemoglobin, arterial oxygen saturation, and oxygen consumption.

LABELING EXERCISE 1: PORTS AND LUMENS OF A PULMONARY ARTERY CATHETER

Place the term in the correct location.

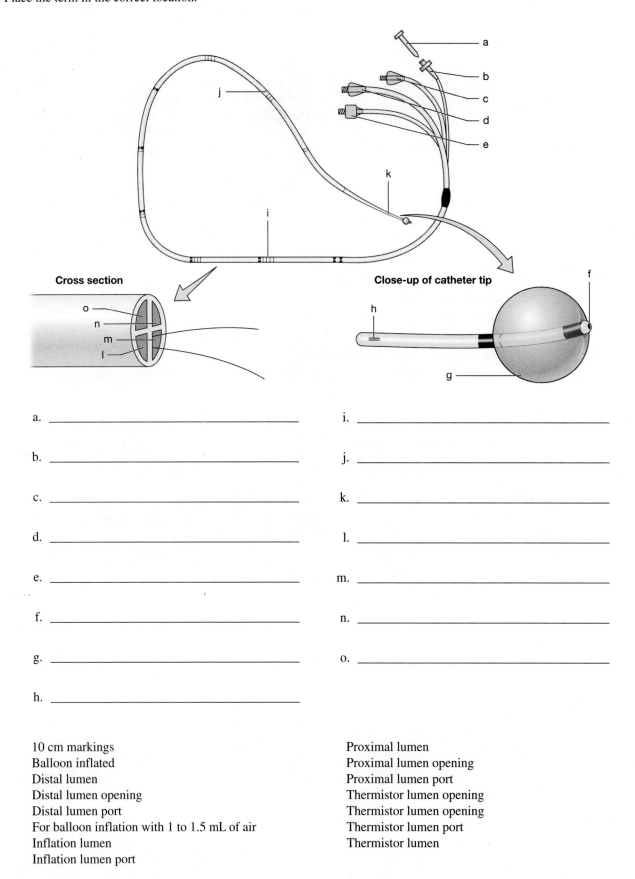

a. _____

b. _____

c. _____

d. _____

e. _____

f. _____

g. _____

h. _____

i. _____

j. _____

k. _____

l. _____

m. _____

n. _____

o. _____

10 cm markings
Balloon inflated
Distal lumen
Distal lumen opening
Distal lumen port
For balloon inflation with 1 to 1.5 mL of air
Inflation lumen
Inflation lumen port

Proximal lumen
Proximal lumen opening
Proximal lumen port
Thermistor lumen opening
Thermistor lumen opening
Thermistor lumen port
Thermistor lumen

LABELING EXERCISE 2: POSITION OF PULMONARY ARTERY CATHETER DURING PAOP

Place the term in the correct location.

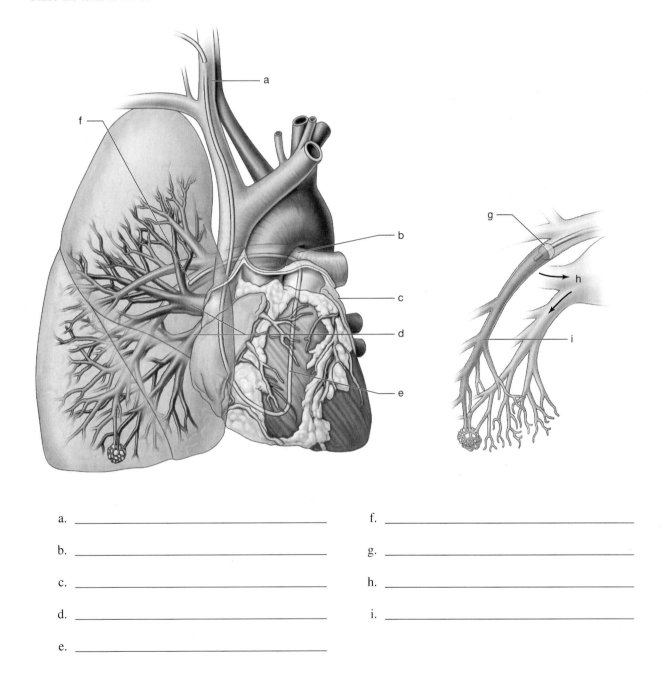

a. _____

b. _____

c. _____

d. _____

e. _____

f. _____

g. _____

h. _____

i. _____

Catheter (in right ventricle)
Catheter tip
Column of blood
Inflated balloon
Left atrial pressure

Left atrium
Right internal jugular vein
Right pulmonary artery
Right pulmonary veins

NCLEX-RN® REVIEW QUESTIONS

24-1. A patient is being admitted to the postanesthesia care unit after having a kidney transplant. The patient has a central venous pressure monitoring device. When stable, the nurse should prepare to transfer this patient to:
1. The cardiovascular ICU.
2. The general surgical ICU.
3. A cardiac step down unit.
4. A unit that is best equipped to support the patient's needs.

24-2. After the insertion of a hemodynamic monitoring device, the nurse is concerned about the quality of the tracing signal. This information could mean a malfunction of which of the following components of the system?
1. Transducer
2. Tubing
3. Location
4. Solution

24-3. A patient needs an arterial line placed. However, the medical staff is having difficulty accessing the preferred artery. Which of the following sites could be used instead?
1. Femoral
2. Subclavian
3. Internal jugular
4. External jugular

24-4. The pressures of a patient with a pulmonary artery catheter are systolic pressure of 26 mm Hg, diastolic pressure of 4 mm Hg, pulmonary artery systolic pressure of 24 mm Hg, and pulmonary artery diastolic pressure of 12 mm Hg. What do these pressures suggest to the nurse?
1. The catheter needs to be adjusted.
2. These values are normal.
3. The patient is dehydrated.
4. The patient is fluid overloaded.

24-5. The monitor of a patient with an arterial line is alarming *low pressure*. Which of the following should the nurse do first?
1. Discontinue the vasopressive medication.
2. Notify the physician.
3. Reposition the limb with the arterial line.
4. Manually assess the patient's blood pressure.

24-6. With hemodynamic monitoring, it has been determined that a patient has a reduced afterload. The nurse realizes this finding will:
1. Increase the workload of the heart.
2. Increase myocardial oxygen demands.
3. Increase stroke volume.
4. Decrease stroke volume.

24-7. A patient with a central venous pressure monitor is demonstrating a waveform with two distinct positive waves. The nurse realizes this tracing indicates:
1. The patient is becoming hypotensive.
2. The patient is registering a normal wave pattern but the *c* wave is not visible.
3. The pulmonic valve is not closing.
4. The patient is fluid volume overloaded.

CHAPTER 25

PREOPERATIVE NURSING

OUTCOME-BASED LEARNING OBJECTIVES

25-1. Describe the components and significance of preoperative assessments.

25-2. Identify critical preoperative assessment findings that require further intervention.

25-3. Discuss the elements of preoperative preparation.

25-4. Prioritize nursing interventions for the preoperative patient.

25-5. Develop a teaching plan for the preoperative patient.

25-6. Identify and discuss areas of future research relevant to the preoperative patient.

CHAPTER OUTLINE

  I. Categories of Surgery
    A. Common Surgical Suffixes
  II. Perioperative Nursing and Perioperative Nursing Practice Standards
            COLLABORATIVE MANAGEMENT
            NURSING MANAGEMENT
    A. Nursing Assessment of the Preoperative Patient
      1. Age
      2. Allergies
      3. Current Health Problem
      4. Type of Surgery Planned
      5. Plans for Autologous Blood Donation
      6. Family History
      7. Past Medical History
      8. Past Surgical History and Experience with Anesthesia
      9. Current Medications
     10. Current Herbal Medications and Nutritional Supplements

KEY TERMS MATCHING EXERCISE

Write the letter of the correct definition in the space next to each term.

Term

_____ 1. cosmetic surgery
_____ 2. curative procedures
_____ 3. diagnostic procedures
_____ 4. elective procedures
_____ 5. emergent (emergency) surgery
_____ 6. exploratory surgery
_____ 7. holding area
_____ 8. palliative procedures
_____ 9. perioperative
_____ 10. preoperative health evaluation
_____ 11. reconstructive surgery
_____ 12. same-day admission
_____ 13. urgent procedures

Definition

a. Surgeries performed for the purpose of diagnosing a condition.

b. Surgeries performed for the primary purpose of curing a condition.

c. An evaluation done within 30 days of a planned operation and must be documented in the patient's chart per the Joint Commission requirements.

d. A hospital process in which the patient is not hospitalized prior to a surgical procedure but instead reports directly to the reception area of the operating room from home.

e. A physical space located adjacent to the operating room where patients wait prior to an operation.

f. Surgeries performed for the primary purpose of alleviating symptoms rather than effecting a cure.

g. Surgery performed for the primary purpose of improving physical appearance.

h. Surgeries that must be performed sooner rather than later.

i. Surgery that must be performed suddenly without advanced planning.

j. Procedure for which the timing is determined by the patient and the surgeon.

k. Surgery performed for the purpose of rebuilding tissues or body structures to achieve a more normal function and appearance.

l. A broad term that refers to the time period surrounding a surgical procedure. It includes the preoperative, intraoperative, and postoperative time periods.

m. Surgery performed for the purpose of identifying abnormalities when the diagnosis of a condition is not established beforehand.

NAME THE SUFFIX

For each definition, provide the correct suffix and one example of how it appears in a word.

14. Surgical creation of permanent opening   Suffix _____   Example _____

15. Surgical repair or reconstruction of   Suffix _____   Example _____

16. Removal of, surgical excision to remove   Suffix _____   Example _____

17. Use of a scope to view an area, looking into   Suffix _____   Example _____

18. Surgical repair or suture of   Suffix _____   Example _____

19. Surgical incision of or cutting into   Suffix _____   Example _____

SHORT ANSWER QUESTIONS

20. Explain the importance of individualizing preoperative education.

   _____

   _____

21. Explain why preoperative fasting is critical to a successful surgery.

   _____

   _____

22. Why are breathing exercises often prescribed preoperatively?

   _____

   _____

23. What benefits do relaxation response exercises provide for the surgical patient?

   _____

   _____

24. What are the increased surgical risks for smokers?

   _____

   _____

25. What assessments are included in the patient history during the preoperative assessment?

   _____

   _____

RISK FACTORS FOR POSTOPERATIVE NAUSEA AND VOMITING

Check the risk factors associated with postoperative nausea and vomiting.

_____ Gender (women more than men)

_____ History of nausea and vomiting with a previous surgery

_____ History of phlebitis

_____ History of motion sickness

_____ Age 55 and over

_____ Age under 55

_____ Smoker

_____ Nonsmoker

_____ Use of certain inhalation anesthetics (volatile anesthetic gases and nitrous oxide)

_____ Absolute iron deficiency

_____ Human immunodeficiency virus (HIV) infection

_____ Use of opioid analgesics

_____ High alcohol consumption

_____ Type of surgery (gynecologic, abdominal, and those on the ear or eye)

_____ Longer surgeries

NCLEX-RN® REVIEW QUESTIONS

25-1. A patient with a pacemaker is going to have surgery to repair a torn leg tendon. Which of the following should the nurse assess for this patient?
  1. If the patient has a magnet to turn the unit off
  2. The date the unit was interrogated
  3. If the patient stopped all medications the morning of the surgery
  4. If the patient had preoperative pulmonary function tests completed

25-2. A patient with type 1 diabetes is being prepared preoperatively for a hernia repair. The nurse realizes that which of the following should be done for this patient?
  1. Preoperative pulmonary function tests
  2. Be alert for increased sensitivity to anesthesia.
  3. Provide the routine doses of insulin.
  4. Strict monitoring of blood glucose levels

25-3. Prior to taking a patient into the operating room, the nurse anesthetist provides a dose of Versed. The purpose for this medication is to:
  1. Reduce the risk of atrial fibrillation.
  2. Decrease gastric acid production.
  3. Reduce pain.
  4. Smooth induction of anesthesia.

25-4. The nurse is planning preoperative care for a patient with a sensory disorder. Which of the following should be included in the care for this patient?
  1. Document preoperative skin status.
  2. Ensure adequate hydration.
  3. Encourage mobility.
  4. Assess pain frequently.

25-5. A preoperative patient is being instructed on ambulation after the surgical procedure. Which of the following would be beneficial for the nurse to include in these instructions?
  1. The patient could always refuse to ambulate.
  2. The patient could sit on the side of the bed instead of ambulate.
  3. Ambulation is important to increase circulation to all body areas and speed the release of anesthesia from the body.
  4. Turning and repositioning the body every two hours is as good as ambulation.

25-6. A preoperative patient wants to know why he has to quit smoking before the surgery. Which of the following should the nurse respond to this patient?
  1. Cigarettes rob the body of needed oxygen and nutrients needed for good circulation and wound healing after the surgery.
  2. There's no real evidence to support smoking cessation before the surgery.
  3. Doctors don't like anyone to smoke.
  4. It's okay if you smoke a few cigarettes the weeks before the surgery.

INTRAOPERATIVE NURSING

OUTCOME-BASED LEARNING OBJECTIVES

26-1. Discuss the sequence of events for the patient from the beginning of surgery to arrival in the postanesthesia care unit.

26-2. Differentiate the roles of the surgical team.

26-3. Describe the interplay between each team member in the success of the surgical intervention.

26-4. Prioritize nursing interventions to maximize patient safety in the operating room.

26-5. Evaluate effective nursing measures for patient advocacy in the operating room.

26-6. Prioritize the nursing care of patients experiencing selected intraoperative complications.

26-7. Differentiate the role of the certified nurse and the anesthesiologist for the anesthetized patient.

CHAPTER OUTLINE

I. Guidance for Professional Practice
II. Surgical Team
   A. Surgeon
   B. Anesthesia Care Provider
   C. Nurses
      1. Perioperative Nursing Education
         HEALTH PROMOTION
III. Surgical Areas
   A. Presurgical or Preoperative Holding Area
      1. Preoperative Operating Room Checklist
   B. Operating Room
IV. Patient Preparation
V. Surgical Approaches
      1. The Future of Surgery: Natural Orifice Translumenal Endoscopic Surgery
VI. Anesthesia
      1. Inhalation Agents

  2. Intravenous Agents
  3. Muscle Relaxants
   a. Complications of General Anesthesia
   b. Malignant Hyperthermia
  4. Other Complications
  5. Regional Anesthesia
   a. Spinal Anesthesia
   b. Epidural Anesthesia
    i. Complications of Spinal or Epidural Anesthesia
   c. Peripheral Nerve Blocks
    NURSING MANAGEMENT
     ASSESSMENT
     NURSING DIAGNOSES
     PLANNING
     OUTCOMES AND EVALUATION PARAMETERS
     INTERVENTIONS AND RATIONALES
  6. Preventing Wrong Site Surgery
  7. Surgical Time-Out
  8. Intraoperative Patient Record
  9. Protecting the Patient from Infection
  10. Positioning the Patient to Prevent Injury
  11. Preventing the Retention of Foreign Objects
  12. Estimating Blood Loss
  13. Latex Allergy
 VII. Postanesthesia Care Unit
 VIII. Gerontological Considerations

KEY TERMS MATCHING EXERCISE

Write the letter of the correct definition in the space next to each term.

Term

_____ 1. scrub nurse
_____ 2. circulating nurse
_____ 3. intraoperative
_____ 4. conscious sedation
_____ 5. general anesthesia
_____ 6. malignant hyperthermia (MH)
_____ 7. epidural anesthesia
_____ 8. Bier block
_____ 9. spinal anesthesia
_____ 10. intrathecal anesthesia
_____ 11. regional anesthesia
_____ 12. peripheral nerve block

Definition

a. The production of complete unconsciousness, muscular relaxation, and absence of pain sensation.

b. Nurse in the operating room whose duties are performed outside the sterile field.

c. The production of insensibility of a part by interrupting the sensory nerve conductivity of any region of the body by local injection of a medication.

d. A type of regional anesthesia in which an anesthetic agent is injected in the epidural space.

e. An anesthesia technique in which a local anesthetic is injected into the subarachnoid space and directly into the cerebrospinal fluid. Also called *intrathecal anesthesia*.

f. Nurse in the operating room who works directly with the surgeon within the sterile field, passing instruments, sponges, and other items needed during the surgical procedure.

g. Process in which an IV catheter is inserted in the extremity at the most distal site possible. A pneumatic tourniquet is applied proximal to the surgical site and inflated higher than the patient's systolic blood pressure. When a local anesthetic (lidocaine) is injected intravenously, the obstruction of blood by the tourniquet prevents it from leaving the surgical area.

h. A rare but life-threatening metabolic complication of anesthesia that usually occurs during the induction phase but could occur any time during surgery.

i. An anesthesia technique in which a local anesthetic is injected into or around a nerve plexus to produce anesthesia of a selected area without inducing a systemic effect.

j. During surgery.

k. A type of anesthesia in which a local anesthetic agent is inserted into the spinal fluid by penetrating the spinal dura.

l. A minimally depressed level of consciousness and satisfactory analgesia that allows the patient to retain the ability to maintain an airway independently and to respond to physical stimulation and verbal commands, obtained through the administration of a combination of pharmacologic agents.

SHORT ANSWER QUESTIONS

13. Describe the primary responsibilities of the perioperative nurse in the operating room.

_____

_____

_____

_____

14. What role does the scrub nurse play in the operating room?

_____

_____

15. What are the benefits of waterless over traditional surgical hand preparation?

_____

_____

16. What are the advantages of laparoscopic surgery over open surgery?

_____

_____

_____

_____

17. Describe the surgical time-out and its purpose.

_____

_____

_____

_____

18. What nursing interventions will decrease the risk of infection?

_____

_____

19. Why it is especially important to monitor glucose levels in elderly patients during surgery?

_____

_____

_____

_____

20. What should be done to prevent foreign objects from being left in the patient upon completion of surgery?

_____

_____

TRUE OR FALSE?

21. _____ T/F A registered nurse first assistant assists the circulating nurse in overseeing general needs of the surgical team.
22. _____ T/F The certified registered nurse anesthetist works under the supervision of the scrub nurse.
23. _____ T/F The perioperative nurse ensures that all information on the preoperative checklist is correct and complete and communicates that information to the surgical team.
24. _____ T/F Traditional surgical hand preparation is more effective than waterless surgical hand preparation but takes more time.
25. _____ T/F During laparoscropic surgery carbon dioxide is used to inflate the abdomen in order to provide space to view and perform the surgery.
26. _____ T/F Why inhaled anesthetic agents work is not completely understood.
27. _____ T/F Fentanyl is more potent than morphine and is the most commonly used analgesic in anesthesia.
28. _____ T/F Peripheral nerve blocks affect skeletal muscle and they are used in surgery to facilitate endotracheal intubation and to provide optimal operating conditions.
29. _____ T/F To reduce the incidence of spinal headache, patients are positioned into an upright position and treated with hydration and analgesics.
30. _____ T/F To prevent wrong-site surgery, AORN guidelines call for the word "no" to be written on the wrong side or site.

NCLEX-RN® REVIEW QUESTIONS

26-1. At the completion of a surgical procedure, a patient will be transferred to the PACU. Which of the following is a focus of nursing care for the patient in this area?
    1. Medicate for latex allergy.
    2. Safely recover from anesthesia.
    3. Estimate blood lost during the surgical procedure.
    4. Validate correct surgical counts.

26-2. A CRNA is providing pre-anesthesia medications to a patient scheduled for a surgical procedure. The care provider responsible for the activities completed by the CRNA would be the:
   1. Anesthesiologist.
   2. Surgeon.
   3. Scrub nurse.
   4. RNFA.

26-3. At the beginning of a surgical procedure, a decision was made to change the approach to resecting a portion of the patient's colon. Because of this decision, changes were made to the surgical instruments and type of anesthesia to provide to the patient. The individual who most likely made this decision would have been the:
   1. Scrub nurse.
   2. Anesthesiologist.
   3. Surgeon.
   4. CRNA.

26-4. After lumbar spinal fusion surgery, the patient tells the nurse that her right arm is weak and feels "numb and tingly." The nurse realizes this patient might be experiencing:
   1. Brachial plexus nerve injury.
   2. A side effect of anesthesia.
   3. A side effect of pain medication.
   4. A blood clot in the brachial artery.

26-5. Prior to the beginning of surgery, the patient tells the nurse to make sure that nothing happens to her religious medal pinned to her hospital gown. During the surgery, the gown is removed and the pin cannot be located. Which of the following should the nurse do?
   1. Complete an occurrence report.
   2. Tell a surgical assistant to search for the hospital gown and the medal.
   3. Ask that all linen be examined before being removed from the surgical suite to locate the medal.
   4. There is nothing that can be done.

26-6. A postoperative patient begins to complain of an occipital headache after having spinal anesthesia. Which of the following can be done to help this patient?
   1. Assist with early ambulation.
   2. Assist to a sitting, upright position.
   3. Restrict fluids.
   4. Provide pain medications and keep well hydrated.

26-7. The anesthesiology directs a care provider to provide pre-anesthesia medications to a patient in the holding area. The care provider most likely to administer this medication would be the:
   1. CRNA.
   2. Perioperative nurse.
   3. Respiratory therapist.
   4. RN first assistant.

CHAPTER 27

POSTOPERATIVE NURSING

OUTCOME-BASED LEARNING OBJECTIVES

27-1. Prioritize nursing diagnoses and interventions for the patient in the postanesthesia care unit.

27-2. Discuss criteria for moving patients through the phases of recovery.

27-3. Discuss the assessment, prevention, and nursing management of common postoperative problems.

27-4. Develop a teaching plan for the discharge of a patient after surgery.

27-5. Identify and discuss areas of future research relevant to the care of the postoperative patient.

EXPLORE **mynursingkit**™

PEARSON

MyNursingKit is your one stop for online chapter review materials and resources. Prepare for success with additional NCLEX®-style practice questions, interactive assignments and activities, web links, animations and videos, and more!

Register your access code from the front of your book at **www.mynursingkit.com**

CHAPTER OUTLINE

I. Nursing Management

NURSING MANAGEMENT OF THE PATIENT IN THE POSTANESTHESIA CARE UNIT

COLLABORATIVE MANAGEMENT

ASSESSMENT

NURSING DIAGNOSES AND EXPECTED OUTCOMES

INTERVENTIONS, RATIONALES, AND EVALUATION

IMPAIRED GAS EXCHANGES

RISK FOR IMBALANCED FLUID VOLUME

RISK FOR DECREASED CARDIAC OUTPUT

RISK FOR IMBALANCED BODY TEMPERATURE: HYPOTHERMIA

READINESS FOR ENHANCED COMFORT: NAUSEA AND VOMITING PAIN

ANXIETY

A. Discharge from the Postanesthesia Care Unit

B. Ambulatory Surgery Discharge

C. Transfer to an Inpatient Unit

NURSING MANAGEMENT OF THE POSTOPERATIVE PATIENT ON THE CLINICAL UNIT

COLLABORATIVE MANAGEMENT

   D. Preventing Postoperative Complications
      1. Atelectasis and Pneumonia
      2. Abdominal Distention, Ileus, and Risk for Constipation
      3. Urinary Retention
      4. Wound Infection
         a. Wound Dehiscence and Evisceration
         b. Wound Drains
         c. Venous Thromboembolism
 II. Gerontological Considerations

HEALTH PROMOTION

III. Research

KEY TERMS MATCHING EXERCISE

Write the letter of the correct definition in the space next to each term.

Term

_____ 1. fast-tracking

_____ 2. postanesthesia care unit (PACU)

_____ 3. surveillance

_____ 4. airway obstruction

_____ 5. hypoxemia

_____ 6. laryngospasm

_____ 7. hypothermia

_____ 8. normothermia

_____ 9. ileus

_____ 10. intermittent pneumatic compression devices

_____ 11. graduated compression stockings

Definition

a. A normal body temperature.

b. Devices used to apply intermittent compression of the calf muscle, thereby increasing venous return.

c. A condition in which peristalsis does not return as expected postoperatively and the bowel remains hypoactive.

d. A core body temperature of less than 96.8°F (36°C) or a condition, regardless of body temperature, in which a person experiences shivering, peripheral vasoconstriction, piloerection, and feelings of cold.

e. Obstruction that occurs most often because medications used in anesthesia cause the muscles to relax.

f. Occurs when the muscles of the larynx contract forcefully, causing a closure or partial closure of the airway.

g. Insufficient oxygen content in the blood.

h. The systematic and continuous assessment of patients for the recognition and management of potentially catastrophic events.

i. Term used to describe a situation in which a patient is transferred from the operating room to the postanesthesia care unit (PACU) phase II, bypassing PACU phase I. Fast-tracking is possible when surgical techniques are minimally invasive and anesthesia is of a short duration.

j. Elastic stockings that apply varying degrees of pressure on the lower leg with the greatest exertion of pressure at the ankle and the lowest pressure at the thigh (or knee in shorter stockings).

k. A physical space located adjacent to the operating room where patients are monitored closely as they recover from anesthesia.

SHORT ANSWER QUESTIONS

12. Describe postanesthesia phases I and II of the postoperative patient.

_____

_____

_____

13. Why is cultural consideration especially important in regard to pain management?

_____

_____

14. Assessments of what areas does the PACU nurse perform when the patient first arrives in the PACU?

_____

_____

15. Explain how the patient should be positioned upon arrival in the PACU and what changes may be made during the time there.

_____

_____

16. What are the common nursing diagnoses in the postoperative patient in the PACU?

_____

_____

_____

17. Describe the impact of regular nursing rounds on patient use of the call light in hospitals.

_____

_____

18. Explain how ambulation aids the postoperative patient.

_____

_____

19. How and why is bowel function affected by surgery?

_____

_____

20. What are the symptoms of surgical site infections, both for superficial incisions and deep incisions?

_____

_____

_____

_____

_____

TRUE OR FALSE?

21. _____ T/F For the first 2 hours after surgery, the patient may be placed on high levels of oxygen (e.g., FIO2 greater than 80%) to destroy pathogens and reduce the risk of surgical-site infections.

22. _____ T/F Respiratory complications, especially the need for upper airway support, are the most frequent postoperative problem in the PACU.

23. _____ T/F Patients are required to be able to void and to take oral fluids prior to discharge.

24. _____ T/F A temperature of 36°C (96.8°F) must be reported to the surgeon immediately.

25. _____ T/F Early ambulation is one of the most important interventions that can assist in recovery from anesthesia and surgery.

26. _____ T/F Among the surgeries with a higher risk of postoperative pulmonary complications are neurosurgery, emergency surgery, and surgeries lasting more than 2 hours.

27. _____ T/F Elevating the head of the bed 30 to 90 degrees lowers the diaphragm, thus facilitating chest expansion and decreasing the risk of postoperative pulmonary complications.

28. _____ T/F Among the risk factors for wound dehiscence and evisceration are obesity, high serum albumin, and diarrhea.

29. _____ T/F The purpose of inserting a wound drain is to prevent infection or abscess.

30. _____ T/F The postoperative patient is at risk for deep vein thrombosis (DVT) because anesthesia vasodilates vessels, leading to stasis and decreased venous return.

NCLEX-RN® REVIEW QUESTIONS

27-1. A postoperative patient in the PACU begins to complain of increasing pain that had previously been controlled. Which of the following should the nurse do?
   1. Administer more pain medications.
   2. Contribute the increase in pain to anxiety.
   3. Investigate the location and intensity of pain.
   4. Administer a placebo.

27-2. The nurse is using the Post Anesthesia Recovery Score to determine if a postoperative patient can be transferred to another care area. Which of the following would indicate that the patient can be transferred?
   1. Score of 8 after 2 hours in the PACU.
   2. Score of 4 after 1 hour in the PACU.
   3. Score of 2 after 30 minutes and a score of 6 after 1 hour in the PACU.
   4. Score of 4 after 30 minutes and a score of 7 after 1 hour in the PACU.

27-3. The nurse is caring for a postoperative patient with a Class II wound. Which of the following should the nurse do to prevent this patient from developing an infection?
   1. There is nothing the nurse can do. This patient has a 40% chance of developing an infection.
   2. Provide antibiotics since this patient has a 10% chance of developing an infection.
   3. Remove the first bloody dressing and replace with a clean dressing.
   4. Keep the wound covered up to 48 hour postoperatively with a sterile dressing.

27-4. A postoperative patient is preparing to go home. Which of the following should the nurse include in this patient's discharge instructions?
   1. Avoid lifting anything heavier than 10 pounds.
   2. Stop taking the antibiotics when the wound is no longer pink or inflamed.
   3. Resume normal activities of daily living.
   4. Return to the gym for daily workouts as energy permits.

27-5. The nurse is planning a research project to find evidence to support rationales for common nursing interventions performed after surgery. Which of the following research topics would provide this information for the nurse?
   1. Factors influencing nurses' decisions in weaning patients off oxygen postoperatively.
   2. Factors influencing the use of "alternative" nursing interventions in preventing postoperative complications.
   3. Effectiveness of nonpharmacological interventions in reducing postoperative pain.
   4. Effectiveness of alternative interventions in reducing postoperative pulmonary complications.

CHAPTER 28

Nursing Assessment of Patients with Neurological Disorders

OUTCOME-BASED LEARNING OBJECTIVES

28-1. Correlate the anatomic and physiological aspects of the nervous system with the neurological examination.

28-2. Explain the importance of history taking in the neurological assessment.

28-3. Categorize the cranial nerves with common functional deficits seen in neurological disease.

28-4. Describe the components of the mental status exam and methods to complete the assessment.

28-5. Explain the rationale for and methods of measuring and documenting muscle stretch reflexes.

28-6. Explain the methods of assessing the presence of pathologic reflexes and the method of documentation.

28-7. Explain the normal age-related differences in the neurological examination of the elderly patient.

CHAPTER OUTLINE

I. Anatomy and Physiology of the Nervous System
   A. Central Nervous System
   B. Peripheral Nervous System
   C. Autonomic Nervous System

II. Health History
   A. Biographic and Demographic Information
   B. Presenting Problem
   C. History of Presenting Problem
   D. Past Medical History
      1. Childhood Diseases and Immunizations
      2. Major Illness
      3. Medications
      4. Allergies

KEY TERMS MATCHING EXERCISE

Write the letter of the correct definition in the space next to each term.

Term

_____ 1. Battle's sign

_____ 2. gingival hyperplasia

_____ 3. raccoon eyes

_____ 4. masked facies

_____ 5. oculocephalic reflex

_____ 6. dysconjugate gaze

_____ 7. decorticate posturing

_____ 8. oculovestibular reflex

_____ 9. decerebrate posturing

_____ 10. fasciculation

Definition

a. Reflex eye movement that stabilizes images on the retina during head movement by producing an eye movement in the direction opposite to the head movement that maintains the visual field or a more-or-less steady gaze. Also called *doll's eye reflex.*

b. Bogginess of the temporal or postauricular region of the head, which indicates fracture of the basilar area of the skull.

c. Eyes moving separately from each other in the cardinal fields of gaze.

d. The characteristic posture of a person with a lesion at or above the upper brainstem. The person is rigidly still with arms flexed, fists clenched, and legs extended.

e. The characteristic posture of an individual with decerebrate rigidity. The extremities are stiff and extended, and the head is retracted.

f. Immobile, expressionless facial appearance commonly seen in Parkinson's disease.

g. Reflex that stabilizes images on the retina during head movement by producing an eye movement in the direction opposite that of the head movement.

h. Excessive proliferation of normal cells of the gingiva.

i. Ecchymosis over the orbit of the eyes that is indicative of a basilar skull fracture. Also called *raccoon sign.*

j. Involuntary contraction or twitching of a group of muscles or muscle fibers, visible under the skin.

KEY TERM CROSSWORD PUZZLE

Complete the crossword puzzle below using key terms.

Across:

1. Abnormal protrusion of the eyeball; may be due to thyrotoxicosis, tumor of the orbit, orbital cellulitis, leukemia, or aneurysm.
4. An exaggerated feeling of depression and unrest without apparent cause; a mood of general dissatisfaction, restlessness, anxiety, discomfort, and unhappiness.
6. The loss or impairment of the sense of smell.
7. Drooping of the upper eyelid, generally due to paralysis.
8. Paired or joined eyes moving in tandem in the cardinal fields of gaze.
9. Normal, nondepressed, reasonably positive mood.
11. The disorder of speech and language due to cerebral dysfunction.
12. Inequality of the size of the pupils; may be congenital or associated with aneurysms, head trauma, diseases of the nervous system, brain lesion, paresis, or locomotor ataxia.
15. A constant, involuntary tremor, oscillation, or jerky movement of the eyeball; the movement may be in any direction.

Down:

2. Indifferent; showing a lack of emotion.
3. Abnormal smallness of the head, often seen in mental retardation.
5. Abnormally large head size; found in acromegaly, hydrocephalus, rickets, osteitis deformans, leontiasis ossea, myxedema, leprosy, and pituitary disturbances.
7. A downward displacement of the eyeball in exophthalmic goiter or in inflammatory conditions of the orbit.
10. The space between the junction of two neurons in a neural pathway where the termination of the axon of one neuron comes into proximity with the cell body or dendrites of another.
13. A nerve cell; the structural and functional unit of the nervous system.
14. An exaggerated feeling of well-being.
16. The awareness of posture, movement, and changes in equilibrium and the knowledge of position, weight, and resistance of objects in relation to the body.

LABELING EXERCISE 1: TWO NEURONS WITH A SYNAPSE BETWEEN

Place the term in the correct location.

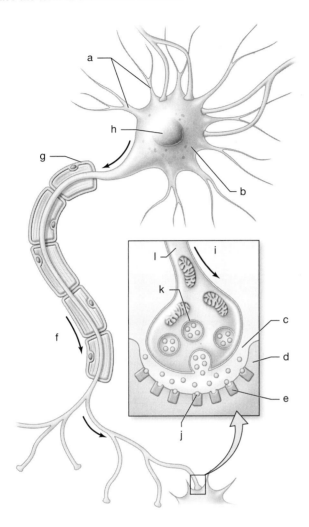

a. _____

b. _____

c. _____

d. _____

e. _____

f. _____

g. _____

h. _____

i. _____

j. _____

k. _____

l. _____

Axon
Cell body
Dendrites
Direction of impulse
Myelin sheath
Nerve impulse

Nucleus
Neurotransmitter
Receiving dendrite
Receptor
Synaptic cleft
Vesicle

LABELING EXERCISE 2: BRAIN AND SPINAL CORD

Place the term in the correct location.

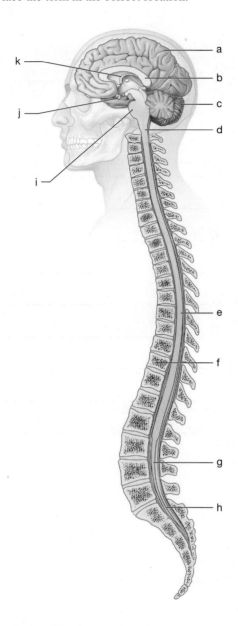

a. _____

b. _____

c. _____

d. _____

e. _____

f. _____

g. _____

h. _____

i. _____

j. _____

k. _____

Body of fornix
Brain stem
Cauda equina
Cerebellum
Cerebrum
Corpus callosum

Dura mater
Pituitary gland
Pons varolii
Spinal cord
Vertebral column

LABELING EXERCISE 3: DORSAL ASPECT OF BRAIN WITH CRANIAL NERVES

Place the term in the correct location.

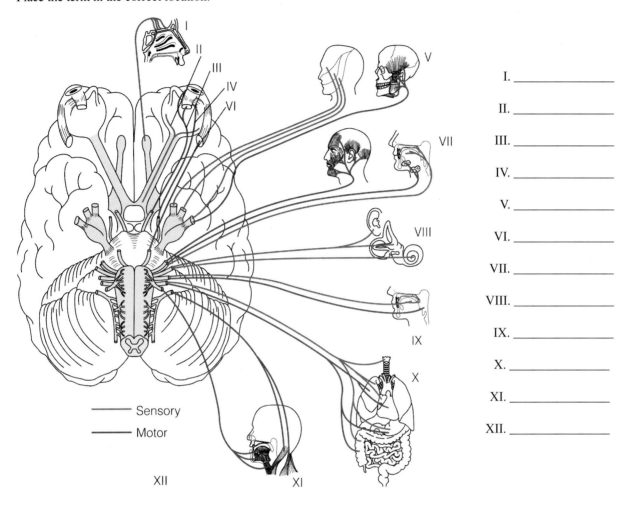

Sensory

Motor

I. _____

II. _____

III. _____

IV. _____

V. _____

VI. _____

VII. _____

VIII. _____

IX. _____

X. _____

XI. _____

XII. _____

Abducens
Accessory
Facial
Glossopharyngeal
Hypoglossal
Oculomotor

Olfactory
Optic
Trigeminal
Trochlear
Vagus
Vestibuocochlear

NCLEX-RN® REVIEW QUESTIONS

28-1. A patient has been diagnosed with crushed vertebrae at level L5-S1. The nurse realizes the patient will have which of the following effects from the injury?
1. The patient will be paralyzed from the waist to the legs.
2. The patient will be paralyzed from the chest to the legs.
3. The patient will be paralyzed from the neck to the legs.
4. The patient's effects will depend upon which nerves in the cauda equine have been injured.

28-2. The nurse is completing the social history on a patient being admitted for a neurological disturbance. The purpose of this history will be to:
1. Determine any family members with neurological disorders.
2. Determine if high-risk behaviors are routinely practiced.
3. Document the use of any herbal remedies.
4. Complete a list of current illnesses.

28-3. During the assessment of a patient the nurse notes ptosis. Which of the following cranial nerves would be responsible for this finding?
1. Optic
2. Trigeminal
3. Vestibulocochlear
4. Oculomotor, trochlear, and abducens

28-4. The nurse is assessing a patient's orientation. Which of the following would be the best to assess orientation to time?
1. Ask the patient to name the city in which he or she lives.
2. Ask the patient to state his or her full name.
3. Ask the patient to say the current day of the week.
4. Ask the patient to say where he or she is at the present time.

28-5. A patient is having increasing thigh weakness. Which of the following reflexes would the nurse most likely assess for this patient's problem?
1. Biceps
2. Triceps
3. Patellar
4. Achilles

28-6. The nurse, assessing for the presence of a grasp reflex, finds the reflex absent. How should the nurse document this finding?
1. +4
2. +3
3. +
4. −

28-7. The achilles reflex is significantly reduced in an elderly patient. The nurse realizes this finding could be indicative of:
1. Pathology.
2. A normal finding.
3. The onset of a neurological disease.
4. A disease affecting the motor neurons.

CHAPTER 29

ACUTE BRAIN DISORDERS

OUTCOME-BASED LEARNING OBJECTIVES

29-1. Describe basic pathophysiology of increased intracranial pressure as presented in this chapter.

29-2. List possible signs or symptoms of increased intracranial pressure.

29-3. Explain the rationale of nursing interventions in caring for patients with increased intracranial pressure.

29-4. Identify various types and causes of head trauma according to level of injury.

29-5. Compare and contrast differences between bacterial meningitis and viral meningitis, including causes, signs and symptoms, diagnostic evaluation, and treatment.

29-6. Identify and distinguish between the major types of brain tumors: intra-axial, extra-axial, and metastatic.

29-7. Explain treatment options for brain tumors.

29-8. Explain the role of the nurse in family teaching of patients with acute brain disorders.

EXPLORE **mynursingkit**

MyNursingKit is your one stop for online chapter review materials and resources. Prepare for success with additional NCLEX®-style practice questions, interactive assignments and activities, web links, animations and videos, and more!

Register your access code from the front of your book at **www.mynursingkit.com**

CHAPTER OUTLINE

I. Intracranial Pressure
  A. Monro-Kellie Doctrine
  B. Pathophysiology
  C. Compensatory Mechanisms
    1. Cerebral Blood Flow
    2. Cerebral Perfusion Pressure
  D. Increased Intracranial Pressure
  E. Cerebral Edema
  F. Herniation Syndromes
    1. Cingulate Herniation
    2. Transtentorial Herniation
    3. Uncal Herniation

4. Laboratory and Diagnostic Procedures
5. Medical Management
      NURSING MANAGEMENT
         ASSESSMENT
         INTERVENTIONS AND RATIONALES
         EVALUATION
      COLLABORATIVE MANAGEMENT
  D. Future Directions
IV. Brain Tumors
  A. Epidemiology
  B. Etiology
  C. Classification of Brain Tumors
    1. Intra-Axial Tumors
      a. Astrocytomas
        i. Glioblastoma Multiforme
      b. Oligodendrogliomas
      c. Ependymomas
    2. Extra-Axial Tumors
      a. Meningiomas
      b. Schwannomas
      c. Pituitary Adenomas
    3. Metastatic Tumors
      a. Epidemiology and Etiology
      b. Clinical Manifestations
      c. Laboratory and Diagnostic Procedures
  D. Medical Management
    1. Surgical Excision
    2. Radiation Therapy
    3. Stereotactic Radiosurgery
    4. Chemotherapy
      NURSING MANAGEMENT
         ASSESSMENT
         INTERVENTIONS AND RATIONALES
      COLLABORATIVE MANAGEMENT
      HEALTH PROMOTION
  E. Future Directions
V. Hydrocephalus
  A. Clinical Manifestations
  B. Laboratory and Diagnostic Procedures
  C. Medical Management
      NURSING MANAGEMENT
VI. Seizures
  A. Epidemiology and Etiology
  B. Clinical Manifestations
    1. Status Epilepticus
  C. Laboratory and Diagnostic Procedures
  D. Medical Management
      NURSING MANAGEMENT
         ASSESSMENT
         INTERVENTIONS AND RATIONALES
      COLLABORATIVE MANAGEMENT
VII. Systemic Response to Acute Brain Disorders
  A. Respiratory Effect
  B. Cardiovascular Effect
  C. Gastrointestinal Effect

D. Metabolic Effect
E. Hematologic Effect
VIII. Gerontological Considerations for Acute Brain Disorder
IX. Rehabilitation

KEY TERMS MATCHING EXERCISE 1

Write the letter of the correct definition in the space next to each term.

Term

_____ 1. intracranial pressure (ICP)
_____ 2. Monro-Kellie doctrine
_____ 3. cerebral perfusion pressure (CPP)
_____ 4. vasodilatory cascade
_____ 5. vasogenic edema
_____ 6. cerebral edema
_____ 7. traumatic brain injury (TBI)
_____ 8. comminuted skull fracture
_____ 9. depressed skull fracture
_____ 10. linear skull fracture

Definition

a. An increase in water content of the brain; swelling.

b. Doctrine that provides the foundation for understanding the implications of increased intracranial pressure. Incompressible structures within the cranial vault are in a state of volume equilibrium, such that any increase of the volumes of one component (i.e., blood, CSF, or brain tissue) must be compensated by a decrease in the volume of another. If this cannot be achieved, pressure will rise, and once the expandable reserve of the intracranial space is exhausted, small changes in volume can lead to precipitous increases in pressure.

c. The fragmented interruption of the skull resulting from multiple linear fractures.

d. An acute brain disorder characterized by an injury to the brain secondary to trauma.

e. A series of events triggered by hypoxia, resulting in increased intracranial pressure.

f. A condition characterized by an alteration in vascular permeability with disruption of the blood–brain barrier.

g. A simple break in the continuity of the skull with no displacement of bone.

h. The pressure exerted by cerebrospinal fluid within the ventricles.

i. Displacement of a comminuted skull fracture.

j. The pressure gradient that drives cerebral blood flow.

KEY TERMS MATCHING EXERCISE 2

Write the letter of the correct definition in the space next to each term.

Term

_____ 11. subdural hematoma (SDH)
_____ 12. diffuse axonal injury (DAI)
_____ 13. second-impact syndrome
_____ 14. postconcussion syndrome
_____ 15. cerebral infarction
_____ 16. cerebral ischemia
_____ 17. intra-axial tumors
_____ 18. metastatic tumors
_____ 19. extra-axial tumors
_____ 20. meningiomas

Definition

a. Tumors originating from the supporting structures of the brain.

b. Tumors originating from the meninges.

c. A primary injury of diffuse white matter that results in tearing or shearing of axons and small blood vessels.

d. Bleeding between the dura and the arachnoid layers of the meninges.

e. A condition in which brain tissue is oxygen deprived.

f. Tumors that originate somewhere else in the body and migrate to another organ.

g. A condition that may follow mild head injury.

h. Tumors originating from glial cells; found mostly in white matter.

i. A condition characterized by a second concussion that occurs before the brain completely recovers from the first concussion.

j. A condition in which brain tissue dies due to lack of oxygen.

WORD SEARCH

First identify the word from its definition. Then find and circle it in the puzzle below.

21. _____ Tumors that are at the original site where they first arose.

22. _____ The ability of the brain to change its vessel size to accommodate changes in intracranial pressure.

23. _____ A localized infection carried from other sites of the body and extending into the cerebral tissue.

24. _____ Inflammation of the meninges caused by a bacterial pathogen.

25. _____ A recognized collection of symptoms that result from a mild head injury.

26. _____ An injury to soft tissue caused by trauma; a bruise.

27. _____ Inflammation of brain tissue.

28. _____ The displacement of brain structures under pressure, causing compression and damage of brain tissue.

29. _____ Abnormal genes inherited from parents.

30. _____ Tumors of the Schwann cells (nerve sheath tumor).

31. _____ The body's response that can result from a primary injury.

32. _____ Refers to mechanical injury to the brain.

33. _____ Bleeding into the space between the skull and the dura.

34. _____ Meningeal irritation.

35. _____ Tumors originating from the ependymal cells of the cerebral ventricles.

36. _____ The accumulation of intracellular water, causing brain swelling.

37. _____ A series of events that occurs as a compensatory mechanism in response to cerebral hypoxia.

38. _____ The measurement of blood flow in the brain.

39. _____ Inflammation of the meninges due to a viral pathogen.

40. _____ Combination of widening pulse pressure, bradycardia, and irregular respiratory patterns; may indicate increasing intracranial pressure.

A	E	P	I	D	U	R	A	L	H	E	M	A	T	O	M	A	D	E	R
B	A	C	T	E	R	I	A	L	M	E	N	I	N	G	I	T	I	S	U
P	R	I	M	A	R	Y	T	U	M	O	R	S	B	N	A	T	L	U	E
E	Y	A	O	D	U	R	E	T	B	P	O	N	G	I	E	R	P	M	B
A	R	M	I	E	A	T	D	U	L	R	Y	Z	I	O	E	A	N	S	T
R	U	E	U	N	P	I	O	A	W	I	C	R	E	A	X	O	D	I	O
O	J	D	N	C	A	E	R	R	E	X	L	F	K	E	T	I	N	G	S
C	N	E	A	E	J	B	N	T	E	O	N	P	W	O	D	I	W	N	A
S	I	C	R	P	T	G	S	D	S	G	Q	O	L	O	A	T	O	I	M
A	Y	I	E	H	F	W	C	E	Y	G	U	A	I	R	G	I	S	N	O
E	R	X	L	A	Z	A	F	Z	S	M	N	L	D	S	Z	R	X	E	N
M	A	O	P	L	T	R	E	X	D	S	O	I	A	K	U	M	A	M	N
P	D	T	U	I	S	I	Q	Y	W	G	Y	M	H	T	P	T	E	B	A
S	N	O	I	T	A	T	U	M	E	N	E	G	A	S	I	M	N	U	W
B	O	T	A	I	O	N	K	A	D	I	L	C	A	S	U	O	A	O	H
A	C	Y	T	S	R	U	E	E	O	N	O	I	S	S	U	C	N	O	C
P	E	C	C	H	M	Y	R	U	J	N	I	Y	R	A	M	I	R	P	S
I	S	C	H	E	M	I	A	C	A	S	C	A	D	E	A	T	S	S	A
W	P	E	W	O	L	F	D	O	O	L	B	L	A	R	B	E	R	E	C
V	I	R	A	L	M	E	N	I	N	G	I	T	I	S	R	A	C	H	K

TRUE OR FALSE?

41. _____ T/F Early signs of increased intracranial pressure are usually alterations in the patient's level of consciousness (LOC) and may be subtle, such as restlessness or slight confusion, or catastrophic, presenting as coma or even death.

42. _____ T/F Women are more likely than men to sustain traumatic brain injuries.

43. _____ T/F Monitoring of ICP is recommended for postconcussive syndrome since cerebral edema may be present.

44. _____ T/F For patients with meningitis, dexamethasone given early in treatment is beneficial and may help prevent vasogenic edema.

45. _____ T/F Treatment for brain abscess includes surgical drainage of the abscess and administering the appropriate antibiotics and steroids.

46. _____ T/F A benign brain tumor will not continue to grow and therefore does not require treatment.

47. _____ T/F Hydrocephalus can occur with virtually any neurological condition.

48. _____ T/F All types of seizure involve some loss of consciousness.

49. _____ T/F Acute brain disorder rarely causes systemic abnormalities apart from neurological problems.

50. _____ T/F Traumatic brain injury in the elderly carries a higher percentage of mortality and morbidity than other age groups.

NCLEX-RN® REVIEW QUESTIONS

29-1. Initial mechanisms to compensate for pressure changes in any of the components (tissue, CSF, blood) of the brain would include which of the following?
 1. Increasing production of CSF
 2. Expansion of brain tissue
 3. Blocking the autoregulation of cerebral blood flow
 4. Increasing absorption of CSF

29-2. Early signs of increased intracranial pressure may include which of the following?
 1. Changes in the optic nerve (CN VIII) may result in ringing in the ears.
 2. Decorticate movement observable in the arms
 3. Complaints of a "different" headache and projectile vomiting
 4. Cushing's triad

29-3. The nursing management for the client with increased intracranial pressure involves assessment of respiratory, cardiovascular, metabolic, and neurological processes. Desired parameters to avoid complications include which of the following? Select all that apply.
 1. Pulse oximetry should be used with supplemental oxygen to maintain saturations of 90% or greater.
 2. Normocapnia levels (PaCO$_2$ levels of 35–40 mm Hg)
 3. Euglycemic levels of 80–120 mg/dL
 4. Normothermia and interventions for body temperatures >99.5°F rectally

29-4. An adult client is admitted to the ER following an automobile accident and having sustained a scalp laceration. The client's head wound was bleeding profusely and was bandaged at the scene by emergency personnel. The client is currently stable. The nurse is aware that before wound closure is initiated, which of the following activities is a priority?
 1. A complete neurological assessment to rule out cerebral contusion
 2. A CAT scan of the head to rule out skull fracture
 3. A cerebral arteriogram to identify which vessel has been ruptured
 4. A skull series to determine the presence of hematomas

29-5. It is important for the nurse to utilize laboratory data to differentiate between bacterial and viral meningitis. Which of the following is true concerning bacterial meningitis?
 1. In the spinal fluid, protein levels will be high and glucose levels will be low.
 2. In the spinal fluid, the color will be clear.
 3. In the spinal fluid, the protein and glucose levels will be low.
 4. The spinal fluid will be bloody.

29-6. Which of the following statements describe the characteristics of benign tumors of the brain?
 1. Benign tumors are nonmalignant and are easily removed by surgery.
 2. Benign tumors are self-limiting and do not influence the function of surrounding tissues.
 3. Benign tumors may be surgically difficult to remove and may compress vital structures.
 4. Benign tumors do not progress into malignant tumors.

29-7. Special concerns with the use of chemotherapy in the treatment of brain tumors include:
 1. Brain tissue, due to increased lymph flow, has an improved mechanism to remove cellular debris.
 2. Chemotherapy is the treatment of choice because all these drugs readily cross the blood–brain barrier.
 3. Malignant cells are homogenous and are consistent in their sensitivity to chemotherapeutic agents.
 4. A flexible approach due to the changing resistance patterns to specific drugs.

29-8. The focus for the nurse in teaching families of patients with acute brain disorders is:
 1. Limited to teaching the early detection of cognitive impairment.
 2. Different from that of other long-term care patients because of the early implementation of rehabilitative therapies
 3. To provide answers to questions honestly as they arise, educate them about the treatment plan, and involve them in discussions of the rehabilitation process.
 4. Geared to offering the family a realistic perspective of the limited abilities of the patient.

CHAPTER 30

CARING FOR THE PATIENT WITH CEREBRAL VASCULAR DISORDERS

OUTCOME-BASED LEARNING OBJECTIVES

30-1. Identify and distinguish between the different types of stroke and their reported impact on rehabilitation and recovery to a functional status.

30-2. Describe the basic pathophysiology of each type of identified stroke.

30-3. Explain the events of the ischemic cascade as it relates to the pathophysiology of stroke.

30-4. Compare and contrast the different medical management options for the treatment of ruptured aneurysms.

30-5. Explain nursing interventions associated with management of vasospasm.

CHAPTER OUTLINE

I. Stroke
  A. Epidemiology
  B. Etiology and Classification
    1. Ischemic Strokes
      a. Thrombotic Strokes
      b. Embolic Strokes
      c. Lacunar Strokes
      d. Transient Ischemic Attacks
    2. Hemorrhagic Strokes
  C. Pathophysiology
    1. Ischemic Strokes
    2. Hemorrhagic Strokes
  D. Clinical Manifestations
  E. Laboratory and Diagnostic Procedures
  F. Medical Management of Ischemic Strokes

G. Surgical Management of Ischemic Strokes
    1. Carotid Endarterectomy
    2. Endovascular Procedures
    3. Revascularization
H. Medical Management of Hemorrhagic Strokes

II. Cerebrovascular Malformations
  A. Cerebral Aneurysms
    1. Epidemiology
      a. Familial Aneurysms
    2. Etiology
    3. Location and Classification of Aneurysms
    4. Pathophysiology
    5. Clinical Manifestations
      a. Ruptured Aneurysms
      b. Unruptured Aneurysms
    6. Risk Factors for Subarachnoid Hemorrhage (SAH)
    7. Laboratory and Diagnostic Procedures
    8. Medical Management
      a. Unruptured Aneurysms
      b. Ruptured Aneurysms
    9. Complications of Subarachnoid Hemorrhage
      a. Rebleeding
      b. Cerebral Vasospasm
      c. Hyponatremia
      d. Seizures
      e. Hydrocephalus
  B. Arteriovenous Malformations
    1. Epidemiology and Etiology
    2. Pathophysiology
    3. Classification of AVMs
    4. Clinical Manifestations
    5. Laboratory and Diagnostic Procedures
    6. Medical Management
  C. Cavernous Malformations
    1. Epidemiology and Etiology
      a. Familial Form of Cavernous Malformations
    2. Pathophysiology
    3. Clinical Manifestations
    4. Laboratory and Diagnostic Procedures
    5. Medical Management

        NURSING MANAGEMENT OF CEREBRAL VASCULAR DISEASES
           ASSESSMENT
           PLANNING
           INTERVENTIONS AND RATIONALES
        COLLABORATIVE MANAGEMENT

III. Rehabilitation
        HEALTH PROMOTION
IV. Future Directions

KEY TERMS MATCHING EXERCISE 1

Write the letter of the correct definition in the space next to each term.

Term

_____ 1. transient ischemic attack (TIA)

_____ 2. cardiogenic embolism

_____ 3. carotid endarterectomy (CEA)

_____ 4. percutaneous angioplasty

_____ 5. fusiform aneurysms

_____ 6. familial intracranial aneurysms

_____ 7. subarachnoid hemorrhage (SAH)

Definition

a. The use of mechanical widening when opening blood vessels other than coronary arteries.

b. A condition characterized by bleeding into the space below the arachnoid space.

c. Blood clots from cardiac sources.

d. Elliptically shaped aneurysm.

e. Surgical procedure to correct carotid stenosis by opening the carotid artery, removing plaque, and restoring blood flow in the lumen.

f. An episode of neurological deficits resulting from temporary ischemia that produces strokelike symptoms but no lasting damage. It occurs when the blood supply to part of the brain is briefly interrupted. Also referred to as a *warning stroke* or *ministroke*.

g. The presence of proven aneurysms in two or more family members among first- and second-degree relatives.

KEY TERMS MATCHING EXERCISE 2

Write the letter of the correct definition in the space next to each term.

Term

_____ 8. posterior circulation

_____ 9. cerebral salt wasting

_____ 10. arteriovenous malformation (AVM)

_____ 11. cavernous malformation

_____ 12. Spetzler-Martin AVM grading scale

_____ 13. Fisher grading scale

_____ 14. Hunt-Hess classification

Definition

a. A scale to grade arteriovenous malformations (AVMs) based on the degree of surgical difficulty in removing them.

b. A mass of abnormal blood vessels in which arterial blood flows directly into the venous system.

c. Refers to circulation in the arteries in the posterior portion of the circle of Willis.

d. Grading scale for subarachnoid hemorrhage referring to the amount of blood on a CT scan.

e. Electrolyte abnormality characterized by loss of sodium and loss of extracellular fluid volume.

f. Grading scale for subarachnoid hemorrhage.

g. Low-flow, cluster-type nodular lesion, not separated by brain tissue.

KEY TERM CROSSWORD PUZZLE

Use key terms to complete the crossword puzzle below.

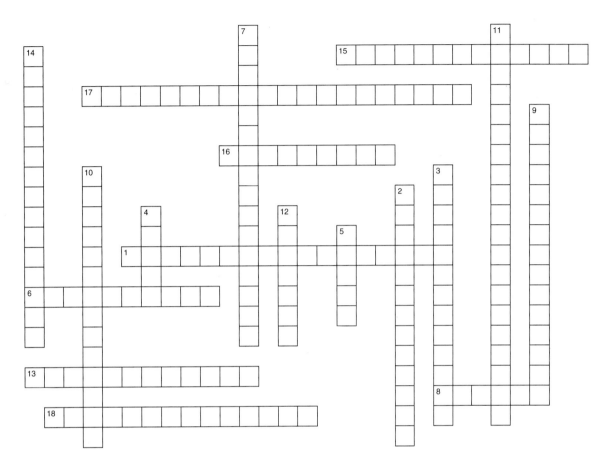

Across:

1. Injury to the cells after blood supply to an ischemic area is restored.
6. An area of dead tissue.
8. Syndrome characterized by a set of neurological deficits that fit a known vascular region.
13. Endovascular procedure in which an aneurysm is obliterated by filling it with a glue-type substance.
15. The development of atherosclerosis.
16. Refers to the transient narrowing of an artery, causing decreased blood flow.
17. Therapy that inhibits platelet adhesion and aggregation.
18. A triad of medical treatments for vasospasm.

Down:

2. Thrombosis of a small penetrating artery, resulting in ischemia and infarction of deep white matter of the brain.
3. Saccular-shaped aneurysm.
4. A device used to secure a widened arterial lumen; it is inserted permanently inside the coronary artery, compressing plaque and providing structural support of the vessel.
5. Refers to the focus of an arteriovenous malformation.
7. A balloon-like outpouching, or widening, of an artery.
9. A series of events that occur as a compensatory mechanism in response to cerebral hypoxia.
10. Coating of the walls of small arteries with a lipid substance, causing narrowing of the arterial lumen.
11. Describes the areas of the brain supplied by the right and left carotid arteries and their branches, including circulation in the arteries in the anterior portion of the circle of Willis.
12. An endovascular procedure in which an aneurysm is filled with a soft coil.
14. Therapies used to arrest the sequence of events that occur during the ischemic cascade.

SHORT ANSWER QUESTIONS

15. What are the risk factors for stroke?

_____

_____

_____

_____

16. What are the risk factors for aneurysm?

_____

_____

_____

_____

17. What complications can occur with subarachnoid hemorrhage?

_____

_____

_____

_____

18. What are the nursing implications for patients being treated for stroke?

_____

_____

_____

_____

19. What can the nurse advise patients to do to reduce their risk of stroke?

_____

_____

_____

_____

_____

_____

_____

_____

_____

LABELING EXERCISE: CIRCLE OF WILLIS

Place the term in the correct location.

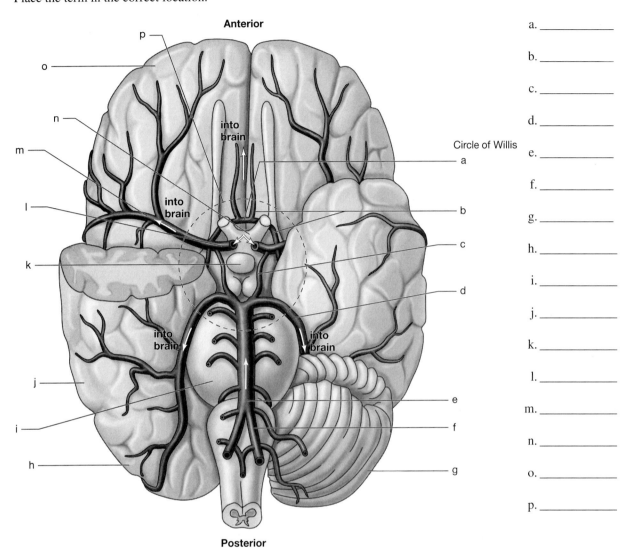

a. _____

b. _____

c. _____

d. _____

e. _____

f. _____

g. _____

h. _____

i. _____

j. _____

k. _____

l. _____

m. _____

n. _____

o. _____

p. _____

Anterior cerebral artery
Anterior communicating artery
Basilar artery
Cerebellum
Frontal lobe
Internal carotid artery
Middle cerebral artery
Occipital lobe

Optic chiasma
Pituitary gland
Pons
Posterior cerebral artery
Posterior communicating artery
Temporal lobe
The circle of Willis
Vertebral artery

NCLEX-RN® REVIEW QUESTIONS

30-1. Which of the following accurately reflects the characteristics of an ischemic stroke?
   1. The strokes are hemorrhagic in nature.
   2. The signs and symptoms, though acute, resolve without permanent disability.
   3. The strokes are commonly caused by atherosclerosis.
   4. Clients experiencing this type of stroke are usually younger.

30-2. In the following selections, identify the process that cannot cause a brain attack.
   1. Plaque formation that alters the internal diameter of a cerebral artery
   2. Embolus that separated from a deep venous thrombosis in the left leg
   3. Thrombus formation as a result of plaque formation.
   4. Lipohyalinosis, a vascular abnormality, caused by hypertension

30-3. In describing the ischemic cascade process, the nurse understands that:
   1. Tissues that surround the necrotic area have themselves undergone anoxia.
   2. Ischemic cascade further extends the area of infarction.
   3. This tissue may be reperfused, but its ability to function has been permanently impaired.
   4. The penumbra of a stroke is the necrotic core.

30-4. Nurses play a crucial role in the management of a patient with vasospasm associated with subarachnoid hemorrhage. When the patient is treated with Triple–H therapy, the nurse must continuously assess for the complications, which include:
   1. Assessing renal output to detect the onset of cerebral salt wasting.
   2. Assessing lung and heart sounds to detect fluid overload.
   3. Detection of the nidus, which can warn of impending seizure onset.
   4. Monitoring for focal seizure onset as these warn of a dire complication.

30-5. When diagnostic testing has found that both endovascular coiling and neurosurgical clipping are treatment options, the choice is based upon which of the following factors?
   1. Endovascular coiling is associated with a longer length of hospital stay.
   2. Neurosurgical clipping is associated with a higher survival and lower morbidity rates one year after procedure.
   3. Endovascular coiling is associated with the client being able to return to activities of normal living and work earlier than patients who had undergone neurosurgical clipping.
   4. There is little difference in either treatment option other than the availability of an interventional neuroradiologist.

CHAPTER 31

CARING FOR THE PATIENT WITH CHRONIC NEUROLOGICAL DISORDERS

OUTCOME-BASED LEARNING OBJECTIVES

31-1. Distinguish among the neurodegenerative disorders of Alzheimer's disease, Parkinson's disease, multiple sclerosis, amyotrophic lateral sclerosis, and myasthenia gravis by describing the etiology and pathophysiology of each disorder.

31-2. Compare and contrast the presenting signs and symptoms of each of the neurodegenerative disorders discussed in the chapter.

31-3. Develop a generalized plan of care for each of the neurodegenerative disorders discussed.

31-4. Develop a comprehensive discharge teaching plan for each of the neurodegenerative disorders discussed.

31-5. Describe generalized health promotion needs for each neurodegenerative disorder discussed.

31-6. Explain gerontological implications for each neurodegenerative disorder discussed.

31-7. Evaluate research implications for nursing practice when caring for persons with a neurodegenerative disorder.

CHAPTER OUTLINE

   I. Alzheimer's Disease and Related Dementias
      A. Epidemiology and Etiology
      B. Pathophysiology
      C. Clinical Manifestations
         1. Preclinical AD
         2. Mild AD
         3. Moderate AD
         4. Severe AD
      D. Laboratory and Diagnostic Procedures
      E. Other Forms of Dementia

F. Medical Management
   1. Drug Therapy
   2. Treating Behavioral Symptoms
   3. Potential Treatments Undergoing Research
G. Gerontological Considerations
     NURSING MANAGEMENT
     COLLABORATIVE MANAGEMENT
H. Discharge Priorities
     HEALTH PROMOTION
II. Parkinson's Disease
A. Epidemiology and Etiology
B. Pathophysiology
C. Clinical Manifestations
   1. Primary Symptoms
   2. Secondary Symptoms
   3. Autonomic Symptoms
   4. Neuropsychiatric Symptoms
   5. Disease Progression
D. Laboratory and Diagnostic Procedures
E. Medical Management
   1. Dopaminergic Drugs
   2. Anticholinergic Drugs
   3. COMT Inhibitors
   4. Other Medications
   5. Surgical Approaches
F. Gerontological Considerations
     NURSING MANAGEMENT
     COLLABORATIVE MANAGEMENT
G. Discharge Priorities
     HEALTH PROMOTION
III. Multiple Sclerosis
A. Epidemiology and Etiology
B. Pathophysiology
C. Clinical Manifestations
D. Laboratory and Diagnostic Procedures
E. Medical Management
   1. Disease-Modifying Drugs
   2. Relapse Management
   3. Symptom Management
F. Gerontological Considerations
     NURSING MANAGEMENT
     COLLABORATIVE MANAGEMENT
G. Discharge Priorities
     HEALTH PROMOTION
IV. Amyotrophic Lateral Sclerosis
A. Epidemiology and Etiology
B. Pathophysiology
C. Clinical Manifestations
D. Laboratory and Diagnostic Procedures
E. Medical Management
     NURSING MANAGEMENT
     COLLABORATIVE MANAGEMENT
F. Discharge Priorities
     HEALTH PROMOTION

V. Myasthenia Gravis
    A. Epidemiology and Etiology
    B. Pathophysiology
    C. Clinical Manifestations
    D. Laboratory and Diagnostic Procedures
    E. Medical Management
        1. Drug Therapy
        2. Plasmapheresis
        3. Intravenous Immunoglobulin Therapy
              NURSING MANAGEMENT
                ASSESSMENT
                NURSING DIAGNOSIS
                PLANNING
                OUTCOMES AND EVALUATION PARAMETERS
                INTERVENTIONS AND RATIONALES
    F. Discharge Priorities
VI. Research

KEY TERMS MATCHING EXERCISE

Write the letter of the correct definition in the space next to each term.

Term

_____ 1. Alzheimer's disease (AD)

_____ 2. Parkinson's disease (PD)

_____ 3. mild cognitive impairment (MCI)

_____ 4. hypokinetic dysarthria

_____ 5. postural instability

_____ 6. on–off phenomena

_____ 7. L'Hermite's sign

_____ 8. amyotrophic lateral sclerosis (ALS)

_____ 9. myasthenia gravis

_____ 10. myasthenic crisis

_____ 11. cholinergic crisis

Definition

a. Electric shock–like sensation throughout the body, elicited by flexing the neck.

b. Diminished postural reflexes, which contribute to difficulty maintaining balance.

c. A rare, progressive neurological disease characterized by loss of motor neurons.

d. A chronic, progressive, irreversible brain disorder found most frequently in adults ages 65 and older.

e. Speech difficulty as a result of slowed, rigid muscles of tongue, mouth, and throat; associated with Parkinson's disease.

f. A disease of the basal ganglia characterized by a slowing down in the innervation and execution of movement, increased muscle tone rigidity, tremors at rest, and impaired postural reflexes.

g. A life-threatening exacerbation of myasthenia gravis that requires mechanical ventilation.

h. A chronic autoimmune neuromuscular disorder in which acetylcholine receptors at the neuromuscular junction are destroyed.

i. A life-threatening condition associated with myasthenia gravis; results from excess acetylcholine.

j. A term used to describe memory loss that appears greater than what is expected for a patient's age.

k. Abrupt fluctuations in movement ability associated with Parkinson's disease.

KEY TERM CROSSWORD

Complete the puzzle below using key terms.

Across:

1. Decreased facial expression due to rigid facial muscles.
4. Disease in which the immune system attacks the nerve tissues in the central nervous system, causing damage to the neurons, which disrupts the body's ability to send signals and causes symptoms.
5. Small, cramped handwriting.
9. A failure of muscle coordination, resulting in loss of balance and coordination, as well as speech difficulties including dysarthria or slurred and scanning speech.
10. A soft, white coating that surrounds and protects nerve fibers.
11. An abnormal physical sensation such as prickling, tingling, or numbness.
12. A specialized protein that is a key component of the neurofibrillary tangles associated with Alzheimer's disease.
14. Involuntary contraction or twitching of a group of muscles or muscle fibers, visible under the skin.
15. Slowed movement; primary symptom of Parkinson's disease.

Down:

2. A neurotransmitter critical to the process of memory formation.
3. A neurotransmitter necessary for ease of movement; loss of this is a key factor in Parkinson's disease.
6. An excitatory neurotransmitter implicated in cell death.
7. Precursor to dopamine; key drug used to treat Parkinson's disease.
8. Soft, muffled voice.
13. Structure located in the midbrain beneath the basal ganglia.
16. Abnormal stiffness or inflexibility associated with Parkinson's disease.
17. Involuntary, writhing movements that may involve limbs, trunk, face, and neck; results from overstimulation of dopamine receptors. Condition characterized by areas of abnormal heart contractility where muscle movement is impaired.
18. A general term for brain dysfunction characterized by a decline in cognition and memory that causes loss of ability to carry out activities of daily living and communicate with others, ultimately resulting in death.

SHORT ANSWER QUESTIONS

12. What are the causes of dementia?

_____

_____

_____

_____

_____

_____

_____

13. What risk factors are associated with Alzheimer's disease?

_____

_____

_____

_____

14. What risk factors are associated with Parkinson's disease?

_____

_____

_____

_____

15. What causes multiple sclerosis?

_____

_____

_____

_____

16. What are the risk factors for multiple sclerosis?

_____

_____

_____

_____

_____

_____

17. What causes amyotrophic lateral sclerosis (ALS)?

_____

18. Describe the pathophysiology of amyotrophic lateral sclerosis.

_____

_____

_____

_____

19. Describe the pathophysiology of myasthenia gravis.

_____

_____

_____

_____

20. Describe the needs of caregivers of patients with neurodegenerative disorders.

_____

_____

_____

_____

_____

_____

TRUE OR FALSE?

21. _____ T/F Treatment for vascular dementia, Lewy body dementia, or frontotemporal dementia is the same, but all are different from treatment for Alzheimer's disease.

22. _____ T/F Deep brain stimulation is a viable treatment option for Alzheimer's disease.

23. _____ T/F Multiple sclerosis occurs most frequently in women over 60.

24. _____ T/F Researchers suspect that the damaging effects of AD on the brain start 10 to 20 years before signs of the disease begin to show.

25. _____ T/F Bradykinesia is often the most prominent and disabling symptom of Parkinson's disease, causing difficulty with walking, changing positions, and speaking and swallowing.

26. _____ T/F Cognitive function degenerates along with the muscles in amyotrophic lateral sclerosis.

27. _____ T/F Relapses in patients with multiple sclerosis can be triggered by excessive exertion, extreme temperatures, infections, hot baths, fever, emotional stress, and pregnancy.

28. _____ T/F Loss of acetylcholine (ACh), a neurotransmitter vital for the transmission of nerve impulses to skeletal muscles, is involved in Alzheimer's disease and myasthenia gravis.

29. _____ T/F Plasmapheresis may be used when a patient with myasthenia gravis is in crisis or not adequately responding to other therapy.

30. _____ T/F Exposure to sunlight, viral illness, surgery, immunization, emotional stress, menstruation, and physical factors might trigger or worsen exacerbations of amyotrophic lateral sclerosis.

NCLEX-RN® REVIEW QUESTIONS

31-1. The nurse is preparing to administer edrophonium chloride to a patient. The nurse realizes this medication is used to:
1. Treat Alzheimer's disease.
2. Improve muscle spasms in multiple sclerosis.
3. Reduce muscle rigidity in Parkinson's disease.
4. Help diagnose myasthenia gravis.

31-2. The nurse is caring for a patient with muscle spasticity, reduced muscle strength, paralysis, and atrophy; however, the patient has an intact memory and cognitive functioning. This patient is demonstrating signs of which of the following disorders?
1. ALS
2. Multiple sclerosis
3. Parkinson's disease
4. Myasthenia gravis

31-3. The nurse is planning the care for a patient with myasthenia gravis. Which of the following would support the goals of care for this patient?
1. Keep NPO.
2. Provide with anti-emetic medication for nausea and vomiting.
3. Assess gag and cough reflex every 4 hours.
4. Provide oxygen for shortness of breath as necessary.

31-4. A patient with ALS is being discharged to home. Which of the following should the patient and family receive as instruction to maximize the patient's respiratory status?
1. Do not lie down after meals.
2. Use blinking instead of talking.
3. Eat foods slowly and in small bites.
4. Balance activity with rest periods.

31-5. A patient with Parkinson's disease asks the nurse about stem cell research and other advances to cure the disorder. Which of the following should the nurse instruct this patient?
1. Spiritual and psychological counseling would be a better investment of time and energy.
2. Family members would benefit from stress management and coping strategy teaching sessions.
3. A regular exercise program and healthy eating habits are the best approaches to use.
4. Some patients choose to participate in clinical research studies as a way of advancing science while managing their condition with the latest, most promising treatments.

31-6. A patient with Parkinson's disease tells the nurse that she's worried about her 80-year-old husband's ability to care for her as she gets older. Which of the following would be an appropriate response for the nurse to make to this patient?
1. That's not something that you should be worried about.
2. You are so healthy now that I'm sure you won't be a burden to your husband.
3. Would you like to talk about things that can help you and your husband?
4. I'll get the doctor for you so you can talk with him about your concerns.

31-7. The nurse who provides care to patients with neurodegenerative disorders is planning to research information on the Internet. In which of the following categories would this research be the most applicable?
1. Complementary alternative approaches
2. Patient/family education
3. Caregivers
4. Emotional and psychological

CHAPTER 32

CARING FOR THE PATIENT WITH SPINAL CORD INJURIES

OUTCOME-BASED LEARNING OBJECTIVES

32-1. Compare and contrast the most common causes of acute spinal cord injury in persons under the age of 65 as opposed to persons over the age of 65.

32-2. Differentiate between a complete and an incomplete spinal cord injury.

32-3. Explain three complications of spinal cord injury and strategies to prevent these complications.

32-4. Discuss the psychosocial impact of spinal cord injury on the patient and family.

32-5. Identify rehabilitative needs and goals for discharge for the patient who has experienced a spinal cord injury.

32-6. Select three nursing diagnoses and apply the nursing process in the care of the patient who has experienced a spinal cord injury.

CHAPTER OUTLINE

I. Epidemiology
II. Etiology
    A. Spinal Tumors
III. Pathophysiology
    A. Classification
        1. Complete Spinal Cord Injury
        2. Incomplete Spinal Cord Injury
            a. Central Cord Syndrome
            b. Anterior Cord Syndrome
            c. Brown-Sequard Syndrome
            d. Cauda Equina Syndrome
            e. Spinal Cord Injury Without Radiographic Abnormality
    B. Primary Mechanisms of Injury
    C. Types of Injury

D. Primary Injury
E. Secondary Injury
   1. Autonomic Hyperreflexia
IV. Clinical Manifestations
  A. Cardiovascular
  B. Pulmonary
  C. Gastrointestinal
  D. Genitourinary
  E. Integumentary
V. General Evaluation and Management
  A. Prehospital
  B. Emergency Department
   1. Initial Assessment
  C. Acute Care Hospital
VI. Laboratory and Diagnostic Procedures
VII. Medical Management
VIII. Surgical Management
    NURSING MANAGEMENT
    PHYSICAL ASSESSMENT AND INTERVENTIONS
    PSYCHOSOCIAL ASSESSMENT AND INTERVENTION
    REHABILITATION
    COLLABORATIVE MANAGEMENT
  A. Gerontological Considerations
    HEALTH PROMOTION
IX. Research

KEY TERMS MATCHING EXERCISE 1

Write the letter of the correct definition in the space next to each term.

Term

_____ 1. spinal cord injury (SCI)
_____ 2. afferent
_____ 3. efferent
_____ 4. complete spinal cord injury
_____ 5. paraplegia
_____ 6. quadriplegia
_____ 7. tetraplegia
_____ 8. incomplete spinal cord injury
_____ 9. cauda equina syndrome
_____ 10. hyperflexion injuries
_____ 11. myelopathy
_____ 12. odontoid process

Definition

a. The toothlike projection of C2 (cervical spine), which sits behind the anterior portion of the ring of C1.

b. *Greek*: Paralysis of both upper and lower extremities.

c. The bundle of nerve roots in the lower portion of the spinal canal, below the conus medullaris, which when compressed or inflamed causes symptoms of pain, altered reflexes, decreased strength, and decreased sensation. When extreme, can cause paralysis of the lower extremities, bowel and bladder dysfunction, and loss of the Achilles reflex; most commonly seen with large disk herniations at L4/L5, causing mass effect on the nerve roots as they descend through the spinal canal.

d. Ability to transport toward a center; for example, a sensory nerve that carries impulses from the peripheral nervous system to the central nervous system.

e. Paralysis of the lower half of the body including both lower extremities and loss of bowel and bladder function.

f. Preservation of some degree of motor and/or sensory function below the level of a spinal injury.

g. Ability to transport away from a central organ or section; conducts impulses from the brain or spinal cord to the periphery.

h. Motor, sensory, and reflex abnormalities due to an abnormality of the spinal cord.

   i. Injury to the spinal cord that results in impairment or loss of motor, sensory, and autonomic functions.
   j. Increased flexion of a joint from trauma.
   k. Permanent loss of all neurological function below the level of injury.
   l. *Latin*: Paralysis of all four extremities.

KEY TERMS MATCHING EXERCISE 2

Write the letter of the correct definition in the space next to each term.

Term

_____ 13. spondylitic disease
_____ 14. compression injuries
_____ 15. rotational injuries
_____ 16. areflexia
_____ 17. contusion
_____ 18. hyperreflexia
_____ 19. neurogenic shock
_____ 20. transection
_____ 21. spinal shock
_____ 22. autonomic hyperreflexia
_____ 23. spinal precautions

Definition

a. Occurs in spinal cord injuries above T6 thoracic spine and results in interruption of the sympathetic change, causing bradycardia, hypotension, and vasodilation of the peripheral vascular system.
b. Injuries resulting from extreme lateral flexion or flexion-rotation of the spine, causing disruption of the posterior spinal ligaments and spinal instability.
c. A condition consisting of inflammation and degenerative changes of the spine including formation of osteophytes, calcification and hypertrophy of the ligaments, and degeneration of the intervertebral disks.
d. An injury to soft tissue caused by trauma; a bruise.
e. Methods of immobilizing the spine and moving patients to prevent or avoid additional spinal injury.
f. Loss of reflexive activity.
g. Injuries that occur when pressure is applied to the spinal cord as a result of mass effect from bone fragments, disk herniation, tumor, abscess, or blood clot.
h. A syndrome characterized by severe hypertension, bradycardia, vasoconstriction below the level of injury, and vasodilation above the level of injury resulting from unchecked stimulation of the sympathetic nervous system triggered by a noxious stimulus.
i. Exaggeration of the deep tendon reflexes.
j. A period of flaccid paralysis and absent reflexes lasting up to 6 weeks after spinal cord injury.
k. Cutting across.

NURSING DIAGNOSES RELATED TO SPINAL CORD INJURY

Provide the possible nursing diagnoses associated with each assessment.

24. Neurological Status

   _____

   _____

25. Pulmonary Function

   _____

   _____

26. Cardiovascular Status

_____

_____

27. Peripheral Tissue Perfusion

_____

_____

28. Gastrointestinal Function

_____

_____

29. Urinary Elimination

_____

_____

30. Pain

_____

_____

31. Psychosocial State

_____

_____

32. Adaptation

_____

_____

LABELING EXERCISE 1: VENTRAL AND DORSAL NERVE ROOTS

Place the term in the correct location.

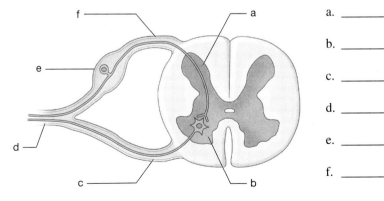

a. _____

b. _____

c. _____

d. _____

e. _____

f. _____

Anterior horn   Spinal nerve
Posterior horn   Ventral root
Dorsal root ganglion   Dorsal root

LABELING EXERCISE 2: SPINAL COLUMN

Place the term in the correct location.

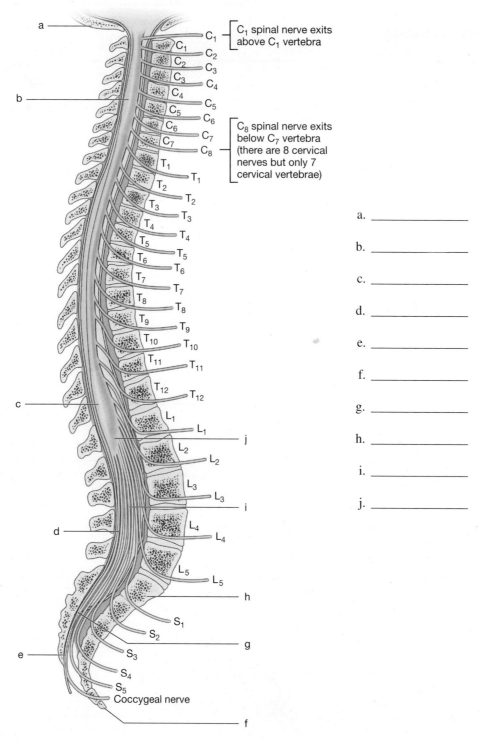

a. _____

b. _____

c. _____

d. _____

e. _____

f. _____

g. _____

h. _____

i. _____

j. _____

Base of skull
Cauda equina
Cervical enlargement
Coccyx
Conus medullaris (termination of spinal cord)

External terminal filum (dural part)
Internal terminal filum (pial part)
Lumbar enlargement
Sacrum
Termination of dural sac

NCLEX-RN® REVIEW QUESTIONS

32-1. The nurse is teaching a group of nursing students about the causes of spinal cord injury. Which of the following statements made by the students indicates the need for further teaching?
1. "Nontraumatic spinal cord injuries are most likely to occur in persons older than 30 years."
2. "Motor vehicle collisions are the most common cause of spinal cord injury in people under 65."
3. "Most spinal cord injuries in persons older than 65 years can be associated with a fall injury."
4. "Sports and recreation–related spinal cord injuries usually occur in persons under 30 years old."

32-2. The patient has experienced a complete spinal cord injury at the second thoracic vertebra. Which of the following signs and symptoms would the nurse expect to find in this patient? Select all that apply.
1. Tetraplegia
2. Loss of bladder function
3. Loss of biceps reflex
4. Intact sensation below the waist
5. Intact sensation to the shoulders
6. Loss of motor function in the hands
7. Loss of knee jerk reflex

32-3. Which of the following statements best describes appropriate prophylaxis for some of the most common complications following spinal cord injury?
1. Use of incentive spirometry and chest physiotherapy to aid in increased respiratory function and airway clearance that can decrease pulmonary embolism development
2. Use of a nasogastric tube during the acute phase of care to decompress the stomach and minimize abdominal distension in order to decrease the risks of vomiting and aspiration
3. Use of good nutritional measures like increased fiber and fluid intake to promote wound healing and good skin integrity, thereby reducing pressure ulcer formation
4. Use of frequent clean intermittent catheterizations and accurate postvoid residual measurements to ensure adequate bladder emptying and prevention of neurogenic shock

32-4. Which statement made by the student nurse would indicate the need for further instruction regarding the psychosocial impact of spinal cord injury?
1. "The patient and his or her family should have access to resources that provide support in dealing with the physical and psychological changes from spinal cord injury."
2. "Because of the stress placed on the patient after spinal cord injury, she or he may experience a wide range of feelings including denial, anger, grief, hopelessness, and depression."
3. "The nurse should carefully monitor the patient for signs of inadequate coping such as increased incorporation into social interactions and maintaining good eye contact."
4. "Loss of body image and independence, lifestyle changes, and loss of control over the immediate environment are some of the changes that cause stress for these patients."

32-5. The nurse is providing discharge instructions to the patient with spinal cord injury and the family. Which of the following statements made by the patient would indicate the need for further instruction?
1. "The proper use of adaptive equipment and transfer strategies will help keep me from getting hurt."
2. "Using clean intermittent catheterization will help prevent constipation and autonomic hyperreflexia."
3. "The rehabilitation will help me become more independent and aid my transition back into the community."
4. "Changing positions and bathing frequently helps protect my skin and prevent pressure ulcer formation."

32-6. When providing care for the patient with a C6 spinal cord injury, which interventions are most important for the nurse to implement first?
1. Auscultate bowel sounds and obtain a dietary consult.
2. Apply antiembolic hose and administer prophylactic anticoagulant medications.
3. Administer humidified oxygen and monitor hemodynamic status.
4. Maintain spinal precautions and institute pulmonary toilet.

CHAPTER 33

NURSING ASSESSMENT OF PATIENTS WITH RESPIRATORY DISORDERS

OUTCOME-BASED LEARNING OBJECTIVES

33-1. Compare and contrast normal and adventitious breath sounds.

33-2. Defend the importance of obtaining information on recent travel as a component of the patient history.

33-3. Describe the relationship of data obtained from the review of a patient's social and occupational history with risk for pulmonary disease.

33-4. Describe the essential components of a physical assessment of the pulmonary system.

33-5. Compare and contrast adjuncts used during physical assessment of the pulmonary system.

CHAPTER OUTLINE

I. Anatomy and Physiology of the Pulmonary System
II. History
   A. Biographic and Demographic Data
   B. Chief Complaint
      1. Presenting Symptoms
   C. Past Medical History
      1. Childhood Diseases and Immunizations
      2. Previous Illnesses and Hospitalizations
      3. Diagnostic Procedures or Surgeries
      4. Medications
      5. Allergies
      6. Use of Oxygen or Ventilatory Assist Devices
      7. Cough and Sputum Production
   D. Family Health History
   E. Risk Factors
      1. Cigarette Smoking
      2. Inactivity

        3. Cardiovascular Disease

        4. Obesity

        5. Substance Abuse

        6. Trauma

     F. Social History

        1. Occupation

        2. Culture

        3. Environment

        4. Habits

        5. Exercise

        6. Nutrition

        7. Travel and Area of Residence

III. Physical Examination

     A. Inspection

        1. General Appearance

           a. Mentation

           b. Rate, Depth, and Rhythm of Respirations

           c. Thoracic Size and Shape

           d. Thoracic Expansion and Symmetry

           e. Use of Accessory Muscles

        2. Color and Appearance of Skin and Extremities

           a. Pallor

           b. Cyanosis

        3. Neck Inspection

     B. Palpation of Skin and Extremities

        1. Edema

        2. Skin Temperature and Moisture

        3. Clinical Reference Points

        4. Chest Excursion

        5. Tactile Fremitus

        6. Tenderness

        7. Crepitus

     C. Auscultation of the Lungs

        1. Normal Breath Sounds

           a. Tracheal Breath Sounds

           b. Bronchial Breath Sounds

           c. Bronchovesicular Breath Sounds

           d. Vesicular Breath Sounds

        2. Adventitious Breath Sounds

           a. Crackles

           b. Wheezes

           c. Stridor

           d. Pleural Friction Rub

     D. Percussion

     E. Pain

     F. Genetic Considerations

     G. Gerontological Considerations

HEALTH PROMOTION

IV. Respiratory Monitoring

     A. Pulse Oximetry

     B. Peak Flow

     C. Arterial Blood Gas

        1. Capnography

V. Summary

KEY TERMS MATCHING EXERCISE 1

Write the letter of the correct definition in the space next to each term.

Term

_____ 1. dyspnea
_____ 2. accessory muscles
_____ 3. tachypnea
_____ 4. hyperpnea
_____ 5. tracheal deviation
_____ 6. bradypnea
_____ 7. fremitus
_____ 8. subcutaneous emphysema
_____ 9. bronchial breath sounds
_____ 10. bronchovesicular breath sounds

Definition

a. Air that escapes into the subcutaneous tissue. Also referred to as *crepitus*.

b. A respiratory rate of less than 12 breaths per minute.

c. Shifting of the tracheal position to the right or left of midline due to the push or pull of thoracic structures.

d. Refers to both the increased rate and depth of respiration associated with metabolic acidosis. It is sometimes referred to as *Kussmaul's breathing*.

e. Subjective feeling of shortness of breath or difficulty breathing.

f. The sternocleidomastoid, scalene, and trapezius muscles, which are normally not necessary to respiration, but are utilized by patients who require extra effort to move air in and out of the lungs.

g. Rapid respiratory rate.

h. Breath sounds normally heard over the right or left bronchus of the lung.

i. Breath sounds normally heard between the bronchus and the smaller airways.

j. Tactile vibration felt over airways.

KEY TERMS MATCHING EXERCISE 2

Write the letter of the correct definition in the space next to each term.

Term

_____ 11. tracheal breath sounds
_____ 12. adventitious breath sounds
_____ 13. crackles
_____ 14. pleural friction rubs
_____ 15. vesicular breath sounds
_____ 16. wheezes
_____ 17. crepitus
_____ 18. resonance
_____ 19. capnography

Definition

a. A low-pitched, clear, hollow tone of long duration. It is commonly heard over the lungs.

b. Breath sounds auscultated over the trachea; they are normally loud and high pitched.

c. When auscultating the lungs, common abnormal, short popping sounds heard on inspiration; caused by the movement of fluid or exudates.

d. Air that escapes into the subcutaneous tissue. Also known as *subcutaneous emphysema*.

e. Breath sounds normally heard over most of the chest wall from the movement of air in small airways distal to the bronchioles.

f. Abnormal lung sound indicating a pathologic process.

g. Harsh leathery sound created from inflamed pleural surfaces rubbing against each other.

h. Use of a device to measure exhaled or end-tidal carbon dioxide.

i. High-pitched musical sounds created by air moving over mucous strands.

TRUE OR FALSE?

20. _____ T/F   The primary risk factor for the development of pulmonary disease is cigarette smoking.

21. _____ T/F   Oral infections can travel to the pulmonary tree to cause abscess formation or pneumonia.

22. _____ T/F   The trapezius, scalenus, and sternomastoid muscles may be smaller in patients with COPD.

23. _____ T/F   Edema of the lower extremities is generally related to right heart or heart failure.

24. _____ T/F   Breath sounds are best auscultated with the patient in a supine position.

25. _____ T/F   If the blood pH is elevated (alkalosis), excessive oxygen is delivered to tissues.

26. _____ T/F   Absence of wheezing in a patient with asthma exacerbation indicates lack of airflow and impending respiratory arrest.

27. _____ T/F   Adventitious breath sounds represent pathologic conditions of the heart or lungs, and indicate the presence of airway spasm, fluid, or secretions that disrupt airflow.

28. _____ T/F   Only 20% of children with cystic fibrosis will reach adulthood.

29. _____ T/F   Physiological changes of aging can cause ineffective coughing.

LABELING EXERCISE 1: RIBS AND INTERSPACES IN RESPIRATORY ASSESSMENT

Place the term in the correct location.

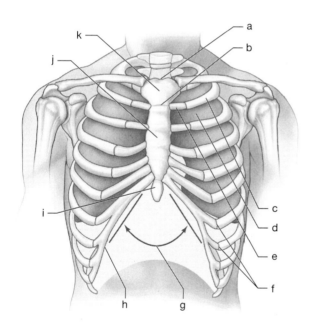

a. _____

b. _____

c. _____

d. _____

e. _____

f. _____

g. _____

h. _____

i. _____

j. _____

k. _____

2nd costal cartilage
2nd interspace
2nd rib
Body of sternum
Costal angle
Costal margin

Costochondral junctions
Manubrium of sternum
Sternal angle
Suprasternal notch
Xiphoid process

LABELING EXERCISE 2: LOBES OF THE LUNGS (ANTERIOR)

Place the term in the correct location.

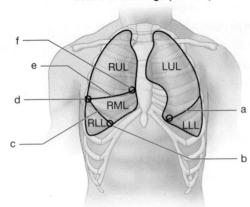

Lobes of the lungs (anterior)

a. _____

b. _____

c. _____

d. _____

e. _____

f. _____

4th rib
5th rib midaxillary line
6th rib midclavicular line
Horizontal fissure
Left oblique fissure
Right oblique fissure

LABELING EXERCISE 3: LOBES OF THE LUNGS (POSTERIOR)

Place the term in the correct location.

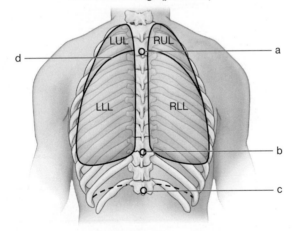

Lobes of the lungs (posterior)

a. _____

b. _____

c. _____

d. _____

T3
T10
T12
Oblique fissure

NCLEX-RN® REVIEW QUESTIONS

33-1. During the auscultation of a patient's lungs, the nurse asks the patient to hold his breath. This assessment technique is useful to determine which of the following adventitious breath sounds?
1. Crackles
2. Wheezes
3. Bronchovesicular
4. Pleural friction rub

33-2. A patient comes into the emergency department with signs of acute respiratory distress. The nurse learns that the patient is a smoker and arrived in Denver a few days ago. Why is this information important to the nurse when planning this patient's care?
1. It helps to determine where to access smoking cessation classes for the patient.
2. It helps to determine if the patient is a resident of the city.
3. It helps when figuring out if the patient's insurance will cover the emergency department visit.
4. It helps to determine why the patient is experiencing acute respiratory distress at this time.

33-3. During the assessment of a patient who is demonstrating signs of a respiratory disorder, the nurse learns that the patient is a hair stylist. This information is important because:
1. It could indicate exposure to occupational vapors or fumes.
2. It could determine this patient's socioeconomic status.
3. It could help indicate this patient's overall state of health.
4. It could indicate the number of hours the patient stands while at work.

33-4. While palpating a patient's thorax, the nurse asks the patient to say the word "ninety-nine." The nurse detects an increase in vibrations which could indicate:
1. Unilateral airway obstruction.
2. Penumothorax.
3. Pleural effusion.
4. Pneumonia.

33-5. The nurse is providing care to a patient in the intensive care unit. Which of the following can the nurse use to assess if the patient can have the endotracheal tube removed?
1. Pulse oximetry
2. Capnography
3. Peak flow meter
4. Arterial blood gas

CHAPTER 34

CARING FOR THE PATIENT WITH UPPER AIRWAY DISORDERS

OUTCOME-BASED LEARNING OBJECTIVES

34-1. Compare and contrast nursing management of the most common facial fractures.

34-2. Explain nursing care for a patient with sinus disease.

34-3. Differentiate the essential components for developing a teaching plan for patients with infections of the upper airway.

34-4. Discuss the implications of the loss of the senses of smell, sight, and taste in patients with upper airway disorders and disfigurement.

34-5. Compare and contrast the nursing management of patients with partial versus total airway obstruction.

34-6. Identify the risk factors of head and neck cancer.

34-7. Explain the nursing management of a patient with head and neck cancer in the acute care setting related to airway, wounds, pain, and nutrition.

CHAPTER OUTLINE

I. Structural, Traumatic, and Deformity Disorders of the Nose and Facial Structures
   A. Nasal Fractures
      1. Epidemiology and Etiology
      2. Laboratory and Diagnostic Procedures
      3. Clinical Manifestations
         NURSING MANAGEMENT
   B. Septal Deviation
      1. Epidemiology and Etiology
      2. Pathophysiology and Clinical Manifestations
      3. Medical Management
         NURSING MANAGEMENT

3. Laboratory and Diagnostic Procedures
4. Medical Management
   NURSING MANAGEMENT

III. Disorders of the Pharynx and Oral Cavity
   A. Sleep Apnea
      1. Etiology, Epidemiology, Pathophysiology, and Clinical Manifestations
      2. Diagnostic Studies
      3. Medical Management
         a. Tracheotomy
            NURSING MANAGEMENT
   B. Oral Cavity Disorders
      1. Etiology and Clinical Manifestations of Hairy Tongue
      2. Etiology and Clinical Manifestations of Dental Caries
      3. Etiology, Pathophysiology, Clinical Manifestations, and Medical Management of Ludwig's Angina
      4. Dental Abscess
         a. Pathophysiology
         b. Epidemiology and Etiology
         c. Laboratory and Diagnostic Procedures
         d. Clinical Manifestations
         e. Medical Management
            NURSING MANAGEMENT
      5. Etiology, Pathophysiology, and Clinical Manifestations of Tonsillitis
      6. Etiology and Clinical Manifestations of Peritonsillar Abscess
      7. Etiology of Pharyngitis
      8. Etiology, Clinical Manifestations, and Medical Management of Epiglottitis

IV. Disorders Related to the Larynx and Trachea
   A. Anatomy and Physiology of the Larynx
   B. Etiology, Epidemiology, Pathophysiology
      1. Vocal Cord Paralysis
      2. Clinical Manifestations
      3. Laboratory and Diagnostic Procedures
      4. Medical Management
         NURSING MANAGEMENT
            ASSESSMENT
            OUTCOMES AND EVALUATION PARAMETERS
            INTERVENTIONS AND RATIONALES
            EVALUATION
   C. Etiology, Epidemiology, and Pathophysiology of Laryngeal Disorders
   D. Etiology, Pathophysiology, and Medical Management of Acute Laryngitis
   E. Etiology, Pathophysiology, and Medical Management of Chronic Laryngitis
      1. Medical Management
         HEALTH PROMOTION
   F. Etiology and Clinical Manifestations of Edema of the Larynx
      1. Medical and Nursing Management
   G. Etiology, Pathophysiology, Clinical Manifestations, and Medical Management of Vocal Cord Pathology
   H. Etiology, Pathophysiology, Clinical Manifestations, and Medical Management of Vocal Cord Polyps
   I. Etiology, Pathophysiology, Clinical Manifestations, and Medical Management of Laryngeal Papillomas
   J. Etiology, Pathophysiology, Clinical Manifestations, and Medical Management of Laryngeal Spasm
   K. Etiology and Clinical Manifestations of Laryngeal Injury
      1. Laboratory and Diagnostic Procedures and Medical Management
   L. Laryngopharyngeal Reflux Disease
      1. Etiology, Pathophysiology, and Clinical Manifestations
      2. Laboratory and Diagnostic Procedures
      3. Medical Management

KEY TERMS MATCHING EXERCISE

Write the letter of the correct definition in the space next to each term.

Term

_____ 1. continuous positive airway pressure (CPAP)
_____ 2. otolaryngology (otorhinolaryngology)
_____ 3. mucormycosis
_____ 4. peritonsillar abscess
_____ 5. pharyngitis
_____ 6. laryngeal spasm
_____ 7. laryngopharyngeal reflux disease (LPRD)
_____ 8. panendoscopy
_____ 9. myocutaneous flap
_____ 10. tracheostomy

Definition

a. A fungal infection often seen in the sinuses of patients with diabetes who do not have good glycemic control.

b. Procedure that delivers air into a patient's airway through a specially designed nasal mask or pillows.

c. An abnormal reflexive response to a laryngeal insult.

d. A rare complication of tonsillitis in which the infection spreads to the tissue around the tonsillar capsule.

e. Surgical procedure to evaluate the upper aerodigestive tract, locate the organ of origin, and obtain a cellular diagnosis.

f. The study of ear, nose, and throat disorders.

g. Refers to the making of a semipermanent or permanent opening into the trachea, and to the opening itself.

h. A piece of tissue, muscle or skin, used in reconstructive surgery; may be used for reconstructing breasts, large lateral temporal, scalp, or intraoral defects, and defects involving the trunk and chest wall.

i. Inflammation of the pharynx caused by upper respiratory infection, which causes a sore throat.

j. Inflammation of the laryngopharynx as a result of gastric reflux into the pharynx and larynx.

KEY TERM CROSSWORD

Complete the crossword puzzle below using key terms.

Across:

1. A collection of symptoms predominantly in the nose and eyes that occur after exposure to airborne particles of dust, dander, or the pollens of certain seasonal plants in people who are allergic to these substances.
4. An acute or recurrent infection of the tonsils.
6. Dehiscent wound that traverses between two different tissue planes; a communication between two areas such as the oral cavity and the skin.
7. A permanent surgical airway with removal of the larynx, usually for cancer.
9. Bleeding from the nose.
10. The loss or impairment of the sense of smell.
13. Term used to refer to the process of weaning a patient toward the goal of removing a tracheostomy tube.
14. Surgical procedure to remove nodal disease in conjunction with the central part of the cancer surgery.
17. Without a voice.
18. Condition that occurs when the normal vibration of the vocal cords is disrupted.

Down:

2. Small saclike growths inside the nasal cavity and sinuses.
3. A disruption in the lymph system into the tissues of the neck and chest.
5. A raspy noise heard in the upper airway as a result of air attempting to move through a narrowed opening.
8. A condition in which the tongue is covered with hairlike papilla due to the overgrowth of the fungus Candida albicans or Aspergillus niger.
11. A temporary surgical airway into the trachea.
12. Inflammation of the larynx and/or vocal cords.
15. Infection or inflammation of the sinuses.
16. Infection and inflammation of the epiglottis and surrounding supraglottic structures often resulting in airway obstruction. Usually caused by Haemophilus influenzae type B.
19. A disorder in which a person stops breathing for more than 10 seconds, typically more than 20 to 30 times in an hour.
20. A deep neck infection involving the sublingual, submandibular, and submental spaces; usually the result of a dental abscess.

SHORT ANSWER QUESTIONS

11. How do the symptoms of allergic rhinitis and those of sinusitis differ?

_____

_____

12. What are the risk factors for mucormycosis?

_____

_____

_____

13. Describe the treatment options for sleep apnea.

_____

_____

_____

14. Describe the interventions the nurse can perform to help the patient with vocal cord paralysis.

_____

_____

_____

15. What are the risk factors for head and neck cancer?

_____

_____

_____

LABELING EXERCISE 1: ANATOMICAL RELATIONSHIP BETWEEN NASAL BONES, CARTILAGE, AND SEPTUM

Place the term in the correct location.

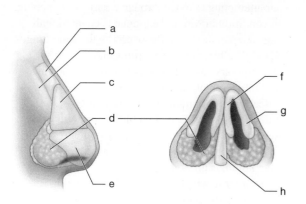

a. _____

b. _____

c. _____

d. _____

e. _____

f. _____

g. _____

h. _____

Fibroareolar tissue
Frontal process of maxilla
Lateral crus
Medial and lateral crusa of lower lateral cartilage

Medial crus
Nasal bone
Septal cartilage
Upper lateral cartilage

LABELING EXERCISE 2: SITES OF SINUSITIS

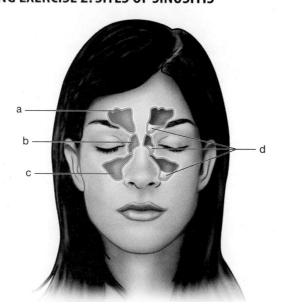

a. _____

b. _____

c. _____

d. _____

Ethmoid sinus
Frontal sinus

Maxillary sinus
Sinusitis

NCLEX-RN® REVIEW QUESTIONS

34-1. The nurse is implementing cerebrospinal fluid leak precautions on a patient with a facial fracture. These precautions are most likely indicated for a fractured:
1. Temporal bone.
2. Mandible.
3. Facial frontal.
4. Transverse.

34-2. The nurse is caring for a patient recovering from sinus surgery. Which of the following should be included in this patient's care plan?
1. Dental consultation for sore gums and teeth
2. Physical therapy consultation for cautious swimming
3. Antihistamines and antibiotic therapy for future symptoms
4. Postoperative wound care and avoidance of activities that caused the chronic infection

34-3. A patient is being treated for nonallergic rhinitis. Which of the following should the nurse instruct this patient?
1. Wash bed linens every two weeks.
2. Avoid animal dander.
3. Take antihistamines as prescribed.
4. Avoid excessive humidity and standing water.

34-4. A patient with mucormycosis says she "looks ugly" and wishes she were dead. Which of the following should the nurse respond to this patient?
1. At least you are alive.
2. It's not so bad.
3. I realize you feel badly about your appearance but the doctor did talk with you about plans to correct the scarring.
4. You could always wear a veil or mask.

34-5. A patient begins to complain of acute shortness of breath and air hunger after receiving a new medication. Which of the following should the nurse do to assist this patient?
1. Place the bed in the flat position.
2. Assist the patient to ambulate.
3. Elevate the head of the bed and support respirations.
4. Provide fluids to thin secretions.

34-6. A middle-aged male patient tells the nurse that his father had head and neck cancer and he hopes that he doesn't develop the disease later in life. Which of the following should the nurse instruct this patient?
1. Have genetic testing done to determine the chances of developing the disease.
2. There is nothing that can be done to avoid developing the disease since his father had it.
3. Avoid alcohol and tobacco products since using these items increases the risk of developing the disease.
4. Limit fruit and vegetable intake.

34-7. A patient is recovering from neck resection surgery for cancer. Which of the following should be included in this patient's plan of care regarding nutritional support?
1. Assess ability to swallow before providing oral foods/fluids.
2. Insert nasogastric tube for prn nutritional support.
3. Restrict fluids.
4. Keep NPO for 5 days.

CHAPTER 35

CARING FOR THE PATIENT WITH LOWER AIRWAY DISORDERS

OUTCOME-BASED LEARNING OBJECTIVES

35-1. Differentiate between restrictive and obstructive lung diseases.

35-2. Compare and contrast the etiology, pathophysiology, clinical manifestations, nursing management, and prevention of the various pulmonary infections and inflammatory disorders.

35-3. Explain the etiology, pathophysiology, and nursing management of COPD, chronic bronchitis, asthma, cystic fibrosis, pulmonary embolism, and cor pulmonale.

35-4. Compare and contrast the etiology and nursing management for patients with a variety of chest trauma and thoracic injuries.

35-5. Discuss the etiology, pathophysiology, and nursing management for patients with lung cancer and lung transplant.

35-6. Discuss the etiology, pathophysiology, and nursing management of occupational lung diseases.

CHAPTER OUTLINE

B. Influenza
   1. Epidemiology
   2. Pathophysiology
   3. Clinical Manifestations
      NURSING MANAGEMENT
   4. Medical Management and Health Promotion
C. Pneumonia
   1. Epidemiology
   2. Etiology
   3. Pathophysiology
      a. Community-Acquired Pneumonia
         i. Types of Community-Acquired Pneumonia
      b. Hospital-Acquired Pneumonia
   4. Clinical Manifestations
   5. Laboratory and Diagnostic Procedures
   6. Medical Management
      NURSING MANAGEMENT
D. Discharge Priorities
      HEALTH PROMOTION
E. Pulmonary Fungal Infections
   1. Etiology and Epidemiology
   2. Pathophysiology
   3. Clinical Manifestations
   4. Laboratory and Diagnostic Procedures
   5. Medical Management
      NURSING MANAGEMENT
         ASSESSMENT
         OUTCOMES AND EVALUATION PARAMETERS
         INTERVENTIONS AND RATIONALES
F. Pulmonary Tuberculosis
   1. Epidemiology
   2. Etiology
   3. Pathophysiology
   4. Clinical Manifestations
   5. Laboratory and Diagnostic Procedures
   6. Medical Management
      NURSING MANAGEMENT
      HEALTH PROMOTION
G. Atypical Mycobacterium
   1. Epidemiology and Etiology
   2. Clinical Manifestations
   3. Medical Management
H. Lung Abscess
   1. Epidemiology and Etiology
   2. Clinical Manifestations
   3. Laboratory and Diagnostic Procedures
   4. Medical Management
      NURSING MANAGEMENT
         ASSESSMENT
         NURSING DIAGNOSES
         OUTCOMES
         INTERVENTIONS AND RATIONALES
         EVALUATION

KEY TERMS MATCHING EXERCISE 1

Write the letter of the correct definition in the space next to each term.

Term

_____ 1. acute bronchitis

_____ 2. influenza

_____ 3. pneumonia

_____ 4. metered-dose inhaler (MDI)

_____ 5. lung abscess

_____ 6. emphysema

_____ 7. asthma

_____ 8. chronic bronchitis

_____ 9. chronic obstructive pulmonary
           disease (COPD)

_____ 10. polycythemia vera

_____ 11. cystic fibrosis (CF)

_____ 12. hemoptysis

_____ 13. atelectasis

Definition

a. Hypersecretion of mucus and chronic productive cough that continues at least 3 months of the year for at least 2 consecutive years.

b. An inflammatory process that results in edema of interstitial lung tissue and extravasation of fluid into the alveoli, thus causing hypoxemia.

c. Inflammation of the tracheobronchial tree, usually in association with a respiratory infection.

d. A chronic disease in which the process of transportation of salt and water across cell membranes is disturbed, leading to production of unusually thick mucus that blocks bodily passages, particularly in the digestive and respiratory systems. This disorder affects all exocrine glands.

e. A contagious disease that is caused by the influenza virus.

f. A disease with multiple precipitating factors resulting in reversible airflow obstruction.

g. A disease state characterized by airflow limitation that is not fully reversible.

h. A device that helps deliver a specific amount of medication to the lungs, usually by supplying a short burst of aerosolized medicine that is inhaled by the patient. It is commonly used to treat asthma, chronic obstructive pulmonary disease, and other respiratory disorders.

i. Collapse or airless condition of the alveoli caused by hypoventilation and obstruction of airways by secretions.

j. An area of pulmonary infection with parenchymal necrosis.

k. Coughing up of blood from the lower respiratory tract.

l. A hematocrit value that is elevated beyond normal values; frequent occurrence in chronic hypoxemia.

m. A disease of the airways that involves destruction of the alveolar walls.

KEY TERMS MATCHING EXERCISE 2

Write the letter of the correct definition in the space next to each term.

Term

_____ 14. pulmonary embolism (PE)

_____ 15. cor pulmonale

_____ 16. pleural effusion

_____ 17. flail chest

_____ 18. pneumothorax

_____ 19. pulmonary contusion

_____ 20. hemothorax

_____ 21. near drowning

_____ 22. carbon monoxide poisoning

_____ 23. coal miner pneumoconiosis

_____ 24. asbestosis

_____ 25. occupational asthma

_____ 26. silicosis

Definition

a. Enlargement of the right ventricle in response to pulmonary hypoxia; literally means "heart of the lungs."

b. Partial or complete collapse of the lung.

c. Abnormal accumulation of fluid in the pleural space.

d. Occurs when an individual breathes carbon monoxide fumes that have built up in an enclosed space.

e. Disease that results from exposure to free crystalline silica in mines, foundries, blasting operations, stone, clay, and glass manufacturing.

f. Occurs when a person sustains two or more rib fractures in two or more places such that the ribs are no longer attached to the thoracic cage, resulting in a free or floating segment of chest wall.

g. The presence of a thrombus or blood clot in the pulmonary vessels, which obstructs blood flow and impedes gas exchange.

h. Occurs when a worker experiences asthmatic symptoms upon exposure to substances that trigger an asthma attack.

i. Condition that connotes survival for at least 24 hours after submersion.

j. Occurs when blunt thoracic trauma is applied through the chest wall to the parenchyma, causing disruption of alveolar capillary networks and usually resulting in hypoxemia; initially a hemorrhage into the lung tissue followed by alveolar and interstitial edema.

k. Diffuse lung fibrosis caused by exposure to asbestos.

l. Partial or complete collapse of the lung due to blood in the pleural space.

m. A chronic lung disease leading to pulmonary fibrosis. It is caused by inhalation of coal dust.

SHORT ANSWER QUESTIONS

27. What can trigger acute bronchitis?

_____

_____

28. Contrast the symptoms of pneumonia with the symptoms of an intrinsic lung disease.

_____

_____

_____

_____

29. Describe the potential risk factors for idiopathic pulmonary fibrosis.

   _____

   _____

30. Explain what distinguishes chronic obstructive pulmonary disease from chronic bronchitis or emphysema alone.

   _____

   _____

   _____

   _____

31. What diagnostic tests are prescribed for patients suspected of having asthma?

   _____

   _____

32. What are the most common risk factors for pulmonary embolism?

   _____

   _____

   _____

   _____

33. Describe the most common presenting symptoms for pulmonary hypertension.

   _____

   _____

34. What are the primary nursing roles for a patient diagnosed with cor pulmonale?

   _____

   _____

35. What are some of the most prevalent known risk factors for lung cancer?

   _____

   _____

   _____

   _____

36. What are the medical treatment options for occupational lung diseases?

   _____

TRUE OR FALSE?

37. _____ T/F Both bronchitis and pneumonia are effectively treated with antibiotics.

38. _____ T/F Most restrictive (interstitial) lung diseases are initiated by some type of injury to the alveolar epithelium, followed by an inflammatory process that involves the alveoli and interstitium of the lung.

39. _____ T/F Prognosis for most cases of idiopathic pulmonary fibrosis diagnosed in the early stages of the disease is complete recovery within one year.

40. _____ T/F Sarcoidosis is believed to occur when a person's immune system overreacts to an unknown toxin, drug, or pathogen that enters the body through the airways.

41. _____ T/F The primary cause of COPD is exposure to tobacco smoke.

42. _____ T/F Medical management of asthma is comprised of three treatment components: (1) objective measures of lung function, (2) environmental control measures and avoidance of risk factors, and (3) compressive pharmacologic therapy.

43. _____ T/F Cystic fibrosis is one of the most common inherited diseases among Caucasians.

44. _____ T/F One of the symptoms of cor pulmonale is a friction rub, which is described as a rubbing, grating, harsh, dry, and scratchy sound heard over the area of pleural inflammation.

45. _____ T/F Pulse oximetry is one of the best methods of confirming carbon dioxide poisoning.

46. _____ T/F Indications for lung transplant include AAT deficiency, bronchiectasis, cystic fibrosis, emphysema, idiopathic pulmonary fibrosis, interstitial lung disease, and pulmonary hypertension.

LABELING EXERCISE: PLEURAL EFFUSION

Place the term in the correct location.

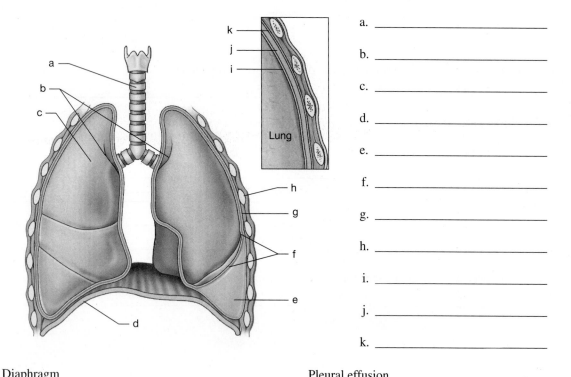

a. _____

b. _____

c. _____

d. _____

e. _____

f. _____

g. _____

h. _____

i. _____

j. _____

k. _____

Diaphragm
Hilum
Lung
Rib
Parietal pleura
Parietal pleura

Pleural effusion
Pleural space
Trachea
Visceral pleura
Visceral pleura

NCLEX-RN® REVIEW QUESTIONS

35-1. A patient with a 30-year history of cigarette smoking is seen in the clinic for a chronic cough and increasing amounts of thick sticky secretions. The nurse realizes this patient most likely is demonstrating signs of:
1. Asthma.
2. Cystic fibrosis.
3. Idiopathic pulmonary fibrosis.
4. Chronic bronchitis.

35-2. A patient is admitted with low-grade fever, night sweats, increasing cough, blood-streaked sputum, general malaise, and weight loss. Which of the following should the nurse do until a diagnosis has been made for this patient?
1. Wear a face mask when completing the assessment.
2. Begin measuring intake and output.
3. Encourage the family to stay with the patient.
4. Provide a meal; try to help the patient change clothes.

35-3. A patient with cystic fibrosis is being discharged. Which of the following would be beneficial to instruct a family member regarding the care this patient will need once at home?
1. Promote patient independence with activities of daily living.
2. Perform chest physiotherapy twice a day.
3. Encourage the patient to return to work as soon as possible.
4. Provide schedule for weaning breathing treatment.

35-4. A patient comes into the emergency department with a hemothorax. Which of the following should the nurse be prepared to do?
1. Immediately transfer the patient to the operating room.
2. Assess vital signs and hemodynamic status.
3. Transfer the patient to the intensive care unit.
4. Assign an unlicensed assistive personnel to monitor vital signs.

35-5. The nurse is planning care for a lung transplant patient. Which of the following should be included in this care?
1. Provide respiratory therapy weaning schedule.
2. Take maximum infection control precautions.
3. Medicate for pain over the transplanted lung site.
4. Discontinue intake and output.

35-6. A patient with black lung becomes more short of breath when talking about his employment history in the coal mines. What can the nurse do to help with the shortness of breath?
1. Place the patient in a supine position.
2. Provide oxygen and help with focused breathing.
3. Encourage the patient to restrict fluids.
4. Encourage the patient to talk through the frustration.

CHAPTER 36

CARING FOR THE PATIENT WITH COMPLEX RESPIRATORY DISORDERS

OUTCOME-BASED LEARNING OBJECTIVES

36-1. Describe the etiology, incidence, and types of acute respiratory failure as seen by nurses in acute care settings.

36-2. Define pulmonary edema and state three of the common etiologies of pulmonary edema that are seen in practice.

36-3. Differentiate between noncardiogenic pulmonary edema and cardiogenic pulmonary edema, as it relates to patient symptomology.

36-4. Distinguish between acute respiratory distress syndrome (ARDS) and acute lung injury (ALI) in patients presenting in an acute care setting.

36-5. Identify the common ventilator modes and important nursing implications for each mode.

36-6. Define PEEP and state two complications of this therapy.

36-7. List the equipment needed for intubation, and explain how the equipment is used with a patient.

36-8. Review the procedure for suctioning and state two important nursing implications related to conducting this procedure.

36-9. State two indications for insertion of a chest tube in a patient in an acute care setting.

CHAPTER OUTLINE

    I. Respiratory Physiology
       A. Oxyhemoglobin Dissociation Curve
          1. Shunts and the Oxyhemoglobin Dissociation Curve
       B. Ventilation/Perfusion Mismatching
   II. Acute Respiratory Failure
       A. Epidemiology and Etiology
       B. Pathophysiology

KEY TERMS MATCHING EXERCISE 1

Write the letter of the correct definition in the space next to each term.

Term

_____ 1. surfactant

_____ 2. perfusion

_____ 3. shunt

_____ 4. ventilation

_____ 5. hypoventilation

_____ 6. acute respiratory failure (ARF)

_____ 7. alveolar ventilation (VA)

_____ 8. anatomic dead space

_____ 9. dead space ventilation (VD)

_____ 10. hypoxemia

Definition

a. A condition defined as a failure of gas exchange.

b. Insufficient oxygen content in the blood.

c. Area in the transporting airways or upper airways and bronchi that results when no gas exchange occurs.

d. The movement of blood carrying oxygen.

e. Decreased ventilation, which causes an increased $PaCO_2$; exists when there is a higher than normal level of carbon dioxide in the blood. Also referred to as *hypercapnia*.

f. The cumulative gas exchange that takes place within each alveolus.

g. The portion of the tidal volume that is not participating in gas exchange.

h. Surface-active agent that promotes alveolar stability.

i. The movement of air between the atmosphere and the alveoli accomplished by respirations or the ability of the lungs to remove carbon dioxide.

j. A hole or passage that allows movement of fluid from one part of the body to another.

KEY TERMS MATCHING EXERCISE 2

Write the letter of the correct definition in the space next to each term.

Term

_____ 11. acute pulmonary edema

_____ 12. cardiogenic pulmonary edema (CPE)

_____ 13. fraction of inspired oxygen (FiO$_2$)

_____ 14. negative pressure pulmonary edema (NPPE)

_____ 15. neurogenic pulmonary edema (NPE)

_____ 16. noncardiogenic pulmonary edema (NCPE)

_____ 17. high-altitude pulmonary edema (HAPE)

_____ 18. acute lung injury (ALI)

_____ 19. acute respiratory distress syndrome (ARDS)

_____ 20. ventilation/perfusion mismatching (V/Q)

Definition

a. A disorder caused by attempts to ventilate a person with an apparent airway obstruction. Also called *postobstruction pulmonary edema* and *airway obstruction pulmonary edema.*

b. Sometimes used when referring to acute respiratory distress syndrome, but is less severe.

c. The amount expressed as a number of oxygen in a gas mixture, 0 (0%) to 1 (100%). For example the FiO$_2$ of normal room air is 0.21 (21%).

d. Usually there is a near equal relationship of ventilation (V.) to perfusion (Q.) in the lungs. The formula V./Q., where ventilation is 4 L/min and perfusion is 5 L/min, explains this relationship. Normal ventilation to perfusion equals 4/5 or 0.8. fraction of inspired oxygen (FiO$_2$).

e. An abnormal accumulation of fluid in the lungs.

f. A rare type of pulmonary edema that develops after a neurological insult to the central nervous system.

g. A progressive form of respiratory failure that leads to alveolar capillary inflammation and damage.

h. An abnormal accumulation of fluid in the lungs caused by a noncardiac etiology.

i. An abnormal accumulation of fluid in the lungs caused by cardiac failure; results from increased hydrostatic pressures in the pulmonary capillary bed secondary to increased pulmonary venous pressure.

j. Type of pulmonary edema that develops in persons who rapidly ascend to heights greater than 2,500 to 3,000 meters (8,202 to 9,842 feet).

KEY TERMS MATCHING EXERCISE 3

Write the letter of the correct definition in the space next to each term.

Term

_____ 21. air-mask-bag unit (AMBU)

_____ 22. minute ventilation (V$_E$)

_____ 23. noninvasive positive pressure ventilation (NPPV)

_____ 24. BiPAP

_____ 25. barotrauma

_____ 26. volutrauma

_____ 27. endotracheal tube

_____ 28. ventilated-associated pneumonia (VAP)

Definition

a. Procedure for delivering breaths to a patient without placement of an artificial airway, such as an endotracheal or tracheostomy tube.

b. Alveoli damage caused by the increased pressure resulting from use of a ventilator. Physical injury or rupture of tympanic membrane, resulting from changing air pressure.

c. Pneumonia that develops in mechanically ventilated patients after more than 48 hours of intubation, with no clinical evidence of pneumonia at the time of intubation.

d. A measurement of how much air the lungs move in 1 minute; it is equal to respiratory rate times tidal volume. A normal resting respiratory rate and a normal resting tidal volume of about 500 mL yield a normal minute ventilation of 6 L/min.

e. Tube used to deliver oxygen that is placed in the trachea.

      f. A device used to deliver oxygen via a mask when a patient is not adequately ventilating or oxygenating.

      g. Lung damage caused by increased volume that causes overdistention of alveoli.

      h. Stands for *bi-level positive airway pressure*, which is a breathing apparatus that helps people get more air into their lungs. The air is delivered through a mask that can be set at two different pressures, one for inhaling (IPAP or inspiratory positive airway pressure) and another for exhaling (EPAP or expiratory airway pressure).

COMPLETE THE SENTENCE

29. One of the physiological effects of aging on the pulmonary system includes decreased effectiveness of _____.

30. Respiratory failure can be divided into three main categories, based on etiology: _____ respiratory failure, _____ respiratory failure, and failure of the respiratory centers in the _____ _____ _____.

31. To treat life-threatening hypoxemia that does not respond to supplemental oxygen, _____ _____ is necessary.

32. Acute pulmonary edema is caused by failure of the _____ or _____.

33. Acute respiratory distress syndrome is caused by _____ to the _____ _____ _____ that allows fluids, proteins, and cell products to flow into the alveoli.

34. During acute respiratory distress syndrome the lung is filled with more water than air, so one goal is to increase _____ _____ _____.

35. Patients who are intubated have a 3 to 10 times greater risk of developing _____ than patients who are not intubated.

36. The most serious potentially fatal complication of noninvasive positive pressure ventilation is _____.

37. The research has provided evidence that patients who might benefit from noninvasive positive pressure ventilation are those with _____, those with _____ _____ _____ failure, and those who are _____.

38. Caring for a patient with a tracheostomy involves the major intervention of _____ to prevent airway injury and cause minimal discomfort.

TRUE OR FALSE?

39. _____ T/F A PaO_2 of less than 60 mmHg and an arterial saturation of oxygen (SaO_2) of less than 90% while breathing room air is representative of hypoxemic respiratory failure.

40. _____ T/F Seizures, cerebral hemorrhage, and head injury are common precipitating factors in the development of neurogenic pulmonary edema.

41. _____ T/F The most common cause of NPPE is laryngospasm during intubation or after extubation.

42. _____ T/F Transfusion-related lung injury only occurs in patients with preexisting respiratory ailments.

43. _____ T/F   A primary cause of cardiogenic pulmonary edema is acute lung injury.
44. _____ T/F   Patients with acute respiratory distress syndrome usually die from multiple-organ failure complications rather than from the respiratory failure.
45. _____ T/F   The functional residual capacity of the lungs increases during the acute exudative phase of acute respiratory distress syndrome.
46. _____ T/F   An endotracheal tube located in the mouth produces many of the complications of patients with respiratory failure who require intubation.
47. _____ T/F   Patients who are on noninvasive positive pressure ventilation can communicate, eat, and require very little, if any, sedation.
48. _____ T/F   Medication administered via the aerosolized route must be dosed at a higher rate and has a number of adverse side effects.

LABELING EXERCISE 1: ALVEOLI WITH BRONCHIOLES

Place the term in the correct location.

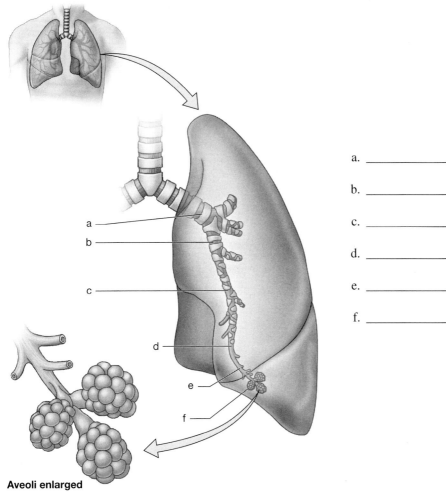

Aveoli enlarged

a. _____

b. _____

c. _____

d. _____

e. _____

f. _____

Alveoli
Bronchiole
Primary bronchus

Secondary bronchus
Terminal bronchiole
Tertiary bronchus

LABELING EXERCISE 2: ALVEOLAR-CAPILLARY MEMBRANE

Place the term in the correct location.

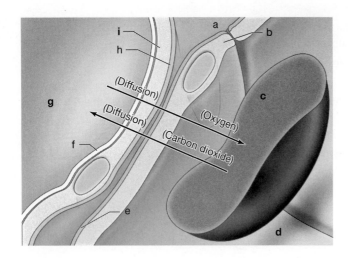

a. _____

b. _____

c. _____

d. _____

e. _____

f. _____

g. _____

h. _____

i. _____

Alveolar epithelium
Alveolus
Capillary
Capillary basement membrane
Capillary endothelium

Epithelial basement membrane
Fluid and surfactant layer
Interstitial space
Red blood cell

NCLEX-RN® REVIEW QUESTIONS

36-1. After reviewing a patient's arterial blood gas results, the nurse determines the patient is demonstrating hypercapneic respiratory failure. Which of the following conditions is most closely related to this type of respiratory failure?
   1. Pneumothorax
   2. Obesity
   3. Guillain-Barre syndrome
   4. Myasthenia gravis

36-2. A patient diagnosed with acute pulmonary edema develops a cough. Which of the following will the patient most likely demonstrate?
   1. Tenacious green sputum
   2. Pink frothy sputum
   3. Rust-brown sputum
   4. Clear thin sputum

36-3. The nurse is planning care for a group of patients. Which of the following would be at greatest risk for developing noncardiogenic pulmonary edema?
   1. A factory worker admitted after inhaling a toxin and developing respiratory distress
   2. A patient with end stage cardiomyopathy
   3. A patient being treated for hemolytic anemia
   4. A patient with diverticulitis

36-4. The nurse is planning the care for patients in the intensive care unit. Which of the following patients is at the greatest risk for developing ARDS?
1. A patient with angina pectoris
2. A patient with diabetic ketoacidosis
3. A patient with aspiration pneumonia
4. A patient with a fractured femur

36-5. A patient who has just been intubated requires high PEEP. The nurse realizes that with an increase in PEEP, the patient is at risk for the development of:
1. Pneumonia.
2. Pneumothorax.
3. Increased cardiac output.
4. Hypoxia.

36-6. The nurse is developing a plan of care for a patient who is intubated and has 5 cm of PEEP. Which of the following would be a priority for the nurse to assess in this patient?
1. Assess bilateral breath sounds every 2–4 hours in order to identify a possible pneumothorax.
2. Monitor intake and output every four hours to assess for signs of renal failure.
3. Listen for adventitious lung sounds every 4 hours for signs of hypovalemia.
4. Assess the need to sedate the client to prevent spontaneous respirations.

36-7. The nurse is gathering the supplies needed to intubate a patient. Which of the following would not be used for this procedure?
1. Laryngoscope blade
2. Nonsterile gloves
3. Oil-soluble lubricant
4. Suction equipment

36-8. The nurse has instructed the spouse of a patient with a tracheostomy on how to perform suctioning. Which of the following would indicate that the spouse is able to perform the suctioning?
1. Donning sterile gloves in preparation for suctioning
2. Hyperoxygenating the patient with 50% oxygen prior to suctioning
3. Placing the head of the bed in a low Fowler's position prior to suctioning
4. Applying suction when passing the catheter into the patient's tracheostomy

36-9. The nurse is planning care for a group of patients. Which of the following patients should the nurse assess first?
1. A patient who is to receive postural drainage every four hours
2. A patient being discharged who needs instruction in the use of a metered dose inhaler
3. A patient with a chest tube with bubbling in the water seal chamber
4. A patient wearing oxygen who has an oxygen saturation of 90%

CHAPTER 37

NURSING ASSESSMENT OF PATIENTS WITH CARDIOVASCULAR DISORDERS

OUTCOME-BASED LEARNING OBJECTIVES

37-1. Compare and contrast the significance of cardiovascular assessment findings.

37-2. Evaluate the relationship of current health status and the presence of cardiac risk factors.

37-3. Describe the relationship of clinical manifestations to data obtained from the review of a patient's social history.

37-4. Describe the essential components of a cardiovascular physical assessment.

CHAPTER OUTLINE

   I. Anatomy and Physiology of the Cardiovascular System
      A. Cardiac Valves
      B. Cardiac Circulatory System
  II. Physiology of the Cardiovascular System
      A. Cardiac Cycle
      B. Autonomic Nervous System
         1. Receptors and Neurotransmitters
 III. History
      A. Biographic and Demographic Data
      B. Chief Complaint
         1. Presenting Symptoms
            a. Specific Cardiovascular Clinical Manifestations
      C. Past Medical History
         1. Childhood Illnesses and Immunizations
         2. Previous Illnesses and Hospitalizations

        3. Diagnostic/Interventional Cardiac Procedures or Surgeries
        4. Medications
        5. Cultural Considerations
        6. Allergies
    D. Family History
    E. Risk Factors
    F. Social History
        1. Occupation
        2. Culture
        3. Environment
        4. Habits
        5. Exercise
        6. Nutrition
        7. Personal Factors
IV. Physical Examination
    A. Inspection of Skin and Extremities
        1. General Appearance
           a. Mentation
        2. Color and Appearance of Skin and Extremities
           a. Cyanosis
           b. Pallor
           c. Nail Beds
        3. Neck Veins
           a. Jugular Venous Distention
           b. Jugular Venous Pressure
           c. Abdominojugular Reflux
    B. Palpation of Skin and Extremities
        1. Edema
        2. Skin Tugor
        3. Capillary Refill
        4. Arterial Pulses
    C. Inspection and Palpation of the Precordium
        1. Clinical Reference Points
        2. Point of Maximal Impulse (PMI)
        3. Heaves and Thrills
    D. Auscultation of the Precordium
        1. Requirements for Auscultation
        2. Normal Heart Sounds: S_1 and S_2
           a. Distinguishing S_1 from S_2
           b. Split Heart Sounds: Split S_1 and Split S_2
           c. Extra Heart Sounds
           d. S_3
           e. S_4
           f. Summation Gallop
           g. Pericardial Friction Rubs
        3. Abnormal Heart Sounds: Murmurs
           a. Murmur Etiology
           b. Innocent Murmurs
    E. Gender Implications/Gender Differences
    F. Gerontological Considerations
V. Critical Thinking Related to Cardiovascular Assessment
VI. Implications for Health Promotion

VII. Cardiovascular Monitoring
 A. Assessment of Heart Rate
 B. Assessment of Blood Pressure
  1. Classification of Blood Pressure
  2. Health Promotion: Preventing Hypertension
 C. Assessment of Oxygen Delivery
VIII. Summary

KEY TERM CROSSWORD

Complete the crossword puzzle below using key terms.

Across:

1. Temporary dizziness or loss of consciousness caused by low blood pressure and insufficient blood flow.
4. The sound heard with a stethoscope of blood flowing through a narrowed blood vessel that is outside the heart.
6. Abnormal heart sounds produced by turbulent blood flow.
10. Palpable sustained lifts of the chest wall due to forceful cardiac contractions.
11. An awareness of the beating of the heart.
12. The need to get up at night to urinate.

Down:

2. Subjective feeling of shortness of breath or difficulty breathing.
3. Bluish-tinged skin or mucous membranes due to deoxygenated hemoglobin in blood vessels close to the skin.
5. Palpable vibratory sensations from turbulent blood flow across cardiac valves due to cardiac murmurs.
7. Accumulation of fluid in the intercellular spaces that causes swelling of tissue.
8. The elasticity and mobility of the skin; reflects the skin's hydration status.
9. Shortness of breath relieved by sitting or standing erect.
13. Technique of listening to the sounds produced by different body areas.

SHORT ANSWER QUESTIONS

1. What are the most common cardiovascular symptoms that patients present to health care professionals?

   _____

   _____

2. What are the modifiable risk factors for cardiovascular disorders?

   _____

   _____

3. What is the difference between jugular venous distention (JVD) and jugular venous pressure (JVP)?

   _____

   _____

4. What is the assessment of the abdominojugular reflux used to detect?

   _____

   _____

5. Explain S_1 and S_2 heard during auscultation.

   _____

   _____

LABELING EXERCISE 1: DIAGRAM OF THE HEART IN CHEST

Place the term in the correct location.

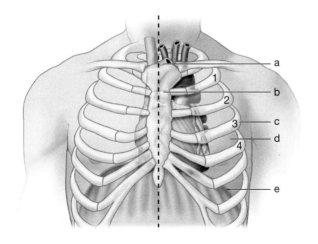

a. _____

b. _____

c. _____

d. _____

e. _____

3rd rib
Angle of Louis
Diaphragm
Intercostal space
Suprasternal notch

LABELING EXERCISE 2: LAYERS OF THE HEART

Place the term in the correct location.

Transverse section of the heart

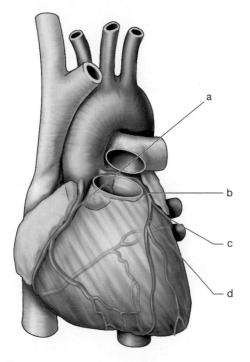

a. _____

b. _____

c. _____

d. _____

e. _____

f. _____

g. _____

Cavity of pericardial sac
Endocardium
Epicardium
Myocardium
Parietal
Visceral
Serous pericardium

LABELING EXERCISE 3: CORONARY ARTERIES

Place the term in the correct location.

a. _____

b. _____

c. _____

d. _____

Circumflex coronary artery
Left anterior descending coronary artery
Left main coronary artery
Right coronary artery

LABELING EXERCISE 4: CLINICAL REFERENCE POINTS FOR PALPATION

Place the term in the correct location.

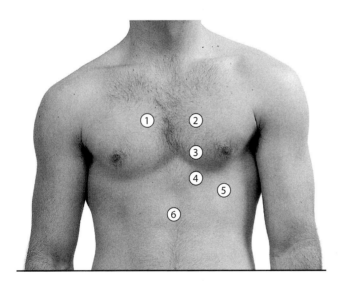

a. _____

b. _____

c. _____

d. _____

e. _____

f. _____

Left sternal border (LSB), 2nd ICS
LSB, 3rd ICS
LSB, 4th ICS
Midclavicular line (MCL), 5th ICS
Point of maximal impulse
Right sternal border (RSB), 2nd intercostal space (ICS)

LABELING EXERCISE 5: CARDIAC BLOOD FLOW PATH

Place the term in the correct location.

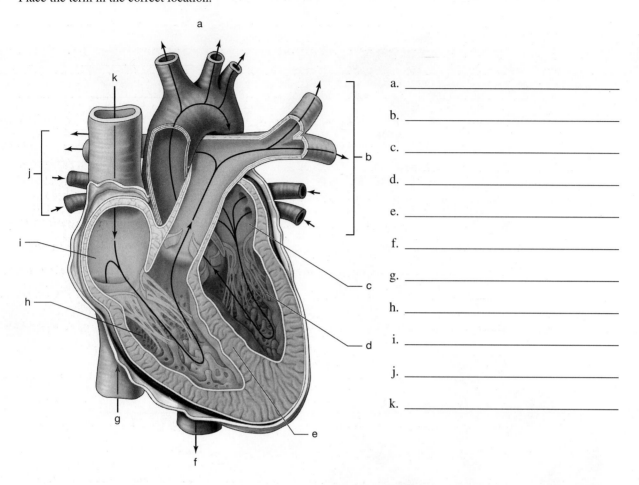

a. _____

b. _____

c. _____

d. _____

e. _____

f. _____

g. _____

h. _____

i. _____

j. _____

k. _____

Cardiac blood flow paths
Interventricular septum
Left atrium
Left ventricle
Pulmonary circulation
Pulmonary circulation

Right atrium
Right ventricle
Systemic atrial circulation
Systemic venous circulation
Systemic venous circulation

NCLEX-RN® REVIEW QUESTIONS

37-1. When determining if a patient meets the criteria for a diagnosis of metabolic syndrome, the nurse checks which assessment findings?
1. Blood pressure, waist circumference, and pulse rate
2. Triglyceride level, waist circumference, and HDL level
3. LDL, HDL, and triglyceride levels
4. HDL level, fasting glucose level, and liver enzymes

37-2. The nurse concludes that which of the following family history data contributes the greatest cardiovascular risk to a patient?
1. An 86-year-old parent has had a stroke.
2. A younger sibling has been diagnosed with multiple sclerosis.
3. A 50-year-old sibling has hypertension.
4. A parent died of peptic ulcer disease.

37-3. A patient seen in the clinic has a blood pressure of 134/86. The nurse should provide which information to the patient?
1. Health-promoting lifestyle modifications
2. Recommendations to begin antihypertensive therapy
3. Recommendation to have the blood pressure rechecked in one week
4. Dietary modifications to eliminate all salt

37-4. The nurse suspects a patient may have a pericardial friction rub when a squeaky muffled sound is heard on auscultation of the heart. To help confirm the suspicion the nurse should auscultate heart sounds while the patient:
1. Is lying on the right side.
2. Lies flat on the back.
3. Is leaning forward.
4. Takes a deep breath.

CHAPTER 38

Nursing Interpretation of the Electrocardiogram

OUTCOME-BASED LEARNING OBJECTIVES

38-1. Describe the configuration of the normal electrocardiogram (ECG).

38-2. Identify and calculate heart rate, rhythm, PR interval, QRS complex, and QT interval for normal and abnormal cardiac rhythms.

38-3. Discuss the etiology and significant ECG features of the following dysrhythmia classifications: sinus, atrial, junctional, block, ventricular, and asystole.

38-4. Interpret the significance of each of the dysrhythmias and formulate nursing responsibilities for each dysrhythmia.

CHAPTER OUTLINE

I. Anatomy of the Heart
   A. Cardiac Conduction System
   B. Sinoatrial (SA) Node
   C. Intra-Atrial Pathways
   D. Atrioventricular (AV) Node and AV Junction
   E. Bundle of His and Bundle Branches
   F. Purkinje Network Fibers
   G. Cardiac Cells
      1. Automaticity
      2. Excitability
      3. Conductivity
      4. Contractility
   H. Electrolytes Affecting Cardiac Function
   I. Cardiac Depolarization and Repolarization
   J. Summary of the Cardiac Conduction System
   K. Cardiac Waveform and Time Intervals Measured on ECG

KEY TERMS MATCHING EXERCISE 1

Write the letter of the correct definition in the space next to each term.

Term

_____ 1. cardiac depolarization

_____ 2. Bachmann bundle

_____ 3. graph paper

_____ 4. fill time

_____ 5. action potential

_____ 6. ECG waveform

_____ 7. cardiac conduction system

_____ 8. intra-atrial pathways

_____ 9. resting membrane potential

_____ 10. relative refractory period

Definition

a. The difference in electrical charge, or voltage, between the inside and outside of a cardiac cell.

b. Part of the electrical conduction system of the heart composed of a group of intra-atrial fibers contained in the left atrium that conduct electrical impulses from the SA node to the left atrium.

c. Period of time needed for blood to enter the heart between contractions.

d. Muscle contraction of the heart resulting from electrolyte exchange in the cardiac cells.

e. Conduction system unique to the myocardium that is composed of specialized cells that enable it to generate and transmit action potentials without stimulation from the nervous system. The specialized cells are concentrated in the sinoatrial and atrioventricular nodes, and the Purkinje network.

f. Part of the electrical conduction system of the heart that consists of the internodal pathways and the Bachmann bundle.

g. Paper specifically designed and used to measure various calculations related to the electrical activity of the heart; it is arranged as a series of horizontal and vertical lines and is standardized to allow for consistency in ECG tracing analysis.

h. Period when depolarization is almost complete, and corresponds with the top and the downslope of the T wave on an ECG tracing.

i. Response of the resting membrane potential to a stimulus that exceeds the membrane threshold value. Carries signals along the muscle cell and conveys information from one cell to another, resulting in cardiac muscle depolarization.

j. Movement away from the baseline, or the isoelectric line, on an ECG tracing on graph paper.

KEY TERMS MATCHING EXERCISE 2

Write the letter of the correct definition in the space next to each term.

Term

_____ 11. cardiac repolarization

_____ 12. negative deflection

_____ 13. atrial dysrhythmia

_____ 14. junctional dysrhythmia

_____ 15. ventricular dysrhythmia

_____ 16. pulseless electrical activity (PEA)

_____ 17. isoelectric line

_____ 18. absolute refractory period

_____ 19. paroxysmal junctional
          tachycardia (PJT)

_____ 20. bundle branch block

Definition

a. Discontinuity of conduction (complete or incomplete) in one branch of the bundle of His that affects normal transmission of the impulse through the ventricles. When one bundle is blocked, the ventricles depolarize asynchronously.

b. Dysrhythmia resulting from an irritable focus in the functional tissue that fires off before the SA node has had a chance to, or because the SA node has failed to fire.

c. Any waveform that goes below the isoelectric line on ECG graph paper.

d. An irritable focus in the AV junction that assumes the pacemaker role by discharging impulses more rapidly than the SA node. Begins and ends abruptly.

e. Process whereby a depolarized cell is polarized, causing a return to the resting membrane potential. Also referred to as the recovery phase.

f. Period of time during which a cardiac cell is unable to respond to any stimulus and cannot spontaneously depolarize.

g. Straight line on the ECG graph paper that marks the beginning and ending point of all waves. Also referred to as the *baseline*.

h. Dysrhythmia that generally results from an irritable focus in the atria that fires off an electrical impulse before the SA node has had a chance to fire in a normal fashion.

i. Absence of a detectable pulse and blood pressure in the presence of electrical activity in the heart as evidenced by some type of ECG rhythm other than ventricular fibrillation or ventricular tachycardia. It is not an actual rhythm, but represents a clinical condition wherein the patient is clinically dead, despite the fact that some type of organized rhythm appears on the ECG monitor.

j. Dysrhythmia that originates in the ventricle and is caused by ectopic or irritable foci in the wall of the ventricle. These are the most serious types of dysrhythmia.

WORD SEARCH

First identify the word from its definition. Then find and circle it in the puzzle below.

21. _____ Special cells and fibers that make up the electrical conduction system of the heart. Also called *nodes*.

22. _____ Atrial contraction, which augments the blood supply going to the ventricles and ultimately cardiac output.

23. _____ Anterior and posterior pathways that branch off the heart's left bundle branch.

24. _____ Term that applies to the emergence of a pacemaker that is lower in the heart and sustains a heart rate when the SA node fails.

25. _____ Ability of pacemaker cells to generate their own electrical impulses without depending on nervous system stimulation external to the heart.

26. _____ Electrically charged components derived from the molecules of electrolytes.

27. _____ A negatively charged ion.

28. _____ Term that encompasses a broad range of abnormalities, including disorders of impulse generation and conduction, failure of pacemakers, and a susceptibility to paroxysmal or chronic atrial tachycardia.

29. _____ A positively charged ion. Major cations affecting cardiac function are potassium (K), sodium (Na), and calcium (Ca).

30. _____ An adhesive pad that contains conducting gel and is connected to a cardiac monitor by lead wires.

31. _____ On an ECG tracing, the point at which the QRS meets the ST segment.

32. _____ A heartbeat originating from a site other than the primary cardiac pacemaker tissue. Also called *arrhythmia* and *ectopic focus*.

33. _____ Ability of an electrical cell to respond to a stimulus. All cardiac cells possess this property. Also referred to as *irritability*.

34. _____ Refers to the imaginary line drawn between the positive and negative electrodes.

35. _____ Ability of the cardiac cell to accept and then transmit a stimulus to other cardiac cells.

36. _____ A mechanical function that enables the cardiac cells to shorten and cause the muscle to contract in response to an electrical stimulus. Also referred to as *rhythmicity*.

37. _____ Premature ventricular contraction that occurs every other beat.

38. _____ An ECG pattern from sources outside the heart; creates an abnormal pattern on ECG graph paper. This interference causes the baseline or isoelectric line to become fuzzy; this fuzzy baseline is referred to as 60 cycle.

39. _____ Complete termination of ventricular activity with no measurable cardiac electrical activity. Represents cardiac standstill from massive cardiac muscle damage.

40. _____ Independent function of the atria and the ventricles.

41. _____ ECG leads that have electrodes with opposite polarity, one positive and one negative.

42. _____ A rapid, regular atrial rhythm with a rate of about 300 beats per minute.

43. _____ A heartbeat originating from a site other than the primary cardiac pacemaker tissue. Also called *dysrhythmia*.

S	A	I	I	A	T	R	I	A	L	F	L	U	T	T	E	R	Y	T	F
P	I	P	L	U	Y	T	Y	T	Y	U	I	B	L	N	E	A	A	E	R
O	B	C	E	E	A	R	S	F	S	S	T	I	W	R	U	S	A	D	R
K	C	I	K	L	A	I	R	T	A	Y	E	G	I	Y	P	T	D	D	R
T	S	E	U	S	N	D	Q	W	R	S	S	E	U	I	A	J	B	O	P
N	A	W	R	T	I	U	A	U	T	R	C	M	C	V	M	P	I	U	Y
O	S	U	Y	E	O	N	A	X	T	A	A	I	S	F	G	O	P	H	X
I	Y	A	T	D	N	R	U	P	I	T	P	N	C	A	T	I	O	N	Y
T	S	L	I	O	T	P	N	S	L	S	E	Y	P	L	O	N	L	T	T
A	T	A	L	R	M	O	A	E	S	U	L	A	R	R	E	T	A	A	I
I	O	N	I	T	R	A	I	U	A	Y	R	K	J	I	E	S	R	S	L
C	L	A	B	C	S	J	T	E	R	T	N	W	K	P	A	R	L	L	I
O	E	E	A	E	O	N	W	I	S	E	L	D	N	U	B	N	E	R	T
S	A	U	T	L	I	U	A	J	C	S	W	W	R	I	U	O	A	N	C
S	P	A	I	E	T	I	O	K	U	I	O	N	R	O	N	E	D	I	A
I	S	L	C	W	L	T	R	R	A	T	T	O	R	O	M	P	S	T	R
D	A	T	X	D	Y	S	R	H	P	C	S	Y	I	A	L	E	I	A	T
V	T	A	E	C	T	O	P	I	C	F	O	C	U	S	E	S	T	E	N
A	R	T	I	F	A	C	T	D	Y	S	R	H	Y	T	H	M	I	A	O
R	A	R	P	E	T	T	R	Y	T	I	V	I	T	C	U	D	N	O	C

KEY TERM CROSSWORD

Complete the crossword puzzle below using key terms.

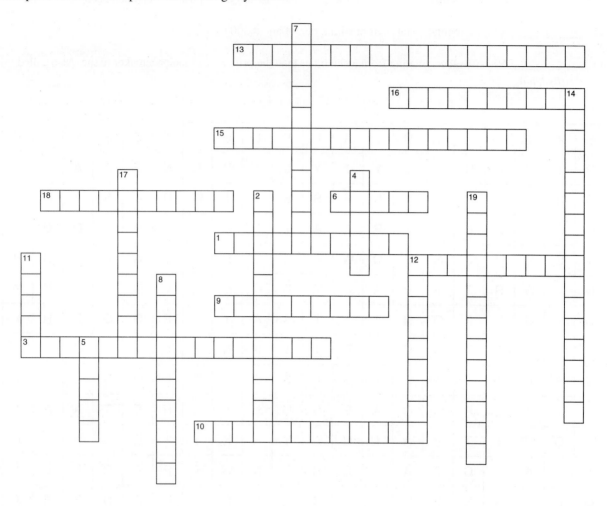

Across:

1. Part of the cardiac cycle; represents time from atrial depolarization to ventricular depolarization on an ECG tracing. Sometimes referred to as the PRI or PR segment.

3. Rapid firing of the sinus node at rates of more than 100 beats per minute at rest. There may be a compensatory response to a decreased cardiac output state.

6. Represents ventricular recovery or repolarization in the cardiac cycle; often referred to as the resting phase of the cycle.

9. Standard surface ECG with 12 leads, 3 bipolar and 9 unipolar.

10. Premature ventricular contraction that occurs every fourth beat.

12. Point at which a stimulus will produce a cell response or depolarization.

13. Any waveform that goes above the isoelectric line on ECG graph paper.

15. Period of time that ensures the cardiac muscle is totally relaxed before another action potential or depolarization can be initiated.

16. A unit of electrical voltage or potential difference equal to one thousandth of a volt.

18. Part of the cardiac cycle; is measured from the Q wave to the end of the T wave.

Down:

2. Lead with one positive electrode and one indifferent zero reference point; consists of standard leads and augmented limb leads.
4. Part of the cardiac cycle; represents atrial contraction or depolarization on an ECG tracing.
5. Follows the T wave in the cardiac cycle and is present only in some people on an ECG tracing.
7. Momentary cessation of sinus impulse formation, causing a pause in the cardiac rhythm followed by spontaneous resumption of electrical activity. This dysrhythmia may be referred to as sinus pause.
8. Part of the cardiac cycle; represents ventricular contraction or depolarization on an ECG tracing.

11. Special cells and fibers that make up the electrical conduction system of the heart.
12. Premature ventricular contraction that is evidenced every third beat.
14. Situation in which the SA node is firing at a heart rate of less than 60 beats per minute. Often called sinus brady.
17. Interval between the end of the QRS complex and the beginning of the T wave on an ECG tracing.
19. Cardiac cell found in the electrical conduction system, which lies in the heart wall and septum. It generates and conducts impulses.

LABELING EXERCISE: ELECTRICAL CONDUCTION SYSTEM OF THE HEART

Define the term. Then place the term on the appropriate blank of the illustration.

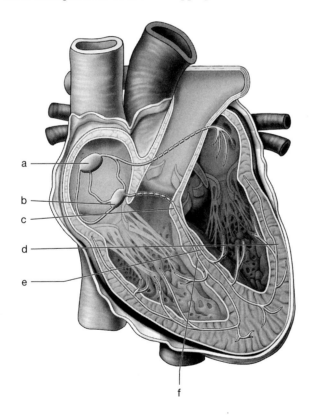

a. _____

b. _____

c. _____

d. _____

e. _____

f. _____

atrioventricular (AV) node:

_____

_____

bundle of His:

_____

_____

left bundle branch:

_____

_____

Purkinje network fibers:

_____

_____

right bundle branch:

_____

_____

sinoatrial (SA) node:

_____

_____

CARDIAC WAVEFORM AND TIME INTERVALS MEASURED ON ECG

Using the illustration as a reference, explain what the terms below represent.

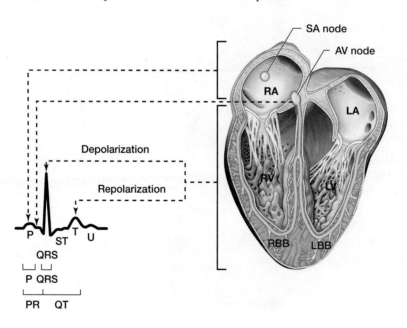

P wave:

_____

_____

PR interval:

_____

_____

QRS complex:

_____

_____

J point:

_____

_____

ST segment:

_____

_____

T wave:

_____

_____

U wave:

_____

_____

RHYTHM STRIP IDENTIFICATION

Record the name of the correct rhythm strip on the line beneath the image.

Rhythm Strips of Normal and False Patterns

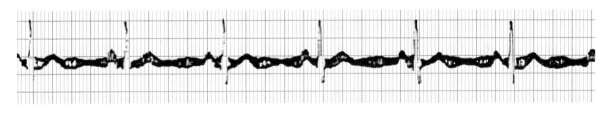

a. _____

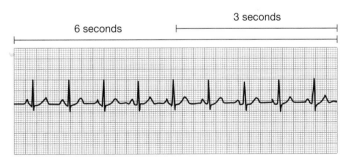

P Wave: Present 1 P wave/QRS complex; PR Interval: 0.18 second;
QRS Complex: 0.06 second; QT Interval 0.36 second; Heart Rate:
Atrial: 90 beats per minute (bpm); Ventricular: 90 bpm; Rhythm:
Regular, Ectopic Beats: None

b. _____

Rhythm Strips of Dysrhythmias

Sinus Dysrhythmias

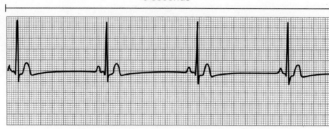

P Wave: Present, 1 P wave/QRS Complex; PR Interval: .16 second;
QRS Complex: 0.08 second; QT Interval: 0.32 second; Heart Rate: Atrial:
40 bpm; Ventricular: 40 bpm; Rhythm: Regular; Ectopic Beats: None

c. _____

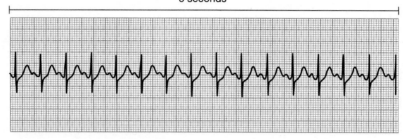

P Wave: Present, 1/QRS Complex; PR Interval: 0.14 second; QRS Complex: 0.08
second; QT Interval: 0.36 second; Heart Rate: Atrial: 140 bpm, Ventricular: 140 bpm;
Rhythm: Regular; Ectopic Beats None

d. _____

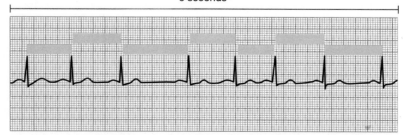

P Wave: Present 1/QRS Complex; PR Interval: 0.18 second; QRS Complex: 0.08
second; QT Interval: 0.40 second; Heart Rate: Atrial: 80 bpm, Ventricular: 80 bpm;
Rhythm: Irregular; Ectopic Beats: None

e. _____

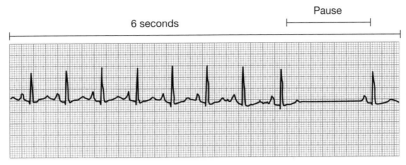

P Wave: Present 1/QRS Complex; PR Interval: 0.20 second; QRS Complex: 0.10 second; QT Interval: 0.40 second; Heart Rate: Atrial: 90 bpm, Ventricular: 90 bpm; Rhythm: Regular except for the pause; Ectopic Beats: None
Conclusion: Sinus arrest (pause)

f. _____

Atrial Dysrhythmias

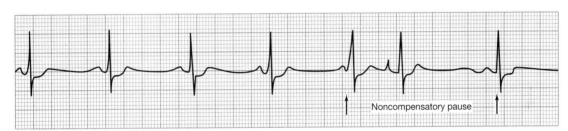

P Wave: Premature; PR Interval: 0.16 second; QRS Complex: 0.10 second; QT interval: 0.40 second; Heart Rate: Atrial: 70 bpm; Ventricular: 70 bpm; Rhythm: Regular except for premature beats. Ectopic Beat PAC. Conclusion: One premature atrial contraction.

g. _____

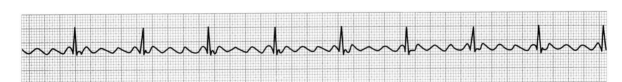

P Wave: None, flutter waves; PR interval: None; QRS Complex: 0.08 second; QT Interval: unable to obtain; Heart Rate: Atrial: about 300 bpm, Ventricular: 90 bpm; Rhythm: Regular; Ectopic Beats: Flutter waves.

h. _____

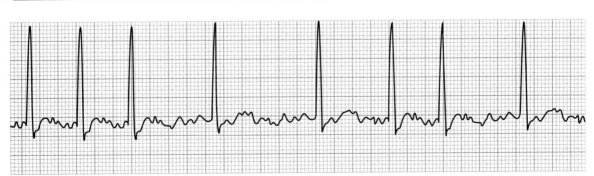

P Wave: None; PR Interval: None; QRS Complex: 0.10 second; QT Interval: unable to obtain; Heart Rate: Ventricular: 80 bpm; Rhythm: Irregular; Ectopic Beats: f waves.

i. _____

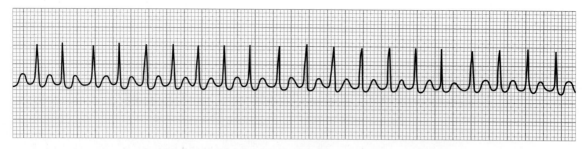

P Wave: None; PR Interval: None; QRS Complex: 0.10 second; QT Interval: unable to obtain; Heart Rate: ⟶ Atrial rate rapid, Ventricular: 200 bpm; Rhythm: Regular; Ectopic Beats: Depends on pacemaker site.

j. _____

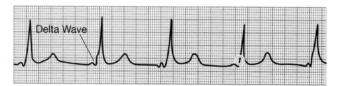

P Wave: Present and irregular; PR Interval: 0.12 second;
QRS Complex: 0.16 second. QT Interval 0.52 second,
40-50 bpm, Ventricular: 40-50 bpm; Rhythm: Regular
Ectopic Beats: None.

k. _____

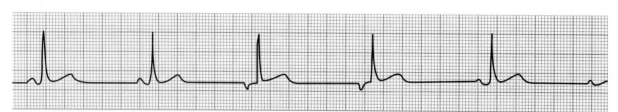

P Wave: Multifocal; PR Interval: 0.16 second; QRS Complex: 0.06 second; QT Interval: 0.04 second; Heart Rate: Atrial: Approximately
60 bpm; Ventricular: 50 bpm; Rhythm: Irregular; Ectopic Beats; Multifocal P waves.

l. _____

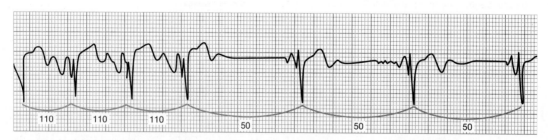

P Wave: Present, but variable configuration; PR Interval: 0.14 second; QRS Complex: 0.08 second; QT Interval: 0.40 second;
Heart Rate: Atrial: 60 bpm, Ventricular: 60 bpm; Rhythm: Irregular; Ectopic Beats: May occur with slow rate.

m. _____

Junctional Dysrhythmias

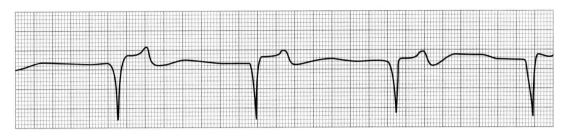

P Wave: None, or buried in QRS Complex; PR Interval: Not measurable; QRS Complex: 0.10 second; QT Interval: 0.40 second; Heart Rate: Atrial: Not measurable, Ventricular: 40 bpm; Rhythm: Regular; Ectopic Beats: None.

n. _____

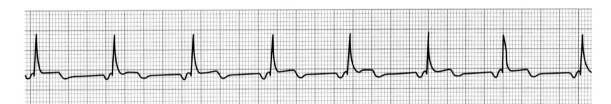

P Wave: Inverted and regular; PR Interval: 0.14–0.16 second; QRS Complex: 0.08 second: QT Interval: 0.44 second; Heart Rate: Atrial: 80 bpm, Ventricular: 80 bpm; Rhythm: Regular: Ectopic Beats: none.

o. _____

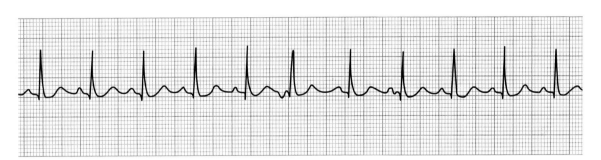

P Wave: Present and regular except for premature beat; PR Interval: 0.16 second; QRS Complex: 0.08 second; second; Heart Rate: Atrial: 110 bpm, Ventricular: 110 bpm; Rhythm: Regular except for premature beats: Ectopic Beats: none

p. _____

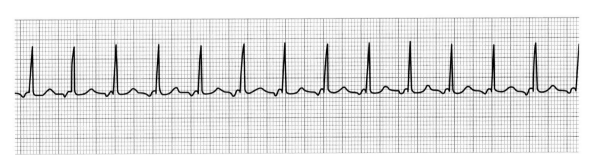

P Wave: Inverted and regular; PR Interval: 0.08 second; QRS Complex: 0.06 second; QT Interval: 0.32 second; Heart Rate: Atrial: 130 bpm, Ventricular: 130 bpm. Rhythm: Regular; Ectopic Beats: None.

q. _____

Conduction Block Dysrhythmias

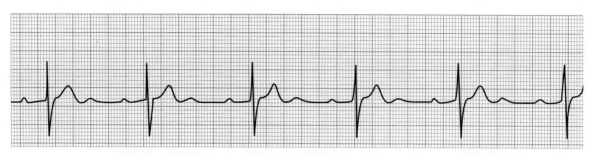

P Wave: Present and regular; PR Interval: 0.24 second; QRS Complex: 0.06 second; QT Interval: 0.40 second; Heart Rate: Atrial: 60 bpm, Ventricular: 60 bpm; Rhythm: Regular; Ectopic Beats: None.

r. _____

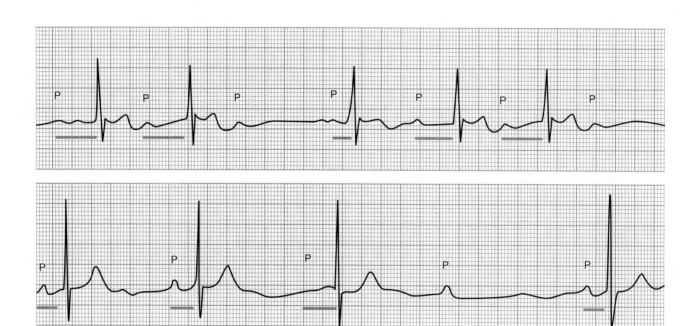

P Waves: Present and regular; PR Interval: Progressively prolonged until one P wave is not conducted and the sequence begins again; QRS Complex: 0.10 second; QT Interval: 0.42–0.60 second; Heart Rate: Atrial: 70 bpm, Ventricular 50 bpm; Rhythm: Atrial: Regular, Ventricular: Irregular due to dropped beat; Ectopic Beats: None. Conclusion: Mobitz I/Wenckeback Second-Degree Heart Block.

s. _____

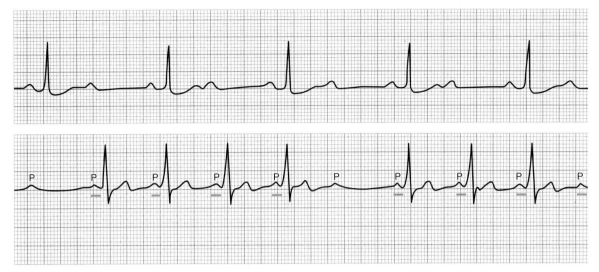

P Waves: Present and regular; PR Interval: 0.24 second; QRS Complex: 0.06 second; QT Interval: 0.48 second; Heart Rate: Atrial: 100 bpm, Ventricular 50 bpm; Rhythm: Atrial: Regular, Ventricular: Irregular due to dropped beat; Ectopic Beats: None.

t. _____

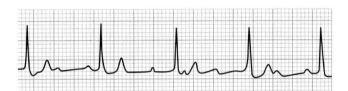

P Waves: Present and regular; PR Interval: None; QRS Complex: 0.12 second; QT Interval: 0.38 second; Heart Rate: Atrial: 90 bpm, Ventricular: 40–50 bpm; Rhythm: Regular; Ectopic Beats: None.

u. _____

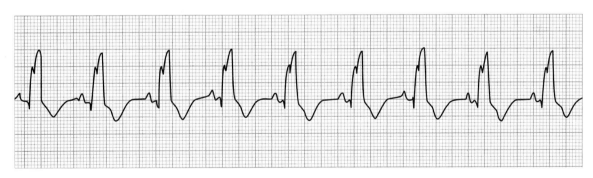

P Wave: Normal sinus rhythm; PR Interval: 0.16 second; QRS Complex: 0.20 second; QT Interval: 0.40 second. Heart Rate: Atrial: 90 bpm, Ventricular: 90 bpm; Rhythm: Atrial: Regular, Ventricular: Regular; Ectopic Beats: None.

v. _____

Ventricular Dysrhythmias

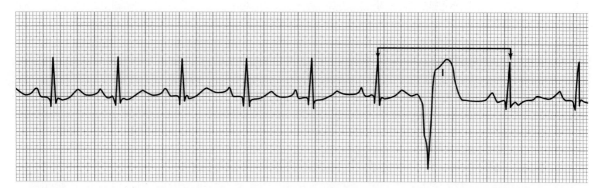

P Wave: Present and regular, except where absent (PVC); PR Interval: 0.20 second; QRS Complex: 0.08 second; QT Interval: 0.42 second; Heart Rate: Atrial: 70 bpm, Ventricular: 80 bpm; Rhythm: Atrial: Regular, Ventricular: Regular except for premature beat; Ectopic Beats: One PVC.

w. _____

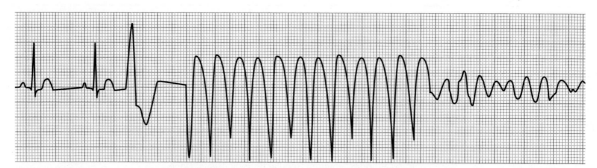

P Wave: Two normal P waves present; PR Interval: Not discernable during dysrhythmia; QRS Complex: Wide and distorted during dysrhythmia; QT Interval: Not discernable during dysrhythmia; Heart Rate: Atrial: Not discernable, Ventricular: Rapid; Rhythm: Both regular and irregular; Ectopic Beats: PVCs, ventricular tachycardia/fibrillation.

x. _____

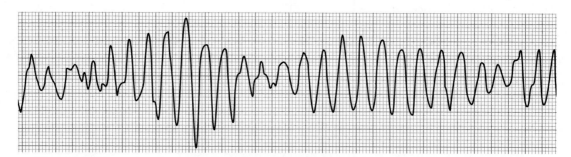

P Waves: Not discernable; PR Interval: Not discernable; QRS Complex: Wide, distorted, and varying heights; QT Interval: not discernable; Rate: Rapid; Rhythm: Both regular and irregular; Ectopic Beats: All.

y. _____

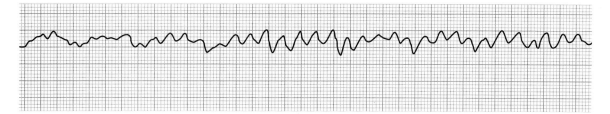

P Waves: Not discernable; PR Interval: Not discernable; QRS Complex: Wide, distorted, and varying heights; QT Interval not discernable; Heart Rate: Not discernable; Ectopic Beats: All.

z. _____

NCLEX-RN® REVIEW QUESTIONS

38-1. The nurse has just completed an electrocardiogram for a patient and realizes that which of the following should be reviewed first?
  1. Assess the QRS complex.
  2. Assess the QT interval.
  3. Assess the P wave.
  4. Assess the heart rate.

38-2. A patient with a low blood pressure has an electrocardiogram with 15 PQRST complexes without ectopi. The nurse believes this patient is demonstrating:
  1. Sinus tachycardia.
  2. A wandering atrial pacemaker.
  3. Sick sinus syndrome.
  4. Premature junctional contraction.

38-3. A patient in heart failure is demonstrating a pulse rate of 50, dizziness, and generalized weakness. Which of the following should be done to help this patient?
  1. Begin vagal maneuvers.
  2. Prepare the patient for temporary pacemaker insertion.
  3. Provide oxygen and plan to administer atropine.
  4. Prepare to administer amiodarone.

38-4. A patient's heart rhythm has changed from Mobitz Type I/Wenkebach to Mobitz Type II. Which of the following should the nurse do to help this patient?
  1. Nothing. Continue to observe this patient's rhythm.
  2. Administer magnesium.
  3. Prepare to administer amiodarone.
  4. Prepare for a temporary pacemaker insertion.

CHAPTER 39

DIAGNOSTIC AND INTERVENTIONAL THERAPIES FOR CARDIOVASCULAR DISORDERS

OUTCOME-BASED LEARNING OBJECTIVES

39-1. Define sensitivity and specificity as they relate to diagnostic testing.

39-2. Describe the major noninvasive and invasive diagnostic tests to detect coronary disease.

39-3. Identify the appropriate screening test and associated nursing management for a given patient population.

39-4. Compare and contrast major advantages and limitations for each test.

39-5. Prioritize the nursing management for patients receiving percutaneous coronary interventional procedures.

CHAPTER OUTLINE

I. Diagnostic Procedures
   A. Electrocardiogram
   B. Echocardiography
   C. Transesophageal Echocardiography
   D. Stress Echocardiography
   E. Exercise Testing
      1. Indications
      2. Protocols and Patient Preparation
      3. Interpretation
   F. Radionuclide Imaging
      1. Perfusion Imaging
   G. Cardiac Magnetic Resonance Imaging
   H. Positron-Emission Tomography
   I. Electron Beam Computed Tomography

KEY TERMS MATCHING EXERCISE 1

Write the letter of the correct definition in the space next to each term.

Term

_____ 1. electrocardiogram

_____ 2. transesophageal echocardiography (TEE)

_____ 3. metabolic equivalent (MET)

_____ 4. myocardial perfusion imaging (MPI)

_____ 5. ECG single photon emission computed tomography (SPECT)

_____ 6. myocardial viability

_____ 7. magnetic resonance imaging (MRI)

_____ 8. electron beam computed tomography (EBCT)

_____ 9. cardiac catheterization

_____ 10. percutaneous coronary intervention (PCI)

Definition

a. Use of a radioactive tracer and a gamma camera to detect blood flow to the myocardium.

b. The use of devices to either remove plaque or alter its morphology in the catheterization laboratory, including atherectomy devices, lasers, and intracoronary stents.

c. Technique that uses radiofrequency pulses from a large, powerful magnet to temporarily disrupt the normal spin of certain atoms within the body.

d. Procedure that uses an electron gun and a stationary tungsten target to rapidly (about 90 seconds) acquire multiple images of the heart during a single breath hold.

e. Surface recording of the electrical activity of the heart.

f. Echocardiogram performed using a miniaturized transducer advanced down the esophagus.

g. Term applied to areas of the myocardium that appear to have normal functioning as well as areas that appear dysfunctional (hibernating or stunned) that might improve with revascularization.

h. A measure of oxygen consumption. One MET is the energy requirement for a person at rest while sitting: around 3.5 mL of oxygen per kilogram of body weight per minute.

i. A nuclear medicine technique that uses radiopharmaceuticals, a rotating camera, and a computer to produce images representing slices through the body in different planes.

j. A term used to describe a variety of invasive procedures used to identify atherosclerotic disease as well as provide anatomic and hemodynamic information about the heart and great vessels using radiopaque catheters.

KEY TERMS MATCHING EXERCISE 2

Write the letter of the correct definition in the space next to each term.

Term

_____ 11. percutaneous transluminal coronary angioplasty (PTCA)

_____ 12. electrophysiology study (EPS)

_____ 13. automated external defibrillator (AED)

_____ 14. biphasic defibrillation

_____ 15. monophasic defibrillation

_____ 16. implantable cardioverter defibrillator (ICD)

_____ 17. temporary transvenous pacing

_____ 18. pacemaker sensitivity

_____ 19. transcutaneous pacing (TCP)

_____ 20. cardiac resynchronization therapy (CRT)

Definition

a. A small, lightweight device that can recognize and treat ventricular fibrillation.

b. Treatment of coronary artery disease (CAD) using expandable balloons to crack (tear or rupture) atherosclerotic plaque, thereby enlarging the lumen of the coronary artery.

c. Therapy that uses atrial synchronized biventricular pacemakers.

d. Device that can automatically terminate the potentially lethal dysrhythmias of ventricular tachycardia and ventricular fibrillation. Currently these devices are incorporated into cardiac pacemakers.

e. An invasive procedure that involves placing multiple multipolar catheter electrodes into the venous and sometimes the arterial side of the heart in order to evaluate the electrical activity of the heart and to identify areas of initiation and propagation of dysrhythmias.

f. Amount of electrical activity the pacemaker will sense or "hear"; measured in millivolts (mV).

g. Procedure that involves insertion of a pacemaker wire through a major vein, such as the internal jugular, subclavian, or femoral. The pacemaker wire is then advanced into the heart for pacing.

h. Traditional means by which electrical voltage is delivered to patients in ventricular tachycardia and fibrillation.

i. Defibrillation procedure that delivers a charge in one direction for half of the shock and in the opposite direction for the second half.

j. Procedure that delivers an electrical stimulus directly through the chest wall.

KEY TERM CROSSWORD

Complete the crossword puzzle below using key terms.

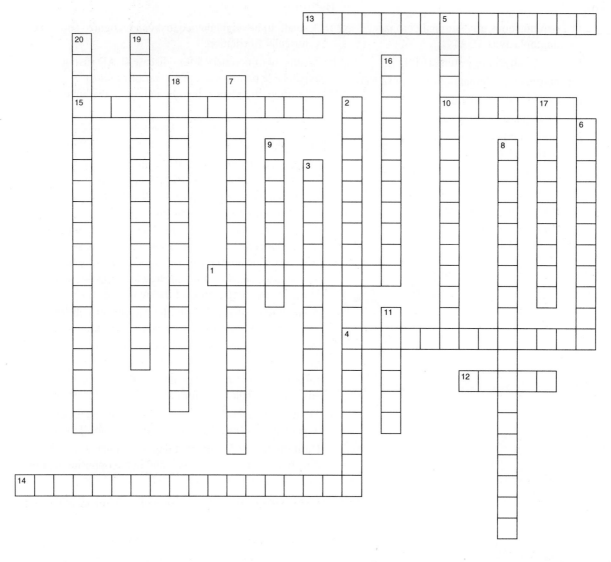

Across:

1. Imaging technology that displays images of a single plane (slice) of the heart.
4. The use of localized radiation within the coronary artery to increase the size of the lumen of the artery.
10. Term used to indicate that sufficient voltage has been put out by a pacemaker to make a myocardial contraction occur.
12. A device used to secure a widened arterial lumen; it is inserted permanently inside the coronary artery, compressing plaque and providing structural support of the vessel.
13. A cardiovascular stress test combining exercise (either physical or pharmacologic) and electrocardiographic and blood pressure monitoring.
14. Ability of a diagnostic test to predict the presence or absence of disease.
15. The timed delivery of an electrical current to depolarize cardiac muscle in order to terminate tachyarrhythmias, atrial tachycardia, rapid atrial fibrillation, atrial flutter, and junctional tachycardia.

Down:

2. The likelihood that a disease is actually present in a patient after testing (a positive test indicates disease).
3. Basically the same as cardioversion in that electrical voltage is delivered to cause depolarization of the myocardium to terminate unwanted rhythms, except it is done in an emergency situation.
5. The noninvasive assessment of the structures and function of the heart and great vessels utilizing high-frequency (ultrasound) sound waves.

Down, continued

6. Describes the ability of a test to identify patients with disease; calculated by dividing the number of true positive tests by the sum of true positives plus false negatives.

7. The likelihood that a disease is actually present in a patient before testing.

8. Detailed, noninvasive imaging of the heart using 16-slice helical scanners, accompanied by ECG gating and iodinated contrast.

9. Destruction of a specific area of the myocardium through localized delivery of chemicals or electrical energy.

11. Dividing the cardiac cycle into segments so that images viewed in cine mode allow the clinician to evaluate wall motion and systolic thickening in all areas of the left ventricle.

16. Describes the frequency with which a test is normal in subjects who are free of disease; calculated by dividing the number of true negatives in the population by the sum of true negatives plus false positives.

17. Accumulation of smooth muscle cells at the site of the original percutaneous coronary intervention that occurs because of an artery's response to injury.

18. Ambulatory electrocardiogram monitoring for an extended period of time.

19. An electronic device that is capable of delivering an electrical stimulus to the heart.

20. Blood flow to the heart muscle.

TRUE OR FALSE?

21. _____ T/F Stress echocardiography can be performed using exercise equipment or a pharmacologic agent to increase the heart rate.

22. _____ T/F The 12-lead electrocardiogram can be used to assess electrolyte abnormalities.

23. _____ T/F Magnetic resonance imaging (MRI) is the most common application of nuclear imaging techniques.

24. _____ T/F A disadvantage of cardiac magnetic resonance imaging is the relatively high exposure to radiation.

25. _____ T/F An advantage of multislice helical CT is its ability to visualize the lumen of the coronary artery with high detail.

26. _____ T/F Information obtained from doing a left heart catheterization is adequate for evaluation of a patient's coronary artery disease.

27. _____ T/F Intracoronary stents have significantly increased the occurrence of restenosis in patients who have undergone percutaneous coronary interventions.

28. _____ T/F Cardiac catheterization is contraindicated for a patient with severe congestive heart failure.

29. _____ T/F The Holter monitor is used to detect silent myocardial ischemia, as well as other conditions.

30. _____ T/F The electrophysiology study is used only for diagnostic purposes.

LABELING EXERCISE: PACEMAKER COMPONENTS

Place the term in the correct location.

a. _____

b. _____

c. _____

d. _____

e. _____

f. _____

g. _____

h. _____

Anode
Cathode
Implantable generator
Pacemaker lead
Left atrium
Left ventricle
Right atrium
Right ventricle

NCLEX-RN® REVIEW QUESTIONS

39-1. A patient asks the nurse if the negative results of a diagnostic test are to be believed because he is aware of the likelihood of errors. Which of the following should the nurse review with this patient?
   1. The calculation of false positives to false negatives
   2. Information about the specificity of the diagnostic test
   3. The calculation of true positives and false negatives
   4. The calculation of true positives divided by false positives

39-2. A patient scheduled for a coronary intravascular ultrasound tells the nurse that he doesn't know what it is. Which of the following should the nurse explain to this patient?
   1. It provides a complete view of the insides of the coronary arteries.
   2. It is used to break plaque within an artery.
   3. It measures pressures within the left side of the heart.
   4. It measures the functioning of the right side of the heart.

39-3. An elderly patient prescribed a cardiac glycoside is experiencing vision changes and nausea. The nurse should be prepared to assist or conduct which of the following diagnostic tests to help this patient?
   1. Echocardiogram
   2. Cardiac catheterization
   3. ECG
   4. Stress test

39-4. A patient comes into the emergency department with chest pain. Which of the following cardiac nuclear studies can be done to help in the diagnosis of this patient?
   1. Technetium-99   3. Thallium-201
   2. TEE   4. SPECT

39-5. The nurse is preparing to discharge a patient recovering from a cardiac catheterization. Which of the following should be included in this patient's discharge instructions?
   1. Avoid heavy lifting for about a week.
   2. Resume normal activities of daily living.
   3. Bright red bleeding from the site is normal.
   4. Keep the dressing on the site for a week.

CHAPTER 40

CARING FOR THE PATIENT WITH CORONARY ARTERY DISEASE

OUTCOME-BASED LEARNING OBJECTIVES

40-1. Discuss the epidemiological factors of coronary artery disease (CAD) and define the risk factors.

40-2. Define and identify the etiology and pathophysiology of CAD/ischemic heart disease and explain the nursing assessment data and interventions used when evaluating a patient with angina pectoris.

40-3. Differentiate the three criteria used to evaluate ischemic heart disease and identify the pathologic significance of each criterion.

40-4. Compare and contrast the pathogenesis of unstable angina, a non–Q wave, subendocardial, non–ST segment elevation myocardial infarction (MI), and a Q wave, transmural, ST segment elevation (MI).

40-5. Identify the complications of an MI and discuss the variables that affect the prognosis of the patient with an MI.

40-6. Identify which clinical manifestations and diagnostic findings are an indication for coronary artery bypass graft surgery (CABG).

40-7. Identify three possible complications of CABG and discuss nursing interventions that potentially reduce the incidence of these complications.

PEARSON
EXPLORE **mynursingkit**™

MyNursingKit is your one stop for online chapter review materials and resources. Prepare for success with additional NCLEX®-style practice questions, interactive assignments and activities, web links, animations and videos, and more!

Register your access code from the front of your book at **www.mynursingkit.com**

CHAPTER OUTLINE

  I. Coronary Artery Anatomy
  II. Epidemiology of Coronary Artery Disease
 III. Etiology of Coronary Artery Disease
 IV. Pathophysiology of Coronary Artery Disease
    A. Atherogenesis
      1. Stage I Lesion
      2. Stage II Lesion
      3. Stage III Lesion
    B. Inflammation and Atherogenesis
    C. Pathophysiology of Myocardial Injury and Death

IX. Medical Management of Coronary Artery Disease
   A. Medical Management of Acute Coronary Syndrome
      1. Pharmacologic and Nonpharmacologic Treatment of Acute Coronary Syndrome
         a. Activity Progression
         b. Reducing Autonomic Stress Responses
         c. Intra-Aortic Balloon Pump
         d. Beta- (B-) Adrenèrgic Blocking (B-blockers) Agents
         e. Angiotensin-Converting Enzyme Inhibitors
         f. Angiotensin II Receptor Blockers in Myocardial Infarction
         g. Nitrate Therapy
         h. Vasodilator Therapy to Relieve Vasoconstriction or Vasospasm
         i. Thrombolytic Agents
         j. Anticoagulation Therapy
   B. Medical Management of Complications of Acute Myocardial Infarction
      1. Recurrent Chest Pain from Ischemia
      2. Pericarditis
      3. Heart Failure
      4. Cardiogenic Shock
      5. Dysrhythmias
         a. Supraventricular Tachycardia
         b. Bradycardia
         c. Ventricular Dysrhythmias
      6. Infarct Expansion, Ventricular Remodeling
      7. Left Ventricular Aneurysm and Thrombus Formation
      8. Mitral Valve Disruption
      9. Ventricular Free Wall Rupture
     10. Ventricular Septal Defect (VSD)
             NURSING MANAGEMENT
             COLLABORATIVE MANAGEMENT
             HEALTH PROMOTION AND DISCHARGE PLANNING
 X. Gerontological Considerations
XI. Coronary Artery Bypass Graft Surgery
   A. Indications
   B. Standard Operative Techniques
      1. New Surgical Techniques
   C. Postoperative Considerations
             NURSING MANAGEMENT
               NURSING DIAGNOSES
               ASSESSMENT
               OUTCOMES AND EVALUATION PARAMETERS
               PLANNING AND INTERVENTIONS WITH RATIONALES
               HEALTH PROMOTION
XII. Research

KEY TERMS MATCHING EXERCISE 1

Write the letter of the correct definition in the space next to each term.

Term

_____ 1. coronary artery disease (CAD)
_____ 2. tunica adventitia
_____ 3. arteriosclerosis
_____ 4. atherosclerosis
_____ 5. acute coronary syndrome (ACS)

Definition

a. An elevated cholesterol and/or triglyceride level in the blood that is a modifiable risk factor for the development of coronary artery disease.

b. Syndrome collectively described by unstable angina, non–ST segment elevation myocardial infarction (MI), and ST segment elevation MI.

_g_ 6. cardiac risk factors
_d_ 7. myocardial hibernation
_h_ 8. myocardial stunning
_f_ 9. hypercholesterolemia
_a_ 10. hyperlipidemia

c. Thickening, reduced elasticity, and calcification of arterial walls.

d. Condition in which myocardial tissue undergoes cellular structural changes and progressive apoptosis (cell death) in response to prolonged cardiac ischemia.

e. The outer layer of an artery; flexible stratum that consists of fibrous tissue made of collagen and elastic fibers surrounded by collagen bundles.

f. An increased cholesterol level in the blood.

g. Habits, lifestyles, and/or genetic factors that predispose an individual to the development of coronary artery disease.

h. A temporary dysfunction that occurs in response to artery occlusion of short duration (artery spasm) or transient global hypoperfusion during a limited low-flow state such as shock.

i. A progressive atherosclerotic disorder of the coronary arteries that results in narrowing or complete occlusion of the vessel lumen.

j. The development of atherosclerosis.

KEY TERMS MATCHING EXERCISE 2

Write the letter of the correct definition in the space next to each term.

Term

_j_ 11. low-density lipoproteins
_e_ 12. high-density lipoproteins
_a_ 13. triglycerides
_f_ 14. metabolic syndrome
_i_ 15. variant, Prinzmetal, or vasospastic angina
_g_ 16. myocardial infarction (MI)
_c_ 17. unstable angina
_h_ 18. sudden cardiac death (SCD)
_b_ 19. troponin I
_d_ 20. troponin T

Definition

a. A form of fat derived from fats in food and produced by the body from other sources such as carbohydrates.

b. A protein complex found in cardiac muscle, along with troponin T.

c. A transitory syndrome falling between stable angina and myocardial infarction wherein thrombus forms in an area of arterial stenosis, but is subsequently fully or partially lysed by endogenous antithrombotic mechanisms.

d. A protein complex found in cardiac muscle, along with troponin I.

e. A type of lipoprotein that binds to cholesterol to transport it back to the liver; lipoproteins may actually remove excess cholesterol from plaque in the arteries.

f. The diagnosis given when a patient has a cluster of cardiac risk factors, including having three out of the five following conditions: abdominal obesity, high triglycerides, low HDL-C, high blood pressure, and high fasting glucose ($\geq$100 mg/dL).

g. The loss of myocytes or myocardial cell death as a result of prolonged ischemia.

h. Type of cardiac arrest most often associated with abrupt coronary artery occlusion from plaque disruption over severely stenotic lesions in the setting of poorly developed collateral circulation.

i. Condition characterized by a vasospasm occurring at a single or multiple sites in major coronary arteries and their large branches.

j. A type of lipoprotein that transports cholesterol and triglycerides from the liver to peripheral tissues.

KEY TERM CROSSWORD

Complete the crossword puzzle using key terms.

Across:

1. The middle layer of an artery that consists of multiple layers of smooth muscle cells and connective tissue made up of elastic fibers, collagen, and proteoglycans.
4. A protocol for empirical treatment of patients with suspected myocardial infarction. Cited in the Advanced Cardiac Life Support guidelines. Stands for morphine, oxygen, nitroglycerin, and aspirin.
5. Blood clot that forms in a blood vessel and remains at the site of formation.
7. A dense connective tissue matrix in the inner lining of an artery that is formed when smooth muscle cells secrete collagen, elastin, and glycosaminoglycans.
9. Layer of an artery that consists of a monolayer of connecting endothelial cells and a lamina of connective tissue and smooth muscle cells.

10. A protein complex found in cardiac and skeletal muscle.
13. When referring to coronary artery stenosis, the term used to describe a lesion that occupies the whole circumference.
14. A heme-containing, oxygen-binding protein that is exclusive to striated and nonstriated muscle. Because of its very small molecular weight, it is released into interstitial fluid as early as 2 hours following damage to muscle tissue.
15. Condition characterized by areas of abnormal heart contractility where muscle movement is impaired.
20. An enzyme found in high concentrations in the heart and skeletal muscle and in smaller concentrations in the brain.

Down:

2. The result of transient subtotal occlusion of a coronary artery with reduced coronary blood flow resulting from plaque disruption and ensuing pathophysiological processes.
3. A steroid molecule produced primarily by the liver that is essential for the formation and maintenance of cell membranes.
6. Condition characterized by an accumulation in the inner lining of an artery of a plaque of cholesterol and other constituents.
8. Refers to myocardial injury associated with ST segment elevation on the ECG.

11. Tissue hypoxia resulting from reduced blood flow to the tissues.
12. Condition characterized by areas of abnormal heart contractility where there is loss of or no muscle movement.
16. When discussing plaque buildup in a coronary artery, the term used to describe a lesion that occupies part of a vessel wall.
17. Cell swelling as a result of changes in membrane permeability.
18. Condition characterized by areas of abnormal heart contractility where muscle movement is hypoactive.
19. Transient chest pain due to myocardial ischemia.

SHORT ANSWER QUESTIONS

21. Explain the cause of plaque accumulation in the inner lining of an artery.

_____

_____

_____

_____

22. What are the differences among stage I, stage II, and stage III lesions in a coronary artery?

_____

_____

_____

_____

23. What are the modifiable risk factors for coronary artery disease?

_____

_____

_____

_____

24. Why is it important to obtain a 12-lead ECG while a patient is still having chest pain?

_____

_____

_____

_____

25. What are clinical manifestations of acute coronary syndrome (ACS)?

_____

_____

_____

_____

26. What laboratory and diagnostic tests are done to diagnose ACS?

_____

_____

_____

_____

27. What are the five strategies for patients with ACS aimed at increasing oxygen supply to ischemic myocardium?

_____

_____

_____

_____

28. Name the pharmacologic and nonpharmacologic methods commonly used to treat patients with ACS.

_____

_____

_____

_____

29. What complications can arise after acute myocardial infarction (AMI)?

_____

_____

_____

_____

30. What is the primary requirement that must be met in order for coronary artery bypass grafting (CABG) to be indicated?

_____

_____

_____

_____

TRUE OR FALSE?

31. _____ T/F   Coronary artery disease (CAD) is the leading cause of death in both males and females of white, African American, Hispanic, American Indian, and Asian Pacific Island ethnicities.

32. _____ T/F   Because women present with CAD at an older age, they have a lesser risk of overall mortality and developing serious complications than men do.

33. _____ T/F   Reductions in myocardial blood supply, especially in times of increased demand, are the cause of stable angina, unstable angina (UA), myocardial infarction (MI), and sudden cardiac death (SCD).

34. _____ T/F   When the plaque buildup in the artery becomes significant enough to cause ischemia that result in clinical manifestations, the result is acute coronary syndrome.

35. _____ T/F   Hormone replacement therapy is a deterrent to the development of coronary artery disease.

36. _____ T/F   The optimal target goal for low-density lipoprotein cholesterol (LDL-C) is less than 150 mg/dL.

37. _____ T/F   If high-density lipoprotein cholesterol (HDL-C) level is higher than the target level, an increased LDL-C level is negated.

38. _____ T/F   Strong evidence suggests that treating systolic high blood pressure can decrease the likelihood of developing heart disease or having a stroke.

39. _____ T/F   The risk level of cardiovascular adverse events in males and females approaches that of nonsmokers within 2 to 3 years of smoking cessation.

40. _____ T/F   Regular exercise (at least 5 times/week lasting at least 30 minutes) of moderate intensity (brisk walking) decreases heart attack risk by 10% to 50% in both men and women.

41. _____ T/F   Angina indicates that coronary artery disease is present and that an acute cardiac event is imminent.

INCREASE OR DECREASE?

42. Factors that _____ HDL-C are smoking cessation by 10%, exercise, and weight reduction.

43. Factors that _____ LDL-C are trans fatty acids, saturated fats, and cholesterol.

44. Factors that _____ LDL-C are polyunsaturated fatty acids, monounsaturated fatty acids, soluble fiber, soy protein, and weight reduction.

45. Factors that _____ triglycerides are excess body weight, reduced physical activity, increased intake of sugar and refined carbohydrates, and increased alcohol intake.

46. Factors that _____ HDL-C are smoking, trans fatty acids, sedentary lifestyle, obesity, and low-fat/high-carbohydrate diet.

47. Factors that _____ triglycerides are exercise, weight reduction, and reduced carbohydrate consumption.

LABELING EXERCISE 1: NORMAL ARTERY LAYERS

Place the term in the correct location.

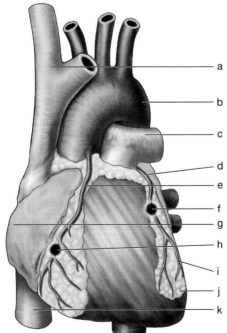

a. _____

b. _____

c. _____

d. _____

Internal elastic lumina
Tunica adventitia
Tunica intima
Tunica media

LABELING EXERCISE 2: THROMBOSIS IN A CORONARY ARTERY

Place the term in the correct location.

a. _____

b. _____

c. _____

d. _____

e. _____

f. _____

g. _____

h. _____

i. _____

j. _____

k. _____

Aorta
Atherosclerosis w/thrombosis
Coronary thrombosis
Fat
Inferior vena cava
Left coronary artery

Left ventricle
Pulmonary trunk
Right coronary artery
Right ventricle
Superior vena cava

NCLEX-RN® REVIEW QUESTIONS

40-1. The nurse plans to provide teaching to a patient who has which of the following modifiable risk factors for coronary heart disease:
   1. The patient eats a high-protein diet.
   2. The patient is 50 pounds overweight.
   3. The patient is a 52-year-old male.
   4. The patient's mother died of a myocardial infarction.

40-2. A patient is being evaluated for a diagnosis of stable angina. Which comment made by the patient would support this diagnosis?
   1. "This pain often comes and goes."
   2. "I only get the pain if I walk more than two blocks."
   3. "I have had this pain for the past three days."
   4. "The pain did not go away when I took nitroglycerin."

40-3. The nurse is teaching a patient with vasospastic angina about ways to prevent this type of chest pain. The nurse teaches the patient to avoid:
   1. Ingesting large meals.
   2. Exposure to very hot temperatures.
   3. Excessive exercise.
   4. Drinking any alcoholic beverages.

40-4. A patient is admitted to the emergency department with acute chest pain and is being evaluated for acute coronary syndrome. The nurse suspects the patient is in the early stages of an acute myocardial infarction, MI, when the electrocardiogram, EKG, shows:
   1. Hyperacute T wave peaking.
   2. ST segment depressions.
   3. T wave inversions.
   4. Left bundle branch block.

40-5. A patient admitted to the emergency department with complaints of chest pain displays ST segment elevations on the electrocardiogram, EKG. The nurse plans interventions, recognizing these are indicative of:
   1. Normal EKG patterns.
   2. Subendocardial injury.
   3. Transmural injury.
   4. Pericardial inflammation.

40-6. A patient with an ST segment elevation MI is being evaluated for coronary artery bypass graft, CABG, surgery following a failed angioplasty. The nurse plans to assess the patient for which of the following clinical manifestations that will qualify the patient for this surgery:
   1. Persistent chest pain
   2. Bradycardia
   3. Systolic pressure greater than 140 mmHg
   4. Frequent episodes of dyspnea

40-7. Because a patient recovering from a coronary artery bypass graft, CABG, is at risk of developing a pulmonary embolus, the nurse plans the following interventions postoperatively:
   1. Ambulation in the hall
   2. Limiting out of bed activity to the patient's room
   3. Providing a bedside commode
   4. Encouraging patient to drink fluids

CHAPTER 41

CARING FOR THE PATIENT WITH CARDIAC INFLAMMATORY DISORDERS

OUTCOME-BASED LEARNING OBJECTIVES

41-1. Compare and contrast the etiology, pathophysiology, clinical manifestations, and medical and nursing management for the four inflammatory/infectious disorders.

41-2. Integrate the etiology, pathophysiology, clinical manifestations, and treatment for valve stenosis, regurgitation, and mitral valve prolapse.

41-3. Explain the rationale and type of preventive therapy necessary for patients with valve disease.

41-4. Differentiate valve repair and replacement procedures in terms of patient care and education needs.

41-5. Compare and contrast the four types of cardiomyopathy in terms of etiology, pathophysiology, clinical manifestations, and medical and nursing management.

41-6. Apply nursing diagnoses and the nursing process to the care of the patient with inflammatory and structural heart disease.

CHAPTER OUTLINE

I. Inflammatory Disorders
  A. Rheumatic Heart Disease
    1. Epidemiology and Etiology
    2. Pathophysiology
    3. Clinical Manifestations
    4. Laboratory and Diagnostic Procedures
    5. Medical Management
        NURSING MANAGEMENT
        HEALTH PROMOTION
  B. Pericarditis
    1. Epidemiology and Etiology
    2. Pathophysiology

3. Clinical Manifestations
4. Laboratory and Diagnostic Procedures
5. Medical Management
  NURSING MANAGEMENT
  ASSESSMENT
  NURSING DIAGNOSIS
  OUTCOMES AND EVALUATION PARAMETERS
  PLANNING, INTERVENTIONS, AND RATIONALES
  HEALTH PROMOTION
C. Myocarditis
  1. Epidemiology and Etiology
  2. Pathophysiology
  3. Clinical Manifestations
  4. Laboratory and Diagnostic Procedures
  5. Medical Management
    NURSING MANAGEMENT
    ASSESSMENT
    NURSING DIAGNOSIS
    OUTCOMES AND EVALUATION PARAMETERS
    PLANNING, INTERVENTIONS, AND RATIONALES
    HEALTH PROMOTION
D. Endocarditis
  1. Epidemiology and Etiology
  2. Pathophysiology
  3. Clinical Manifestations
  4. Laboratory and Diagnostic Procedures
  5. Medical Management
    NURSING MANAGEMENT
    ASSESSMENT
    NURSING DIAGNOSIS
    OUTCOMES AND EVALUATION PARAMETERS
    PLANNING, INTERVENTIONS, AND RATIONALES
    HEALTH PROMOTION
    COLLABORATIVE MANAGEMENT
II. Structural Heart Disease
  A. Cardiac Valvular Disorders
    1. Valvular Stenosis
    2. Valvular Regurgitation
  B. Mitral Valve Diseases
    1. Mitral Valve Stenosis
      a. Epidemiology/Etiology/Pathophysiology
      b. Clinical Manifestations
    2. Mitral Valve Regurgitation
      a. Epidemiology/Etiology/Pathophysiology
      b. Clinical Manifestations
    3. Mitral Valve Prolapse
      a. Epidemiology/Etiology/Pathophysiology
      b. Clinical Manifestations
  C. Aortic Valve Disease
    1. Aortic Valve Stenosis
      a. Epidemiology/Etiology/Pathophysiology
      b. Clinical Manifestations
    2. Aortic Valve Regurgitation
      a. Epidemiology/Etiology/Pathophysiology
      b. Clinical Manifestations

3. Tricuspid Valve Disease
   a. Epidemiology/Etiology/Pathophysiology
   b. Clinical Manifestations
4. Pulmonic Valve Disease
   a. Epidemiology/Etiology/Pathophysiology
   b. Clinical Manifestations
D. Clinical Management for Valve Disorders
   1. Laboratory and Diagnostic Procedures for Cardiac Valve Disease
   2. Medical Management
      a. Invasive Management of Valve Disease
         i. Annuloplasty
         ii. Valvuloplasty
         iii. Percutaneous Transluminal Balloon Valvuloplasty
         iv. Prosthetic Heart Valves
            a. Mechanical Valves
            b. Biological Valves
            NURSING MANAGEMENT
            HEALTH PROMOTION
            COLLABORATIVE MANAGEMENT
E. Cardiomyopathy
   1. Dilated Cardiomyopathy
   2. Epidemiology and Etiology
   3. Pathophysiology
   4. Clinical Manifestations
   5. Laboratory and Diagnostic Procedures
   6. Medical Management
      NURSING MANAGEMENT
F. Hypertrophic Obstructive Cardiomyopathy
   1. Epidemiology and Etiology
   2. Pathophysiology
   3. Clinical Manifestations
   4. Laboratory and Diagnostic Procedures
   5. Medical Management
      NURSING MANAGEMENT
         ASSESSMENT
         OUTCOMES AND EVALUATION PARAMETERS
         PLANNING, INTERVENTIONS, AND RATIONALES
G. Restrictive Cardiomyopathy
   1. Epidemiology and Etiology
   2. Pathophysiology
   3. Clinical Manifestations
   4. Laboratory and Diagnostic Procedures
   5. Medical Management
      NURSING MANAGEMENT
H. Arrhythmogenic Right Ventricular Cardiomyopathy
   1. Epidemiology and Etiology
   2. Pathophysiology
   3. Clinical Manifestations
   4. Laboratory and Diagnostic Procedures
   5. Medical Management
      NURSING MANAGEMENT
         HEALTH PROMOTION FOR THE CARDIOMYOPATHIES
         COLLABORATIVE MANAGEMENT
      a. End-of-Life Issues with Cardiomyopathy
      b. National Guidelines for Cardiomyopathy
I. Gerontological Considerations
J. Research

KEY TERMS MATCHING EXERCISE 1

Write the letter of the correct definition in the space next to each term.

Term

_____ 1. rheumatic heart disease

_____ 2. tricuspid valve regurgitation

_____ 3. pulsus paradoxus

_____ 4. Dressler's syndrome

_____ 5. pericardial window

_____ 6. constrictive pericarditis

_____ 7. cardiac tamponade

_____ 8. pericardial effusion

_____ 9. pericardial friction rub

_____ 10. Beck's triad

Definition

a. Bleeding into the pericardial sac. As the accumulation of blood increases, it compresses the atria and ventricles, decreasing venous return and filling pressure, which leads to decreased cardiac output, myocardial hypoxia, and cardiac failure.

b. An inflammatory disease of the heart that causes long-term damage, scarring, and malfunction of the heart valves.

c. An excess buildup of pericardial fluid that is a threat to normal cardiac function. The fluid buildup is the result of an accumulation of infectious exudates or toxins and/or blood.

d. Occurs when the pericardial layers adhere to each other as a result of fibrosis of the pericardial sac.

e. Classic assessment findings for the patient with cardiac tamponade, consisting of decreased blood pressure, muffled heart sounds, and jugular venous distention.

f. Inability of a heart valve to completely close, resulting in a backflow of blood from the right ventricle to the right atrium.

g. An opening in the pericardial sac that allows fluid from effusion and tamponade to drain.

h. A greater than 10 mmHg drop in systolic blood pressure during inspiration.

i. A grating, scraping, squeaking, or a crunching sound that is the result of friction between the roughened, inflamed layers of the pericardium.

j. Condition characterized by fever, pericarditis, chest pain, and pericardial and pleural effusions. Believed to be an autoimmune response, it occurs in 5% to 15% of patients 1 to 4 weeks after a myocardial infarction.

KEY TERMS MATCHING EXERCISE 2

Write the letter of the correct definition in the space next to each term.

Term

_____ 11. dilated cardiomyopathy

_____ 12. hypertrophic cardiomyopathy

_____ 13. pericardiectomy

_____ 14. restrictive cardiomyopathy

_____ 15. infective endocarditis

_____ 16. valvular regurgitation

_____ 17. mitral valve prolapse

_____ 18. mitral valve regurgitation

_____ 19. aortic valve regurgitation

_____ 20. arrhythmogenic right ventricular cardiomyopathy (ARVC)

Definition

a. An inability of the mitral valve to close due to an abnormality in the structure and function of the valve.

b. An electrical disturbance that develops when the muscle tissue in the right ventricle is replaced with fibrous scar and fatty tissues.

c. A disorder of the sarcomere, the contractile element of the cardiac muscle; characterized by left ventricular and occasionally right ventricular hypertrophy, with greater hypertrophy occurring in the septum. Also referred to as *idiopathic hypertrophic subaortic stenosis (IHSS)*.

d. An infection of the cardiac endocardial layer of the heart, which may include one or more heart valves, the mural endocardium, and/or a septal defect; previously known as bacterial endocarditis.

e. A disorder characterized by endometrial scarring that usually affects one or both ventricles and restricts filling of blood, resulting in systolic dysfunction. The ventricle has normal wall thickness, but the walls are rigid, producing elevated filling pressures and dilated atria.

f. Incomplete closure of the aortic valve, which causes blood to regurgitate back into the left ventricle through a valve; results from abnormal valve cusps or aortic root.

g. Removal of the pericardial sac to allow fluid to drain from around the heart.

h. Occurs when one or more of the valve leaflets bulge or prolapse into the left atrium during systole. This prolapse of the valve results in valve regurgitation.

i. Inability of a heart valve to completely close, resulting in a backflow of blood through the incompetent valve orifice into the previous chamber.

j. A disorder of the myocardium characterized by dilation and impaired contraction of one or more ventricles; the most common form of cardiomyopathy.

WORD SEARCH

First identify the word from its definition. Then find and circle it in the puzzle below.

21. _____ Occurs when the mitral valve assumes an abnormal funnel shape due to thickening and shortening of the valve structures as a result of calcification. Contractures develop between the junctions or commissures (leaflets) of the valve.

22. _____ A surgery done to correct valve regurgitation by repairing the enlarged annulus.

23. _____ The fibrous ring at the junction of the cardiac valve leaflets and the muscular wall.

24. _____ The site where cardiac valve leaflets meet each other.

25. _____ Surgical procedure used to separate fused heart valve leaflets.

26. _____ A surgical procedure to repair torn or damaged leaflets, chordae tendineae, or papillary muscle.

27. _____ Commercially manufactured heart valves.

28. _____ A valve obtained from human cadaver donations; used primarily to replace the aortic and pulmonic valves.

29. _____ Valve obtained from the patient's own pulmonic valve and pulmonary artery. Also called *autologous valve*.

30. _____ Valve obtained from other species, most commonly from pigs (porcine valves), although cow valves (bovine) also are used. Also referred to as *xenografts*.

31. _____ Another name for allograft valve.

32. _____ Diseases of the myocardial muscle fibers that result in progressive structural and functional abnormalities of the myocardium.

33. _____ Inflammation of all three layers of the heart: the endocardium, myocardium, and pericardium.

34. _____ A focal or diffuse inflammation of the myocardium or heart muscle; an uncommon disorder that is frequently associated with pericarditis.

35. _____ Inflammation of the pericardial sac due to an inflammatory process in which the two layers of the pericardium become inflamed and roughened, causing fluid to build up.

36. _____ A narrowing of the aortic valve orifice, which results in an obstruction to blood flow from the left ventricle to the aorta during systole.

M	M	Y	O	C	A	R	D	I	T	I	S	A	C	E	D	F	G	B	A
A	I	E	A	U	T	O	G	R	A	F	T	V	A	L	V	E	I	C	O
E	A	T	C	E	C	F	G	A	H	I	M	B	J	L	M	V	E	P	R
V	B	C	R	H	H	O	M	O	G	R	A	F	T	V	A	L	V	E	T
L	A	D	H	A	A	I	M	J	N	O	P	N	A	L	J	A	G	R	I
A	A	L	J	N	L	N	T	M	R	U	A	T	S	A	C	V	F	I	C
V	E	I	V	N	L	V	I	Q	I	V	R	W	X	B	V	L	N	C	V
T	S	U	L	U	N	N	A	C	T	S	E	Y	A	P	L	A	W	A	A
F	A	H	C	L	L	G	D	L	A	Y	S	Z	U	Q	I	C	A	R	L
A	I	M	L	O	E	O	T	Q	V	L	C	U	W	A	S	I	G	D	V
R	O	A	N	P	M	S	P	O	Z	E	V	Z	R	S	E	G	A	I	E
G	A	F	P	L	A	M	F	L	Y	R	S	A	T	O	H	O	N	T	S
O	B	N	R	A	C	X	I	W	A	Y	A	T	L	I	T	L	A	I	T
L	O	E	J	S	U	E	H	S	O	S	C	P	E	V	E	O	D	S	E
L	A	C	M	T	D	I	Q	S	S	V	T	M	O	N	E	I	M	J	N
A	E	G	L	Y	N	A	U	L	P	U	L	Y	A	M	O	B	E	Y	O
F	A	H	A	I	R	O	S	E	G	R	R	E	B	E	C	S	F	B	S
P	A	N	C	A	R	D	I	T	I	S	I	E	G	A	D	Z	I	E	I
A	B	E	C	A	R	D	I	O	M	Y	O	P	A	T	H	I	E	S	S

SHORT ANSWER QUESTIONS

37. What are the clinical manifestations of acute rheumatic fever?

_____

_____

_____

_____

38. What is a pericardial friction rub?

_____

_____

39. What are the three diseases that affect the mitral valve?

_____

_____

40. What is the most sensitive diagnostic test for valve disease, and why is it superior to other diagnostic tests?

_____

_____

_____

41. Describe the classifications and types of cardiomyopathies.

_____

_____

_____

TRUE OR FALSE?

42. _____ T/F Only infections of the pharynx initiate and reactivate rheumatic fever.

43. _____ T/F Myocarditis can be caused by viral, bacterial, and fungal infections.

44. _____ T/F Acute infective endocarditis (IE) is usually caused by organisms of low virulence that have a limited ability to infect other organs.

45. _____ T/F Among the risk factors for infective endocarditis are recent dental surgery and bleeding gums.

46. _____ T/F A stenotic valve is one that is unable to close normally, causing a backward flow of blood, while a regurgitant valve is unable to open normally, causing an impedance of blood flow.

47. _____ T/F Dyspnea, angina, fatigue, and syncope, which increase with exertion, are among the clinical manifestations of aortic valve stenosis.

48. _____ T/F With hypertrophic cardiomyopathy (HCM) the walls of the ventricle hypertrophy or remodel with a marked increase in the chamber size.

49. _____ T/F Restrictive cardiomyopathy is characterized by endocardial scarring that usually affects one or both ventricles and restricts filling of blood, resulting in systolic dysfunction.

50. _____ T/F Because arrhythmogenic right ventricular cardiomyopathy (ARVC) is reported more frequently among athletes compared to other groups of people, it is generally believed that sporting activities are a primary cause of the condition.

LABELING EXERCISE 1: LAYERS OF THE HEART WALL

Place the term in the correct location.

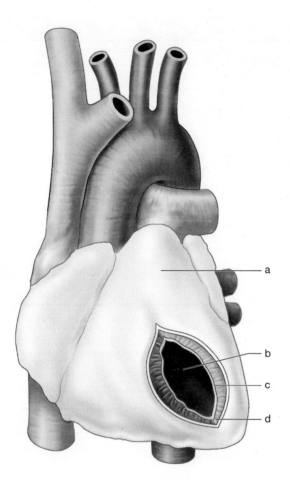

a. _____

b. _____

c. _____

d. _____

Endocardium (lining)
Interior of chamber
Myocardium (muscle)
Pericardium (covering)

LABELING EXERCISE 2: CARDIAC VALVES, CHORDAE TENDINEAE, AND PAPILLARY MUSCLE

Place the term in the correct location.

a. _____

b. _____

c. _____

d. _____

e. _____

f. _____

g. _____

Aortic valve
Chordae tendineae
Mitral valve
Papillary muscle

Pulmonic valve
Tricuspid valve
Vessels in lungs

NCLEX-RN® REVIEW QUESTIONS

41-1. When performing an assessment the nurse auscultates a pericardial friction rub. The patient should also be assessed for:
  1. Chest pain.
  2. A systolic murmur.
  3. Bradycardia.
  4. Atrial fibrillation.

41-2. When assessing the patient with aortic valve regurgitation, AVR, the nurse can expect to find the following clinical manifestation:
  1. A diastolic murmur
  2. A narrow pulse pressure
  3. Frequent spikes of temperature
  4. Intolerance to cold

41-3. A patient with aortic valve disease is started on a nitrate. When explaining how this drug will reduce myocardial oxygen demand, the nurse understands:
  1. They decrease preload and dilate coronary arteries.
  2. They decrease afterload and increase coronary workload.
  3. Atrial fibrillation will be reduced and heart rate decreased.
  4. Cardiac conduction is slowed and heart rate is decreased.

41-4. A patient has been given discharge instructions following a mechanical valve replacement. The nurse determines further instruction is needed when the patient states:
1. "I will need to have my blood checked for clotting ability on a regular basis."
2. "I plan to begin an exercise program in cardiac rehabilitation."
3. "I ordered a Medic Alert bracelet to identify me as taking a blood thinner."
4. "I will avoid having any invasive procedure since I could bleed to death."

41-5. When preparing a patient with cardiomyopathy for discharge, the nurse should provide which instructions?
1. Avoid taking any nitroglycerin-type drugs.
2. Avoid strenuous activity and space activities throughout the day.
3. Restrict fluid intake to only liquids with meals.
4. Anticipate monthly appointments for weight checks.

41-6. A patient with mitral valve regurgitation reports experiencing fatigue and activity intolerance. The nurse instructs the patient to:
1. Eliminate all fats from the diet.
2. Include some sedentary activities in the daily schedule.
3. Avoid doing any type of housework.
4. Restrict calories to avoid overworking the heart.

CHAPTER 42

CARING FOR THE PATIENT WITH HEART FAILURE

OUTCOME-BASED LEARNING OBJECTIVES

42-1. Evaluate the etiology, incidence, and prevalence of heart failure.

42-2. Distinguish between systolic and diastolic dysfunction.

42-3. Describe the pathophysiology of heart failure and the compensatory neurohormonal responses that occur.

42-4. Compare and contrast right-sided versus left-sided symptoms of heart failure.

42-5. Evaluate the diagnostic workup used to determine the presence of heart failure.

42-6. Describe a comprehensive treatment plan including the medical, device, and surgical components of treatment, using the multidisciplinary team approach.

42-7. Describe the self-management concepts necessary for patients with heart failure.

42-8. Compare and contrast potential comorbidities associated with heart failure.

42-9. Describe components of end-of-life care for end-stage heart failure.

CHAPTER OUTLINE

  I. Epidemiology
    A. Mortality
    B. Medical Impact
    C. Economic Impact
  II. Pathophysiology
  III. Etiology
    A. Systolic Dysfunction
    B. Diastolic Dysfunction

C. Neurohormonal Response
   1. Sympathetic Nervous System Activation
   2. Renin-Angiotensin-Aldosterone System Activation
   3. Other Hormone Activation and Cytokine Release
IV. Course of Heart Failure
   A. Chronic Heart Failure
   B. Stages of Heart Failure
      1. Stage A
      2. Stage B
      3. Stage C
      4. Stage D
   C. New York Heart Association Classification System
   D. Diagnosing Heart Failure
      1. History
V. Clinical Manifestations
   A. Laboratory and Diagnostic Procedures
   B. Hemodynamic Monitoring
VI. Medical Management
   A. Pharmacologic Management
      1. Angiotensin-Converting Enzyme (ACE)
      2. Angiotensin II Receptor Blockers (ARB)
      3. Beta-Adrenergic Blockers
      4. Diuretics
      5. Digitalis
      6. Aldosterone Antagonists
      7. Antiarrhythmic/Dysrhythmic Agents
      8. Anticoagulant and Antiplatelet Agents
      9. Inotropic, Vasopressor, and Vasodilator Therapeutic Agents
      10. Medications for Select Patients
      11. Complementary and Alternative Therapies
   B. Device Therapies for Heart Failure
      1. Cardiac Resynchronization Therapy
      2. Implantable Cardioverter Defibrillators
         NURSING MANAGEMENT
   C. Percutaneous and Surgical Treatments for Coronary Artery Disease
      1. Percutaneous Coronary Interventions
      2. Coronary Artery Bypass Graft Surgery
   D. Other Surgical Treatments for Systolic Heart Failure
      1. Valve Replacement or Repair
      2. Cardiac Transplantation
      3. Mechanical Assist Devices
      4. Investigational Surgical Therapies
VII. Acute Decompensated Heart Failure
         NURSING MANAGEMENT
         COLLABORATIVE MANAGEMENT
            HOSPITAL CLINICAL PATHWAY
            HEALTH PROMOTION
               MEDICATIONS
               ACTIVITY
               WEIGHT
               DIET
               SYMPTOMS
               FAMILY/SIGNIFICANT OTHER SUPPORT
               LIFESTYLES AND HABITS
               HEART FAILURE RESOURCES FOR PATIENTS AND FAMILIES

KEY TERMS MATCHING EXERCISE 1

Write the letter of the correct definition in the space next to each term.

Term

_____   1. heart failure

_____   2. left ventricular ejection
            fraction (LVEF)

_____   3. systolic dysfunction

_____   4. biventricular heart failure

_____   5. diastolic dysfunction

_____   6. left-sided heart failure

_____   7. right-sided heart failure

_____   8. hypertrophy

_____   9. cardiomegaly

_____ 10. New York Heart Association (NYHA)
            classification system

_____ 11. crackles

Definition

a. Impaired ventricular function with volume overload and decreased contractility.

b. The proportion of blood ejected during each ventricular contraction compared with the total ventricular filling volume.

c. An abnormal cardiac condition characterized by impairment of the right side of the heart and congestion and elevated pressure in the systemic veins and capillaries.

d. A functional classification system that categorizes cardiac patients' subjective degree of symptoms into NYHA classes I through IV.

e. An abnormal cardiac condition characterized by the impairment of the left side of the heart and elevated pressure and congestion in the pulmonary veins and capillaries.

f. A complex and debilitating clinical syndrome in which there is loss or dysfunction of the cardiac muscle or an inability of the ventricle to fill or eject blood.

g. Enlargement of the heart.

h. Impaired relaxation, preventing the heart from filling appropriately at normal preload pressures.

i. When auscultating the lungs, common abnormal, short, popping sounds heard on inspiration; caused by the movement of fluid or exudates.

j. An increase in the size of an organ caused by an increase in the size of the cells and tissues rather than the number of cells.

k. A global inability of the heart muscle to pump blood effectively from both ventricles, compromising forward flow leading to right and left heart failure symptoms.

KEY TERMS MATCHING EXERCISE 2

Write the letter of the correct definition in the space next to each term.

Term

_____ 12. jugular venous distention (JVD)

_____ 13. tachypnea

_____ 14. ascites

_____ 15. hepatojugular reflux

_____ 16. pitting

_____ 17. S3 (third heart sound)

_____ 18. S4 (fourth heart sound)

_____ 19. euvolemia

_____ 20. apnea

_____ 21. hypopnea

_____ 22. polysomnography

Definition

a. Term used when the body is in a state of equal fluid balance, without fluid retention.

b. Multichannel electrophysiological recording used to detect disturbances of breathing during sleep.

c. Increased blood pressure in the jugular vein that reflects the volume and pressure of venous blood, when volume overload is present.

d. Abnormal third heart sound in the cardiac cycle; often heard when the ventricles are volume overloaded.

e. Rapid respiratory rate.

f. Cessation of airflow for more than 10 seconds.

g. An abnormal intraperitoneal accumulation of fluid containing large amounts of protein and electrolytes.

h. A reduction but not complete cessation of airflow to less than 50% of normal.

i. Abnormal fourth heart sound heard in the cardiac cycle; often heard with heart failure and hypertension.

j. An increase in jugular venous pressure when pressure is applied over the abdomen; is suggestive of right-sided heart failure.

k. An indention that remains for a short time after pressing edematous skin with the finger.

SHORT ANSWER QUESTIONS

23. What factors have contributed to the escalation of the rate of heart disease in the United States?

_____

_____

24. What risk factors for heart failure are not modifiable?

_____

_____

25. What are the symptoms of right-sided heart failure and left-sided heart failure?

_____

_____

_____

_____

26. What are the clinical manifestations of heart failure?

_____

_____

_____

_____

27. What are the treatment goals for chronic heart failure?

_____

_____

_____

_____

_____

28. Name four percutaneous coronary interventions (PCIs) used to treat heart failure.

_____

_____

_____

29. What surgical techniques other than coronary artery bypass graft (CABG) can be used to treat heart failure?

_____

_____

_____

_____

30. What general health promotion strategies should the nurse present to the patient with heart failure?

_____

_____

_____

31. Discuss heart failure as it relates to gender.

_____

_____

_____

_____

32. What are end-stage treatment options for the patient with heart failure?

_____

_____

TRUE OR FALSE?

33. _____ T/F Heart failure is a chronic condition and, with suboptimal or lack of treatment, will lead to progressive cardiac dysfunction, progressive symptoms, and eventually death.

34. _____ T/F Results from a lipid panel can determine whether the etiology or the exacerbation of heart failure is related to hypo- or hyperthyroidism.

35. _____ T/F Although a number of pharmacologic treatments have been shown to improve outcomes in patients with heart failure, the prognosis of these patients remains poor.

36. _____ T/F The least effective method to relieve heart failure symptoms is to remove excess fluid with loop diuretics.

37. _____ T/F Garlic, ginseng, and *ginkgo biloba* may alter antiplatelet and anticoagulant effects, so those taking aspirin, other antiplatelet agents, or warfarin should be cautioned about bleeding.

38. _____ T/F Coronary artery bypass graft surgery is recommended when there is a high likelihood that revascularization will decrease the amount of ischemic myocardium by improving blood flow and thereby improving cardiac muscle function.

39. _____ T/F Not taking prescribed medications at all or as directed can be a major factor in bringing on acute decompensated heart failure.

40. _____ T/F Episodes of apnea and hypopnea while sleeping may result in oxygen saturation.

41. _____ T/F Patients who have their hypertension treated have demonstrated as high as a 71% risk reduction for developing heart failure.

42. _____ T/F Cardiovascular disease has killed more men than women since 1984.

NCLEX-RN® REVIEW QUESTIONS

42-1. The nurse teaches a patient recently diagnosed with heart failure the importance of adhering to medication, diet, and lifestyle changes because the patient is at risk to:
 1. Develop diabetes.
 2. Suffer sudden death.
 3. Experience a myocardial infarction.
 4. Develop hypertension.

42-2. The nurse explains to a patient with systolic heart failure that the heart muscle:
 1. Has become weak and enlarged.
 2. Is stiff and unable to relax between contractions.
 3. Quivers and does not beat in a regular rhythm.
 4. Has lost the ability to sense electrical impulses.

42-3. Because the sympathetic nervous system (SNS) is activated in response to the decreased cardiac output seen in heart failure, the nurse can expect the following clinical manifestations in the patient:
 1. Decrease in blood pressure
 2. Decrease in lung sounds
 3. Increase in gastric motility
 4. Increase in heart rate

42-4. The nurse concludes the following assessment findings are indicative of right-sided failure in a patient with heart failure:
 1. Paroxysmal nocturnal dyspnea.
 2. Difficulty concentrating.
 3. Jugular venous distention.
 4. Basilar lung crackles.

42-5. A patient seen in the emergency department with symptoms of heart failure has extremely elevated levels of brain naturietic peptide (BNP). The nurse plans interventions based on determining the patient is at risk for:
1. Hypotension
2. Increased mortality
3. Liver failure
4. Ventricular dysrhythmias

42-6. The nurse explains to the family of a patient with Stage D heart failure that treatment at this stage may necessitate the following:
1. A heart transplant
2. Insertion of a pacemaker
3. Frequent blood transfusions
4. Use of an implantable cardiac defibrillator

42-7. The nurse teaching a patient with heart failure about weight management includes the following information:
1. Keep a diary of weekly weights.
2. Report weight gains or losses of 10 pounds from "goal weight."
3. Omit a diuretic dose if you experience a 2 pound weight loss.
4. Call your health care provider if you gain 2 pounds or more overnight.

42-8. Which nursing action would best help to empower a patient to deal with depression associated with heart failure?
1. Help the patient to understand the treatment plan that has been developed.
2. Suggest the patient speak with another person who has heart failure.
3. Offer to call the patient's spiritual advisor.
4. Suggest the patient request a prescription for antidepressant medications.

42-9. The nurse concludes that a patient with advanced stage of heart failure has a poor prognosis when the following manifestations are present:
1. Creatinine is 2.3 mg/dL.
2. Serum sodium is 140 mEq/L.
3. Heart rate is 60.
4. Hemoglobin is 15 gm/dL.

CHAPTER 43

CARING FOR THE PATIENT WITH PERIPHERAL VASCULAR DISORDERS

OUTCOME-BASED LEARNING OBJECTIVES

43-1. Describe the risk factors and clinical findings in peripheral arterial disease.

43-2. Develop a nursing care plan for the patient with peripheral arterial disease.

43-3. Compare and contrast the clinical findings and management of Raynaud's disease and Buerger's disease.

43-4. Discuss signs and symptoms of common potential complications of endovascular repair and surgery of the aorta, and appropriate nursing interventions for each.

43-5. Identify the risk factors, diagnosis, medical management, and nursing care for deep venous thrombosis.

43-6. Explain the actions of commonly used anticoagulants and antiplatelet agents used for patients with peripheral arterial disease and nursing management of the patient receiving them.

43-7. Identify the risk factors, diagnosis, medical management, and nursing care for varicose veins.

43-8. Identify the risk factors, diagnosis, medical management, and nursing care for aortic aneurysm and aortic dissection.

CHAPTER OUTLINE

  I. Anatomy and Physiology Review
 II. Peripheral Arterial Disease
    A. Etiology and Epidemiology
    B. Pathophysiology
    C. Clinical Manifestations
    D. Diagnostic Procedures
    E. Medical Management

F. Surgical Management
> **NURSING MANAGEMENT**
> **ASSESSMENT**
> **NURSING DIAGNOSES**
> **INTERVENTIONS, OUTCOMES, AND EVALUATION PARAMETERS**
> **COLLABORATIVE MANAGEMENT**
> **HEALTH PROMOTION**

G. Complications

III. Raynaud's Disease
A. Etiology and Epidemiology
B. Pathophysiology
C. Clinical Manifestations
D. Diagnosis
E. Medical Management and Surgical Management
F. Complications
> **NURSING MANAGEMENT**
> **HEALTH PROMOTION**

IV. Buerger's Disease (Thromboangiitis Obliterans)
A. Etiology and Epidemiology
B. Pathophysiology
C. Clinical Manifestations
D. Diagnosis, Medical Management, and Surgical Management
E. Complications
> **NURSING MANAGEMENT**
> **HEALTH PROMOTION**

V. Thoracic Outlet Syndrome

VI. Carotid Artery Disease
A. Etiology and Epidemiology
B. Pathophysiology
C. Clinical Manifestations
D. Diagnosis
E. Medical Management
F. Surgical Management
> **NURSING MANAGEMENT**
> **ASSESSMENT**
> **NURSING DIAGNOSES**
> **INTERVENTIONS, OUTCOMES, AND EVALUATION PARAMETERS**
> **HEALTH PROMOTION**

VII. Subclavian Steal Syndrome

VIII. Renovascular Disease
A. Etiology and Epidemiology
B. Pathophysiology
C. Clinical Manifestations
D. Diagnosis
E. Medical and Surgical Management
> **HEALTH PROMOTION AND COMPLICATIONS**
> **NURSING MANAGEMENT**

IX. Aortic Aneurysm
A. Etiology and Epidemiology
B. Pathophysiology
C. Clinical Manifestations
D. Diagnosis
E. Medical Management
F. Surgical Management

G. Complications

KEY TERMS MATCHING EXERCISE 1

Write the letter of the correct definition in the space next to each term.

Term

_____ 1. intermittent claudication (IC)

_____ 2. paresthesia

_____ 3. peripheral arterial disease (PAD)

_____ 4. ankle-brachial index (ABI)

_____ 5. aortic coarctation

_____ 6. sympathectomy

_____ 7. thromboangiitis obliterans (TAO)

_____ 8. carotid endarterectomy (CEA)

_____ 9. transient ischemic attack (TIA)

_____ 10. stenosis

Definition

a. Excision of a portion of the sympathetic division of the autonomic division of the autonomic nervous system.

b. An episode of neurological deficits resulting from temporary ischemia that produces strokelike symptoms but no lasting damage. It occurs when the blood supply to part of the brain is briefly interrupted. Also referred to as a *warning stroke* or *ministroke*.

c. Disease that affects the arteries of the extremities.

d. A chronic inflammatory vascular occlusive disease most common in men who smoke. Also known as *Buerger's disease.*

e. An abnormal physical sensation such as prickling, tingling, or numbness.

f. Narrowing of the lumen of the aorta.

g. Exercise-induced leg pain.

h. Narrowing of the lumen of a blood vessel.

i. Ratio of arterial pressure at the ankle to the pressure at the brachial artery; used to predict the severity of peripheral arterial disease that may be present. A decrease in the ABI result with exercise is a sensitive indicator that significant pulmonary arterial disease is probably present.

j. Surgical procedure to correct carotid stenosis by opening the carotid artery, removing plaque, and restoring blood flow in the lumen.

KEY TERMS MATCHING EXERCISE 2

Write the letter of the correct definition in the space next to each term.

Term

_____ 11. aneurysm

_____ 12. endoleaks

_____ 13. aortic dissection (AD)

_____ 14. deep venous thrombosis (DVT)

_____ 15. lymphedema

_____ 16. varicose veins

_____ 17. pulmonary embolism (PE)

_____ 18. venous thromboembolism (VTE)

_____ 19. Virchow's triad

_____ 20. Unna's boot

_____ 21. lymphangitis

Definition

a. The formation of a blood clot within a deep vein, commonly in the thigh or calf.

b. Localized diseased segment of an artery that becomes thin and dilated because of degenerative changes in the tunica media layer.

c. An acute inflammation of the lymphatic channels.

d. A rigid bandage that prevents edema while promoting healing; it is worn for several days at a time. Commonly used to treat venous ulcers.

e. Continued leakage of blood into the aneurysmal sac.

f. The three factors that contribute to thrombosis: damage to the venous wall, a change in flow, and blood hypercoagulability.

g. Edema due to the obstruction of the lymphatics.

h. Weakening of the layers inside the aorta, which can result in tears in the aortic wall and leakage of blood into the chest or abdomen.

i. Includes the disorders of deep venous thrombosis and pulmonary embolism.

j. The presence of a thrombus or blood clot in the pulmonary vessels, which obstructs blood flow and impedes gas exchange.

k. Dilated, tortuous, superficial veins most commonly seen in the lower extremities.

COMPLETE THE SENTENCE

22. _____ _____, also called _____ _____ _____, is the most common symptom of peripheral arterial disease.

23. _____ _____ is caused by a transient spasm of the small cutaneous and subcutaneous arteries and arterioles, which results in a decreased blood flow to the affected extremity.

24. The diagnosis of Buerger's disease, or thromboangiitis obliterans, is based on clinical findings, and criteria for its diagnosis include _____ _____, onset before age 50, ischemic ulcers, and pain.

25. Thoracic outlet syndrome may be due to an extra _____ _____ or an old fracture of the _____, which reduces the space of the outlet.

26. Subclavian steal syndrome can occur in the patient following coronary artery bypass grafting when a(n) _____ is not corrected prior to use of the internal mammary artery as a bypass, causing the patient to have recurrent angina.

27. The most common surgery performed for patients with renovascular disease is _____ _____.

28. Once a(n) _____ is initiated, it will grow larger as the tension on the vessel wall increases and if left untreated, it may rupture.

29. Most patients with aortic dissection present with sudden, sharp, shifting chest or back pain that can mimic acute _____ _____, _____ _____, or ruptured _____ _____ _____.

30. Some patients with _____ _____ may have no symptoms, whereas other patients experience sensations of heaviness, tiredness, itching, burning, or aching in their leg(s).

31. _____ can progress to fibrosis and irreversible tissue damage.

LABELING EXERCISE 1: THE LYMPHATIC SYSTEM

Place the term in the correct location.

Regional lymph nodes:

a. _____

b. _____

c. _____

d. _____

e. _____

f. _____

g. _____

h. _____

i. _____

j. _____

Aorta
Axillary nodes
Cervical nodes
Cisterna chyli
Entrance of thoracic duct into left subclavian vein

Inguinal nodes
Internal jugular vein
Lymphatic collecting vessels
Right lymphatic duct
Thoracic duct

LABELING EXERCISE 2: MAJOR ARTERIES OF THE BODY

Place the term in the correct location.

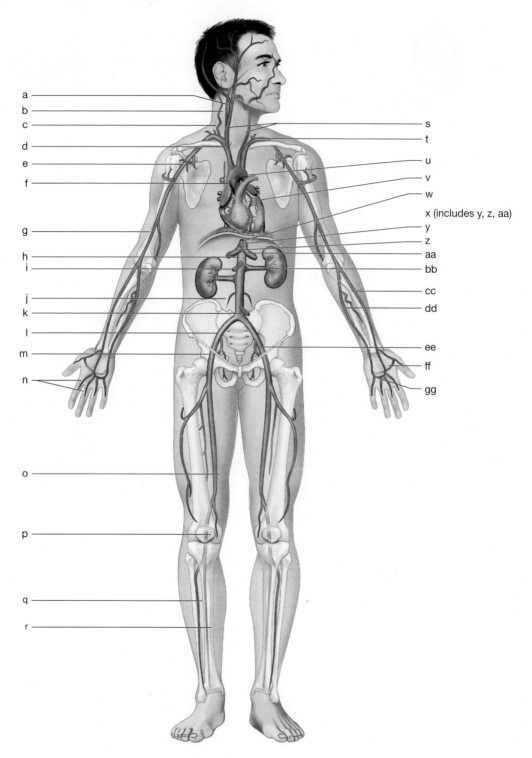

a. _____

b. _____

c. _____

d. _____

e. _____

f. _____

g. _____

h. _____

i. _____

j. _____

k. _____

l. _____

m. _____

n. _____

o. _____

p. _____

q. _____

r. _____

s. _____

t. _____

u. _____

v. _____

w. _____

x. _____

y. _____

z. _____

aa. _____

bb. _____

cc. _____

dd. _____

ee. _____

ff. _____

gg. _____

Abdominal aorta
Anterior tibial artery
Aortic arch
Ascending aorta
Axillary artery
Brachial artery
Brachiocephalic artery
Branches of celiac trunk
Common carotid arteries
Common hepatic artery
Common iliac artery
Coronary artery
Deep palmar arch
Digital arteries
External carotid artery
External iliac artery
Femoral artery

Gonadal artery
Inferior mesenteric artery
Internal carotid artery
Internal iliac artery
Left gastric artery
Popliteal artery
Posterior tibial artery
Radial artery
Renal artery
Splenic artery
Subclavian artery
Superficial palmar arch
Superior mesenteric artery
Thoracic aorta
Ulnar artery
Vertebral artery

LABELING EXERCISE 3: MAJOR VEINS OF THE BODY

Place the term in the correct location.

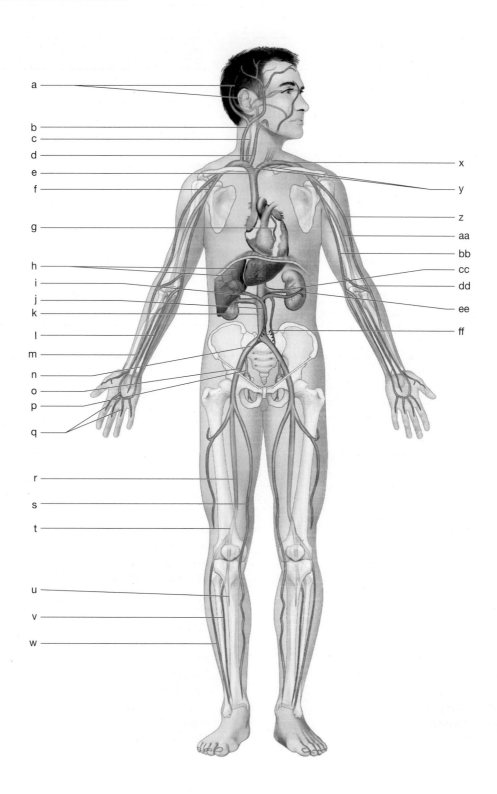

a. _____

b. _____

c. _____

d. _____

e. _____

f. _____

g. _____

h. _____

i. _____

j. _____

k. _____

l. _____

m. _____

n. _____

o. _____

p. _____

q. _____

r. _____

s. _____

t. _____

u. _____

v. _____

w. _____

x. _____

y. _____

z. _____

aa. _____

bb. _____

cc. _____

dd. _____

ee. _____

ff. _____

Anterior tibial vein
Axillary vein
Basilic vein
Brachial vein
Cephalic vein
Common iliac vein
Digital veins
Dural sinuses
External iliac vein
External jugular vein
Femoral vein
Great cardiac vein
Great saphenous vein
Hepatic portal vein
Hepatic veins
Inferior mesenteric vein

Inferior vena cava
Internal iliac vein
Internal jugular vein
Median cubital vein
Peroneal vein
Popliteal vein
Posterior tibial vein
Radial vein
Renal vein
Right and left brachiocephalic veins
Splenic vein
Subclavian vein
Superior mesenteric vein
Superior vena cava
Ulnar vein
Vertebral vein

LABELING EXERCISE 4: PERIPHERAL PULSES

Place the term in the correct location.

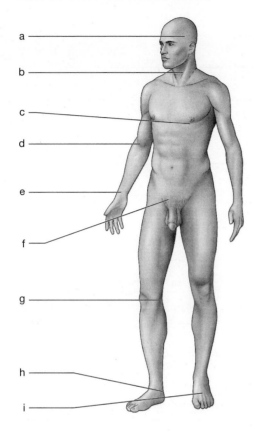

a. _____

b. _____

c. _____

d. _____

e. _____

f. _____

g. _____

h. _____

i. _____

Apical
Brachial
Carotid
Dorsalis pedis
Femoral

Popliteal
Posterior tibial
Radial
Temporal

NCLEX-RN® REVIEW QUESTIONS

43-1. A patient is seen for a wound on his great toe. Which of the following findings would indicate to the nurse that the wound is an arterial ulceration?
1. Large amount of exudate
2. Wound base pale
3. Wound borders irregular
4. Wound shallow

43-2. The nurse is evaluating the plan of care for a patient with peripheral arterial disease. Which of the following findings would indicate the patient has sufficient perfusion to the extremities?
1. Patient is able to discuss disease process, risk factors, and current treatment plan.
2. Patient verbalizes adherence to and compliance with treatment plan.
3. Patient verbalizes understanding of disease, management, and prevention.
4. Patient has warm extremities, palpable pulses, reduction in pain, and prevention of ulceration.

43-3. A patient doesn't believe she has Raynaud's disease because the problem "comes and goes." Which of the following should the nurse respond to this patient?
1. Drinking alcohol makes the symptoms better.
2. Caffeinated drinks lessens the symptoms of the disease.
3. You should have the symptoms all the time.
4. The fingers do appear normal between attacks.

43-4. While assessing a patient who has just had surgery to repair an abdominal aortic aneurysm, the nurse sees a drop in the patient's blood pressure. What should be done?
1. Increase the intravenous fluids.
2. Alert the physician and prepare to administer vasoactive medications.
3. Elevate the head of the bed.
4. Alert the physician and prepare to administer vasodilator medications.

43-5. An obese patient is admitted with an edematous and red left calf. Which of the following diagnostic tests would be the most beneficial to aid in the diagnosis of this patient?
1. Homan's sign
2. CT scan
3. MRI
4. Duplex ultrasound

43-6. A patient with type 2 diabetes is prescribed Trental. Which of the following should the nurse instruct this patient?
1. Take the medication on an empty stomach.
2. Remind your doctor that you are on this medication if you ever need to take insulin for the diabetes.
3. Muscle pain is common with this medication.
4. Avoid taking this medication with grapefruit juice.

43-7. A patient is being discharged after having ablation surgery for varicose veins. Which of the following should the nurse include in this patient's discharge instructions?
1. The need to rest in a sitting position
2. How to gradually increase tolerance for being in a standing position
3. A weaning program for compression stockings
4. The development of a walking program and weight reduction strategies

43-8. During an admission assessment the patient says to the nurse, "I just felt something rip in my chest and my back is really hurting." Which of the following should the nurse do?
1. Continue with the assessment.
2. Help the patient readjust his or her posture in bed to help with the back pain.
3. Call for help and stay with the patient.
4. Find out if the patient is due for his or her medications.

CHAPTER 44

NURSING ASSESSMENT OF PATIENTS WITH GASTROINTESTINAL, RENAL, AND URINARY DISORDERS

OUTCOME-BASED LEARNING OBJECTIVES

44-1. Compare and contrast the significant subjective and objective data that pertain to the gastrointestinal and urinary systems obtained during history taking.

44-2. Identify the four components of the physical exam.

44-3. Describe techniques used during the physical assessment of the gastrointestinal and urinary systems.

44-4. Differentiate abnormal from normal findings of the physical assessment of the gastrointestinal and urinary systems.

44-5. Describe key aspects that should be included when documenting the physical examination.

CHAPTER OUTLINE

I. Anatomy and Physiology
   A. Gastrointestinal System
      1. Related Structures
   B. Urinary System
II. History
   A. Biographic and Demographic Data
      1. Cultural Considerations
   B. Chief Complaint
      1. Present Symptoms
      2. Duration of Symptoms
      3. Exacerbation or Diminishment of Symptoms
      4. What Is Wrong? What Is Feared?

C. Past Medical History
    1. Childhood Illnesses and Immunizations
    2. Previous Illnesses and Hospitalizations
    3. Diagnostic Procedures and Surgeries
    4. Sexual History
    5. Medications
    6. Allergies
D. Family History
E. Social History
    1. Habits
    2. Recent Travel
III. Physical Examination
  A. Inspection
  B. Auscultation
  C. Percussion
  D. Palpation
IV. Adjunctive Physical Examinations
  A. Rebound Tenderness
  B. Iliopsoas Sign
  C. Obturator Sign
  D. Murphy's Sign
V. Radiologic Testing
  A. Computed Tomography Scan of the Abdomen and Pelvis
  B. Ultrasound
  C. Kidney-Ureter-Bladder (KUB) Versus Three-Way Abdominal Films
  D. Barium Enema
IV. Invasive Procedures
  A. Colonoscopy and Endoscopy
  B. Endoscopic Retrograde Cholangiopancreatography
VI. Common Laboratory Studies
VII. Gerontological Considerations
VIII. Summary

KEY TERMS MATCHING EXERCISE 1

Write the letter of the correct definition in the space next to each term.

Term

_K_ 1. immunoglobulin A
_d_ 2. antrum
_H_ 3. cardia
_g_ 4. cardioesophageal
_b_ 5. esophagus
_L_ 6. GERD, gastroesophageal reflux disease
_e_ 7. peristalsis
_a_ 8. pharyngoesophageal
_i_ 9. retroperitoneal space
_j_ 10. anal canal
_F_ 11. colon
_C_ 12. rectum

Definition

a. Pertaining to the pharynx and the esophagus.

b. The muscular tube that carries swallowed foods and liquids from the pharynx to the stomach.

c. The lower part of the large intestine between the sigmoid colon and the anal canal.

d. Any nearly closed cavity or chamber.

e. A progressive wavelike movement that occurs involuntarily in hollow tubes of the body.

f. The large intestine from the end of the ileum to the anal canal that surrounds the anus.

g. Pertaining to the junction of the esophagus and the stomach.

h. The upper orifice of the stomach connecting with the esophagus.

i. Area behind the peritoneum and outside the kidney.

j. The last part of the large intestine situated between the rectum and the anus. It is about 2.5 to 4 cm long.

k. A diverse group of plasma proteins, made of polypeptide chains; one of the primary mechanisms for protection against diseases.

l. A common condition in which acid from the stomach flows back into the esophagus, causing discomfort and, in some cases, damage to the esophageal lining.

KEY TERMS MATCHING EXERCISE 2

Write the letter of the correct definition in the space next to each term.

Term

_e_ 13. intussusception

_h_ 14. pyloric stenosis

_b_ 15. barium enema

_i_ 16. colonoscopy

_f_ 17. endoscopic retrograde cholangiopancreatography (ERCP)

_j_ 18. flexible sigmoidoscopy

_g_ 19. gastroparesis

_d_ 20. renal calculi

_l_ 21. ventral hernia

_k_ 22. tympany

_a_ 23. iliopsoas

_c_ 24. KUB

Definition

a. Refers to three muscles of the abdomen—psoas major, psoas minor, and iliacus—that pass from the abdomen through the pelvis and are partially responsible for hip flexion.

b. Type of enema used to obtain an x-ray of the large intestines. Radiographs are taken after the patient receives barium sulphate through an enema tube.

c. Abbreviation for a radiograph that is also known as a "plain film of the abdomen." The radiograph helps to determine position, size, and structure of the kidneys and urinary tract. It is useful in evaluating for the presence of calculi and masses. This is also an excellent test for intestinal obstruction because it shows the air in the colon nicely.

d. Kidney stones.

e. The slipping of one part of an intestine into another part just below it.

f. Radiograph following injection of a radiopaque material into the papilla of Vater.

g. Delayed emptying of food from the stomach into the small bowel.

h. Narrowing of the pyloric orifice. In adults, frequently results from peptic ulcer disease, malignant compression of the gastric outlet, or pneumatosis intestinalis.

i. Visualization of the lower gastrointestinal tract, usually through the insertion of an endoscope through the anus.

j. A sigmoidoscope that uses fiber optics to inspect the sigmoid colon.

k. (1) A high-pitched, drum-like tone of medium duration. It is commonly heard over the air-filled intestines. (2) Abdominal distention with gas.

l. A hernia through the abdominal wall.

TRUE OR FALSE?

25. _____ T/F   Bowel sounds mean very little in the context of an abdominal examination.

26. _____ T/F   The patient history should be completed quickly so that the physical examination may begin, since that is more significant in determining a diagnosis.

27. _____ T/F   When percussing the abdomen, there should be a hollow sound, similar to that of tapping on a watermelon, over the epigastric area and sometimes over the bowels.

28. _____ T/F   The correct order for the physical examination of the abdominal area is inspection, percussion, palpitation, and auscultation.

29. _____ T/F   The KUB test is useful in evaluating for the presence of calculi and masses but ineffective for detecting obstruction.

30. _____ T/F   The colonscopy and endoscopy instruments are inserted through the rectum.

31. _____ T/F   In cases of trauma, the CT scan is not the best test for visualizing injury to hollow organs, such as the bowel or bladder.

32. _____ T/F   When there is intra-abdominal inflammation or disease of the kidneys, movement of the iliopsoas causes pain.

33. _____ T/F   In an older adult who is obese, the nurse may be able to visualize peristalsis when the patient is lying supine.

34. _____ T/F   An elevated serum amylase is an indication of pancreatic inflammation.

LABELING EXERCISE 1: ORGANS OF THE GASTROINTESTINAL (GI) SYSTEM

Place the term in the correct location.

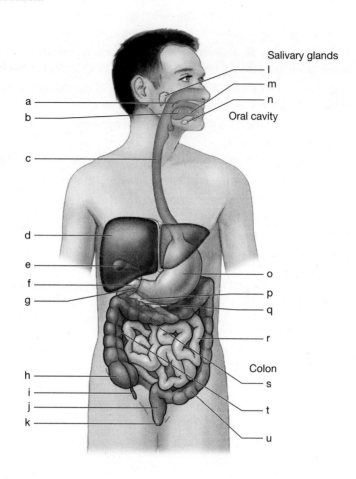

a. _____

b. _____

c. _____

d. _____

e. _____

f. _____

g. _____

h. _____

i. _____

j. _____

k. _____

l. _____

m. _____

n. _____

o. _____

p. _____

q. _____

r. _____

s. _____

t. _____

u. _____

Anus	Duodenum	Pancreatic duct	Submandibular
Appendix	Esophagus	Parotid	Tongue
Ascending colon	Gallbladder	Pharynx	Transverse colon
Cecum	Ileum (small intestine)	Rectum	
Common bile duct	Liver	Stomach	
Descending colon	Pancreas	Sublingual	

LABELING EXERCISE 2: THE STOMACH

Place the term in the correct location.

a. _____

b. _____

c. _____

d. _____

e. _____

f. _____

g. _____

h. _____

i. _____

j. _____

k. _____

Cardia
Circular layer
Duodenum
Esophagus
Fundus
Greater curvature

Lesser curvature
Longitudinal layer
Oblique layer
Pyloric sphincter valve
Rugae

LABELING EXERCISE 3: THE PANCREAS AND GALLBLADDER

Place the term in the correct location.

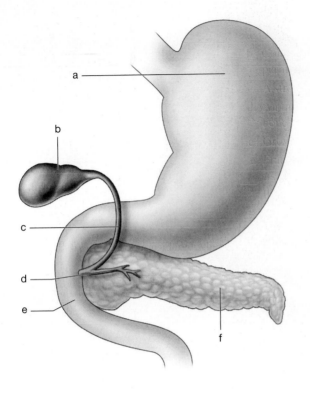

a. _____

b. _____

c. _____

d. _____

e. _____

f. _____

Common bile duct
Duodenum
Gallbladder
Stomach
Pancreas
Pancreatic duct

LABELING EXERCISE 4: ABDOMINAL MUSCLES

Place the term in the correct location.

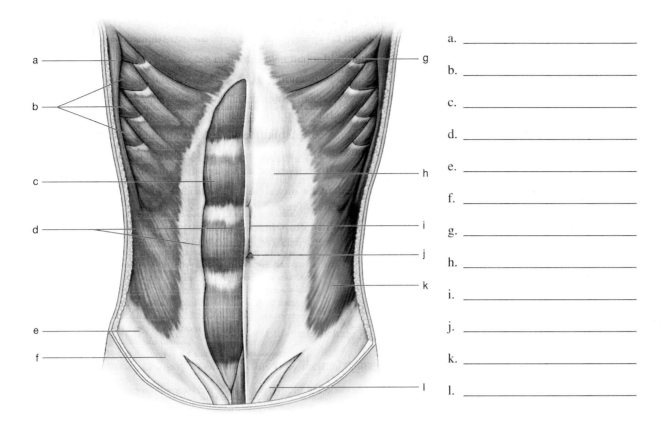

a. _____

b. _____

c. _____

d. _____

e. _____

f. _____

g. _____

h. _____

i. _____

j. _____

k. _____

l. _____

External abdominal oblique
Iliac crest
Inguinal canal
Inguinal ligament
Latissimus dorsi
Linea alba

Pectoralis major
Rectus abdominus
Rectus abdominis covered by sheath
Rectus sheath (cut edges)
Serratus anterior
Umbilicus

LABELING EXERCISE 5: THE RENAL SYSTEM

Place the term in the correct location.

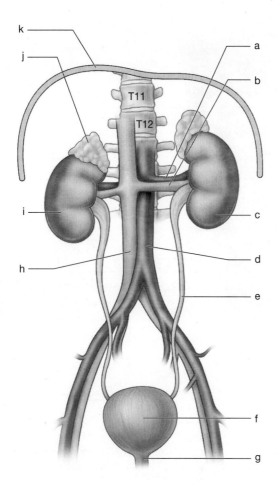

a. _____

b. _____

c. _____

d. _____

e. _____

f. _____

g. _____

h. _____

i. _____

j. _____

k. _____

Adrenal gland   Renal artery

Aorta   Renal vein

Bladder   Right kidney

Diaphragm   Ureter

Inferior vena cava   Urethra

Left kidney

NCLEX-RN® REVIEW QUESTIONS

44-1. A patient comes into the clinic with complaints of ongoing abdominal cramping and diarrhea. Which of the following should the nurse ask this patient during the interview?
1. Where do you work?
2. What did you eat recently?
3. What type of water do you have?
4. What type of daily exercise do you do?

44-2. The nurse is examining a patient's abdomen. Which of the following should be done after inspection?
1. Percussion
2. Auscultation
3. Deep palpation
4. Light palpation

44-3. The nurse is preparing to perform an abdominal examination on a patient. Which of the following should the nurse do?
1. Avoid pulsatile areas around the umbilicus because it could be an aortic aneurysm.
2. Ask the patient if there are any painful areas on the abdomen.
3. Expect not to be able to palpate the right kidney.
4. Expect to find the lower liver margin at the level of the lower right rib cage if the patient has cirrhosis.

44-4. A postoperative patient has loud bowel sounds; however, the bowel is distended. Which of the following do these findings suggest?
1. Acute pancreatitis
2. Fluid volume overload
3. The nurse palpated before listening to the bowel sounds.
4. The bowels are not functioning in a coordinated pattern.

44-5. The nurse is conducting a physical examination on a patient. Which of the following should the nurse include in the documentation of this examination?
1. The history of the chief complaint is so important to the differential diagnosis that the nurse should prepare for this part of the assessment through a structured interview.
2. Document only pertinent data reflecting interview and examination data that reflect pathologic processes.
3. Develop a systematic approach to document core questions and a head-to-toe examination.
4. To avoid forgetting relevant data, the nurse should pause the examination between systems for note taking and documentation.

CHAPTER 45

CARING FOR THE PATIENT WITH GASTROINTESTINAL DISORDERS

OUTCOME-BASED LEARNING OBJECTIVES

45-1. Describe the different causes of stomatitis and related nursing care.

45-2. Compare and contrast pathophysiology, clinical manifestations, and treatment with related nursing care of patients with peptic ulcer disease (PUD) and gastroesophageal reflux disease (GERD).

45-3. Develop a teaching plan for patients with celiac disease.

45-4. Analyze the similarities and differences between different types of inflammatory bowel disease.

45-5. List the risk factors for developing GERD.

45-6. Delineate nursing care for a patient with colon cancer.

45-7. Describe the different intestinal tubes and related nursing care for patients with intestinal obstruction.

45-8. Discuss the clinical manifestations of the complications of gastric surgery.

45-9. Outline the nursing care of a patient with an ileostomy, colostomy, and continent ileostomy.

CHAPTER OUTLINE

I. Disorders of the Mouth and Esophagus
   A. Stomatitis
      1. Pathophysiology
      2. Etiology
         a. Viral Causes
         b. Bacterial Causes
         c. Fungal Causes
         d. Traumatic Causes

5. Medical Management
   a. Medications
   b. Lifestyle Modifications
   c. Surgery
      NURSING MANAGEMENT
      HEALTH PROMOTION
B. Cancer of the Stomach
   1. Pathophysiology
   2. Clinical Manifestations
      a. Diagnostic Procedures
   3. Medical Management
      a. Surgery
      b. Radiation/Chemotherapy
         NURSING MANAGEMENT
         HEALTH PROMOTION
C. Malabsorption/Maldigestion Syndromes
   1. Celiac Disease (Sprue)
      a. Pathophysiology
      b. Clinical Manifestations
         i. Diagnostic Procedures
      c. Medical Management
         NURSING MANAGEMENT
   2. Lactose Intolerance
      a. Diagnostic Procedures
   3. Medical Management
      NURSING MANAGEMENT
   4. Pancreatic Insufficiency
      NURSING MANAGEMENT
   5. Short Bowel Syndrome
   6. Medical Management
      NURSING MANAGEMENT
   7. Intestinal Obstruction
      a. Pathophysiology
      b. Clinical Manifestations
         i. Diagnostic Procedures
   8. Medical Management
      NURSING MANAGEMENT
D. Diverticular Disease
   1. Pathophysiology/Etiology
   2. Clinical Manifestations
      a. Diagnostic Procedures
   3. Medical Management
      a. Dietary Modifications
      b. Drug Therapy
      c. Rest
      d. Surgery
         NURSING MANAGEMENT
         HEALTH PROMOTION
E. Inflammatory Bowel Disease
   1. Epidemiology
   2. Pathophysiology
      a. Genetic Links
      b. Immune Response
         i. Immune Response to Bacteria
         ii. The Epithelium and Immune Response

3. Ulcerative Colitis
4. Crohn's Disease
5. Clinical Manifestations
   a. Diagnostic Procedures
      i. Endoscopy
      ii. Radiography
      iii. Blood Tests
6. Medical Management
   a. Drug Therapy
   b. Diet Therapy
   c. Surgery
      NURSING MANAGEMENT
F. Colon Cancer
  1. Pathophysiology/Etiology
  2. Clinical Manifestations
   a. Diagnostic Procedures
  3. Medical Management
   a. Surgery
   b. Chemotherapy and Radiation Therapy
      NURSING MANAGEMENT
G. Research

KEY TERMS MATCHING EXERCISE 1

Write the letter of the correct definition in the space next to each term.

Term

_d_ 1. herpetic stomatitis
_a_ 2. aphthous stomatitis (contact stomatitis)
_e_ 3. oral candidiasis
_j_ 4. Vincent's stomatitis
_g_ 5. anti-infectives
_i_ 6. gastroesophageal reflux
_c_ 7. histamine₂ (H2)-receptor blockers
_h_ 8. lower esophageal sphincter (LES)
_b_ 9. proton pump inhibitor (PPI)
_f_ 10. rolling (paraesophageal) hernia

Definition

a. A common ulcerative condition limited to the oral cavity. Also known as *canker sores*.

b. Drug that blocks the proton pump in the stomach, thus reducing gastric acid secretion.

c. Drugs that block the H2-receptors located in the gastrointestinal tract and reduce acid secretion.

d. Inflammation of the oral cavity caused by the herpes simplex virus.

e. An overgrowth of the yeast-like fungus *Candida albicans*.

f. A protrusion of the greater curvature of the stomach through the esophageal hiatus.

g. Drugs that are used to treat infections and include antibiotics, antivirals, and antifungals.

h. An area at the distal end of the esophagus that prevents the movement of gastric juice into the esophagus.

i. The backflow of gastric contents into the lower end of the esophagus.

j. An acute bacterial infection of the gingiva oral mucous membranes caused most often by the bacteria *Borrelia vincentii*. Also known as *acute necrotizing stomatitis* or *trench mouth*.

KEY TERMS MATCHING EXERCISE 2

Write the letter of the correct definition in the space next to each term.

Term

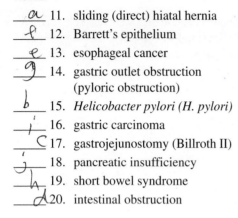

_a_ 11. sliding (direct) hiatal hernia

_f_ 12. Barrett's epithelium

_e_ 13. esophageal cancer

_g_ 14. gastric outlet obstruction (pyloric obstruction)

_b_ 15. *Helicobacter pylori (H. pylori)*

_i_ 16. gastric carcinoma

_c_ 17. gastrojejunostomy (Billroth II)

_j_ 18. pancreatic insufficiency

_h_ 19. short bowel syndrome

_d_ 20. intestinal obstruction

Definition

a. Occurs when a portion of the fundus of the stomach moves upward through the esophageal hiatus into the thoracic cavity.

b. A bacterium that infects the stomach and duodenum and is associated with peptic ulcers.

c. Procedure in which a larger distal portion of the stomach is removed than with the gastroduodenostomy (Billroth I) procedure, and the remainder is anastomosed to the jejunum.

d. The impairment of the forward movement of intestinal contents by mechanical causes (tumors), adhesions, or functional causes (surgery, anesthesia, medications); can occur anywhere from the pylorus to the rectum.

e. Cancer that occurs anywhere in the esophagus, but more often occurs in the middle and distal portions; is usually squamous cell carcinoma.

f. Columnar epithelial tissue that replaces the normal squamous epithelium in the esophagus after prolonged exposure to gastric juice. It is resistant to gastric acid, supports the healing of the esophagus, and is premalignant.

g. Results from edema, inflammation, or scarring and obstructs the flow of gastric contents from the stomach to the duodenum. Also called *pyloric obstruction*.

h. Syndrome in which the surface of the small intestine is reduced as a result of surgical resection of the small bowel, typically because of tumors, Crohn's disease, infarction, trauma, or radiation.

i. Cancer in the stomach, most commonly in the antrum and distal portions; is usually an adenocarcinoma.

j. A deficiency of pancreatic enzymes resulting in malabsorption of nutrients.

KEY TERMS MATCHING EXERCISE 3

Write the letter of the correct definition in the space next to each term.

Term

_____ i. 21. diverticular disease

_____ f. 22. inflammatory bowel disease (IBD)

_____ i 23. ulcerative colitis (UC)

_____ g 24. continent ileostomy (Kock ileostomy
or Kock pouch)

_____ d 25. ileal pouch anal anastomosis (IPAA)

_____ c 26. adenomatous polyps

_____ e 27. C-reactive protein (CRP)

_____ b 28. carcinoembryonic antigen (CEA)

_____ a 29. Crohn's disease

Definition

a. An inflammatory bowel disease that involves all layers (transmural) of the intestinal wall and can occur anywhere from the mouth to the anus, but commonly affects the ileum.

b. A glycoprotein found in embryonic gastrointestinal epithelium, but also found in tumors of the adult gastrointestinal tract. It is used to detect colon cancer, most specifically adenocarcinoma.

c. Polyps that result from a mutation on chromosome 5. They are long thin projections of tissue arising from the mucosal epithelium and are considered premalignant tissue. Most colorectal cancers develop from this type of polyp.

d. Procedure in which the entire colon, including the rectum, is removed and a pouch formed from the terminal ileum, which is then attached to the anus.

e. A protein released from the liver in response to local inflammation or tissue injury; useful as a marker for inflammation and colon cancer.

f. An immunologic disease that results in idiopathic intestinal inflammation; includes Crohn's disease and ulcerative colitis.

g. During ileostomy surgery, the procedure in which the terminal ileum is folded back on itself and the inner wall removed, thereby forming a reservoir and a nipple valve that prevents leakage of fecal contents through the stoma.

h. Disorder that involves chronic inflammation of the mucosal and submucosal layers of the colon and rectum.

i. Disease in which abnormal saclike outpouchings (diverticula) of the intestinal wall occur anywhere in the gastrointestinal tract except the rectum, but usually occurring in the distal large intestine.

KEY TERM CROSSWORD

Complete the crossword puzzle below using key terms.

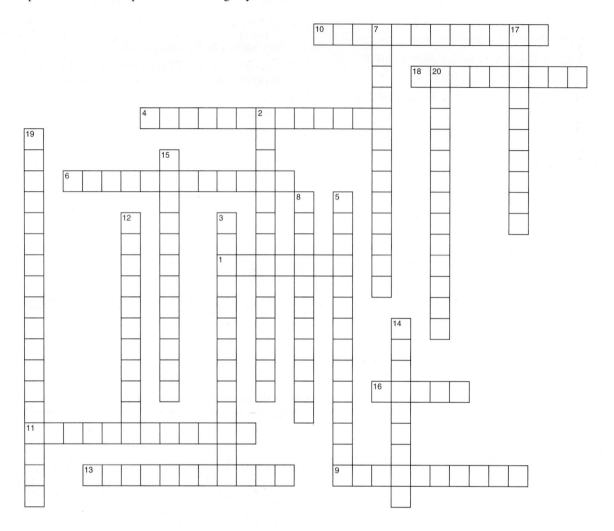

Across:

1. An enzyme that breaks down lactose, a sugar found in milk.
4. An autoimmune disorder involving a sensitivity to gluten, a protein found in wheat, that results in an immune-mediated response that causes a histologic change in the villi of the small intestine.
6. An erosion of the stomach lining that develops most often in the antrum, which is adjacent to the body of the stomach.
9. Generalized inflammation of the oral mucosa; it is classified according to the etiology.
10. The failure of chemical processes such as inadequate pancreatic enzymes or bile salts.
11. Lack of hydrochloric acid in the stomach.
13. Disease in which malignant tissue arises from the cells in the colon; it is frequently associated with adenomatous polyps.
16. Botulism toxin that has been purified and is injected into the lower esophageal sphincter to relax the muscle.
18. A motor disorder of the esophagus that is characterized by failure of the lower esophageal sphincter to relax properly and by impaired peristalsis.

Down:

2. The presence of one or more diverticula.
3. The failure of the small intestine to absorb nutrients from digested food.
5. Inflammation of a diverticulum.
7. An erosion of the duodenal lining resulting from *Helicobacter pylori* infection and hypersecretion of acid and pepsin.
8. Feces that have a high fat content. The stool is typically foul-smelling, greasy, and floats.
12. A generic term used for any ulceration in the digestive surfaces of the upper GI tract.
14. Procedure in which a stoma is formed from the ileum. If permanent, the entire colon is removed and fecal material is collected in an external collection bag.

15. Protrusion of the upper portion of the stomach into the thorax through the esophageal hiatus.
17. Cancer that arises from the flat cells that line the oral cavity and is slow growing; most often squamous cell carcinoma.
19. Results from a deficiency of lactase, the enzyme responsible for the breakdown of lactose, at the brush border of the small intestine, resulting in malabsorption.
20. An inflammatory bowel disease that involves all layers (transmural) of the intestinal wall and can occur anywhere from the mouth to the anus, but commonly affects the ileum.

SHORT ANSWER QUESTIONS

30. What can cause stomatitis?

_____

_____

31. Describe the treatment of choice for oral cancer.

_____

_____

32. Describe the symptoms of hiatal hernia.

_____

_____

33. What factors increase the risk of developing gastroesophageal reflux disease (GERD)?

_____

_____

34. What contributes to the development of esophageal cancer?

_____

_____

_____

_____

35. What are the clinical manifestations of gastric carcinoma?

_____

_____

36. What diagnostic procedure is used to detect lactose intolerance?

_____

_____

37. What foods should be avoided by a person with diverticular disease?

_____

_____

_____

38. Describe the differences between Crohn's disease and ulcerative colitis (UC).

_____

_____

_____

39. Describe dietary factors that may contribute to the development of colorectal cancer.

_____

_____

_____

TRUE OR FALSE?

40. _____ T/F Patients who report an allergy to latex may be susceptible to developing contact stomatitis if the nurse uses latex gloves when examining the oral mucosa.

41. _____ T/F The death rate for oral cancer is lower than the death rates for cancer of the brain, liver, testes, kidney, or skin cancer (malignant melanoma).

42. _____ T/F Surgery is the treatment of choice for hiatal hernia.

43. _____ T/F Surgery to treat GERD involves decreasing the pressure in the lower esophagus in order to prevent reflux of gastric contents.

44. _____ T/F Esophageal dilation using a balloon catheter is the usual treatment for achalasia.

45. _____ T/F Gastric ulcers are associated with increased acid secretion.

46. _____ T/F Refined foods contribute significantly to the development of diverticular disease.

47. _____ T/F About 20% to 30% of patients with diverticulitis require surgical treatment.

48. _____ T/F More patients with ulcerative colitis have surgery than patients with Crohn's disease.

49. _____ T/F Most types of colon cancer grow quickly, without symptoms in the early stages.

NCLEX-RN® REVIEW QUESTIONS

45-1. A patient with severe stomatitis has anorexia secondary to pain from the ulcers. The nurse implements the following interventions to assist the patient with eating:
    1. Administer ordered antibiotic one hour prior to meals.
    2. Have patient rinse mouth with full-strength peroxide prior to eating.
    3. Have patient rinse mouth with a warm sodium bicarbonate solution.
    4. Ensure patient rinses with viscous lidocaine prior to eating.

45-2. The nurse identifies the following risk factors for peptic ulcers in a patient with peptic ulcer disease. Select all that apply.
    1. Occasional intake of alcohol
    2. A history of *H. pylori* gastritis
    3. Frequent use of NSAIDS
    4. Daily use of a proton pump inhibitor
    5. Consumption of a high-fat diet

45-3. The nurse is assisting a patient newly diagnosed with celiac disease in menu selection. The nurse suggests which menu item?
    1. Roast beef sandwich
    2. Beef barley soup
    3. Creamed corn
    4. All-bran muffin

45-4. A patient with ulcerative colitis has been started on sulfasalazine (Azulfidine). Prior to administering the first dose, the nurse should obtain which information?
    1. Determine if patient is allergic to penicillin.
    2. Determine if patient is pregnant.
    3. Check if patient is on any beta blockers.
    4. Obtain a baseline temperature.

45-5. The nurse teaches the patient with GERD to control or reduce symptoms by doing the following:
    1. Be sure to eat three full meals a day.
    2. Lie down for 30 minutes after eating.
    3. Drink 16 ounces of room-temperature fluids with each meal.
    4. Eat your last meal or snack at least 2 hours before going to sleep.

45-6. A patient has had a colonscopy, which was negative for signs of colon cancer. When the patient indicates plans to have the test repeated next year, the nurse responds:
    1. "Be sure a tissue biopsy is also done."
    2. "That's correct. Be sure to schedule one yearly."
    3. "You might schedule a sigmoidoscopy since they only have to be done every 5 years."
    4. "A colonoscopy only needs to be done every 5–10 years if it was negative."

45-7. A patient with a bowel obstruction has a nasogastric tube (NG) connected to intermittent suction for intestinal decompression. The nurse should assess the patient for which imbalances?
    1. Hyperkalemia
    2. Hypernatremia
    3. Fluid volume deficit
    4. Metabolic acidosis

45-8. A patient experiencing episodes of dumping syndrome expresses frustration and is discouraged. The nurse offers the following comment.
    1. "You need to strictly adhere to the dietary modifications or you will always have these symptoms."
    2. "The dumping syndrome often subsides in 6 to 12 months."
    3. "It must be difficult not being allowed to have any sweets."
    4. "You will adjust to the symptoms over time and be able to anticipate when they will occur."

45-9. Three days following a colon resection for cancer the patient expresses concern that only gas is coming out of the colostomy. The nurse responds:
    1. "Passing gas is a very good sign the bowel is working."
    2. "It may take a few weeks until stool is formed."
    3. "You may need to have medication to stimulate the bowel."
    4. "You will need to restrict your activity until stool begins to form."

CHAPTER 46

CARING FOR THE PATIENT WITH HEPATIC AND BILIARY DISORDERS

OUTCOME-BASED LEARNING OBJECTIVES

46-1. Describe the different types of hepatitis virus and the mode of transmission for each one.

46-2. Discuss the clinical manifestations of hepatitis.

46-3. Compare and contrast pathophysiology, clinical manifestations, and treatment with related nursing care of patients with cirrhosis.

46-4. Outline the nursing care of a patient with hepatic encephalopathy.

46-5. Delineate nursing care for a patient with liver cancer.

46-6. List the risk factors for gallbladder disease.

46-7. Compare and contrast the nursing care for patients with an open cholecystectomy and a laparoscopic cholecystectomy.

46-8. Analyze the similarities and differences between acute and chronic pancreatitis.

46-9. Discuss the causes, clinical manifestations, and treatment for pancreatic cancer.

46-10. Develop a teaching plan for patients with pancreatitis.

PEARSON

EXPLORE mynursingkit™

MyNursingKit is your one stop for online chapter review materials and resources. Prepare for success with additional NCLEX®-style practice questions, interactive assignments and activities, web links, animations and videos, and more!

Register your access code from the front of your book at **www.mynursingkit.com**

CHAPTER OUTLINE

  I. Disorders of the Liver
     A. Hepatitis
        1. Etiology
           a. Viral Causes
              i. Hepatitis A
              ii. Hepatitis B
              iii. Hepatitis C

iv. Hepatitis D
v. Hepatitis E
vi. Hepatitis G
2. Pathophysiology
3. Clinical Manifestations
a. Prodromal Phase
b. Icteric Phase
c. Convalescent Phase
4. Diagnostic Procedures
5. Medical Management
a. Preventive Drug Treatment
b. Supportive Treatment
c. Complementary Therapies
NURSING MANAGEMENT
HEALTH PROMOTION
ASSESSMENT
INTERVENTIONS
B. Cirrhosis
1. Pathophysiology
2. Clinical Manifestations
3. Complications
a. Portal Hypertension
b. Hepatic Encephalopathy
c. Hepatorenal Syndrome
4. Diagnostic Procedures
5. Medical Management
a. Treatment for Ascites
i. Medical Treatment
b. Treatment for Hepatic Encephalopathy
c. Treatment for Esophageal Varices
d. Treatment for Hepatorenal Syndrome
e. Surgical Treatment for End-Stage Liver Disease
NURSING MANAGEMENT
ASSESSMENT
INTERVENTIONS
HEALTH PROMOTION
C. Liver Cancer
1. Pathophysiology
2. Clinical Manifestations
3. Diagnostic Tests
4. Medical Management
NURSING MANAGEMENT
II. Disorders of the Gallbladder
A. Cholelithiasis
1. Etiology and Epidemiology
2. Pathophysiology
3. Clinical Manifestations
B. Cholecystitis
1. Pathophysiology
2. Clinical Manifestations
C. Biliary Dyskinesia
1. Diagnostic Procedures
2. Medical Management
a. Dietary and Lifestyle Management
b. Surgery

          c. Medications
          d. Ultrasound Therapy
          e. Complementary Therapy
              NURSING MANAGEMENT
                  ASSESSMENT
                  INTERVENTIONS
                      HEALTH PROMOTION
III. Disorders of the Exocrine Pancreas
    A. Pancreatitis
        1. Acute Pancreatitis
            a. Pathophysiology
            b. Clinical Manifestations
        2. Chronic Pancreatitis
            a. Pathophysiology
            b. Clinical Manifestations
        3. Diagnostic Tests for Acute Pancreatitis
        4. Diagnostic Tests for Chronic Pancreatitis
        5. Medical Management of Acute Pancreatitis
            a. Medications
            b. Surgery
        6. Medical Management of Chronic Pancreatitis
            a. Medications
            b. Surgery
                NURSING MANAGEMENT
                    ASSESSMENT
                    NURSING DIAGNOSES AND INTERVENTIONS
                        HEALTH PROMOTION
    B. Cancer of the Pancreas
        1. Pathophysiology
        2. Clinical Manifestations
        3. Diagnostic Tests
        4. Medical Management
    C. Research

KEY TERMS MATCHING EXERCISE 1

Write the letter of the correct definition in the space next to each term.

Term

  c   1. carboxypeptidase
  d   2. cholecystokinin
  b   3. viral hepatitis
  f   4. hepatitis A virus (HAV)
  a   5. hepatitis B virus (HBV)
  j   6. hepatitis C virus (HCV)
  g   7. hepatitis D virus (HDV)
  i   8. hepatitis E virus (HEV)
  h   9. serum immunoglobulin G (IgG)
  e   10. serum immunoglobulin M (IgM)

Definition

a. A DNA virus that causes hepatitis and is transmitted sexually and parenterally.

b. Inflammation of the liver caused by several viruses: HAV, HBV, HCV, HDV, and HEV.

c. An enzyme that breaks away the end amino acids on protein molecules.

d. A hormone secreted by the gastrointestinal mucosa that stimulates the gallbladder to eject bile and the pancreas to secrete alkaline fluid.

e. An antibody produced by the body in response to an antigen; usually present during the acute phase of an infection.

f. An RNA virus that causes hepatitis and is transmitted mainly through contaminated food and water.

g. An RNA virus that occurs only in the presence of HBV.

h. An antibody produced by the body that is an indicator of long-term immunity or resolving infection.

i. An RNA virus that is transmitted mostly through the fecal–oral route and is endemic in Southeast Asia and parts of Africa.

j. An RNA virus that causes hepatitis and is transmitted mainly parenterally. The majority of the cases develop chronic hepatitis.

KEY TERMS MATCHING EXERCISE 2

Write the letter of the correct definition in the space next to each term.

Term

_____ 11. alanine aminotransferase (ALT)

_____ 12. alkaline phosphatase (ALP)

_____ 13. aspartate aminotransferase (AST)

_____ 14. convalescent phase

_____ 15. gamma-glutamyltransferase (GGT)

_____ 16. icteric phase

_____ 17. lactic dehydrogenase (LDH)

_____ 18. prodromal phase

_____ 19. hepatic encephalopathy

_____ 20. hepatorenal syndrome

Definition

a. An intracellular enzyme present in many cells, but high concentrations are found in the liver. The enzyme is released in response to liver injury.

b. A result of an increased level of circulating neurotoxins. The most abundant neurotoxin, ammonia, is the end product of protein digestion.

c. In viral hepatitis, the phase that occurs approximately 6 to 8 weeks after exposure to the virus and lasts up to 10 weeks when liver function returns to normal. Also called the *recovery phase*.

d. The phase of acute hepatitis in which jaundice occurs, usually 1 to 2 weeks after the prodromal phase.

e. An enzyme found mostly in the liver and bone. It is released when liver injury or inflammation occurs and when abnormal osteoblastic activity is present in the bone.

f. The phase of acute hepatitis that occurs between exposure to the virus and the appearance of jaundice. It is characterized by fatigue, anorexia, malaise, nausea, vomiting, and a headache; often mistaken for the flu.

g. An enzyme released from hepatocytes when liver injury occurs.

h. Syndrome characterized by azotemia occurring in a patient with liver failure.

i. An enzyme found in the liver, heart, skeletal muscle, and kidneys that is released when cellular injury occurs.

j. An enzyme found mostly in the liver that is released when cellular damage occurs.

KEY TERMS MATCHING EXERCISE 3

Write the letter of the correct definition in the space next to each term.

Term

_g_ 21. caput medusae

_b_ 22. primary biliary cirrhosis

_j_ 23. sclerosing cholangitis

_f_ 24. choledocholithiasis

_d_ 25. cholelithiasis

_i_ 26. cholecystitis

_h_ 27. biliary dyskinesia

_a_ 28. cholecystectomy

_c_ 29. magnetic resonance cholangiopancreatography (MRCP)

_e_ 30. pancreaticoduodenal (Whipple) resection

Definition

a. Surgical removal of the gallbladder either through an open incision or with a laparoscope.

b. An autoimmune disease in which there is inflammation and destruction of the intrahepatic biliary system, resulting in fibrosis.

c. A noninvasive imaging test used to detect bile duct stones and pancreatic duct obstruction.

d. Disorder in which stones form in the gallbladder that may be composed of cholesterol or calcium.

e. A radical surgical procedure to treat pancreatic cancer that involves removal of the head of the pancreas, the duodenum, the distal portion of the stomach, part of the jejunum, and the lower half of the common bile duct.

f. A gallstone in the common bile duct.

g. A term used to describe the engorged, tortuous, and visible blood vessels radiating from the umbilicus in patients with severe liver disorders. In mythology, Medusa's hair was a tangle of snakes.

h. Motility disorders of the gallbladder.

i. Inflammation of the gallbladder; most commonly caused by gallstones.

j. An inflammatory disorder of the biliary tract that leads to fibrosis and strictures in the biliary system.

WORD SEARCH

First identify the word from its definition. Then find and circle it in the puzzle below.

31. _____ An enzyme mainly in the pancreas; aids in the digestion of carbohydrates.

32. _____ Refers to low serum albumin, which most often results from liver damage.

33. _____ The formation of glucose from noncarbohydrate organic molecules (i.e., lactate, glycerol, and amino acids); it is a function of the liver.

34. _____ Varicose veins in the distal esophagus that result most often from portal hypertension, a complication of cirrhosis of the liver.

35. _____ Increased pressure in the hepatic circulation that is a complication of cirrhosis.

36. _____ The portion of the pancreas that secretes enzymes or digestion into the duodenum.

37. _____ Cancer of the gallbladder.

38. _____ An enzyme that aids in the breakdown of large protein molecules by breaking the interior bonds of the amino acids.

39. _____ A substance produced in the liver containing bile salts, cholesterol, bilirubin, electrolytes, and water. It is concentrated and stored in the gallbladder, where it is released in response to a meal to aid in the emulsification and absorption of dietary fat.

40. _____ Small channels adjacent to the hepatocytes that move bile toward the common bile duct.

41. _____ Pertaining to the cells of the liver.

42. _____ A product in the breakdown of hemoglobin. It is conjugated by the hepatocytes and is excreted in bile.

43. _____ A flapping tremor of the hands when the arms are outstretched; believed to be caused by the accumulation of substances normally detoxified by the liver.

44. _____ An inflammatory disease of the liver in which normal structure and function are disrupted.

45. _____ Black or maroon, sticky, foul-smelling feces resulting from the digestion of blood.

46. _____ A treatment for esophageal varices in which a bleeding vessel is sclerosed with a chemical agent.

47. _____ Removal of ascites fluid from the abdomen.

48. _____ Inflammation of the pancreas.

49. _____ A rare tumor of the islets of Langerhans in the pancreas.

50. _____ An enzyme secreted by the pancreas that hydrolyzes triglycerides, cholesterol, and phospholipids.

51. _____ A pancreatic enzyme that hydrolyzes the interior bonds of large protein molecules.

52. _____ Feces that have a high fat content. The stool is typically foul-smelling, greasy, and floats.

53. _____ Cells that line the liver sinusoids and are phagocytic.

H	S	E	X	O	C	R	I	N	E	P	A	N	C	R	E	A	S	I	P
C	Y	T	S	B	D	B	C	A	G	E	I	A	N	C	A	E	C	A	O
G	H	P	E	O	G	E	H	K	M	O	B	P	I	L	L	K	L	F	R
B	L	Y	O	A	P	I	J	A	R	W	V	T	B	F	P	U	E	O	T
D	I	U	M	A	T	H	L	N	E	S	A	Q	U	H	H	P	R	S	A
A	G	L	C	O	L	O	A	O	T	U	S	X	R	Y	A	F	O	A	L
R	E	A	E	O	T	B	R	G	Q	E	W	R	I	N	A	F	T	E	H
A	B	F	I	C	N	R	U	R	E	J	F	A	L	P	M	E	H	A	Y
L	S	C	E	A	A	E	Y	M	H	A	B	L	I	H	Y	R	E	B	P
U	I	A	G	D	I	N	O	P	I	E	L	I	B	D	L	C	R	S	E
L	S	C	H	K	M	A	A	G	S	N	A	V	A	C	A	E	A	I	R
L	E	B	J	A	N	Q	S	L	E	I	E	N	A	E	S	L	P	X	T
E	T	S	L	M	E	F	I	G	I	N	N	M	G	R	E	L	Y	I	E
C	N	A	T	R	Y	P	S	I	N	C	E	D	I	L	I	S	B	R	N
O	E	M	A	C	H	O	O	B	A	H	U	S	M	A	J	C	A	E	S
T	C	O	B	D	F	L	H	N	E	O	N	L	I	P	A	S	E	T	I
A	A	D	P	A	N	C	R	E	A	T	I	T	I	S	E	B	A	S	O
P	R	U	C	E	A	I	R	L	K	C	A	D	F	M	H	C	G	A	N
E	A	P	A	F	G	J	I	B	E	A	F	M	E	L	E	N	A	D	A
H	P	A	M	O	N	I	C	R	A	C	O	I	G	N	A	L	O	H	C

TRUE OR FALSE?

54. ___F___ T/F Anyone in a high-risk group, such as health care workers, day care workers, injection drug users, or male homosexuals, should be vaccinated against hepatitis C.

55. ___T___ T/F Nursing interventions for hepatitis are primarily supportive and include education about rest, diet, and disease transmission.

56. ___T___ T/F Continued alcohol use causes inflammation in the liver, which can lead to necrosis, fibrosis, regenerative nodules, and structural changes.

57. ___F___ T/F The onset of symptoms for cirrhosis, which include fatigue, weakness, anorexia, and weight loss, occur early in the disease.

58. ___T___ T/F Preventing or minimizing complications of cirrhosis is accomplished through holistic care that addresses physical, spiritual, and psychosocial aspects of the patient.

59. ___T___ T/F Survival prospects for patients with liver cancer are less than 6 months.

60. ___F___ T/F Cholelithiasis is generally symptom free for the first 6 months of the disease.

61. ___F___ T/F Removal of the gallbladder, or cholecystectomy, is done only for patients with bililary dyskinesia.

62. ___T___ T/F Pain in the upper right quadrant is the predominant symptom of cholecystitis.

63. ___T___ T/F In cases of pancreatitis, the pancreas begins to digest itself.

LABELING EXERCISE 1: LIVER AND BILIARY SYSTEM

Place the term in the correct location.

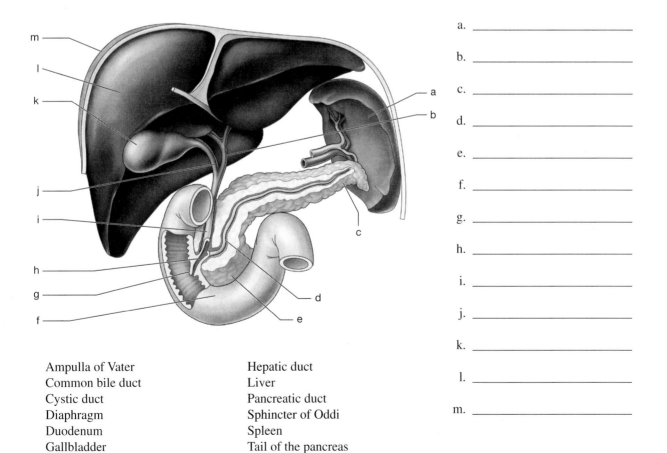

a. _____

b. _____

c. _____

d. _____

e. _____

f. _____

g. _____

h. _____

i. _____

j. _____

k. _____

l. _____

m. _____

Ampulla of Vater
Common bile duct
Cystic duct
Diaphragm
Duodenum
Gallbladder
Head of the pancreas

Hepatic duct
Liver
Pancreatic duct
Sphincter of Oddi
Spleen
Tail of the pancreas

LABELING EXERCISE 2: (A) EXTRAHEPATIC BILE PASSAGES, GALLBLADDER, AND PANCREATIC DUCTS. (B) ENTRY OF THE PANCREATIC AND BILE DUCTS INTO THE HEPATOPANCREATIC AMPULA, THEN INTO THE DUODENUM

Place the term in the correct location.

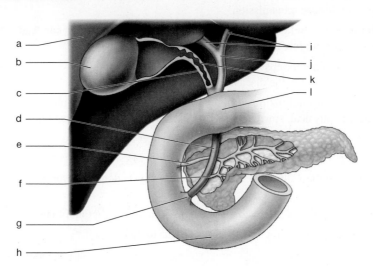

a. _____

b. _____

c. _____

d. _____

e. _____

f. _____

g. _____

h. _____

i. _____

j. _____

k. _____

l. _____

Drawing A

Accessory pancreatic duct
(Common) bile duct
Cystic duct
Duodenum
Gallbladder
Hepatopancreatic ampulla
Liver
Main pancreatic duct
Pylorus
Right and left hepatic ducts
Common hepatic duct
Spiral valve in cystic duct

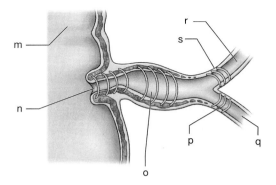

m. _____

n. _____

o. _____

p. _____

q. _____

r. _____

s. _____

Drawing B

Bile duct
Descending part of duodenum
Hepatopancreatic ampulla
Major duodenal papilla
Pancreatic duct
Sphincter of bile duct
Sphincter of pancreatic duct

LABELING EXERCISE 3: PORTAL CIRCULATION

Place the term in the correct location.

a. _____

b. _____

c. _____

d. _____

e. _____

f. _____

g. _____

h. _____

i. _____

j. _____

k. _____

l. _____

m. _____

Coronary (gastric)
Cystic
Hepatic veins
Inferior mesenteric
Inferior vena cava
Left gastroepiploic
Pancreatic

Portal
Pyloric
Right gastroepiploic
Short gastric
Splenic
Superior mesenteric

NCLEX-RN® REVIEW QUESTIONS

46-1. A patient recently diagnosed with hepatitis C denies being an IV drug user or having multiple sex partners. The nurse identifies the most likely cause of exposure was the following:
    1. Insertion of a central venous catheter two months ago
    2. A kidney transplant five years ago
    3. Eating unwashed fruit on a recent trip to Mexico
    4. Treatment with intravenous antibiotics for six weeks

46-2. During the icteric phase of hepatitis the nurse will expect the patient to report the following:
    1. Urinary frequency
    2. Constipation
    3. Pruritis
    4. Headaches

46-3. A patient admitted with Laennec's cirrhosis has the following laboratory values: sodium is 133 mEz/L; potassium is 3.6 mEq/L; albumin is 2.3 mEq/L; and bilirubin is 2.0 gm/dL. On assessment the nurse expects the following findings:
1. Confusion
2. Irregular pulse
3. Dark-colored urine
4. Asterixis

46-4. A patient with Laennec's cirrhosis and hepatic encephalopathy has been receiving lactulose, Cephulac, for two days. When evaluating the desired effect of the medication, the nurse expects the patient to:
1. Demonstrate an improvement in cognitive abilities.
2. Become drowsy and relaxed.
3. Have an increase in appetite.
4. Report having diarrhea and expelling flatus frequently.

46-5. Which of the following would be considered as risk factors for the development of liver cancer? Select all that apply.
1. A patient with a history of alcoholism
2. A patient being treated for hepatitis C
3. A patient who is receiving proton pump inhibitors for GERD
4. A patient who received multiple blood transfusions following a motor vehicle accident
5. A patient diagnosed with hepatitis A 10 years ago

46-6. The nurse determines a patient is at increased risk for gallbladder disease following hospitalization for which condition?
1. Bariatric surgery
2. Acute myocardial infarction
3. Hepatitis B infection
4. Colon resection

46-7. The nurse is caring for a patient who has had an open cholecystectomy. The nurse places highest priority on which nursing activity?
1. Turning and repositioning frequently
2. Having patient do isometric leg exercises
3. Assisting patient to choose foods low in fat
4. Ambulating patient in the hall

46-8. A patient with acute pancreatitis was medicated with an intravenous opioid analgesic 30 minutes ago but continues to have abdominal pain. Which nursing intervention would be most appropriate?
1. Position the patient on the left side.
2. Place the patient in a recumbent position.
3. Assist the patient to assume a knee-chest position.
4. Provide a diversionary activity such as reading.

46-9. The nurse reviews the patient's history and physical and identifies which risk factors for pancreatic cancer?
1. Adherence to a vegetarian diet the past 20 years
2. Abdominal radiation for gallbladder diseases
3. Treatment for diabetes insipidus
4. A body mass index, BMI, of 22

46-10. The nurse includes the following in the teaching plan of a patient with chronic pancreatitis:
1. "You will need to restrict intake of alcohol."
2. "Continue to restrict your activities for the next 2 months."
3. "It is important to eat a high-fat, high-protein diet."
4. "You may need to take medications to reduce gastric acidity."

CHAPTER 47

CARING FOR THE PATIENT WITH RENAL AND URINARY DISORDERS

OUTCOME-BASED LEARNING OBJECTIVES

47-1. Discuss the function of the kidney in relation to regulating fluid, electrolyte, and acid–base balance.

47-2. List common diagnostic tests used to determine kidney function and related diseases.

47-3. Identify the major diseases of the kidney.

47-4. Discuss complications of kidney-related diseases.

47-5. Recognize the signs and symptoms associated with urinary tract disorders.

47-6. Compare and contrast the underlying principles of hemodialysis and peritoneal dialysis.

CHAPTER OUTLINE

I. Physiology
II. Disorders of the Kidney
   A. Acute Glomerulonephritis
      1. Laboratory and Diagnostic Procedures
      2. Goodpasture's Syndrome
      3. Alport Syndrome
      4. Medical Management
         NURSING MANAGEMENT
   B. Chronic Glomerulonephritis
      1. Laboratory and Diagnostic Procedures
      2. Medical Management
         NURSING MANAGEMENT
            ASSESSMENT
            NURSING DIAGNOSES
            PLANNING

KEY TERMS MATCHING EXERCISE 1

Write the letter of the correct definition in the space next to each term.

Term

_h_ 1. Bowman's capsule

_b_ 2. erythropoietin

_e_ 3. glomerulus

_a_ 4. nephron

_d_ 5. renin

_g_ 6. azotemia

_e_ 7. hematuria

_c_ 8. oliguria

Definition

a. The functional unit of the kidney.

b. Hormone that stimulates the production of red blood cells.

c. Decreased urine output of less than 400 mL in a 24-hour period.

d. An enzyme produced in the kidneys that converts angiotensinogen to angiotensin, which is an enzyme that helps elevate blood pressure.

e. The presence of blood in the urine.

f. A compact tuft of capillaries in which blood is filtered.

g. An increase in blood urea nitrogen (BUN) caused when the kidneys are unable to excrete normally.

h. A thin, double-walled capsule encasing the glomerulus.

KEY TERMS MATCHING EXERCISE 2

Write the letter of the correct definition in the space next to each term.

Term

___b___ 9. proteinuria

___g___ 10. suppurative

___c___ 11. anasarca

___f___ 12. anuria

___h___ 13. Kussmaul's respirations

___e___ 14. hyperkalemia

___d___ 15. end-stage renal disease (ESRD)

___a___ 16. staghorn calculus

Definition

a. A calculus or stone that remains in the renal pelvis and becomes so large that it fills the pelvis completely, blocking the flow of urine.

b. The presence of protein in the urine.

c. Total body edema.

d. A patient is considered to have this disease when the loss of filtration ability reaches approximately seven-eighths, at which point the survival of the patient depends on dialysis or, if an acceptable candidate, a kidney transplant.

e. An excess of potassium in the blood.

f. Total loss of urine production.

g. Pertaining to the formation of pus.

h. Deep, sighing respirations. Also called *hyperpnea*.

SHORT ANSWER QUESTIONS

17. How is polycystic kidney disease diagnosed?

_____

_____

18. What are the risk factors for renal carcinoma?

_____

_____

19. What is the purpose of continuous renal replacement therapy when used for acute renal failure?

_____

_____

20. What genetic considerations are risk factors for renal failure?

_____

_____

TRUE OR FALSE?

21. ___T___ T/F   Acute glomerulonephritis usually occurs within 1 to 3 weeks after an untreated pharyngitis.
22. ___T___ T/F   Hypertension often accompanies chronic glomerulonephritis.
23. ___F___ T/F   Pyelonephritis is more common in men because they have a longer urethra than women.
24. ___F___ T/F   Hydronephrosis is nonsymptomatic, except for fatigue and general malaise.
25. ___T___ T/F   The first sign of acute tubular necrosis (ATN) may be decreased urine output.
26. ___T___ T/F   If the body is unable to excrete the urea from the kidney, it accumulates and toxicity develops.
27. ___F___ T/F   Taking calcium in pill form may decrease the risk of developing calculi.
28. ___F___ T/F   An important intervention in treating cystitis is to decrease fluids to avoid pressure.
29. ___T___ T/F   Treatment for overactive bladder may include medications to relax the bladder muscles.
30. ___T___ T/F   Tests for bladder cancer should be performed on the patient with gross, painless, intermittent hematuria.

COMPLETE THE SENTENCE

31. Medical treatment for glomerulonephritis includes _____ to reduce extracellular fluid and _____ if needed.

32. An important part of nursing care for the patient with chronic glomerulonephritis is the prevention of

    _____.

33. If a pyelonephritis infection is not severe, the kidney can heal but will form _____ _____ that tends to contract and cause the kidney to shrink and become granular, making it less efficient.

34. The most common causes of obstruction in the ureter, bladder, or uretha are an enlarged _____

    _____, _____ _____, and _____ _____.

35. If untreated, polycystic kidney disease can lead to _____ _____.

36. In approximately 75% of renal infarctions, the vessel that becomes occluded is the _____ _____.

37. It is important for the nurse to teach the patient undergoing nephrectomy about postoperative _____

    _____.

38. _____ _____ _____ is the most common form of intrinsic renal failure and accounts for the majority of acute renal failure admissions to the hospital.

39. For the patient with chronic renal failure, the nurse includes education about avoiding _____, avoiding

    _____ _____, and avoiding _____ _____.

40. Renal and ureteral calculi may form anywhere in the urinary tract but most commonly develop in the

    _____ _____, or _____ of the kidneys and are generally referred to as _____

    _____.

LABELING EXERCISE 1: THE KIDNEY AND NEPHRON

Place the term in the correct location.

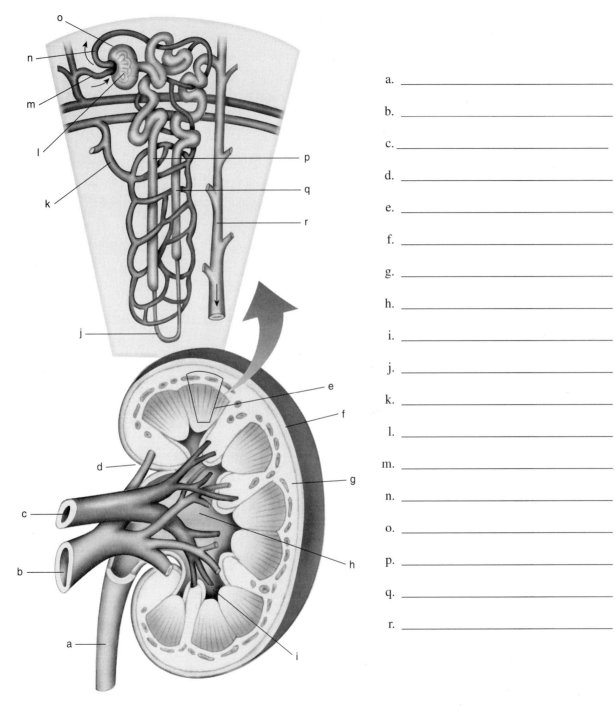

a. _____

b. _____

c. _____

d. _____

e. _____

f. _____

g. _____

h. _____

i. _____

j. _____

k. _____

l. _____

m. _____

n. _____

o. _____

p. _____

q. _____

r. _____

Afferent arteriole	Proximal tubule
Bowman's capsule	Pyramid in renal medulla
Calyx	Renal artery
Collecting tubule	Renal capsule
Distal tubule	Renal cortex
Efferent arteriole	Renal pelvis
Glomerulus	Renal vein
Hilum of kidney	Ureter
Loop of Henle	Vein

NCLEX-RN® REVIEW QUESTIONS

47-1. When caring for a patient with chronic renal failure the nurse anticipates which electrolyte imbalance will be found in the patient's laboratory values?
1. Potassium level of 3.2 mEq/L
2. Phosphorus level of 4.9 mg/dL
3. Chloride level of 98 mg/dL
4. Calcium level of 9.2 mg/dL

47-2. The nurse anticipates which of the following abnormalities will be found in the urinary workup of a patient with glomerulonephritis?
1. Increased glucose
2. Red blood cells
3. *E. coli*
4. Increased creatinine clearance

47-3. A patient is being evaluated for polycystic kidney disease. The nurse determines which symptom would best support this diagnosis?
1. Ankle edema
2. Complaints of lumbar pain
3. Frequent urinary tract infections
4. Urgency with urination

47-4. A patient with chronic renal failure begins to complain of pleuritic chest pain and a pericardial friction rub is auscultated. The nurse anticipates the following treatment will be ordered:
1. Patient will be put on compete bed rest.
2. Dialysis will be performed.
3. A pericardial window will be done.
4. Antibiotic therapy will be initiated.

47-5. A patient has been diagnosed with having calcium oxalate calculi. The nurse suggests that the patient pick another menu item when the patient chooses which food?
1. Cream of mushroom soup
2. Orange juice
3. Pork chop
4. Strawberry shortcake

47-6. A patient who has been conducting home peritoneal dialysis tells the nurse that his return fluid has been "pink" in color. Which of the following should the nurse do?
1. Instruct the patient that this outflow is normal.
2. Assess the patient for other signs of infection.
3. Assess for any changes in the patient's diet.
4. Remind the patient to use clean technique when performing the procedure.

CHAPTER 48

NURSING ASSESSMENT OF PATIENTS WITH REPRODUCTIVE DISORDERS

OUTCOME-BASED LEARNING OBJECTIVES

48-1. Describe the structures and function of the male and female reproductive systems.

48-2. Identify pertinent subjective and objective data related to the reproductive systems and information about the sexual function that should be obtained.

48-3. Identify risk factors for reproductive system disorders.

48-4. Differentiate normal from abnormal findings obtained from the physical assessment for males and females.

48-5. Describe age-related changes in the male and female reproductive systems.

48-6. Discuss the implications for health promotion related to the reproductive systems of females and males.

CHAPTER OUTLINE

I. Female Reproductive System
  A. Physiology of the Menstrual Cycle
II. Male Reproductive System
  A. Physiology of Male Reproduction
III. History
  A. Biographical and Demographic Data
  B. Chief Complaint
    1. Current Medications
    2. Allergies
  C. Past Medical History
    1. Childhood Illnesses and Immunizations
    2. Previous Illnesses and Hospitalizations
    3. Diagnostic Procedures and Surgeries

   4. Menstrual History
   5. Obstetric History
   6. Sexual History and Risks for Sexually Transmitted Infection
  D. Family History
  E. Social History
   1. Cigarette Smoking and Substance Abuse
   2. Domestic Violence
 IV. Physical Examination
  A. Female Examination
   1. Breasts
   2. External Genitalia
   3. Vagina and Cervix
   4. Uterus and Adnexa
   5. Rectum
  B. Male Examination
   1. External Genitalia
   2. Hernia and Inguinal Lymph Nodes
   3. Prostate
 V. Gerontological Considerations
 VI. Health Promotion
  A. National Guidelines for Disease Screening and Self-Examination
 VII. Summary

KEY TERMS MATCHING EXERCISE 1

Write the letter of the correct definition in the space next to each term.

Term

_____ 1. galactogenesis

_____ 2. lactation

_____ 3. oxytocin

_____ 4. progesterone

_____ 5. prolactin

_____ 6. endometriosis

_____ 7. hypospadias

_____ 8. menarche

_____ 9. molimenal

Definition

a. Breast-feeding.

b. Formation of breast milk from nutrients available from the bloodstream.

c. Symptoms of menstruation.

d. Steroid hormone produced by the ovaries and the placenta. It is responsible for uterine changes in the second half of the menstrual cycle.

e. Beginning of menstruation or first menses.

f. Condition in which endometrial-like cells are found outside the uterus. During the menstrual cycle, these cells respond to hormone production and may swell and bleed. In response, the body will surround these lesions with scar tissue, which can form adhesions on the area of attachment.

g. Peptide hormone produced in the hypothalamus but secreted by the posterior pituitary gland. It causes uterine contraction and stimulates breast milk production.

h. Opening of the urinary meatus on the ventral or bottom of the penis, between the penis and scrotum.

i. Peptide hormone produced by the anterior pituitary gland. Stimulates breast development and breast milk during and after pregnancy.

KEY TERMS MATCHING EXERCISE 2

Write the letter of the correct definition in the space next to each term.

Term

_____ 10. lithotomy

_____ 11. friable

_____ 12. cremasteric reflex

_____ 13. chancres

_____ 14. cryptorchidism

_____ 15. hydrocele

_____ 16. varicocele

_____ 17. andropause

Definition

a. Easily damaged.

b. Ulcers of syphilis.

c. Position in which the patient lies on the back with the legs flexed at the hips and knees and the legs spread widely at the hip.

d. Condition in which testicles rise in the scrotum to the abdominal cavity when the thigh is stroked or the room is cold.

e. Undescended testicle(s).

f. Varicosities of the veins of the scrotum.

g. A decrease in testosterone associated with aging.

h. Swelling of the scrotum caused by fluid collection.

SHORT ANSWER QUESTIONS

18. What are the five areas of concern in the prevention of sexually transmitted infection?

_____

_____

_____

_____

_____

_____

19. What cultural considerations should be employed for genital examinations?

_____

_____

_____

_____

_____

20. What gerontological considerations should be employed for genital examinations of older adults?

_____

_____

_____

_____

_____

LABELING EXERCISE 1: THE FEMALE BREAST

Place the term in the correct location.

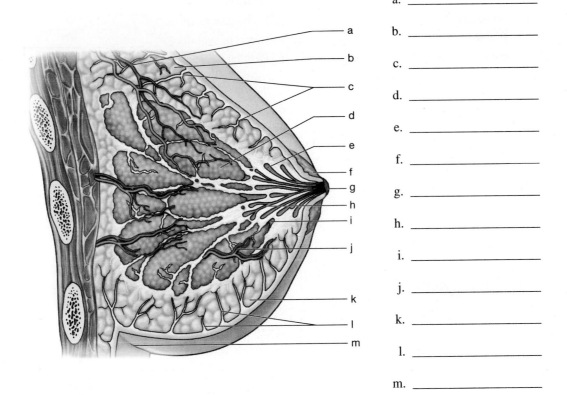

a. _____

b. _____

c. _____

d. _____

e. _____

f. _____

g. _____

h. _____

i. _____

j. _____

k. _____

l. _____

m. _____

Adipose tissue (lobules of fat)
Alveolar duct
Ampulla
Areola
Branches of intercostals and internal thoracic artery
Cooper's ligaments
Cooper's ligaments (suspensory)

Glandular tissues (alveolar glands)
Inframammary fold
Lactiferous ducts
Nipple
Subcutaneous fat of the breast
Thoracic branch of axillary artery

LABELING EXERCISE 2: FEMALE INTERNAL GENITALIA

Place the term in the correct location.

a. _____

b. _____

c. _____

d. _____

e. _____

f. _____

g. _____

h. _____

i. _____

j. _____

k. _____

Bladder
Cervix
Infundibulo-pelvic ligament
Ovaries
Oviducts
Rectouterine cul-de-sac

Rectum
Round ligaments
Urethra
Uterus
Vagina

LABELING EXERCISE 3: MALE GENITALIA

Place the term in the correct location.

a. _____

b. _____

c. _____

d. _____

e. _____

f. _____

g. _____

h. _____

i. _____

j. _____

Epididymis
Glans penis
Penis
Prostate
Pubic bone

Scrotum
Seminal vesicle
Testicle
Urinary bladder
Vas deferens

NCLEX-RN® REVIEW QUESTIONS

48-1. A male patient is concerned that prostate problems will affect his ability to father children. Which of the following should the nurse instruct this patient?
1. All sperm is produced in the vas deferens.
2. The prostate does not have a role in the ability to father children.
3. Sperm does pass through the prostate to be mixed with fluid to aid in ejaculation.
4. The third lobe of the prostate gland has a role in the ability to produce sperm.

48-2. While asking a patient about alcohol intake during a health interview, the patient responds, "Why do you need to know that?" Which of the following should the nurse do?
1. Change the subject.
2. Document the patient's noncompliance with the interview.
3. Tell the patient that nurses are just inquisitive.
4. Utilize the questions in the CAGE assessment.

48-3. During the assessment of a 20-year-old male, the nurse learns of illicit drug and alcohol use. Which of the following should the nurse assess in this patient related to his illicit drug and alcohol use?
1. Blood pressure
2. Nutritional status
3. Sexual partner history
4. Smoking history

48-4. While assessing a female patient's genitalia the nurse notes a relaxation of the posterior vaginal wall over the rectum. This finding would indicate:
1. A normal finding.
2. Cystocele.
3. Sign of abuse.
4. Rectocele.

48-5. A male patient tells the nurse that his wife is complaining that his penis "is getting smaller." Which of the following can the nurse explain to this patient?
1. A lower testosterone level is the cause for your wife's complaint.
2. Your wife's vagina is just getting longer.
3. An increase in exercise will help.
4. Eating a diet rich in calcium will help.

48-6. An 82-year-old female patient without a family history of reproductive cancer believes that she should no longer have annual Pap smears. Which of the following should the nurse instruct this patient?
1. Pap smears are indicated for all women every year.
2. Having a Pap smear means that any cancer can be caught early for treatment.
3. Pap smears are just a way of life for women, regardless of their age.
4. Discuss this with your doctor to see if they are really necessary at your age.

CHAPTER 49

CARING FOR THE PATIENT WITH FEMALE REPRODUCTIVE DISORDERS

OUTCOME-BASED LEARNING OBJECTIVES

49-1. Differentiate the cause, mode of transmission, prevention, and treatment of sexually transmitted infections.

49-2. Discuss risk factors, diagnosis, and treatment of breast cancer.

49-3. Describe the procedure for a breast self-examination.

49-4. Differentiate the pathophysiology of the most common female reproductive disorders.

49-5. Discuss the medical treatment and nursing care for the most common female reproductive disorders.

49-6. Discuss the common causes and treatment of infertility and the related nursing care.

49-7. Discuss common diagnostic surgical procedures related to female reproductive disorders.

49-8. Describe key components of the interview of a patient who has been victimized by intimate partner violence.

CHAPTER OUTLINE

I. Sexually Transmitted Infections
  A. Sexually Transmitted Infections Characterized by Cervicitis
    1. Chlamydia Infections
      a. Lymphogranuloma Venereum
    2. Gonorrhea
    3. Etiology, Epidemiology, and Pathophysiology of Pelvic Inflammatory Disease
      a. Clinical Manifestations of Pelvic Inflammatory Disease
      b. Medical Management of Pelvic Inflammatory Disease
      c. Health Promotion for Diseases Characterized by Cervicitis

C. Etiology, Epidemiology, Pathophysiology, Clinical Manifestations, and Medical Management of Cystocele and Rectocele

D. Etiology, Epidemiology, Pathophysiology, Clinical Manifestations, and Treatment of Uterine Prolapse

E. Etiology, Epidemiology, Pathophysiology, Clinical Manifestations, and Medical Management of Ectopic Pregnancy

F. Reproductive System Cancers

G. Etiology, Epidemiology, Pathophysiology, Clinical Manifestations, and Treatment of Orgasmic Dysfunction

H. Etiology, Epidemiology, Pathophysiology, Clinical Manifestations, and Treatment of Dyspareunia

> **NURSING MANANAGEMENT**
>
> **NURSING DIAGNOSES**
>
> **OUTCOMES**
>
> **PLANNING AND INTERVENTION**
>
> **HEALTH PROMOTION FOR FEMALE REPRODUCTIVE DISORDERS**

IV. Menstrual Disorders

A. Etiology, Epidemiology, Pathophysiology, Clinical Manifestations, and Medical Management of Amenorrhea

B. Etiology, Epidemiology, Pathophysiology, Clinical Manifestations, and Treatment of Polycystic Ovary Syndrome

C. Etiology, Epidemiology, Pathophysiology, Clinical Manifestations, and Treatment of Dysmenorrhea

D. Etiology, Epidemiology, Pathophysiology, Clinical Manifestations, and Treatment of Menorrhagia

E. Etiology, Epidemiology, Pathophysiology, Clinical Manifestations, and Treatment of Metrorrhagia

F. Etiology, Epidemiology, Pathophysiology, Clinical Manifestations, and Treatment of Premenstrual Syndrome

G. Etiology, Epidemiology, Pathophysiology, Clinical Manifestations, and Treatment of Premenstrual Dysphoric Disorder

> **NURSING MANAGEMENT**
>
> **ASSESSMENT OF PMS AND PMDD**
>
> **PLANNING FOR EXPECTED OUTCOMES AND CARE FOR PMS AND PMDD**
>
> **INTERVENTIONS FOR PMS AND PMDD**
>
> **EVALUATION OF PMS AND PMDD**

H. Etiology, Epidemiology, Pathophysiology, Clinical Manifestations, and Treatment of Toxic Shock Syndrome

I. Etiology, Epidemiology, Pathophysiology, and Medical Management of Menopause

V. Diagnostic and Surgical Procedures

A. Etiology, Epidemiology, Pathophysiology, and Medical Management of Infertility

B. Etiology, Epidemiology, Pathophysiology, and Medical Management of Abortion

VI. Diagnostic and Surgical Procedures

A. Hysterectomy

B. Mammoplasty

1. Breast Augmentation
2. Breast Reduction
3. Mastopexy
4. Breast Reconstruction
   a. Tissue Expanders and Implant Reconstruction
   b. Tissue Transfer Reconstruction
   c. Nipple-Areolar Reconstruction

C. Papanicolaou (Pap) Smears

VII. Interpersonal Violence

VIII. Gerontological Considerations

IX. Research

KEY TERMS MATCHING EXERCISE 1

Write the letter of the correct definition in the space next to each term.

Term

_____ 1. lymphogranuloma venereum (LGV)
_____ 2. pelvic inflammatory disease (PID)
_____ 3. genital herpes
_____ 4. genital warts
_____ 5. human papillomavirus (HPV)
_____ 6. bacterial vaginosis (BV)
_____ 7. trichomoniasis
_____ 8. fibrocystic breast
_____ 9. breast cancer
_____ 10. mammography

Definition

a. The most common bacterial infection in women of childbearing age. The cause is not clearly understood.

b. A sexually transmitted infection caused by *Chlamydia trachomatis*. It is a rare condition, with only 200 cases reported each year.

c. A low-dose x-ray procedure that allows visualization of the internal structure of the breast.

d. An increase in glandular and fibrous tissues in the breast; characterized by small, nodular cysts that are palpable in the breast.

e. An infection of the internal reproductive organs, including the fallopian tubes. It is a very common and a very serious complication of many sexually transmitted infections. The highest risk is seen in women of childbearing age who are sexually active.

f. Sexually transmitted, cauliflower-like growths in the genital, anal, and vaginal areas. Also called *genital warts*.

g. An incurable condition caused primarily by the herpes simplex virus; it can be treated with antiviral drugs.

h. A sexually transmitted protozoan infection caused by *Trichomonas vaginalis*.

i. The formation of a malignant glandular tumor, which over time destroys normal breast tissue and can spread to other parts of the body.

j. Sexually transmitted, cauliflower-like growths in the genital, anal, and vaginal areas. Also called *human papillomavirus*.

KEY TERMS MATCHING EXERCISE 2

Write the letter of the correct definition in the space next to each term.

Term

_____ 11. fibroid tumor
_____ 12. endometriosis
_____ 13. dysmenorrhea
_____ 14. menorrhagia
_____ 15. metrorrhagia
_____ 16. premenstrual dysphoric disorder (PMDD)
_____ 17. premenstrual syndrome (PMS)
_____ 18. perimenopause
_____ 19. bladder suspension
_____ 20. hysterectomy

Definition

a. The time during which periods may increase, decrease, and become irregular as the function of the ovaries waxes and wanes.

b. A surgical procedure to remove the uterus.

c. Growths arising from the tissue of the uterine muscle; they develop slowly in women 25 through 40 years of age.

d. A severe form of premenstrual syndrome that includes five or more symptoms of depression for most of the time during the last week of the luteal phase and begins to remit within a few days after onset of the follicular phase of the menstrual cycle.

e. Painful menstruation.

f. Condition in which endometrial-like cells are found outside the uterus. During the menstrual cycle, these cells respond to hormone production and may swell and bleed. In response, the body will surround these lesions with scar tissue, which can form adhesions on the area of attachment.

g. A procedure designed to correct urinary incontinence. It is done to suspend the bladder and correct urinary incontinence that is often caused by weakened ligaments due to childbirth. Also called a *Burch procedure*.

h. Heavy bleeding during a menstrual period.

i. A complex, often misunderstood condition, involving physical, psychological, and behavioral symptoms associated with the menstrual cycle.

j. Bleeding between menstrual periods.

KEY TERM CROSSWORD

Complete the crossword puzzle below using key terms.

Across:

1. Inflammation of the breast tissue; occurs most frequently in breast-feeding women. Microorganisms invade the tissue through some portal of entry, such as a crack, fissure, or duct.
4. The ending of a pregnancy before the age of fetal viability.
5. Condition in which the uterus is unable to remain high in the vaginal canal and begins to protrude into the vagina; can occur if the structures supporting the uterus are weakened during childbirth.
6. Implantation of the products of conception outside the uterine endometrium.
8. A common fungal infection caused by the *Candida* species of fungus; more commonly known as a yeast infection.
9. Occurs when the posterior vaginal wall is weakened and the rectum bulges into the vagina.
12. Most frequently reported sexually transmitted infection in the United States. It is caused by *Chlamydia trachomatis* and is treatable with antibiotics.
13. A sexually transmitted infection (STI) that is caused by the *Treponema pallidum* bacterium; has been called the "great imitator" because its symptoms often mimic those of other STIs.
15. Breast pain.
16. Difficulty reaching orgasm.
18. Removal of a cancerous growth and a small amount of surrounding normal tissue.
19. A bacterial, sexually transmitted infection that is rare outside the tropics.

Down:

2. Removal of the entire breast (total) or a modified radical mastectomy, which is removal of the entire breast along with the surrounding lymph nodes.
3. Occurs when the wall between the bladder and the anterior vagina weakens, often as a result of childbirth, and the bladder protrudes into the vaginal vault.
7. A test in which the health care provider looks at the cells of the cervix through a special magnifying scope that is placed near the opening of the speculum that is inserted into the vagina.
10. Painful intercourse; can be a result of several factors such as endometriosis or menopause.
11. Sexually transmitted infection that is caused by the bacterium *Neisseria gonorrhoeae*, which infects the warm moist environment of the reproductive tract, along with any other mucous membranes in the body.
14. A device that, when inserted into the vagina, will help support the vaginal walls, reducing the bulging of those walls into the vagina.
17. Condition in which the vaginal muscles at the introitus contract very tightly, making vaginal penetration painful.

SHORT ANSWER QUESTIONS

21. How is gonorrhea diagnosed in a female?

22. What are the risk factors for pelvic inflammatory disease?

23. What infections cause ulcers in the genital area of females?

24. What infections of the female reproductive tract cause vaginitis?

_____

_____

25. What are five risk factors for breast cancer?

_____

_____

26. What are the risk factors for uterine fibroid tumors?

_____

_____

27. What nursing diagnoses are associated with endometriosis?

_____

_____

28. What can cause ectopic pregnancy?

_____

_____

29. What medical complications apart from reproductive issues are caused by polycystic ovary syndrome?

_____

_____

30. How is toxic shock syndrome diagnosed?

_____

_____

TRUE OR FALSE?

31. _____ T/F   Most women infected with chlamydia are asymptomatic.
32. _____ T/F   About one-third of the forms of HPV cause genital tract cancers, including cervical cancer.
33. _____ T/F   *Candida flora* is not transmitted through oral or genital contact.
34. _____ T/F   Fibrocystic changes in the breast are related to increased risk of breast cancer.
35. _____ T/F   Exercise is a preventive measure for developing breast cancer.
36. _____ T/F   Nothing can be done to prevent cystocele and retocele.
37. _____ T/F   Amenorrhea can occur when a woman exercises excessively.
38. _____ T/F   Polycystic ovary syndrome is the most common cause of infertility.
39. _____ T/F   Although black cohosh is considered helpful with symptoms of menopause, studies showed that it has little to no effect on menopause-related depression and anxiety.
40. _____ T/F   The primary difference between premenstrual syndrome and premenstrual dysphoric disorder is the degree of severity of the symptoms.

NCLEX-RN® REVIEW QUESTIONS

49-1. A female patient is complaining of burning with urination, itching, and a white cheesy vaginal discharge. Which of the following should the nurse ask this patient to aid in the diagnosis of the patient's problem?
1. Age of first sexual intercourse experience
2. Recent use of antibiotics
3. Recent new sexual partner
4. Presence of genital sores

49-2. A patient with breast cancer is having a lumpectomy and radiation for treatment. The nurse realizes this patient will most likely:
1. Need chemotherapy to totally eliminate the disease.
2. Need breast reconstructive surgery.
3. Have the same survival rate as someone with a mastectomy.
4. Have a poor prognosis.

49-3. The nurse is instructing a 20-year-old female patient on self–breast examination. This instruction should include:
1. Perform the exam on days 4 to 7 of the menstrual cycle.
2. Lying down is the only position to use to truly palpate the breasts.
3. Nipple discharge is normal.
4. Expect the breasts to have dimples.

49-4. A patient diagnosed with endometriosis says she doesn't know what caused the disease. Which of the following should the nurse instruct this patient?
1. The disease is caused by uterine muscle growths.
2. The disease is caused by weak posterior vaginal walls.
3. The disease is caused by uterine cells attaching to other organs, causing scarring.
4. The disease is caused by the bladder protruding into the vagina.

49-5. During an assessment, a female patient tells the nurse that she fears for her marriage because sexual intercourse hurts ever since she went through menopause. Which of the following should the nurse respond to this patient?
1. Would you like to talk to a psychiatrist?
2. I'm sure your husband is not pleased.
3. Have you tried using lubricating gels to help decrease the pain?
4. Every woman goes through this. It passes.

49-6. A female patient is having difficulty conceiving because of highly acidic cervical secretions. The nurse realizes that which of the following reproductive treatments might be indicated for this patient?
1. ICSI
2. ZIFT
3. GIFT
4. IVF-ET

49-7. A female patient is scheduled for a colposcopy. Which of the following should the nurse instruct this patient prior to the procedure?
1. Avoid sexual intercourse for 24 to 48 hours before the procedure.
2. Take nothing by mouth after midnight.
3. An intramuscular pain medication injection will be provided immediately before the procedure.
4. Expect to be hospitalized for at least one day.

49-8. A female victim of personal violence has been discharged from the emergency room. Which of the following should the nurse do to be most helpful to this patient at this time?
1. Provide discharge instructions.
2. Provide the telephone number of the local police station.
3. Arrange for a family client or friend to take the patient to his or her home.
4. Provide self-defense instructions.

CHAPTER 50

CARING FOR THE PATIENT WITH MALE REPRODUCTIVE DISORDERS

OUTCOME-BASED LEARNING OBJECTIVES

50-1. Identify the most common male reproductive disorders.

50-2. Discuss the etiology, pathophysiology, clinical manifestations, and treatments of testicular, penile, and prostatic disorders.

50-3. Interpret diagnostic test results for male reproductive disorders.

50-4. Identify nursing management goals when caring for males with reproductive disorders.

50-5. Apply nursing diagnoses and nursing process to the care of the male patient with testicular and prostatic cancer.

50-6. Discuss health education, health promotion, and disease prevention specific for male health.

CHAPTER OUTLINE

I. Testicular Disorders
   A. Epididymitis: Etiology
      1. Clinical Manifestations
      2. Medical Management
         NURSING MANAGEMENT
   B. Orchitis: Etiology
      1. Clinical Manifestations
      2. Medical Management
         NURSING MANAGEMENT
   C. Testicular Torsion: Epidemiology and Etiology
      1. Clinical Manifestations
      2. Medical Management
         NURSING MANAGEMENT

D. Hydrocele: Epidemiology and Etiology
  1. Clinical Manifestations
  2. Medical Management
       NURSING MANAGEMENT
E. Spermatocele: Etiology, Epidemiology, and Clinical Manifestations
  1. Medical Management
F. Varicocele: Epidemiology and Etiology
  1. Clinical Manifestations
  2. Medical Management
G. Undescended or Mispositioned Testicles: Epidemiology, Etiology, and Clinical Manifestations
  1. Medical Management
H. Testicular Cancer: Etiology and Epidemiology
  1. Pathophysiology
  2. Clinical Manifestations
  3. Diagnostic Testing and Staging
  4. Medical Management
       NURSING MANAGEMENT
       NURSING INTERVENTIONS AND HEALTH PROMOTION
       HEALTH PROMOTION
II. Prostate Disorders
  A. Prostatitis: Etiology
    1. Clinical Manifestations
    2. Laboratory and Diagnostic Procedures
    3. Medical Management
         NURSING MANAGEMENT
  B. Benign Prostatic Hyperplasia
    1. Etiology and Epidemiology
    2. Pathophysiology
    3. Clinical Manifestations
    4. Laboratory and Diagnostic Procedures
    5. Medical Management
        a. Medication and Treatments
        b. Surgery
           NURSING MANAGEMENT
  C. Cancer of the Prostate: Etiology and Epidemiology
    1. Pathophysiology
    2. Clinical Manifestations
    3. Diagnostic Testing and Staging
    4. Medical Management
         NURSING MANAGEMENT
         COLLABORATIVE MANAGEMENT
III. Penile Disorders
  A. Phimosis and Paraphimosis
  B. Peyronie's Disease
  C. Urethral Structure
  D. Epispadias
  E. Hypospadias: Etiology
  F. Penile and Scrotal Injuries
  G. Cancer of the Penis
IV. Sexual Functioning
  A. Erectile Dysfunction
    1. Etiology and Epidemiology
    2. Laboratory and Diagnostic Procedures
    3. Medical Management
         COLLABORATIVE MANAGEMENT

B. Male Infertility
C. Andropause
1. Diagnostic and Laboratory Procedures
2. Medical Management
NURSING MANAGEMENT
D. Vasectomy
V. Inguinal Hernia
1. Medical Management
NURSING MANAGEMENT
VI. Sexually Transmitted Infections
VII. Gerontological Considerations
VIII. Research

KEY TERMS MATCHING EXERCISE 1

Write the letter of the correct definition in the space next to each term.

Term

_____ 1. epididymitis
_____ 2. orchitis
_____ 3. testicular torsion
_____ 4. orchiectomy
_____ 5. orchiopexy
_____ 6. spermatocele
_____ 7. gynecomastia
_____ 8. impotence
_____ 9. prostatitis

Definition

a. Twisting of the spermatic cord.
b. Male breast enlargement due to a hormonal imbalance.
c. Refers to problems associated with ejaculation or orgasm, in addition to erectile dysfunction.
d. Surgical removal of the testes.
e. Inflammation of the long, tubular structure that connects and carries sperm from the testicle to the vas deferens.
f. Surgical fixation of a testis.
g. Inflammation of the prostate gland.
h. Inflammation of one or both testes.
i. Painless, sperm-containing cysts found on the testicle.

KEY TERMS MATCHING EXERCISE 2

Write the letter of the correct definition in the space next to each term.

Term

_____ 10. benign prostatic hyperplasia (BPH)
_____ 11. hydronephrosis
_____ 12. retrograde ejaculation
_____ 13. prostatectomy
_____ 14. paraphimosis
_____ 15. Peyronie's disease
_____ 16. phimosis
_____ 17. erectile dysfunction (ED)

Definition

a. The inability to achieve or maintain an erection sufficient to allow intercourse.
b. Condition in which the foreskin is retracted, but cannot be returned to its normal position covering the glans.
c. Collection of urine in the pelvis of the kidney from obstructed outflow.
d. Term applied to age-related benign enlargement of the prostate gland where there is no cancerous growth involved.
e. The inability to retract the foreskin over the penile glans.
f. Condition in which plaque forms on the erectile tissue of the penis, primarily in middle-aged or older men.
g. Backward ejaculation of semen into the bladder.
h. Removal of the prostate and seminal vesicles.

KEY TERMS MATCHING EXERCISE 3

Write the letter of the correct definition in the space next to each term.

Term

_____ 18. penectomy

_____ 19. priapism

_____ 20. spermatogenesis

_____ 21. bioavailable testosterone

_____ 22. direct inguinal hernia

_____ 23. hernia

_____ 24. indirect inguinal hernia

_____ 25. vasectomy

Definition

a. A persistent erection.

b. Removal of part of or the entire penis.

c. Male sterilization surgery.

d. Protrusion of an anatomic structure through the wall that normally contains it.

e. Production of mature male germ cells.

f. Occurs when abdominal contents herniate through a weak point in the fascia of the abdominal wall and into the inguinal canal.

g. Occurs when abdominal contents protrude through the deep inguinal ring.

h. Free testosterone and testosterone that is loosely bound to albumin.

COMPLETE THE SENTENCE

26. Medical management of testicular torsion is _____ _____.

27. The most common form of cancer in the Caucasian male between the ages of 15 and 34 is _____ cancer.

28. Risk factors for prostate cancer are age over _____, _____ _____ ethnicity, family history, _____-_____ diet and _____ consumption, body weight, and _____.

29. With the advent of _____-_____ _____ as a screening tool, many men with asymptomatic, early prostate cancer have been identified.

30. Urinary _____ and _____ may develop from urethral stricture.

31. More than 95% of penile carcinomas are _____ _____ _____.

32. Spinal cord injuries, _____, _____, _____, and complications of _____ _____ are organic causes of erectile dysfunction.

33. Treatment for hernia requires _____ and, if strangulated, _____ _____.

34. Genital warts are a presenting sign of _____ _____.

35. _____ _____ are a presenting sign of herpes, primary syphilis, chancroid, granuloma inguinale, lymphogranuloma, and venereum.

LABELING EXERCISE: EXTRASCROTAL TESTICULAR SITES

Place the term in the correct location.

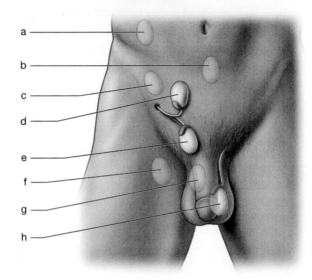

Ectopic testes
Cryptorchism

a. _____

b. _____

c. _____

d. _____

e. _____

f. _____

g. _____

h. _____

Abdominal   Normal
Femoral   Perineal
High scrotal   Superficial inguinal
Intracanalicular   Suprapubic

NCLEX-RN® REVIEW QUESTIONS

50-1. A male patient undergoing radiation therapy for testicular cancer develops acute scrotal swelling. The nurse realizes this patient is most likely experiencing:
   1. Testicular torsion.
   2. Hydrocele.
   3. Orchitis.
   4. Epididymitis.

50-2. A patient is diagnosed with acute prostatitis. The nurse realizes this patient will most likely demonstrate which of the following symptoms:
   1. Hypotension
   2. Tachycardia
   3. Dyspnea
   4. Hematuria

50-3. A patient with epididymitis has an elevated white blood cell count. The nurse realizes this diagnostic test result is most likely because of:
   1. Systemic disease.
   2. An inflammatory process.
   3. An upper respiratory infection.
   4. A urinary tract infection.

50-4. The nurse is planning discharge teaching for a patient with chronic prostatitis. Which of the following should be included in these instructions?
   1. Avoid alcohol.
   2. Take antibiotics until the symptoms disappear.
   3. Limit fluids.
   4. Reduce protein intake.

50-5. The nurse is planning the discharge for a patient recovering from a prostatectomy. Which of the following should be included to address the patient's knowledge of self-care?
   1. Resume normal activities of daily living.
   2. Increase oral intake at the rate of 2 to 3 quarts per day.
   3. Go to the nearest emergency room if experiencing urinary incontinence.
   4. Follow up with physician in 3 months.

50-6. A 45-year-old male tells the nurse that he doesn't want to have to take medication for erectile dysfunction. Which of the following should the nurse respond to this patient?
   1. There is no way to avoid erectile dysfunction.
   2. More than 80% of men over the age of 40 experience erectile dysfunction.
   3. It only happens to men with respiratory problems.
   4. Stay healthy, don't smoke, and avoid alcohol.

CHAPTER 51

NURSING ASSESSMENT OF PATIENTS WITH ENDOCRINE DISORDERS

OUTCOME-BASED LEARNING OBJECTIVES

51-1. Identify the components of the endocrine system.

51-2. Explain the general structure and function of hormones.

51-3. Explain the concept of hormonal regulation as it relates to the hypothalamus, pituitary, thyroid, parathyroid, adrenals, gonads, and pancreas glands.

51-4. Explain subjective and objective data related to the general assessment of the endocrine system.

51-5. Discuss the purpose, preparation, and nursing functions related to diagnostic testing of the endocrine system.

PEARSON
EXPLORE **mynursingkit**™

MyNursingKit is your one stop for online chapter review materials and resources. Prepare for success with additional NCLEX®-style practice questions, interactive assignments and activities, web links, animations and videos, and more!

Register your access code from the front of your book at **www.mynursingkit.com**

CHAPTER OUTLINE

I. Anatomy and Physiology Review
   A. General Structure and Function of Hormones
   B. Hormone Classification and Function
   C. General Hormone Regulation
      1. Hypothalamus Gland
      2. Pituitary Gland
II. Assessment
   A. Health History
      1. Health Assessment Across the Adult Life Span
   B. Current Health Problems
   C. Physical Examination
III. Specific Hormonal Functions and Assessment of Hormonal Imbalances
   A. Growth Hormone
      1. Assessment
      2. Laboratory and Diagnostic Procedures

KEY TERMS MATCHING EXERCISE

Write the letter of the correct definition in the space next to each term.

Term

_____ 1. endocrine

_____ 2. receptors

_____ 3. autocrine functioning

_____ 4. circadian rhythm

_____ 5. infradian rhythm

_____ 6. negative feedback

_____ 7. paracrine functioning

_____ 8. positive feedback

Definition

a. Rhythmic repetition of cycles lasting for more than a 24-hour period; an example is the female menstrual cycle.

b. Bioregulation of one cell type that influences the activity of an adjacent cell type by secreting chemicals that diffuse into the tissue and act specifically on cells in that area.

c. Secretion of cells that act to influence only their own growth.

d. Glands that secrete directly into the bloodstream.

e. Process by which a deviation from normal is reinforced or accelerated, producing an increased stimulus. For example, uterine contraction stimulates oxytocin secretion, which brings about increased contractions and increased oxytocin.

f. Structure in a cell membrane or within a cell that combines with a hormone to alter an aspect of the functioning of the cell.

g. A compensatory mechanism by which homeostasis is achieved in which the endocrine glands respond to a decrease in hormone levels, leading to gland stimulation and increased hormone production. When a normal level of hormone is reached, it feeds back to suppress the stimulating hormone and a normal state occurs.

h. Pertinent to events that occur at approximately 24-hour intervals.

SHORT ANSWER QUESTIONS

9. What are the glands that make up the endocrine system?

_____

_____

10. What five mechanisms are responsible for abnormalities of endocrine function?

_____

_____

11. What are the symptoms associated with abnormal levels of growth hormone?

_____

_____

12. What are the symptoms associated with abnormal levels of antidiuretic hormone?

_____

_____

13. What is the role of the gonads in endocrine function?

_____

_____

14. Describe the two major disorders that may be caused by adrenal cortex malfunction.

_____

_____

_____

15. What are the symptoms of hypothyroidism?

_____

_____

_____

16. How is pancreatic function connected to diabetes mellitus?

_____

_____

_____

17. How is diabetes mellitus diagnosed?

_____

_____

18. Why is patient history the most important part of data collection with endocrine disorders?

_____

_____

LABELING EXERCISE: GENERAL FEEDBACK LOOP

Place the term in the correct location.

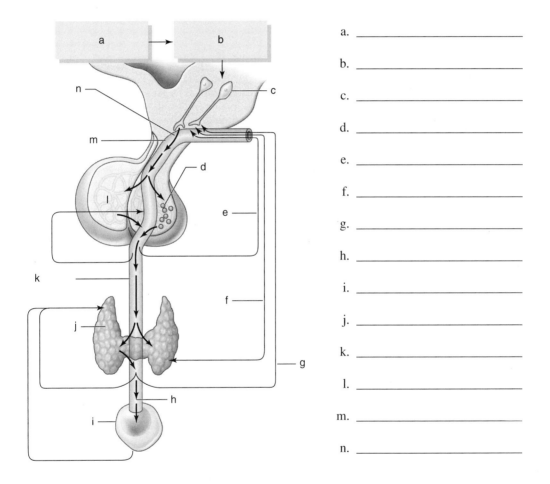

a. _____

b. _____

c. _____

d. _____

e. _____

f. _____

g. _____

h. _____

i. _____

j. _____

k. _____

l. _____

m. _____

n. _____

Central nervous system
Effector cells or physiologic effects
External and internal stimuli
General circulation
Hypothalamic portal veins
Hypothalamus neurosecretory cells
Long feedback loop

Pituitary
Releasing factor
Short feedback loop
Short feedback loop
Stimulating hormones
Target gland
Target hormone

NCLEX-RN® REVIEW QUESTIONS

51-1. The nurse is providing care to a patient with many health problems. Which of the following care issues could impact the patient's endocrine functioning?
1. Hearing deficit
2. Increased intracranial pressure
3. Low blood pressure
4. Renal calculi

51-2. A patient says, "I take a medicine that causes the hormones in my body to work better." The nurse realizes this patient is describing:
1. Metabolic activation of a hormone in peripheral tissue.
2. A hormone in an active form.
3. A feedback system.
4. Paracrine functioning.

51-3. A patient is diagnosed with the inability to produce glucagon. The nurse realizes this patient is experiencing a disorder in which of the following pancreatic cells?
1. Alpha
2. Beta
3. Delta
4. F

51-4. During a physical assessment, the nurse notes a patient is having difficulty swallowing. This finding could indicate:
1. Enlarged thyroid.
2. Hyperglycemia.
3. Addison's disease.
4. Pituitary tumor.

51-5. A patient's glucose tolerance test is 212 mg/dL. The nurse realizes this finding is consistent with which of the following?
1. Physiological stress
2. Diabetes mellitus
3. Insulinomas
4. Addison's disease

CHAPTER 52

CARING FOR THE PATIENT WITH GLANDULAR AND HORMONAL DISORDERS

OUTCOME-BASED LEARNING OBJECTIVES

52-1. Describe the anatomic location and function of the endocrine glands, including the physiological effects of the hormones that each gland produces.

52-2. Compare the common pathophysiological syndromes caused by under- and overproduction of hormones for each of the endocrine glands, including the thyroid, parathyroid, hypothalamus and pituitary, and adrenal glands.

52-3. Identify clinical manifestations, treatment, and nursing interventions for hypo- and hypermetabolic conditions.

52-4. Describe the complex neurological and immunologic effects of common glandular disorders.

52-5. Develop a plan of care for patients with each of the common endocrine gland disorders, including the patient teaching and discharge needs.

52-6. Describe the potential gerontological implications for each glandular disorder.

52-7. Identify implications for nursing research when caring for persons with glandular disorders.

CHAPTER OUTLINE

  I. Endocrinology
     A. Hormones
        1. Hormone Production
     B. Endocrine Disorders
     C. The Effect of Aging on the Endocrine System
 II. Disorders of the Thyroid Gland

6. Medical Management
    NURSING MANAGEMENT
    DISCHARGE PRIORITIES
    HEALTH PROMOTION
D. Hypermetabolic Disorders of the Anterior Pituitary Gland: Prolactinomas and Acromegaly
    1. Epidemiology and Etiology
    2. Pathophysiology of Hyperpituitary Disorders
    3. Risk Factors
    4. Clinical Manifestations
    5. Laboratory and Diagnostic Procedures
    6. Medical Management
        NURSING MANAGEMENT
        NURSING DIAGNOSIS
        INTERVENTIONS AND RATIONALES
        DISCHARGE PRIORITIES
    7. Gerontological Considerations
        HEALTH PROMOTIONS
E. Disorders of the Posterior Pituitary Gland
F. Hypometabolic Disorders of the Posterior Pituitary
    1. Epidemiology and Etiology
    2. Pathophysiology and Risk Factors
        a. Neurogenic Diabetes Insipidus
        b. Nephrogenic Diabetes Insipidus
        c. Gestational Diabetes Insipidus
        d. Dipsogenic Diabetes Insipidus
    3. Clinical Manifestations
    4. Laboratory and Diagnostic Procedures
    5. Medical Management
        NURSING MANAGEMENT
        DISCHARGE PRIORITIES
G. Hypermetabolic Disorder of the Posterior Pituitary: SIADH
    1. Epidemiology and Etiology
    2. Pathophysiology
    3. Clinical Manifestations
    4. Laboratory and Diagnostic Procedures
    5. Medical Management
        NURSING MANAGEMENT
        DISCHARGE PRIORITIES
        COLLABORATIVE MANAGEMENT
    6. Complementary and Alternative Approaches
VIII. Disorders of the Adrenal Gland
A. Hypometabolic Adrenal Disorders: The Adrenal Cortex
    1. Epidemiology and Etiology
    2. Pathophysiology
    3. Clinical Manifestations
    4. Laboratory and Diagnostic Procedures
    5. Medical Management
        NURSING MANAGEMENT
        DISCHARGE PRIORITIES
        COLLABORATIVE MANAGEMENT
B. Hypermetabolic Disorders of the Adrenal Cortex: Cushing's Syndrome
    1. Epidemiology and Etiology
    2. Pathophysiology
    3. Clinical Manifestations

4. Laboratory and Diagnostic Procedures
5. Medical Management
    NURSING MANAGEMENT
        ASSESSMENT
        NURSING DIAGNOSIS
        PLANNING
        OUTCOMES AND EVALUATION PARAMETERS
        INTERVENTIONS AND RATIONALE
        EVALUATION
        DISCHARGE PRIORITIES
C. Hypermetabolic Disorders of the Adrenal Cortex: Hyperaldosteronism
    1. Pathophysiology, Risk Factors, and Clinical Picture
    2. Laboratory and Diagnostic Procedures
    3. Medical Management
        NURSING MANAGEMENT
D. Hypermetabolic Disorder of the Adrenal Medulla: Pheochromocytoma
    1. Pathophysiology, Risk Factors, and Clinical Picture
    2. Laboratory and Diagnostic Procedures
        MEDICAL MANAGEMENT
        NURSING MANAGEMENT
            HEALTH PROMOTION IN HYPERMETABOLIC ADRENAL DISORDERS
        COLLABORATIVE MANAGEMENT
    3. Cultural and Genetic Considerations for Adrenal Disorders
IX. Research

KEY TERMS MATCHING EXERCISE 1

Write the letter of the correct definition in the space next to each term.

Term

_____ 1. negative feedback
_____ 2. chronic lymphocytic thyroiditis
_____ 3. diabetes insipidus (DI)
_____ 4. thyrotoxicosis
_____ 5. exophthalmos
_____ 6. hyperparathyroidism
_____ 7. hypoparathyroidism
_____ 8. Trousseau's sign
_____ 9. osteitis fibrosa cystica
_____ 10. hypopituitarism

Definition

a. A critical, hypermetabolic condition in which excess production of thyroid hormones threatens physiological stability and well-being.

b. Contraction of the muscles when the nerves are mildly compressed; for example, inflating a blood pressure cuff and keeping it above systolic will induce carpal spasms.

c. A compensatory mechanism by which homeostasis is achieved in which the endocrine glands respond to a decrease in hormone levels, leading to gland stimulation and increased hormone production. When a normal level of hormone is reached, it feeds back to suppress the stimulating hormone and a normal state occurs.

d. A hypermetabolic condition in which the parathyroid gland produces an excess of parathyroid hormone.

e. A complication of hypoparathyroidism in which the bone softens and becomes deformed or forms cysts.

f. An autoimmune condition characterized by high titers of the circulating antibodies thyroid peroxidase and thyroglobulin that destroy thyroid cells and may lead to hypothyroidism. It is the most common thyroid disease in the United States. Also known as *Hashimoto's thyroiditis*.

g. A hypometabolic condition in which the secretion of pituitary hormones is inadequate.

h. A hypometabolic condition in which the parathyroid gland fails to produce adequate parathyroid hormone.

i. A hypometabolic disorder of the adrenal gland in which there is excretion of a large volume of dilute urine due to deficiency of antidiuretic hormone (ADH) or an inability of the kidneys to respond to ADH.

j. Abnormal protrusion of the eyeball; may be due to thyrotoxicosis, tumor of the orbit, orbital cellulitis, leukemia, or aneurysm.

KEY TERMS MATCHING EXERCISE 2

Write the letter of the correct definition in the space next to each term.

Term

_____ 11. panhypopituitarism

_____ 12. Hashimoto's thyroiditis

_____ 13. psychogenic polydipsia

_____ 14. syndrome of inappropriate antidiuretic hormone (SIADH)

_____ 15. Addisonian crisis (adrenal crisis)

_____ 16. adrenal insufficiency

_____ 17. primary adrenal insufficiency

_____ 18. secondary adrenal insufficiency

_____ 19. Cushing's syndrome

_____ 20. pheochromocytoma

Definition

a. A hypermetabolic state in which there is a chronic excess of corticosteroid hormones for a variety of reasons.

b. Condition in which there is inadequate secretion of all the hormones of the anterior pituitary.

c. Condition in which the pituitary gland has insufficient secretion of ACTH, resulting in insufficient cortisol production by the adrenal glands.

d. Condition in which the body fails to produce an adequate amount of adrenal hormones.

e. Condition in which 90% of the adrenal gland has been destroyed, resulting in an absence of adrenal hormones.

f. A tumor (usually benign) that originates from the adrenal medulla.

g. An autoimmune condition characterized by high titers of the circulating antibodies thyroid peroxidase and thyroglobulin that destroy thyroid cells and may lead to hypothyroidism. It is the most common thyroid disease in the United States. Also known as *chronic lymphocytic hypothyroidism.*

h. A rare, life-threatening disease in which a deficiency of adrenal hormones is exacerbated by stress or trauma.

i. A hypermetabolic state of the adrenal glands in which antidiuretic hormone is produced in excess, leading to the retention of fluid and hyponatremia.

j. Condition in which excessive thirst occurs for psychogenic, rather than organic, reasons.

KEY TERM CROSSWORD

Complete the crossword puzzle below using key terms.

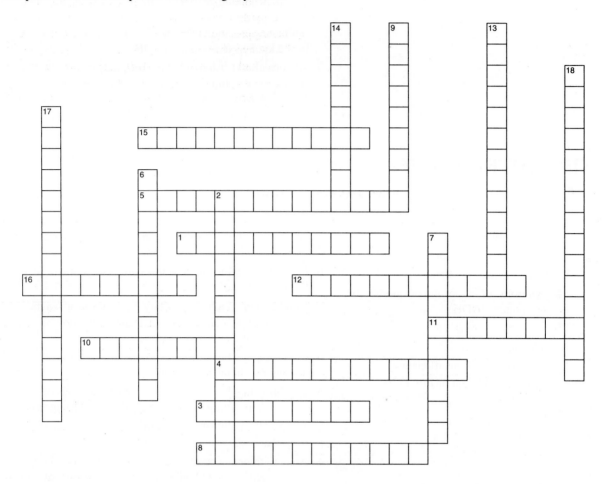

Across:

1. Abnormal growth of thyroid tissue.
3. A substance in a food or a drug that inhibits the production of thyroid hormone.
4. Spasm of facial muscles; latent tetany, which can be demonstrated by tapping the inferior portion of the zygoma, resulting in facial spasms.
5. A metabolic condition in which the thyroid gland fails to produce adequate thyroid hormones.
8. A rare, life-threatening complication of hypothyroidism.
10. Abnormal enlargement of the thyroid gland.
11. A long-term consequence of hypothyroidism in which the facial features are coarsened and changed by puffiness, periorbital edema, and a mask-like appearance.
12. The spontaneous flow of milk in a breast unassociated with childbirth or nursing.

15. A life-threatening, hypermetabolic condition in which excess production of thyroid hormones causes serious cardiac disorders.
16. Condition caused by the congenital absence or atrophy of the thyroid gland, resulting in hypothyroidism and characterized by mental deficiency, large tongue, puffy facial features, and dwarfism.

Down:

2. Full or partial surgical removal of the thyroid gland.
6. Inflammation of the thyroid gland.
7. A hypermetabolic condition of the pituitary gland, characterized by enlargement of the extremities, particularly the hands, feet, and other body parts such as the face.
9. Condition brought on by overproduction of pituitary growth hormone in youth before the long bones have closed. Characterized by abnormal height.

Down, continued

13. A hypermetabolic condition caused by an autoimmune disease in which the thyroid gland produces too much thyroid hormone.
14. Appearing to function as a normal thyroid gland.
17. A hypermetabolic condition in which the thyroid gland produces and the body responds to an excess production of thyroid hormones.
18. A rare condition caused by severe or total deficiency of hormones produced by the adrenal cortex.

SHORT ANSWER QUESTIONS

21. What is the primary function of the thyroid gland?

22. What are the risk factors for hypothyroidism?

23. What are the symptoms of hypothyroidism?

24. What are the symptoms of hyperthyroidism?

25. What is the leading cause of Addison's disease?

TRUE OR FALSE?

26. _____ T/F   The pineal gland is responsible for melatonin production.

27. _____ T/F   Signs and symptoms of thyroid disorders are easy to recognize.

28. _____ T/F   Changes in hormone metabolism and hormone levels, slowed response of target cells to hormones, and changes in physiological body rhythms such as menstruation occur due to aging.

29. _____ T/F   Thyroid disease is much more common in females than in males.

30. _____ T/F   Antithyroid drugs, such as propylthiouracil (PTU) and methimazole (Tapazole, Carbimazole), may be used in both the initial and long-term treatment of hypothyroidism.

31. _____ T/F   Supplementation with calcium and vitamin D is the primary treatment of hypoparathyroidism.

32. _____ T/F   The intervention of choice for hyperparathyroidism is minimally invasive surgery.

33. _____ T/F   Pharmacologic intervention is the primary treatment for acromegaly and other hyperpitutitary disorders.

34. _____ T/F   Diabetes insipidus can be of four types: neurogenic, nephrogenic, gestational, or dipsogenic.

35. _____ T/F   The adrenal glands produce hormones that are essential to the body's sexual response and general adaptation to sexual functioning.

COMPLETE THE SENTENCE

36. Hormones produced by the _____ glands, also known as ductless glands, are secreted internally into the blood, whereas hormones secreted by the _____ system are secreted through ducts or tubes.

37. The most common cause of hyperthyroidism is _____ _____ .

38. The parathyroid glands regulate the blood calcium level within a very narrow range to maintain the effective functioning of the body's _____ and _____ .

39. The most common cause of pituitary disorders is _____ _____ .

40. Adrenal glands secrete hormones which help regulate _____ _____ , regulate _____ , and supplement other _____ .

LABELING EXERCISE: LOCATION OF THE ENDOCRINE GLANDS IN THE MALE AND FEMALE BODIES

Place the term in the correct location.

a. _____

b. _____

c. _____

d. _____

e. _____

f. _____

Adrenal glands
Ovaries (female)
Pancreas
Pituitary gland
Thyroid and parathyroid glands
Testes (male)

NCLEX-RN® REVIEW QUESTIONS

52-1. A patient is diagnosed with a decreased melatonin level. The nurse realizes this patient could demonstrate an alteration in:
1. Immune system.
2. Insulin.
3. Testosterone.
4. Circadian rhythm.

52-2. A patient is diagnosed with diabetes insipidus. The nurse realizes this patient is experiencing a disorder in which of the following glands?
1. Adrenal cortex
2. Adrenal medulla
3. Posterior pituitary
4. Thyroid

52-3. A patient tells the nurse that he gets "dizzy" when he stands up too fast and doesn't understand why his skin appears tan when he rarely spends any time in the sun. The nurse realizes this patient is describing symptoms of which of the following disorders?
1. Cushing's syndrome
2. Addison's disease
3. Hyperaldosteronism
4. Pheochromocytoma

52-4. A patient is diagnosed with a low calcium level. Which of the following should the nurse assess in this patient?
1. Ambulation
2. Muscle strength
3. Hand grasps
4. Chvostek's sign

52-5. The nurse is preparing discharge instructions for a patient with adrenal insufficiency. These instructions should include:
1. Hormone replacement therapy for several weeks.
2. Vomiting is expected.
3. See your physician immediately with any flu-like symptoms.
4. Diarrhea is a side effect of medications.

52-6. The nurse is providing care to an older patient recovering from surgery for hyperpituitarism. Which of the following should the nurse instruct this patient?
1. Do not drive until vision is restored.
2. Expect all symptoms to resolve immediately.
3. You might experience occasional diarrhea.
4. Muscle weakness will resolve in time.

52-7. A female patient with a family history of endocrine disorders wants to know if her infant daughter will develop any of the disorders. Which of the following should the nurse respond to this patient?
1. There's really nothing that can be done.
2. Have you talked with your doctor about genetic screening tests?
3. That's really unlikely.
4. I wouldn't worry about that now.

CHAPTER 53

CARING FOR THE PATIENT WITH DIABETES

OUTCOME-BASED LEARNING OBJECTIVES

53-1. Discuss the epidemiology of diabetes and pre-diabetes (impaired glucose tolerance and impaired fasting glucose).

53-2. Differentiate between the classifications of pre-diabetes and diabetes as they relate to clinical manifestations and health care management.

53-3. Compare and contrast the pathophysiology of pre-diabetes and diabetes.

53-4. Identify the major acute and chronic complications associated with diabetes.

53-5. Identify risk factors for adults associated with the development of pre-diabetes and diabetes.

53-6. Discuss the pharmacologic and nutritional management of diabetes as contrasted between diabetes type 1 and type 2.

53-7. Discuss the role of physical activity and exercise in the prevention and treatment of diabetes.

53-8. Describe the clinical signs and symptoms, diagnosis, medical therapy, nursing assessment, and management of diabetes.

53-9. Compare and contrast the clinical signs and symptoms, diagnosis, treatment, nursing assessment, and management of diabetic ketoacidosis, hyperglycemic hyperosmolar syndrome, and hypoglycemia.

53-10. Describe the prevention, progression, clinical signs and symptoms, nursing assessment, and management of lower extremity disease as it relates to diabetes.

PEARSON
EXPLORE **mynursingkit**™

MyNursingKit is your one stop for online chapter review materials and resources. Prepare for success with additional NCLEX®-style practice questions, interactive assignments and activities, web links, animations and videos, and more!

Register your access code from the front of your book at **www.mynursingkit.com**

CHAPTER OUTLINE

  I. Epidemiology and Etiology of Diabetes and Other Forms of Glucose Intolerance
     A. Cultural and Ethnic Considerations of Diabetes Development
 II. Normal Physiology of Fuel Metabolism
III. Pathophysiology and Fuel Metabolism in Diabetes
     A. Physiological Manifestations of Systemic Complications of Diabetes Mellitus
        1. Diseases of Heart and Vessels
        2. Kidney Disease

      3. Blindness and Other Visual Disorders

      4. Neuropathy

      5. Complications of Pregnancy

      6. Diabetic Ketoacidosis

      7. Hyperosmolar Hyperglycemic Syndrome

      8. Hypoglycemia

IV. Risk Factors and Pathophysiology of Type 1 Diabetes

    A. Genetics

    B. Environmental

    C. Autoimmunity

    D. Sequence in the Development of Type 1 Diabetes

    E. Relationship Between Environmental Triggers and Beta-Cell Destruction

V. Risk Factors and Pathophysiology of Type 2 Diabetes

    A. Genetics

    B. Ethnicity

    C. Racial Admixture

    D. Family History

    E. Diet

    F. Obesity

    G. Physical Inactivity

    H. Urbanization

    I. Socioeconomic Status and Education

    J. Intrauterine Environment

    K. Sequence in the Development of Type 2 Diabetes

VI. Clinical Manifestations

VII. Laboratory and Diagnostic Procedures

    A. Blood Glucose Levels

    B. Oral Glucose Tolerance Tests

    C. Self-Monitoring of Blood Glucose

    D. Continuous Blood Glucose Monitoring

    E. Hemoglobin A_{1c} Test

    F. Glycated Serum Proteins

    G. Urinary Glucose

    H. Urinary and Blood Ketones

    I. Diabetes Diagnosis

VIII. Medical Management

    A. Pharmaceutical Management of Hyperglycemia

      1. Insulin Preparations

        a. Time Profile of Insulin Preparations

          i. Rapid-Acting Insulin

          ii. Short-Acting Insulin

          iii. Intermediate-Acting Insulin

          iv. Long-Acting Insulin

        b. Premixed Insulins

        c. Incretin Mimetics

        d. Amylin Analog

      2. Insulin Delivery Devices

        a. Insulin Pumps

      3. Oral Diabetes Medications

        a. Sulfonylureas

        b. Meglitinides

        c. Alpha-Glucosidase Inhibitors

        d. Biguanides

        e. Thiazolidinediones

        f. Dipeptidyl Peptidase-4 Inhibitors

KEY TERMS MATCHING EXERCISE 1

Write the letter of the correct definition in the space next to each term.

Term

_____ 1. hyperglycemia

_____ 2. pancreatic beta cells

_____ 3. type 1 diabetes mellitus

_____ 4. gestational diabetes mellitus (GDM)

_____ 5. impaired fasting glucose (IFG)

_____ 6. impaired glucose tolerance (IGT)

_____ 7. latent autoimmune diabetes in adults (LADA)

_____ 8. maturity onset diabetes of the young (MODY)

_____ 9. type 2 diabetes mellitus

Definition

a. Type of diabetes characterized by insulin resistance and decreased insulin secretion.

b. Type of diabetes characterized by the destruction of pancreatic beta cells.

c. Cells in the pancreatic islets of Langerhans that produce insulin.

d. A category of pre-diabetes in which the fasting glucose level is > 100 mg/dL but < 126 mg/dL.

e. Diabetes that has early onset (usually before the age of 25); it is inherited in an autosomal dominant manner and more closely resembles type 2 diabetes rather than type 1.

f. A category of pre-diabetes in which the blood glucose level following an oral glucose load of 75 grams is > 140 mg/dL but < 200 mg/dL.

g. A specific type of diabetes that occurs during pregnancy in women who had no history of diabetes prior to the pregnancy.

h. An autoimmune form of diabetes that affects adults.

i. Elevated blood glucose levels.

KEY TERMS MATCHING EXERCISE 2

Write the letter of the correct definition in the space next to each term.

Term

_____ 10. pancreatic polypeptide

_____ 11. counterregulatory hormones

_____ 12. insulin resistance

_____ 13. Diabetes Control and Complications Trial (DCCT)

_____ 14. diabetic ketoacidosis (DKA)

_____ 15. hyperosmolar hyperglycemic nonketotic syndrome (HHS)

_____ 16. honeymoon period

_____ 17. molecular mimicry

_____ 18. Diabetes Prevention Program (DPP)

Definition

a. A complex peptide hormone secreted by the pancreatic islet cells whose role is not completely understood.

b. A process in which peptides from proteins, such as viruses, become structurally similar to self-peptides and activate T-cell autoimmunity.

c. A transient period of time when newly diagnosed patients with type 1 diabetes have restoration of insulin production and thus a reduced requirement for exogenous insulin.

d. Hormones that antagonize the actions of insulin. Examples include glucagon, cortisol, growth hormone, and catecholamines.

e. Unresponsiveness of anabolic processes to the normal effects of insulin and possibly tissue insensitivity to insulin.

f. An acute emergent complication of diabetes (usually type 1 diabetes) primarily characterized by hyperglycemia, dehydration, and metabolic acidosis.

g. A landmark research study in the United States and Canada which demonstrated that intensive management of type 1 diabetes (aimed at normal blood glucose levels) resulted in decreased occurrence and progression of development of microvascular complications (i.e., retinopathy, neuropathy, nephropathy).

h. An emergent complication of diabetes characterized by serum hyperosmolarity, hyperglycemia, and dehydration.

i. A major clinical research trial of patients with pre-diabetes that clearly demonstrated that lifestyle modification was superior to pharmacologic therapy with metformin (an oral diabetes medication) in preventing diabetes.

KEY TERMS MATCHING EXERCISE 3

Write the letter of the correct definition in the space next to each term.

Term

_____ 19. oral glucose tolerance test (OGTT)

_____ 20. glycated serum proteins (GSPs)

_____ 21. hemoglobin A_{1C} (Hb A_{1C}) test

_____ 22. United Kingdom Prospective Diabetes Study (UKPDS)

_____ 23. continuous subcutaneous insulin infusion (CSII)

_____ 24. dawn phenomenon

_____ 25. medical nutrition therapy (MNT)

_____ 26. hypoglycemic unawareness

_____ 27. diabetic peripheral neuropathy (DPN)

Definition

a. A method of exogenous insulin delivery that uses an external "insulin pump," which allows for programmed delivery of insulin into subcutaneous tissue.

b. A chronic complication of diabetes in which the nerves outside the spinal cord are damaged.

c. A test in which the glycemic response to a prescribed dose of oral glucose is used to determine glucose tolerance status (i.e., normal glucose tolerance, impaired glucose tolerance, or diabetes).

d. Refers to a series of stable minor hemoglobin components formed nonenzymatically from the glycosylation of the hemoglobin molecule. Sometimes also referred to as *glycohemoglobin, glycosylated hemoglobin,* or *A1C.*

e. Meal planning approaches for patients with diabetes that combine clinical evidence, cultural, social, and ethnic approaches, and patient motivation.

f. A test of short-term blood glucose control (14 to 20 days) obtained by measuring the glycosylation of total serum proteins or glycosylation of albumin.

g. Condition that results from altered counterregulation, particularly deficient glucagon and epinephrine responses to hypoglycemia. This results in a loss of autonomic nervous system symptoms; for instance, tachycardia, palpitations, and tremors are absent.

h. Situation in which a patient has fasting hyperglycemia that is not related to nocturnal hypoglycemia and rebound hyperglycemia.

i. A large clinical research study in Great Britain of patients with type 2 diabetes which concluded that tight glucose control (i.e., maintaining blood glucose levels close to normal ranges) results in decreased microvascular complications.

KEY TERM CROSSWORD

Complete the crossword puzzle below using key terms.

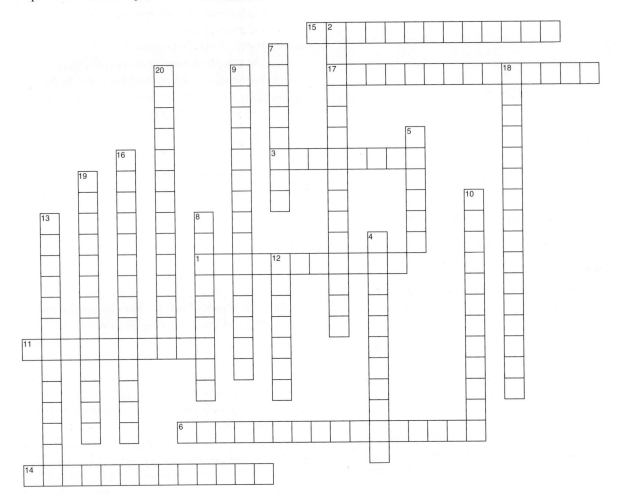

Across:

1. A condition of glucose intolerance ranging between normal glucose tolerance and overt diabetes.
3. A starch polysaccharide that is stored in the liver and muscles of humans and can be hydrolyzed to glucose.
6. Small amounts of protein (30 to 299 mg/24 hours) in the urine.
11. A biochemical pathway that results in the generation of high-energy compounds (e.g., ATP and NADH).
14. Pertaining to the large blood vessels of the arterial and venous system (e.g., coronary arteries).
15. A response to the use of exogenous insulin, which results in nocturnal hypoglycemia. This is often referred to as rebound hyperglycemia.
17. Nutritional components such as vitamins or minerals that are needed in small quantities by living organisms.

Down:

2. Excessive urination caused by the presence of certain substances (such as glucose) in the renal tubules.
4. Condition in which an excessive amount of ketones is produced during diabetic ketoacidosis (DKA); it is the cause of metabolic acidosis during DKA.
5. A compound that is structurally similar to another with some slight differences in composition.
7. A hormone produced by the alpha cells of the pancreas.
8. Breakdown of triglycerides to free fatty acids and glycerol.
9. The formation of glucose from noncarbohydrate organic molecules (i.e., lactate, glycerol, and amino acids); it is a function of the liver.
10. Decreased blood glucose levels.

12. A hormone produced by the beta cells of the pancreas that has multiple effects. Insulin is necessary for glucose transport into insulin-sensitive tissues and storage of carbohydrates, fats, and protein.
13. Normal blood glucose levels.
16. The conversion of glycogen to glucose.
18. A class of medications that enhances glucose dependent insulin secretion from the pancreatic β-cell resulting in a reduction in postprandial glucose levels.
19. Pertaining to the small blood vessels of the arterial and venous system.
20. Nutritional components such as protein, carbohydrates, and fat that are needed in large quantities by living organisms.

SHORT ANSWER QUESTIONS

28. Complications from diabetes can cause changes that result in what chronic conditions?

_____

_____

29. What factors play a part in the development of type 1 diabetes?

_____

_____

30. Describe the risk factors for development of type 2 diabetes.

_____

_____

_____

_____

31. What causes lower extremity amputations to occur in patients with diabetes?

_____

_____

_____

32. How does the use of insulin drips in hospital settings for non-DKA or non-HHS patients impact nursing care?

_____

_____

_____

_____

TRUE OR FALSE?

33. _____ T/F   Individuals with pre-diabetes are at increased risk for developing type 2 diabetes.

34. _____ T/F   Over 10% of adults in the United States over 20 years of age have diabetes.

35. _____ T/F   Plasma insulin levels increase and glucagon levels decrease as blood glucose levels rise during the fed state.

36. _____ T/F   Diabetes remains the leading cause of new cases of blindness among adults 20 to 74 years old.

37. _____ T/F   Type 2 diabetes appears to result from an interaction between genetics, environment, and autoimmunity.

38. _____ T/F   Obesity is strongly associated with the development of type 1 diabetes.

39. _____ T/F   *Tachycardia* (increased heart rate) occurs as a result of dehydration and volume depletion in the patient with diabetes.

40. _____ T/F   Self-monitoring of blood glucose involves measuring blood glucose levels several times each week using portable glucose meters.

41. _____ T/F   The increased risk of infections in patients with chronic hyperglycemia can result in infections, such as pyelonephritis, with decline in renal function.

42. _____ T/F   Supplemental therapy using herbs such as *Coccinia indica* and *vanadium* will increase insulin secretion in type 1 diabetes.

COMPLETE THE SENTENCE

43. Glucagon, cortisol, growth hormone, epinephrine, and norepinephrine are referred to as _____ because their actions oppose the effects of _____.

44. The abnormalities of fuel metabolism associated with diabetes result from a(n) _____ in insulin and a(n) _____ in glucagon and other counterregulatory hormones.

45. Clinical signs and symptoms of type 1 diabetes generally originate from _____ and _____; in type 2, clinical signs and symptoms originate from _____.

46. The _____ _____ _____ _____ system measures glucose levels in interstitial fluid every 10 seconds and provides an average blood glucose level every 5 minutes.

47. The development of _____ _____ is marked by abrupt changes in mental status, abnormal neurological signs, progression to coma, and brain herniation and death.

NCLEX-RN® REVIEW QUESTIONS

53-1. The nurse understands the current epidemic of diabetes involves:
   1. The United States only.
   2. A greater prevalence in females than males in the United States.
   3. A decline in incidence among Mexican Americans.
   4. A decrease in occurrence in children.

53-2. A 54-year-old patient who takes oral hypoglycemic medication to control blood sugar levels is hospitalized for pneumonia and is given insulin to regulate blood sugars. The nurse identifies that the patient has which type of diabetes?
   1. Type 1
   2. Type 2
   3. Latent autoimmune diabetes in adults
   4. Hyperosmolar hyperglycemic syndrome

53-3. A patient who developed gestational diabetes with the last two pregnancies expresses concern that she will become diabetic and need to take insulin. The nurse offers the following explanation:
1. "Your risk may be increased by 50%, so you can do things to maintain a healthy lifestyle."
2. "There is no association between gestational diabetes and type 1 diabetes."
3. "Unfortunately you probably will develop diabetes when you are older."
4. "You will most likely develop type 2 diabetes, but you may not need to take insulin."

53-4. The nurse instructs a patient with type 1 diabetes to include which measures to reduce the risk of developing diabetic nephropathy?
1. Restrict foods high in potassium.
2. Have an annual test for microalbuminuria.
3. Avoid drinking excessive amounts of water.
4. Eat a diet low in fat and fiber.

53-5. The nurse determines a patient is most likely in the second stage of developing type 2 diabetes when the following clinical manifestations are seen:
1. Fasting blood sugar is 130 mg/dL.
2. Postprandial blood sugar is 190 mg/dL.
3. Patient loses 4 pounds in one week.
4. Patient complains of frequent muscle cramps.

53-6. A patient has taken the prescribed dose of a meglitinide oral hypoglycemic agent before lunch and has only eaten 20% of the meal. The nurse should plan to assess the patient for:
1. A drop in blood pressure.
2. Bradycardia.
3. Irritability.
4. Hot, flushed skin.

53-7. A patient with type I diabetes with significant peripheral neuropathy asks the nurse which type of exercise would be best to engage in. The nurse suggests:
1. "Walking at a moderate pace would be good for circulation."
2. "Bicycling can provide an aerobic exercise that is safe for you."
3. "Short episodes of vigorous aerobic activity such as rowing would be good."
4. "Stationary activity such as weight lifting helps to improve muscle strength."

53-8. Sixty minutes after receiving a meglitinide drug, which was given prior to lunch, a patient with type 2 diabetes becomes shaky and complains of palpitations. The nurse determines the reaction is caused by the following:
1. The patient consumed the lunch too quickly.
2. The blood sugar is low secondary to the medication's effect.
3. The dose of the drug was probably insufficient to meet the patient's carbohydrate intake.
4. The medication should be given after meals, not before.

53-9. The nurse should assess the patient with diabetic ketoacidosis (DKA) being treated with large doses of regular insulin for which change in laboratory values?
1. Decrease in creatinine level
2. Decrease in potassium level
3. Increase in sodium level
4. Increase in phosphorus level

53-10. When teaching a patient about proper diabetic foot care the nurse includes the following:
1. "Soak your feet in warm sudsy water for 20 minutes daily."
2. "Walking barefoot around your house is good for strengthening the foot muscles."
3. "Apply lotion to dry feet, especially between the toes, every day."
4. "Trim the toenails straight across and file the edges smooth."

CHAPTER 54

NURSING ASSESSMENT OF PATIENTS WITH MUSCULOSKELETAL DISORDERS

OUTCOME-BASED LEARNING OBJECTIVES

54-1. Identify basic anatomy and physiology of the musculoskeletal system.

54-2. Analyze the process of obtaining a history on the musculoskeletal system.

54-3. Identify the general guidelines required for a musculoskeletal examination.

54-4. Identify the process of assessment of the following structures: temporomandibular joint, shoulders, elbows, wrists, hands, fingers, neck, spine, hips, knees, ankles, and feet, as well as assessment of gait.

54-5. Compare and contrast normal and abnormal findings associated with the temporomandibular joint, shoulders, elbows, wrists, hands, fingers, neck, spine, hips, knees, ankles, feet, and gait.

54-6. Compare and contrast the normal and abnormal range of motion for the temporomandibular joint, shoulders, elbows, wrists, hands, fingers, neck, spine, hips, knees, ankles, feet, and gait.

CHAPTER OUTLINE

I. Anatomy and Physiology of the Musculoskeletal System
   A. Bones
   B. Muscles
   C. Cartilage
   D. Ligaments
   E. Tendons
   F. Joints
II. History
   A. Biographical and Demographic History
      1. Cultural Considerations

B. Chief Complaint
C. Past Medical History
III. Physical Examination
  A. General Guidelines for Musculoskeletal Assessment
  B. Inspection
  C. Palpation
  D. Range of Motion
  E. Testing Muscle Strength
IV. Head-to-Toe Musculoskeletal Assessment
  A. Temporomandibular Joint
  B. Shoulders
  C. Elbows
  D. Wrists
  E. Hands and Fingers
  F. Neck and Spine
    1. Range of Motion of the Neck
    2. Range of Motion of the Spine
  G. Hip
    1. Range of Motion in the Hip
  H. Knees
    1. Range of Motion of the Knee
  I. Ankles and Feet
  J. Gait (Ambulation)
V. Gerontological Considerations
  A. Assessing the Elderly Patient
VI. Documentation
  A. Nursing Diagnoses
        HEALTH PROMOTION
VII. Summary

KEY TERMS MATCHING EXERCISE

Write the letter of the correct definition in the space next to each term.

Term

_____ 1. range of motion (ROM)
_____ 2. Bouchard's nodes
_____ 3. boutonniére deformity
_____ 4. carpal tunnel syndrome
_____ 5. interphalangeal joint
_____ 6. metacarpophalangeal joints
_____ 7. Dupuytren's contracture
_____ 8. ankylosing spondylitis
_____ 9. degenerative joint disease
_____ 10. pathologic fractures

Definition

a. Hard, painless nodules at the joints of the fingers; may indicate osteoarthritis (progressive loss of cartilage at a joint).

b. Movement of a joint within its normal range.

c. Difficulty or an inability to extend the ring or fifth finger.

d. Flexion of the proximal interphalangeal joint.

e. Progressive loss of cartilage at a joint.

f. Joints at the knuckles.

g. Compression of the median nerve in the carpal tunnel, just below the palm dorsally.

h. Fractures that occur without trauma due to bone thinning.

i. Joints between the fingers.

j. A type of arthritis that affects the spine and the sacroiliac joint.

KEY TERM CROSSWORD

Complete the crossword puzzle below using key terms.

Across:

1. Device required by a patient to assist with ambulation (e.g., cane, crutches, walker).
3. Front plane of the body.
5. Sac containing synovial fluid that cushions joints during movement.
6. Movement of a body part toward the midline (center) of the body.
7. Abnormal sounds (grating, snapping, crackling, rattling) emanating from a joint while in movement.
8. Small aggregation of cells formed in response to injury or inflammation.
9. Used for measuring a patient's range of motion.
11. Back plane of the body.
12. Present at birth or prenatally.

Down:

1. Movement of a body part away from the midline (center) of the body.
2. Displacement of a bone from its normal position in a joint.
4. Involuntary muscle movements of a body part or limb.
10. Hard, painless nodules at the joints of the fingers; may indicate osteoarthritis.
13. Walking
14. Shortening of a muscle attached to a joint.
15. An infection of the flexor tendon sheaths.
16. Involuntary contraction or twitching of a group of muscles or muscle fibers, visible under the skin.
17. Inflammation of the big toe, dorsum, ankles, heels, or elbows.
18. Unequal

COMPLETE THE SENTENCE

11. Bones in the human body can be classified into three types: (1) _____ bones, which have a tubular shaft and articular surfaces, or surfaces that form a joint, at each end; (2) _____ bones, which are thin with broad surfaces; and (3) _____ or _____ bones that vary in size and shape.

12. Biographical data obtained from the patient should include _____, _____, _____, and _____ _____.

13. During the physical examination, the nurse compares each joint for _____ and _____, and assesses the patient's ability to move the joint through its normal full _____ _____ _____.

14. The nurse assesses muscle strength by applying _____ and assigning a numerical grade from _____ to _____.

15. Part of the musculoskeletal assessment involves feeling the area for increased _____, observing for _____, and palpating for _____ around a joint.

16. While the patient performs range of motion tasks, the nurse palpates the joints for _____ and questions the patient regarding any associated _____.

17. To assess for carpal tunnel syndrome, the patient is asked to perform _____ _____, _____ _____, and _____ _____.

18. When assessing the knee, pain and abnormal or decreased ROM may indicate a(n) _____ injury or _____ tear to the anterior or posterior _____ _____ and the medial and lateral _____ ligaments.

19. During range of motion assessments a complaint of _____ is always an abnormal finding.

20. _____, _____, and skeletal _____ _____ tend to decrease as people age.

LABELING EXERCISE 1: LIGAMENTS OF THE KNEE JOINT

Place the term in the correct location.

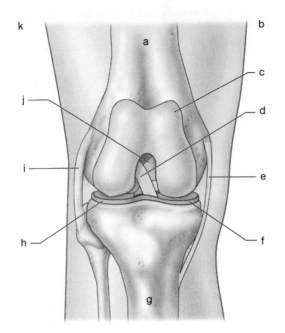

a. _____

b. _____

c. _____

d. _____

e. _____

f. _____

g. _____

h. _____

i. _____

j. _____

k. _____

Anterior cruciate ligament (ACL)
Articular cartilage
Femur
Inner side of the knee
Lateral collateral ligament (LCL)
Lateral meniscus

Medial collateral ligament (MCL)
Medial meniscus
Outer side of the knee
Posterior cruciate ligament (PCL)
Tibia

LABELING EXERCISE 2: KNEE JOINT

Place the term in the correct location.

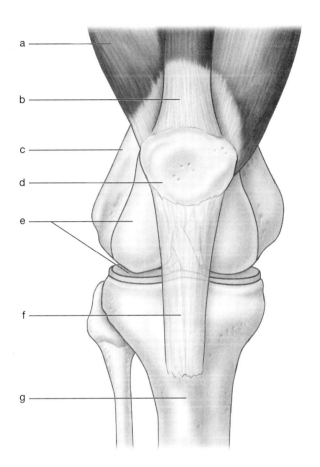

a. _____

b. _____

c. _____

d. _____

e. _____

f. _____

g. _____

Cartilage   Patellar ligament
Femur   Tendon
Quadricep muscle   Tibia
Patella

NCLEX-RN® REVIEW QUESTIONS

54-1. A patient is seen in the emergency department for a dislocated shoulder. The nurse realizes that the anatomy structure injured in this patient would be the:
   1. Tendon.
   2. Joint.
   3. Cartilage.
   4. Ligament.

54-2. While assessing a patient with neck and arm pain, the nurse learns that the patient works as a billing manager for a physician's office. The patient's occupation would be considered as which part of the patient's history?
   1. Demographic
   2. Biographic
   3. Social
   4. Chief complaint

54-3. The nurse documents that the patient's deltoid muscles are bilaterally graded as a 5. The musculoskeletal system area that this nurse has just assessed on this patient would be:
1. Range of motion.
2. Palpation.
3. Inspection.
4. Muscle strength.

54-4. During the assessment of a patient's musculoskeletal status the nurse checks for the bulge sign. The body area that the nurse is currently assessing would be the:
1. Knee.
2. Hip.
3. Ankle.
4. Elbow.

54-5. While observing a patient's gait, the nurse notes unequal leg length. This finding could be indicative of:
1. Muscle deformity.
2. Scoliosis.
3. Hip fracture.
4. Degenerative joint disease.

54-6. While assessing a patient's range of motion, the nurse conducts the Phalen's test. The nurse is assessing which area of the patient's musculoskeletal status?
1. Wrist
2. Hip
3. Elbow
4. Ankle

CHAPTER 55

CARING FOR THE PATIENT WITH MUSCULOSKELETAL DISORDERS

OUTCOME-BASED LEARNING OBJECTIVES

55-1. Compare and contrast the etiology, pathophysiology, clinical manifestations, and medical and nursing management for bone diseases.

55-2. Explain the rationale and type of preventive therapy necessary for patients with bone disease.

55-3. Describe the unique treatment and prevention needs of the gerontological population.

55-4. Compare and contrast the etiology, pathophysiology, clinical manifestations, and medical and nursing management for muscular diseases.

55-5. Differentiate between the five types of myopathies, various treatment modalities, and nursing care of a patient diagnosed with a myopathy.

55-6. Discuss the causative factors, treatment modalities, and nursing care related to a patient diagnosed with fibromyalgia.

EXPLORE

PEARSON

mynursingkit™

MyNursingKit is your one stop for online chapter review materials and resources. Prepare for success with additional NCLEX®-style practice questions, interactive assignments and activities, web links, animations and videos, and more!

Register your access code from the front of your book at **www.mynursingkit.com**

CHAPTER OUTLINE

I. Bone Physiology
   A. Characteristics
   B. Bone Tissue
      1. Bone Cells
      2. Bone Remodeling–Modeling Process
   C. Material Properties of Bone
   D. Bone Tissue and Hormones
II. Bone Disorders
   A. Osteoporosis
      1. Epidemiology
      2. Etiology and Pathophysiology

c. Medical Management
    i. Medications
    ii. Exercise
    iii. Diet
      (a) Nursing Implications Regarding Diet
    iv. Physical Therapy
    v. Occupational Therapy
    vi. Braces and Standing Walkers
d. Research
4. Myotonic Muscular Dystrophy
    a. Clinical Manifestations
    b. Laboratory and Diagnostic Procedures
    c. Medical Management
5. Research
6. Limb Girdle Muscular Dystrophy
7. Facioscapulohumeral Disease
8. Oculopharyngeal Muscular Dystrophy
    NURSING MANANGEMENT FOR THE PATIENT WITH MUSCULAR DYSTROPHY
    COLLABORATIVE MANAGEMENT
9. Gerontological Considerations
B. Myopathies
  1. Clinical Manifestations
  2. Medical Management
  3. Types of Myopathies
    a. Congenital Myopathy
    b. Hypokalemic Myopathy
      i. Clinical Manifestations
      ii. Medical Management
    c. Mitochondrial Myopathy
      i. Medical Management
    d. Steroid-Induced Myopathy
      i. Medical Management
  4. Inflammatory Myopathies
    a. Polymyositis
      i. Clinical Manifestations
      ii. Laboratory and Diagnostic Procedures
      iii. Medical Management
    b. Dermatomyositis
      i. Clinical Manifestations
      ii. Laboratory and Diagnostic Procedures
      iii. Medical Management
    c. Inclusion Body Myositis
      i. Clinical Manifestations
      ii. Medical Management
    NURSING MANAGEMENT
      ASSESSMENT
  5. Gerontological Considerations for Patients with a Myopathy
C. Rhabdomyolysis
  1. Clinical Manifestations and Diagnosis
  2. Complications
  3. Medical Management
    NURSING MANAGEMENT

KEY TERMS MATCHING EXERCISE 1

Write the letter of the correct definition in the space next to each term.

Term

_____ 1. endoskeletal

_____ 2. osteology

_____ 3. periosteum

_____ 4. cancellous (trabecular) bone

_____ 5. compact (cortical) bone

_____ 6. Haversian canals

_____ 7. lamellar bone

_____ 8. subchondral bone

_____ 9. modeling

_____ 10. osteoblasts

_____ 11. osteoclasts

_____ 12. osteocytes

Definition

a. Mature bone.

b. Bone with a hard outer casing and an interior that is porous, spongy, and meshwork-like in structure.

c. Pertaining to the cartilaginous and bony skeleton of the body.

d. The smooth tissue at the ends of bones that is covered with cartilage.

e. Fibrous membrane that covers bone.

f. Mature osteoblasts that maintain the bony matrix and participate in the dynamic task of releasing calcium into the bloodstream.

g. Any cells that form bone within the body.

h. Bone that is resistant to compression, is dense, and is laid down in concentric layers.

i. Canals located in cortical bone; they contain one or two capillaries and nerve fibers that serve as the transport system for nutrients.

    j. Large cells formed in bone marrow and originating from macrophage-like cells; designed to absorb and remove unwanted bone tissue, causing the bone to be "remodeled" or "destroyed."

    k. The process by which bone growth occurs and where there is a higher rate of bone formation relative to bone loss.

    l. The study of bones and the bone structure of the human body.

KEY TERMS MATCHING EXERCISE 2

Write the letter of the correct definition in the space next to each term.

Term

_____ 13. osteoid
_____ 14. osteoporosis
_____ 15. kyphosis
_____ 16. lordosis
_____ 17. scoliosis
_____ 18. electromyelogram (EMG)
_____ 19. hypotonia
_____ 20. dermatomyositis
_____ 21. Gottron's sign
_____ 22. perivascular
_____ 23. transcutaneous electrical nerve stimulation (TENS)

Definition

a. Progressive inflammatory muscle condition that occurs with inflammatory skin changes.

b. Low-voltage electrical stimulation through the skin; used to relieve pain.

c. Curvature of the spine that creates a stooped-over "humpback" appearance.

d. A skeletal disease that is characterized by low bone mass and deterioration of the bone tissue. This continued deterioration results in bone fragility and susceptibility to fractures.

e. Reddish raised rash or papules over the knuckles.

f. Lateral curvature of the spine.

g. Situated around a blood vessel.

h. Excessive inward curvature of the spine.

i. The absence of muscle tone, resulting in flaccidity of the muscles.

j. A graphic recording that tests the contraction of muscles that have been electrically stimulated.

k. Type I collagen and noncollagenous protein osteocalcin.

SHORT ANSWER QUESTIONS

24. What glands secret hormones that impact bone tissue?

_____

_____

25. What can influence the amount of bone mineral density lost through aging?

_____

_____

26. Why does bone loss occur after menopause?

_____

_____

27. Describe the two kinds of osteomyelitis.

_____

_____

_____

_____

28. What are the clinical manifestations of osteitis deformans, or Paget's disease?

_____

_____

29. What should be the primary focus of nursing care for the patient with bone cancer?

_____

_____

30. What complications can occur with Duchenne or Becker muscular dystrophy?

_____

_____

_____

_____

31. What are the patient teaching and discharge priorities for muscular dystrophy?

_____

_____

_____

_____

32. What can cause rhabdomyolysis?

_____

_____

_____

_____

33. What are idiopathic muscle cramps and what causes them?

_____

_____

_____

_____

TRUE OR FALSE?

34. _____ T/F   Aging causes the periosteum to become thinner, decreasing vascularity.

35. _____ T/F   Cancellous or trabecular bone provides about 80% of the skeletal mass.

36. _____ T/F   Caucasians have the least bone mass, and African Americans have the most.

37. _____ T/F   Testing for osteoporosis, especially in females, should start at age 50 and men at age 70 and older, and be repeated every 2 years.

38. _____ T/F   Adults over the age of 30 years and children ages 15 years or younger are at a higher risk for developing bone tumors.

39. _____ T/F   Osteosarcoma has a greater incidence in females than males and the tumor most often develops in the extremeties.

40. _____ T/F   Genetics play the key role in whether a child develops muscular dystrophy (MD).

41. _____ T/F   A child with Duchenne muscular dystrophy usually outgrows it by the teens or early 20s.

42. _____ T/F   Weakness of limbs is the main sign of generalized myopathy.

43. _____ T/F   Patients with Eaton-Lambert syndrome complain of muscle fatigue primarily in the leg and trunk muscles.

LABELING EXERCISE 1: BONE TISSUES

Place the term in the correct location.

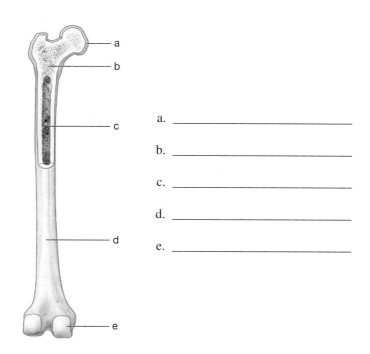

a. _____

b. _____

c. _____

d. _____

e. _____

Cancellous tissue
Compact tissue
Marrow
Subchondral tissue
Subchondral tissue

LABELING EXERCISE 2: CORTICAL AND CANCELLOUS BONE

Place the term in the correct location.

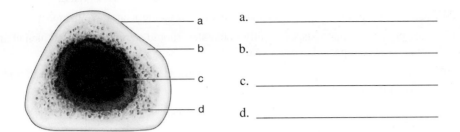

a. _____

b. _____

c. _____

d. _____

Compact bone (cortical)
Marrow
Periosteum
Spongy bone (cancellous)

LABELING EXERCISE 3: COMPACT AND CANCELLOUS BONE WITH HAVERSIAN CANAL

Place the term in the correct location.

a. _____

b. _____

c. _____

d. _____

e. _____

f. _____

g. _____

h. _____

i. _____

**Compact bone & spongy
(cancellous bone)**

Canaliculi
Haversian canal
Lacunae containing osteocytes
Lamellae
Osteon

Osteon of compact bone
Periosteum
Trabeculae of spongy bone
Volkmann's canal

NCLEX-RN® REVIEW QUESTIONS

55-1. Endocrine glands that produce hormones which influence bone growth include the:
Select all that apply.
1. Pituitary gland.
2. Parathyroid gland.
3. Thyroid gland.
4. Adrenal glands.
5. Thymus gland.
6. Parotid gland.

55-2. Choose the correct statement regarding preventive care for osteoporosis.
1. Testing for osteoporosis in females should start at age 50.
2. Men require serum testing rather than assessing bone density.
3. Medicare will not reimburse for preventive care for osteoporosis.
4. Bone mineral density tests are recommended to be done annually.

55-3. Regarding hip fracture statistics among older adults, which statement is accurate?
1. Hip fracture incidence is equal between males and females.
2. 20% of older people who sustain a hip fracture die within a year.
3. Two years following a hip fracture, most people will return to full mobility.
4. The risk for hip fracture declines after the age of 80.

55-4. Exaggerated curvature of the spine is prevalent in young adults with Duchenne muscular dystrophy. Which term describes a lateral curvature of the spine?
1. Lordosis
2. Kyphosis
3. Dystropsis
4. Scoliosis

55-5. The nurse recognizes which of the following as a priority goal when working with an older person who has a myopathy?
1. Fatigue
2. Economic status
3. Safety
4. Emotional welfare

55-6. In addition to pain reduction, patients using the drug pregabalin (Lyrica) also have improvement with:
1. Mood.
2. Appetite.
3. Sleep.
4. Energy.

CHAPTER 56

CARING FOR THE PATIENT WITH MUSCULOSKELETAL TRAUMA

OUTCOME-BASED LEARNING OBJECTIVES

56-1. Describe the incidence, prevalence, and prevention strategies for musculoskeletal trauma.

56-2. Explain the pathophysiological stages of bone healing.

56-3. Compare and contrast the various types of fractures and methods for fracture treatment.

56-4. Apply nursing diagnoses and the nursing process to the care of the patient with musculoskeletal trauma.

56-5. Discuss potential complications related to musculoskeletal trauma.

56-6. Identify research implications for nursing practice in caring for the musculoskeletally injured patient.

CHAPTER OUTLINE

I. Etiology
>   HEALTH PROMOTION
II. Pathophysiology
  A. Contusions
  B. Sprains and Strains
    1. Medical Management
>   NURSING MANAGEMENT
>   ASSESSMENT
>   NURSING DIAGNOSES
>   OUTCOMES AND EVALUATION PARAMETERS
>   PLANNING, INTERVENTIONS, AND RATIONALES
>   HEALTH PROMOTION
  C. Dislocations
    1. Etiology
    2. Clinical Manifestations

KEY TERMS MATCHING EXERCISE 1

Write the letter of the correct definition in the space next to each term.

Term

_____ 1. avulsion fracture

_____ 2. contusion

_____ 3. ligament

_____ 4. physes

_____ 5. PRICE

_____ 6. sprain

_____ 7. strain

_____ 8. avascular necrosis (AVN)

_____ 9. dislocation

_____ 10. diaphysis

_____ 11. epiphysis

_____ 12. fractures

Definition

a. Shaft of a long bone, between both metaphysis.

b. Condition in which bone tissue dies due to a temporary or permanent loss of blood supply to the bone.

c. A strong fibrous band of connective tissue.

d. An injury to the muscle belly or its tendon attachment to bone.

e. Growth plates.

f. Fracture that occurs when a ligament is pulled away from its attachment point at the bone and takes a small piece of the bone with it.

g. The end of the bone beyond the physis.

h. Acronym for *protection* (immobilize and prevent weight bearing), *rest*, *ice*, *compression*, and *elevation*.

i. Displacement of a bone from its normal position in a joint.

j. Discontinuities in bone that may be complete or incomplete.

k. An injury to a ligament.

l. An injury to soft tissue caused by trauma; a bruise.

KEY TERMS MATCHING EXERCISE 2

Write the letter of the correct definition in the space next to each term.

Term

_____ 13. metaphysis

_____ 14. Buck's boots traction

_____ 15. burst fracture

_____ 16. cast

_____ 17. chance fracture

_____ 18. skin traction

_____ 19. external fixation

_____ 20. skeletal traction

_____ 21. intramedullary (I-M) rodding

_____ 22. open reduction internal fixation (ORIF)

_____ 23. compartment syndrome

_____ 24. fasciotomy

Definition

a. Fracture that occurs when an axial load is placed on the spine and vertebrae.

b. An area of widening between the diaphysis and physis.

c. A method of fracture fixation that entails sliding a metal rod down the medullary canal of a long bone.

d. Incisions made to release skin and muscle coverings.

e. Treatment that entails placement of a skeletal pin through the bone, which is then attached to a weighted cord to maintain proper alignment of the fractured bone.

f. A foam boot used for traction.

g. A fracture through the body and posterior elements of the vertebrae of the spine; caused by forward flexion, causing a distraction injury.

h. A rigid circumferential encasement device made of plaster or fiberglass.

i. An acute problem following injury or surgery caused when pressure within the muscles builds to dangerous levels. The resulting increased pressure within the fascial compartment impairs blood supply.

j. A treatment in which the bones or bone ends of a fracture are held in place by skeletal pins. The pins are screwed into the bone and attached to a frame worn on the outside of the body.

k. A treatment in which a fracture is exposed by an incision in the skin directly over the fracture. Implants such as plates (strips of metal), screws, and wires are placed directly on or in the bone to anatomically stabilize a fracture.

l. Treatment that uses straps or foam boots secured to the lower extremity attached to a weighted cord that is pulling no more than 6 pounds to maintain proper alignment of the fractured bone.

COMPLETE THE SENTENCE

25. _____ are similar in nature to _____, but they occur at the ligaments (strong fibrous bands of connective tissue) that attach bone to bone.

26. Classification of fractures by direction of fracture include _____, _____, _____, _____, _____, _____, and _____.

27. Initial assessment of an extremity fracture includes observation for _____, _____ in the skin, and a thorough assessment of _____ and sensory status distal to the extremity.

28. Organs that can be injured during a trauma with pelvic fracture are the _____ and _____, _____, _____, and _____ system.

29. The most important factors that direct management of pelvic injury are the patient's _____ status and stability of the _____ _____.

30. Patients with musculoskeletal trauma may have _____ issues and need to use _____ _____.

31. Patients who sustain multiple trauma have increased _____ needs to heal tissue injuries.

32. The "five Ps" of compartment syndrome are _____ out of proportion to the injury or with passive stretch of the muscle within that compartment, _____, _____ _____ refill, _____, and _____ in the affected extremity.

33. The compression that occurs with cast syndrome or superior mesenteric artery syndrome impedes the blood flow to the _____, causing _____ and eventually _____ of the gastrointestinal tract and vessel walls that can result in hemorrhage and death.

34. _____ and _____ fractures are the most common types of fractures in elderly patients.

LABELING EXERCISE 1: ANKLE LIGAMENTS AND INVERSION INJURY

Place the term in the correct location.

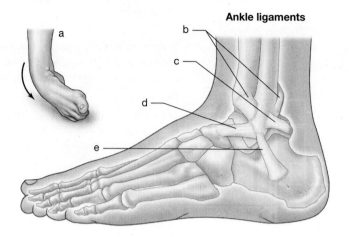

Ankle ligaments

a. _____

b. _____

c. _____

d. _____

e. _____

Anterior talofibular ligament
Calcaneofibular ligament
Inversion injury
Posterior talofibular ligament
Tibiofibular ligaments

LABELING EXERCISE 2: LONG BONE

Place the term in the correct location.

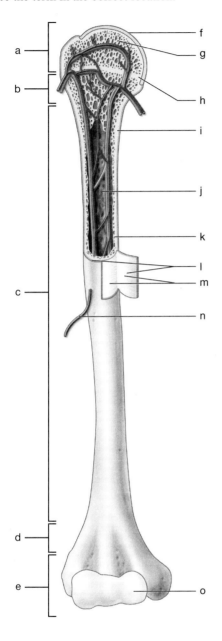

a. _____

b. _____

c. _____

d. _____

e. _____

f. _____

g. _____

h. _____

i. _____

j. _____

k. _____

l. _____

m. _____

n. _____

o. _____

Articular cartilage
Articular cartilage
Compact bone
Diaphysis
Distal epiphysis
Endosteum
Epiphyseal line
Medullary cavity (contains yellow bone marrow in adult)

Metaphysis
Metaphysis
Nutrient artery through nutrient foramen
Perforating fibers
Periosteum
Proximal epiphysis
Spongy bone (contains red bone marrow)

LABELING EXERCISE 3: VASCULAR ANATOMY OF THE PELVIS

Place the term in the correct location.

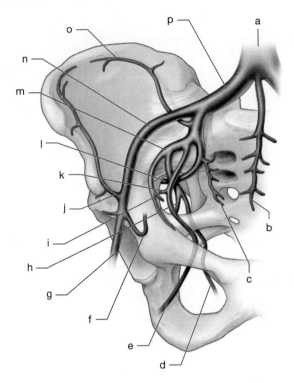

a. _____

b. _____

c. _____

d. _____

e. _____

f. _____

g. _____

h. _____

i. _____

j. _____

k. _____

l. _____

m. _____

n. _____

o. _____

p. _____

Aorta
Common femoral artery
Common iliac artery
Deep iliac circumflex artery
External iliac artery
Iliolumbar artery
Inferior epigastric artery
Inferior gluteal artery

Internal iliac artery
Lateral sacral artery
Middle sacral artery
Obturator artery
Pudendal artery
Sciatic artery
Superior gluteal artery
Vesicular arteries

LABELING EXERCISE 4: LIGAMENTS OF THE PELVIS

Place the term in the correct location.

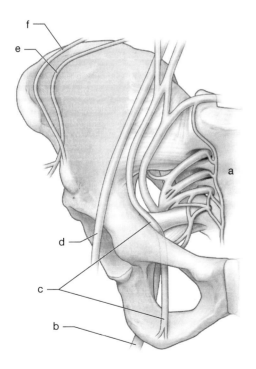

a. _____

b. _____

c. _____

d. _____

Iliolumbar ligament
Sacroiliac ligament
Sacrospinous ligament
Sacrotuberous ligament

LABELING EXERCISE 5: NEUROANATOMY OF THE PELVIS

Place the term in the correct location.

a. _____

b. _____

c. _____

d. _____

e. _____

f. _____

Femoral nerve
Ilioinguinal nerve
Lateral femoral cutaneous nerve
Lumbosacral plexus
Obturator nerve
Sciatic nerve

NCLEX-RN® REVIEW QUESTIONS

56-1. The nurse is planning an educational offering with a local parent-teacher group. Which of the following would be an appropriate topic to include regarding musculoskeletal injuries?
1. Reasons to complete homework at a reasonable hour
2. Need to get adequate sleep
3. Good nutrition
4. Alcohol consumption and motor vehicle accidents

56-2. A patient with a fractured leg asks the nurse how long it will be before he is able to resume his normal activities. Which of the following should the nurse respond to this patient?
1. 2 to 4 weeks
2. 4 to 8 weeks
3. Within 3 months
4. Within 6 months

56-3. A patient is diagnosed with a comminuted fracture of his right tibia. The nurse realizes that this fracture is being classified according to:
1. Appearance.
2. Apposition.
3. Angulation.
4. Mechanism of injury.

56-4. The nurse is providing care to a patient with a long leg cast. Which of the following findings would indicate compromised circulation?
1. Swelling of the toes
2. Drainage on the cast
3. Increased temperature
4. Foul odor

56-5. A patient recovering from a fractured ulna is complaining of pain out of proportion to the injury. Which of the following does this indicate to the nurse?
1. Dependency on narcotics
2. Fear
3. Anxiety
4. Compartment syndrome

56-6. A patient recovering from a traumatic amputation is demonstrating signs of post-traumatic stress disorder. The nurse realizes this disorder is most likely associated with:
1. Substance abuse.
2. Unemployment.
3. An individual's age at the time of injury.
4. Wishful thinking as a coping mechanism.

CHAPTER 57

CARING FOR THE PATIENT DURING MUSCULOSKELETAL SURGICAL PROCEDURES

OUTCOME-BASED LEARNING OBJECTIVES

57-1. List components of the neurovascular assessment appropriate for a patient who has had orthopedic surgery.

57-2. Discuss the types of precautions required to prevent hip dislocation in the postoperative hip replacement patient.

57-3. Describe the nursing actions appropriate for a patient with symptoms of complications, including compartment syndrome.

57-4. Describe the appropriate use of assistive devices utilized for orthopedic patients.

57-5. Discuss the importance of optimal pain control in the postoperative orthopedic patient.

EXPLORE

PEARSON

mynursingkit™

MyNursingKit is your one stop for online chapter review materials and resources. Prepare for success with additional NCLEX®-style practice questions, interactive assignments and activities, web links, animations and videos, and more!

Register your access code from the front of your book at **www.mynursingkit.com**

CHAPTER OUTLINE

   I. Preoperative Assessment of the Orthopedic Surgical Patient
      A. Clinical Manifestations
      B. Past Medical History
      C. Medications
      D. Allergies
      E. Prior Surgeries and Hospitalizations
      F. Cardiovascular Disease
      G. Pulmonary Disease
      H. Diabetes
      I. Functional Status
      J. Genetic Factors
      K. Occupational History
      L. Culture
  II. Anesthetic

III. Surgical Procedures
    A. Upper Extremity Surgery
        1. Rotator Cuff Repair
        2. Shoulder Arthroplasty
        3. Shoulder Subluxation and Dislocation Repair
        4. Elbow Repair
            a. Elbow Dislocation
        5. Carpal Tunnel Repair
        6. Wrist Arthroplasty
        7. Postoperative Assessment
    B. Total Hip Arthroplasty
        1. Postoperative Assessment
    C. Pelvic Surgery
    D. Knee Surgery
        1. Anterior Cruciate Ligament (ACL) Repair
        2. Knee Arthroplasty
        3. Meniscus Repair
        4. Postoperative Assessment
    E. Amputation
        1. Postoperative Assessment
    F. Spinal Surgery
        1. Postoperative Assessment
    G. Ankle and Foot Surgeries
        1. Tendon Injuries
        2. Ankle Arthroscopy
        3. Ankle Reconstruction
        4. Ankle Arthroplasty
        5. Postoperative Assessment
        6. Surgical Management for the Foot
               NURSING MANAGEMENT
    H. Neurovascular Assessment
    I. Pain Management
    J. Appearance of Surgical Site and Dressing
    K. Surgical Tubes and Drains
    L. Therapeutic Modalities
    M. Exercise
    N. Discharge Planning
        1. Environment
IV. Complications
    A. Respiratory Insufficiency
    B. Venous Thromboembolism
    C. Compartment Syndrome
    D. Pressure Ulcers
    E. Infection
    F. Joint Dislocation
    G. Heterotrophic Ossification
    H. Osteonecrosis or Avascular Necrosis
            COLLABORATIVE MANAGEMENT
               HEALTH PROMOTION
V. Research

KEY TERMS MATCHING EXERCISE

Write the letter of the correct definition in the space next to each term.

Term

_____ 1. arthroplasty

_____ 2. total joint replacement

_____ 3. osteolysis

_____ 4. amputation

_____ 5. discectomy

_____ 6. laminectomy

_____ 7. arthrodesis

_____ 8. continuous passive motion device

_____ 9. fat embolus

_____ 10. compartment syndrome

_____ 11. heterotrophic ossification (OS)

_____ 12. osteonecrosis

Definition

a. Surgical fusion of bone.

b. An acute problem following injury or surgery caused when pressure within the muscles builds to dangerous levels. The resulting increased pressure within the fascial compartment impairs blood supply.

c. Surgery to remove a diseased disk.

d. The death of bone tissue.

e. A diseased or injured joint that is surgically removed and replaced with an orthosis.

f. Restoration of a joint either by total joint replacement surgery or by resurfacing bone and removing damaged bone and cartilage.

g. Surgical removal of an anatomic part.

h. Machine into which an extremity is placed to perform continuous passive range of motion.

i. Destruction of implanted synthetic or cement components of repaired bone segments.

j. The development of bone tissue in areas where bone tissue is not normally present.

k. The removal of a vertebral posterior arch intended to remove a lesion or herniated disk.

l. Fat that enters the circulatory system after the fracture of a long bone.

SHORT ANSWER QUESTIONS

13. What are the clinical manifestations of rotator cuff injury?

_____

_____

_____

_____

_____

14. What causes carpal tunnel syndrome?

_____

_____

_____

_____

15. What discharge planning and patient education should be done for patients who have undergone total hip arthroplasty?

_____

_____

_____

_____

16. What can cause tears in the anterior cruciate ligament (ACL)?

_____

_____

17. What causes bunions to form and why are they more predominant in women?

_____

_____

_____

_____

18. What prevention education can nurses do to prevent elders from having musculoskeletal injuries and the consequent surgery?

_____

_____

_____

_____

COMPLETE THE SENTENCE

19. _____, _____ _____ _____, and _____are the three major complaints associated with musculoskeletal conditions that cause the patient to seek surgical care.

20. The most common surgical procedure used to treat arthritis of the acromioclavicular joint is a(n) _____ _____.

21. To immobilize and retain alignment, upper and lower extremity surgeries frequently utilize _____, _____ _____, _____, and _____ postoperatively.

22. Simple fractures of the pelvis that are not displaced are considered to be _____ _____ and do not require fixation.

23. About one quarter of people with back pain have a(n) _____ _____, and the most common site of back pain is in the _____ _____.

LABELING EXERCISE 1: SHOULDER ANATOMY

Place the term in the correct location.

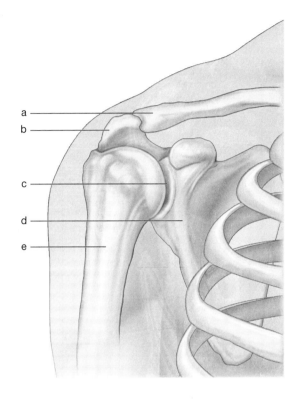

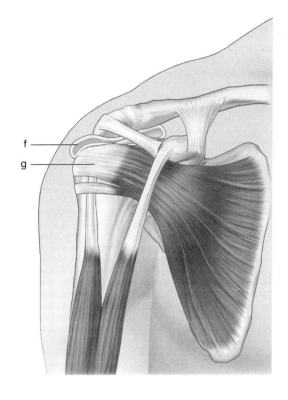

Drawing A

a. _____

b. _____

c. _____

d. _____

e. _____

Drawing B

f. _____

g. _____

Acromion
Bursa
Clavicle
Humerus
Rotator cuff
Scapula
Socket

LABELING EXERCISE 2: KNEE ANATOMY

Place the term in the correct location.

a. _____

b. _____

c. _____

d. _____

e. _____

f. _____

g. _____

h. _____

i. _____

Anterior cruciate ligament (ACL)
Articular cartilage
Femur
Lateral collateral ligament (LCL)
Lateral meniscus
Medial collateral ligament (MCL)
Medial meniscus
Posterior cruciate ligament (PCL)
Tibia

NCLEX-RN® REVIEW QUESTIONS

57-1. Which of the following statements indicates that a nurse is not certain about the techniques to assess the musculoskeletal neurovascular status?
1. "Obtaining vital signs with the neurovascular assessment is a good idea."
2. "Checking for parathesia or paralysis of the extremity is necessary."
3. "Perform the assessment on the affected extremity only to avoid unnecessary pain."
4. "The nurse reviews motor, sensory, and circulation function during the assessment."

57-2. Following a hip replacement procedure, which statement made by a patient regarding postoperative precautions requires clarification?
1. "I'm looking forward to riding home in my new little sports car."
2. "Sitting on my beanbag chair isn't possible for a while."
3. "Someone else will have to help me tie my athletic shoes."
4. "Getting an elevated toilet seat from the medical supply store is required."

57-3. A patient is wearing a long leg cast and tells the nurse, "The pain behind my knee is killing me. It's at an eleven on the pain scale of zero to ten." What action should the nurse take?

1. Elevate the leg on several pillows to promote circulation.
2. Give the patient the strongest analgesic currently ordered.
3. Contact the orthopedic surgeon with this information.
4. Ask the patient if the extremity feels cool under the cast.

57-4. The nurse on an orthopedic unit is consulting with a discharge planner. They are determining what type of assistive devices a patient will need following a total hip replacement. Which of the following would be advisable for most patients? Select all that apply.

1. A comfortable recliner
2. Raised toilet seat
3. Shower bench
4. Sock aid and long-handled shoe horn
5. Wheelchair

57-5. When performing a pain assessment on a postoperative patient who underwent total knee replacement, the expected description of the pain would be which of the following?

1. Dull
2. Radiating to the toes
3. Sharp
4. Burning

CHAPTER 58

CARING FOR THE PATIENT WITH ARTHRITIS AND CONNECTIVE TISSUE DISORDERS

OUTCOME-BASED LEARNING OBJECTIVES

58-1. Differentiate autoimmune disease from connective tissue disease.

58-2. Utilize the nursing process when planning care for each autoimmune disease.

58-3. Compare and contrast the etiology, pathophysiology, clinical manifestations, nursing management, and prevention of the various types of arthritis.

58-4. Identify the four highest priority nursing diagnoses for rheumatoid arthritis and osteoarthritis.

58-5. Describe nursing management for patients experiencing gout.

58-6. Compare and contrast the clinical manifestations and nursing management of each of the following connective tissue diseases: (a) myositis, (b) polymyositis, and (c) dermatomyositis.

EXPLORE  PEARSON

MyNursingKit is your one stop for online chapter review materials and resources. Prepare for success with additional NCLEX®-style practice questions, interactive assignments and activities, web links, animations and videos, and more!

Register your access code from the front of your book at **www.mynursingkit.com**

CHAPTER OUTLINE

KEY TERMS MATCHING EXERCISE 1

Write the letter of the correct definition in the space next to each term.

Term

_____ 1. osteoarthritis (OA)

_____ 2. subcutaneous nodules

_____ 3. rheumatoid arthritis (RA)

_____ 4. dactylitis

_____ 5. enthesitis

_____ 6. psoriatic arthritis

_____ 7. gouty arthritis

_____ 8. tophi

Definition

a. Chronic condition that accompanies aging, affecting the weight-bearing joints most commonly; is the most common form of arthritis.

b. Chronic inflammatory process that affects the peripheral joints and surrounding muscles, ligaments, tendons, and blood vessels.

c. Accumulation of uric acid crystals in the cartilage of the earlobe.

d. An inflammatory process associated with psoriasis.

e. A uniform swelling of the soft tissues between the metacarpophalangeal and interphalangeal joints.

f. Condition in which there is an imbalance in purine metabolism, which increases uric acid in the joints by the formation of uric acid crystals.

g. Upon palpitation, discomfort at the site of the attachment of bone to the tendon.

h. Small, nontender swellings found over bony prominences on the hands and feet.

KEY TERMS MATCHING EXERCISE 2

Write the letter of the correct definition in the space next to each term.

Term

_____ 9. circinate balanitis

_____ 10. reactive arthritis

_____ 11. ankylosing spondylitis

_____ 12. septic arthritis

_____ 13. systemic lupus erythematosus (SLE)

_____ 14. Lyme disease

_____ 15. Sjögren's syndrome

_____ 16. myositis

Definition

a. A type of arthritis caused by a reaction to an infection somewhere else in the body. Also called *Reiter's syndrome* or *undifferentiated spondyloarthropathy*.

b. A bacterial infection that affects the organs and joints; transmitted by black-legged ticks.

c. An uncommon disease in which the immune system inflames the body's own healthy muscle tissue.

d. Inflammation surrounding the circular muscle around the penis.

e. The most destructive form of acute arthritis; can result from trauma, direct inoculation of bacteria during joint surgery, spread of infection from another part of the body (hematogenous), or when an infection from an adjacent bone extends through the cortex into the joint space. Also called *nongonococcal bacterial arthritis*.

f. An autoimmune disease in which the immune system attacks and destroys the glands that produce tears and saliva.

g. An example of a systemic type III hypersensitivity autoimmune disease characterized by damage to joints and soft organs as a result of the effects of autoantibodies and antibody–antigen activity (immune complex responses).

h. A type of arthritis that affects the spine and the sacroiliac joint.

SHORT ANSWER QUESTIONS

17. What causes osteoarthritis?

_____

_____

_____

_____

18. What are the desired nursing outcomes for patients with rheumatoid arthritis?

_____

_____

19. What causes reactive arthritis?

_____

_____

_____

_____

20. In addition to medication, what is important in treating ankylosing spondylitis?

_____

_____

21. Who is most at risk for septic arthritis?

_____

_____

TRUE OR FALSE?

22. _____   T/F   Initially, the best treatment for osteoarthritis in weight-bearing joints is rest.

23. _____   T/F   Rheumatoid arthritis can be cured through use of corticosteroids.

24. _____   T/F   Methotrexate has been the drug of choice for psoriatic arthritis.

25. _____   T/F   Gouty arthritis is caused by an accumulation of uric acid crystals in the joints.

26. _____   T/F   Patients with septic arthritis present with multiple swollen and painful joints.

27. _____   T/F   A diagnostic test commonly used for systemic lupus erythematosus is for anticitrulline antibody.

28. _____   T/F   Diffuse scleroderma is a severe and progressive disease with early onset of organ involvement including the gastrointestinal tract, heart, lungs, and kidneys.

29. _____   T/F   Early symptoms of Lyme disease include fatigue, malaise, lethargy, headache, stiff neck, myalgias, arthralgias, and regional or generalized lymphadenopathy.

30. _____   T/F   The most common symptoms of Sjögren's syndrome are dry eyes and dry mouth.

31. _____   T/F   Myositis may be triggered by a tick bite, injury, infection, or an autoimmune disease.

COMPLETE THE SENTENCE

32. Tests to detect the presence of osteoarthritis include three different radiologic techniques: _____ _____ of the affected joint, _____ _____, and _____ _____ _____.

33. Rheumatoid arthritis is thought to be a(n) _____ disorder that not only involves tissue hypersensitivity but also has a(n) _____ component.

34. Environmental factors that have been associated with the development of psoriasis and psoriatic arthritis include both _____ and _____ infections, and _____.

35. Any patient with _____ who also complains of joint discomfort should be evaluated for psoriatic arthritis.

36. Reducing the consumption of alcohol and meat is one way to control _____ _____.

37. In addition to medication, treatment for the patient with reactive arthritis includes _____ _____ to promote range of motion in the affected joints and specific range-of-motion exercises to reduce _____ and promote _____.

38. For a person genetically susceptible to _____ _____ _____, predisposing factors can be physical or mental stress, exposure to sunlight or ultraviolet light, viral or streptococcal infections, pregnancy, and abnormal estrogen metabolism.

39. Medical management of scleroderma focuses on _____ control and improving the patient's _____ _____ _____.

40. In the United States, _____ _____ is heavily concentrated in the areas of the Northeast, Southeast, and West Coast.

41. A laboratory test that can assist with the diagnosis of myositis is the _____ _____.

NCLEX-RN® REVIEW QUESTIONS

58-1. A patient tells the nurse she has "a common connective tissue disease." The nurse realizes this patient is most likely describing:
1. Arthritis.
2. Gout.
3. Rheumatoid arthritis.
4. Psoriatic arthritis.

58-2. Which of the following should the nurse include in the plan of care for a patient with ankylosing spondylitis?
1. Limit activity.
2. Reduce the use of extremities as necessary.
3. Encourage independence with physical and occupation therapy.
4. Provide care according to symptom exacerbation.

58-3. An 85-year-old patient is admitted with an upper respiratory infection and a swollen left knee. The nurse realizes this patient could be experiencing:
1. Reactive arthritis.
2. Gout.
3. Osteoarthritis.
4. Septic arthritis.

58-4. The nurse has completed the assessment of a patient with rheumatoid arthritis. Which of the following nursing diagnoses would be applicable to this patient?
   1. *Activity Intolerance* related to fatigue
   2. *Knowledge, Deficient*
   3. *Fluid Volume, Excess*
   4. *Nutrition, Imbalanced: More than Body Requirements*

58-5. The nurse is planning care for a patient with gout. Which of the following should be included to assist with pain management?
   1. Monitor complete blood count.
   2. Apply ice as tolerated.
   3. Apply heat as tolerated.
   4. Massage the affected limb.

58-6. A 13-year-old female patient is diagnosed with juvenile myositis. The nurse realizes this disease process is most likely:
   1. Osteoarthritis.
   2. A combination of other types of myositis.
   3. Rheumatoid arthritis.
   4. Lupus erythematosus.

CHAPTER 59

NURSING ASSESSMENT OF PATIENTS WITH IMMUNOLOGIC AND INFLAMMATORY DISORDERS

OUTCOME-BASED LEARNING OBJECTIVES

59-1. Describe the function of the organs, tissues, and cellular components of the immune system.

59-2. Compare and contrast the significance of self antigens versus non-self antigens and immune tolerance.

59-3. Compare and contrast cell-mediated and humoral immunity in relationship to the type of lymphocytes involved, response to antigens, and role in immune protection.

59-4. Compare and contrast the actions of cytokines, lymphokines, interleukins, interferons, complement, and tumor necrosis factor on immune function.

59-5. Explain the action and significance of acquired immune response through immunizations.

59-6. Explain the action and significance of antigen presentation in B-cell activation, stimulation of immunoglobulin production, and secondary immune response.

59-7. Discuss the effects of aging on the immune system.

59-8. Apply the assessment skills of inspection, palpation, percussion, and auscultation in evaluating body systems and determining the status of immune function.

CHAPTER OUTLINE

  I. Anatomy of the Immune System
    A. Bone Marrow
      1. Granulocytes
        a. Neutrophils
        b. Basophils
        c. Eosinophils

2. Nongranulocytes
    a. Monocytes
    b. Lymphocytes
  B. Lymphatic System
    1. Tonsils and Adenoids
    2. Spleen
II. Physiology of the Immune System
  A. Natural Immunity
    1. Physical and Chemical Barriers
      a. Skin
      b. Mucous Membranes
      c. Gastric pH
      d. Toll Receptors
    2. Self Versus Non-Self
    3. Immune Tolerance
    4. Inflammatory Response
  B. Acquired Immunity
    1. Cellular Immune Response
      a. T Lymphocytes
        i. T-Helper Cells
        ii. Suppressor T Cells
        iii. Natural Killer Cells
      b. Cytokines and Lymphokines
        i. Interleukins
        ii. Interferons
        iii. Tumor Necrosis Factor
        iv. Tissue Factor
    2. Complement Proteins and Function
    3. Humoral Immune Response
      a. B Lymphocytes
      b. Antibodies and Plasma Cells
      c. Antibody Functions
      d. Antigen Presentation and Recognition
      e. Memory B Cells
  C. Immunizations
    1. National Guidelines for Immunization
  D. Effects of Age on the Immune System
    1. Gerontological Considerations
  E. Genetic Implications
III. Assessment of the Immune System
  A. Patient History
    1. Pain
    2. Past Medical History
    3. Medication History
    4. Family History
    5. Social History
  B. Physical Assessment
    1. Inspection
    2. Palpation
    3. Percussion
    4. Auscultation
    5. Integumentary Assessment
    6. Neurological Assessment
    7. Cardiovascular Assessment
    8. Respiratory and Chest Assessment

9. Gastrointestinal Assessment
10. Genitourinary System
11. Musculoskeletal Assessment
12. Common Laboratory and Diagnostic Exams of the Immune System
    a. Laboratory Tests
    b. Immune Function Tests
    c. Computerized Axial Tomography
          HEALTH PROMOTION
C. Summary

KEY TERMS MATCHING EXERCISE 1

Write the letter of the correct definition in the space next to each term.

Term

_____ 1. immune tolerance

_____ 2. lymphatic system

_____ 3. natural immunity

_____ 4. toll receptors

_____ 5. acquired immunity

_____ 6. active acquired immunity

_____ 7. B lymphocytes

_____ 8. human leukocyte antigens (HLAs)

_____ 9. cell-mediated immune response

_____ 10. T-helper cells

Definition

a. The circulatory system of the immune system that is comprised of the lymph vessels, lymph nodes, and lymph tissue and functions to drain lymph fluid (chyle) from throughout the body and return it to venous circulation in the chest.

b. The ability of the immune system to differentiate self from non-self and tolerate all self antigens while retaining the ability to mount an immune response to non-self antigens.

c. Type of immunity that occurs after birth and includes antibodies, immune-competent T cells and B cells, and cytokines that act to remove antigens that are considered non-self.

d. Genetic protein markers on the cell wall of white blood cells that alert the immune system to the appropriateness of a cell belonging to the system.

e. Part of the natural immune response; microcellular receptors on the surface of many types of immune and tissue cells that are able to initiate immune responses when pieces of bacterial cell walls attach to them.

f. Type of immunity that is the responsibility of a group of body organs, cells, and chemicals that are present at birth or shortly after.

g. Type of white blood cell that make antibodies against antigens, perform the role of antigens in presenting cells, and eventually develop into memory cells after activation by antigen interaction.

h. A type of T cell that is identified and named by the kind of receptor that is on its surface, a CD4 receptor (cluster of differentiation receptor 4).

i. Type of immunity that involves the production of antibodies by the immune system in response to specific foreign antigens, such as bacteria.

j. Immune responses that are initiated through specific antigen recognition by the T cells; important in identifying and destroying cells that are already infected and providing protection against fungi, and has major involvement in rejection of transplant tissues, tumor immunity, and hypersensitivity reactions.

KEY TERMS MATCHING EXERCISE 2

Write the letter of the correct definition in the space next to each term.

Term

_____ 11. tissue factor (TF)

_____ 12. tumor necrosis factor (TNF)

_____ 13. humoral immune response

_____ 14. immunoglobulin

_____ 15. antigen–antibody complex

_____ 16. deoxyribonucleic acid (DNA)

_____ 17. fragment antigen binding (FAB) portion

_____ 18. fragment crystalline (FC) portion

_____ 19. primary immune response

_____ 20. secondary immune response

Definition

a. The section of an antibody that is capable of attaching to the cell membrane of infected or mutant cells or of foreign pathogens (bacteria, viruses) and assisting macrophages to eliminate them.

b. Mechanism by which organisms gain immunity to previously encountered substances; involves B lymphocytes and antibody-mediated immunity.

c. Cytokine that is important in immune function and inflammation; released by a variety of injured tissue cells, macrophages, and platelets; stimulates platelets to stick together and form the beginning of a clot to stop bleeding when injury occurs.

d. The section of an antibody that is capable of being shaped to receive a specific antigen.

e. The first exposure to a specific antigen; results in creation of B memory cells, which provide lifelong protection against the specific antigen.

f. A small peptide produced by a variety of cells, including granulocytes and lymphocytes; critical in the stimulation of the initial inflammatory response, specifically the activity of macrophages and granulocytes; also stimulates cells to initiate programmed apoptosis when mutations occur, which is important in inhibiting tumor development and growth.

g. The attachment of the FAB portion of an antibody to an antigen, resulting in the stimulation of a strong immune response. Attracts other phagocytic cells such as neutrophils and macrophages to help eliminate the antigen; stimulates creation of B memory cells for long-term protection.

h. A complex protein present in the chromosomes of the nuclei of cells that is the basis of heredity and the carrier of genetic information for all organisms except RNA viruses.

i. Second exposure to a specific antigen that triggers a stronger and quicker immune response than the first exposure, with production of greater amounts of antibodies due to the presence of memory B cells; results in a milder set of clinical symptoms or no observable response to the pathogen because the immune system quickly eliminates the pathogen.

j. A diverse group of plasma proteins, made of polypeptide chains; one of the primary mechanisms for protection against diseases.

WORD SEARCH

First identify the word from its definition. Then find and circle it in the puzzle below.

21. _____ Any foreign substance (bacterium, virus, protein) that elicits an immune response.

22. _____ The protective process of response to a foreign substance.

23. _____ Lymphatic system drainage; a milky fluid comprised of serous fluid, white cells, and fatty acids, arising from the interstitial fluid of the gastrointestinal tract. It contains a high proportion of fat and proteins.

24. _____ White blood cell that is produced in the bone marrow and develops into a lymphocyte or monocyte; does not contain granules in its cytoplasm.

25. _____ Lymph tissue that filters debris from the breakdown of cells, bacteria, viruses, and fungal antigens located throughout the body.

26. _____ Programmed cell death in a multicellular organism; process by which cells can self-destruct when infected or mutated.

27. _____ White blood cells that are produced in the bone marrow and develop into plasma cells that are responsible for the creation and release of antibodies and development of long-term immune protection.

28. _____ Receptors on cells that are not recognized as unique to that individual.

29. _____ Receptors on cells that are recognized as unique to that individual.

30. _____ White blood cells that are vital to initiating and regulating an immune response; produced in the bone marrow and mature and differentiate into various types of T cells in the thymus and other lymphatic tissue such as CD4 (cluster of differentiation, a type of receptor), CD8, T-memory, and T-suppressor cells. They are a crucial part of the immune response because they function as the regulatory cells of the immune system and are responsible for initiating and controlling immune processes such as phagocytosis, cytokine/lymphokine secretion, and activation of B cells.

31. _____ Lymphocytes that, when active, divide rapidly and secrete small proteins called cytokines that regulate or assist in the immune response.

32. _____ The movement of white blood cells to an area of inflammation or infection in response to the release of chemical mediators from neutrophils, macrophages, T cells, and injured tissue.

33. _____ Chemical signals released by white blood cells (predominately T cells) that act as messages between cells and instruct immune cells to proliferate, differentiate, or alter activities; more than 100 different kinds have been identified.

34. _____ Protein made and released by T cells when the invading organism is a virus; functions to protect other cells from viral attack and stimulates the immune response; also inhibits the growth of certain tumor cells.

35. _____ Chemical message produced by lymphocytes that enables the cells of the immune system to communicate and stimulate or slow an immune response. The various types of IL include IL-1 and IL-6, which are pro-inflammatory and stimulate B-cell production, whereas others, such as IL-12 and IL-13, help slow and inhibit the immune and inflammatory responses.

36. _____ Cytokines that are made by lymphocytes; act as chemical messengers between cells and instruct immune cells to proliferate, differentiate, or alter activities. The major lymphokines are interleukins and interferons.

37. _____ A chemical coating of an antigen by cytokines or antibodies that makes that cell more attractive to phagocytes.

38. _____ Proteins made by B cells and found in the plasma that are capable of attaching to antigens and stimulating immune responses.

39. _____ A group of proteins in the blood that stimulates the inflammatory response and serves as a primary chemical mediator of the antigen–antibody reactions of the B-cell immune response.

40. _____ The surrounding and attaching of antibodies to an antigen, causing the antigens to clump together and stimulate the immune cells to locate the complex and consume it or destroy it.

41. _____ A substance formed when antibodies attach to antigens to destroy them.

42. _____ Action of antibodies that involves the process of changing the charge or shape of the antigen and blocking its ability to attach to another cell.

43. _____ Differentiated B cells that are found in the plasma and are responsible for production of specific antibodies or immunoglobulins.

44. _____ One of the actions of antibodies; occurs when an immune complex falls or precipitates out of circulation and is more easily located by neutrophils and monocytes for phagocytosis.

45. _____ The process of stimulating the immune system to create active immunity for protection against a disease by injection with a live or killed vaccine. Often used interchangeably with *vaccination* or *inoculation*.

46. _____ A preparation that contains an infectious agent (live or killed) or its components; administered to stimulate the production of antibodies that can prevent infection or create resistance to infection from that agent; a type of acquired artificial immunity.

47. _____ Impaired or absent ability to react to common antigens.

T	L	Y	M	P	H	O	C	Y	T	E	A	Y	D	O	B	I	T	N	A
N	A	N	O	P	S	O	N	I	Z	A	T	I	O	N	E	F	C	A	B
E	O	O	C	R	D	E	G	H	O	C	P	L	J	I	A	D	H	N	G
U	L	N	E	T	N	E	M	E	L	P	M	O	C	S	P	E	K	E	A
T	B	S	G	I	A	R	E	S	O	K	A	B	P	E	Q	T	L	R	V
R	D	E	I	R	G	T	N	O	I	T	A	N	I	T	U	L	G	G	A
A	S	L	C	M	A	R	S	L	L	E	C	B	G	R	O	U	F	Y	C
L	L	F	A	I	M	N	L	Y	M	P	H	N	O	D	E	S	H	E	C
I	L	A	E	B	N	U	U	Y	A	E	Y	D	J	C	B	E	I	S	I
Z	E	N	N	H	F	T	N	L	M	I	L	H	T	C	E	L	L	S	N
A	C	T	E	T	L	C	E	E	O	P	E	B	A	G	Q	F	C	A	E
T	A	I	D	G	I	B	E	R	C	C	H	E	M	O	T	A	X	I	S
I	M	G	M	F	H	G	O	S	F	O	Y	O	U	D	O	N	E	T	F
O	S	E	C	M	K	A	E	P	C	E	M	T	K	H	A	T	C	G	A
N	A	N	I	J	U	G	I	N	R	T	R	P	E	I	L	I	K	V	D
A	L	B	S	D	A	N	E	H	C	F	A	O	L	P	N	G	A	O	B
D	P	R	E	C	I	P	I	T	A	T	I	O	N	E	S	E	C	E	E
I	M	M	U	N	I	Z	A	T	I	O	N	L	J	O	X	N	S	R	A
C	A	E	G	P	H	E	I	C	Y	T	O	K	I	N	E	S	O	G	I
A	F	D	E	B	A	I	N	T	E	R	L	E	U	K	I	N	D	A	C

SHORT ANSWER QUESTIONS

48. Why are the stem cells in bone marrow so important?

_____

_____

49. Why is maintaining skin integrity important to health and survival?

_____

_____

50. How does immune tolerance develop?

_____

_____

_____

_____

51. How does aging affect the immune response?

_____

_____

_____

_____

52. What serum tests are done to evaluate the function of the immune system?

_____

_____

_____

_____

TRUE OR FALSE?

53. _____ T/F   The bone marrow, the spleen, and the lymphatic system including lymph nodes and lymphatic circulation make up the immune system.

54. _____ T/F   All of the components of natural immune function—the organs, cells, and secretions of the body that provide protection from foreign proteins, chemicals, and other non-self particles—are present at birth.

55. _____ T/F   Lysozymes, acidic pH of the stomach, and toll receptors all function as chemical barriers in the natural immune system.

56. _____ T/F   The cellular immune response is initiated by red blood cells called B cells.

57. _____ T/F   All adults should be given pneumococcal vaccine to prevent pneumonia caused by *Streptococcus pneumoniae*.

58. _____ T/F   Plasma cells are differentiated B cells that are found in the plasma and are responsible for production of specific antibodies.

59. _____ T/F   Because environmental substances rarely affect the action of the immune system, history of exposure is of little consequence in the patient history.

60. _____ T/F   Infection in the face, neck, or head may be evident in the lymph nodes of the neck, which may be swollen, tender, and red.

61. _____ T/F   Enlarged lymph nodes should not be palpated during the physical examination because of pain.

62. _____ T/F   Percussion is an important part of the physical examination because it can reveal fluid accumulation, tenderness, or the existence of a mass or infection.

LABELING EXERCISE: LYMPHATIC SYSTEM WITH LYMPH NODES

Place the term in the correct location.

a. _____

b. _____

c. _____

d. _____

e. _____

f. _____

g. _____

h. _____

i. _____

j. _____

k. _____

l. _____

Adenoid
Appendix
Bone marrow
Heart
Large intestine
Lymphatics
Lymph node
Peyer's patch in small intestine
Spleen
Thoracic duct
Thymus
Tonsil

NCLEX-RN® REVIEW QUESTIONS

59-1. A patient is demonstrating signs of the immune response. The nurse realizes that which of the following is responsible for beginning this response?
    1. Lymph nodes   3. Spleen
    2. T cells   4. B cells

59-2. A patient's body is able to recognize self-cells. The nurse realizes this ability is considered:
    1. Antigen formation.   3. Immune intolerance.
    2. Antibody formation.   4. Immune tolerance.

59-3. A patient tells the nurse that when she "gets a cold," the symptoms are minor and last only a few hours to a day. The nurse realizes this patient's response to a virus is because of:
    1. T-helper 1 cells.   3. T-helper 2 cells.
    2. Suppressor T cells.   4. Null cells.

59-4. A patient is diagnosed with a viral infection. Which of the following elements is the most beneficial to this patient's immune functioning?
    1. Complement   3. Interleukins
    2. Tumor necrosis factor   4. Interferons

59-5. A patient tells the nurse that he doesn't need a flu shot because he had one last year. Which of the following should the nurse respond to this patient?
    1. The virus that causes the flu changes each year so a new flu shot is recommended.
    2. Thank you for letting me know.
    3. You should probably have the pneumonia vaccine instead.
    4. The flu shot doesn't do anything to prevent the flu anyway.

59-6. A patient tells the nurse that "this is only the second time I've ever been stung by a bee but it's much worse that the first time." The nurse realizes this patient's immune response is most likely because of:
    1. Primary immune response.   3. Secondary immune response.
    2. T cell activation.   4. Immunization.

59-7. The nurse is admitting an elderly patient with an autoimmune disorder. Which of the following could explain the reason for this disorder?
    1. Delayed hypersensitivity response
    2. Decreased primary and secondary production of antibodies
    3. Increased auto-antibody production
    4. Decreased percentage of suppressor T cells

59-8. The nurse is going to assess the neurological status of a patient with an infection. Which of the following should be included in this assessment?
    1. Extra ocular movements   3. Hand grasps
    2. Hearing   4. Facial symmetry

59-9. A patient is having a CD4 count conducted. The nurse realizes this laboratory value is used to determine:
    1. The number of antibodies made to parts of the patient's cell's nuclei.
    2. The time it takes red cells to precipitate out of serum.
    3. The total number of T helper lymphocytes.
    4. Acute inflammation and tissue destruction.

CHAPTER 60

CARING FOR THE PATIENT WITH IMMUNE RESPONSE DISORDERS

OUTCOME-BASED LEARNING OBJECTIVES

60-1. Differentiate the nursing management for patients with immune hypersensitivity responses and immune deficiencies.

60-2. Compare and contrast the immune hypersensitivity response related to allergy, autoimmune, and alloimmune disorders.

60-3. Compare and contrast the pathophysiology, clinical manifestations, and laboratory data for the human immunodeficiency virus (HIV) and acquired immune deficiency syndrome (AIDS).

60-4. Prioritize the nursing management of the patient with HIV/AIDS to decrease the incidence of opportunistic infections.

CHAPTER OUTLINE

I. Immune Hypersensitivities: Allergic, Autoimmune, and Alloimmune Responses
  A. Mechanism of Hypersensitivity Immune Response
    1. Type I IgE-Mediated Hypersensitivity
    2. Type II Cytotoxic Specific Reaction
      a. Blood Transfusion Reactions
    3. Type III Immune Complex–Mediated Reaction
    4. Type IV Cell-Mediated Reactions
  B. Immune Hypersensitivity
  C. Allergy Etiology and Epidemiology
  D. Pathophysiology of Allergy Reactions
  E. Clinical Manifestations of Allergic Response
    1. Skin Allergies
    2. Latex Allergy

B. Secondary Immune Deficiencies
C. Human Immunodeficiency Virus and Acquired Immunodeficiency Syndrome
   1. Etiology
   2. Epidemiology
   3. Transmission
      a. Sexual Transmission
      b. Contaminated Needle Transmission
      c. Contaminated Blood Products
      d. Perinatal Transmission
      e. Transmission to Health Care Workers
   4. Pathophysiology
      a. Stages of HIV/AIDS
   5. Clinical Manifestations of HIV/AIDS
      a. Opportunistic Infections and Malignancies
      b. *Pneumocystis carinii* Pneumonia
         i. *Mycobacterium Tuberculosis*
         ii. Hepatitis Virus B and C
         iii. *Mycobacterium Avium* Complex
         iv. Wasting Syndrome
         v. Candidiasis
         vi. Herpes Zoster and Herpes Simplex
      c. Other Infectious Organisms and Disease Processes
      d. Oncologic Manifestations
   6. Medical Management
   7. Laboratory and Diagnostic Procedures
      a. Antiretroviral Drug Therapy for HIV Infection
      b. Treatment of Opportunistic Infections and Symptom Management
         NURSING MANAGEMENT
            TREATMENT CHOICE ISSUES
            DISCHARGE PRIORITIES
            ONGOING CARE
            HEALTH PROMOTION
         COLLABORATIVE MANAGEMENT
D. Research Topics Related to the Immune Deficiencies

KEY TERMS MATCHING EXERCISE 1

Write the letter of the correct definition in the space next to each term.

Term

_____ 1. alloimmune response

_____ 2. autoimmune response

_____ 3. immediate hypersensitivity reaction

_____ 4. immune hypersensitivity response

_____ 5. primary immune deficiency

_____ 6. secondary immune deficiencies

_____ 7. type-specific hypersensitivity reactions

_____ 8. delayed hypersensitivity reaction

_____ 9. tissue-specific antigens

_____ 10. type I (IgE-mediated) allergic reaction

_____ 11. type II (tissue-specific–mediated) hypersensitivity reaction

Definition

a. Involve IgG and IgM antibody–antigen immune complexes; tissue-specific antigens on the surface of cells are not recognized as self by the immune system and are attacked and damaged or destroyed.

b. Occurs when the body fails to recognize self cells or proteins and mounts an immune response against the self.

c. Proteins located in the cell membrane of some tissues such as blood, nerves, lungs, and kidneys that are involved in type II tissue-specific–mediated hypersensitivity reactions.

d. Impaired immune responses that result from a nongenetic cause such as aging, malnutrition, malignancies, immunosuppressive drug therapy, and infections such as the human immunodeficiency virus.

e. A hypersensitivity response of the immune system to antigens from another human; usually occurs when tissue is transplanted or grafted.

f. Occurs when the immune system responds to an antigen over several hours to days. An example is contact dermatitis.

g. Involve the production of antigen-specific IgE antibodies after exposure to a foreign antigen or allergen; most common of the immune hypersensitivity disorders.

h. Occurs when the immune system overresponds to an antigen, either from the environment, from the individual himself, or from another individual. Disorders fall into three broad categories based on the triggering antigen: allergy, autoimmune, and alloimmune.

i. Four specific mechanisms of overreactive immunologic response (types I, II, III, and IV) to environmental allergens, self antigens, or antigens from another human.

j. An excessive response of the immune system that occurs in seconds to hours after exposure to an antigen. A systemic anaphylaxis is one example.

k. Results from genetic abnormalities in immune system development and causes partial or total immune system dysfunction.

KEY TERMS MATCHING EXERCISE 2

Write the letter of the correct definition in the space next to each term.

Term

_____ 12. type III (immune complex–mediated) reaction

_____ 13. type IV (cell-mediated) hypersensitivity reaction

_____ 14. autoimmune diseases

_____ 15. autoantibodies

_____ 16. autoantibody tests

_____ 17. human leukocyte antigens (HLAs)

_____ 18. systemic lupus erythematosus (SLE)

_____ 19. acute graft rejection

_____ 20. chronic graft rejection

_____ 21. graft versus host disease (GVHD)

_____ 22. host versus graft disease (HVGD)

Definition

a. T-cell–mediated immune response, instead of an antibody response. The response is delayed, with the onset of symptoms 24 to 48 hours after antigen exposure. One example is poison ivy reaction.

b. Tests that measure the amount or presence of antibodies to self proteins. Examples include the antinuclear antibody test and anti-IgG serum test.

c. A type of alloimmune hypersensitivity response that involves transplanted organs or tissues; occurs when a recipient's immune system reacts against the foreign antigens on the cells of the graft.

d. Involve IgG and IgM antibody–antigen immune complexes; differentiated from type II reactions in that such reactions are soluble in plasma and circulate in the blood and are not localized at a tissue-specific surface. The traveling antibody–antigen complexes can deposit in tissue or joints and precipitate phagocytosis and inflammation.

e. Genetic protein markers on the cell wall of white blood cells that alert the immune system to the appropriateness of a cell belonging to the system.

f. Occurs months to years after graft transplant and involves the slow, progressive failure of a transplanted organ.

g. Diseases that result from hypersensitivity responses and produce tissue damage and destruction. Examples include Goodpasture's syndrome and systemic lupus erythematosus.

h. An alloimmune response in which the grafted tissue initiates an immune response against tissue of the host or recipient of the grafted tissue. An example is seen in transplanted bone marrow.

i. A type IV cell-mediated immune response that occurs between 2 weeks and 1 month after transplant. This occurs when a recipient's T cells are activated against unmatched HLA antigens in the transplanted tissue.

j. An example of a systemic type III hypersensitivity autoimmune disease characterized by damage to joints and soft organs as a result of the effects of autoantibodies and antibody–antigen activity (immune complex responses).

k. An antibody produced in response to a self protein. Antinuclear antibodies, antibodies that bind to the nucleus of cells and result in cell destruction, are one example.

KEY TERMS MATCHING EXERCISE 3

Write the letter of the correct definition in the space next to each term.

Term

_____ 23. hyperacute rejection

_____ 24. acquired immunodeficiency syndrome (AIDS)

_____ 25. human immunodeficiency virus (HIV)

_____ 26. opportunistic infections (OIs)

_____ 27. CD4+ T cells

_____ 28. reverse transcriptase

_____ 29. acute retroviral syndrome

_____ 30. AIDS indicator conditions

_____ 31. HIV antibody positive status

_____ 32. *Pneumocystis carinii* pneumonia (PCP)

_____ 33. Kaposi's sarcoma

_____ 34. highly active antiretroviral drug therapy (HAART)

Definition

a. A group of generalized symptoms seen in some individuals during the period of primary infection with the human immunodeficiency virus (1 to 3 months). Symptoms include fever, malaise, lymphadenopathy, and skin rash.

b. Infections from microorganisms that are not usually considered pathogens, but cause disease if the immune system is impaired.

c. Occurs within the first hours after transplant when the recipient has a preexisting antibody to the antigen in the graft tissue. Blanching of the graft is one of the earliest signs of rejection.

d. An individual's status when enough HIV antibodies have been produced in response to infection by the HIV virus to be measured by antibody serology, usually after 3 weeks to 3 months.

e. Combination therapy that has the greatest effect in controlling HIV proliferation and minimizing the development of drug resistance. Antiretroviral drugs are grouped according to the mechanism of action against HIV.

f. An enzyme present in some classes of virus, including HIV, that is capable of replicating DNA from RNA, the reverse of normal replication of DNA.

g. A malignancy involving the endothelial layer of blood and lymphatic vessels. Kaposi's is the most common cancer associated with AIDS.

h. The infective agent responsible for causing AIDS; it is a retrovirus that infects CD4 T cells and fatally impairs immune function.

i. Indicates an HIV-infected individual has been diagnosed with opportunistic infections such as *Pneumocystis carinii* pneumonia or AIDS-defining cancer, such as Kaposi's sarcoma, or that the individual's CD4 count has fallen below 200 mL/μL.

j. T lymphocytes with cluster of differentiation 4 (CD4) receptors. The HIV particle can attach and enter T-helper (CD4) cells via the CD4 receptor.

k. The disease resulting from infection by the human immunodeficiency virus; manifested by loss of T cells and opportunistic infections.

l. An opportunistic fungal respiratory infection that can be seen in severely immune-compromised hosts.

SHORT ANSWER QUESTIONS

35. What are clinical examples for each of the four types of immune hypersensitivity response?

_____

_____

36. What are risk factors for respiratory allergies?

_____

_____

_____

_____

37. What causes a loss of immune tolerance?

_____

_____

_____

_____

38. What are the symptoms of systemic lupus erythematosus?

_____

_____

_____

_____

39. What are the key concepts in preventing alloimmune hypersensitivity response?

_____

_____

40. What are the common causes of secondary immunodeficiency?

_____

_____

_____

_____

41. Describe the role of antiretroviral drug therapy for HIV infection.

_____

_____

_____

_____

42. What secondary cancers are included in the CDC's classification of AIDs diseases?

_____

_____

43. Why is early detection of HIV infection so difficult?

_____

_____

_____

_____

44. In addition to exposure to infected body fluids through sexual contact, how is HIV infection transmitted?

_____

_____

_____

_____

KEY TERM CROSSWORD

Complete the crossword puzzle below using key terms.

Across:

1. A severe form of type I hypersensitivity response that is systemic. Symptoms can include hives, severe bronchoconstriction, and loss of airway.
4. The number of HIV viral particles in a sample of blood, expressed as copies. Used to monitor the virulence of HIV infection.
6. A specific and sensitive serum test that measures the presence of antibodies to HIV; generally done as a confirmation test when enzyme immunoassay tests for HIV are positive.
7. Deficiencies that occur when all or some part of the immune system fails to develop or is damaged through disease processes and, thus, cannot mount an appropriate immune response.
9. Antigens created by the developing fetal immune system while it is in the process of eliminating autoreactive lymphocytes.
11. A round area of redness surrounding the wheal of an allergic reaction on the skin.
13. The process of introducing small amounts of a triggering allergen to an allergic individual in increasing amounts over time. The goal is to reduce the severity of the allergic response.
14. The time between actual HIV infection and when HIV tests can detect the presence of the virus or antibodies to the virus in blood; usually 1 to 6 months.
16. A treatment used in some autoimmune diseases that involves removing blood from the body and filtering antibodies out of the plasma. The red blood cells and fluids are returned to the body.
18. An antigen, or protein, from the external environment. Common allergens include dust, food, pollen, and pet dander.

Down:

2. A protein produced by mast and other cells. Its release results in vasodilation and bronchoconstriction.
3. The process of producing antibodies to an antigen present in the body.
5. A form of type I hypersensitivity reaction that occurs when an allergen attaches to IgE antibodies. IgE antibodies attach to mast cells and result in degranulation and release of histamine.
8. A small, round, serous-filled raised blister on the skin that is the result of exposure to an allergen.
10. A class of antibodies produced by the B-lymphocyte plasma cells in response to exposure to a foreign antigen or allergen.
12. Introduction of small amounts of various allergens into the skin of an allergic individual through either intradermal injection or a scratch or "prick test" technique to detect a triggering allergen.
15. A chronic inflammatory skin disorder characterized by dry skin related to water loss in the epidermis and decreased skin lipid levels.
17. A class of synthetic steroid hormones that decreases the inflammatory response and suppresses immune activity; used to prevent graft rejection.
19. Occurs when the immune system overresponds to an antigen from the external environment, such as with skin allergies, latex allergies, food allergies, and anaphylactic reaction.
20. Involves the loss of lean tissue from increased protein metabolism, changes in metabolic rate, and anorexia and diarrhea. It is a hallmark of AIDS-related disease.

TRUE OR FALSE?

45. _____ T/F The four types of immune response can be seen in allergic, autoimmune, and alloimmune antigen reaction.
46. _____ T/F Anaphylactic reactions usually occur in 12 to 18 hours.
47. _____ T/F Latex allergy can produce a response within minutes after exposure or up to 48 hours after exposure.
48. _____ T/F Recognition of self-antigens is vital for normal immune function because it prevents the immune system from destroying the host.
49. _____ T/F Genetic factors play no part in autoimmune disease.
50. _____ T/F Immunosuppressive drug therapy is the focal point of alloimmune medical treatment.
51. _____ T/F HIV-2 involves a slower, milder progression to AIDS than HIV-1, with increased infectiousness at the end of the disease process.

52. _____ T/F HIV cannot be cured but it can be prevented by an HIV vaccine.

53. _____ T/F Candidiasis is a fungal opportunistic infection that occurs in the mouth in virtually all patients with AIDS.

54. _____ T/F CD4+ cells have more CD4 receptor sites than other types of cells and are therefore the primary targets of infection by HIV.

LABELING EXERCISE: HIV INFECTING CD4+ T CELL

Place the term in the correct location.

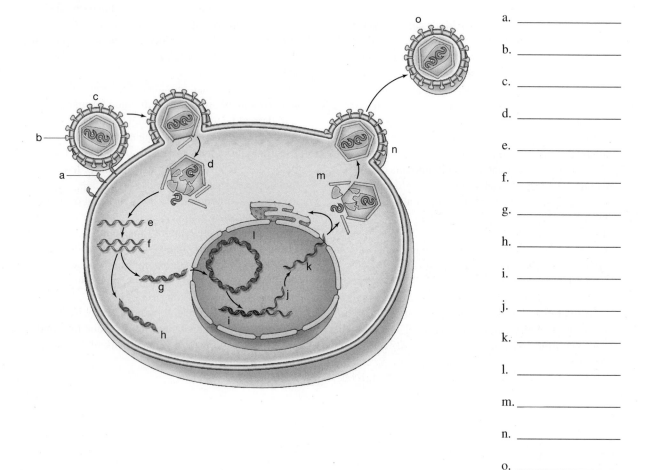

a. _____

b. _____

c. _____

d. _____

e. _____

f. _____

g. _____

h. _____

i. _____

j. _____

k. _____

l. _____

m. _____

n. _____

o. _____

Budding particle
cDNA
CD4 receptor T4 molecule
Double-stranded circularized DNA
Double-stranded DNA
Genomic RNA
gp120
HIV

Host chromosome
Mature virion
Postviral DNA
Protein synthesis and processing
Reverse transcriptase
Unintegrated DNA
Viral mRNA

NCLEX-RN® REVIEW QUESTIONS

60-1. When the nurse suspects the patient has developed an immune hypersensitivity response, the clinical picture may be based on which of the following characteristics?
1. The immune system loses self-tolerance and immune deficiencies result.
2. Hypersensitive reactions are determined by the type of antigen, the time sequence of the reaction, and the immunological response.
3. The primary mechanism of a hypersensitive response is a genetic disorder that occurred during the embryonic development of the immune system.
4. Hypersensitive responses are usually the result of opportunistic infections, which activate a primary response from the T and B cells.

60-2. In differentiating immune hypersensitivity responses that result from an autoimmune mechanism and those resulting from an allergic or alloimmune mechanism, which of the following characteristics apply?
1. The primary trigger for a hypersensitive reaction is a genetic defect.
2. The origin of an alloimmune reaction is from the host's DNA.
3. The trigger for an autoimmune response is a self-antigen.
4. Once activated, the hypersensitive response is identical regardless of trigger.

60-3. Which of the following differentiate Acquired Immune Deficiency Syndrome (AIDS) from Human Immunodeficiency Virus (HIV)?
1. HIV is the end disease manifestation of AIDS.
2. AIDS is a syndrome of opportunistic infections that occurs as a final stage in clients infected with HIV.
3. HIV transmission does not occur upon contact with infected body fluids that have lymphocytes that can harbor HIV.
4. AIDS precedes HIV and allows for the progression of the virus' entry into the host's lymphocytes.

60-4. The client with HIV/AIDS will benefit from nursing management activities to decrease the incidence of opportunistic infections. Which of the following does not work toward this purpose?
1. Subjective assessment to promote the early detection of infection from any body region
2. Start antibiotics prior to obtaining cultures to ensure the appropriate therapy is initiated in a timely manner.
3. Health care providers and family members wash hands before and after patient contact to reduce the risk of opportunistic infection cross contamination.
4. Encourage hydration and maintenance of weight to support the immune system.

CHAPTER 61

CARING FOR THE PATIENT WITH INFLAMMATORY RESPONSE, SHOCK, AND SEVERE SEPSIS

OUTCOME-BASED LEARNING OBJECTIVES

61-1. Compare and contrast the etiologies of anaphylactic, cardiogenic, hypovolemic, neurogenic, and septic shock.

61-2. Describe the cellular alterations that occur in shock.

61-3. Describe the body's response to shock.

61-4. Identify the factors that place a patient at risk of developing shock.

61-5. Discuss the emergency care of the patient in shock, including identification of the underlying cause, management of the patient's airway, breathing, and circulation, and selected pharmacologic interventions.

61-6. Describe the acute care of the patient in shock, including oxygen management, circulatory management, nutritional management, skin care, and pain and sedation management.

61-7. Compare and contrast systemic inflammatory response syndrome (SIRS), sepsis, and severe sepsis based on the definitions used by the American College of Chest Physicians/Society of Critical Care Medicine.

61-8. Prioritize the treatment of the patient with SIRS and identify strategies to prevent the development of SIRS.

61-9. Understand the etiologies, epidemiology, and management of multiple organ dysfunction syndrome (MODS) as an end result of shock and severe sepsis.

61-10. Prioritize the treatment of the patient with MODS and identify strategies to prevent the development of MODS.

CHAPTER OUTLINE

I. Shock
   A. Epidemiology
   B. Etiology
      1. Anaphylactic Shock
      2. Cardiogenic Shock

3. Hypovolemic Shock
4. Neurogenic Shock
5. Septic Shock
C. Pathophysiology
D. Medical Management
   1. The Emergency Period of Shock Care
      a. Prehospital Care and Transport
      b. Emergency Department Care
      c. Fluid Resuscitation
      d. Pharmacologic Support
      e. Pain Management
      f. Additional Interventions
   2. Acute Care Period of Shock
      NURSING MANAGEMENT
      COLLABORATIVE MANAGEMENT
E. Gerontological Considerations
II. Systemic Inflammatory Response, Sepsis, and Severe Sepsis
   A. Epidemiology and Etiology
   B. Pathophysiology
   C. Clinical Manifestations
   D. Laboratory and Diagnostic Procedures
   E. Medical Management
      NURSING MANAGEMENT
      COLLABORATIVE MANAGEMENT
III. Multiple Organ Dysfunction Syndrome
   A. Etiology
   B. Pathophysiology
   C. Clinical Manifestations and Diagnosis
   D. Laboratory and Diagnostic Procedures
   E. Medical Management
      NURSING MANAGEMENT
      HEALTH PROMOTION
IV. Research
V. Summary

KEY TERMS MATCHING EXERCISE

Write the letter of the correct definition in the space next to each term.

Term

_____ 1. systemic inflammatory response syndrome (SIRS)

_____ 2. insulin resistance (IR)

_____ 3. septic shock

_____ 4. systemic vascular resistance

_____ 5. ischemia reperfusion injury

_____ 6. end-organ perfusion

_____ 7. sepsis

_____ 8. severe sepsis

_____ 9. protein C

_____ 10. multiple organ dysfunction syndrome (MODS)

Definition

a. A multifactorial process that occurs when anaerobic metabolism is initiated by hypoperfusion and hypoxia that leads to an oxygen deficit in endothelial, parenchymal, or immune competent cells.

b. Clinical syndrome that is defined by the presence of infection and a systemic inflammatory response.

c. A systemic response of the immune system that can be triggered by both infectious and noninfectious causes.

d. Sepsis with one or more organ system dysfunction.

e. Unresponsiveness of anabolic processes to the normal effects of insulin and possibly tissue insensitivity to insulin.

f. The blood perfusion of the end organs such as the integumentary system.

g. The arterial systolic pressure; normal is 900 to 1,400 dyn·s/cm^5.

h. Diagnosed when two or more organ systems fail.

i. A normal component of the coagulation system.

j. In adults, refers to a state of acute circulatory failure characterized by persistent hypotension unexplained by other causes. In pediatric patients, defined as a tachycardia with signs of decreased perfusion. Hypotension is a late sign in children.

SHORT ANSWER QUESTIONS

11. What are the causes of cardiogenic shock?

_____

_____

_____

_____

12. Describe the overall goal of shock management.

_____

_____

_____

_____

13. What nursing diagnoses apply to a patient care plan for shock?

_____

_____

_____

_____

14. What are the clinical manifestations of septic shock in children?

_____

_____

_____

_____

15. In collaboration with other health care providers, the nurse is responsible for what aspects of care for the patient with sepsis?

_____

_____

_____

_____

TRUE OR FALSE?

16. _____ T/F Anaphylactic shock results from an antigen–antibody reaction.

17. _____ T/F Diabetic ketoacidosis can cause septic shock.

18. _____ T/F Impaired oxygen and glucose use are at the core of shock syndrome.

19. _____ T/F Treatment for shock through reperfusion can cause secondary tissue damage and organ dysfunction.

20. _____ T/F Pain medications for patients experiencing shock should not be given because they can cause hypotension and respiratory depression.

21. _____ T/F The patient with systemic inflammatory response syndrome (SIRS) or sepsis will ultimately progress to septic shock and/or multiple organ dysfunction syndrome (MODS).

22. _____ T/F Sepsis is the 10th leading cause of death in the United States and the leading cause of death in noncardiac care units.

23. _____ T/F A patient suspected of being in septic shock who is hypothermic is in an advanced stage of sepsis and at great risk of dying.

24. _____ T/F Mortality from multiple organ dysfunction syndrome has decreased considerably in the past few decades due to improved methods for patient support.

25. _____ T/F For patients with multiple organ dysfunction syndrome (MODS), it is the body's own defense mechanisms that ultimately contribute to organ compromise and failure.

COMPLETE THE SENTENCE

26. Loss of blood, plasma, or other body fluids can cause _____ shock.

27. _____ shock results in hypotension and perfusion abnormalities.

28. Before transporting the patient with shock, only critical interventions such as _____ _____ should be performed.

29. In cases of suspected pelvic fractures, profound hypotension, or hemorrhage, _____ _____ _____ may be used before the patient arrives at the hospital.

30. The PRIO system of staging sepsis includes five categories: _____, _____, _____, _____, and _____ _____.

31. Three principal actions occur within the body with sepsis: _____, _____, and _____.

32. After stabilizing the airway, breathing, and circulation of a patient with septic shock, the major focus of resuscitation is to prevent _____ and _____ and to identify the _____ of the sepsis.

33. One of the most important practices for the nurse caring for the patient with shock is diligent _____ _____.

34. The primary focus for the management of MODS is to _____ _____ _____ _____.

35. Tachycardia related to pain and anxiety increases _____ and _____ due to the stress imposed on the body by pain.

NCLEX-RN® REVIEW QUESTIONS

61-1. A patient is admitted with a gunshot wound to the abdomen. The nurse realizes that care must focus on preventing which of the following types of shock?
1. Anaphylactic
2. Cardiogenic
3. Neurogenic
4. Hypovolemic

61-2. A patient in shock is demonstrating signs of hypovolemia. The nurse realizes this is because of:
1. Undiagnosed bleeding.
2. Metabolic alkalosis.
3. Water moving into the cells.
4. Pre-renal failure.

61-3. A patient has a sudden decrease in urine output. Which of the following would be the reason why the nurse suspects this patient is demonstrating signs of shock?
1. Respiratory alkalosis
2. Inadequate blood flow to the gastrointestinal tract
3. Increase in circulating neutrophils
4. Shift of sodium into the cells to conserve fluid

61-4. The nurse is planning care for a group of patients. Which of the following is at risk for developing shock?
1. 20-year-old female with asthma
2. 44-year-old female with hypothyroidism
3. 56-year-old male with atrial fibrillation
4. 76-year-old male receiving chemotherapy who has a pressure ulcer

61-5. A fluid challenge for a patient in shock was unsuccessful and the patient is now demonstrating signs of end-organ failure. Which of the following should be provided to this patient?
1. Inotropics
2. Steroids
3. Vasopressors
4. Recombinant human activated protein C

61-6. The nurse is planning care for a patient in shock experiencing a nutritional deficit. Which of the following should be included in this plan of care?
1. Stay with the patient during three large meals.
2. Suggest that a feeding tube should be inserted for supplementation.
3. Place a large-bore intravenous access device for hyperalimentation.
4. Determine the patient's food preferences and arrange to have those foods provided.

61-7. A patient is diagnosed with an infection and is demonstrating signs of kidney failure. The nurse realizes this patient is exhibiting:
1. Sepsis.
2. Systemic inflammatory response.
3. Severe sepsis.
4. Septic shock.

61-8. A patient is demonstrating signs of an infection. Which of the following should be done to prevent the onset of systemic inflammatory response?
1. Change the dressing on a red and inflamed CVP insertion site.
2. Obtain blood cultures.
3. Pack a draining wound.
4. Apply a dry dressing over a necrotic pressure ulcer.

61-9. A patient is in septic shock. Which of the following would indicate a progression to multi-system organ failure in this patient?
1. Hypoglycemia
2. Decreased heart rate
3. Paralytic ileus
4. Decreased right arterial pressure

61-10. The nurse is planning care for a patient at risk for developing MODS. Which of the following should be included in this plan of care?
1. Use clean technique when changing venous access devices.
2. Wash hands prior to providing any care to the patient.
3. Encourage family to visit.
4. Provide a flu inoculation and pneumonia vaccine.

CHAPTER 62

NURSING ASSESSMENT OF PATIENTS WITH HEMATOLOGIC DISORDERS

OUTCOME-BASED LEARNING OBJECTIVES

62-1. Explain how the hematologic system functions in an adult.

62-2. Describe the types, characteristics, and functions of blood cells.

62-3. Explain how the process of coagulation works in the event of an injury.

62-4. Describe appropriate nursing assessment/ responsibilities related to the hematologic system in the adult patient.

62-5. Describe laboratory tests used to evaluate the hematologic system.

62-6. Distinguish between normal and abnormal test results for the hematologic system.

62-7. Discuss the meaning of "shift to the left."

CHAPTER OUTLINE

I. Anatomy and Physiology of the Hematologic System
  A. Bone Marrow
  B. Types of Blood Cells
    1. Erythrocytes (Red Blood Cells)
    2. Leukocytes (White Blood Cells)
      a. Lymphocytes
      b. Basophils
      c. Neutrophils
      d. Eosinophils
      e. Monocytes and Tissue Macrophages
    3. Thrombocytes (Platelets)
  C. Lymphatic System
  D. Spleen

E. Liver
F. Normal Clotting Mechanism: Hemostasis
   1. Primary Hemostasis
   2. Secondary Hemostasis
   3. Coagulation Factors and the Cascade System
G. History
   1. Biographic and Demographic Data
   2. Chief Complaint
      a. Presenting Symptoms
   3. Past Medical History
   4. Family History
H. Risk Factors
 II. Physical Examination
  A. Inspection
   1. Skin
   2. Head and Neck
   3. Chest
   4. Abdomen
  B. Laboratory and Diagnostic Procedures
   1. Automated Blood Cell Analysis: Complete Blood Count
      a. Erythrocyte Evaluation
      b. Leukocyte Evaluation
      c. Platelet Evaluation
   2. Coagulation Studies
   3. Bone Marrow Examination
 III. Gerontological Considerations
 IV. Implications for Health Promotion
  V. Critical Thinking Related to the Hematologic System
 VI. Summary

KEY TERMS MATCHING EXERCISE

Write the letter of the correct definition in the space next to each term.

Term

_____ 1. red blood cell (RBC)
_____ 2. white blood cell (WBC)
_____ 3. humoral immune response
_____ 4. reticuloendothelial system (RES)
_____ 5. lymphatic system
_____ 6. absolute neutrophil count (ANC)
_____ 7. mean corpuscular hemoglobin (MCH)
_____ 8. mean corpuscular hemoglobin concentration (MCHC)
_____ 9. mean corpuscular volume (MCV)
_____ 10. red blood cell distribution width (RDW)

Definition

a. Amount of hemoglobin per red blood cell.

b. The circulatory system of the immune system that is comprised of the lymph vessels, lymph nodes, and lymph tissue and functions to drain lymph fluid (chyle) from throughout the body and return it to venous circulation in the chest.

c. A direct measurement of the homogeneity (consistency) of red blood cell size.

d. A type of blood cell involved in protecting the body against foreign matter.

e. Part of the immune system; consists of the phagocytic cells located in reticular connective tissue, primarily monocytes and macrophages.

f. Concentration of hemoglobin in each red blood cell.

g. Mechanism by which organisms gain immunity to previously encountered substances; involves B lymphocytes and antibody-mediated immunity.

h. A useful measurement that reveals that proportion of the white blood cells that can be utilized in first response immune interactions; the most accurate measurement of circulating neutrophils within white blood cells.

i. Measure of the size of a red blood cell.

j. A type of blood cell that transports oxygen and carbon dioxide. Also called an *erythrocyte*.

KEY TERM CROSSWORD

Complete the crossword puzzle below using key terms.

Across:

1. The ratio of the volume of erythrocytes (red blood cells) to that of the whole blood.
5. Mature white cell; the two types of lymphocytes are T lymphocytes (T cells) and B lymphocytes (B cells).
7. The formation and development of blood cells.
11. A component of the white blood cell differential; actual function is not well known.
13. Lymphatic system drainage; a milky fluid comprised of serous fluid, white cells, and fatty acids, arising from the interstitial fluid of the gastrointestinal tract.
14. Primary phagocytic defense; responds to bacteria, inflammation, injury, infection, and foreign objects.
16. White blood cell with numerous granules in the cytoplasm; granulocytes are divided into neutrophils, eosinophils, and basophils.
17. Acts as a phagocyte in inflammatory conditions, particularly allergic reactions.
18. The oxygen-carrying pigment of the erythrocytes, formed by the developing erythrocyte in bone marrow.

Down:

2. The branch of biology (physiology), pathology, clinical laboratory, internal medicine, and pediatrics that is concerned with the study of blood, the blood-forming organs, and blood diseases.
3. A biconcave, immature red blood cell disk without a nucleus.
4. White blood cell.
6. Platelet.
8. Thrombocyte of blood that is small and colorless with no nucleus, which assists in blood clotting by adhering to other platelets and to damaged epethelium. Also called blood platelet, thrombocyte.
9. Primitive cell in the bone marrow from which mature blood cells derive.
10. The protein portion of blood that remains when cells have been removed.
12. The largest of the white blood cells and makes up about 3% to 8% of the total leukocyte count.
15. Red blood cell.
18. Cessation of bleeding; a complex process that changes blood from a fluid to a solid state.

SHORT ANSWER QUESTIONS

11. What are the components of the hematologic system?

_____

_____

12. What are the categories of leukocytes?

_____

_____

13. What is the purpose of lymphocytes and how do they accomplish it?

_____

_____

14. Describe the process of primary and secondary hemostasis.

_____

_____

_____

_____

15. What can cause a decreased erythrocyte count?

_____

_____

_____

_____

TRUE OR FALSE?

16. _____ T/F Bone marrow makes up about 4% to 5% of a person's body weight.

17. _____ T/F All skeletal bones produce stem cells throughout the life span.

18. _____ T/F Leukocytes make up about 40% of the total blood volume.

19. _____ T/F With age, RBCs become tougher, allowing them to pass through narrow capillaries without sustaining damage.

20. _____ T/F Normally reticulocytes account for approximately 1% of the circulating red blood cells.

21. _____ T/F Fatigue, weakness, and shortness of breath are common symptoms of problems with the erythrocytes of their hematologic system.

22. _____ T/F Hemoglobin, which enables RBCs to carry out their primary function of oxygen transport, varies from 10 to 17 g/dL.

23. _____ T/F The absolute neutrophil count (ANC) provides the proportion of the white blood cells that can be utilized in first response immune interactions.

24. _____ T/F One indication that a patient may be bleeding internally is a platelet level above 30,000.

25. _____ T/F Older adults are more vulnerable to problems with clotting and infection fighting, due to their decreased amount of red bone marrow.

NCLEX-RN® REVIEW QUESTIONS

62-1. The nurse understands that the main purposes of the hematologic system are to:
1. Transport oxygen and wastes to their respective locations and to carry immunological products that aid the body's defense against infection.
2. Help regulate and maintain body temperature and to collect and return interstitial fluid to the blood, which assists in preserving fluid balance.
3. Maintain the appropriate blood volume in every organ of the body and to regulate and control all the body fluid electrolytes and pH levels.
4. Remove any toxic substances from the body and to help protect the body against infection and disease by producing lymphocytes.

62-2. The nurse realizes that which of the following are associated with the erythrocytes? Select all that apply.
1. Contain one-third oxygen-carrying hemoglobin by volume.
2. Immature cells have no nucleus.
3. Lifespan of five to nine days.
4. Terminally differentiated.
5. 5,000 to 10,000 cells per micro-litre of blood.
6. Broken down by the spleen into bilirubin and iron.
7. Helps remove senescent cells from circulation.
8. Mature in the bursa of Fabricius.

62-3. For which of the following patients might the nurse anticipate a bone marrow examination?
1. The patient with RBC 5.2×10^6 cells/mm^3
2. The patient with PLT 620,000/microliter
3. The patient with MCV 90 microliters per mm^3
4. The patient with HGB 16 g/dL

62-4. The patient's laboratory test results are reported to the nurse: WBC 1,100/microliter, RBC 4.6×10^6 cells/mm^3, HGB 14g/dL, PLT 150,000/microliter. Which of the following nursing actions should be performed first?
1. Obtain a set of vital signs and prepare the patient for bone marrow examination.
2. Administer prophylactic antibiotic medications and obtain blood culture specimens.
3. Place the patient on neutropenic precautions and notify the physician of the results.
4. Bathe the patient with bacteriostatic soap and administer steroid medications.

62-5. Certain bleeding disorders, such as hemophilia, are caused from deficiencies in one or more of the factors involved in the clotting cascade. Therefore, as it relates to the normal mechanism for hemostasis in the adult patient, it is imperative the nurse understands that:
1. Factor VIII, Ca^+, and adenosine diaphosphate combine to change fibrinogen into fibrin.
2. Thrombin and factor V eventually create the mesh that traps platelets and forms a clot.
3. Active factor XII and active factor XI start a cascade that ultimately activates factor X.
4. Factor X and platelet thromboplastic factor aid in the activation of prothrombin activator.

62-6. Which of the following problems within the patient's past medical history would warrant further diagnostic hematologic workup?
1. Appendectomy three years ago
2. Urinary tract infection currently
3. Partial colectomy six months ago
4. Pre-hypertension for one year

62-7. Which of the following statements made by a nurse indicates the need for a review of "a shift to the left"?
1. "It shows an increase in the total white blood cell count because of a rise in band and blast cells."
2. "It can quantify the efficacy of interaction between the hemoglobin molecule and the erythrocyte."
3. "It may indicate insufficient host defenses if it occurs with a normal white blood cell count."
4. "It might be a premature sign of an undetected infection in an otherwise healthy individual."

CHAPTER 63

CARING FOR THE PATIENT WITH BLOOD DISORDERS

OUTCOME-BASED LEARNING OBJECTIVES

63-1. Describe the physiology of hematopoiesis, thrombopoiesis, and hemostasis.

63-2. Explain the pathophysiological alterations in erythropoiesis, thrombopoiesis, and hemostasis that give rise to specific hematologic disorders.

63-3. Compare and contrast the causes, the therapeutic management, and clinical presentation of the various types of anemias and hemostasis disorders.

63-4. Analyze laboratory values, correlating to physical signs and symptoms, and distinguish between various hematologic disorders.

63-5. Explain appropriate nursing interventions for the management of thrombocytopenia.

63-6. Compare and contrast the hallmark clinical presentation of bleeding disorders versus clotting disorders.

PEARSON

EXPLORE **mynursingkit**™

MyNursingKit is your one stop for online chapter review materials and resources. Prepare for success with additional NCLEX®-style practice questions, interactive assignments and activities, web links, animations and videos, and more!

Register your access code from the front of your book at **www.mynursingkit.com**

CHAPTER OUTLINE

I. Hematopoiesis: Development of Blood Cells
   A. Anemia
   B. Etiology and Classifications of Generalized Anemia
      1. Normal Physiology of Red Blood Cell Development
         a. Erythropoiesis
         b. Hemoglobin Development
      2. Clinical Presentation of Generalized Anemia
         a. Laboratory and Diagnostic Procedures
            i. Complete Blood Count
         b. Severity of Anemia

B. Disorders of Secondary Hemostasis
   1. Hemophilia
      a. Pathophysiology
      b. Clinical Presentation
         i. Physical Manifestations
         ii. Alterations in Laboratory Values
      c. Medical Management
           NURSING MANAGEMENT
C. Complex Disease of the Clotting Cascade: Disseminated Intravascular Coagulation
   1. Pathophysiology
   2. Clinical Presentation
      a. Physical Manifestations
      b. Alterations in Laboratory Values
   3. Medical Management
           NURSING MANAGEMENT
D. Aplastic Anemia
   1. Pathophysiology
   2. Clinical Presentation
   3. Medical Management
           NURSING MANAGEMENT
IV. Research
V. Summary

KEY TERMS MATCHING EXERCISE 1

Write the letter of the correct definition in the space next to each term.

Term

_____ 1. erythropoietic stem cells (proerythroblast)

_____ 2. hematopoietic stem cell (HSC)

_____ 3. megakaryocytic stem cells

_____ 4. myeloid progenitor cell

_____ 5. 2,3-diphosphoglycerate (2,3-DPG)

_____ 6. deoxyhemoglobin

_____ 7. iron deficiency anemia (IDA)

_____ 8. absolute iron deficiency

_____ 9. functional iron deficiency

_____ 10. megaloblastic anemia

_____ 11. hemoglobinopathies

_____ 12. sickle cell anemia

Definition

a. Substance produced by red blood cells during hypoxic states that sustains the deoxyhemoglobin configuration.

b. Physiological state characterized by failure to supply enough iron for erythropoiesis despite sufficient quantities.

c. Chronic erythrocyte disorder characterized by misshapen "sickle-shaped" red blood cells resulting from malfunctioning hemoglobin molecules.

d. Physiological state indicating insufficient amounts of total body iron.

e. The earliest of four stages in development of the normoblast. Ancestor cell giving rise to red blood cells.

f. Configuration of hemoglobin stimulated by hypoxic states and characterized by rapid release of oxygen to peripheral tissues.

g. Bone marrow cell that is the precursor to all hematologic cell types.

h. Red blood disorders characterized by abnormal hemoglobin.

i. Most common cause of anemia, resulting from insufficient iron in the diet.

j. Ancestor cell that gives rise to granulocytes and monocytes.

k. Ancestor cells that eventually develop into platelets.

l. Anemia resulting from impaired DNA synthesis of the red blood cells' ancestor cells.

KEY TERMS MATCHING EXERCISE 2

Write the letter of the correct definition in the space next to each term.

Term

_____ 13. hemolytic anemia

_____ 14. glucose-6-phosphate dehydrogenase (G6PD) deficiency

_____ 15. hereditary spherocytosis (HS)

_____ 16. autoimmune hemolytic anemia

_____ 17. heparin-induced thrombocytopenia (HIT)

_____ 18. von Willebrand's disease

_____ 19. vitamin B_{12} (cobalamin)

_____ 20. aplastic anemia

_____ 21. Schilling test

_____ 22. hemophilia

_____ 23. hemostasis

_____ 24. thalassemia

Definition

a. The most common enzyme deficiency contributing to hemolytic anemia. Enzymatic deficiencies in erythrocytes increase the red blood cells' sensitivity and susceptibility to oxidative stress. Deficiencies in the enzyme are genetically encoded and relatively common especially in persons of African American and Mediterranean descent.

b. Group of diseases characterized by increased red blood cell destruction.

c. Class of hematologic disorders characterized by genetic inheritance of a mutated hemoglobin-coding gene; characterized by increased hemolysis.

d. Red blood cell disorder characterized by destruction of cells by antibodies of the host.

e. A relatively rare disorder characterized by severe pancytopenia (low or absent red blood cells, white blood cells, and platelets) in both the periphery and bone marrow.

f. Genetic disorder resulting from mutated genes controlling Factor VIII or Factor IX; characterized by uncontrolled bleeding.

g. Hemolytic anemia disorder characterized by insufficient red blood cell membrane proteins.

h. Drug-induced, immune-mediated thrombocytopenia; caused by exposure to heparin therapy.

i. Procedure to identify anemia due to malabsorption.

j. Essential nutrient found in animal proteins; responsible for the activation of folate iron.

k. Most common inherited bleeding disorder; characterized by deficiencies in von Willebrand factor.

l. Cessation of bleeding; a complex process that changes blood from a fluid to a solid state.

WORD SEARCH

First identify the word from its definition. Then find and circle it in the puzzle below.

25. _____ The branch of biology (physiology), pathology, clinical laboratory, internal medicine, and pediatrics that is concerned with the study of blood, the blood-forming organs, and blood diseases.

26. _____ The formation and development of blood cells.

27. _____ Maturation process of blood cells during which cell generations gain increasing specialization; begins with the hematopoietic stem cell and goes to the fully mature peripheral cell.

28. _____ Disorder that results when the total body red blood cell volume is decreased; usually measured by hemoglobin, hematocrit, and red blood cell count.

29. _____ Physiological state of decreased blood oxygen levels.

30. _____ The oxygen-carrying pigment of the erythrocytes, formed by the developing erythrocyte in bone marrow.

31. _____ Physiological state of decreased oxygen availability due to cardiac or pulmonary causes.

32. _____ In development, a parent cell that gives rise to a distinct cell lineage by a series of cell divisions. Like stem cells, progenitor cells have a capacity to differentiate into a specific type of cell. In contrast to stem cells, however, they are already far more specific: They are pushed to differentiate into their "target" cell.

33. _____ Process of red blood cell development.

34. _____ Hormone that stimulates the production of red blood cells.

35. _____ Physiological state of decreased oxygen availability due to decreased concentration of hemoglobin or red blood cells.

36. _____ Black or maroon, sticky, foul-smelling feces resulting from the digestion of blood.

37. _____ Shedding of the outer layer of epidermis (skin or mucosa).

38. _____ A form of iron in the body acting as a supply reservoir.

39. _____ Term describing red blood cells that are paler in color than normal, suggesting iron deficiencies.

40. _____ Term describing red blood cells that are smaller in size than normal.

41. _____ Protein concentrated in the small intestine; responsible for transportation of iron from the gut to target cells.

42. _____ Hormone produced in the liver that is responsible for iron supply regulation.

43. _____ Pertaining to a molecular form that can be readily used by the body.

44. _____ Form of dietary iron that is common in red meats and fish.

45. _____ Form of dietary iron available in vegetables, cereals, and fortified food.

46. _____ Amount of iron in a food substance that is available for absorption from the digestive tract.

47. _____ Naturally occurring, water-soluble form of vitamin B critical for red blood cell formation.

48. _____ Large, immature red blood cells.

49. _____ Chemical secreted by the gastric mucosa required for vitamin B_{12} absorption.

50. _____ Anemia caused by insufficiencies in intrinsic factor.

51. _____ Hormone produced by the liver and kidneys; responsible for stimulating thrombopoiesis.

C	E	R	Y	T	H	R	O	P	O	I	E	T	I	N	A	B	D	H	N
I	P	R	O	G	E	N	I	T	O	R	C	E	L	L	S	C	A	E	O
T	E	A	Y	T	H	R	O	M	B	O	P	O	I	E	T	I	N	P	R
Y	R	E	E	T	A	L	O	F	G	H	E	M	E	I	R	O	N	C	I
C	N	A	R	D	H	E	M	O	G	L	O	B	I	N	B	C	A	I	E
O	I	G	N	I	R	R	E	F	S	N	A	R	T	G	D	E	A	D	M
R	C	E	A	B	H	I	O	H	E	M	A	T	O	L	O	G	Y	I	E
C	I	J	K	A	I	X	O	P	Y	H	C	I	X	O	P	Y	H	N	H
I	O	A	H	D	M	H	L	F	O	P	N	I	T	I	R	R	E	F	N
M	U	K	N	O	E	I	Y	R	D	I	O	A	C	H	B	A	M	E	O
I	S	E	P	G	W	S	U	P	V	E	E	C	N	O	D	N	A	U	N
B	A	I	M	E	N	A	X	Q	O	S	G	S	H	M	I	E	T	L	A
A	N	E	M	I	C	H	Y	P	O	X	I	A	I	R	P	L	O	E	G
H	E	M	O	S	I	D	E	R	I	N	I	N	A	S	O	E	P	H	D
A	M	H	C	B	I	O	A	V	A	I	L	A	B	L	E	M	O	F	B
F	I	E	R	O	T	C	A	F	C	I	S	N	I	R	T	N	I	J	A
O	A	D	L	R	N	O	R	I	L	A	T	N	E	M	E	L	E	C	E
J	B	P	A	M	T	G	K	N	O	I	T	A	M	A	U	Q	S	E	D
A	E	N	I	N	O	I	T	A	I	T	N	E	R	E	F	F	I	D	C
G	H	C	L	R	D	E	A	M	E	G	A	L	O	B	L	A	S	T	A

TRUE OR FALSE?

52. _____ T/F Hematopoietic stem cells are capable of differentiating into one of many types of cells but cannot develop into any cell in the body.

53. _____ T/F The chemical and cellular signals that trigger the process of hematopoiesis are being studied for use in medications.

54. _____ T/F The main function of hemoglobin is to produce the myeloid progenitor cell.

55. _____ T/F The complete blood count typically includes the following laboratory values pertinent to the study of red blood cells: hemoglobin (Hgb), hematocrit (Hct), red blood cells, reticulocyte mean corpuscle volume (MCV), and mean corpuscle hemoglobin (MCH).

56. _____ T/F Hematocrit and hemoglobin values increase with excessive hydration (hemodilution), anemia, and hemorrhage.

57. _____ T/F Iron deficiency anemia occurs when iron is depleted through inadequate diet, blood loss, reallocation of iron stores, or malabsorption, failing to meet the needs of erythropoiesis.

58. _____ T/F Anemia can be caused by chronic diseases such as cancer, chronic kidney failure, autoimmune disorders, and infectious diseases such as acquired immunodeficiency syndrome (AIDS).

59. _____ T/F The target range for hemoglobin and hematocrit are Hgb 11 g/dL (Hct 33%) to Hgb 12 g/dL (Hct 36%).

60. _____ T/F Megaloblastic anemia progresses quickly, with symptoms typical to all anemias manifesting within a week.

61. _____ T/F Diet plays a minor role in iron deficiency anemia but is a significant factor in megaloblastic anemia.

62. _____ T/F Patients with alpha-thalassemias and beta-thalassemia minor are usually asymptomatic and usually do not require medical intervention.

63. _____ T/F An increase in red blood cells and serum haptoglobin are characteristic of hemolytic anemia.

64. _____ T/F Defects in the red blood cell membrane can cause hemolytic anemia.

65. _____ T/F Thrombocytopenia is a life-threatening condition when the platelet count falls below 70,000 uL.

66. _____ T/F Clot formation is affected in primary and secondary hemostasis by von Willebrand's disease.

COMPLETE THE SENTENCE

67. Anemia can be triggered either by (1) loss of _____ _____, (2) altered production of _____, or (3) altered (increased) destruction of _____ _____ _____.

68. Although cellular growth requires many elements, _____, _____, and _____ play particularly pivotal roles in erythropoiesis.

69. Anemia may cause manifestations in the _____ system, the _____ system, and the _____ system.

70. Nursing care for the patient presenting with anemia focuses on _____ of complications secondary to decreased oxygen-carrying capacity and thorough _____ to identify underlying etiologies.

71. Blood loss of 40% can cause _____ _____ to become rapidly overwhelmed with symptoms of _____ imminent.

72. The immediate goal of treatment for acute blood loss is prevention of _____ _____ and _____.

73. Management for sickle cell anemia centers on avoiding sickle cell crisis through maintenance of _____ _____, maintenance of _____, and prevention of _____.

74. _____ are proteins present in the bloodstream that, when activated, help facilitate the next step of the _____ _____.

75. Management of thrombocytopenia includes avoiding medications such as _____ that have _____ activity.

76. Nursing care for the patient with hemophilia focuses on reduction of _____ _____ and on management of the administration of the _____ _____.

LABELING EXERCISE: ERYTHROPOIESIS

Place the term in the correct location.

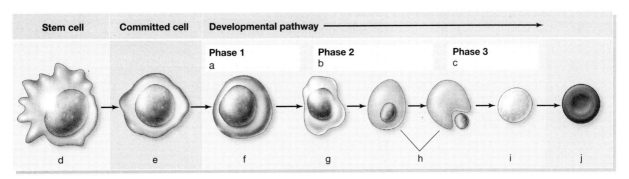

a. _____   f. _____

b. _____   g. _____

c. _____   h. _____

d. _____   i. _____

e. _____   j. _____

Early erythroblast   Late erythroblast
Ejection of nucleus   Normoblast
Erythrocyte   Proerythroblast
Hemocytoblast   Reticulocyte
Hemoglobin accumulation   Ribosome synthesis

NCLEX-RN® REVIEW QUESTIONS

63-1. A patient comes into the emergency department with bleeding from a severe hand wound from a kitchen knife. The nurse realizes that which of the following hemostasis phases is occurring?
1. Clotting cascade
2. Soft platelet plug
3. Contact activation
4. Fibrinolysis

63-2. The nurse is planning care for a patient receiving radiation for bone cancer. Which of the following is this patient at risk for developing?
1. Fluid volume deficit
2. Fluid volume overload
3. Bleeding
4. Sensory perception disorder

63-3. A patient tells the nurse that he thinks he has Alzheimer's because he's been "tripping while walking" and has periods of confusion and memory loss. The nurse realizes this patient is demonstrating signs of:
1. Iron deficiency anemia.
2. Anemia from acute blood loss.
3. Vitamin B_{12} deficiency.
4. Anemia of chronic disease.

63-4. A patient is admitted with fatigue and jaundice. Which of the following diagnostic values would indicate a diagnosis of hemolytic anemia?
1. Increase in lactate dehydrogenase
2. Decrease in serum AST
3. Decrease in reticulocyte count
4. Increase in plasma haptoglobin

63-5. A patient is admitted with thrombocytopenia. Which of the following should be included in this patient's plan of care?
   1. No intramuscular or subcutaneous injections
   2. Rectal temperature every 4 hours
   3. Encourage independence with activities of daily living
   4. Provide rectal suppository for nausea

63-6. A patient's platelet count is 49,500/mm^3. The nurse realizes this patient is at risk for:
   1. Prolonged postoperative bleeding.
   2. Bleeding when brushing the teeth.
   3. Cranial bleeding.
   4. Pericardial space bleeding.

CHAPTER 64

CARING FOR THE PATIENT WITH CANCER

OUTCOME-BASED LEARNING OBJECTIVES

64-1. Identify the prevalence and incidence of cancer, list the common risk factors, and describe the correlation to development of malignancy.

64-2. Discuss the pathophysiology of cancer.

64-3. Compare and contrast the five common types of solid tumor cancer (prostate, breast, colorectal, lung, and brain) and cancers of the hematopoietic and lymphatic system.

64-4. Develop a detailed nursing plan of care for patients with cancer of the prostate, breast, colon or rectum, lung, brain, hematopoietic system, and lymphatic system.

64-5. Describe current treatment approaches to fatigue, nutrition, and pain and the importance of improving quality of life for patients with cancer.

64-6. Discuss the rationale for treatment modalities such as surgery, radiation therapy, chemotherapy, biotherapy, and transplantation.

EXPLORE **mynursingkit**
PEARSON

MyNursingKit is your one stop for online chapter review materials and resources. Prepare for success with additional NCLEX®-style practice questions, interactive assignments and activities, web links, animations and videos, and more!

Register your access code from the front of your book at **www.mynursingkit.com**

CHAPTER OUTLINE

F. Route of Tumor Spread
   1. Direct
   2. Metastatic
G. Health Promotion: Prevention, Screening, and Detection
H. Definitions
   1. Cancer Screening
   2. Cancer Prevention
   3. Screened Individual
   4. Target Population
I. Risk Factors
   1. Age
   2. Hormones
   3. Immune Dysfunction
   4. Drugs and Chemicals
   5. Tobacco
   6. Nutrition and Physical Activity
   7. Sexual Activity
   8. Alcohol
   9. Radiation
   10. Viruses
   11. Psychosocial
III. Diagnosing Cancer
   A. History and Physical
IV. Commonly Occurring Cancers
   A. Cancers of the Hematopoietic and Lymphatic Systems
V. Cancer Treatment Modalities
   A. Surgery
      1. Primary Treatment
      2. Adjuvant Treatment
      3. Salvage Treatment
      4. Palliative Treatment
      5. Combination Treatment
      6. Reconstructive Treatment
      7. Preoperative Care
         NURSING MANAGEMENT
   B. Radiation Therapy
      1. Administration of Radiation Therapy
         a. External Radiation Therapy
         b. Photodynamic Therapy
         c. Internal Radiation Therapy
      2. Radiation Precautions
      3. Radiation Side Effects
         NURSING MANAGEMENT
   C. Chemotherapy
      1. Principles of Chemotherapy
      2. Classification
      3. Administration and Safe Handling
         a. Safety Concerns
         b. Dose Calculations
         c. Administration
      4. Chemotherapy Side Effects and Toxicities
         a. Gastrointestinal System Effects
         b. Genitourinary System Effects
         c. Cardiopulmonary System Effects
         d. Hematopoietic System Effects

e. Reproductive System Effects
f. Neurological System Effects
g. General Effects
   NURSING MANAGEMENT
   COLLABORATIVE MANAGEMENT
D. Biotherapy
   NURSING MANAGEMENT
E. Transplantation: Bone Marrow and Peripheral Blood Stem Cell
   1. Indications for Transplantation
   2. Types of Bone Marrow Transplantation
   3. Sources of Transplantation
      a. Peripheral Blood Stem Cells
      b. Bone Marrow Harvesting
      c. Umbilical Cord Blood
   4. The Transplantation Process
F. Complications of Transplantation
   NURSING MANAGEMENT
VI. Cancer Emergencies
VII. Living with Cancer: Supportive Therapies and Symptom Management
   A. Nutrition
      1. Nutritional Support
   B. Fatigue
      1. Influencing Factors
   C. Cancer Pain
   D. Alternative Care Programs
VIII. Quality of Life Throughout the Cancer Continuum
 IX. Gerontological Considerations
  X. Discharge Planning
 XI. Research
   A. Clinical Trials

KEY TERMS MATCHING EXERCISE 1

Write the letter of the correct definition in the space next to each term.

Term

_____ 1. cancer
_____ 2. incidence
_____ 3. prevalence
_____ 4. survival
_____ 5. neoplasm
_____ 6. carcinogenesis
_____ 7. benign
_____ 8. carcinoma *in situ*

Definition

a. Lacking malignant cells.

b. The number of newly diagnosed cases of cancer in a specific time period in a defined population.

c. Disorder in which neoplasms have not invaded the basement membrane of the epithelial site, thus the surrounding tissues are left untouched by malignant cells.

d. Observation of persons with cancer over time and the likelihood of their dying over several time periods; a link between incidence and mortality data.

e. Pertaining to the production of cancer.

f. The measurement of all cancer cases at a designated point in time.

g. New growth.

h. Common term for all malignant neoplasms.

KEY TERMS MATCHING EXERCISE 2

Write the letter of the correct definition in the space next to each term.

Term

_____ 9. malignant

_____ 10. staging

_____ 11. metastasis

_____ 12. radiation

_____ 13. biopsy

_____ 14. lymphoma

_____ 15. palliative

_____ 16. anorexia

Definition

a. The portion of the tumor classification system that describes the extent of the tumor and evidence of metastasis throughout the body.

b. The alleviation (not curative) of suffering from symptoms.

c. Loss of appetite.

d. Containing cancerous cells.

e. Malignancy of the lymphatic system.

f. A portion of tissue examined for the presence of abnormal cells.

g. The spread of cancerous cells beyond the tumor to distant sites.

h. Waves and particles of energy that cause mutation of cells' DNA, which can weaken the cells' defense against a carcinogen or cause cell death.

KEY TERMS MATCHING EXERCISE 3

Write the letter of the correct definition in the space next to each term.

Term

_____ 17. cytokines

_____ 18. absolute neutrophil count (ANC)

_____ 19. nadir

_____ 20. biotherapy

_____ 21. allogeneic bone marrow

_____ 22. autologous BMT

_____ 23. bone marrow transplantation

_____ 24. peripheral blood stem cell (PBSC) transplantation

_____ 25. engraftment

_____ 26. mortality

Definition

a. Treatment with agents whose origin, mostly mammal, is from biologic sources and/or affecting biologic responses.

b. A useful measurement that reveals that proportion of the white blood cells that can be utilized in first response immune interactions.

c. Transplantation of stem cells located in peripherally circulating blood.

d. The number of deaths from cancer in a specific period of time and within an identified population.

e. Chemical signals released by white blood cells (predominately T cells) that act as messages between cells and instruct immune cells to proliferate, differentiate, or alter activities; more than 100 different kinds have been identified.

f. Establishment of new bone marrow.

g. Procedure in which hematopoietic cells from the bone marrow of one person are transferred into another person; used to treat a variety of diseases.

h. The point at which the lowest blood count is reached.

i. Procedure in which bone marrow is collected from the patient and frozen. It is then reinfused into the patient following high-dose chemotherapy, with or without radiation.

j. Bone marrow from a histocompatible donor.

MATCHING: TNM SYSTEM OF TUMOR CLASSIFICATION AND STAGING

Match the classification with its correct meaning.

Abbreviation

_____ 27. T0

_____ 28. Tis

_____ 29. T1

_____ 30. T2

_____ 31. T3

_____ 32. T4

_____ 33. N0

_____ 34. N1

_____ 35. N2, 3, 4

_____ 36. M0

_____ 37. M1, 2, 3

Meaning

a. No evidence of disease in lymph nodes.

b. No evidence of a primary tumor or lesion.

c. No evidence of metastasis.

d. Advanced lesion spreading into adjacent organs.

e. Carcinoma *in situ.*

f. Evidence of disease in regional lymph nodes but not likely metastatic.

g. Worsening degrees of metastatic involvement, including distant lymph nodes and functional impairment.

h. Localized lesion with deep growth into adjacent structures.

i. Increasing involvement of regional lymph nodes.

j. Lesion contained in organ of origin.

k. Advanced lesion limited to a region of the original organ.

SHORT ANSWER QUESTIONS

38. How does a grade 1 tumor differ from a grade 4 tumor?

_____

_____

39. Describe the exogenous risk factors for cancer.

_____

_____

_____

_____

40. What are the seven warning signs of cancer?

_____

_____

41. What is considered primary treatment for cancer and what is its goal?

_____

_____

_____

_____

42. What are the benefits of radiation therapy?

_____

_____

_____

_____

43. What is the purpose of chemotherapy?

_____

_____

44. What body systems experience side effects caused by chemotherapy?

_____

_____

_____

_____

45. What causes fatigue in patients undergoing being treated for cancer?

_____

_____

46. Why are artificial hydration and nutrition for patients with cancer considered controversial therapies?

_____

_____

47. Why are gerontological issues related to cancer treatment being given more attention?

_____

_____

_____

_____

TRUE OR FALSE?

48. _____ T/F Cancer cells reproduce faster than normal cells.
49. _____ T/F Diet and exercise play a significant role in cancer prevention.
50. _____ T/F Patients undergoing radiation treatment often lose their appetite during treatment and for many weeks after treatment ends.
51. _____ T/F Chemotherapeutic agents are administered only through arterial routes to avoid tissue damage.
52. _____ T/F Nurses must determine the best route of delivery for the chemotherapeutic agents through ongoing patient assessment.
53. _____ T/F Agents used in biotherapy originate mostly with mammals.
54. _____ T/F Bone marrow transplants can come from the recipient's own bone marrow or that of a histocompatible donor.
55. _____ T/F Factors that are examined when assessing a bone marrow or stem cell donor are histocompatibility, health status, gender, and age.
56. _____ T/F Cancer cachexia can be present in patients who have adequate caloric and protein intake.
57. _____ T/F Up to 50% of cancer patients with pain fail to achieve adequate relief.

COMPLETE THE SENTENCE

58. The three stages of cellular change that occur with cancer are _____, _____, and _____.

59. _____ are responsible for killing more Americans than alcohol, vehicle crashes, suicide, AIDS, homicide, and illegal drugs combined.

60. The total dose of radiation prescribed is delivered daily in fractionalized amounts in order to maximize _____ _____ _____ and to minimize _____ to surrounding tissue and allow for repair to begin.

61. The main difficulties encountered in the development of chemotherapeutic agents are the presence of _____ _____ and _____ _____.

62. Drugs that can reduce or eliminate _____ and _____ are an essential part of the treatment plan for patients receiving chemotherapeutic agents.

63. In addition to antiemetic drugs to reduce gastrointestinal side effects of chemotherapy, nurses can suggest other interventions such as _____ _____, _____ _____, and altering the patient's _____.

64. Patients who have experienced cancer may have a greater appreciation of _____, improved _____ relationships, enhanced _____, and healthier _____.

65. The three categories of need for patient teaching and discharge priorities for cancer patients are treatment _____ _____ and _____, _____ _____, and _____.

NCLEX-RN® REVIEW QUESTIONS

64-1. A patient says to the nurse, "It seems like everyone I know is getting cancer." The nurse realizes that the incidence of cancer is related to:
   1. The measurement of all cancer cases at a particular point in time.
   2. The number of deaths from cancer in a specific period of time and within an identified population.
   3. The observation of persons with cancer over time and the likelihood of their dying over several time periods.
   4. The number of newly diagnosed cases of cancer in a specific time period in a defined population.

64-2. A patient is diagnosed with prostate cancer. The nurse realizes this patient's disease was potentiated by which of the following growth factors?
   1. Epidermal
   2. Platelet-derived
   3. Insulin-like
   4. Fibroblast

64-3. A male patient is admitted with a 3-week history of nausea, vomiting, and weight loss. He can't remember how he arrived at the hospital and says his vision has been "changing." The nurse realizes this patient could be demonstrating signs of which type of cancer?
   1. Colon
   2. Prostate
   3. Melanoma
   4. Brain

64-4. A patient with cancer is at risk of bleeding. Which of the following should the nurse include in this patient's plan of care?
   1. Apply pressure to all venipuncture sites for at least 5 minutes.
   2. Measure rectal temperature every 4 hours.
   3. Use mouthwash after toothbrushing.
   4. Use a firm toothbrush.

64-5. A patient being treated for cancer is experiencing nausea and vomiting. Which of the following can the nurse do to assist this patient?
   1. Provide meals that are high in carbohydrates.
   2. Administer antiemetics and appetite stimulants prior to meals.
   3. Limit meals to 3 times per day.
   4. Encourage fluid intake prior to meal times.

64-6. A patient being treated for cancer is scheduled for a bone marrow transplant. The nurse realizes this treatment is needed to:
   1. Prevent surgery.
   2. Reduce the amount of chemotherapy the patient will need.
   3. Avoid the use of radiation.
   4. Increase the effects of chemotherapy and radiation.

CHAPTER 65

NURSING ASSESSMENT OF PATIENTS WITH INTEGUMENTARY DISORDERS

OUTCOME-BASED LEARNING OBJECTIVES

65-1. Discuss the structure and function of the skin.

65-2. Obtain a health history relative to assessment of the skin, hair, and nails.

65-3. Collect subjective and objective data relative to assessment of the skin, hair, and nails.

65-4. Utilize correct techniques of physical exam when assessing the skin, hair, and nails.

65-5. Distinguish between normal and abnormal assessment findings in the skin, hair, and nails.

65-6. Describe skin lesions by morphologic classification.

65-7. Identify biologic and cultural variations in assessment of the skin.

CHAPTER OUTLINE

   I. Anatomy and Physiology of the Skin
      A. Skin Layers
         1. Epidermis
         2. Dermis
         3. Subcutaneous Tissue
         4. Blood and Lymph Supply, Sebaceous Glands, and Innervation
  II. Gerontological Considerations
      A. Physiological Impact of Ultraviolet Rays
 III. History
      A. Biographic and Demographic Data
      B. Chief Complaint
      C. Presenting Symptoms

KEY TERMS MATCHING EXERCISE

Write the letter of the correct definition in the space next to each term.

Term

_____ 1. edema

_____ 2. turgor

_____ 3. configuration

_____ 4. discrete lesion

_____ 5. distribution

_____ 6. ecchymosis

_____ 7. linear lesion

_____ 8. morphologic classification

_____ 9. primary lesion

Definition

a. Loss of hair, which can be a result of familial patterns of baldness, disease, medications, or a pathologic condition.

b. Lesions that appear as red or purple pigmented.

c. Refers to the pattern of arrangement or position of lesions.

d. A lesion that is initially dark red or purple, but gradually fades to yellowish green before it disappears.

e. Examination of superficial skin lesions with a diascope.

f. An individual or separate lesion.

g. Classification of skin lesions in terms of type of lesion (primary, secondary, or vascular), size, shape or configuration, color, texture, elevation or depression, and pedunculation.

_____ 10. secondary lesion

_____ 11. vascular lesion

_____ 12. diascopy

_____ 13. alopecia

h. Accumulation of fluid in the intercellular spaces that causes swelling of tissue.

i. A description of the lesions on the skin according to location or body region affected.

j. Lesion that forms a line.

k. Lesion that results from a change in the primary lesion or external trauma to the primary lesion.

l. Lesion that results from the initial reaction to a pathologic condition.

m. The elasticity and mobility of the skin; reflects the skin's hydration status.

TRUE OR FALSE?

14. _____ T/F   The more melanin an individual has, the lighter the skin and hair and the more susceptible the skin is to sun damage.

15. _____ T/F   Subcutaneous tissue, which is composed of loose connective tissue and fat cells, is considered part of the skin.

16. _____ T/F   The lymphatic system is located in the dermis and helps combat skin infections.

17. _____ T/F   Older adults have drier, scalier skin because they often lack adequate hydration.

18. _____ T/F   Dark-skinned people have no risk of damage from the sun because of the increased amount of protective pigment.

19. _____ T/F   Men have a higher risk of developing skin cancer than women.

20. _____ T/F   Palpation of the skin during an examination is used to assess skin temperature, texture, thickness, moisture, turgor, edema, and lesions.

21. _____ T/F   A wart is an example of a nodule.

22. _____ T/F   Sunscreen should be applied 15 to 30 minutes prior to sun exposure.

23. _____ T/F   A diet deficient in protein may prevent adequate wound healing.

LABELING EXERCISE: SKIN LAYERS

Place the term in the correct location.

a. _____

b. _____

c. _____

Dermis
Epidermis
Hypodermis

NCLEX-RN® REVIEW QUESTIONS

65-1. A patient tells the nurse that she tans easily. The nurse realizes that the skin layer responsible for melanocyte production is the:
1. Epidermis.
2. Dermis.
3. Subcutaneous tissue.
4. Sebaceous glands.

65-2. A patient says that she "got badly sunburned" on top of "taking medication for bronchitis." This information would be applicable to which area of the health history skin assessment?
1. Childhood illnesses
2. Medications
3. Immunizations
4. Allergies

65-3. A patient is diagnosed with MRSA. The nurse should focus on which area of the skin assessment?
1. Exercise
2. Habits
3. Nutrition
4. Culture

65-4. When assessing the temperature of a patient's skin, the nurse should:
1. Wear sterile gloves.
2. Use the dorsal surface of the hand.
3. Begin with the patient's hands.
4. Assess and complete one side of the patient, then assess the other side.

65-5. While assessing a patient's hair, the nurse notes patchy hair loss. This finding could be indicative of:
1. A scalp infection.
2. Cigarette smoking.
3. Medications.
4. A systemic infection.

65-6. The nurse palpates a fluid-filled sac on a patient's forearm. This finding would be considered as a:
1. Bulla.
2. Cyst.
3. Nodule.
4. Tumor.

65-7. The nurse documents that a patient has carotenemia. This patient is exhibiting:
1. A yellowish stain in the skin.
2. A bluish tinge in the skin.
3. Purplish blue-black areas of the skin.
4. Generalized red skin.

CHAPTER 66

CARING FOR THE PATIENT WITH SKIN DISORDERS

OUTCOME-BASED LEARNING OBJECTIVES

66-1. Differentiate the etiology, pathophysiology, and interventions for infections of the skin.

66-2. Identify preventive measures for skin disorders.

66-3. Identify the impact of the environment on the skin.

66-4. Describe the signs and symptoms, diagnostic tests, and treatment of skin disorders.

66-5. Develop a nursing plan of care for a patient with a skin disorder.

66-6. Differentiate the psychological and physical implications for the patient with a skin disorder.

66-7. Describe the effects of aging on the skin.

CHAPTER OUTLINE

I. Nails
   A. Brittle Nails
      1. Treatment of Brittle Nails
   B. Nail Infections
   C. Nail Trauma or Loss
II. Hair
III. Skin
   A. Sunlight
      1. Health Promotion Related to Sun Protection
   B. Nonmalignant Disorders Related to Sun Exposure
      1. Etiology, Epidemiology, and Pathophysiology of Photodermatitis
         a. Clinical Manifestations of Photodermatitis
      2. Etiology, Epidemiology, Clinical Manifestations, and Treatment of Actinic Keratosis
   C. Etiology, Epidemiology, and Pathophysiology of Contact Dermatitis
      1. Diagnosis, Clinical Manifestations, and Treatment of Contact Dermatitis
   D. Etiology, Epidemiology, Pathophysiology, and Clinical Manifestations of Urticaria

KEY TERMS MATCHING EXERCISE 1

Write the letter of the correct definition in the space next to each term.

Term

_____ 1. androgenetic alopecia

_____ 2. androgenic alopecia

_____ 3. actinic keratosis

_____ 4. contact dermatitis

_____ 5. photodermatitis

_____ 6. atopic dermatitis

_____ 7. pilosebaceous follicles

_____ 8. acne vulgaris

_____ 9. café-au-lait spot

_____ 10. solar lentigo

_____ 11. dermatofibromas

Definition

a. A skin disorder caused by the sun that leads to proliferation of abnormal, dystrophic cells.

b. A common, inflammatory adverse reaction to sunlight in which the individual sunburns more easily than usual or develops papular or vesicular lesions with exposure to the sun.

c. Loss of hair related to excessive androgen production that causes a decrease in size of the hair follicles, leading to hair loss in central and frontal areas.

d. Common, fibrous, tumor-like nodules of the skin.

e. Pigmented macules that are light brown in color.

f. An inflammation of the skin related to exposure to an irritant or allergen in the environment.

g. A sebaceous cyst containing hair follicles.

h. Lesions that develop due to a familial tendency and chronic sun exposure in Caucasians older than 60 years of age. They are macules that are darker and larger than freckles and do not fade during winter. Commonly referred to as *age spots* or *liver spots*.

i. A chronic skin disorder with an increased production of sebum from the sebaceous glands and the formation of comedones that plug the pores.

j. A chronic inflammatory skin disorder characterized by dry skin related to water loss in the epidermis and decreased skin lipid levels.

k. Physiological baldness in which androgen levels are normal; however, there is a genetic predisposition to balding.

KEY TERMS MATCHING EXERCISE 2

Write the letter of the correct definition in the space next to each term.

Term

_____ 12. Neurofibromatosis

_____ 13. seborrheic keratosis

_____ 14. dermatophyte

_____ 15. necrotizing fasciitis (NF)

_____ 16. Stevens–Johnson syndrome (SJS)

_____ 17. toxic epidermal necrolysis (TEN)

_____ 18. blepharoplasty

_____ 19. rhinoplasty

_____ 20. rhytidectomy

_____ 21. dermabrasion

_____ 22. liposuction

Definition

a. A fungus parasite on the skin.

b. Part of the same syndrome of diseases as Stevens–Johnson syndrome, but it is a more severe form of the disorder and is life threatening with more extensive skin detachment.

c. An infection of the superficial fascia or the connective tissue surrounding muscle and subcutaneous tissue leading to necrosis.

d. An autosomal dominant inherited disorder characterized by the formation of tumors of the peripheral nerves over the entire body.

e. A benign epidermal lesion seen predominantly in the middle-aged and elderly populations.

f. Process of removing the epidermis and upper dermis of the skin so that the skin can regenerate into a smooth surface.

g. Surgical procedure to fix ptosis or drooping of the eyelid.

h. Common type of cosmetic surgery, the purpose of which is to remove subcutaneous fat.

i. Surgical excision of skin to eliminate wrinkles of the face.

j. A severe, acute, self-limiting skin reaction to infection or to certain medications; affects the epidermal layer of the skin and mucous membranes.

k. Plastic surgery of the nose.

KEY TERM CROSSWORD

Complete the crossword puzzle below using key terms.

Across:

1. Viral epidermal eruptions caused by human papilloma virus. Also known as warts.
2. A chronic, noncontagious inflammatory skin disorder; characterized by erythematous papules and plaques with silver-white scales that are sharply demarcated.
3. A common, contagious skin infection caused by *Staphylococcus aureus* and/or group A beta-hemolytic streptococcus that is characterized by vesicles that rupture and form yellow crusts.
4. Contagious skin disease caused by a mite; commonly found in underdeveloped countries and places where there is overcrowding and poor hygiene.
5. Infestation with lice.
8. Benign tumor consisting of fat cells.
10. Well-circumscribed malformations of the skin. Also known as moles.
11. Inflammation of the folds of tissue surrounding the fingernail.
12. The eggs of a louse.
15. A diffuse inflammatory process of the dermis and subcutaneous tissue layers characterized by erythema, edema, and pain; usually caused by staphylococcus or streptococcus infections.
16. Inflammation of the hair follicles.
17. Raised, erythematous, intensely pruritic plaques or wheals that are surrounded by a white halo. Also known as hives.

Down:

1. Condition leading to a localized loss of melanocytes and, thus, patches of depigmentation.
4. A viral infection that occurs because of the reactivation of latent varicella zoster virus or the virus that causes chickenpox. Also known as herpes zoster.
6. An infection of the skin composed of a cluster of boils caused by *Staphylococcus aureus*.
7. Abnormal growth of hair, especially in women.
9. A form of cellulitis characterized by inflammation and redness of the skin due to group A hemolytic streptococci.
13. Deep linear crack or furrow in the continuity of the epidermis.
14. A boil or a walled-off, deep, painful, firm inflammation of the skin that contains pus.
18. A common fungal infection caused by the *Candida* species of fungus; more commonly known as a yeast infection.

SHORT ANSWER QUESTIONS

23. What is the SMART acronym and its significance?

_____

_____

24. What can cause urticaria?

_____

_____

25. What skin lesions are associated with aging?

_____

_____

_____

26. What causes psoriasis?

_____

_____

27. What causes herpes zoster and how is it activated?

_____

_____

_____

_____

28. Who is most at risk for tinea?

_____

_____

29. What symptoms should alert the nurse to the presence of necrotizing fasciitis (NF)?

_____

_____

_____

_____

30. What nursing diagnoses are possible for NF?

_____

_____

_____

_____

31. What are the clinical manifestations of Stevens–Johnson syndrome?

_____

_____

_____

_____

32. What cultural considerations should be included in preoperative planning for cosmetic surgery?

_____

_____

_____

_____

TRUE OR FALSE?

33. _____ T/F Toenails and fingernails can be disfigured by systemic disease, exposure to toxic agents, nutritional deficiencies, infection, and trauma.

34. _____ T/F Alopecia is associated with low self-esteem and poor body image.

35. _____ T/F Poison ivy creates an irritant reaction that causes contact dermatitis.

36. _____ T/F Hypertrophic and keloid scars occur more frequently when the injury occurs over the sternum, anterior chest, shoulder, upper lip, earlobe, and neck.

37. _____ T/F Melanomas occur as the result of a recent blistering sunburn.

38. _____ T/F Dangerous reactions to bee and wasp stings occur more commonly in children under 18.

39. _____ T/F Ointments penetrate the skin more than creams and may be too occlusive for rashes with exudates or in intertriginous areas.

40. _____ T/F Necrotizing fasciitis (NF) is difficult to diagnose because the symptoms are many and varied.

41. _____ T/F Stevens–Johnson symdrome (SJS) occurs most commonly in adults over 50.

42. _____ T/F The patient undergoing a rhytidectomy will continue to look younger by approximately 10 years for the rest of her life, even as aging progresses.

COMPLETE THE SENTENCE

43. The ABCD method instructs the nurse to assess for these four characteristics: A _____, B _____ _____, C _____ _____, and D _____ _____ _____ _____ _____ _____.

44. Pressure ulcers occur most commonly on the _____ and in the _____ area.

45. Wet dressings or compresses often use _____ solution, _____ _____, or _____ _____ creams.

46. The cause of Stevens–Johnson syndrome (SJS) is most commonly an adverse reaction to _____ or a(n) _____.

47. In addition to its role in improving facial lines, Botox injections are also used to improve thick bands in the _____, to combat _____ _____, to treat _____, and as a pain reliever for _____ patients.

NCLEX-RN® REVIEW QUESTIONS

66-1. An 18-month-old baby is diagnosed with impetigo. Which of the following should the nurse instruct the mother of this baby?
   1. Systemic antibiotics are the only treatment.
   2. There are no special precautions to take.
   3. Do not take the baby to day care until the condition has healed.
   4. The baby should have oatmeal baths.

66-2. A patient with a history of pruritis asks the nurse what she could do to prevent it from reoccurring. Which of the following could the nurse instruct this patient?
   1. Wear dark clothing.
   2. Avoid skin lotions.
   3. Avoid excessive bathing.
   4. Avoid sun exposure.

66-3. The nurse is planning to instruct a patient on skin protection and sun exposure. Which of the following could the nurse use to assist in this instruction?
   1. The mnemonic COLD
   2. The mnemonic SMART
   3. The contents of a bottle of sunscreen
   4. Statistics of the onset of skin cancer after sun exposure

66-4. A patient is admitted with the diagnosis of necrotizing fasciitis day 3. The nurse realizes this patient will most likely demonstrate which of the following symptoms?
   1. Flu-like symtoms
   2. Skin blisters with purple foul-smelling exudate
   3. Gangrene
   4. Fever

66-5. A patient with a skin disorder has a poor appetite and will not take fluids by mouth. Which of the following should the nurse do to assist this patient?
   1. Monitor intake and output.
   2. Place on a fluid restriction.
   3. Ask the physician for an order for intravenous fluid replacement therapy.
   4. Begin a calorie count.

66-6. A patient tells the nurse that she had flu symptoms after starting a new medication. In a few days, she started developing skin blotches and her skin was "falling off." The nurse realizes this patient is describing:
   1. Hives.
   2. Stevens–Johnson syndrome.
   3. Psoriasis.
   4. Necrotizing fasciitis.

66-7. A 50-year-old female patient tells the nurse that she doesn't understand why she has so many facial wrinkles when others at the same age do not. Which of the following should the nurse respond to this patient?
   1. It's because of smoking, genetics, and sun exposure.
   2. It's because of a poor diet.
   3. It's because of over-bathing.
   4. It's because of vitamin deficiencies.

CHAPTER 67

CARING FOR THE PATIENT WITH WOUNDS

OUTCOME-BASED LEARNING OBJECTIVES

67-1. Compare and contrast the clinical manifestations of the three phases of wound healing.

67-2. Describe wound characteristics and nursing documentation that are required in a periodic wound assessment.

67-3. Describe key factors that are relative to the prevention of pressure ulcers.

67-4. Compare and contrast wound classifications and respective treatments.

67-5. Evaluate therapies and their benefits with respect to wound healing.

67-6. Understand the psychosocial and liability factors pertaining to wound care.

67-7. Describe how research in wound care will lead to better efficiency and outcomes with evidence-based practice.

CHAPTER OUTLINE

I. Physiology of Wound Healing
   A. Phase One: Homeostasis/Inflammatory Phase
   B. Phase Two: Proliferation
   C. Phase Three: Remodeling
II. Wound Healing Assessment
   A. Vascular System: Macro and Micro
   B. Venous System
III. Risk Factors That Impact Wound Healing
   A. Nutrition and Hydration
   B. Infection
   C. Comorbidities
   D. Medications
   E. Stress
   F. Glucose Control and Diabetic Management

KEY TERMS MATCHING EXERCISE 1

Write the letter of the correct definition in the space next to each term.

Term

_____ 1. collagen synthesis
_____ 2. epithelialization
_____ 3. granulation tissue
_____ 4. inflammatory phase
_____ 5. senile purpura
_____ 6. acute wounds
_____ 7. chronic wounds
_____ 8. iatrogenic wounds
_____ 9. traumatic wounds
_____ 10. hemosiderin staining

Definition

a. A phase of wound healing that begins at the time of the injury or surgery. The purpose of this phase is to prepare the site for growth of new tissue.

b. Recent wounds that are either traumatic or iatrogenic in etiology that progress through the stages of wound healing normally.

c. Multistep process in which fibrin proteins form a matrix to support the newly forming tissue.

d. Occurs when the heme part of the red blood cell is deposited in the tissues as red blood cells get trapped and accumulate due to venous congestion. As the red blood cell dies, the heme is deposited and a brownish hue staining color results.

e. Tiny, round granule-like nodules that become beefy, red, and moist because of the dense revascularization process.

f. Process by which a wound closes from its margins, covering the defect with a layer of new skin.

g. Intravenous puncture sites, incisions, radiation-induced skin damage, and grafts that occurred while a patient was in the hospital.

h. A type of hemorrhaging under the skin that occurs most frequently in the elderly because their blood vessels are thinner and more fragile than those of younger people.

i. Abrasions, blisters, cuts, bites, stab wounds, gunshot wounds, and first- and second-degree burns.

j. Wounds that do not follow the expected sequence of repair in a timely and uncomplicated manner.

KEY TERMS MATCHING EXERCISE 2

Write the letter of the correct definition in the space next to each term.

Term

_____ 11. basement membrane
_____ 12. primary intention
_____ 13. secondary intention
_____ 14. tertiary or third intention
_____ 15. hyperbaric oxygen therapy (HBOT)
_____ 16. interface pressure
_____ 17. hypergranulation
_____ 18. impaired wound healing
_____ 19. wound dehiscence
_____ 20. wound evisceration

Definition

a. The separation of sutures or staples along the incision in a previously closed wound.

b. The pressure between a bony prominence and a surface such as a hospital bed or seating surface.

c. The protrusion of organs from a wound site.

d. In the granulation process, healing that occurs when major tissue defects gradually close by epithelialization and contracture formation, and then form scar tissue.

e. A thin, acellular layer between the dermis and epidermis that acts as scaffolding for the epidermis. Blood supply and nutrients reach the epidermis by passing through this layer.

f. A wound that is surgically closed or one with smooth, closely aligned margins.

g. The formation of soft, pink, fleshy projections as the body attempts to heal an enlarged wound track.

h. Refers to intermittent treatment of the entire body with 100% oxygen at greater than normal atmospheric pressures.

i. The disruption of the normal biochemical repair or regeneration process.

j. Healing that occurs in wounds that have not been sutured in a timely manner or have broken down and been sutured later.

WORD SEARCH

First identify the word from its definition. Then find and circle it in the puzzle below.

21. _____ The tendency toward stability within an organism; it is the first reaction toward that stability when a wound occurs.

22. _____ Process in which stimulated endothelial cells multiply and form tubular structures differentiating into arterioles or venules.

23. _____ Small cells that migrate along the fibrin network to produce the connective tissue and collagen fibers.

24. _____ A group of extracellular polypeptides (secreted by platelets and macrophages) that affect cell growth, reproduction, movement, or function.

25. _____ Granulocytes, macrophages, and lymphocytes, which are attracted to an injured site by the complement factors and antigens.

26. _____ The process by which phagocytes absorb and enzymatically degrade foreign matter and devitalized tissue.

27. _____ A long-chain fatty acid that regulates platelet aggregation and controls inflammation.

28. _____ The fourth and final phase of wound healing that begins about 3 weeks after the injury and can still be in progress 6 months to 2 years later.

29. _____ Protrusions in the fifth layer of the epidermis that extend down into the dermis and help anchor the epidermis to the dermis. Also called *epidermal ridges*.

30. _____ A type of hemorrhaging under the skin that occurs most frequently in the elderly because their blood vessels are thinner and more fragile than those of younger people.

31. _____ A skin condition characterized dry, pruritic, cracked, or fissured skin with scaling and flaking.

32. _____ Recent wounds that are either traumatic or iatrogenic in etiology that progress through the stages of wound healing normally.

33. _____ Wounds that do not follow the expected sequence of repair in a timely and uncomplicated manner.

34. _____ A localized injury to the skin and/or underlying tissue, usually over a bony prominence, as a result of pressure or pressure in combination with shear and/or friction.

35. _____ An area of swelling or mass of blood confined to an organ, tissue, or space, due to a broken blood vessel.

36. _____ A mass caused by the accumulation of serum within a tissue or organ. It is similar to a hematoma except that instead of a collection of blood it is a collection of serous fluid.

S	T	S	A	L	B	O	R	B	I	F	D	A	E	A	C	I	B	J	B
C	H	R	G	N	F	R	E	C	L	U	E	R	U	S	S	E	R	P	A
E	D	O	E	H	G	L	K	E	M	R	E	T	E	P	E	G	S	H	C
P	E	T	M	M	L	I	N	A	P	L	N	F	O	H	N	J	A	E	I
R	H	C	G	E	O	E	O	G	B	Q	M	P	I	A	I	B	G	R	C
O	B	A	M	A	O	D	O	G	E	P	A	D	R	G	L	O	Q	H	E
S	D	F	G	M	J	S	E	F	E	L	E	S	W	O	E	T	E	Z	N
T	I	H	A	O	P	C	T	L	H	N	N	K	U	C	P	W	V	S	D
A	C	T	E	T	C	B	T	A	I	D	E	Z	M	Y	U	G	E	O	E
G	A	W	K	A	G	Y	N	W	S	N	O	S	L	T	R	X	A	C	T
L	H	O	B	M	F	H	T	I	B	I	G	P	I	E	P	C	W	I	D
A	O	R	Q	E	A	O	D	O	M	S	S	A	J	S	U	A	B	S	K
N	I	G	P	H	U	V	E	C	S	Y	E	Y	X	T	R	Q	C	L	E
D	M	L	E	S	G	O	F	X	L	I	F	M	E	Z	A	P	U	A	N
I	H	B	I	U	X	E	R	O	S	I	S	W	B	E	Y	R	E	F	I
N	O	R	C	S	D	R	T	W	L	Z	O	S	V	J	K	G	W	P	M
D	E	A	F	K	N	B	G	N	T	U	Q	A	C	M	T	A	H	O	B
J	L	D	M	Q	E	T	P	U	N	F	H	Y	J	R	I	D	V	E	N
A	F	G	I	A	N	O	S	D	N	U	O	W	C	I	N	O	R	H	C
C	B	A	M	O	R	E	S	I	J	E	H	K	A	L	C	F	B	A	D

SHORT ANSWER QUESTIONS

37. What are the three phases of wound healing and their main purposes?

_____

_____

_____

_____

38. How does stress impact wound healing?

_____

_____

_____

_____

39. How does diabetes promote development of ulcers?

_____

_____

_____

_____

40. Why is compression recommended for venous ulcers?

_____

_____

_____

_____

41. Explain the difference between partial and full thickness wounds.

_____

_____

42. How does the Braden scale for predicting pressure sore risk work?

_____

_____

_____

_____

43. Describe the four methods of débridement.

_____

_____

_____

_____

44. What are the benefits of moist wound healing?

_____

_____

_____

_____

45. What should be considered when selecting a wound care dressing?

_____

_____

_____

_____

46. What are the risk factors for dehiscence?

_____

_____

_____

_____

47. What are the nursing diagnoses related to wound healing?

_____

_____

_____

_____

TRUE OR FALSE?

48. _____ T/F The remodeling phase of wound healing begins as soon as the bleeding stops and can last for up to 2 years.

49. _____ T/F All factors that contribute to healing hinge on the health of the vascular system.

50. _____ T/F People who are 75 years or older have more difficulty with wound healing than younger people.

51. _____ T/F Vasculitic ulcers occur more often in men than in women and are among the most painful type of ulcer.

52. _____ T/F Maceration is when excessive moisture destroys the skin's integrity and leaves the skin layers suboptimal.

53. _____ T/F Only mild skin cleansers should be used on wounds during change of dressings.

54. _____ T/F Hyperbaric oxygen therapy treatments last from 20 to 60 minutes.

55. _____ T/F Honey is often a successful topical agent for use in healing chronic wounds.

56. _____ T/F Active drains are usually placed in a stab wound near an incision site to provide a conduit that functions by gravity for the removal of this drainage.

57. _____ T/F The law requires the patient to bear responsibility for the prevention of pressure ulcers during a hospital stay.

NCLEX-RN® REVIEW QUESTIONS

67-1. A patient with cancer has been receiving steroids. The nurse realizes that this patient could experience an alternation in which phase of wound healing?
1. Homeostasis
2. Inflammatory
3. Proliferation
4. Remodeling

67-2. A patient's wound has clear drainage. The nurse would document this finding as being:
1. Serous.
2. Serosanguineous.
3. Sanguineous.
4. Purulent.

67-3. The nurse is planning care for a patient prone to pressure ulcer development. Which of the following should be included when determining appropriate body care for this patient?
1. Plan sufficient time for a daily morning bath.
2. Bathe with hot water.
3. Avoid the use of skin moisturizers.
4. Do not massage bony prominences or use friction while bathing.

67-4. A patient is admitted with a venous ulcer on his left lower extremity. The nurse realizes this patient will most likely be treated with:
1. Surgery.
2. Compression.
3. Debridement.
4. Moist dressing.

67-5. A patient was admitted with a draining leg wound. Currently the wound is dry and the edges are well approximated. Which of the following should be used to treat this patient's wound?
1. Debridement
2. A dry dressing
3. Keep the wound open to air
4. A moist wound dressing

67-6. A patient recovering from surgery refuses to move out of bed but tells the nurse that his sacrum is sore. Which of the following should the nurse do to help this patient?
1. Provide the patient with pain medication.
2. Suggest that he sit on the side of the bed and dangle his legs.
3. Discuss discharge planning needs with the patient.
4. Begin vigilant pressure ulcer prevention care.

67-7. A group of nurses are trialing the use of several different wound care products. The results of this trial will impact:
1. Healing rates.
2. Patient comfort.
3. Wound infection rates.
4. Wound appearance.

CHAPTER 68

CARING FOR THE PATIENT WITH BURN INJURIES

OUTCOME-BASED LEARNING OBJECTIVES

68-1. Differentiate between the three classifications of burn injury: mild, moderate, and major.

68-2. Compare and contrast the causes, incidence, prevalence, types, and prevention of burn injuries.

68-3. Describe the pathophysiological response of burn injury at the tissue and organ level.

68-4. Compare and contrast the three periods of burn care.

68-5. Describe the significance and components of burn severity assessment including size and depth of injury, impact of patient's age on injury, part of the body burned, and past medical history.

68-6. Describe the components of a comprehensive burn treatment plan for each of the three periods of burn care, including fluid resuscitation, pain management, wound care, surgical management, contracture prevention, nutritional needs, and emotional adjustment.

68-7. Describe the discharge teaching needed to facilitate an optimal recovery and return to society.

68-8. Identify the potential complications associated with each period of burn injury.

CHAPTER OUTLINE

I. Epidemiology
II. Etiology
    A. Types of Burn Injury
        1. Thermal Burns
        2. Scald Burns
        3. Electrical Burns
        4. Radiation Burns
        5. Chemical Burns
        6. Inhalation Injury
    B. Health Promotion
III. Pathophysiology of Tissue Injury
    A. Tissue Injury
    B. Systemic Injury

C. Organ Injury
1. Cardiac Response
2. Pulmonary Response
3. Gastrointestinal Response
4. Renal Response
5. Immune Response
6. Integumentary Response
7. Multisystem Dysfunction
IV. Periods of Burn Injury Management
A. Emergency Phase
1. Prehospital Care and Transport
2. Emergency Department Care
3. Burn Center Criteria
a. Admission to a Burn Center
4. Admission Assessment
5. Clinical Manifestations and Determinants of Burn Wound Severity
a. Burn Size
b. Burn Depth
c. Age
d. Past Medical History
e. Part of Body Burned
6. Laboratory and Diagnostic Evaluation
a. Red Blood Cells
b. Leukocytes
c. Platelets
7. Medical Management
a. Fluid Resuscitation
i. Fluid Resuscitation Assessment
b. Pain Management
i. Alternative Therapies for Pain Management
NURSING MANAGEMENT
COLLABORATIVE MANAGEMENT
B. Acute Phase
1. Wound Care
a. Cleansing
b. Wound Débridement
c. Shaving, Culturing, and Photographs
d. Escharotomies
e. Fasciotomy
f. Application of Topical Antibiotics/Dressing
g. Special Care Sites
h. Temporary Dressings
i. Biologic Dressings
ii. Biosynthetic Dressings
iii. Synthetic Dressings
i. Infection Assessment
j. Hyperbaric Oxygen Therapy
2. Surgical Management
a. Burn Wound Excision
b. Burn Wound Closure
i. Harvesting of Skin
ii. Donor-Site Care
iii. Alternative Skin Covering

3. Promoting and Maintaining Normal Mobility
   a. Positioning
   b. Splinting
   c. Exercise Program
4. Nutritional Requirements
   NURSING MANAGEMENT
   COLLABORATIVE MANAGEMENT
C. Rehabilitative Phase
   1. Scar and Contracture Formation
   2. Exercise Program
      a. Functional Skills
      b. Stretching Exercises
      c. Scar Massage
   3. Pressure Dressing and Garments
   4. Functional and Cosmetic Reconstruction
   5. Psychological Recovery
   6. Pain Management
   7. Nutritional Requirements
   8. Discharge Priorities
   9. Health Promotion
   10. Occupational Recovery
       NURSING MANAGEMENT
       NURSING DIAGNOSIS
       COLLABORATIVE MANAGEMENT
V. Complications of Burn Injuries
VI. Gerontological Considerations
VII. Research

KEY TERMS MATCHING EXERCISE 1

Write the letter of the correct definition in the space next to each term.

Term

_____ 1. inhalation injury

_____ 2. scald burns

_____ 3. thermal burns

_____ 4. chemical burns

_____ 5. radiation burns

_____ 6. full-thickness injury

_____ 7. partial-thickness injury

_____ 8. zone of coagulation

_____ 9. zone of hyperthermia

Definition

a. Area where the amount of injury to the tissue is the greatest.

b. The outermost portion of an injured area where cell damage is minor.

c. Type of thermal injury that occurs from contact with hot foods or liquids, including steam.

d. Burns that usually result from overexposure to the sun or are associated with radiation treatment for cancer.

e. Injury from flames; the most common type of burn injury.

f. An injury that extends into the underlying structures and organs.

g. Injury in which the epidermis and part of the dermis are destroyed.

h. Burns that occur when the skin is in contact with caustic chemical compounds such as strong acids, alkalis, or organic compounds.

i. Inhalation of smoke, causing injury to the lungs.

KEY TERMS MATCHING EXERCISE 2

Write the letter of the correct definition in the space next to each term.

Term

_____ 10. zone of stasis

_____ 11. eschar

_____ 12. Lund-Browder formula

_____ 13. rule of nines

_____ 14. escharotomies

_____ 15. allograft

_____ 16. autografting

_____ 17. biologic dressing

_____ 18. biosynthetic dressing

Definition

a. Incisions made through burn tissue to relieve the constricting effects of the edema that accompanies circumferential injuries.

b. Grafting of the patient's own skin to somewhere else on the patient's body.

c. Formula for determining burn size that divides the body into percentage areas.

d. Nonviable burned tissue.

e. A combination of biologic and synthetic materials that are effective as temporary covering for a variety of wounds.

f. Area surrounding the zone of coagulation that has potentially viable but injured cells.

g. Divides the body into seven areas, which represent 9% or multiples of 9% of the body surface area; used to determine burn size.

h. Heterografts such as pigskin or allografts obtained from living or deceased humans.

i. Grafting of skin to a wound that was harvested from human cadavers.

KEY TERMS MATCHING EXERCISE 3

Write the letter of the correct definition in the space next to each term.

Term

_____ 19. donor site

_____ 20. heterografts

_____ 21. full-thickness skin graft

_____ 22. meshed skin graft

_____ 23. split-thickness skin graft

_____ 24. sheet skin grafts

_____ 25. hypertrophic scar

_____ 26. keloid scar

Definition

a. Split-thickness grafts that have not been meshed.

b. Hypertrophic scar tissue that extends beyond the wound edges.

c. An area on the body where skin is surgically harvested to use for covering burn wounds.

d. Grafting of skin that is surgically removed by excising the entire thickness of the donor skin to the level of the subcutaneous tissue, typically 0.025 to 0.30 inch thick.

e. Scar tissue that is an overgrowth of dermal tissue that remains within the boundaries of the wound.

f. Biologic dressings made from animals such as pigs.

g. Grafting of a partial layer of skin, including the epidermis and part of the dermis.

h. Procedure of cutting holes in harvested skin, which allows it to be stretched over a greater surface area.

SHORT ANSWER QUESTIONS

27. Explain what burn shock is and its role in burns.

_____

_____

_____

_____

28. What is the ABCDEF format used for the initial assessment of a patient with burns during prehospital care?

_____

_____

_____

_____

29. What areas are examined or considered when performing a fluid resuscitation assessment?

_____

_____

_____

_____

30. What temporary dressings are used for burn wounds?

_____

_____

_____

_____

31. Explain why good nutrition is especially important for adequate healing of burn wounds.

_____

_____

_____

_____

TRUE OR FALSE?

32. _____ T/F Pneumonia is the most common infection among hospitalized patients with burns.

33. _____ T/F Thermal burns tend to be deeper than other kinds of burn injuries.

34. _____ T/F Children playing with matches and cigarette lighters account for approximately 35% of all burn injuries.

35. _____ T/F All organs are impacted by a major burn injury, regardless of the source.

36. _____ T/F Renal blood flow and filtration rates increase after a major burn injury as a result of fluid shifts.

37. _____ T/F A patient with electrical burns meets the criteria for admission to a burn center even if the burn is less than 10% of the total body surface area.

38. _____ T/F Full-thickness injuries (third degree) are the most painful when even lightly touched.

39. _____ T/F The acute period of burn management begins when the patient is hemodynamically stable, usually 2 or 3 days after sustaining the injury, and ends with closure of the burn wounds.

40. _____ T/F The rehabilitative phase begins when there is less than 20% open wound, which may be as early as 2 weeks or as long as several years after the burn injury.

41. _____ T/F   Elderly patients with burns suffer from greater morbidity and mortality than do younger patients with similar burn extents.

COMPLETE THE SENTENCE

42. Burns occur as a result of exposure to _____ (thermal); direct contact with _____, _____, or _____; and _____.

43. The three zones of injury in wounds caused by thermal damage are the zone of _____, the zone of _____, and the zone of _____.

44. Blood flow to the GI tract immediately after a burn is affected by the release of _____ from the sympathetic nervous system and _____, a potent vasoconstrictor.

45. Keeping the burn patient warm is difficult because of loss of _____ _____, but it is important to prevent shivering, which increases _____ and _____ needs.

46. Burn size is estimated by using one of two common formulas, the _____ _____ _____ and the _____-_____ formula.

LABELING EXERCISE: SKIN LAYERS OF PARTIAL-THICKNESS VERSUS FULL-THICKNESS INJURY

Place the term in the correct location.

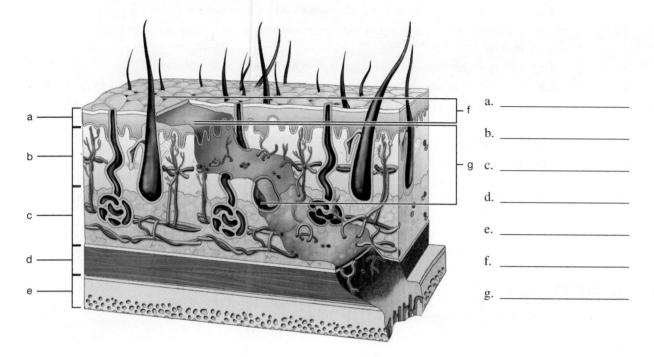

a. _____

b. _____

c. _____

d. _____

e. _____

f. _____

g. _____

Bone
Dermis
Epidermis
Full

Muscle
Partial
Subcutaneous tissue

NCLEX-RN® REVIEW QUESTIONS

68-1. Which of the following patients has a moderate burn injury?
1. A 94-year-old with lung cancer and congestive heart failure with a 15% TBSA partial-thickness thermal burn injury to the face and anterior torso
2. A 20-year-old with diabetes mellitus and HIV with 2% TBSA full-thickness and 10% TBSA partial-thickness chemical burn injuries to the back
3. A 40-year-old with high cholesterol and GERD with a 20% TBSA partial-thickness thermal burn injury to both upper extremities and the chest
4. A 67-year-old with eczema and asthma with 12% TBSA full-thickness and 8% TBSA partial-thickness scald burns to the abdomen and perineum

68-2. A nurse is teaching a class on injury prevention to a group of new mothers. Which of the following statements made by one of the participants indicates a clear understanding of the content regarding burn injury prevention?
1. "The best way to prevent electrical fires is to avoid smoking cigarettes in bed."
2. "Many thermal injuries in children can be avoided by using plastic outlet covers."
3. "Using tanning beds instead of exposure to the sun can prevent radiation burns."
4. "Chemicals must be locked up and away from children to avert chemical burns."

68-3. Which of the following changes may be seen after a major burn injury? Select all that apply.
   1. Increased pulmonary vascular resistance
   2. Serum hypokalemia
   3. Congestive heart failure
   4. Localized vasoconstriction
   5. Decreased release of Hageman factor
   6. Intravascular hypovolemia
   7. Increased T-cell production

68-4. As it relates to the acute care phase of burn care, the nurse understands that:
   1. The physically stable patient is frequently more aware of the ramifications of the injury and often requires psychological and physical restorative therapies.
   2. Strict wound care regimens that include aseptic cleansing and debridement are instituted to prevent further tissue injury and sepsis from wound infection.
   3. Application of cool normal saline–soaked towels to the burned areas for prolonged periods of time may contribute to further skin injury and hypothermia.
   4. Older patients have an increased risk of complications because they have a greater surface area to body mass ratio, causing a higher risk for hypovolemic shock.

68-5. Which of the following would be important when considering burn injury severity? Select all that apply.
   1. "Rule of Nines"
   2. The patient's age
   3. Blood glucose
   4. Parkland formula
   5. Past medical history
   6. Time burn occurred
   7. Urine output
   8. Depth of injury

68-6. The patient has just been admitted to the burn unit with a 75% full-thickness thermal burn injury, and the physician has written new admission orders. Which of the following interventions should the nurse carry out first?
   1. Administer glutamine granules per duotube.
   2. Infuse lactated ringers IV at 175 mL/hr.
   3. Apply silver sulfadiazine to open wounds.
   4. Give 10 mg morphine IV prior to dressings.

68-7. When planning the discharge home of the patient who has been badly burned, it is appropriate that the nurse include which of the following recommendations?
   1. Taper calorie intake once your ideal body weight has been achieved to avoid obesity.
   2. Contact the Occupational Safety and Health Administration for vocational counseling.
   3. Prevent rubbing healed burn areas because this could cause shearing and breakdown.
   4. Ensure pressure garments fit properly by wearing them until the scar begins to tingle.

68-8. Complications often occur in patients with burns. Which of the following complications might be most closely associated with the rehabilitative period of burn care? Select all that apply.
   1. Hypovolemic shock
   2. Psychological problems
   3. Congestive heart failure
   4. Wound infections
   5. Grieving and denial
   6. Contracture and scars
   7. Loss of function
   8. Immunosuppression

CHAPTER 69

NURSING ASSESSMENT OF THE PATIENT WITH SENSORY DISORDERS

OUTCOME-BASED LEARNING OBJECTIVES

69-1. Differentiate normal from abnormal findings of a physical assessment of the ear, nose, and throat.

69-2. Identify the subjective and objective history data related to ear, nose, and throat disorders that need to be obtained.

69-3. Identify the risk factors for ear, nose, and throat disorders.

69-4. Describe the psychosocial impact of disorders of the ear, nose, and throat and how it impacts nursing care.

66-5. Describe the purpose, nursing responsibility, and significance of results of diagnostic exams of the ear, nose, and throat.

CHAPTER OUTLINE

I. Anatomy and Physiology of the Ear, Nose, and Throat
   A. Ear
   B. Nose
   C. Oral Cavity
   D. Neck
II. History
   A. Biographic and Demographic History
   B. Chief Complaint and Presenting Symptoms
   C. Past Medical History
      1. Childhood Diseases and Immunizations
      2. Previous Illnesses and Hospitalizations
      3. Medications
      4. Allergies
      5. Cough and Sputum Production

D. Family Health History
E. Social History
   1. Occupational and Recreational
   2. Cultural Considerations
   3. Environmental Exposures
   4. Habits
   5. Travel
III. Ear
  A. Current Health and Risk Factors
  B. Current Issue
   1. Hearing Loss
   2. Otalgia
   3. Tinnitus
   4. Vertigo
   5. Hearing Loss, Tinnitus, Vertigo, and Medications
   6. Infection or Drainage
   7. Barotrauma
  C. Physical Examination
   1. Inspection and Monitoring
   2. Palpation
   3. Hearing Tests
   4. Auscultation
   5. Ear Monitoring Equipment
  D. Health Promotion
IV. Nose and Paranasal Sinuses
  A. Current Health and Risk Factors
  B. Current Issue
   1. Pain
   2. Headache
   3. Difficulty Breathing
   4. Bleeding or Drainage
   5. Trauma
   6. Sense of Smell
   7. Sneezing
   8. Sleep Patterns/Obstructive Sleep Apnea
  C. Physical Examination
   1. Inspection
   2. Palpation
  D. Percussion
   1. Nose and Paranasal Sinuses Monitoring Equipment
  E. Health Promotion
V. Mouth
  A. Current Health and Risk Factors
  B. Current Issue
   1. Fetid Breath
   2. Poor Dentition
   3. Infection and Inflammation
   4. Trismus
  C. Physical Examination
   1. Inspection
  D. Health Promotion

VI. Lips
   A. Current Health and Risk Factors
      1. Hydration
      2. Color
      3. Ulcerations, Lesions, or Bleeding
      4. Infections
   B. Physical Inspection
      1. Palpation

HEALTH PROMOTION

VII. Gingiva and Teeth
   A. Current Health and Risk Factors
   B. Physical Examination
      1. Inspection
   C. Health Promotion
VIII. Buccal Mucosa
   A. Current Health and Risk Factors
   B. Physical Examination
      1. Inspection
      2. Palpation
   C. Health Promotion
IX. Tongue
   A. Current Health and Risk Factors
      1. Sense of Taste
   B. Physical Examination
      1. Inspection
      2. Palpation
      3. Tongue Monitoring Equipment
   C. Health Promotion
X. Pharynx and Larynx
   A. Current Health and Risk Factors
   B. Change in Voice
   C. Physical Examination
      1. Inspection
      2. Palpation
      3. Auscultation
      4. Pharynx and Larynx Monitoring Equipment
   D. Health Promotion
XI. Summary

KEY TERMS MATCHING EXERCISE 1

Write the letter of the correct definition in the space next to each term.

Term

_____ 1. cerumen

_____ 2. conductive hearing loss

_____ 3. sensorineural hearing loss

_____ 4. epistaxis

_____ 5. tinnitus

_____ 6. ototoxicity

_____ 7. otalgia

_____ 8. vertigo

Definition

a. Type of hearing loss attributed to damage to the eighth cranial nerve.

b. A hearing screening test that distinguishes whether hearing loss in an ear is conductive or sensorineural.

c. Earwax.

d. Subjective sensation of spinning; dizziness; the illusion of rotational movement, tilting, and swaying with feelings of imbalance during standing or walking; symptom of a balance disorder.

_____ 9. barotrauma

_____ 10. pneumatoscope

_____ 11. Weber test

e. Type of hearing loss in which sound waves cannot reach the inner ear for processing and interpretation; caused by diseases such as external ear infections.

f. Bleeding from the nose.

g. Harmful effect on the eighth cranial nerve or organs of hearing and balance.

h. An otoscope with a bulb attachment that can be used to introduce air into the ear canal and middle ear to test for ruptured tympanic membrane.

i. A buzzing, roaring, or ringing in the ears.

j. Alveoli damage caused by the increased pressure resulting from use of a ventilator. Physical injury or rupture of tympanic membrane, resulting from changing air pressure.

k. Ear pain.

KEY TERMS MATCHING EXERCISE 2

Write the letter of the correct definition in the space next to each term.

Term

_____ 12. caloric test

_____ 13. Rinne test

_____ 14. Romberg test

_____ 15. Schwabach test

_____ 16. voice whisper test

_____ 17. allergic rhinitis

_____ 18. anosmia

_____ 19. obstructive sleep apnea (OSA)

_____ 20. fetid breath

_____ 21. trismus

Definition

a. Disorder of sleep with habitual snoring characterized by brief periods of breathing cessation or a marked reduction in tidal volume with a minimum of five episodes per hour during sleep with excessive daytime somnolence.

b. Tests hearing for air and bone conduction by using an activated tuning fork on the mastoid process.

c. Restricted movement of the jaw.

d. Assesses abnormal nystagmus, tinnitus, or hearing loss as a result of vestibular dysfunction from 8 cranial nerve lesions by inserting water into the ear.

e. Assesses inner ear balance, proprioceptive ability, and visual and cerebellar system function by asking the patient to maintain an upright posture when arms are held out in front, with eyes open and eyes closed.

f. Halitosis or foul or putrid breath.

g. A hearing test that measures conduction of sound by bone when placing an activated tuning fork on the right and left mastoid sequentially.

h. Inflammation of the nasal mucosa caused by an allergic substance such as pollen.

i. The loss or impairment of the sense of smell.

j. A hearing test in which the examiner stands 1 to 2 feet in back of the patient and whispers.

TRUE OR FALSE?

22. _____ T/F A history of alcohol use is strongly associated with head and neck cancer.

23. _____ T/F Objective tinnitus is a condition that only the afflicted person can hear.

24. _____ T/F Inflammation and edema from eustachian tubes extending to the nasal mucosa may obstruct airflow between the middle ear and nose.

25. _____ T/F The sense of smell diminishes slightly with age.

26. _____ T/F Oxygen saturation should be maintained between 87% and 95% for individuals with normal lung function.

27. _____ T/F A musty smell to the breath, or fetor hepaticus, is the result of end-stage renal disease.

28. _____ T/F Poor nutrition and hydration are revealed in problems with the gingiva, lips, and tongue.

29. _____ T/F Palpable lymph nodes should be soft to rubbery, freely mobile, distinct, round, and nontender.

30. _____ T/F The most important implication for oral health promotion measures that patients can take is to avoid the use of any tobacco products and minimize the use of alcohol.

31. _____ T/F A person with cheilosis may need to be referred to cardiac rehabilitation to maximize cardiac efficiency.

LABELING EXERCISE 1: OUTER, MIDDLE, AND INNER EAR

Place the term in the correct location.

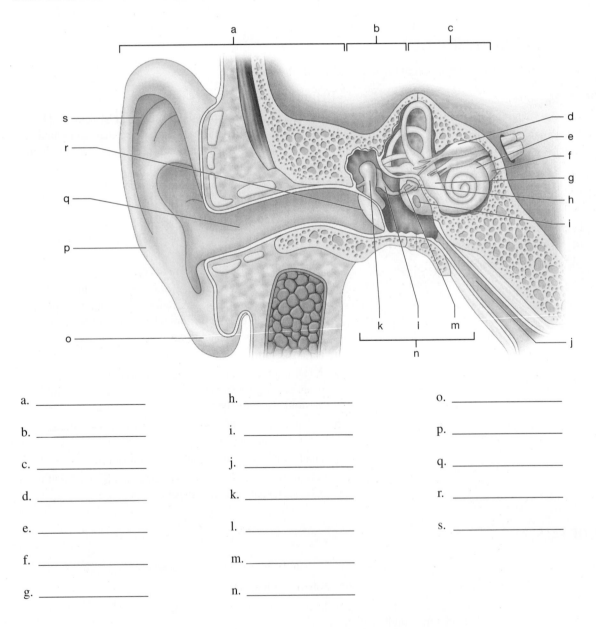

a. _____   h. _____   o. _____

b. _____   i. _____   p. _____

c. _____   j. _____   q. _____

d. _____   k. _____   r. _____

e. _____   l. _____   s. _____

f. _____   m. _____

g. _____   n. _____

Auditory (eustachian) tube
Auricle
Cochlea
Cochlear nerve
External auditory canal
Helix
Incus
Inner ear (labyrinth)
Lobe
Mallous

Middle ear
Ossicles
Outer ear
Oval window
Round window
Stapes
Tympanic membrane (eardrum)
Vestibular nerve
Vestibule

LABELING EXERCISE 2: THE NOSE

Place the term in the correct location.

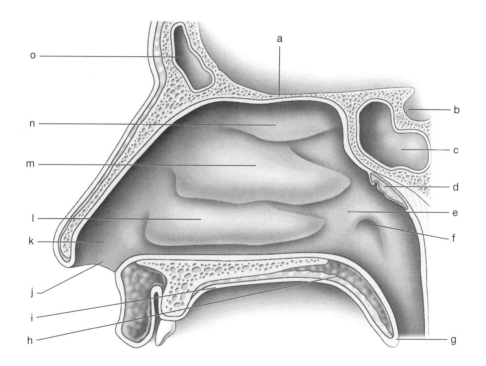

a. _____

b. _____

c. _____

d. _____

e. _____

f. _____

g. _____

h. _____

i. _____

j. _____

k. _____

l. _____

m. _____

n. _____

o. _____

Anterior naris
Cribriform plate of ethmoid bone
Frontal sinus
Hard palate
Inferior turbinate

Middle turbinate
Opening of auditory (eustachian) tube
Pharyngeal tonsil
Posterior naris
Sella turcica

Soft palate
Sphenoid sinus
Superior turbinate
Uvula
Vestibule

LABELING EXERCISE 3: STRUCTURES OF THE MOUTH

Place the term in the correct location.

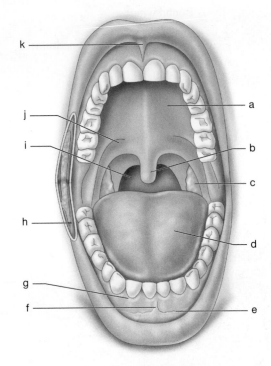

a. _____

b. _____

c. _____

d. _____

e. _____

f. _____

g. _____

h. _____

i. _____

j. _____

k. _____

Buccinator muscle
Dorsum of tongue
Frenulum of lower lip
Frenulum of upper lip
Gingiva
Hard palate

Palatine tonsil
Posterior wall of oropharynx
Soft palate
Uvula
Vestibule of mouth

LABELING EXERCISE 4: THE NECK

Place the term in the correct location.

a. _____

b. _____

c. _____

d. _____

e. _____

f. _____

g. _____

h. _____

Common carotid artery

Cricoid cartilage

Cricothyroid ligament

Cricothyroid muscle

Cupula (dome) of pleura

Medial margin of sternocleidomastoid muscle

Thyroid cartilage

Thyroid gland

NCLEX-RN® REVIEW QUESTIONS

69-1. An elderly patient tells the nurse that "the flowers in the garden don't smell the same as they used to." The nurse realizes this patient's sense of smell is:
1. Altered because of a sinus infection.
2. Altered because of an obstruction.
3. Decreased due to normal aging.
4. Decreased due to nasal polyps.

69-2. A patient tells the nurse that her hearing "has gotten worse over the years" after being treated with antibiotics for tuberculosis. The nurse realizes this patient's hearing loss is most likely because of:
1. Long-term use of herbal remedies.
2. Old age.
3. Ototoxicity.
4. The use of over-the-counter preparations.

69-3. A patient has small lesions on both corners of the mouth. The nurse realizes this finding could indicate:
1. A riboflavin deficiency.
2. Merkel cell carcinoma.
3. A deficiency in the clotting mechanism.
4. A congenital disorder.

69-4. The daughter of an elderly patient tells the nurse that her mother is losing weight and doesn't eat meals with the family anymore. Which of the following should the nurse assess in this patient?
1. Cognitive status
2. Swallowing ability
3. Nutritional status
4. Current medications

69-5. During a physical assessment, the nurse notes that the patient does not gag when the back of the mouth is touched with a tongue blade. This finding could be indicative of:
1. Hypogeusia.
2. Ageusia.
3. Vagus nerve paralysis.
4. An alteration in swallowing which could lead to respiratory issues.

CHAPTER 70

CARING FOR THE PATIENT WITH HEARING AND BALANCE DISORDERS

OUTCOME-BASED LEARNING OBJECTIVES

70-1. Identify and define the major structures included in the sense of hearing.

70-2. Compare and contrast the two mechanisms of hearing.

70-3. Distinguish the three types of hearing loss.

70-4. Apply health promotion strategies to prevent hearing loss in all age groups.

70-5. Compare and contrast the three different pathologic causes for a hearing disorder.

70-6. Discuss discharge priorities for a patient with a hearing disorder.

70-7. Explain specific aspects of the nursing management for a geriatric patient with a hearing disorder.

70-8. Apply the nursing process to a patient with a hearing disorder.

CHAPTER OUTLINE

I. Anatomy and Physiology of the Ear
   A. Mechanism of Hearing
II. Etiology and Epidemiology of Hearing Impairment
III. Pathophysiology and Treatment of Hearing Impairment or Loss
   A. Hearing Loss in the Newborn
   B. Hearing Loss in Children
   C. Hearing Loss in Adults
   D. Hearing Loss in Older Adults
   E. Noise-Induced Hearing Loss
   F. Acoustic Neuroma
   G. Balance and Equilibrium

KEY TERMS MATCHING EXERCISE 1

Write the letter of the correct definition in the space next to each term.

Term

_____ 1. air conduction
_____ 2. bone conduction
_____ 3. conductive hearing loss
_____ 4. mixed hearing loss
_____ 5. sensorineural hearing loss
_____ 6. exostosis
_____ 7. myringotomy
_____ 8. otitis externa
_____ 9. otosclerosis

Definition

a. Type of hearing loss attributed to damage to the eighth cranial nerve.

b. Abnormal bone growth within the middle ear that causes hearing loss.

c. Surgical procedure in which tubes are placed in the ears to facilitate drainage and prevent the buildup of pressure within the inner ear and prevent ear infections.

d. Process of sound waves reaching the inner ear for interpretation.

e. Type of hearing loss that is both conductive and sensorineural in cause.

f. Inflammation/infection of the external ear canal.

g. Type of hearing loss in which sound waves cannot reach the inner ear for processing and interpretation; caused by diseases such as external ear infections.

h. A condition of the ear canal in which the bony lining under the skin develops a number of lumps that grow into the tube. Also called *surfer's ear*.

i. Process of sound vibrations reaching the inner ear for interpretation.

KEY TERMS MATCHING EXERCISE 2

Write the letter of the correct definition in the space next to each term.

Term

_____ 10. stapedectomy
_____ 11. tympanoplasty
_____ 12. mastoidectomy
_____ 13. mastoiditis
_____ 14. otitis media
_____ 15. ototoxic
_____ 16. presbycusis
_____ 17. tinnitus
_____ 18. acoustic neuroma

Definition

a. Removal of the stapes bone and its replacement to restore hearing.

b. Inflammation/infection of the middle ear.

c. A benign tumor of the eighth cranial (acoustic) nerve.

d. A buzzing, roaring, or ringing in the ears.

e. Something that, if ingested, causes damage to the auditory nerve, affecting hearing.

f. Surgical repair of the eardrum or bones of the middle ear in an effort to restore hearing.

g. Infection of the mastoid bone.

h. Hearing loss caused by changes in the middle and inner ear due to the aging process.

i. Surgical procedure in which the mastoid process is excised in the event of infection.

KEY TERMS MATCHING EXERCISE 3

Write the letter of the correct definition in the space next to each term.

Term

_____ 19. noise-induced hearing loss (NIHL)

_____ 20. labyrinthectomy

_____ 21. labyrinthitis

_____ 22. vertigo

_____ 23. vestibular nerve dissection

_____ 24. Ménière's disease

_____ 25. frequency

_____ 26. decibel (dB)

_____ 27. pitch

Definition

a. Organ of balance within the middle ear.

b. Surgical procedure in which the labyrinth is excised to eradicate vertigo; results in complete hearing loss to the ear.

c. Describes frequency; low pitch is 100 Hz and high pitch is 10,000 Hz.

d. Inner ear disorder that affects hearing and balance.

e. Hearing loss caused by noises or sounds at a high decibel level for long periods of time.

f. A measurement of sound. Sounds typically range from 0 to 140 dB or greater.

g. The number of sound waves emanating per second; measured in Hertz (Hz). Hearing frequencies from 500 to 2,000 Hz are needed to understand everyday speech.

h. Surgical procedure to cut the vestibular nerve in the event of constant vertigo or dizziness.

i. Subjective sensation of spinning; dizziness; the illusion of rotational movement, tilting, and swaying with feelings of imbalance during standing or walking; symptom of a balance disorder.

SHORT ANSWER QUESTIONS

28. Name the three types of hearing loss and give an example of each.

_____

_____

_____

_____

29. What are the clinical manifestations of benign paroxysmal positional vertigo?

_____

_____

_____

_____

30. What is the treatment for tinnitus?

_____

_____

_____

_____

31. How do cochlear implants work?

_____

_____

_____

_____

32. What are the common causes of hearing loss in the elderly?

_____

_____

_____

_____

COMPLETE THE SENTENCE

33. Until the eustachian tube changes in size and angle, children are more susceptible than adults to _____

_____.

34. Noise-induced hearing loss (NIHL) is seen most frequently after an individual has had a prolonged exposure to noise or sound at the level of _____ to _____ dB or a sudden exposure to sound/noise at greater than _____ dB.

35. The term _____ _____ is often used to describe the symptoms associated with vertigo.

36. The three characteristics used to assess a person's ability to hear are _____, _____, and

_____.

37. If flushing the ear does not remove impacted cerumen, the patient is instructed to place _____

_____ in the ear 3 times per day for 2 days to soften it.

LABELING EXERCISE 1: ANATOMICAL STRUCTURES OF THE EAR

Place the term in the correct location.

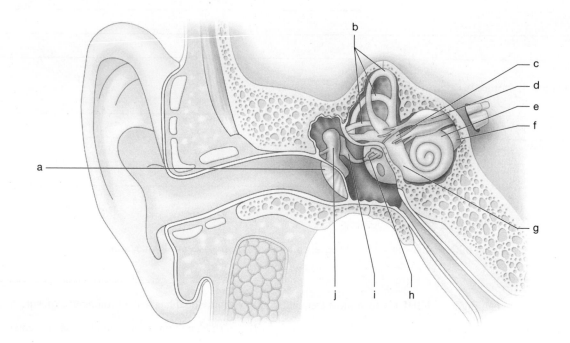

a. _____   f. _____

b. _____   g. _____

c. _____   h. _____

d. _____   i. _____

e. _____   j. _____

Cochlea
Cochlear nerve
Incus
Malleus
Saccule

Semicircular canals
Stapes
Tympanic membrane (eardrum)
Utricle
Vestibular nerve

LABELING EXERCISE 2: ANATOMICAL STRUCTURES OF BALANCE

Place the term in the correct location.

a. _____

b. _____

c. _____

d. _____

e. _____

f. _____

g. _____

Cochlea
Horizontal canal
Posterior canal
Saccule

Superior canal
Utricle
Vestibule

NCLEX-RN® REVIEW QUESTIONS

70-1. A patient with a history of ruptured eardrums tells the nurse that she was told that one of her bones in her ear malfunctions. The nurse realizes this patient is describing an alteration in which of the following structures?
 1. Incus
 2. Stapes
 3. Cochlea
 4. Malleus

70-2. A patient tells the nurse that he heard a very loud buzzing noise while lying on the table to have a CT scan of his head done. The nurse realizes this patient is describing which mechanism of hearing?
 1. Bone conduction
 2. Air conduction
 3. Middle ear conduction
 4. Acoustic nerve conduction

70-3. A patient has been experiencing progressive hearing loss that he was told was because of antibiotics he had taken as a child. The nurse realizes this patient is most likely experiencing which type of hearing loss?
 1. Sensorineural
 2. Conductive
 3. Mixed
 4. Interpretive

70-4. A 12-year-old child has experienced otitis media four times in the last year. Which of the following should the nurse instruct this patient and his parents?
1. Make sure the entire course of antibiotics are completed.
2. Always keep your appointments to have your ears checked.
3. Everyone should have an annual hearing test completed.
4. Ongoing episodes of otitis media could lead to permanent hearing loss.

70-5. A 10-year-old patient is scheduled for a myringotomy. The nurse realizes this procedure is used to most likely treat which of the following causes of a hearing disorder?
1. Mechanical
2. Inflammatory
3. Obstructive
4. Mixed

70-6. A patient was admitted with an acute onset of a hearing deficit because of an industrial accident. Which of the following should be included in this patient's discharge planning?
1. Nutritional needs
2. Resumption of normal activities of daily living
3. A return-to-work plan
4. Counseling on future occupational needs and choices

70-7. A healthy elderly patient tells the nurse that she's just waiting to die because she can't hear anymore and she knows that hearing is "the last sense to go." Which of the following should the nurse say or do for this patient?
1. Leave the patient to rest alone.
2. Agree with the patient and ask if there's anything that can be done at this time.
3. Suggest the choices of a hearing aid or other devices or procedures that can help return the sense of hearing.
4. Ask the patient if there's anyone in particular that she would like the nurse to contact.

70-8. A patient with a hearing deficit tells the nurse that she doesn't understand what's going on with her health. Which of the following should the nurse do to help this patient?
1. Ask the physician to talk with the patient.
2. Provide the patient with educational materials.
3. Shout into one of the patient's ears that she will talk with her when she gets some time.
4. Face the patient, speak in a low tone, and answer the patient's questions.

CHAPTER 71

CARING FOR THE PATIENT WITH VISUAL DISORDERS

OUTCOME-BASED LEARNING OBJECTIVES

71-1. Identify the normal basic anatomy and physiology of the eye.

71-2. Perform basic assessment, tests, and examination of the eye in obtaining meaningful data for management and treatment.

71-3. Describe different types of visual and ocular conditions and problems.

71-4. Apply nursing diagnoses, nursing process, and patient teaching associated with the visual and ocular problems of adults.

71-5. Discuss and provide meaningful resources for patients with visual and ocular problems.

CHAPTER OUTLINE

   I. Anatomy and Physiology Overview
   A. Orbit and Ocular Adnexa
   B. Eye Structures
      1. Uveal Tract
      2. Lens
      3. Vitreous Body
      4. Retina
  II. Visual Assessment
   A. Initial Examination
 III. Visual Impairment
   A. Refraction
      1. Emmetropia
      2. Ametropia
         a. Myopia
         b. Hyperopia
         c. Astigmatism
         d. Presbyopia

B. Strabismus
1. Adult Strabismus
2. Diplopia
3. Amblyopia
4. Phoria
5. Tropia
6. Nystagmus
C. Macular Degeneration
1. Drusen
2. Dry Age-Related Macular Degeneration
3. Wet Age-Related Macular Degeneration
4. Disciform Scar
5. Laboratory and Diagnostic Procedures and Medical Management
   NURSING MANAGEMENT
   COLLABORATIVE MANAGEMENT
   HEALTH PROMOTION
D. Diabetic Retinopathy
1. Epidemiology, Etiology, and Risk Factors
2. Pathophysiology and Clinical Manifestations
3. Laboratory and Diagnostic Procedures
4. Medical Management
   NURSING MANAGEMENT
   ASSESSMENT AND NURSING DIAGNOSES
   OUTCOMES AND EVALUATION PARAMETERS
   PLANNING AND INTERVENTIONS
   COLLABORATIVE MANAGEMENT
   HEALTH PROMOTION
E. Glaucoma
1. Epidemiology and Etiology
2. Pathophysiology
3. Open-Angle Glaucoma
4. Ocular Hypertension
5. Low-Tension Glaucoma
6. Secondary Glaucoma
7. Acute Angle-Closure Glaucoma
8. Clinical Manifestations
9. Laboratory and Diagnostic Procedures
10. Medical Management
    NURSING MANAGEMENT
    ASSESSMENT AND NURSING DIAGNOSES
    OUTCOMES AND EVALUATION PARAMETERS
    PLANNING AND INTERVENTIONS
    COLLABORATIVE MANAGEMENT
    DISCHARGE PRIORITIES AND HEALTH PROMOTION
F. Cataracts
1. Immature Cataracts
2. Cataract Surgical Implications
   a. Cataract Surgery
   b. Postoperative Cataract Care
   NURSING MANAGEMENT
IV. Infections and Inflammation
A. Dry Eye Syndrome
B. Blepharitis

    C. Conjunctivitis
       1. Viral Conjunctivitis
       2. Allergic Conjunctivitis
       3. Bacterial Conjunctivitis
    D. Uveitis
    E. Bullous Keratopathy
    F. Corneal Ulcer
    G. Trachoma
    H. Preseptal Cellulitis
    I. Orbital Cellulitis

DISCHARGE PRIORITIES AND HEALTH PROMOTION

    J. Endophthalmitis
       1. Clinical Manifestations
       2. Diagnostic and Laboratory Procedures and Medical Management
  V. Eye Trauma and Injury
    A. Epidemiology and Etiology
    B. Pathophysiology with Clinical Manifestations and Medical Management
       1. Chemical Burns
       2. Central Retinal Artery Occlusion
       3. Open Globe
       4. Laboratory and Diagnostic Procedures

NURSING MANAGEMENT

    C. Eye Urgencies
       1. Penetrating or Perforating Trauma
       2. Blunt Trauma
       3. Neovascular Glaucoma
       4. Ocular Flashes and Floaters
       5. Retinal Vascular Occlusions
       6. Sudden Vision Loss
    D. Eyelid Laceration
  VI. Retinal Detachment
    A. Posterior Vitreous Detachment
    B. Retinal Breaks
    C. Vitreous Hemorrhage
    D. Nonrhegmatogenous and Rhegmatogenous Detachment
       1. Retinal Detachment Surgical Implications
          a. Cryopexy
          b. Vitrectomy
  VII. Eye Tumors or Neoplasms
    A. Benign Eye Tumors
       1. Nevus
       2. Hypertrophy of Retinal Pigment Epithelium
       3. Lymphoid Hyperplasia
       4. Papilloma
       5. Seborrheic Keratosis
       6. Xanthelasma
       7. Telangiectasis
    B. Precancerous Eye Tumors
       1. Actinic Keratosis
       2. Melanocytic Nevus
    C. Malignant Eye Tumors
       1. Basal Cell Carcinoma
       2. Squamous Cell Carcinoma

3. Intraocular Lymphoid
4. Intraocular Choroidal Metastasis Tumor
5. Merkel Cell Carcinoma
6. Kaposi's Sarcoma
7. Orbital Tumors

NURSING MANAGEMENT AND HEALTH PROMOTION

VIII. Gerontological Considerations
IX. Cultural Considerations
X. Genetic Considerations
XI. Ethical Issues
XII. Research
XIII. Summary

KEY TERMS MATCHING EXERCISE 1

Write the letter of the correct definition in the space next to each term.

Term

_____ 1. accommodation

_____ 2. emmetropia

_____ 3. ametropia

_____ 4. astigmatism

_____ 5. amblyopia

_____ 6. contrast sensitivity (CS)

_____ 7. legal blindness

_____ 8. macular degeneration (MD)

_____ 9. metamorphopsia

_____ 10. nystagmus

Definition

a. The best-corrected visual acuity of 20/200 or a visual field of 20 degrees or less in both eyes.

b. A general term used to indicate a refractive error that can usually be corrected with glasses, contact lenses, or possibly refractive surgery.

c. The condition of the normal eye when parallel rays are focused exactly on the retina and vision is perfect. Normal refractive error or vision without any corrective optical devices.

d. An optical defect.

e. Disorder in which a person has an eye with decreased or impaired vision with no obvious anatomic explanation, usually from childhood. Also known by the lay term *lazy eye*.

f. The deterioration and mottling of the macula through the course of time.

g. A constant, involuntary tremor, oscillation, or jerky movement of the eyeball; the movement may be in any direction.

h. The ability of the lens to focus up close or near; to focus a clear image on the retina.

i. Condition characterized by vision distortion, that is, when straight lines, such as door frames or posts, look crooked or irregular.

j. The function of being able to distinguish subtle gradations of grayish patterns between targets and background.

KEY TERMS MATCHING EXERCISE 2

Write the letter of the correct definition in the space next to each term.

Term

_____ 11. diabetic retinopathy (DR)

_____ 12. retinopathy

_____ 13. cotton-wool spots (CWS)

_____ 14. flame-shaped hemorrhages

_____ 15. acute angle-closure glaucoma (AACG)

_____ 16. foreign body sensation (FBS)

_____ 17. hypopyon

_____ 18. central retinal artery occlusion (CRAO)

_____ 19. open globe

_____ 20. retinal detachment

Definition

a. White layer of inflammatory cells in the anterior chamber.

b. An open eyeball with a laceration, penetrating injury, or intraocular foreign body; usually results from blunt trauma or projectile injury.

c. Disorder characterized by the angle in the anterior chamber closing suddenly as a result of iris blockage; prevents aqueous flow through the trabecular meshwork, causing the intraocular pressure to rise suddenly, usually to greater than 40 mmHg.

d. Blockage of the central retinal artery, usually by an embolism. Its symptom is sudden, painless, unilateral blindness.

e. Degenerative changes in the retina.

f. A feeling in the eye of a "gritty" feeling, as if something is in the eye.

g. Soft exudates that appear as white cotton spots in the nerve fiber layer of the retina; caused by lack of blood supply to the tissue.

h. Retinal hemorrhages that occur in the nerve fiber layer.

i. Disorder characterized by weakened and damaged blood vessels (capillaries) that result in edema from leaking capillaries that hemorrhage.

j. The separation of the sensory retinal layers from the retinal pigment epithelium, where subretinal fluid collects in the potential space.

KEY TERM CROSSWORD

Complete the crossword puzzle below using key terms.

Across:

1. Deposits of various size, shape, consistency, refractive index, and motility within the eye's vitreous humor, which is normally transparent.
3. The opacity of the natural crystalline lens.
6. A defect in vision caused by an imperfection in the eye (often the eyeball is too short).
7. Individuals see nearby objects clearly, but distant objects appear blurred.
8. Condition where the eye exhibits a progressively diminished ability to focus on near objects with age; also recognized as a symptom of aging.
11. Seeing double vision, when one object appears as two.
12. Sudden bright light; flashes appear as sparks or minuscule strands of light, almost like streaks of lightning that occur when the vitreous gel bumps, rubs, or tugs against the retina.
13. A tendency toward a functional deviation or defect that results from a break in visual fusion by covering an eye.
15. A collection of blood cells in the anterior chamber of the eye.

Down:

2. Deviation from the normal.
4. A condition in which an individual's eyes do not look at the same object together. Also referred to as cross eyed.
5. A group of diseases of the optic nerve involving loss of retinal ganglion cells in a characteristic pattern of optic neuropathy.
9. Yellowish, round, slightly elevated, different-sized subretinal pigment epithelial deposits in the macula.
10. Deviation of an eye from the normal position with respect to the line of vision when the eyes are open.
14. Inward deviation of the eye.

SHORT ANSWER QUESTIONS

21. What are the potential contraindications for refractive surgery?

_____

_____

_____

_____

22. What causes presbyopia?

_____

_____

_____

_____

23. What are the risk factors for age-related macular degeneration?

_____

_____

_____

_____

24. How is glaucoma diagnosed?

_____

_____

_____

_____

25. What are the signs and symptoms of cataracts?

_____

_____

_____

_____

26. Describe the three types of conjunctivitis.

_____

_____

_____

_____

27. What causes orbital cellulitis?

_____

_____

_____

_____

28. What causes endophthalmitis?

_____

_____

_____

_____

29. What are the clinical manifestations of retinal detachment?

_____

_____

_____

_____

30. Describe the signs of ocular tumors.

_____

_____

_____

_____

TRUE OR FALSE?

31. _____ T/F Adults with normal eye function should have a dilated eye examination every year.

32. _____ T/F Intraocular pressure can be assessed by palpation over the eyelid.

33. _____ T/F Four of the leading causes of visual impairment are macular degeneration, diabetic retinopathy, glaucoma, and cataracts.

34. _____ T/F Most adult onset of strabismus is the result of head trauma, especially if one is unconscious for a long period of time.

35. _____ T/F Family history, diabetes, and being very farsighted can put one at greater risk for developing glaucoma.

36. _____ T/F Risk factors that may accelerate cataract growth are ultraviolet light, strain from reading with inadequate light, alcohol, high-fat diet, and corticosteroid therapy.

37. _____ T/F The most common causative organisms in adults for orbital cellulitis are staphylococci and streptococci from bacterial sinusitis.

38. _____ T/F An intraocular foreign body should be left in place and stabilized until medical management can be determined.

39. _____ T/F Nevi located near the corneosceral limbus on the iris should be surgically removed as soon as possible.

40. _____ T/F Color blindness is a hereditary condition.

LABELING EXERCISE: THE HUMAN EYE

Place the term in the correct location.

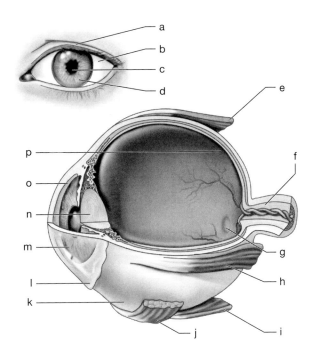

a. _____

b. _____

c. _____

d. _____

e. _____

f. _____

g. _____

h. _____

i. _____

j. _____

k. _____

l. _____

m. _____

n. _____

o. _____

p. _____

Conjunctiva
Cornea
Eyelid
Inferior oblique muscle
Inferior rectus muscle
Iris
Iris
Lens

Macula
Medial rectus muscle
Optic nerve
Pupil
Retina
Sclera
Sclera
Superior rectus muscle

NCLEX-RN® REVIEW QUESTIONS

71-1. A patient tells the nurse that he has been having more difficulty seeing in the night. The nurse realizes that which of the following eye structures is responsible for night vision?
  1. Retinal pigment epithelium
  2. Optic disc
  3. Vitreous body
  4. Photoreceptor layer of the retina

71-2. While conducting an alternating cover test for phoria, the nurse notes that a patient's just uncovered eye is eso. This finding would indicate:
  1. The just uncovered eye moves inward.
  2. The just uncovered eye moves outward.
  3. The just uncovered eye has steady fixation.
  4. Vertical phoria.

71-3. A patient tells the nurse that she needed laser treatment to her eyes one time because her blood sugar reading was 9%. The nurse realizes this patient is describing which of the following?
  1. Cataracts
  2. Glaucoma
  3. Diabetic retinopathy
  4. Retinal detachment

71-4. The nurse is planning care for a patient who has had surgery to remove a cataract. Which of the following should be included in this patient's discharge instructions?
  1. Use the prescribed eyedrops for approximately 4 weeks.
  2. Be examined for corrective lenses within 1 week.
  3. Use prescribed eyedrops for 1 day.
  4. The eye patch will need to be worn for at least 12 weeks.

71-5. The daughter of a patient diagnosed with macular degeneration and loss of central vision asks the nurse what she can do to make sure she doesn't develop the same eye condition. Which of the following can the nurse provide to this patient?
  1. Wear sunglasses and hats to prevent sunlight exposure.
  2. Take antioxidant vitamins.
  3. Take an aspirin a day.
  4. Ask your physician for a prescription to take a medication called a statin.

CHAPTER 72

DISASTER AND BIOTERRORISM NURSING

OUTCOME-BASED LEARNING OBJECTIVES

72-1. Define terrorism.

72-2. Describe the historical use of various agents.

72-3. Discuss various chemical agents, signs and symptoms, and treatment.

72-4. Compare and contrast biologic agents, signs and symptoms, and treatment.

72-5. Delineate the signs and symptoms of radiation illness.

72-6. Apply the principles of an incident command system in the hospital setting during a WMD event.

72-7. Describe the role of DMAT, DMORT, and the Strategic National Stockpile.

72-8. Apply critical incident stress principles to WMD events.

EXPLORE **mynursingkit**™

PEARSON

MyNursingKit is your one stop for online chapter review materials and resources. Prepare for success with additional NCLEX®-style practice questions, interactive assignments and activities, web links, animations and videos, and more!

Register your access code from the front of your book at **www.mynursingkit.com**

CHAPTER OUTLINE

I. Terrorism
- A. Targets
- B. Historical Use of Various Agents
    1. Chemical Agents
    2. Biologic Agents
    3. Radiologic Agents
    4. Explosive Agents
- C. Planning for Disasters
- D. National Standards of Nursing Education

II. Types of Events
- A. Personal Protective Equipment
    1. Level A
    2. Level B
    3. Level C
    4. Level D
- B. Decontamination

III. Chemical Agents
  A. Spread

NURSING MANAGEMENT OF THE PATIENT EXPOSED TO CHEMICAL AGENTS
COLLABORATIVE MANAGEMENT

  B. Routes of Entry
    1. Ingestion
    2. Inhalation
    3. Injection
    4. Dermal Exposure
  C. Nerve Agents
    1. Sarin (GB)
    2. Soman (GD)
    3. Tabun (GA)
    4. V Agent (VX)
  D. Vesicants
    1. Mustard
    2. Lewisite
    3. Phosgene Oxime
  E. Blood Agents
  F. Choking Agents (Asphyxiates)
    1. Ammonia
    2. Chlorine
    3. Phosgene
  G. Irritants
    1. Tear Gas (CS)
    2. Pepper Spray (OC)
  H. Other Agents
IV. Biologic Agents

NURSING MANAGEMENT OF WMD INFECTION
COLLABORATIVE MANAGEMENT

  A. Spread
    1. Aerosol Route
    2. Oral Route
    3. Injection
    4. Dermal Exposure
    5. Vector Transmission
  B. Bacteria
    1. Anthrax
      a. Cutaneous Anthrax
      b. Inhalation Anthrax
      c. Gastrointestinal Anthrax
    2. Brucellosis
    3. Plague
      a. Bubonic Plague
      b. Septicemic Plague
      c. Pneumonic Plague
    4. Tularemia
      a. Typhoidal Tularemia
      b. Ulceroglandular Tularemia
      c. Oropharyngeal Tularemia
    5. Q Fever
  C. Viruses
    1. Smallpox
    2. Venezuelan Equine Encephalitis
    3. Viral Hemorrhagic Fevers

D. Toxins
  1. Botulinum
  2. Staphylococcal Enterotoxin B
  3. Ricin
  4. Trichothecene Mycotoxins
V. Radiologic Agents
  NURSING MANAGEMENT OF THE PATIENT EXPOSED TO RADIOLOGIC AGENTS
  COLLABORATIVE MANAGEMENT
  A. Devices
  B. Types of Radiation
  1. Exposure
  2. Ionizing Radiation
  3. Routes of Entry
  C. Radiation Exposure
  D. Acute Radiation Syndrome
  1. Prodromal Phase
  2. Latent Phase
  3. Illness Phase
  4. Recovery or Death
VI. Explosions
  A. Blast Injuries
VII. How These Events Affect the Health Care System
  A. WMD as Medical Disasters
  B. Specific Problems
  C. Problems After the Initial Response
VIII. National Incident Command System
  A. Hospital Incident Command System
  1. Organization
  2. Sections
  B. START Triage
IX. National Resources
  A. Strategic National Stockpile
  1. Organization
  2. Push Packs
  3. Vendor Managed Inventory
  4. Technical Support
  B. National Disaster Medical System
  1. Disaster Medical Assistance Teams
    a. Types of DMAT Teams
    b. Deployment
  2. Disaster Mortuary Operational Response Teams
    a. Services
X. Critical Incident Stress Management
  A. Stress
  1. Common Signs of Stress
  2. Critical Incident
  B. Crisis Intervention and Critical Incident Stress Management
  1. Health Care Workers
    a. Demobilization
    b. Critical Incident Defusing
    c. Critical Incident Stress Debriefing
  2. Community
XI. Summary

KEY TERMS MATCHING EXERCISE

Write the letter of the correct definition in the space next to each term.

Term

_____ 1. biologic agent

_____ 2. hot zone

_____ 3. warm zone

_____ 4. cold zone

_____ 5. chemical agent

_____ 6. blister agent

_____ 7. nerve agents

_____ 8. choking agent

_____ 9. incapacitating agent

_____ 10. riot control agent

_____ 11. vomiting agent

_____ 12. radiologic agents

_____ 13. critical incident stress management

Definition

a. Chemical agent that can cause redness and irritation of the skin and blistering. Also called a *vesicant*.

b. The area of highest contamination in a decontamination area. Also called the *red zone* or the *exclusion zone*.

c. Chemical agents that cause vomiting.

d. The zone where no one is allowed without first being decontaminated. Also called the *green zone* or the *support zone*.

e. A comprehensive approach to the management of stress and critical incidents.

f. Viruses, bacteria, and toxins that can be weaponized to cause disease, illness, and/or death.

g. Chemicals that inactivate acetylcholinesterase at the receptor site. They cause symptoms of SLUDGE'M (*s*alivation, *l*acrimation, *u*rination, *d*efecation, *g*astric upset, *e*mesis, and *m*iosis).

h. Chemicals that can be used as weapons to cause injury, illness, and death. They are roughly divided by their mechanism of action into blood agents, blister agents, choking agents, irritants, and nerve agents.

i. Agents that generally cause pain, burning, lacrimation, or discomfort upon exposure to mucous membranes. Also called an *irritant*.

j. The zone where actual decontamination takes place. Also called the *yellow zone* or the *contamination reduction corridor*.

k. Chemical agents that decrease acetylcholine at nerve synapses. They work in the opposite manner of nerve agents.

l. Chemicals that cause injury, illness, and death by damaging the lungs. Also called an *asphyxiate*.

m. Agents that are a source of alpha, beta, or gamma radiation that can be used as a weapon.

KEY TERM CROSSWORD

Complete the crossword puzzle below using key terms.

Across:

1. Agents that generally cause pain, burning, lacrimation, or discomfort upon exposure to mucous membranes. Also called riot control agents.
6. Acronym for a device that can release radiation into the environment.
8. Acronym that describes equipment designed to protect the wearer from various hazards.
9. Acronym for a system of policies and procedures within a framework that allows for safe and effective management during a disaster.
10. Acronym for an international organization coordinated by Vanderbilt University whose goal is to teach nursing groups about emergency preparedness.
11. Acronym for a formal event run by trained counselors to assist those involved in a critical incident to better cope with the incident.
12. Acronym for a national repository of pharmaceutical agents, vaccines, medical supplies, and equipment that can be delivered to the site of a large-scale disaster to augment local and state resources.
13. An act designed to disrupt daily life and cause terror and panic.
14. The ability of a chemical agent to remain in an area. In general, the agent would have a low vapor pressure and a high vapor density.
16. The reduction or removal of contaminating agents.

Down:

2. A stressful incident that is so markedly distressing and powerful as to overcome a person's normal feelings of control and coping.
3. Material produced by living organisms that has chemical properties that can cause injury, illness, and death.
4. Acronym for a team of volunteers that can assist with handling mass casualties in time of disaster.
5. Chemical agent that can cause redness and irritation of the skin and blistering. Also called a blistering agent.
7. Acronym suggested for common use by the Department of Justice to describe weapons of mass destruction.
15. Acronym for an acute illness caused by irradiation of the whole body. The phases of the illness are prodromal, latent, illness, and recovery or death.
17. Acronym for weapons of mass destruction, which are agents that can cause massive damage and injury.
18. Acronym for a group of volunteer health care professionals and ancillary staff that can provide emergency medical services and relief in times of disaster.
19. Acutely swollen and usually painful lymph node seen in plague near the site of the flea bite.
20. Chemical agents that cause injury, illness, and death by damaging the lungs. Also called choking agents.

SHORT ANSWER QUESTIONS

14. Explain why some disaster incidents are not immediately recognized as having taken place.

_____

_____

_____

_____

15. What are some of the problems associated with personal protective equipment?

_____

_____

_____

_____

16. How are chemical agents spread, and what are the routes of entry?

_____

17. Describe the signs and symptoms seen with nerve agents.

_____

_____

_____

_____

18. Why would the release of a biologic agent have a greater impact on the health care system than release of a chemical agent?

_____

_____

19. What parts of the body are most likely to be affected in a primary blast injury?

_____

20. Why is including the use of media important when planning a WMD event?

_____

TRUE OR FALSE?

21. _____ T/F   After a disaster occurs, the most seriously injured casualties are usually the first to arrive at hospitals.

22. _____ T/F   Level D PPE is regular clothing with no respiratory or skin protection.

23. _____ T/F   Persistent agents, such as mustard and VX, are more useful than nonpersistent agents as tactical agents within a population.

24. _____ T/F   Smallpox is thought to be the most likely biologic agent to be used in a terrorist attack.

25. _____ T/F   Spore-forming bacteria such as anthrax are very stable and may remain in soil and water for years.

26. _____ T/F   All exposure to radiation increases the risk for cancers later in life.

27. _____ T/F   Most deaths from acute radiation syndrome are related opportunistic infections as a result of bone marrow destruction.

28. _____ T/F   The National Incident Management System is for use only in the prevention, preparedness, response, recovery, and mitigation phases of disaster management.

29. _____ T/F   In the START system a yellow tag indicates that the patient is ambulatory, with or without minor injuries, and does not require immediate treatment.

30. _____ T/F   Increasing knowledge and decreasing the perceived stress for health care workers and other emergency service personnel can be done through demobilization, critical incident defusing, and critical incident stress debriefing.

NCLEX-RN® REVIEW QUESTIONS

72-1. Which of the following may be considered an act of "domestic" terrorism?
1. A group of local protestors outside an abortion clinic.
2. A riot following the outcome of a soccer game in Peru.
3. A suicide bomber that targeted a marketplace in Israel.
4. A Marine detonating a bomb inside the Pentagon.

72-2. The nurse attends a seminar on the use of various biological, chemical, radiological and explosive agents throughout history. Which of the following statements by the nurse would indicate a clear understanding of these topics?
1. "Georgi Markov was assassinated when the pellet with which he was shot released sarin into his body."
2. "Pungi sticks used by the Viet Cong caused infected sores, as they were contaminated with human waste."
3. "Biologic experimentation by the Japanese during World War II included chlorine gas and sulfur mustard."
4. "The Chernobyl Nuclear Reactor Unit in the Ukraine accidentally released a large cloud of polonium-210."

72-3. The nurse would expect to implement which of the following interventions when caring for the patient exposed to smallpox? Select all that apply.
1. Immediately institute droplet isolation.
2. Provide the smallpox vaccine.
3. Administer doxycycline and Rifampin.
4. Treat in a screened-in area.
5. Place face-to-face contacts under surveillance.
6. Administer antitoxin as soon as possible.
7. Perform vigorous gastric lavage.

72-4. After exposure to a chemical agent the patient begins experiencing severe eye irritation, headache, hematemesis, hoarseness, and dermal changes. The nurse recognizes the patient could be experiencing signs and symptoms of exposure to:
1. Cyanide.
2. Mustard.
3. V agent.
4. Phosgene.

72-5. Which of the following statements best describes acute radiation syndrome (ARS)?
1. Radiation produces highly reactive free radicals that directly damage proteins, mRNA, and DNA.
2. Those body tissues with higher cell proliferation rates are less susceptible to the effects of radiation.
3. The severity of the symptoms and the duration of each phase increases as the radiation dose goes up.
4. The hematopoietic system contains some of the most radiation-resistant tissues in the human body.

72-6. The Incident Command System has been employed following a bombing at a shopping mall. A patient injured in the incident sustained an obviously open left tibial fracture with minimal active bleeding. Pulses are 2+ in all extremities, capillary refill time is brisk, and the patient is awake, alert, and oriented. Vital signs are HR 96, BP 136/74, RR 22, and pain 8/10. Using the START triage system, the nurse should assign this patient to which of the following categories?
1. Black
2. Green
3. Yellow
4. Red

72-7. Which of the following statements by the nurse regarding the Strategic National Stockpile (SNS) would indicate the need for further instruction?
1. "The receiving site is responsible for providing its own gloves and sharps containers."
2. "The Strategic National Stockpile is part of the Department of Homeland Security."
3. "Supplies are released by the Centers for Disease Control based on a governor's request."
4. "Vaccines, antitoxins, and intravenous antibiotics are all kept in the 12-hour Push Packs."

72-8. The nurse may expect to find which of the following signs and symptoms of stress in the patient after a critical incident? Select all that apply.
1. Near syncope
2. Decreased heart rate
3. Hopelessness
4. Excess sweating
5. Memory problems
6. Withdrawal
7. Coherent thinking

CHAPTER 73

CARING FOR THE PATIENT IN THE EMERGENCY DEPARTMENT

OUTCOME-BASED LEARNING OBJECTIVES

73-1. Explain the practice of emergency nursing.

73-2. Differentiate among the various components of the triage process and determine each component's relevance.

73-3. Compare and contrast patient priority categories.

73-4. Explain the legal issues related to the practice of emergency nursing.

73-5. Describe preparation for emergency nursing practice.

CHAPTER OUTLINE

I. History
II. The Role of the Emergency Department
III. IOM Report and the Future of Emergency Care
IV. Emergency Nursing Roles
    A. Specialty Roles in Emergency Nursing
V. Triage
    A. Types of Triage
    B. Components of Triage
    C. Gerontological Considerations
    D. Triage Urgency Categories
    E. Disaster Triage
VI. Legal Issues
    A. Emergency Medical Treatment and Active Labor Act
        1. Consent
    B. Evidence Collection and Preservation
VII. Preparation for Practice
    A. Discharge Priorities
    B. Health Promotion
VIII. Summary

KEY TERMS MATCHING EXERCISE

Write the letter of the correct definition in the space next to each term.

Term

_____ 1. emergency nursing

_____ 2. triage

_____ 3. Emergency Medical Treatment and Active Labor Act (EMTALA)

_____ 4. forensic evidence

_____ 5. oligoanalgesia

Definition

a. A process that is used to determine the severity of a patient's illness or injury.

b. Results when a patient complains of pain, but no interventions are provided for pain relief.

c. Something that is legally submitted to a court of law as a means of determining the truth related to an alleged crime.

d. The care of individuals of all ages with perceived or actual physical or emotional alterations of health that are undiagnosed or require further interventions.

e. A part of the 1986 COBRA laws and the 1990 OBRA amendment that defines the legal responsibilities of Medicare-participating hospitals in treating individuals who present with emergency medical conditions; ensures that patients have access to emergency services regardless of their ability to pay.

SHORT ANSWER QUESTIONS

6. What are the differences between general consent, informed consent, and implied consent?

_____

_____

_____

_____

7. What emergency nursing roles are open to nurses?

_____

_____

_____

_____

8. What is involved in the "across the room assessment" that is the first part of triage?

_____

_____

_____

_____

9. Why is ongoing reassessment especially important in the emergency department setting?

_____

_____

_____

_____

10. What is the difference between the four- and five-level triage urgency scales?

_____

_____

_____

_____

TRUE OR FALSE?

11. _____ T/F   Emergency departments have become the primary source of health care for the poor and uninsured patient.

12. _____ T/F   The first emergency departments were opened in hospitals in the early 1900s.

13. _____ T/F   The process of triage was established after hospitals began opening emergency departments.

14. _____ T/F   Emergency nursing can be practiced both inside and outside the hospital.

15. _____ T/F   The emergency nurse's intuition plays a part in assessment of patients during triage.

16. _____ T/F   A hospital may never delay an appropriate medical screening examination or further examination or treatment to inquire about the patient's payment method or insurance status.

17. _____ T/F   It is the emergency nurse's responsibility to discern whether a patient's request for pain relief is based on true need or the desire to be medicated for other reasons.

18. _____ T/F   Emergency department nurses are responsible for educating patients on health promotion as well as discharge priorities.

19. _____ T/F   Forensic evidence is something that is legally submitted to a court of law as a means of determining the truth related to a death.

20. _____ T/F   More training and protocols are needed to provide children with the most appropriate care in emergencies.

NCLEX-RN® REVIEW QUESTIONS

73-1. The nurse realizes that the practice of emergency nursing could be explained by which of the following statements?
1. "Emergency nursing is unique because it involves the application of the nursing process to patients of all ages who require immediate care."
2. "The development of this specialty has flourished over the last 90 years, since Florence Nightingale cared for the wounded in Vietnam."
3. "Providing care becomes less challenging in the emergency department as the patient population becomes increasingly more diverse."
4. "Nurses providing emergency care may become certified in their respective field by successfully completing the EMTALA exam."

73-2. The nurse is triaging a pediatric patient who is complaining of abdominal pain. Which of the following would be the best and most comprehensive method of evaluating this patient?
1. EMTALA
2. ACEP
3. CIAMPEDS
4. MVIT

73-3. A patient comes into the emergency department with a complaint of right ankle pain after stepping in a hole 1 hour prior to arrival. The affected ankle is moderately edematous with good pulse, motor, and sensory function distal to the injury, but the patient is unable to weight bear secondary to the pain. Vital signs are HR 95, BP 136/72, RR 20, T 99.1° F, SpO$_2$ 100%, and pain 8 on a 0–10 scale. Based on the five-level Emergency Severity Index system, how should this patient be categorized at triage?
   1. Level I – Resuscitative
   2. Level II – Emergent
   3. Level III – Urgent
   4. Level V – Non-urgent

73-4. The nurse has attended a class on evidence collection and chain of custody for emergency nurses. Which of the following statements made by the nurse would indicate the need for further instruction?
   1. "If possible, wound care should be postponed until photographs are taken."
   2. "Evidence should always be placed in a plastic bag if it is wet or bloody."
   3. "Gloves should be changed frequently to prevent cross contamination."
   4. "The collected evidence should be locked in a secure area until its release."

73-5. The nurse wants to practice emergency nursing. To do this, the nurse understands that it:
   1. Requires a familiarity with a single patient population.
   2. Utilizes an extensive and generalized patient assessment.
   3. Requires little skill in venipuncture or intravenous insertion.
   4. May include caring for patients from various age groups.

CHAPTER 74

CARING FOR THE PATIENT WITH MULTISYSTEM TRAUMA

OUTCOME-BASED LEARNING OBJECTIVES

74-1. Discuss the correlation between mechanism of injury with patient assessment based on an understanding of the kinematics of trauma.

74-2. List the priorities of the primary and secondary surveys.

74-3. Explain the rationale for the tertiary survey.

74-4. Compare and contrast special considerations experienced during the initial resuscitation.

CHAPTER OUTLINE

I. Kinematics of Injury
   A. Motor Vehicle Collisions
      1. Frontal Impact
      2. Side Impact
      3. Rear Impact
      4. Vehicle Rollover
      5. Ejection
   B. Motorcycle Crashes
      1. Frontal Impact
      2. Side Impact
      3. Laying Down of the Motorcycle
   C. Pedestrian Injuries
   D. Falls
   E. Penetrating Injuries
      1. Stab Wounds
      2. Gunshot Wounds
   F. Blast Injuries

KEY TERMS MATCHING EXERCISE 1

Write the letter of the correct definition in the space next to each term.

Term

_____ 1. kinematics
_____ 2. flail chest
_____ 3. pulmonary contusion
_____ 4. massive hemothorax
_____ 5. open pneumothorax
_____ 6. tension pneumothorax
_____ 7. apoptosis

Definition

a. Occurs when a person sustains two or more rib fractures in two or more places such that the ribs are no longer attached to the thoracic cage, resulting in a free or floating segment of chest wall. As a result, during spontaneous ventilation the floating segment moves in the opposite direction or paradoxically to the chest wall. This condition is almost always associated with pulmonary contusion.

b. The predictive patterns of injuries.

c. Occurs when an injury perforates the chest or pleural space. During inspiration air enters the pleural space and becomes trapped. As more air is trapped, the pressure in the pleural space increases, collapsing the lung and causing the mediastinum to shift to the opposite side.

d. Programmed cell death in a multicellular organism; process by which cells can self-destruct when infected or mutated.

e. Occurs when blunt thoracic trauma is applied through the chest wall to the parenchyma, causing disruption of alveolar capillary networks and usually resulting in hypoxemia; initially a hemorrhage into the lung tissue followed by alveolar and interstitial edema.

f. An open communication between the atmosphere and intrathoracic pressure; usually caused by penetrating trauma.

g. An accumulation of 1,500 mL or more of blood in the thoracic cavity.

KEY TERMS MATCHING EXERCISE 2

Write the letter of the correct definition in the space next to each term.

Term

_____ 8. Beck's triad
_____ 9. cardiac tamponade
_____ 10. Battle's sign
_____ 11. FAST examination
_____ 12. hyphema
_____ 13. raccoon eyes
_____ 14. rehabilitation

Definition

a. The multidisciplinary plan of care that maximizes an impaired individual's function by minimizing the deficits to achieve the highest quality of life possible.

b. A collection of blood cells in the anterior chamber of the eye.

c. Focused assessment with sonography for trauma.

d. Bleeding into the pericardial sac. As the accumulation of blood increases, it compresses the atria and ventricles, decreasing venous return and filling pressure, which leads to decreased cardiac output, myocardial hypoxia, and cardiac failure.

e. Classic assessment findings for the patient with cardiac tamponade, consisting of decreased blood pressure, muffled heart sounds, and jugular venous distention.

f. Bogginess of the temporal or postauricular region of the head, which indicates fracture of the basilar area of the skull.

g. Ecchymosis over the orbit of the eyes that is indicative of a basilar skull fracture. Also called *raccoon sign*.

SHORT ANSWER QUESTIONS

15. Why are injuries sustained in a motorcycle crash likely to be more severe than in an automobile collision?

_____

_____

_____

_____

16. What are the most common injuries that result from falls?

_____

_____

_____

_____

17. What are the three phases of blast injury?

_____

_____

_____

_____

18. What is the ABCDE sequence used in the primary survey?

_____

_____

_____

_____

19. What assessments are performed during the secondary survey?

_____

_____

_____

_____

20. What can the nurse do to decrease the risk of coagulopathy in a trauma patient?

_____

_____

_____

_____

TRUE OR FALSE?

21. _____ T/F When in an automobile, positioning the seat belt over the pelvis allows it to receive a load that is 20 to 50 times as great as the weight of the body.

22. _____ T/F Improper positioning of headrests in an automobile can cause cervical spine injury or soft tissue injury to the neck in the case of a rear impact.

23. _____ T/F The driver of a motorcycle is more likely to sustain serious injuries than the passenger in the event of a frontal impact.

24. _____ T/F In the case of a stab wound, it may be helpful to know the gender of the attacker because men tend to stab upward and women tend to stab overhand or downward.

25. _____ T/F In the case of uncontrolled external bleeding, application of a tourniquet is the recommended intervention.

26. _____ T/F Massive transfusion is the replacement of at least one blood volume (~5 liters in an adult) within the first 12 hours of resuscitation.

27. _____ T/F The secondary survey of a trauma patient is done after resuscitative measures have yielded adequate response.

28. _____ T/F The emergency nurse must not assume an unconscious trauma patient to have spinal cord injury.

29. _____ T/F The leading causes of death among adults 65 and over are falls and elder abuse and neglect.

30. _____ T/F Fractures are sometimes missed in elderly patients because their pain perception is decreased.

NCLEX-RN® REVIEW QUESTIONS

74-1. A patient was a restrained driver in a motor vehicle collision with right lateral impact. Vital signs are HR 120, BP 86/60, RR 26, T 97.0, SpO$_2$ 96%, abdominal pain 10. Chest x-ray reveals multiple left lower rib fractures. Which of the following injuries is this patient most likely experiencing?
1. Ruptured spleen
2. Right neck sprain
3. Calcaneus fracture
4. Lacerated liver

74-2. A patient comes into the emergency department after sustaining multiple traumatic injuries. The nurse would conduct in order which of the following for the primary trauma survey?
1. Oxygen administration, obtaining IV access, NGT insertion, log rolling the client
2. Jaw thrust, assessing pupils, controlling external bleeding, applying warm blankets
3. Auscultating breath sounds, obtaining vital signs, abdominal palpation, chin lift
4. Blood product administration, emotional support, past medical history, warming lights

74-3. The nurse is conducting a tertiary survey on a trauma patient. Which of the following should the nurse do to ensure the patient is receiving the best possible treatment and prevent errors that could lead to inpatient trauma death?
1. Overhydrate the patient.
2. Ensure endotracheal tube placement.
3. Check for the halo effect.
4. Check for hyphema.

74-4. A patient comes into the emergency department with uncontrolled bleeding from a traumatic event. Which of the following should be done to ensure adequate fluid resuscitation?
1. Provide aggressive infusion of normal saline.
2. Provide immediate infusion of Ringer's lactate solution.
3. Provide aggressive infusion of crystalloids.
4. Assess the patient's response to fluid resuscitation for adequate perfusion.

ANSWER KEY

Chapter 1 – Preparation for Practice

Key Terms Matching Exercise 1

1.	f	**7.**	g
2.	d	**8.**	c
3.	h	**9.**	e
4.	a	**10.**	k
5.	l	**11.**	j
6.	i	**12.**	b

Key Terms Matching Exercise 2

13.	e	**20.**	g
14.	k	**21.**	h
15.	f	**22.**	c
16.	d	**23.**	b
17.	m	**24.**	j
18.	l	**25.**	i
19.	a		

Short Answer Questions

26. Complementary therapy refers to a therapy used in addition to a conventional therapy. Alternative therapy, sometimes called unconventional therapy, refers to a therapy used instead of conventional or mainstream therapy.

27. The most prevalent deficit of CAM therapies is seen when patients use them instead of conventional therapy and do not seek traditional diagnosis and treatment. People who choose CAM therapies first and continue to use them for symptom treatment may delay diagnosis of treatable cancers as well as a huge array of curable conditions.

28. When assessing patients the nurse should ask if they use any nontraditional therapies and, if so, what their response is to them.

29. Reiki, yoga, and hypnosis can be used as complementary therapies. Herbal medicine may also be considered complementary when used in conjunction with prescribed medical treatment and with the knowledge of the health care provider. Acupuncture is an alternative to traditional methods of relieveing pain.

Note: Answers for 30 and 31 will be different for each student.

NCLEX-RN® Review Questions

Question numbers correspond to Outcome-Based Learning Objectives for this chapter.

1-1. Answer: 2

> **Rationale:** Assessment is the initial step in the nursing process to identify patient problems and desired outcomes in a consistent and efficient manner. Caring is considered to be the most central and unifying concept in nursing. Advocacy at the patient care level is an activity by the nurse to ensure the patient's right to autonomy, free choice, and the ability to make informed decisions.
> **Cognitive Level:** Application
> **Nursing Process:** Implementation
> **Client Need:** Safe, Effective Care Environment; Management of Care

1-2. Answer: 2

> **Rationale:** Adding the aspects of caring enables nursing to meet psychological and spiritual needs. Without caring, nursing is a scientific and technical profession. The physiological needs will be met without the aspects of caring through the utilization of the technical body of knowledge. Ethical and moral needs are personal values.
> **Cognitive Level:** Application
> **Nursing Process:** Assessment
> **Client Need:** Psychosocial Integrity; Coping and Adaptation

1-3. Answer: 2

> **Rationale:** Team nursing is the delivery model in which ancillary and inexperienced staff members work under the direction of a professional nurse. Functional nursing is an adaptation of the industrial model and is work assignment based upon functions and tasks to be completed within a specific time frame. Primary care nursing has a professional nurse assigned to plan and coordinate care from admission to discharge. Total patient care refers to a delivery model in which the nurse assumes total responsibility for meeting the needs of assigned patients during the nurse's time on duty.
> **Cognitive Level:** Application
> **Nursing Process:** Planning
> **Client Need:** Safe, Effective Care Environment; Management of Care

1-4. Answer: 1

> **Rationale:** The industrial nurse's practice focuses on promotion and restoration of health, prevention of illness and injury, and protection from work-related and environmental hazards. The school nurse advances the well-being, academic performance, and lifelong achievement of students. The assisted living nurse provides care to clients whose needs are beyond the scope of home care but do not require the level of services in nursing homes.

Cognitive Level: Application
Nursing Process: Implementation
Client Need: Safe, Effective Care Environment;
Management of Care

1-5. Answer: 1
Rationale: Cultural encounters are the fourth component of Campinha-Bacote's model. Cultural studies encompass a process that would increase cultural knowledge. Cultural diversity refers to the variations among groups of people with respect to habits, values, preferences, beliefs, taboos, behaviors, and social interaction. Culture refers to a complex of learned patterns of behavior, beliefs, and values that can be attributed to a particular group of people.
Cognitive Level: Application
Nursing Process: Evaluation
Client Need: Psychosocial Integrity; Coping and Adaptation

Chapter 2 – Experiential Learning: Skill Acquisition and Gaining Clinical Knowledge

Key Terms Matching Exercise 1

1.	d	5.	a
2.	b	6.	e
3.	g	7.	c
4.	f		

Key Terms Matching Exercise 2

8.	c	12.	e
9.	a	13.	f
10.	g	14.	b
11.	d		

Short Answer Questions

15. Clinical knowledge is the knowledge necessary to perform proficiently in the clinical setting. It includes the recognition of signs and symptoms of physiological and emotional distress and changes in a patient's vital signs, as well as knowing how to perform required tasks. Clinical judgment is reasoning across time about a particular patient. Clinical judgment is a part of clinical knowledge.

16. This distinction is similar to the distinction between scientific and clinical reasoning. Nursing and medicine use techne, such as blood pressure measurements and dosage ranges for medication, but when clinical judgment, relationship, perception (or noticing), timing, and skilled know-how are involved, then phronesis is being used.

17. The quality of learning is quite different for new as opposed to more experienced nurses. Beginners have a level of trust in the environment and in the legitimacy of coworkers' knowledge, which allows them to absorb information as fact. This trust sets up qualities of freedom and exhilaration in learning that are probably only available to those who do not yet comprehend the contingent nature of both the situation and what is known about it. This freedom in learning is furthered because advanced beginners do not yet feel responsible for managing clinical situations with which they are unfamiliar.

18. The Dreyfus model may make you more aware of the many years of nursing practice needed and may help you to be realistic in your assessment of your progress.

True or False?

19.	T	23.	F
20.	F	24.	T
21.	T	25.	T
22.	T		

Nursing Stage of Development

26. Expertise
27. Competent
28. Competent
29. Expertise
30. Novice
31. Proficiency
32. Proficiency
33. Novice
34. Advanced Beginner
35. Expertise

NCLEX-RN® Review Questions

Question numbers correspond to Outcome-Based Learning Objectives for this chapter.

2-1. Answer: 3
Rationale: The novice stage begins in the first year of education to become a nurse. The advanced beginner is a new graduate. There is a level of trust in the environment and legitimacy of coworkers' knowledge. There is freedom with learning, mainly because of no responsibility for situations in which the nurse has no experience. Competency is evidenced by exhilaration with good personal performance as apposed to remorse when performance could have been more precise or effective. Proficiency is evidenced by a change in the perspective of a situation or being able to read and respond to a patient's needs. This nurse was functioning at the level of competent practitioner.
Cognitive Level: Analysis
Nursing Process: Evaluation
Client Need: Physiological Integrity, Physiological Adaptation

2-2. Answer: 3
Rationale: There is a difference between practical knowledge and theoretical knowledge. With practical knowledge, practice is shaped by one's knowledge of the discipline, the science and technology relevant to the situation at hand. Theoretical knowledge is scientific, formal knowledge that is needed prior to the development of practical knowledge. This patient's respiratory and cardiac interventions did not reveal a cause for the onset of lower extremity weakness. Because of the elevated blood pressure, a head CT scan would be needed to rule out a cerebral bleed, which could reveal the cause of lower extremity weakness. This patient's condition could be changing.
Cognitive Level: Analysis
Nursing Process: Implementation
Client Need: Physiological Integrity, Physiological Adaptation

2-3. Answer: 3

Rationale: Clinical knowledge is knowledge necessary to perform proficiently in the clinical setting. Clinical judgment is clinical reasoning, across time, about a particular patient. Techne is something that can be standardized and replicated. Even though the patient has orders to receive an insulin infusion for 4 hours, the patient's laboratory values indicate a drop in blood glucose level. The infusion of insulin appears to no longer be necessary, and the physician should be contacted immediately for updated orders. The patient's changing condition dictates the direction of care needed.

Cognitive Level: Application
Nursing Process: Evaluation
Client Need: Physiological Integrity, Physiological Adaptation

2-4. Answer: 1

Rationale: Phronesis is a form of rationality and skill-based character. It is similar to clinical judgment, which is clinical reasoning across time about a patient. Based upon the patient's vital signs, the nurse should not provide the medication and should notify the physician of the findings. It could be potentially harmful to the patient if the medication were given.

Cognitive Level: Application
Nursing Process: Evaluation
Client Need: Physiological Integrity, Reduction of Risk Potential

2-5. Answer: 4

Rationale: In order to make good clinical judgments, the nurse must be skillful in moral and clinical perception. Even though conceptual knowledge is needed, it is not sufficient to ensure the nurse will notice and correctly identify a change in a patient condition even though the nurse may know conceptually what the formal characteristic of the patient condition is in principle. The nurse should not question the patient's complaint of pain and should administer the prescribed medication. Delaying the medication, calling the physician, or administering a placebo are not within the realm of good moral and clinical judgments for the patient.

Cognitive Level: Application
Nursing Process: Implementation
Client Need: Physiological Integrity, Pharmacological and Parenteral Therapies

2-6. Answer: 1

Rationale: Moral agency is more than the intent to do good or to be a good practitioner. It requires the experiential skill to recognize when an ethical breach in practice has occurred and the social and communication skills to effectively intervene on behalf of the patient. The nurse observing the error should encourage the error to be reported. The nurse should not ignore the situation, report the error to the physician, or report the error to another nurse without additional follow-up.

Cognitive Level: Analysis
Nursing Process: Evaluation
Client Need: Physiological Integrity, Pharmacological and Parenteral Therapies

2-7. Answer: 4

Rationale: The novice is a beginning learner. The competent nurse tries to limit the unexpected through planning and analysis and forecasting the needs of the immediate future. The competent nurse structures the day by goals and plans; however, the nurse is unable to perceive the demands of the situation in response to the patient's

responses and readiness. The proficient nurse has a more differentiated world of practice, feels at home in the situation, and can recognize changes. The expert nurse uses responses based in techne and phronesis to come up with new possibilities and develop intuitive links between seeing and responding to changing events. The nurse who assesses the patient's circulation to the lower extremities before helping the patient to ambulate is functioning at the proficiency level of nursing practice.

Cognitive Level: Application
Nursing Process: Implementation
Client Need: Physiological Integrity, Reduction of Risk Potential

Chapter 3 – Health Care Trends and Regulatory Aspects of Health Care Delivery

Key Terms Matching Exercise 1

1. d		**6.** g	
2. i		**7.** j	
3. b		**8.** a	
4. c		**9.** h	
5. e		**10.** f	

Key Terms Matching Exercise 2

11. b		**16.** f	
12. g		**17.** e	
13. a		**18.** d	
14. j		**19.** c	
15. i		**20.** h	

Short Answer Questions

21. The switch to the DRG payment schedule effectively predetermined the amount that a hospital is reimbursed for the treatment of a Medicare patient diagnosed with a particular condition. DRGs shifted the payment unit from total charges or "days in the hospital" to the patient's diagnosis. The advent of DRGs has served as an incentive for hospitals to place greater emphasis on reducing costs, utilization of services, and length of patient stay. Under the DRG prospective payment system, hospitals and extended care facilities have had to develop length-of-stay (LOS) estimates for a variety of diagnoses. These estimates help determine, on average, the LOS beyond which the facility will not be reimbursed for the patient's care. Patients are sometimes discharged to their homes before it is appropriate, and equipment and services are not always adequate to meet all their needs.

22. Factors to consider include understanding patients' needs, their concerns, and their values; building on the clinical expertise or experience of the professional nurse; and seeking relevant clinical data and best practices. Best practices are defined as proven processes that produce consistent, high-quality results. In nursing there are many sources of knowledge that guide critical thinking about care, including the applicability of nursing interventions and intuition about approaches and interactions with patients. Data and research are also becoming more available through the use of Internet resources in the practice arena.

23. Structure standards focus on the internal characteristics of the organization and its personnel. These standards regulate the environment to ensure quality and answer the question, "Is a structure in place that will allow quality to exist?" Process

standards focus on whether the activities within an organization are being appropriately conducted. These standards target behaviors, activities, interventions, and the sequence of caregiving events. Outcome standards refer to whether the services provided make any difference. These standards address physical health status, mental health status, social and physical functions, health attitudes/knowledge/behavior, utilization of services, and the patient's perception of care.

Complete the Sentence

24. HIPAA (Health Insurance Portability and Accountability Act)
25. Joint Commission
26. Medicare
27. EMTALA (Emergency Medical Treatment and Labor Act)
28. IOM (Institute of Medicine)
29. Leapfrog Group
30. Medicaid
31. OSHA (Occupational Safety and Health Administration)

True or False?

32. T
33. F
34. F
35. T
36. T

NCLEX-RN® Review Questions

Question numbers correspond to Outcome-Based Learning Objectives for this chapter.

3-1. Answer: 3

Rationale: The Joint Commission's patient safety standards took effect in July 2001 and are generally updated and/or expanded on an annual basis. Hospitals must take all of these standards and initiatives into consideration as they plan quality activities and policy/procedure development. The Institute of Medicine provides science-based advice on medicine and health in an effort to improve health. The Leapfrog Group focuses on collecting data about medical errors and setting standards that will reduce errors. A committee for Physician Order Entry does not exist but rather is an initiative of the Leapfrog Group that is aimed at eliminating errors from the process of transcribing physician orders that are handwritten or given verbally.
Cognitive Level: Application
Nursing Process: Planning
Category of Client Need: Safe, Effective Care Environment; Management of Care

3-2. Answer: 1

Rationale: Traditional indemnity insurance indemnifies insured individuals against financial losses for health care costs and individuals are not restricted on which providers they can access. They are reimbursed directly for any costs. Medicare is a national health insurance program for individuals 65 or older, under 65 with disabilities, and those with end stage renal disease. A health maintenance organization (HMO) is a group health care agency that provides basic and supplemental health maintenance and treatment services to voluntary enrollees. A primary care physician (PCP) generally directs care within a network of providers. A self-funded plan is one that has been created by using the Employee Retirement Income Security

Act (ERISA), where companies cover their employees for medical costs instead of providing commercial insurance plans.
Cognitive Level: Analysis
Nursing Process: Evaluation
Category of Client Need: Safe, Effective Care Environment; Management of Care

3-3. Answer: 3

Rationale: Within *Salaries/Wages*, expenses include regular salaries for staff, premium pay such as overtime, benefits, and temporary labor. Benefits can include medical care coverage, vacation/sick time, training/orientation, and travel reimbursement. *Charges* are based on the cost of supplies or services and take into consideration the price paid to the vendor and a mark-up for processing, staff time, and organizational overhead. *Overhead* covers system costs for depreciation of the buildings and equipment, administrative positions and expenses, and interest on loans. Administrative costs are for non–revenue-generating departments such as finance, human resources and housekeeping. *Purchased Services* include maintenance agreements for large equipment, equipment rentals, repair costs, and vendor contracts for services.
Cognitive Level: Application
Nursing Process: Implementation
Category of Client Need: Safe, Effective Care Environment; Management of Care

3-4. Answer: 2

Rationale: Nurses should assess their patients' health care coverage or insurance plan for potential referrals for financial assistance or counseling. Patients may be concerned about their current coverage or may lack coverage altogether. This concern can cause significant stress that may affect the patients' ability to rest and recover. Referrals may be made to the hospital's financial department or social services to assist in resolving any payment or coverage issues.
Cognitive Level: Application
Nursing Process: Implementation
Category of Client Need: Safe, Effective Care Environment; Management of Care

3-5. Answer: 4

Rationale: Structure standards, or measures, focus on the internal characteristics of the organization and its personnel. Process standards focus on whether the activities within an organization are being conducted appropriately. Process measures focus on the behaviors of the provider of care. Process standards look at activities, interventions, and the sequence of caregiving events. Outcome standards refer to whether the services provided by the organization make any difference. They answer questions about the services that nurses provide and whether they make a difference to the patients or to the health status of the population. Outcome standards address physical health status, mental health status, social and physical functioning, health attitudes/knowledge/behavior, utilization of services, and the patient's perception of quality care.
Cognitive Level: Analysis
Nursing Process: Evaluation
Client Need: Safe, Effective Care Environment; Management of Care

3-6. Answer: 1

Rationale: Inspections are generally made on a routine basis by the fire marshal to check for building code compliance and the training of staff to respond to emergency

situations. Inspections also occur whenever there are new regulations or standards, during construction and remodeling, or after any significant structural damage. The Occupational Safety and Health Administration (OSHA) is an agency that oversees environmental safety and works through federal and state partnerships to inspect and enforce safety standards in the workplace. The Centers for Disease Control (CDC) is an agency that focuses on protecting the health and safety of people within and outside of a health care environment by development and application of disease prevention and control, promotion of environmental health, and education. The Joint Commission is the leading accreditation body for the United States and evaluates a health care organization's quality and performance improvement program.
Cognitive Level: Application
Nursing Process: Planning
Category of Client Need: Safe, Effective Care Environment, Safety and Infection Control

3-7. Answer: 4
Rationale: In some situations family members may disagree with the treatment plan and the patient's stated wishes. This can cause a dilemma for the nurse in advocating for the patient and assisting the family through appropriate decision making. The nurse should seek consultation with the physician and an administrative representative of the organization regarding a plan of action. If the patient is not able to advocate for himself, the case may need to be referred to social services or the organization's committee for discussion and counsel.
Cognitive Level: Analysis
Nursing Process: Planning
Category of Client Need: Safe, Effective Care Environment; Management of Care

3-8. Answer: 3
Rationale: There are specific guidelines for documentation that every nurse should follow. The patient should be clearly identified on each record form, or upon accessing the record electronically. Observations should be objective and factual. Opinions regarding care or decisions are not appropriate for the legal record. Entries should be accurate and legible using only approved terms and abbreviations. Observations should be entered as close to the time they occurred as possible. All entries should be authenticated with the name and title of the caregiver.
Cognitive Level: Application
Nursing Process: Implementation
Category of Client Need: Safe, Effective Care Environment; Management of Care

3-9. Answer: 1
Rationale: The Health Insurance Portability and Accountability Act (HIPAA) was created to improve health insurance portability and continuity of coverage for individuals. There are three central goals for this law: to create standards and a framework for health information, to prevent inappropriate access to health information, and to give patients control over their health information and how it is used. This nurse should follow the patient's direction and provide the medical record as requested to the physician family member.
Cognitive Level: Analysis
Nursing Process: Implementation
Category of Client Need: Safe, Effective Care Environment; Management of Care

3-10. Answer: 4
Rationale: This nurse was performing discharge planning. Case managers interface with the nursing staff to help assess discharge needs and to establish a plan for discharge. Discharge planning begins when the patient is admitted and continues to be evaluated throughout the patient's stay. The interface with the staff nurse providing direct care and the case manager is crucial in assessing the need for referral to specialty services, determining financial concerns for ongoing care, and progress toward the discharge goals.
Cognitive Level: Analysis
Nursing Process Step: Assessment
Category of Client Need: Safe, Effective Care Environment; Management of Care

Chapter 4 – Ethical and Legal Guidelines for Nursing Practice

Key Terms Matching Exercise 1

1. i
2. g
3. a
4. e
5. b
6. d
7. f
8. c
9. h
10. j

Key Terms Matching Exercise 2

11. e
12. j
13. f
14. g
15. a
16. i
17. b
18. h
19. c
20. d

Short Answer Questions

21. The eight ethical principles are:
    Autonomy
    Beneficence
    Nonmaleficence
    Veracity
    Justice
    Paternalism
    Fidelity
    Respect for others

22. Questions to be answered might include:
    Did the patient have a living will?
    Did the patient ever verbally convey his wishes in this situation?
    What do the family members believe in regard to end-of-life treatment?
    Do the family members hold any hope of their parent recovering?
    What options do the family members have in this situation?
    Are any of the options out of the question for them?
    Which option seems best to the family members?
    What is required to take that plan of action?

23. Structure standards focus on the internal characteristics of the organization and its personnel. These standards regulate the environment to ensure quality and answer the question, "Is a structure in place that will allow quality to exist?" Process standards focus on whether the activities within an organization are being appropriately conducted. These standards target behaviors, activities, interventions, and the sequence of caregiving events. Outcome standards refer to whether the services provided make any difference. These standards address physical health status, mental

health status, social and physical function, health attitudes/knowledge/behavior, utilization of services, and the patient's perception of care.

24. A breach of contract could result in:
    * Your business or professional reputation could be damaged.
    * You could sever your business or professional relationship with the other party.
    * You could be sued. If sued, you could be forced to spend valuable time away from your business or practice in order to respond to factors of litigation: discovery requests, depositions, court appearances.
    * You could incur legal fees.
    * You could be ordered by the court to perform your obligations under the contract. If you do not obey the court's order, you could be held in contempt of court, fined, and/or imprisoned.
    * You could be forced to pay money damages to the nonbreaching party, in an amount that puts that party in as good a position as it would have been in were it not for the breach.
    * You could be forced to pay punitive damages, which are not limited by the amount of the other party's losses and can be very significant.
    * You could end up spending much more time, money, and mental and physical energy resolving the breach than you would have spent performing your obligations under the contract.

25. The nurse would have to determine whether the girl can be considered an emancipated minor or a mature minor before administering treatment. If the girl is no longer under a parent's control and regulation and is responsible for her own financial affairs, she can be treated as an emancipated minor. This can be the case if the patient is married or in the military. Because the girl is seeking treatment for an infectious disease that can be transmitted to others, she has the right to obtain treatment without informing her parents in most cases. Whether the girl can be considered a mature minor capable of consenting to medical care is dependent on the laws of that state.

True or False?

26.	F	31.	T
27.	F	32.	T
28.	F	33.	T
29.	T	34.	F
30.	F	35.	T

NCLEX-RN® Review Questions

Question numbers correspond to Outcome-Based Learning Objectives for this chapter.

4-1. Answer: 1
    Rationale: Fidelity means keeping one's promises or commitments. Staff members know not to promise to patients commitments that they may not be able to keep. Nurses have multiple fidelity duties to the patient, physician organization, profession, and self, which at times may conflict with one another. Justice concerns the issue that persons should be treated equally and fairly. Respect for others acknowledges the right of individuals to make decisions and to live by these decisions. Nonmaleficence states that one should do no harm.
    Cognitive Level: Analysis
    Nursing Process: Planning
    Client Need: Safe, Effective Care Environment; Management of Care

4-2. Answer: 4
    Rationale: The M stands for "massage the dilemma" by identifying the issues and all the people involved. The O stands for "outline the options" or examining options. The R stands for "resolve the dilemma." The A stands for "act by applying the chosen option." And the L stands for "look back and evaluate" the success of achieving desired outcomes.
    Cognitive Level: Analysis
    Nursing Process: Evaluation
    Client Need: Safe, Effective Care Environment; Management of Care

4-3. Answer: 3
    Rationale: The patient benefit model uses substituted judgment and facilitates decision making for the incompetent patient. The autonomy model facilitates decision making for the competent patient. The social justice model considers broad social issues that may arise within an institution and within this model; many ethics committees hold ethical grand rounds. A nonmalficence model does not exist.
    Cognitive Level: Application
    Nursing Process: Planning
    Client Need: Safe, Effective Care Environment; Management of Care

4-4. Answer: 4
    Rationale: Each state practice act establishes a board of nursing, whose purposes are to ensure enforcement of the act, to regulate those who come under its provisions and prevent those not addressed by the act from practicing nursing, and to protect the public. Nurses have an obligation to continually remain current on issues that affect their practice. Means of remaining current include reading professional nursing journals, accessing the state board of nursing website for changes in the state nurse practice act, and being active in professional nursing organizations. Many states require mandatory continuing education in order to renew the registered nurse license. There are no expectations for nurses to take college-level nursing courses or to retake the state board of nursing examination every five years. Attending staff meetings at hospitals does not ensure competence to provide patient care.
    Cognitive Level: Analysis
    Nursing Process: Assessment
    Client Need: Safe, Effective Care Environment; Management of Care

4-5. Answer: 2
    Rationale: A crime is any act or omission or an act that violates public law either in forbidding or commanding it. Most crimes are established by local, state, and federal governments; thus, criminal laws may vary from state to state. In a criminal case, the state, through a prosecutor, initiates the suit. Contracts are promises that the law will enforce. Contract law is that which governs the formation of these promises or agreements between two or more parties, in relation to a particular subject. Tort law is defined as a wrongful act committed against another person or the person's property. Civil law starts with abstract rules, which judges must then apply to the various cases before them.
    Cognitive Level: Analysis
    Nursing Process: Assessment
    Client Need: Safe, Effective Care Environment; Management of Care

4-6. Answer: 4
>   **Rationale:** There are six elements that must be presented in a successful malpractice suit; all of these factors must be proven before the court will find liability against the nurse and/or institution. These six elements are: duty owed the patient: breach of the duty owed the patient, foreseeability, causation, injury, and damages.
>   **Cognitive Level:** Analysis
>   **Nursing Process:** Evaluation
>   **Client Need:** Safe, Effective Care Environment; Management of Care

4-7. Answer: 2
>   **Rationale:** The minimum requirements that define acceptable practice are considered internal standards. Examples of internal standards include the organization's policy and procedure manual, the individual's job description, and the practitioner's education and skills. External standards are those created by professional and specialty organizations. Accreditation standards, such as those published by The Joint Commission, assist in establishing the acceptable standards of care for health care facilities.
>   **Cognitive Level:** Application
>   **Nursing Process:** Planning
>   **Client Need:** Safe, Effective Care Environment; Management of Care

4-8. Answer: 2
>   **Rationale:** There are two important reasons for national standards of care. With the advent of educational programs and videos, the ability to transport individuals to national conferences or to consult in small, more rural areas, and the use of telemedicine and virtual diagnostics, all areas with health care delivery systems have access to the same information and educational opportunities. A second reason is that all patients have the right to quality health care, whether hospitalized in a small community setting or in a major medical center.
>   **Cognitive Level:** Application
>   **Nursing Process:** Planning
>   **Client Need:** Safe, Effective Care Environment; Management of Care

4-9. Answer: 2
>   **Rationale:** Invasion of privacy is a violation of a person's right to protection against unreasonable and unwarranted interference with his or her personal life. A newer application of invasion of privacy is the recently enacted Health Insurance Portability and Accountability Act of 1996. Defamation of character, also known as libel and slander, is harming another's reputation by diminishing the esteem, respect, goodwill, or level of confidence that others have for that person. Individuals have the right to their good name. Breach of confidentiality, a part of invasion of privacy, concerns facts that are presented in the medical record. Assault is an intentional tort.
>   **Cognitive Level:** Analysis
>   **Nursing Process:** Evaluation
>   **Client Need:** Safe, Effective Care Environment; Management of Care

4-10. Answer: 4
>   **Rationale:** Even though the patient had originally provided informed consent for the procedure, the patient changed her mind. It is the nurse's responsibility to contact his or her immediate supervisor and the responsible physician. Both entities need to be informed of the patient's change of mind.
>   **Cognitive Level:** Application
>   **Nursing Process:** Planning

>   **Client Need:** Safe, Effective Care Environment; Management of Care

4-11. Answer: 1
>   **Rationale:** The rights protection model is where nurses assist patients in asserting their autonomy rights. The values-based decision model is where the nurse assists the patient by discussing her needs and desires and helps the patient make choices that are most consistent with the patient's values, lifestyle, and desires. This model is predicated on sharing information and assisting the individual to become empowered to speak on her own behalf. Using this approach, the patient is assisted to exert her right to autonomy and self-determination. The respect for persons model centers on the inherent human dignity that is deserving of respect. *A Patient's Bill of Rights* enumerates the health care institution's responsibility for providing medically indicated treatment and service, the collaborative nature of health maintenance, and the patient's rights to confidentiality, informed consent, and considerate and respectful care.
>   **Cognitive Level:** Application
>   **Nursing Process:** Planning
>   **Client Need:** Safe, Effective Care Environment; Management of Care

Chapter 5 – Nursing Care Delivery Systems

Key Terms Matching Exercise 1

1.	c	**6.**	h
2.	a	**7.**	e
3.	j	**8.**	d
4.	f	**9.**	g
5.	i	**10.**	b

Short Answer Questions

11. The functional nursing delivery system involves delegating responsibilities to LVN/LPNs and unlicensed assistive personnel, which is a way to provide patient care when the patient-to-staff ratio is higher than usual. It can also be more cost effective. Delegation by an RN requires clinical judgment and knowledge of the applicable state's nurse practice act, which authorizes the scope of responsibility and grants the authority to delegate. All RNs must know how to prioritize patients' needs and assign tasks based on the competency of the personnel, but they also must know how to supervise the personnel and intervene when necessary. The RN must consider qualifications, job descriptions, and competency when delegating tasks to various caregivers. Delegating a task to an individual who is not competent has serious implications for the RN, the RN's license, and the institution should the patient suffer an adverse outcome.

12. The primary care system is structured in such a way that relationship-based care can occur: each nurse has complete responsibility for a fewer number of patients. It embodies principles and values needed for relationship-based care, and allows for collaboration among all care givers and for the development of therapeutic relationships.

13. Current research supports a nursing care delivery system with more RNs involved. The primary nursing model requires a richer mix of RNs, allowing for relationship-based care and collaboration among health care providers.

True or False?

14.	T	**18.**	F
15.	F	**19.**	F
16.	T	**20.**	T
17.	F		

NCLEX-RN® Review Questions

Question numbers correspond to Outcome-Based Learning Objectives for this chapter.

5-1. Answer: 3

Rationale: In team nursing, patients are assigned to a team led by a registered nurse. Other names for team nursing include care partners, modular teams, or patient-focused teams. The case method of nursing care is where the registered nurse is responsible for the patient and has total care responsibility for the patient during the shift worked. Functional nursing is task oriented and nurses perform assigned tasks but are not given a patient assignment. In primary nursing, each patient is assigned to a nurse who has 24-hour responsibility for the nursing care provided to the patient.

Cognitive Level: Analysis
Nursing Process: Assessment
Client Need: Safe, Effective Care Environment, Management of Care

5-2. Answer: 4

Rationale: In primary nursing, each patient is assigned to a nurse who has 24-hour responsibility for the nursing care provided to the patient. In the case method of nursing care, the registered nurse has total care responsibility for the patient during the shift worked. Functional nursing is task oriented and nurses perform assigned tasks but are not given a patient assignment. In team nursing, patients are assigned to a team led by a registered nurse. The team assignments can change daily.

Cognitive Level: Analysis
Nursing Process: Evaluation
Client Need: Safe, Effective Care Environment, Management of Care

5-3. Answer: 3

Rationale: In team nursing, the team leader assigns all patients to team members and may delegate additional tasks according to team members' competence. In the case method care delivery system, the entire caregiving staff are registered nurses. Unlicensed assistive personnel are not used. In functional nursing, a registered nurse is in charge and is responsible for delegating all activities and tasks to all staff for all patients on a care area. In primary nursing, the primary nurse is responsible for the 24-hour plan of care for the patient. Other nurses and unlicensed assistive personnel are considered associate caregivers.

Cognitive Level: Application
Nursing Process: Implementation
Client Need: Safe, Effective Care Environment, Management of Care

5-4. Answer: 2

Rationale: The case method of care delivery is total patient care provided by a complete registered nurse staff. The care delivery systems of team, functional, and primary all have unlicensed assistive personnel and therefore would cost an organization less money to sustain.

Cognitive Level: Analysis
Nursing Process: Assessment

Client Need: Safe, Effective Care Environment, Management of Care

5-5. Answer: 4

Rationale: Advanced practice nurses are used in the primary nursing care delivery system to add clinical expertise and education. In the case method of care delivery, advanced practice nurses and case managers will aid in the coordination of care. Because of the costs associated with advanced practice nurses and case managers, they are most likely not used in a functional care delivery system. Advanced practice nurses and case managers are used as consultants within the team nursing care delivery system.

Cognitive Level: Application
Nursing Process: Implementation
Client Need: Safe, Effective Care Environment, Management of Care

Chapter 6 – Nursing Documentation

Key Terms Matching Exercise

1.	c	**3.**	d
2.	b	**4.**	a

Short Answer Questions

5. The Focus system includes a detailed patient assessment, and the problem is written as a nursing diagnosis, which is similar to the nursing process.

6. The disadvantages of the electronic medical record are:
- Not all health care providers are comfortable with computers.
- Technology and extensive training may be necessary.
- Lack of security measures can threaten patient confidentiality.
- If the system is "down," then information is unavailable unless hard copies are used and readily accessible.
- Initial implementation of the system is expensive.

7. One possibility is: "The patient reported being sleepy due to frequent interruptions during the night. He ate half a piece of toast and nothing else for breakfast."

8. One possibility is: "When I asked the patient how she was feeling, she did not turn to face me and continued to rub her arm. She responded only after I touched her to get her attention."

9. One possibility is: "The patient put her hand to her throat and her chin came forward when she attempted to swallow water. She reported that her throat felt swollen and swallowing was difficult."

10. One possibility is: "The patient drank only 3 ounces water and refused more liquids. He bent over at the waist and said that he had sharp pain in the left abdomen."

True or False?

11.	F	**16.**	T
12.	F	**17.**	T
13.	T	**18.**	F
14.	T	**19.**	T
15.	F	**20.**	F

NCLEX-RN® Review Questions

Question numbers correspond to Outcome-Based Learning Objectives for this chapter.

6-1. Answer: 4

> **Rationale:** The Health Insurance Portability and Accountability Act of 1996 requires the Department of Health and Human Services (DHHS) to adopt standards for electronic health care transactions. DHHS published a Privacy Rule in December of 2000, which set national standards for the protection of health information. The rule affects documentation in that only those health care team members involved with the patient's care, or the patient, have a legal right to review the medical record. Release of patient information without the consent of the patient is a violation of the patient's privacy and a violation of HIPAA. The Joint Commission publishes safety goals that need to be addressed by health care facilities to improve patient care. Medicare does not publish standards; however, if an organization is in HIPAA violation, Medicare funding could be jeopardized. The state boards of nursing control the practice of nursing by developing state nursing practice acts that establish guidelines to ensure safe practice.
> **Cognitive Level:** Analysis
> **Nursing Process:** Implementation
> **Client Need:** Safe, Effective Care Environment; Management of Care

6-2. Answer: 1

> **Rationale:** The patient record is a legal document so the nurse should never document medication administration in advance. The nurse should document only those doses of medication that are being given now.
> **Cognitive Level:** Application
> **Nursing Process:** Implementation
> **Client Need:** Safe, Effective Care Environment; Management of Care

6-3. Answer: 1

> **Rationale:** The CBE system saves time and decreases the amount of documentation needed. Improved communication through standardized terminology is an advantage of an electronic medical record. The Focus system is flexible, centers on the nursing process, and allows the reader to easily locate information about a specific problem. The Problem-Oriented Medical Record uses the SOAP method for documentation.
> **Cognitive Level:** Application
> **Nursing Process:** Implementation
> **Client Need:** Safe, Effective Care Environment; Management of Care

6-4. Answer: 4

> **Rationale:** The development of a nursing plan of care using the nursing process requires critical thinking skills to evaluate findings, identify assumptions, examine alternatives, and understand various points of view. Critical thinking is an integral part of each step of the nursing process. The activities or skills of observation, intuition, and listening are all important skills; however, they are not necessarily used to analyze the data to create this patient's plan of care.
> **Cognitive Level:** Analysis
> **Nursing Process:** Assessment
> **Client Need:** Safe, Effective Care Environment; Management of Care

Chapter 7 – Nursing Process

Key Terms Matching Exercise

1.	h	**6.**	c
2.	a	**7.**	e
3.	g	**8.**	f
4.	b	**9.**	i
5.	j	**10.**	d

Objective or Subjective Data?

11. objective data
12. objective data
13. objective data
14. subjective data
15. objective data
16. objective data
17. subjective data
18. objective data
19. subjective data
20. subjective data

True or False?

21.	T	**24.**	F
22.	F	**25.**	F
23.	T		

Complete the Sentence

26. assessment
27. planning
28. subjective, objective
29. clinical judgments
30. primary; secondary; primary; Secondary

NCLEX-RN® Review Questions

Question numbers correspond to Outcome-Based Learning Objectives for this chapter.

7-1. Answer: 2

> **Rationale:** Interdependent activities are those activities that overlap with other health team members, physicians, social workers, pharmacists, nutritionists, and therapists (physical, speech, occupational) and require coordination and planning with these various health team members. Independent activities are those that nurses perform, prescribe, and/or delegate based on their education and skills. Examples are assessing, analyzing and diagnosing, planning, implementing, and evaluating. Dependent activities are those that are prescribed by the physician and carried out by the nurse. They include implementing the physician's orders to administer medications or treatments. There is not a co-dependent nursing role.
> **Cognitive Level:** Analysis
> **Nursing Process:** Implementation
> **Client Need:** Safe, Effective Care Environment; Management of Care

7-2. Answer: 2

Rationale: Planning is done after the formulation of nursing diagnosis and is prioritized according to the patient's needs. Patient goals and objectives are then established to clearly outline expected outcomes of care. Assessment is defined as reviewing a patient's situation in order to diagnose the patient's problems. Implementation is the "doing" or intervening phase of the nursing process. It involves organization and actual delivery of nursing care, which leads to achievement of stated goals and objectives. Evaluation focuses on the patient's behavioral changes and compares them with the criteria stated in the objectives. It consists of both the patient's status and the effectiveness of the nursing care.

Cognitive Level: Application
Nursing Process: Implementation
Client Need: Health Promotion and Maintenance; Prevention/Early Detection of Health Problems

7-3. Answer: 4

Rationale: To conduct a comprehensive nursing assessment, the nurse must utilize cognitive, affective, and psychomotor skills. Asking the patient questions about his or her current health status is utilizing the cognitive skill. There is no psychosocial skill level utilized to conduct a comprehensive nursing assessment.

Cognitive Level: Analysis
Nursing Process: Implementation
Client Need: Health Promotion and Maintenance; Prevention/Early Detection of Health Problems

7-4. Answer: 3

Rationale: Nursing diagnoses are clinical judgments about an individual, family, or community response to actual or potential health problems and life processes. Nursing diagnoses are different from collaborative problems such as medical diagnoses because nurses' accountability differs for nursing diagnoses and collaborative problems. Nurses ultimately are accountable for formulating nursing diagnoses and intervening appropriately. With regard to a collaborative problem, the nurse is accountable for monitoring changes in the status of the problem and initiating the appropriate interventions, either nurse-prescribed or physician prescribed. Collecting data is an aspect of the nursing assessment. Evaluating care would be done after providing an intervention.

Cognitive Level: Analysis
Nursing Process: Implementation
Client Need: Health Promotion and Maintenance; Prevention/Early Detection of Health Problems

7-5. Answer: 4

Rationale: One aspect of critical thinking is accurate decision making. Newer forms of decision making in clinical areas include the development of critical pathways. Critical pathways identify key events of patient care and expected time frames. Their advantages include improved patient outcomes, streamlined charting, facilitation of quality assessment, improved patient education, and enhanced communication among health care providers. A standardized assessment form would streamline the assessment process. A care plan is created at the completion of the nursing assessment. Evidence-based practice is the careful and practical use of current best evidence to guide health care decisions. This includes clinical practice guidelines that usually are developed nationally by expert researchers, clinicians, and theorists in their areas of excellence.

Cognitive Level: Analysis
Nursing Process: Evaluation
Client Need: Health Promotion and Maintenance; Prevention/Early Detection of Health Problems

Chapter 8 – Role of Research in Nursing Practice

Key Terms Matching Exercise 1

1.	j	**6.**	h
2.	f	**7.**	c
3.	e	**8.**	d
4.	a	**9.**	g
5.	i	**10.**	b

Key Terms Matching Exercise 2

11.	h	**16.**	d
12.	g	**17.**	c
13.	b	**18.**	f
14.	j	**19.**	i
15.	e	**20.**	a

Word Search

21. probability sampling
22. random assignment
23. research
24. variables
25. population
26. setting
27. informatics
28. ethnography
29. sample
30. sampling

31. hypothesis
32. pilot study
33. basic
34. data saturation
35. quota sampling
36. phenomenology
37. power analysis
38. research design
39. grounded theory
40. applied research

A	P	T	R	S	I	S	Y	L	A	N	A	R	E	W	O	P	I	R	T
Q	O	R	E	H	O	N	V	A	R	I	A	B	L	E	S	P	Y	E	R
U	N	O	O	W	E	G	F	C	F	G	I	O	E	L	O	I	E	S	T
O	T	I	R	B	R	A	M	O	W	G	A	S	W	P	Z	L	D	E	R
R	R	G	Q	U	A	R	P	Y	R	H	M	S	U	A	H	O	R	A	L
S	N	R	H	L	N	B	U	S	A	M	P	L	I	N	G	T	O	R	K
S	I	O	T	K	D	E	I	U	B	E	A	Y	W	H	Q	S	Q	C	I
B	L	U	U	P	O	A	Z	L	A	T	M	T	S	X	A	T	U	H	P
A	I	N	R	D	M	R	E	R	I	E	S	F	I	T	E	U	O	D	H
S	H	D	X	S	A	H	V	O	H	T	K	R	S	C	V	D	T	E	E
I	Y	E	T	R	S	B	N	A	U	O	Y	E	W	Y	S	Y	A	S	N
C	P	D	H	B	S	A	M	P	L	E	I	S	A	E	D	B	S	I	O
R	O	T	Z	T	I	E	S	E	O	F	R	E	A	L	I	Y	A	G	M
E	T	H	N	O	G	R	A	P	H	Y	L	A	J	M	A	I	M	N	E
S	H	E	B	Y	N	I	D	H	T	T	A	R	R	E	P	H	P	T	N
E	E	O	W	V	M	U	E	R	O	F	C	P	I	O	L	L	E	O
A	S	R	S	S	E	T	T	I	N	G	S	H	L	R	E	U	I	B	L
R	I	Y	H	E	N	V	A	W	Y	U	O	D	F	O	U	I	N	N	O
C	S	N	O	I	T	A	R	U	T	A	S	A	T	A	D	B	G	D	G
H	I	R	A	P	P	L	I	E	D	R	E	S	E	A	R	C	H	E	Y

Complete the Sentence

41. experimental research
42. nonexperimental research design
43. correlational research design
44. quasi-experimental
45. experimental research design

46. Descriptive research designs
47. quantitative; qualitative
48. Applied
49. Qualitative
50. evidence-based practice

NCLEX-RN® Review Questions

Question numbers correspond to Outcome-Based Learning Objectives for this chapter.

8-1. Answer: 4

Rationale: Basic research is done to extend the knowledge base in a discipline, or to formulate or refine a theory. This would include studying Maslow's hierarchy of needs, the application of Orem's theory to the nursing process, and how certain conditions exist to substantiate a particular nursing theory. Applied research focuses on finding solutions to existing problems such as patients' physiological responses to blood pressure medication.
Cognitive Level: Analysis
Nursing Process: Planning
Client Need: Safe, Effective Care Environment; Management of Care

8-2. Answer: 2

Rationale: Qualitative research describes events as they occur naturally. It is a systematic, subjective approach used to describe life experiences and give them meaning. This type of research uses methods that are more subjective, a smaller sample size, and fewer research controls. The design of the qualitative study tends to evolve over time during the study. Quantitative research is characterized by the collection of numerical values, under a controlled situation, that yield data, which can be generalized. Quantitative research uses subjects that represent certain groups and strives to control as much bias as possible through design decisions.
Cognitive Level: Application
Nursing Process: Implementation
Client Need: Safe, Effective Care Environment; Management of Care

8-3. Answer: 1

Rationale: The design of the qualitative study is not specified in advance but rather evolves over time during the study. This is termed an emergent design—one that becomes clear during the study as the researcher makes decisions about what has been learned. Searching for associations between variables describes a descriptive quantitative study. Searching to find associations between several variables describes a correlational quantitative study. Searching to find the effects of a particular intervention describes an experimental quantitative study.
Cognitive Level: Analysis
Nursing Process: Implementation
Client Need: Safe, Effective Care Environment; Management of Care

8-4. Answer: 3

Rationale: Not all problems are researchable. Problems or questions of a moral or ethical nature are incapable of being researched. There are no right or wrong answers, only points of view that reflect one's values. Because this study is a moral or ethical issue, the other criteria would not be applicable.
Cognitive Level: Analysis
Nursing Process: Assessment
Client Need: Safe, Effective Care Environment; Management of Care

8-5. Answer: 1

Rationale: There are a number of research design strategies that may be employed to answer the research question that has been posed. The one selected must help maximize the possibilities of achieving accurate information in the results.

Cognitive Level: Application
Nursing Process: Planning
Client Need: Safe, Effective Care Environment; Management of Care

8-6. Answer: 4

Rationale: Evidence-based practice extends beyond research utilization; it involves making clinical decisions on the basis of the best possible evidence. Though the best evidence usually comes from rigorous research, evidence-based practice also uses other sources of credible information. The differentiation between research utilization and evidence-based practice is that research utilization is part of evidence-based practice and is a prescribed task of summarizing and using research findings to address a particular practice problem. Evidence-based practice is the careful and practical use of current best evidence to guide health care decisions. Evidence-based practice typically involves weighing various types of evidence, and an evidence hierarchy may be used to rank studies and other information according to the strength of evidence provided.
Cognitive Level: Application
Nursing Process: Planning
Client Need: Safe, Effective Care Environment; Management of Care

8-7. Answer: 1

Rationale: Inherent in the principle of respect for persons are the concepts of autonomy, dignity, uniqueness, freedom, and choice. This principle forms the foundation of the participant's rights to informed consent, privacy, and confidentiality. The principle of justice requires that people be treated fairly. Beneficence is the duty to promote or do good. Nonmaleficence is the ability to not inflict physical or emotional harm.
Cognitive Level: Analysis
Nursing Process: Planning
Client Need: Safe, Effective Care Environment; Management of Care

8-8. Answer: 2

Rationale: There are three points at which the HIPAA privacy regulations will impact nursing research. They are (1) assessing data from a covered entity; (2) creating data; and (3) disclosing data. When obtaining individual health information directly from the subject, the subject must authorize the use of the information. Essential elements of disclosure must be included in the authorization: who will be receiving the information; what further disclosures the researcher anticipates; and what information will be disclosed to the researcher. Data de-identification applies to accessing data. It is inappropriate for the researcher to share information with the organization's research committee members or the patient's physician.
Cognitive Level: Analysis
Process Step: Implementation
Client Need: Safe, Effective Care Environment; Management of Care

8-9. Answer: 2

Rationale: The actual review of a quantitative study divides the critique into four stages of review. Stage 1 refers to a review of the purpose, problem statement, and congruency with design and methodology. Stage 2 focuses on the conduct of the research. Stage 3 refers to studying the findings of a study and assessing if the outcomes and conclusions are believable and supported by the findings. Stage 4 summarizes the overall quality of the study,

identifies the strengths and limitations of the study, and evaluates the contributions of the study to nursing.
Cognitive Level: Application
Nursing Process: Evaluation
Client Need: Safe, Effective Care Environment; Management of Care

Chapter 9 – Health Assessment

Key Terms Matching Exercise 1

1.	c	**6.**	f
2.	h	**7.**	g
3.	a	**8.**	d
4.	i	**9.**	e
5.	b	**10.**	j

Key Terms Matching Exercise 2

11.	i	**16.**	a
12.	j	**17.**	f
13.	d	**18.**	e
14.	c	**19.**	g
15.	h	**20.**	b

Labeling Exercise 1: Apical, bilateral radial, and bilateral pedal pulse locations

a. Brachial artery
b. Radial artery
c. Femoral artery
d. Dorsalis pedis artery
e. Posterior tibial artery
f. Popliteal artery
g. Common carotid artery
h. Temporal artery

Labeling Exercise 2: Palpation

a. Fingertips
b. Finger pads
c. Palmar surface of fingers
d. Metacarpophalangeal joint
e. Palmar surface
f. Ulnar surface
g. Dorsal surface

Labeling Exercise 3: Patient positioning during physical examination

a. Sitting
b. Supine
c. Dorsal recumbent
d. Lithotomy
e. Sims' (posterior view)
f. Prone
g. Knee-chest
h. Standing, bent over examining table

NCLEX-RN® Review Questions

Question numbers correspond to Outcome-Based Learning Objectives for this chapter.

9-1. Answer: 2
   Rationale: Within the Vietnamese culture, the head may be considered sacred and feet profane; do not touch the feet and then the head. Avoiding eye contact is a sign of respect. Using both hands when giving a person something shows respect. Tone of voice should be soft. A loud voice or pointing of the finger is a sign of disrespect.
   Cognitive Level: Application
   Nursing Process: Implementation
   Client Need: Health Promotion and Maintenance; Prevention and/or Early Detection of Health Problems

9-2. Answer: 1
   Rationale: Facilitation is demonstrated by using comments such as "please continue" or nodding one's head to encourage the patient to say more. Explanation is a technique that uses factual information to explain an issue in efforts to clarify it for the patient. Clarification is a technique used to explain ambiguities with information. And empathy is an acknowledgement of the patient's feelings.
   Cognitive Level: Application
   Nursing Process: Implementation
   Client Need: Health Promotion and Maintenance; Prevention and/or Early Detection of Health Problems

9-3. Answer: 3
   Rationale: An awareness of body language is an important factor during the interview. Positive nonverbal messages enhance the relationship with the patient and show attentiveness and acceptance. Examples of positive nonverbal messages are a professional appearance, a relaxed open posture, appropriate eye contact, equal-status seating, a moderate tone of voice and rate of speech, and appropriate touch. Examples of negative nonverbal messages are a tense posture, critical gestures such as pointing or finger tapping, yawning, speaking too quickly, avoiding eye contact by focusing on notes, and inappropriate touch.
   Cognitive Level: Analysis
   Nursing Process: Assessment
   Client Need: Psychosocial Integrity; Coping and Adaptation

9-4. Answer: 2
   Rationale: Tympany is a high-pitched, drum-like tone of medium duration. It is commonly heard over the air-filled intestines. Resonance is a loud, hollow tone of long duration. It is commonly heard over the lungs. Flatness is a soft, high-pitched tone with a short duration. It is heard over muscle and bone. Hyperresonance is a loud, low tone with a longer duration than resonance. It is heard when air is trapped in a space such as the lungs.
   Cognitive Level: Analysis
   Nursing Process: Assessment
   Client Need: Health Promotion and Maintenance; Prevention and/or Early Detection of Health Problems

9-5. Answer: 3
   Rationale: The five components of critical thinking related to health assessment include collection of information, analysis of the situation, generation of alternatives, selection of alternatives, and evaluation. Collection of information begins with the interview and continues throughout the entire health assessment. The second skill is analysis of the situation. During this phase the nurse must distinguish normal from abnormal. The patient's age, gender, genetic background, and culture affect the analysis. The nurse must

utilize laboratory findings, diagnostic tests, charts, and measures related to development and aging. Generation of alternatives includes identifying options and establishing priorities. It begins with identification of options, and then the nurse and patient work together to establish the priorities. The next step is the selection of alternatives. The critical thinking skills needed for this step are the ability to develop outcomes and plans. The outcome is the final result of what the patient will attain, and the plan is the activities that will lead to that outcome. The last step in critical thinking is evaluation. Evaluation requires the nurse to determine if the expected outcomes have been achieved.
Cognitive Level: Analysis
Nursing Process: Planning
Client Need: Health Promotion and Maintenance; Prevention and/or Early Detection of Health Problems

Chapter 10 – The Aging Patient

Key Terms Matching Exercise 1

1.	b	6.	a
2.	e	7.	d
3.	c	8.	h
4.	j	9.	g
5.	i	10.	f

Key Terms Matching Exercise 2

11.	a	16.	g
12.	f	17.	i
13.	c	18.	b
14.	h	19.	e
15.	j	20.	d

Age-Related or Disorder?

21.	age-related	31.	age-related
22.	disorder	32.	age-related
23.	age-related	33.	disorder
24.	age-related	34.	disorder
25.	disorder	35.	age-related
26.	disorder	36.	disorder
27.	age-related	37.	age-related
28.	disorder	38.	disorder
29.	disorder	39.	disorder
30.	age-related	40.	disorder

True or False?

41.	F	46.	T
42.	T	47.	T
43.	F	48.	F
44.	T	49.	F
45.	T	50.	F

NCLEX-RN® Review Questions

Question numbers correspond to Outcome-Based Learning Objectives for this chapter.

10-1. Answer: 4

> **Rationale:** It is prudent to remove any dental appliances such as dentures prior to assessment of the oral mucosa, as cancerous lesions may be hidden beneath these devices. As the pink conjunctiva is exposed during ectropion, it can be mistaken for an eye infection. The ear canal must be free of cerumen and the tympanic membrane must be readily visible on otoscopic exam for an accurate hearing exam result. Cheilosis is a dry scaling of the oral cavity caused by dehydration, poor nutrition, poorly fitting dentures, or medications, and although the geriatric client may have this condition, it does not lead to the normal weakening of the abdominal muscles seen in these same patients.
> **Cognitive Level:** Application
> **Nursing Process:** Evaluation
> **Client Need:** Health Promotion and Maintenance; Prevention and/or Early Detection of Health Problems

10-2. Answer: 2

> **Rationale:** Updates for the pneumococcal vaccine should be received every 6 to 7 years, but the tetanus vaccine is only usually updated every 10 years. Breast self-exams should be performed monthly with mammography done every 1 to 2 years up to the age of 70. The recommendation for colonoscopy for clients over 65 is every 10 years, but fecal occult blood testing should be completed yearly. Current recommendations call for complete hearing and vision screenings and a full eye exam annually.
> **Cognitive Level:** Application
> **Nursing Process:** Evaluation
> **Client Need:** Health Promotion and Maintenance; Prevention and/or Early Detection of Health Problems

10-3. Answer: 1

> **Rationale:** Ketolorac is an anti-inflammatory medication that can worsen asymptomatic pathologic gastrointestinal conditions. Angiotensin converting enzyme (ACE) inhibitors carry a threefold risk of causing angioedema in African American clients. Amiodarone may not only be ineffective in the elderly, but it also increases the risk of these clients developing life-threatening dysrhythmias such as torsades de pointes and prolongation of the QT interval. Disopyramide is highly anticholinergic and may induce

heart failure. It is meperidine that breaks down into potentially harmful metabolites that can cause convulsions or other central nervous system effects. Ticlopidine helps prevent clot formation but is more toxic than aspirin. Trimethobenzamide is an ineffective antiemetic that may cause extrapyramidal side effects.
Cognitive Level: Analysis
Nursing Process: Assessment
Client Need: Health Promotion and Maintenance; Prevention and/or Early Detection of Health Problems

10-4. Answer: 1
Rationale: The patient's recurrent perineal rash, multiple bruises in various stages of healing, and an unkempt appearance strongly suggest possible physical abuse and neglect. The correct action by the nurse or any mandatory reporter in this situation would be to notify the health care provider (since they are at their office) and Adult Protective Services. Nurses should become familiar with their own local laws and facility policies and procedures regarding the handling of elder mistreatment, including notification of law enforcement. This scenario did not include specific possible signs and symptoms of financial exploitation, psychological abuse, or self-neglect. However, the nurse should remember that sometimes the elderly fall victim to more than one type of mistreatment simultaneously. It is not the nurse's job to contact the news media or make implications or allegations regarding abuse or neglect cases.
Cognitive Level: Application
Nursing Process: Implementation
Client Need: Psychosocial Integrity; Psychosocial Adaptation

10-5. Answers: 4, 5, 6
Rationale: An intermediate care facility is for patients who are somewhat independent but require 24-hour supervision and assistance. These facilities are able to help with ADLs, provide special diets, and may receive Medicare and Medicaid payments. These facilities are not able to accept bedbound clients or those with gastrostomy tube feedings or complicated wound care. These clients must utilize the services of a skilled nursing facility. Adult day care programs provide daytime respite for caregivers while fostering socialization among the seniors who participate.
Cognitive Level: Application
Nursing Process: Planning
Client Need: Safe, Effective Care Environment; Management of Care

10-6. Answer: 3
Rationale: The Green House Project provides "home-like" settings within a community of seniors who require assistance with meals or socialization but who fear institutionalization and loss of independence. This option uses a pager system for staff members instead of the traditional call lights and a communal dining table instead

of trays or a dining hall. Skilled nursing care such as IV therapy is available only in skilled care facilities or in the hospital. Adult day care programs provide daytime respite for caregivers while fostering socialization among the seniors who participate. These programs may not be covered by insurance such as Medicare and offer few to no health services.
Cognitive Level: Application
Nursing Process: Planning
Client Need: Safe, Effective Care Environment; Management of Care

10-7. Answer: 2
Rationale: The TTY technology is older and offers fewer advantages than the newer Voice over Internet Protocol. Some improvements include Internet utilization, communication through voice and text and streaming video. There are several new medication administration devices and technologies that provide better assistance for clients with complex medication regimens or problems with forgetfulness. Continuous body monitoring systems are often very expensive, but there are some simpler, more cost-effective solutions. Simple monitoring systems are available that include video cameras and door sensors connected to the cell phones and Internet services of family members, and these systems cost much less than other alternatives. The Internet Health File project allows seniors to maintain and update their health information online and reserve the right to share this data with family or their health care provider.
Cognitive Level: Application
Nursing Process: Assessment
Client Need: Safe, Effective Care Environment; Management of Care

Chapter 11 – Genetics

Key Terms Matching Exercise 1

1.	b	**6.**	c
2.	d	**7.**	i
3.	a	**8.**	h
4.	f	**9.**	g
5.	j	**10.**	e

Key Terms Matching Exercise 2

11.	h	**16.**	j
12.	e	**17.**	b
13.	i	**18.**	a
14.	g	**19.**	c
15.	d	**20.**	f

Word Search

21. sex chromosome
22. mutation
23. nondisjunction
24. karyotype
25. pedigree
26. cytogenetics
27. X-linked dominant
28. X-linked recessive
29. codon
30. exon
31. gamete
32. intron
33. nonsense mutation
34. haploid
35. pharmacogenomics
36. zygote
37. genomics
38. homozygous
39. heterozygous
40. telomere
41. wild type
42. genetic variance
43. gene
44. allele
45. genome

X	N	O	N	S	E	N	S	E	M	U	T	A	T	I	O	N	D	W	Q	U
Z	P	A	I	E	O	H	I	R	P	L	Y	H	E	U	R	T	K	Y	U	P
W	L	S	R	X	L	I	N	K	E	D	R	E	C	E	S	S	I	V	E	H
I	H	C	E	C	L	H	S	A	D	C	S	T	A	E	Y	H	U	K	A	A
L	A	I	G	H	F	I	N	X	I	W	E	E	I	D	O	J	A	P	G	R
D	U	T	V	R	W	E	N	U	G	L	W	R	N	M	R	U	L	I	D	M
T	I	E	V	O	U	O	U	K	R	O	S	O	O	H	P	O	E	F	L	A
Y	X	N	P	M	S	Y	A	I	E	T	N	Z	R	T	I	A	R	N	T	C
P	O	E	A	O	U	R	Y	L	E	D	Y	Y	J	D	A	S	D	A	E	O
E	D	G	T	S	Y	F	J	C	I	G	D	G	E	N	O	M	I	C	S	G
S	C	O	D	O	N	Y	I	S	O	R	I	O	S	O	T	S	C	P	I	E
D	I	T	T	M	E	R	J	U	R	T	G	U	M	U	T	A	T	I	O	N
L	O	Y	K	E	A	U	S	A	O	H	A	S	L	I	E	A	S	A	E	O
U	P	C	Y	U	N	N	O	E	G	E	M	N	N	M	N	E	P	N	E	M
E	A	J	S	C	I	D	R	L	E	U	E	F	O	Y	M	A	J	O	T	I
O	G	E	T	O	G	Y	Z	E	N	A	T	N	X	U	I	K	N	R	R	C
R	H	I	A	C	K	F	O	L	O	C	E	R	E	M	O	L	E	T	U	S
U	O	H	J	K	L	F	A	L	A	G	P	L	H	U	A	D	S	N	S	H
N	E	E	C	N	A	I	R	A	V	C	I	T	E	N	E	G	A	I	G	L

True or False?

46.	T	**51.**	F
47.	F	**52.**	T
48.	F	**53.**	F
49.	T	**54.**	T
50.	F	**55.**	T

Labeling Exercise 1: The Chromosome

a. Nucleus
b. Cell
c. Histones
d. DNA (double helix)
e. Base pairs
f. Telomere
g. Centromere
h. Telomere
i. Chromatid
j. Chromosome

Labeling Exercise 2: Structure of a Chromosome

a. Telomere
b. Sample-loci
c. Q-arm
d. Centromere
e. P-arm

NCLEX-RN® Review Questions

Question numbers correspond to Outcome-Based Learning Objectives for this chapter.

11-1. Answer: 2
Rationale: Understanding the genetic variance between the client's genotype and phenotype is important for appropriate nursing management. It is the mutation or polymorphism of a gene, not the gene itself, that causes a predisposition to a disease. Predictive genetic tests are performed on asymptomatic clients who are at risk for a genetic disorder. Diagnostic genetic tests are performed on clients who are symptomatic. Developing a pedigree in order to recognize important patterns of inheritance and clusters of diseases helps the health care provider to determine a genetic risk assessment.
Cognitive Level: Analysis
Nursing Process: Evaluation
Client Need: Health Promotion and Maintenance; Prevention and/or Early Detection of Health Problems

11-2. Answer: 3
Rationale: Each parent contributes 23 chromosomes to his or her offspring, making 46 total chromosomes or 23 pairs of chromosomes. An extra or third chromosome instead of the normal pair is called a trisomy. Each chromosome contains genes, and each gene pair contains alleles from each parent. Alleles that are identical are homozygous, and those that are different are heterozygous. Down syndrome is a trisomy chromosomal disorder, and chromosomal disorders are not the result of abnormalities of individual genes on the chromosome.
Cognitive Level: Analysis
Nursing Process: Evaluation
Client Need: Health Promotion and Maintenance; Prevention and/or Early Detection of Health Problems

11-3. Answer: 1
Rationale: Although each cell contains the entire genome, most cells only express about 30% of the genes within the genome. Each nucleotide in DNA contains the deoxyribose sugar component instead of the ribose sugar component, which is contained in RNA. Cytosine always binds to guanine in both DNA and RNA, but adenine always binds to thymine to form DNA. Adenine always binds to uracil in RNA only. The purines and pyrimidines bases in DNA always bind in a complementary nature to form polynucleotide chains, which form a double-helix shape.
Cognitive Level: Analysis
Nursing Process: Implementation
Client Need: Health Promotion and Maintenance; Prevention and/or Early Detection of Health Problems

11-4. Answer: 3
Rationale: Single-gene disorders are caused by a mutation in a single gene, not a chromosome or portion of a chromosome. The mutation is a permanent DNA change that affects one or both chromosomes in a pair. The fluorescence in situ hybridization (FISH) method is used to detect very tiny chromosomal deletions, and cri du chat syndrome is a disorder caused by a large, cytogenetically visible deletion. Although thalassemia is an autosomal recessive disorder, one of the types of single-gene disorders, it is rare within the Amish community. Also, any type of carrier screening is often unacceptable in most Amish communities. Complex disorders may be caused by single-gene mutations, but they are not single-gene disorders. They are usually considered disorders of adulthood that are caused by a combination of genetic variations and environmental factors.
Cognitive Level: Analysis
Nursing Process: Evaluation
Client Need: Health Promotion and Maintenance; Prevention and/or Early Detection of Health Problems

11-5. Answer: 1
Rationale: Features such as penetrance and expressivity determine the manifestations of some genetic disorders so that not every individual with the same genotype expresses the same signs and symptoms. The information gathered from a pedigree can help the nurse develop a personalized prevention program for certain chronic conditions or single-gene disorders. The patterns of single-gene disorders are dependent on the chromosomal location of the gene and whether the phenotype is dominant or recessive. Although current age and ethnicity are important when obtaining a pedigree, medical conditions with onset and duration are equally as important.
Cognitive Level: Analysis
Nursing Process: Evaluation
Client Need: Health Promotion and Maintenance; Prevention and/or Early Detection of Health Problems

11-6. Answer: 4
Rationale: Head injury has been investigated as influencing Alzheimer disease but has not been proven a contributor. LDL receptor disorder may lead to familial hypercholesterolemia. Cancers diagnosed after age 40 to 50 are not necessarily associated with inherited susceptibility to cancer. Also, male smokers have an increased relative risk of cancer development over nonsmokers. A recognizable Mendelian inheritance pattern within a family history may suggest inherited cancer susceptibility syndrome.
Cognitive Level: Application
Nursing Process: Planning
Client Need: Health Promotion and Maintenance; Prevention and/or Early Detection of Health Problems

11-7. Answer: 2

Rationale: Gene and stem cell therapies are two applications currently in clinical development for the potential genetic correction of X-linked severe combined immune deficiency and information about diseases such as cancer and Parkinson's, respectively. There are no current human gene therapy products available for commercial use. Polymerase chain reaction and microarray analysis are commonly used genetic testing methods that can analyze nucleic acid and identify subgroups of cancer to stratify for treatment, respectively. Serum cholinesterase sensitivity is a potential genetic related concern that can occur during anesthesia, like malignant hyperthermia. Karotype is a picture of the entire chromosome complement of a cell that aids in identifying individuals with chromosomal disorders such as Down syndrome. Pharmacogenetics focuses on how genetic variation affects the varied responses of medications, and cytochrome P450 enzymes help metabolize certain medications and are directly affected by polymorphisms or DNA variations in the genes that code for them. The benefits of utilizing pharmacogenetic principles and understanding cytochrome P450 enzymes for the client at risk for malignant hyperthermia can help prevent potential harmful effects of anesthetic medications.
Cognitive Level: Analysis
Nursing Process: Planning
Client Need: Physiological Integrity; Physiological Adaptation

Chapter 12 – Stress and Adaptation

Key Terms Matching Exercise 1

1. a
2. f
3. c
4. g
5. j
6. i
7. d
8. h
9. b
10. e

Key Terms Matching Exercise 2

11. d
12. f
13. g
14. i
15. e
16. j
17. a
18. h
19. c
20. b

Complete the Sentence

21. alarm, resistance, exhaustion
22. external stressors
23. developmental, middle age
24. Situational
25. maladaptive coping mechanisms
26. (1) a clear sense of personal values and goals, (2) a strong tendency toward interaction with the environment, (3) a sense of meaningfulness, and (4) an internal rather than an external locus of control
27. sense of coherence
28. primary appraisal
29. secondary appraisal
30. hassles, uplifts

True or False?

31. F
32. T
33. F
34. F
35. T
36. T
37. F
38. T
39. F
40. T

Labeling Exercise: Disorders Caused or Aggravated by Stress

a. Skin disorders: eczema, pruritus, urticaria, psoriasis
b. Respiratory disorders: asthma, hay fever, tuberculosis
c. Cardiovascular disorders: coronary artery disease, essential hypertension, congestive heart failure
d. Gastrointestinal disorders: constipation, diarrhea, duodenal ulcer, anorexia nervosa, obesity, ulcerative colitis
e. Menstrual irregularities
f. Musculoskeletal disorders: rheumatoid arthritis, low back pain, migraine headache, muscle tension
g. Metabolic disorders: hyperthyroidism, hypothyroidism, diabetes
h. Decreased immune response
i. Accident proneness
j. Cancer

NCLEX-RN® Review Questions

Question numbers correspond to Outcome-Based Learning Objectives for this chapter.

12-1. Answer: 2

Rationale: Stress may be caused by internal and external sources. Internal stressors originate within a person. They include lifestyle choices, such as the use of caffeine, an overloaded schedule, negative self-talk, such as self-criticism and overanalyzing, and stressful personality traits, such as perfectionist, workaholic, or pleaser. External stressors originate outside the body. They are precipitated by changes in the external environment. They may be triggered by the actual physical environment, the social environment, the organizational environment, major life events, and other catastrophic events such as hurricanes, floods, and fires. Daily hassles, such as commuting long distances, misplacing keys, and experiencing mechanical breakdowns, also act as external stressors.
Cognitive Level: Analysis
Nursing Process: Assessment
Client Need: Psychosocial Integrity; Coping and Adaptation

12-2. Answer: 2

Rationale: Primary appraisal is the process of evaluating the significance of the transaction as it relates to a person's well-being. A person seeks answers as to the meaning of the situation with regard to his or her well-being. Secondary appraisal is the process of evaluating the significance of the transaction between the person and his or her environment as it relates to available coping resources and options. Primary and secondary appraisals often occur simultaneously and interact with each other in determining stress. Reappraisal develops from the feedback of changes in the person-environment relationship and from reflection about the coping process. Reappraisal allows for changes in the person's evaluation of the event, or a relabeling of the cognitive appraisal. The event may be reappraised and evaluated as nonstressful due to changes in the relationship between the person and the environment.

For example, a hospitalization initially may be deemed stressful by the individual, based on primary and secondary appraisal, but during reappraisal, the situation is evaluated as nonstressful because of changes in the relationship between the person and the environment, such as a positive outcome of improved health from the hospitalization. Sense of coherence refers to how an individual sees the world and his or her life in it. It is a personality characteristic or coping style rater than a response to a specific situation. The three components of SOC are comprehensibility, manageability, and meaningfulness.
Cognitive Level: Analysis
Nursing Process: Evaluation
Client Need: Psychosocial Integrity; Coping and Adaptation

12-3. Answer: 4
Rationale: The shock and countershock phases are both seen in the alarm phase within the general adaptation syndrome. Physical signs and symptoms of the alarm reaction generally are those of the sympathetic nervous system stimulation. They include increased blood pressure, increased heart and respiratory rate, decreased gastrointestinal motility, pupil dilatation, and increased perspiration. The patient also may complain of such symptoms as increased anxiety, nausea, fatigue, anorexia, and weight loss. There are fewer signs and symptoms of the resistance stage. The bodily symptoms of the alarm reaction disappear, and resistance rises above normal. Instead of continuing to lose weight, such as occurred in the alarm phase, the person returns to a "normal" weight. In the exhaustion phase, physical symptoms of the alarm reaction may reappear briefly in a final attempt of the body to survive. This is exemplified by a terminally ill person whose vital signs become stronger just before death. The individual in the stage of exhaustion usually becomes ill and may die if assistance from outside sources is not available. Often this stage can be reversed by external sources of adaptive energy such as medication, blood transfusion, and/or psychotherapy.
Cognitive Level: Analysis
Nursing Process: Implementation
Client Need: Psychosocial Integrity; Coping and Adaptation

12-4. Answer: 2
Rationale: An impaired ability to adapt to physiological and psychological stress may contribute to the pathogenesis of cardiovascular disease as the cardiovascular system is particularly vulnerable to stress. Incidents of acute stress have been associated with a higher risk for serious cardiac events, such as heart dysrhythmias and heart attacks, and even death from such events in people with heart disease. Emotional effects of stress alter the heart rhythms and pose a risk for serious arrhythmias in people with existing heart rhythm disturbances. The nurse should suggest the conversation end.
Cognitive Level: Application
Nursing Process: Implementation
Client Need: Physiological Integrity; Physiological Adaptation

12-5. Answer: 2
Rationale: Even though the detoxifying actions of the liver require free radicals, the liver also detoxifies them. Neither the spleen, colon, nor kidney is responsible for the detoxification of free radicals.
Cognitive Level: Application
Nursing Process: Assessment
Client Need: Physiological Integrity; Physiological Adaptation

12-6. Answer: 2
Rationale: *Ineffective individual coping* is defined as an inability to manage internal or environmental stressors appropriately as a result of inadequate resources. Potential etiologies include disruption of emotional bonds, unsatisfactory support system, sensory overload, and inadequate psychological and physical resources. *Anxiety* is a vague, uneasy feeling of discomfort or dread, the source of which may not be known. There is no evidence to suggest this patient is experiencing *caregiver role strain*. *Decisional conflict* is an uncertainty about course of action to take when the choice involves risk, loss, or challenge to personal life values.
Cognitive Level: Application
Nursing Process: Assessment
Client Need: Psychosocial Integrity; Coping and Adaptation

12-7. Answer: 1
Rationale: Factors that have been found to be successful in reducing stress include exercise, nutrition, rest and sleep, and time management. Regular exercise promotes both physical and emotional health. Physiological benefits include improved muscle tone, improved cardiopulmonary function, and weight control. Psychological benefits include relief of tension, a feeling of well-being, and relaxation. Good nutrition is essential in increasing the body's resistance to stress. A reduction in caffeine, salt, sugar, and fat and increasing vitamins and minerals will minimize the negative effects of stress. Rest and sleep restore the body's energy levels and are an essential element of stress management. There is no evidence to suggest this patient needs a support group or anger management.
Cognitive Level: Analysis
Nursing Process: Implementation
Client Need: Psychosocial Integrity; Coping and Adaptation

Chapter 13 – Psychosocial Issues in Nursing

Key Terms Matching Exercise 1

1.	f	**6.**	g
2.	e	**7.**	d
3.	c	**8.**	i
4.	h	**9.**	j
5.	b	**10.**	a

Key Terms Matching Exercise 2

11.	h	**16.**	g
12.	a	**17.**	c
13.	f	**18.**	i
14.	b	**19.**	d
15.	j	**20.**	e

Therapeutic or Nontherapeutic?

21. **nontherapeutic** "We will work on that together."
22. **nontherapeutic** "Let's discuss what you feel is unfair about the situation."
23. **therapeutic**
24. **nontherapeutic** "Let's talk about your feelings."
25. **nontherapeutic** "You sound upset. Tell me what you are feeling right now."
26. **therapeutic**

27. **therapeutic**
28. **nontherapeutic** "What led up to that situation?"
29. **nontherapeutic** "I will try to answer your questions and clarify some issues regarding your treatment."
30. **nontherapeutic** "Describe what you were feeling just prior to this occurrence."

Short Answer Questions

31. Therapeutic communication is purposeful communication that conveys openness and caring. It consists of those words and actions that enhance the nurse–patient relationship and empower patients to make informed choices about their health care. A therapeutic alliance is one in which the nurse and the patient consciously work together to reach mutually agreed-on goals. The ability to communicate therapeutically is key to the formation of a therapeutic alliance.

32. The term locus of control refers to the perception people have about how much control they exert over the events that happen in their lives. People with an internal locus of control orientation believe that events in their lives are controlled by their own actions and decisions. People with an external locus of control orientation believe that events in their lives are controlled more by fate, luck, and external circumstances.

33. The five stages of grief and mourning depicted by Kubler-Ross are:
    1. Denial—Individuals react with a shocked "No, not me." This is healthy and allows individuals and significant others time to gather coping resources.
    2. Anger—Individuals say "Why me?" or "Why us?" During this stage people sometimes blame others, including God.
    3. Bargaining—Individuals say "Yes me, but. . . ." or "If you just give me enough time to see my daughter married, I'll be ready."
    4. Depression—Individuals say "Yes me." With this acknowledgment of the reality of the situation comes feelings of depression.
    5. Acceptance—Facing the loss or death peacefully. In the case of death, individuals tend to withdraw into themselves.

34. • Validate the presence of the depression. Acceptance by the nurse allows the patient to feel positive about the therapeutic relationship. This helps with healing, decreases isolation, and increases coping ability.
    • Provide emotional support through empathetic listening. Empathetic listening helps to build trust and strengthens the therapeutic relationship.
    • Encourage the expression of feelings both positive and negative. Patients may not fully understand what is happening to them. If they can express feelings freely, the nurse can plan specific actions to assist the patient to see the situation clearly.
    • Avoid excessive cheerfulness and false reassurance. This will not help patients to work through their problems.
    • Encourage the patient to be involved in his or her care. The ability to control aspects of one's life helps to allay feelings of helplessness.
    • Assist the patient in goal setting and problem solving. Patients may be overwhelmed by their situation. Assisting them to view the problem in its component parts will reduce anxiety and assist with effective coping behaviors.
    • Assess for suicidal ideation and if present ensure safety and make a referral. Involve the health care team if you suspect that the patient is suicidal.
    • If necessary, refer for psychotherapy and pharmacological intervention. It is important to ensure safety and prevent patients from harming themselves.

35. • Introductory or orientation phase—The introductory phase begins when the therapeutic relationship is initiated. Introductions take place and the patient is given initial information pertinent to her circumstances.
    • Working phase—During the working phase a therapeutic alliance is established. A therapeutic alliance is one in which the nurse and the patient consciously work together to reach mutually agreed-on goals.
    • Termination phase—During this phase the nurse and patient review what occurred during the working phase and what goals have been met and what progress was made.

Labeling Exercise: Maslow's Hierarchy of Needs

a. Self-actualization
b. Self-esteem
c. Love and belonging
d. Safety and security
e. Physiological needs

NCLEX-RN® Review Questions

Question numbers correspond to Outcome-Based Learning Objectives for this chapter.

13-1. Answer: 4
Rationale: Cognitive theory has impacted the treatment of a broad range of emotional and mental health disorders. It is based on the premise that mental health symptoms are related to how individuals view themselves and the world around them. This theory states that individuals develop a set of core beliefs as a result of interacting with the environment. These beliefs or schemas can be positive or negative. Schemas influence how individuals interpret and evaluate experiences while behaviors are often the result of these interpretations. The cognitive triad is influenced by negative schemas that influence the person to see him- or herself as inadequate, negatively misinterpret an experience, and view the future in a negative way. Being stuck in the cognitive triad leads to the development of cognitive distortions, which in turn may result in the development of mental health symptoms. Assimilation is a concept within Piaget's theory of cognitive development. Holism is a concept within Engel's biopsychosocial model of development.
Cognitive Level: Analysis
Nursing Process: Assessment
Client Need: Psychosocial Integrity; Psychosocial Adaptation

13-2. Answer: 1
Rationale: The introductory phase begins when the therapeutic relationship is initiated. Introductions take place and the patient is given initial information pertinent to his or her circumstance. The nurse starts to develop a trusting relationship. The second phase is called the working phase. It is during this phase that a *therapeutic alliance* is established. A therapeutic alliance is when the nurse and the patient consciously work together toward reaching mutually agreed upon goals. The third phase of the therapeutic nurse–patient relationship is termination. Depending on the nature, length, and intensity of the therapeutic relationship the termination phase can be difficult for patients. Termination is introduced during the initial phase and often discussed during the working phase. During this phase the nurse and patient review what occurred during the working phase and what goals have been met and what progress was made.
Cognitive Level: Analysis

Nursing Process: Implementation
Client Need: Psychosocial Integrity; Coping and Adaptation

13-3. Answer: 4
Rationale: Cultural competence is defined as the nurse continually striving to provide culturally appropriate care to patients and families. Nurses must convey empathy, show respect, build trust, establish rapport, listen actively, provide appropriate feedback, and demonstrate genuine interest. Language differences, differences in the understanding of terminology, and differences in perceptions and expectations also create barriers. The nurse should obtain an interpreter to help establish a communication method with the patient.
Cognitive Level: Analysis
Nursing Process: Planning
Client Need: Psychosocial Integrity; Coping and Adaptation

13-4. Answer: 3
Rationale: The nurse needs to design a teaching plan that will be effective for the patients' learning while taking into consideration individual needs and time constraints. The best approach for these patients would be for the nurse to conduct the training in a group setting.
Cognitive Level: Analysis
Nursing Process: Planning
Client Need: Safe, Effective Care Environment; Management of Care

13-5. Answer: 4
Rationale: Once the crisis is stabilized the nurse can then help the patient problem solve and explore alternatives. It is here that new coping skills can be taught. Teaching new coping skills empowers patients to better handle future crisis events. It is for this reason that crisis is often seen as an opportunity for growth. The nurse provides continual emotional support through this process because the change can be very anxiety producing. The nurse should ask the patient if there are any outstanding problems that still need to be addressed. Assessing vital signs does not help establish rapport. Asking the patient about having had emergency surgery and listing needs and concerns should be done at the beginning of the crisis situation.
Cognitive Level: Application
Nursing Process: Implementation
Client Need: Psychosocial Integrity; Coping and Adaptation

13-6. Answer: 4
Rationale: To provide patient-centered care, power and authority need to be transferred away from the health care professional and toward the patient. Ways in which nurses can demonstrate interpersonal competence and empower patients to become more involved in their health care decisions include answering questions honestly, engaging in mutual goal setting, informing patients in advance of procedures, preparing patients for procedures, letting patients know what to expect, listening to any patient concerns, and not treating adult patients as children.
Cognitive Level: Application.
Nursing Process: Implementation
Client Need: Psychosocial Integrity; Coping and Adaptation

13-7. Answer: 2
Rationale: Anger and anxiety are two emotions that are often related. When individuals feel anxious they also experience accompanying feelings of frustration and helplessness. These feelings in turn can cause individuals to feel powerless to control their own autonomy. Anger develops to a greater or lesser degree as a response to the

feelings of powerlessness and helplessness. Anger is a more powerful feeling that helps individuals feel more in control.
Cognitive Level: Analysis
Nursing Process: Assessment
Client Need: Psychosocial Integrity; Coping and Adaptation

13-8. Answer: 4
Rationale: In panic levels of anxiety, the nurse should not leave the patient and should not ask the patient for explanations. The nurse should not start the chemotherapy as soon as possible but should provide the patient with a period of rest after the attack has ended. The patient should also be referred for further evaluation.
Cognitive Level: Application
Nursing Process: Implementation
Client Need: Psychosocial Integrity; Coping and Adaptation

Chapter 14 – Nutrition

Key Terms Matching Exercise 1

1.	h	6.	f
2.	e	7.	g
3.	b	8.	a
4.	i	9.	d
5.	j	10.	c

Key Terms Matching Exercise 2

11.	g	16.	e
12.	i	17.	d
13.	a	18.	b
14.	c	19.	f
15.	j	20.	h

Complete the Sentence

21. >5%, >10%
22. 6–11 servings of grains, 2–4 servings of fruit, 3–5 servings of vegetables, 2–3 servings of protein, 2–3 servings of dairy
23. 18.5–24.9, 25–29.9, 30
24. anorexia nervosa, bulimia nervosa, eating-disorders-not-otherwise-specified (EDNOS)
25. fruits, vegetables, nuts, low-fat dairy, fat, saturated fat
26. (1) abdominal obesity, (2) high triglycerides, (3) low HDL-C, (4) high blood pressure, and (5) fasting glucose greater than or equal to 110 mg/dL
27. low-sodium
28. whole grains, fruits, vegetables, and low-fat milk products
29. hypoglycemic, hyperglycemic
30. calcium, vitamin D sources

True or False?

31.	F	36.	F
32.	T	37.	T
33.	T	38.	F
34.	F	39.	T
35.	F	40.	F

Therapeutic Lifestyle Changes for Cardiovascular Disease

Lifestyle Component	Recommendation
Diet	Saturated fat: <7% total daily calorie intake
	Trans fatty acids: limit
	Monounsaturated fat: up to 20% total daily calorie intake
	Polyunsaturated fat: up to 10% total daily calorie intake
	Total fat: 25%–35% total daily calorie intake
	Cholesterol: <200 mg/day
	Fiber: 20–30 g/day with consideration given to include 10–25 g soluble fiber daily
	Carbohydrate: 50%–60% of total daily calorie intake
	Protein: approximately 15% of total daily calorie intake
Weight Management	Maintain desirable weight, avoid weight gain, lose weight if indicated.
Physical Activity	Increase physical activity. Energy balance to include at least 200 calories of energy expenditure from moderately intense activity most days.

NCLEX-RN® Review Questions

Question numbers correspond to Outcome-Based Learning Objectives for this chapter.

14-1. Answer: 1

Rationale: A food frequency questionnaire is used to supplement a 24-hour recall, which is often limited in information. Even though a client reports a deficiency of one nutrient in the past 24 hours, overall intake of the nutrient may be satisfactory. Determining if the client is vegetarian will not help to determine calcium intake, since vegetarians can obtain calcium from many sources. Offering the client dairy products assumes there is a calcium deficiency based only on the 24-hour recall. Albumin levels reflect protein status and low levels will cause low calcium levels, but will not provide information related to calcium intake.
Cognitive Level: Application
Nursing Process: Implementation
Client Need: Physiological Integrity: Reduction of Risk Potential

14-2. Answer: 3

Rationale: The National Dietary Guidelines for Americans include: consume a variety of foods within and among the basic food groups while staying within energy needs; control calorie intake to manage body weight; be physically active every day; increase daily intake of fruits and vegetables, whole grains, and nonfat or low-fat milk and milk products; choose fats wisely for good health; choose carbohydrates wisely for good health; choose and prepare foods with little salt; if you drink alcoholic beverages, do so in moderation; keep food safe to eat.
Cognitive Level: Application
Nursing Process: Implementation
Client Need: Health Promotion and Maintenance; Prevention and/or Early Detection of Health Problems

14-3. Answer: 1

Rationale: The local and systemic inflammatory response brought on by the pancreatitis causes hypermetabolism and can increase the catabolic rate by 80% in severe cases. The pancreas is still able to produce enzymes, and if stimulated to do so, leads to autodigestion of the organ. Enteral feedings into the jejunum are often tolerated and do not stimulate the pancreas to produce. Metabolism is increased until inflammation has subsided.
Cognitive Level: Application

Nursing Process: Implementation
Client Need: Physiological Integrity: Physiological Adaptation

14-4. Answer: 2

Rationale: The loss of greater than 10% of body weight will impair wound healing. Maintenance of admission weight would be positive. Sometimes nocturnal feedings are given to supplement what the patient eats during the day. Refusal to eat supplements is not desired, but it is not as great a concern as a 10% body weight loss.
Cognitive Level: Application
Nursing Process: Assessment
Client Need: Physiological Integrity: Reduction of Risk Potential

14-5. Answer: 2

Rationale: Protein intake should only constitute 15% of the total calorie intake. Cholesterol intake should be less than 200 mg/day. Fiber intake should be 20–30 grams daily. Saturated fats should be less than 7% of daily caloric intake.
Cognitive Level: Application
Nursing Process: Assessment
Client Need: Health Promotion and Maintenance; Prevention and/or Early Detection of Health Problems

14-6. Answer: 2

Rationale: TPN solutions contain all the needed vitamin, minerals, and electrolytes, and the nurse must closely monitor levels to ensure they are within normal limits as they may change daily. TPN solutions contain large amounts of glucose; the client should be monitored for hyperglycemia. Some clients may still take oral feedings, depending on their condition. TPN is usually initiated at a rate of at least 50 ml/hour and increased gradually.
Cognitive Level: Application
Nursing Process: Implementation
Client Need: Physiological Integrity: Pharmacological and Parenteral Therapy

14-7. Answer: 3

Rationale: Clients with COPD often fatigue easily and have early satiety when eating, so if the nutrient-dense foods are eaten first, clients will optimize their nutrient intake. They often need to supplement their intake with liquid nutritional supplements, but a protein intake of 2/3 of the daily calories is excessive. Excessive intake of calories should also be avoided as it leads to CO_2 production from the nutrient metabolism.

Cognitive Level: Application
Nursing Process: Implementation
Client Need: Health Promotion and Maintenance;
Prevention and/or Early Detection of Health Problems

Chapter 15 – Pain Assessment and Management

Key Terms Matching Exercise 1

1. i	6. c
2. b	7. a
3. h	8. e
4. f	9. j
5. d	10. g

Key Terms Matching Exercise 2

11. e	16. j
12. h	17. i
13. a	18. b
14. g	19. c
15. f	20. d

Dimensions of Pain

21. physiological	26. physiological
22. cognitive	27. sensory
23. sensory	28. physiological
24. cognitive	29. affective
25. behavioral	30. physiological

Types of Pain

31. breakthrough pain	36. cancer pain
32. neuropathic pain	37. transient pain
33. phantom limb pain	38. recurrent pain
34. acute pain	39. nociceptive pain
35. cancer pain	40. chronic pain

True or False?

41. T	46. F
42. F	47. F
43. T	48. T
44. T	49. T
45. F	50. T

NCLEX-RN® Review Questions

Question numbers correspond to Outcome-Based Learning Objectives for this chapter.

15-1. Answer: 2
   Rationale: Pain is a major problem in this country, often contributing to postoperative complications like delayed wound healing and pneumonia. The lack of specialized treatment facilities, resources, and low health benefit coverage make it more difficult to treat. There are many misconceptions among health care workers, patients, and their families, making pain often more difficult to treat.
   Cognitive Level: Analysis
   Nursing Process: Evaluation

Client Need: Health Promotion and Maintenance;
Prevention and/or Early Detection of Health Problems

15-2. Answer: 1
   Rationale: The Joint Commission has set standards regarding pain management, but these guidelines require accredited health care organizations to educated clients about their rights to receive pain assessment and treatment. Treating the patient with addiction and pain can be an ethical dilemma, but nurses are fundamentally required to relieve the patient's suffering, not withhold pain medications. The patient's subjective reports of pain are always the primary evaluation tool used for treatment of pain. However, as patients are becoming more educated about their rights regarding pain management, their expectations are growing.
   Cognitive Level: Analysis
   Nursing Process: Assessment
   Client Need: Health Promotion and Maintenance;
Prevention and/or Early Detection of Health Problems

15-3. Answer: 2
   Rationale: The *behavioral dimension of pain* includes responses to pain that may be situational, developmental, or learned. Behaviors commonly associated with the expression of pain are both verbal and nonverbal. Grimacing or furrowed brow, guarding, agitation, and avoiding required activities are examples of nonverbal expressions of pain. Verbal expressions of pain include crying, moaning, and verbalization. It is appropriate to expect a patient to demonstrate anxiety in situations that are not familiar to him such as treatment in an emergency department or hospitalization. Patients who have developmental delays will demonstrate behaviors consistent with the situation and their developmental age. When pain is well controlled, pain behaviors alleviate or resolve and patients appear relaxed, calmer, and are able to participate in daily activities. Participation in required activities of recovery is facilitated. Failure to respond to a patient's self-report of pain may encourage the development of learned pain behaviors. Patients who come to understand that unless they appear to be uncomfortable their reports of pain will not be believed may purposefully demonstrate behaviors consistent with pain when clinicians are present.
   Cognitive Level: Analysis
   Nursing Process: Assessment
   Client Need: Psychosocial Integrity; Coping and Adaptation

15-4. Answer: 4
   Rationale: The numeric rating scale, visual analog scale, and behavioral assessment are all unidimensional pain evaluation tools. The patient interview is the only multidimensional pain evaluation tool listed.
   Cognitive Level: Application
   Nursing process: Evaluation
   Client Need: Health Promotion and Maintenance;
Prevention and/or Early Detection of Health Problems

15-5. Answer: 1
   Rationale: Recurrent pain is short in duration but recurs after a pain-free period. Pain associated with a recent event, such as surgery, illness, or trauma, is acute pain. Pain of short duration with complete resolution is known as transient pain. Cancer-related pain is associated with malignancy and sometimes disease progression.
   Cognitive Level: Analysis
   Nursing Process: Evaluation
   Client Need: Physiological Integrity; Physiological Adaptation

15-6. Answer: 3

Rationale: If there are questions regarding the prescription of a medication, the prescribing provider should be contacted for clarification, not the pharmacy. Optimally, opioid agonists, not antagonists, should be used in combination with non-opioid, NSAID, and adjuvant medications. The administration of intramuscular analgesics is usually avoided because of an unreliable absorption rate and rapid fall-off of action. The absorption, distribution, metabolism, and elimination of each prescribed medication should be considered prior to administration.

Cognitive Level: Application
Nursing Process: Planning
Client Need: Physiological Integrity; Pharmacological and Parenteral Therapies

15-7. Answer: 3

Rationale: Although some patients do rely solely on alternative and complementary therapies for pain relief, these and other nonpharmacologic treatments are usually used in conjunction with a medication regimen to fully treat the multidimensional pain experience. A strong support network of friends and family has been shown to improve the patient's overall pain experience and perceptions of pain. Fear of ridicule or dissuasion is a real problem that some patients face when dealing with complementary or alternative treatments. However, nurses should use this as an opportunity to encourage and educate the patient. Continuing any nonmedication treatment that was helpful in the hospital following discharge is the correct thing to do.

Cognitive Level: Analysis
Nursing Process: Evaluation
Client Need: Physiological Integrity; Basic Care and Comfort

15-8. Answer: 1

Rationale: Pain management education should never be standardized but instead be individualized to the client and the family. Allowing the client to make choices within the treatment regimen helps the client develop the feeling of having regained some control, not lost it. Equianalgesia refers to allowing the selection of a dosage of an opioid that is approximately the same potency to another opioid already in use. The selection of medications best suited for nociceptive or neuropathic pain is often directed by the pain's quality. Nursing interventions for pain management do originate from the data gathered from the pain and physical assessments.

Cognitive Level: Analysis
Nursing Process: Planning
Client Need: Physiological Integrity; Physiological Adaptation

15-9. Answer: 4

Rationale: Nurses are vital to the multidisciplinary team. However, financial services can help the client who has monetary needs, requires specialty services, or is unable to return to gainful employment. When the treatment regimen requires technical modalities, pain management services are often utilized. Nurses are to continually assess and treat pain appropriately based on these assessments and prescribed therapies. They often coordinate with the other members regarding the client's condition.

Cognitive Level: Analysis
Nursing Process: Assessment
Client Need: Health Promotion and Maintenance; Prevention and/or Early Detection of Health Problems

Chapter 16 – Substance Abuse

Key Terms Matching Exercise

1. i
2. g
3. a
4. k
5. b
6. f
7. e
8. c
9. j
10. h
11. d

Short Answer Questions

12. Substance abuse is repeated use of a substance despite significant and repeated negative substance-related consequences. Substance dependence is a pattern of substance use that is continued despite significant consequences, usually with physiological tolerance effects and a withdrawal syndrome if the substance is withdrawn. Substance dependence involves addiction, whereas substance abuse does not necessarily imply addiction.

13. A genetic predisposition can provide the base for vulnerabilities to substance abuse, but environment and experiences have an enormous influence on whether those genetics are expressed.

    Adult alcoholism develops as a result of the considerable role genetics plays when the gene pool has alcohol abusers in it. However, family environmental factors do supply a significant platform in terms of how the addiction is allowed to be asserted. Similarly, adult substance abuse has been examined in those who were adopted and had birth parents who were substance abusers. Again, it was found that having the genes for substance abuse does not, in and of itself, guarantee an addicted adult. The environment must interact with the genetics to create the development of highest risk.

14. Characteristic features seen with abuse alcohol include slurred speech, ataxia, slowed reaction times, disinhibition, and interactions including repetitive argumentativeness or profuse apologizing for drinking.

15. The four CAGE questions are:
    1. Have you ever felt that you should **C**ut down on your drinking?
    2. Have people **A**nnoyed you by criticizing your drinking?
    3. Have you ever felt bad or **G**uilty about your drinking?
    4. Have you ever had a drink in the morning as an **E**ye-opener to get rid of a hangover?

16. Delirium tremens (DTs), one symptom of withdrawal, is a condition of severe memory disturbance, agitation, anorexia, and hallucinations. Generally, DTs begin a few days after drinking stops and end within 1 to 5 days.

17. The five stages of the Transtheoretical Model of behavior change are:
    (1) Precontemplation—The patient does not intend to change the health behavior in the near future. This stage usually lasts approximately 6 months. What the nurse sees is an avoidance of communications designed to help change occur.
    (2) Contemplation—The patient does intend to change the health behavior in the next 6 months. There is awareness of the benefits of change, but the barriers and ambivalence are potent and interfere.
    (3) Preparation—The patient intends to make the change within the next month. The patient develops a plan of action with small, important steps taken toward change.
    (4) Action—The patient demonstrates modified risky behavior and makes the change. There is significant risk of reverting

to previous problematic health behaviors. Healthy action requires considerable time and energy.

(5) Maintenance—Work to prevent relapse occurs in this stage. Temptation gradually diminishes over 6 months to 5 years. This stage is meant to extend through the patient's life.

18. Heroin as a drug is not inherently dangerous. Unless there is an accidental overdose, the heroin alone as a substance will not harm the individual. But addiction to heroin exposes the patient to the dangerous and deadly ancillary issues of:
    - Diluting agents (which are likely contaminated)
    - Needle cleanliness
    - Exposure to transmissible diseases such as hepatitis, TB, and HIV
    - Overdose
    - Malnutrition
    - Poisoning by impurities
    - Criminal behaviors necessary to support the addiction, which can put the individual at great risk

19. Alcoholics Anonymous (AA) and Narcotics Anonymous (NA) are spiritual programs based on fellowship among their members. Women for Sobriety (WFS) is another self-help group. Unlike AA/NA, WFS is not based on a spiritual philosophy; instead, the program is based on abstinence. Alcoholics and addicts who were not comfortable in AA but were nevertheless determined to become sober have founded Rational Recovery (RR), a self-help approach that rejects the spiritual approach of AA. RR also rejects the notion that alcoholics and addicts are powerless to stop their addictions, suggesting instead that until now they simply have not chosen to do so.

20. Liver function profiles are often needed to determine whether the liver enzymes are effective or whether the liver is able to competently metabolize medications, as alcohol interferes with the liver's abilities to function adequately. Drug screens (blood and urine) are often needed to determine whether there is evidence of a drug in the blood or urine. The patient may deny use of substances, but drug screens are able to detect their presence. A breathalyzer test is done to detect evidence of alcohol, and the extent of the alcohol, in the expired breath of the patient.

21. Many treatment centers are now incorporating the concept of relapse prevention into their treatment programs. This concept is designed to teach patients how to anticipate relapse. By learning skills to use in high-risk situations, patients gain confidence and the expectation of being able to cope successfully, thus decreasing the probability of relapse.

True or False?

22.	T	27.	T
23.	F	28.	T
24.	T	29.	T
25.	T	30.	F
26.	F	31.	F

NCLEX-RN® Review Questions

Question numbers correspond to Outcome-Based Learning Objectives for this chapter.

16-1. Answer: 1
Rationale: A history of alcoholism carries a strong genetic risk; research indicates children of alcoholics have a fourfold risk of becoming alcoholics. Personality disorders and self-centered behavior are related to psychological issues and are behavioral risk factors for substance abuse. Socioeconomic status reflects sociocultural and environmental risk factors for substance abuse.

Cognitive Level: Application
Nursing Process: Implementation
Client Need: Physiological Integrity: Reduction of Risk Potential

16-2. Answer: 1
Rationale: Within the social-cultural framework, the family provides many roles that can contribute to the problem of substance abuse. An expectation that drinking will be encouraged at family gatherings will pose a great challenge for the client. Having two friends also in recovery programs may be a source of support for the client. His parents not attending NA meetings do not pose as strong a risk as the temptation of alcohol at family gatherings. Refusing to enable drug use by the sibling is a positive factor.

Cognitive Level: Analysis
Nursing Process: Assessment
Client Need: Psychosocial Integrity; Coping and Adaptation

16-3. Answer: 3
Rationale: Long-term use of methamphetamine leads to extensive neural damage, leading to cognitive impairments, psychosis, and inadequate cerebral perfusion. Patients will often have difficulty performing normal activities of daily living, such as combing hair, brushing teeth, etcetera. They do not do repetitive tapping or frequent crying. Their nutritional status is usually poor, due to lack of adequate food intake.

Cognitive Level: Application
Nursing Process: Assessment
Client Need: Physiological Integrity; Physiological Adaptation

16-4. Answer: 4
Rationale: Use of inhalants and solvents can cause serious cardiac arrhythmias, such as ventricular fibrillation, leading to sudden death. They produce CNS excitement, producing euphoria and excitement. They cause an increase in heart rate and respirations. They do not lead to glaucoma.

Cognitive Level: Application
Nursing Process: Implementation
Client Need: Health Promotion and Maintenance; Prevention and/or Early Detection of Health Problems

16-5. Answer: 3
Rationale: The high following PCP ingestion sets in within 5 minutes and lasts 4–6 hours, but effects can last up to 48 hours.

Cognitive Level: Application
Nursing Process: Planning
Client Need: Physiological Integrity; Physiological Adaptation

16-6. Answer: 1
Rationale: The patient with alcoholism often suffers malnutrition secondary to poor eating habits and lack of proper nutrients. Eating 100% of meals is evidence that the patient is actually consuming the food and would be the most appropriate outcome. Even though the patient chooses high-protein foods, that does not guarantee they will be eaten. Requesting between meal snacks is also good, but does not provide evidence that the patient is receiving the best nutrition. The family may provide favorite foods, but that does not guarantee they will be nutritious or eaten.

Cognitive Level: Application
Nursing Process: Planning
Client Need: Physiological Integrity; Physiological Adaptation

16-7. Answer: 1

Rationale: It is most important that the nurse maintain a nonjudgmental attitude, which will help to convey respect to the patient and establish trust. The CAGE instrument is one type of questionnaire, but does not have to be used for every assessment. The nurse does not have to have a witness and a signed consent does not need to be signed.
Cognitive Level: Application
Nursing Process: Implementation
Client Need: Psychosocial Integrity; Psychosocial Adaptation

Chapter 17 – Nursing Management at End of Life

Key Terms Matching Exercise

1. c
2. a
3. e
4. d
5. b

Short Answer Questions

6. Beneficence means to do or promote good. It is different from nonmaleficence, or the duty not to inflict harm. When the duty not to inflict harm conflicts with the duty to provide benefit, there is support for the view that the obligation not to injure others is greater than the obligation to benefit them.

7. The living will, the durable power of attorney for health care, and the directive for organ donation are the advance directives that patients most frequently create. Advance directives lay the groundwork for decision making at the time of acute illness. They give patients peace of mind that their wishes will be followed even if they cannot communicate and provide clear directions for significant others and the health care team regarding the patients' wishes.

8. Opioids are highly effective in relieving dyspnea by depressing respiratory drive; causing vasodilation, which can reduce pulmonary vascular congestion; and producing sedation and euphoria.

9. At the end of life, the use of opioids, benzodiazepines, and other medications in doses high enough to control the patient's symptoms may unintentionally hasten death. This is referred to as double effect, where an action may have two possible effects, one good and one bad. The action is not considered immoral if it is undertaken with the intention of achieving the good effect without intending the bad effect, even though it may be foreseen. At the end of life not administering a drug to relieve symptoms because it may hasten death would be viewed as causing the patient harm and increased suffering.

10. The four types of complicated grief and their characteristics are:
   (1) Exaggerated
      • Response is out of proportion.
      • Response is more intense than expected.
      • The person is disabled with clinical depression or other psychiatric disorders.
   (2) Masked
      • Feelings are expressed as physical symptoms.
      • Feelings are expressed as maladaptive behavior.
      • Feelings are not expressed at all.
      • The person may not realize that symptoms or behaviors are related to the loss.
   (3) Delayed
      • Feelings may not arise until another person is lost.
      • Feelings surrounding the loss are not expressed until the person suffers another loss.

   (4) Chronic
      • The person never reaches resolution with regard to the loss.
      • The reaction to the loss is unusually long.

True or False?

11.	F	16.	F
12.	T	17.	F
13.	T	18.	T
14.	F	19.	F
15.	T	20.	T

NCLEX-RN® Review Questions

Question numbers correspond to Outcome-Based Learning Objectives for this chapter.

17-1. Answer: 1

Rationale: Veracity helps ensure clients make informed decisions based on truthful information; beneficence means to do or promote good. End-of-life, palliative care is always focused on symptomatology rather than cure, and decisions are always made with regard to the best recommendations for the client, not necessarily the family. Ethical decision making does involve a systematic appraisal of each situation using moral principles and ethical theories in order to justify the choice made.
Cognitive Level: Analysis
Nursing Process: Planning
Client Need: Psychosocial Integrity; Coping and Adaptation

17-2. Answer: 3

Rationale: A durable power of attorney for health care, or health care proxy, is appointed by the client to make future medical decisions for the client should he or she become incapacitated. This surrogate does not require the consent of others, family members, or friends in order to make a decision. The living will is a form of advance directive, not a form of durable power of attorney for health care. Veracity describes the health care team's duty to be truthful to the client and family so informed decisions can be made. The advance directive does direct the health care team regarding the types of treatments the client desires should he or she become incapacitated.
Cognitive Level: Application
Nursing Process: Planning
Client Need: Safe, Effective Care Environment; Management of Care

17-3. Answer: 4

Rationale: Reducing lighting and noise helps make the hospital environment more comfortable and peaceful. Opioids such as morphine, Dilaudid (hydromorphone), and Duragesic (fentanyl) are frequently used to treat pain and suffering in dying clients, as they bind to receptor sites in the brain and spinal cord to prevent the neurotransmitters involved in pain transmission from being released. However, the opiate Demerol (meperidine) is not recommended because its metabolite produces potentially toxic effects to the central nervous system, such as seizures. Benzodiazepine medications have synergistic and anticonvulsant effects when combined with opioids, but neuroleptics are helpful for diminishing acute confusional states and delirium. The release of endogenous opioids and ketones subsequent to hypoxia, hypoperfusion, and dehydration may produce analgesia known as starvation euphoria.

Cognitive Level: Analysis
Nursing Process: Planning
Client Need: Physiological Integrity; Physiological Adaptation

17-4.   Answer: 1
   Rationale: Although in some cultures direct eye contact and open expressions of grief are acceptable, in many other cultures they are not. Clients' different cultural beliefs should be respected and the beliefs of the health care team or other cultures should not be forced upon the palliative care client. Many hospitals or other health care facilities have policies regarding body preparation after death, but whenever possible, the health care team should work with the client and family to accommodate individual religious or cultural beliefs.
   Cognitive Level: Application
   Nursing Process: Planning
   Client Need: Psychosocial Integrity; Coping and Adaptation

17-5.   Answer: 2
   Rationale: Many groups and organizations are advocating for increased educational experiences related to end-of-life issues for health care personnel, but being part of a multidisciplinary team does not improve the availability of such programs. Advance directives may provide civil and criminal immunity for health care personnel meeting certain conditions, but solely being part of or using an interdisciplinary approach to palliative care does not. Also, the client's goals of care should guide the utilization of technology in end-of-life care, not vice versa. A collaborative approach does, however, help the client and family achieve a pain-free and meaningful death experience.
   Cognitive Level: Application
   Nursing Process: Planning
   Client Need: Psychosocial Integrity; Coping and Adaptation

17-6.   Answer: 3
   Rationale: Terminal prognosis is not equated with stopping treatment. Patients have the opportunity to participate in their care, but the health care team remains dedicated to the client's treatment. Sometimes radiation therapy is continued or initiated during hospice care when it is required to alleviate pain from tumor growth. Although death is inevitable for everyone, a painful death is not. The provision of hospice care is aimed at comfort instead of cure.
   Cognitive Level: Application
   Nursing Process: Implementation
   Client Need: Psychosocial Integrity; Coping and Adaptation

17-7.   Answer: 4
   Rationale: Medications that produce a double effect, both good and bad side effects, are used in palliative care. However, if administration of these medications is done for the purposes of achieving both the potential good and bad outcomes, then the moral efficacy of giving them should be reviewed. The double action is not considered immoral only if it is done with the intention of achieving the good effect without the intention of achieving the bad effect. Respite care is provided through some hospice services, and bereavement services for a minimum of one year are usually provided through all hospice networks. Although hospice care and palliative care often overlap, and are even used interchangeably by some, the two are similar but unique. In order for the client to experience a minimum amount of pain and distress, anticipatory doses and titration of analgesics and sedatives should be afforded the client during terminal extubation. Withdrawing neuromuscular blockers should be a decision made after the benefits are weighed against the consequences. When care of the client shifts from the curative model to the comfort model, so do

the plans and interventions of the health care team. Beneficence means to do good, and nonmaleficence is the duty not to inflict harm. During the palliative care of a client in the acute care setting, invasive procedures, tests, or treatments must be reevaluated. The decision should be based on whether or not it improves the client's suffering or improves the client's functional status. The greater obligation during palliative care is not to cause more pain or suffering than to benefit the client.
   Cognitive Level: Analysis
   Nursing Process: Assessment
   Client Need: Psychosocial Integrity; Coping and Adaptation

Chapter 18 – Fluid and Electrolytes

Key Terms Matching Exercise 1

1.	j	**6.**	g
2.	f	**7.**	i
3.	e	**8.**	c
4.	h	**9.**	b
5.	a	**10.**	d

Key Terms Matching Exercise 2

11.	f	**16.**	g
12.	b	**17.**	h
13.	a	**18.**	j
14.	e	**19.**	i
15.	d	**20.**	c

Short Answer Questions

21.   Sodium is the most numerous cation in the ECF. It maintains ECF volume through osmotic pressure, regulates acid–base balance by combining with chloride or bicarbonate ions, and conducts nerve impulses via the sodium channels of cells.

22.   Hyperkalemia is likely in cases of severe cellular injury such as crush injuries or burns, renal disease, insulin deficiency (diabetic ketoacidosis or hyperosmolar hyperglycemic nonketotic syndrome), Addison's disease (hypoaldosteronism), or the use of potassium supplements. Symptoms may include irregular pulse, irritability, abdominal distention, cramping, muscle weakness, paresthesia, and arterial blood gases (ABGs) may show metabolic acidosis.

23.   Vitamin D (cholecalciferol), a fat-soluble vitamin, is essential for the absorption of calcium and phosphorus from the gut. Vitamin D deficiency is the most common cause of hypocalcemia.

24.   Potassium is **never** administered by IV push! Too rapid administration of potassium can result in life-threatening dysrhythmias. If potassium is replaced too quickly, hyperkalemia may result.

25.   Clinical manifestations are related to decreased neuromuscular activity, such as those seen in hyperkalemia. Cardiovascular symptoms are hypotension, bradycardia, flushing and sense of warmth, and possible respiratory or cardiac arrest. Gastrointestinal symptoms are nausea and vomiting; neurological symptoms are mental changes (drowsiness), respiratory depression, and decreased deep tendon reflex. Deep tendon reflexes are usually lost at 8 mg/dL, and respiratory failure is likely if the serum level exceeds 10 mg/dL. Coma can occur at a level of 10 mg/dL, and cardiac arrest is possible at levels >15 mg/dL.

True or False?

26.	T	**31.**	T
27.	T	**32.**	T
28.	T	**33.**	F
29.	F	**34.**	T
30.	F	**35.**	T

Food Sources of Electrolytes

36.	b	**39.**	b
37.	f	**40.**	e
38.	a	**41.**	d

NCLEX-RN® Review Questions

Question numbers correspond to Outcome-Based Learning Objectives for this chapter.

18-1. Answer: 4

Rationale: The intracellular fluids (ICF) are fluids that exist within the cell cytoplasm and nucleus. The extracellular fluids (ECF) are fluids that exist outside the cell, such as interstitial fluid between cells, fluid in the bloodstream (serum), cerebrospinal fluid (CSF) in the central nervous system, gastrointestinal secretions, sweat, and urine.
Cognitive Level: Analysis
Nursing Process: Assessment
Client Need: Physiological Adaptation: Physiological Integrity

18-2. Answer: 2

Rationale: The osmolality of blood, as well as 0.9% sodium chloride (normal saline) is 275 to 295 milliosmoles per kilogram (mOsm/kg) of body weight. Thus, the IV fluid is isotonic, which would facilitate restoration of fluid balance with blood loss. Both the dextrose 5% in 0.45% saline and sodium bicarbonate solutions are hypertonic in osmolality, while 0.45% sodium chloride is hypotonic.
Cognitive Level: Analysis
Nursing Process: Planning
Client Need: Physiological Adaptation; Physiological Integrity

18-3. Answer: 2

Rationale: The normal range for potassium is 3.5 to 5.0 millimoles/liter (mEq/L). A K^+ of 6.5 mEq/L is considered hyperkalemic, while the values of 2.9 and 2.5 mEq/L reflect hypokalemia.
Cognitive Level: Analysis
Nursing Process: Evaluation
Client Need: Physiological Adaptation; Reduction of Risk Potential

18-4. Answer: 3

Rationale: There are typically three major reasons for elevated serum calcium: bone malignancy, primary hyperparathyroidism, and drug toxicity from thiazide diuretics, lithium carbonate, and vitamins A and D. Long-term use of cardiac medications is not a cause of an elevated serum calcium level. Malnutrition is not considered as a cause for an elevated serum calcium level.
Cognitive Level: Analysis
Nursing Process: Assessment
Client Need: Physiological Adaptation: Physiological Integrity

18-5. Answer: 1

Rationale: Symptoms of sodium deficit are reduced ability of cells to depolarize and repolarize. As sodium levels drop, neurological changes occur, such as lethargy, headache, confusion, personality changes, apprehension, seizures, and even coma. The question about water intake would be appropriate for hypernatremia as thirst is increased due to the increase in serum sodium and osmolality. Numbness and tingling of the fingers indicates hypocalcemia, while excessive alcohol intake results in hypomagnesemia.
Cognitive Level: Analysis
Nursing Process: Assessment
Client Need: Physiological Adaptation; Physiological Integrity

18-6. Answer: 2

Rationale: As a result of hyperparathyroidism, possible laryngeal spasm can occur, leading to asphyxiation. A tracheotomy tray should be available at the bedside for emergency tracheotomy when patients' calcium levels are severely low. The patient with Cushing's syndrome may have electrolyte imbalances associated with hypernatremia. Excessive alcohol intake can result in a deficit of magnesium. Hyperphosphatemia is primarily due to renal disease and a decreased excretion of phosphorous, as is common with those requiring dialysis.
Cognitive Level: Analysis
Nursing Process: Planning
Client Need: Physiological Adaptation; Physiological Integrity

18-7. Answer: 4

Rationale: Dizziness upon standing reflects orthostatic hypotension, which often accompanies fluid volume deficit. Drinking fluids high in sodium can result in fluid volume excess. A weight gain of 5 pounds in a week is associated with fluid volume excess, and feeling thirsty is not a normal sensation unless the patient is experiencing fluid volume deficit.
Cognitive Level: Application
Nursing Process: Planning
Client Need: Physiological Adaptation; Physiological Integrity

Chapter 19 – Acid–Base Imbalance

Key Terms Matching Exercise 1

1.	d	**6.**	j
2.	f	**7.**	g
3.	h	**8.**	a
4.	e	**9.**	c
5.	b	**10.**	i

Key Terms Matching Exercise 2

11.	g	**18.**	b
12.	i	**19.**	a
13.	d	**20.**	j
14.	m	**21.**	h
15.	f	**22.**	k
16.	e	**23.**	c
17.	l		

Short Answer Questions

24. The four basic categories into which abnormalities in acid and base balance can be grouped are:
    - Respiratory acidosis—excess of carbon dioxide leading to an acid pH
    - Respiratory alkalosis—lower than normal level of carbon dioxide leading to an alkaline pH
    - Metabolic acidosis—excess of hydrogen ion or a deficiency in bicarbonate leading to an acid pH
    - Metabolic alkalosis—excess of bicarbonate leading to an alkaline pH

25. Conditions that can cause acute and chronic respiratory acidosis are:
    Acute Respiratory Acidosis
    CNS Depression—drug overdose; head trauma; encephalitis; stroke
    Neuromuscular Disease—Guillain-Barre syndrome; myasthenic crisis; spinal cord injury
    Airway Disease—status asthmaticus; upper airway obstruction
    Pleural or Chest Wall Abnormalities—pneumothorax; large pleural effusion
    Chronic Respiratory Acidosis
    Impaired Central Ventilatory Drive—central sleep apnea; obesity hypoventilation
    Neuromuscular Disease—amyotrophic lateral sclerosis; muscular dystrophy; poliomyelitis; multiple sclerosis; spinal cord injury
    Airway and Lung Parenchyma Disease—emphysema; chronic bronchitis; interstitial lung disease
    Other—kyphoscoliosis; diaphragmatic paralysis

26. Respiratory alkalosis can be caused by:?
    Central Nervous System—pain, anxiety, psychosis, fever, stroke, meningitis, encephalitis, tumor, trauma, hypoxemia
    Drugs—salicylates, nicotine, progesterone
    Pregnancy
    Sepsis
    Hepatic failure
    Iatrogenic on mechanical ventilation

27. Metabolic acidosis can be caused by:
    Excess H+ Production—lactic acidosis due to tissue hypoxia; ketoacidosis (diabetic, alcoholic, starvation)
    Ingestion of Acids—poisoning with agents such as ethylene glycol (antifreeze) or aspirin
    Inadequate Acid Excretion—renal dysfunction; endocrine disturbances (e.g., hypoaldosteronism)
    Excessive Loss of Bicarbonate—excessive diarrhea; acetazolamide

28. Metabolic alkalosis can be caused by:
    Excessive Loss of H+—protracted vomiting; nasogastric suction
    Acid Shifts into Cells—potassium deficiency
    Excessive Reabsorption of Bicarbonate—hypochloremia; thiazide and loop diuretics

29. The hypercarbic drive is a response to *acute* respiratory acidosis. Chemoreceptors are located on the surface of the medulla in the brainstem. These receptors are termed "central" because they are located within the central nervous system (CNS). These central chemoreceptors are in contact with cerebrospinal fluid (CSF). The level of arterial CO_2 acts on the central chemoreceptors by altering the pH of the CSF, causing the most important single stimulus of ventilation, and this is called the hypercarbic drive.

30. The hypoxic drive responds to low oxygen tension and is triggered by acidosis and hypercapnia. If a person suffers from chronic ventilatory failure, such as a patient with end-stage emphysema that leads to chronically high $PaCO_2$ levels (chronic respiratory acidosis), bicarbonate will cross the blood–brain barrier to buffer the CSF hydrogen ion changes. It takes hours to days for this adaptation to occur. Due to this increased bicarbonate on the brain side of the blood–brain barrier, the central chemoreceptors become less sensitive to changes in the level of CO_2, which results in a decrease in the strength of the ventilatory drive moderated by these central receptors. When this occurs, the only remaining drive to breathe is the stimulation of the peripheral receptors by a low PaO_2, the hypoxic drive.

31. The lungs help to regulate plasma pH on a minute-to-minute basis by regulating the level of carbon dioxide, the respiratory acid. Carbon dioxide is measured as the partial pressure of carbon dioxide in arterial blood, the $PaCO_2$. This level is tightly controlled under normal conditions and kept within a narrow range of 35 to 45 mmHg at sea level. The lungs can either retain or excrete CO_2 by altering the rate and depth of ventilation.

32. The kidneys perform two basic functions to maintain acid–base balance: They secrete hydrogen ions and they restore or reclaim bicarbonate.

33. Normal ABG values are:
    $pH = 7.40 \ (range: 7.35-7.45)$
    $PaCO_2 = 40 \ mEq/L \ (range: 35-45)$
    $\overline{HCO_3} = 22-28 \ mEq/L$

True or False?

34.	F	**39.**	T
35.	T	**40.**	F
36.	T	**41.**	T
37.	F	**42.**	T
38.	T	**43.**	F

Acid and Base Terminology

Acidemia/Acidosis	Alkalemia/Alkalosis
Blood pH < 7.40	Blood pH > 7.40
Caused by loss of base/alkali; increase of acid	Caused by increase of base/alkali; loss of acid
Lowers the 20:1 bicarbonate-to carbonic-acid ratio	Raises the 20:1 bicarbonate- to carbonic-acid ratio
Less base/more acid	More base/less acid

NCLEX-RN® Review Questions

Question numbers correspond to Outcome-Based Learning Objectives for this chapter.

19-1. Answer: 2
Rationale: Carbon dioxide is a potential acid. When it is dissolved in water, it becomes carbonic acid. Carbonic acid then dissociates into hydrogen ion and bicarbonate. In plasma, under normal circumstances, there are 20 parts of

bicarbonate to 1 part carbonic acid, a ratio of 20:1. If this 20:1 ratio is altered in either direction, the plasma pH will change. An increase in carbon dioxide levels will lead to a drop in blood pH.
Cognitive Level: Analysis
Nursing Process: Assessment
Client Need: Physiological Adaptation; Physiological Integrity

19-2. Answer: 4

Rationale: Bones also act as a buffer. The carbonate and phosphate salts in bone provide a long-term supply of buffer. They act as a reserve for alkalis. In acute metabolic acidosis, bone can take up hydrogen ions in exchange for calcium, sodium, and potassium. In chronic metabolic acidosis, calcium carbonate is released from bone as bone crystals dissolve. This situation can lead to the osteodystrophy often seen in chronic renal failure, which is a cause of chronic metabolic acidosis.
Cognitive Level: Analysis
Nursing Process: Assessment
Client Need: Physiological Adaptation; Physiological Integrity

19-3. Answer: 2

Rationale: The tidal volume refers to the total amount of air inhaled and exhaled with each breath. A portion of that volume, however, is in the large conducting airways such as the trachea and bronchi. That volume, referred to as anatomic dead space, does not reach the alveolar airspaces to take part in the exchange of oxygen and carbon dioxide with the blood. The amount of anatomic dead space is estimated as 1 mL/lb of body weight. The remainder of the tidal volume, that portion which does reach the alveoli and participates in gas exchange with capillary blood, is termed alveolar volume. Minute alveolar ventilation is the volume of alveolar air per minute that takes part in gas exchange, transferring oxygen to the blood and removing carbon dioxide from the blood. It is actually this minute alveolar ventilation that determines the $PaCO_2$. Normal minute alveolar ventilation is calculated as: Tidal volume – anatomic dead space = alveolar volume; Respiratory rate $\times$ alveolar volume = minute alveolar ventilation.
Cognitive Level: Application
Nursing Process: Assessment
Client Need: Physiological Adaptation; Physiological Integrity

19-4. Answer: 3

Rationale: The respiratory center located in the medulla in the brainstem controls the rate and depth of ventilation in response to the level of arterial CO_2, denoted as $PaCO_2$. Chemoreceptors located on the surface of the medulla are in contact with cerebrospinal fluid. As the level of $PaCO_2$ rises, the arterial $PaCO_2$ reaches equilibrium with the CO_2 in the CSF. That CO_2 in the CSF combines with water to form carbonic acid. The carbonic acid dissociates into hydrogen ions and bicarbonate. The CSF hydrogen ion diffuses into the medullary tissue and stimulates the chemoreceptors. They, in turn, stimulate the diaphragm and intercostal muscles to increase the rate and depth of ventilation. This increase in minute ventilation will "blow off" excess CO_2, returning it back toward normal, thereby correcting the pH. The reverse happens when there are

abnormally low levels of CO_2. In this state of hyperventilation, the medullary centers slow the rate and depth of ventilation to allow accumulation of CO_2 back toward normal, thereby correcting the pH.
Cognitive Level: Analysis
Nursing Process: Assessment
Client Need: Physiological Adaptation; Physiological Integrity

19-5. Answer: 4

Rationale: In respiratory and metabolic alkalosis, the kidneys retain hydrogen ion and excrete bicarbonate. This metabolic compensation is slow compared to respiratory compensation. It can take hours to days to occur. The average ventilation rate is about 6 L/*minute*, whereas the renal excretion rate is only about 2 L/*day*.
Cognitive Level: Analysis
Nursing Process: Assessment
Client Need: Physiological Adaptation; Physiological Integrity

19-6. Answer: 2

Rationale: The steps to analyze an arterial blood gas results are as follows: Step 1: Assess the pH; Step 2: Assess the $PaCO_2$; Step 3: Assess the bicarbonate and the base excess; Step 4: Evaluate compensation. PaO_2 and minute ventilation are not parts of the arterial blood gas evaluation.
Cognitive Level: Application
Nursing Process: Assessment
Client Need: Physiological Adaptation; Physiological Integrity

19-7. Answer: 4

Rationale: The patient would be at risk for metabolic alkalosis caused by loss of hydrogen from the GI tract. Gastric contents have high concentrations of hydrochloric acid and a smaller amount of potassium chloride. Gastric hydrogen secretion stimulates, and is matched by, pancreatic bicarbonate secretion. When the acid contents of the stomach pass through the pylorus into the duodenum, they stimulate the pancreas to secrete lytic enzymes and bicarbonate. This bicarbonate neutralizes the acidity of the stomach contents. If the patient suffers excessive vomiting or the gastric secretions are removed by nasogastric suction before they can pass into the duodenum, there is no stimulus to the secretion of bicarbonate and it accumulates.
Cognitive Level: Analysis
Nursing Process: Assessment
Client Need: Physiological Adaptation; Physiological Integrity

19-8. Answer: 4

Rationale: Metabolic acidosis occurs when intracellular glucose is inadequate due to starvation or a lack of insulin to move it into the cells. The body breaks down fatty tissue to meet its metabolic needs. Fatty acids are released, which are converted to ketones, causing ketoacidosis. Asking a client about smoking or emphysema would pertain to respiratory acidosis and vomiting is related to metabolic alkalosis.
Cognitive Level: Analysis
Nursing Process: Assessment
Client Need: Physiological Adaptation; Physiological Integrity

19-9. Answer: 1

Rationale: The use of supplemental oxygen in patients with chronic respiratory acidosis must be approached with caution. Because chronic hypercapnea blunts the central hypercarbic drive, these patients' main stimulus to breathe is the peripheral hypoxic drive. These patients breathe because their level of PaO_2 goes down. High levels of supplemental oxygen may blunt this hypoxic drive, leading to a further decrease in ventilation and a worsening of hypercapnea. Acute asthma and panic disorder may result in overventilation, thus respiratory alkalosis. A deviated septum generally would not result in an acid–base imbalance.

Cognitive Level: Analysis
Nursing Process: Planning
Client Need: Physiological Adaptation; Physiological Integrity

Chapter 20 – Infectious Disease

Key Terms Matching Exercise 1

1.	c	**6.**	j
2.	e	**7.**	f
3.	h	**8.**	i
4.	a	**9.**	d
5.	b	**10.**	g

Key Terms Matching Exercise 2

11.	d	**17.**	a
12.	i	**18.**	g
13.	j	**19.**	f
14.	e	**20.**	c
15.	h	**21.**	b
16.	k		

True or False?

22.	T	**27.**	T
23.	T	**28.**	F
24.	F	**29.**	T
25.	F	**30.**	T
26.	F	**31.**	T

Short Answer Questions

32. The five local symptoms of inflammation are:
(1) Redness from increased blood flow to the area
(2) Heat due to increased blood flow to the area
(3) Swelling due to the fluid exudates that form in the interstitial tissue
(4) Pain caused by the pressure of the exudates and release of chemicals that irritate nerve endings
(5) Loss of function related to the pain and swelling

33. The major systemic symptoms of inflammation are (1) fever and (2) leukocytosis.

34. The two types of immune responses are (1) humoral immunity and (2) cellular immunity. The humoral response involves the antigen–antibody reactions, whereas the cellular response involves the reaction of the WBCs.

35. The ten areas to be assessed for an infection during a physical exam are:
(1) Vital signs
(2) Skin and mucous membranes
(3) Head and neck
(4) Lymph nodes
(5) Lungs
(6) Heart
(7) Abdomen
(8) Genitourinary tract
(9) Reproductive system
(10) Nervous system

36. The seven diagnostic tests related to infection are:
(1) WBC count
(2) Erythrocyte sedimentation rate (ESR)
(3) Culture and sensitivity
(4) Gram stain
(5) Febrile agglutinins
(6) Viral antibody tests
(7) Fungal infection

NCLEX-RN® Review Questions

Question numbers correspond to Outcome-Based Learning Objectives for this chapter.

20-1. Answer: 2

Rationale: The five cardinal local symptoms of inflammation are: (1) heat due to increased blood flow; (2) redness from increased blood flow to the area; (3) swelling due to the fluid exudates into the interstitial tissue; (4) pain caused by the pressure of the exudates and release of chemicals that irritate nerve endings; and (5) loss of function related to the pain and swelling.

Cognitive Level: Analysis
Nursing Process: Assessment
Client Need: Physiological Adaptation; Physiological Integrity

20-2. Answer: 4

Rationale: Both advanced age and chronic diseases, such as diabetes mellitus and COPD, make an individual more susceptible to infection. Stress can also be a contributing factor such as with menopause, employment, and adolescent issues.

Cognitive Level: Analysis
Nursing Process: Planning
Client Need: Health Promotion and Maintenance; Prevention and/or Early Detection of Health Problems

20-3. Answer: 3

Rationale: Vehicle transmission occurs when the organism's life is maintained on something outside the reservoir until it is passed to the susceptible host. The vehicle is a nonliving object that is not normally harmful but acts as an intermediary for the infectious agent. With hepatitis B, it may be contaminated blood or blood products or salmonella. Airborne transmission occurs when the organism is expelled from the infected person and remains suspended in the air in tiny droplets no larger than five microns. Contact transmission can occur by direct contact, indirect contact, or droplets. Vector-borne transmission occurs when a disease-producing organism is carried by a living intermediate host that transfers the organism to a susceptible host.

Cognitive Level: Analysis
Nursing Process: Implementation
Client Need: Physiological Adaptation; Physiological Integrity

20-4. Answer: 2

Rationale: The single most important action in the control and prevention of infection is hand washing. Inadequate hand washing is considered the leading cause of health-care-associated infections and the spread of multi-resistant organisms.

Cognitive Level: Application
Nursing Process: Implementation
Client Need: Safe, Effective Care Environment; Safety and Infection Control

20-5. Answer: 3

Rationale: Diseases that were thought to be under control have reemerged due to antibiotic resistance and the development of new strains of pathogens. Tuberculosis is an example of a reemerging disease.

Cognitive Level: Analysis
Nursing Process: Assessment
Client Need: Physiological Adaptation; Physiological Integrity

20-6. Answer: 1

Rationale: Active immunization involves the introduction of live, killed, or attenuated toxin of a disease organism into the body. The immune system responds by producing antibodies. Active immunization provides long-term and possibly lifelong immunity. Some vaccines require boosters to maintain the immunity such as that for influenza. Examples of active immunizations include measles, mumps, hepatitis B and hepatitis A, along with pertussis.

Cognitive Level: Application
Nursing Process: Implementation
Client Need: Health Promotion and Maintenance; Prevention and/or Early Detection of Health Problems

20-7. Answer: 1

Rationale: Hepatitis B is a disease preventable through universal childhood vaccination. The focus for reducing incidence of bacterial meningitis is with young children. Nosocomial infections are problematic with inpatient settings, especially intensive care units. The goal related to peptic ulcer disease is to reduce the number of hospitalizations.

Cognitive Level: Analysis
Nursing Process: Planning
Client Need: Health Promotion and Maintenance; Prevention and/or Early Detection of Health Problems

20-8. Answer: 4

Rationale: The filled specimen cup should be treated as an infectious material and should not be placed on the patient's bedside table once filled. Label the specimen correctly with client information, the source of the specimen, and the time of collection. Most specimens can be refrigerated for a few hours if necessary. Standard precautions, use of a sterile container with a tight-fitting lid, and taking the specimen to the lab immediately are necessary procedures.

Cognitive Level: Application
Nursing Process: Implementation
Client Need: Safe, Effective Care Environment; Safety and Infectious Control

Chapter 21 – Hypertension

Key Terms Matching Exercise 1

1.	b	**5.**	g
2.	a	**6.**	c
3.	d	**7.**	f
4.	e		

Key Terms Matching Exercise 2

8.	f	**12.**	d
9.	b	**13.**	c
10.	g	**14.**	e
11.	a		

Blood Pressure Regulators

Name each system that influences blood pressure change in the body and summarize how it works.

15. Neural Regulation—The pons and medulla of the brain are the neural control centers for the regulation of blood pressure. These areas are where the autonomic nervous system is integrated and modulated and where the vasomotor control center and cardiovascular control center are located. These control centers transmit parasympathetic impulses through the vagus nerve and sympathetic impulses through the spinal cord and peripheral sympathetic nerves to the heart and blood vessels.

16. Arterial Baroreceptors and Arterial Chemoreceptors—Baroreceptors located in the walls of blood vessels are pressure-sensitive receptors that respond to changes in the stretch of the blood vessels by sending impulses to the brain and heart to adjust the heart rate and smooth muscle tone. They respond to changes in arterial pressure (high or low) and signal the central nervous system (CNS). Signals are then transmitted back through baroreceptors to counteract the abnormal changes in the arterial pressure.

17. Mechanisms for Regulating Fluid Volume—Fluid volume throughout the body is maintained through multiple homeostatic mechanisms. Normal fluid volume is the result of a dynamic equilibrium between oral fluids and other dietary intakes and fluid output, which occurs through perspiration, urination, and respiration. The cardiovascular, renal, and respiratory areas are involved as are the pituitary gland, parathyroid glands, and adrenal glands. When changes occur in the osmolarity (i.e., the concentration of the solute), the number of particles in fluid is conserved or eliminated in order to maintain a system homeostatic state.

18. Humoral Regulation—The hormones that play a role in regulating blood pressure include the renin-angiotensin-aldosterone mechanism, vasopressin, and epinephrine and norepinephrine.
    - Renin acts as an enzyme to convert angiotensin I to angiotensin II, which constricts the blood vessels to increase peripheral vascular resistance, increasing blood pressure. Angiotensin II also stimulates the adrenal glands to release aldosterone, which also results in an increase to blood pressure.
    - Vasopressin is released when blood pressure is low or an increase in osmolality occurs. It increases water reabsorption by the kidneys and causes vasoconstriction, increasing blood pressure.
    - Epinephrine and norepinephrine are catecholamines secreted by the adrenal medulla. They work on the alpha and beta receptors, which influence heart rate and contractility, ultimately regulating blood pressure.

Short Answer Questions

19. Factors that can be modified Include:
    - High sodium dietary intake
    - Overweight
    - Excessive alcohol consumption
    - Low potassium intake
    - Smoking

20. Factors that cannot be modified Include:
    - Family history
    - Age
    - Race

21. Organs most often damaged as a result of uncontrolled high blood pressure are the heart, brain, kidney, and retina.

22. The causes of a hypertensive crisis include acute and chronic renal failure, exacerbation of chronic hypertension, sudden withdrawal of antihypertensive medications, and vasculitis.

23. African Americans have twice as high a possibility of developing high blood pressure as do Caucasian Americans. In patients who live in the southeastern portion of the United States as opposed to other parts of the country, the incidence of high blood pressure also is higher. In addition, environmental factors such as obesity, cigarette smoking, sedentary lifestyle, use of illegal drugs, and sodium intake have an impact on blood pressure. Also, a family history of hypertension and heart disease increases the risk for the development of those diseases.

24. Clinical signs and symptoms the patient describes may be nonspecific such as a headache or dizziness, sleepiness, nausea and vomiting, irritability, and visual disturbances. More serious complications may occur when a patient remains undiagnosed

for years. Myocardial infarction, heart failure, cerebral vascular accidents, and renal failure may all be the result of untreated high blood pressure and occur without further warning.

25. When a patient experiences severe stress, the amount of catecholamines is increased. This is frequently referred to as the "fight-or-flight" response. This response increases the blood pressure. Evidence shows the beneficial effects of regular exercise in preventing or ameliorating the stress-induced metabolic and psychological comorbidities. It is believed that exercise reduces the body's sensitivity to stress and also the peripheral actions that influence metabolic functions. Of particular importance are the documented effects of exercise on insulin sensitivity and metabolizing calories for fuel rather than storage. It is concluded that when chronic psychosocial stress accompanies physical inactivity, it contributes to our current epidemic of cardiometabolic and emotional disease. Regular exercise provides a way to prevent and combat this burden.

Classification of Blood Pressure for Adults

Add the appropriate blood pressure readings for each category.

BP Classification	SBP (mmHg)	DBP (mmHg)
Normal	<120	and <90
Prehypertension	120–139	Or 80–89
Stage 1 hypertension	140–159	Or 90–99
Stage 2 hypertension	>160	Or >100

NCLEX-RN® Review Questions

Question numbers correspond to Outcome-Based Learning Objectives for this chapter.

21-1. Answer: 4
    Rationale: Prehypertension is the early phase when the relationship between the blood pressure measurement and the need for health education is the primary focus of care. These B/P readings indicate prehypertension, thus lifestyle changes such as a low fat/sodium diet, weight loss, increasing activity, and healthy methods to handle daily stress would be indicated as the first step in treatment. A beta-blocker would be used for stage I hypertension, increasing potassium would not be necessary unless taking a loop diuretic, and understanding the signs and symptoms of CVA isn't warranted at this level.
    Cognitive Level: Analysis
    Nursing Process: Planning
    Client Need: Health Promotion and Maintenance; Prevention and/or Early Detection of Health Problems

21-2. Answer: 1
    Rationale: The difference between the systolic and diastolic pressure is about 40 mmHg and is called the pulse pressure. The pulse pressure is the ratio of stroke volume (amount of blood ejected with each heart beat) to

compliance of the arterial system (systemic vascular resistance). Ankle-brachial index is a test that measures blood pressure at the ankle and in the arm while a person is at rest to predict peripheral vascular disease. Normal blood pressure is a measurement of the systolic and diastolic readings, not the difference between the two. Stroke volume represents the amount of blood ejected with each heart beat.
Cognitive Level: Analysis
Nursing Process: Assessment
Client Need: Physiological Integrity; Physiological Adaptation

21-3. Answer: 3, 4, 1, 2
Rationale: Age (older than 55 for men and 65 for women) is considered a risk factor for hypertension along with being of male gender. African American individuals have two times greater possibility of developing high blood pressure than Caucasian Americans. Environmental factors such as obesity, cigarette smoking, sedentary lifestyle, use of illegal drugs/excessive alcohol consumption create risk. Stress such as job stresses, economic position, losses and/or gains of any kind, and many other issues of life are risk factors for hypertension. The client in #3 has four risk factors (age, gender, race, and diabetes). The client in #4 has three risk factors (age, gender, excessive alcohol use); the client in #1 has two risk factors (race and job/economic stress); and the client in #2 has one, which is obesity.
Cognitive Level: Analysis
Nursing Process: Assessment
Client Need: Health Promotion and Maintenance; Prevention and/or Early Detection of Health Problems

21-4. Answer: 1
Rationale: ACE inhibitors such as Enalapril (Vasotec) block the conversion of angiotensin I to vasoconstrictor angiotensin II. Since angiotensin II is a potent vasoconstrictor, the primary vasoactive hormone of the renin-angiotensin-aldosterone system, when it is blocked vasodilation occurs, resulting in a decrease in blood pressure. Option #2 describes the action of a calcium-channel blocker, #3 a central alpha agonist, and #4 a vasodilator.
Cognitive Level: Application
Nursing Process: Implementation
Client Need: Physiological Integrity; Pharmacological and Parenteral Therapies

21-5. Answer: 3
Rationale: Individuals living in the southeastern region (sometimes called the Salt Belt) of the United States have a higher percentage of high blood pressure.
Cognitive Level: Analysis
Nursing Process: Assessment

Client Need: Health Promotion and Maintenance; Prevention and/or Early Detection of Health Problems

21-6. Answer: 1
Rationale: Dietary Approaches to Stop Hypertension (DASH) is a diet low in sodium, saturated fat, cholesterol, and total fat. The diet focuses on fruits, vegetables, nuts, and low-fat dairy products. The food choices in #1 are the best example as #2 is high in sodium, #3 high in fat, and #4 high in cholesterol.
Cognitive Level: Application
Nursing Process: Planning
Client Need: Health Promotion and Maintenance; Prevention and/or Early Detection of Health Problems

21-7. Answer: 3
Rationale: Ischemic heart disease is the most common site of target organ damage associated with high blood pressure. Due to prolonged hypertension the coronary arteries are unable to deliver an adequate blood supply to the myocardium. This loss causes the heart muscle to lose its ability to contract sufficiently, resulting in a decreased cardiac output. The shearing force of blood flowing with increased pressure over time causes irregularities in the intima of the lumen of the arteries. This causes an increased buildup of plaque to form, ultimately narrowing the lumen of the artery and decreasing blood flow to the myocardium, resulting in ischemic heart disease. Renal insufficiency, diabetes, and aortic aneurysm are also complications.
Cognitive Level: Application
Nursing Process: Implementation
Client Need: Health Promotion and Maintenance; Prevention and/or Early Detection of Health Problems

Chapter 22 – Infusion Therapy

Key Terms Matching Exercise 1

1.	h	**6.**	b
2.	a	**7.**	e
3.	j	**8.**	g
4.	c	**9.**	d
5.	f	**10.**	i

Key Terms Matching Exercise 2

11.	d	**16.**	b
12.	a	**17.**	g
13.	c	**18.**	f
14.	h	**19.**	j
15.	i	**20.**	e

Word Search

First identify the word from its definition. Then find and circle it in the puzzle below.

21. dwell
22. lumen
23. catheter
24. adapter
25. noncoring needle
26. parenteral
27. septum
28. drip factor
29. dual-channel pump
30. multichannel pump
31. standards of practice
32. bevel
33. gauge

34. filter
35. volumetric pump
36. infusate
37. extravasation
38. air embolism
39. mechanical phlebitis
40. flushing
41. Y set
42. intraosseous therapy
43. stopcock
44. extension set
45. Luer-Lok

Y	P	A	R	E	H	T	S	U	O	E	S	S	O	A	R	T	N	I	A
M	S	I	L	O	B	M	E	R	I	A	C	C	P	T	A	R	R	Y	Y
A	U	E	R	A	F	E	D	T	E	S	N	O	I	S	N	E	T	X	E
F	I	L	T	E	R	S	A	D	T	P	A	R	E	N	T	E	R	A	L
E	C	I	T	C	A	R	P	F	O	S	D	R	A	D	N	A	T	S	D
R	D	A	E	I	T	W	Z	B	T	R	P	O	O	Y	T	R	E	Y	E
N	R	R	A	T	C	A	T	H	E	T	E	R	E	D	X	P	T	C	E
O	I	R	E	A	T	H	E	E	D	S	M	N	E	O	T	R	A	C	N
I	P	A	G	A	N	G	A	U	G	E	S	R	B	U	D	S	S	D	G
T	F	R	N	S	T	A	D	N	O	K	K	E	M	W	S	B	U	I	N
A	A	V	I	E	E	Y	A	P	N	T	V	C	E	R	L	T	F	O	I
S	C	R	H	A	Z	L	P	L	U	E	R	L	O	K	R	I	N	O	R
A	T	S	S	T	A	U	T	E	L	S	L	F	I	C	Q	U	I	P	O
V	O	L	U	M	E	M	E	T	R	I	C	P	U	M	P	T	Y	O	C
A	R	S	L	E	Y	E	R	R	A	R	E	H	U	T	U	O	Y	O	N
R	R	A	F	T	E	N	I	O	S	E	E	T	E	M	M	T	T	E	O
T	D	U	A	L	C	H	A	N	N	E	L	P	U	M	P	A	S	S	N
X	Y	G	E	U	R	E	N	I	L	L	O	U	T	L	O	Y	R	W	R
E	M	E	C	H	A	N	I	C	A	L	P	H	L	E	B	I	T	I	S

Complete the Sentence

46. phlebitis
47. Over-the-needle peripheral-short catheters
48. through-the-needle peripheral-short catheter
49. central vascular access device (CVAD)
50. nontunneled and noncuffed device, tunneled and cuffed device, implanted ports
51. Swan-Ganz catheter *or* pulmonary artery catheter
52. Dialysis, pheresis
53. drop factor
54. electrolytes, serum proteins, blood chemistries
55. distal, upper

Labeling Exercise: Common Veins Used for Intravenous Therapy

Place the term in the correct location.

a. Superior cephalic vein
b. Median veins—cephalic, cubital, and basilic
c. Accessory cephalic veins
d. Basilic vein
e. Median veins
f. Cephalic vein
g. Metacarpal and dorsal vein

NCLEX-RN® Review Questions

Question numbers correspond to Outcome-Based Learning Objectives for this chapter.

22-1. Answer: 3
Rationale: The nurse should adhere to standard precautions and utilize whichever type of gloves would be indicated for the level of care of the patient. The nurse should avoid puncturing the septum. If the septum is punctured, the entire device will need to be surgically removed and replaced. The nurse should use a noncoring needle to access the device.
Cognitive Level: Application
Nursing Process: Implementation
Client Need: Physiological Integrity; Pharmacological and Parenteral Therapies

22-2. Answer: 3
Rationale: Alarms are placed on infusion pumps to alert the nursing staff of a potential problem. Turning the machine on and off until the alarm stops is not appropriate. Turning the alarm off could potentially harm the patient. Removing the fluids from the pump and administering them using gravity could also be harmful to the patient. The nurse should troubleshoot the reason for the "other" alarm and assess the pump's battery level or other indications that the pump is malfunctioning. An infusion pump should never replace safe and thorough nursing care.
Cognitive Level: Analysis
Nursing Process: Implementation
Client Need: Physiological Integrity; Pharmacological and Parenteral Therapies

22-3. Answer: 4
Rationale: There is no evidence to suggest that the patient's access catheter needs to be flushed with normal saline. The SASH technique is the approach used when the access device is used to administer medication. There is also no evidence to suggest the need for a volumetric pump. The nurse should assess the patient's most recent electrolyte levels prior to beginning an infusion with an electrolyte replacement.
Cognitive Level: Analysis
Nursing Process: Assessment
Client Need: Physiological Integrity; Pharmacological and Parenteral Therapies

22-4. Answer: 1
Rationale: When removing a vascular access device, the nurse should document the patient's consent and education, size, length, type of catheter, and condition, condition of the venipuncture site, the dressing applied, the patient's response to the procedure, and the name and title of the nurse.
Cognitive Level: Application
Nursing Process: Implementation
Client Need: Physiological Integrity; Pharmacological and Parenteral Therapies

22-5. Answer: 4
Rationale: Mechanical phlebitis is associated with the catheter, its insertion, and the selected site. Using areas of flexion and a gauge size too large for the intended vein and prescribed therapy can result in the development of mechanical phlebitis. Patient noncompliance as restricting physical activity will enhance the development of phlebitis. There is no evidence to suggest the patient will develop bruising, thrombosis, or an infection at the access device site.
Cognitive Level: Analysis
Nursing Process: Assessment
Client Need: Physiological Integrity; Pharmacological and Parenteral Therapies

Chapter 23 – Blood Administration

Key Terms Matching Exercise

1. b
2. f
3. a
4. e
5. d
6. c

Key Term Crossword

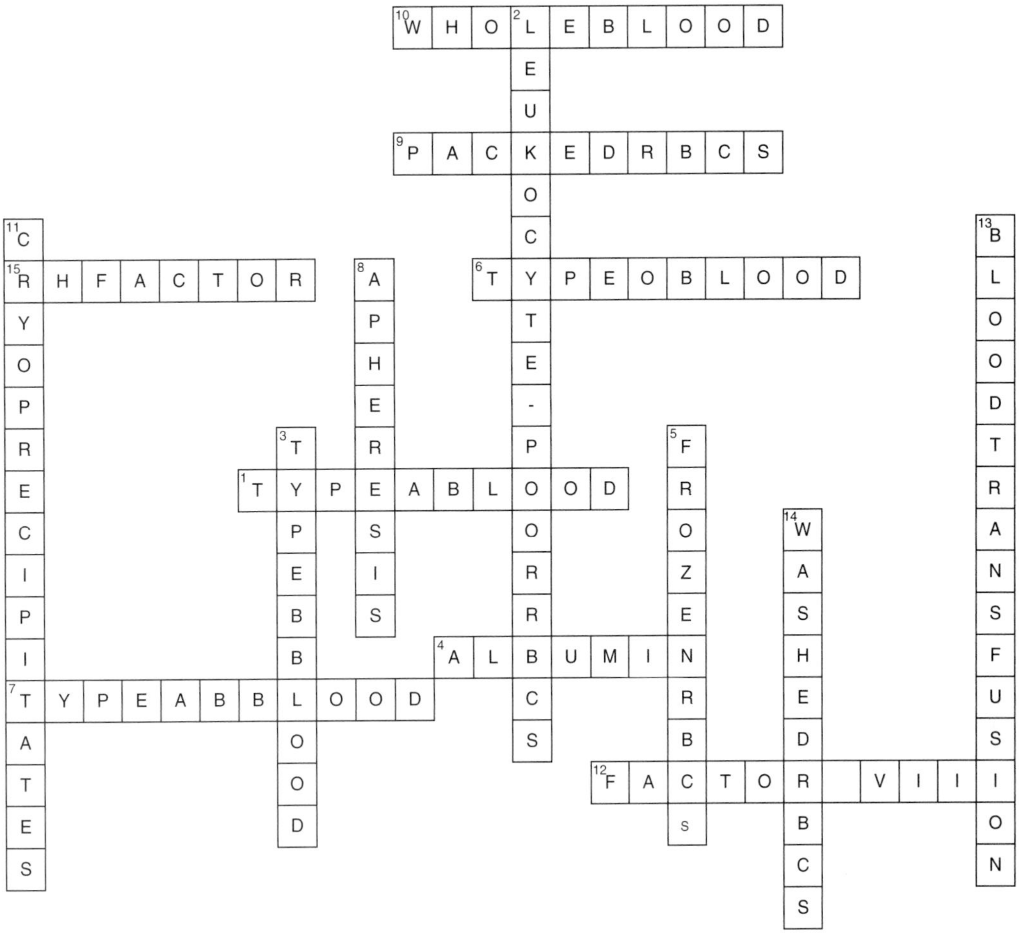
10 WHOLEBLOOD
2 LEUKOCYTE-POORRBCS
9 PACKEDRBCS
11 CRYOPRECIPITATES
15 RHFACTOR
8 APHERESIS
6 TYPEOBLOOD
13 BLOODTRANSFUSION
3 TYPEBBLOOD
1 TYPEABLOOD
5 FROZENRBCS
14 WASHEDRBCS
4 ALBUMIN
7 TYPEABBLOOD
12 FACTOR VIII

True or False?

7. T
8. F
9. F
10. T
11. T
12. T
13. T
14. F
15. F
16. T

Blood Types, Antigens and Antibodies, and Transfusion Types

Complete the missing spaces in the table below.

Blood Type with Antigen	Antibody Produced	Type for Transfusion
Blood type A, Antigen A	Antibody B	Can receive A or O blood
Blood type B, Antigen B	Antibody A	Can receive B or O blood
Blood type AB, Antigen AB	None	Can receive A, B, or O type blood—Universal recipient
Blood type O, No antigens	Antibodies A and B	Can receive O type blood only—Universal donor

NCLEX-RN® Review Questions

Question numbers correspond to Outcome-Based Learning Objectives for this chapter.

23-1. Answer: 4

Rationale: There are specific guidelines for being a blood donor. Reasons for ineligibility as a blood donor include residing in the United Kingdom from 1980–1996 for greater than 3 months, residing in Europe for greater than 5 years, or lived in Africa or had sex with someone who was born or lived in Africa. Also, having a history of intravenous (IV) drug use would also be contraindicated for becoming a blood donor.
Cognitive Level: Application
Nursing Process: Implementation
Client Need: Physiological Integrity; Pharmacology and Parenteral Therapies

23-2. Answer: 3

Rationale: Packed RBCs are the most common blood product administered. Fresh frozen plasma does not contain platelets and does not impact the incidence of transfusion reactions. Fresh frozen plasma is administered through a filter and does cause rapid volume replacement. It restores plasma volume in shock without increasing RBCs.
Cognitive Level: Analysis
Nursing Process: Planning
Client Need: Physiological Integrity; Pharmacology and Parenteral Therapies

23-3. Answer: 2

Rationale: Although bacterial contamination of a blood product is rare, it can occur. The clinical manifestations of bacterial contamination may not occur until the transfusion is complete, or in some cases several hours later depending on the virulence of the infecting organism. Fever, chills, and hypotension are common initial symptoms. Endotoxic shock and even death will occur if the infection is left untreated. Fluid replacement, antibiotics, and blood pressure support is needed immediately to prevent irreversible shock and death. Providing an antipyretic or epinephrine are not appropriate interventions for this patient. Stating that the reaction is normal and expected is an incorrect nursing intervention.
Cognitive Level: Application
Nursing Process: Implementation
Client Need: Physiological Integrity; Pharmacology and Parenteral Therapies

23-4. Answer: 1

Rationale: Remaining with the patient for the first 15 minutes and observing for transfusion reactions is an activity within the implementation phase of blood administration. Assessing for signs of increased tissue perfusion is in the evaluation phase of blood administration. Checking the size and insertion date of the IV catheter is within the planning phase of blood administration. Checking for compatibility of blood product to the patient's blood type is within the assessment phase of blood administration.
Cognitive Level: Application
Nursing Process: Implementation
Client Need: Physiological Integrity; Pharmacology and Parenteral Therapies

23-5. Answer: 4

Rationale: Stopping the transfusion, calling for help, and beginning life-support measures would be appropriate for an acute hemolytic reaction. Obtaining urine and blood samples is appropriate for a febrile nonhemolytic reaction. Administering epinephrine is appropriate for a hemolytic or anaphylactic reaction. The nurse should slow the transfusion, provide an antihistamine, and then resume the transfusion. This is appropriate for an allergic reaction to the blood transfusion.
Cognitive Level: Application
Nursing Process: Implementation
Client Need: Physiological Integrity; Pharmacology and Parenteral Therapies

Chapter 24 – Hemodynamic Monitoring

Key Terms Matching Exercise 1

1.	b	**6.**	h
2.	e	**7.**	j
3.	c	**8.**	a
4.	g	**9.**	d
5.	i	**10.**	f

Key Terms Matching Exercise 1

11.	i	**17.**	l
12.	k	**18.**	b
13.	d	**19.**	c
14.	a	**20.**	e
15.	g	**21.**	f
16.	j	**22.**	h

True or False?

23.	F	**28.**	F
24.	T	**29.**	F
25.	T	**30.**	T
26.	F	**31.**	T
27.	T	**32.**	T

Labeling Exercise 1: Ports and Lumens of a Pulmonary Artery Catheter

a. For balloon inflation with 1 to 1.5 mL of air
b. Inflation lumen port
c. Distal lumen port
d. Proximal lumen port
e. Thermistor lumen port
f. Distal lumen opening
g. Balloon inflated
h. Thermistor lumen opening
i. 10 cm markings
j. Proximal lumen opening
k. Thermistor lumen opening
l. Proximal lumen
m. Thermistor lumen
n. Inflation lumen
o. Distal lumen

Labeling Exercise 2: Position of Pulmonary Artery Catheter During PAOP

a. Right internal jugular vein
b. Right pulmonary artery
c. Left atrium
d. Right pulmonary veins
e. Catheter (in right ventricle)
f. Catheter tip
g. Inflated balloon
h. Left atrial pressure
i. Column of blood

NCLEX-RN® Review Questions

Question numbers correspond to Outcome-Based Learning Objectives for this chapter.

24-1. Answer: 4
   Rationale: Hemodynamic monitoring devices are utilized in a variety of patient care areas including emergency departments, intensive care areas, and intermediate care areas. The level of intervention differs depending on the patient's diagnosis and hemodynamic stability.
   Cognitive Level: Application
   Nursing Process: Planning
   Client Need: Physiological Integrity; Physiological Adaptation

24-2. Answer: 1
   Rationale: After the transducer system is assembled and attached to the catheter, the infusion rate is held constant by the transducer system and the pressure sleeve. The information on the transducer package insert will indicate the constant infusion rate, but 1 to 3 milliliters per hour is common. The transducer converts pressure detected at the catheter tip into an electrical signal. This signal is displayed on a bedside or portable monitor.
   Cognitive Level: Analysis
   Nursing Process: Assessment
   Client Need: Physiological Integrity; Physiological Adaptation

24-3. Answer: 1
   Rationale: The radial artery is the most common site for arterial catheter placement. Other sites such as the brachial, axillary, femoral, dorsalis pedis, and posterior tibial are possible alternatives. For monitoring central venous pressure, the subclavian, internal or external jugular, and femoral veins are potential insertion sites. For a pulmonary artery catheter, an introducer is inserted in either the jugular, subclavian, or femoral vein.
   Cognitive Level: Application
   Nursing Process: Planning
   Client Need: Physiological Integrity; Physiological Adaptation

24-4. Answer: 2
   Rationale: Normal systolic pressures in the right ventricle are between 20 and 30 mm Hg and diastolic pressures are between 0 to 8 mm Hg. The normal pulmonary artery systolic pressure is 20 to 30 mm Hg and the diastolic pressure is 5 to 15 mm Hg. The normal right ventricular systolic pressure and the pulmonary artery systolic pressure are the same.
   Cognitive Level: Analysis
   Nursing Process: Assessment
   Client Need: Physiological Integrity; Physiological Adaptation

24-5. Answer: 4
   Rationale: Each monitor has the ability to alarm to notify the nurse that the blood pressure is too high or too low. After the arterial line is inserted, set the high and low alarm limits. These alarms should never be turned off when the nurse leaves the room. When high or low alarms occur, assess the patient for changes. If changes occur in the arterial waveform, first assess the patient and take a manual cuff pressure. If the cuff pressure varies from the arterial pressure, it is necessary to troubleshoot the equipment by systematically inspecting and, if necessary, tightening all connections and tubing from insertion site to pressure bag.
   Cognitive Level: Application
   Nursing Process: Assessment
   Client Need: Physiological Integrity; Physiological Adaptation

24-6. Answer: 3
   Rationale: Reduced afterload suggests vasodilation of the pulmonary and systemic vasculature. Decreased afterload lessens the workload on the heart and reduces myocardial oxygen requirements. With reduced resistance to ventricular ejection, an increase in stroke volume occurs as the ventricles empty.
   Cognitive Level: Analysis
   Nursing Process: Planning
   Client Need: Physiological Integrity; Physiological Adaptation

24-7. Answer: 2
   Rationale: The normal central venous pressure waveform has three positive waves that correspond to atrial cardiac events. The *a* wave correlates with the P wave or atrial contraction. The next positive wave, the *c* wave, may not be visible on the tracing. The *c* wave reflects retrograde swelling of the tricuspid valve into the right atrium occurring during ventricular contraction. The *v* wave represents atrial filling (diastole) and the increased pressure against the closed tricuspid valve in early diastole. A dicrotic notch is seen in a pulmonary artery waveform and indicates the closure of the pulmonic valve. This will not be seen on a central venous pressure waveform.
   Cognitive Level: Analysis
   Nursing Process: Assessment
   Client Need: Physiological Integrity; Physiological Adaptation

Chapter 25 – Preoperative Nursing

Key Terms Matching Exercise

1. g		8. f
2. b		9. l
3. a		10. c
4. j		11. k
5. i		12. d
6. m		13. h
7. e		

Name the Suffix

14. ostomy; colostomy
15. plasty; rhinoplasty
16. ectomy; colectomy
17. scopy; laparoscopy
18. orraphy; herniorrhaphy
19. otomy; thoracotomy

Short Answer Questions

20. Preoperative education can improve patient outcomes and decrease preoperative anxiety, but it may also create worries in individuals who feel healthy but are scheduled for major elective procedures. Also, in some cultures, preoperative teaching is not a routine part of preoperative care; therefore, teaching can actually increase the patient's anxiety level. This highlights the need to individualize teaching.

21. Patients who will have general anesthesia, regional anesthesia, or conscious sedation are instructed to abstain from food and fluids prior to the operation to reduce the risk of pulmonary aspiration of stomach contents associated with anesthesia. Current guidelines recommend that patients fast from the intake of solid food (i.e., a light meal) for 6 or more hours before procedures and from clear liquids for 2 or more hours.

22. Deep breathing is taught as an intervention to decrease the risk of the postoperative pulmonary complications of hypoxemia, atelectasis, and pneumonia.

23. Although the mechanisms that mediate the relaxation response remain unknown, eliciting the RR reduces volumetric oxygen consumption from rest and counteracts the effects of stress.

24. Smoking damages the mucociliary clearance system, resulting in increased secretions and a higher risk of postoperative atelectasis and pneumonia (Barrera et al., 2005). Smoking increases circulating carboxyhemoglobin, which reduces circulating oxygen, resulting in less oxygen delivery to body tissues. Smoking causes vasoconstriction, a serious concern for patients undergoing cardiac or vascular surgery.

25. Patient history includes age, allergies, current health problem, type of surgery planned, plans for autologous blood donation, family history, past medical history, past surgical history and experiences with anesthesia, current herbal medications and nutritional supplements, current medications, and use of alcohol, cigarettes, and social drugs.

Risk Factors for Postoperative Nausea and Vomiting

Gender (women more than men)
History of nausea and vomiting with a previous surgery
History of motion sickness
Nonsmoker
Use of certain inhalation anesthetics (volatile anesthetic gases and nitrous oxide)
Use of opioid analgesics
Type of surgery (gynecologic, abdominal, and those on the ear or eye)
Longer surgeries

NCLEX-RN® Review Questions

Question numbers correspond to Outcome-Based Learning Objectives for this chapter.

25-1. Answer: 2

Rationale: Preoperative information required for patients with pacemakers includes identification of the underlying cardiac rhythm that necessitates use of the pacemaker and information about the pacemaker itself. All patients with pacemakers need to have the unit interrogated—tested to check battery status, and thresholds for sensing and pacing leads—within 3 months of scheduled surgery. Pacemaker interrogation after surgery is also recommended. A magnet is used to turn off the tachycardia detection on an implanted defibrillator and is usually done the morning of surgery. There is no evidence to suggest that a patient with a pacemaker should not take prescribed medications. Pulmonary function tests would not be indicated for this patient.

Cognitive Level: Application
Nursing Process: Assessment
Client Need: Physiological Integrity; Reduction of Risk Potential

25-2. Answer: 4

Rationale: Poor glucose control is associated with higher rates of surgical site infections. Patients with diabetes also experience slower wound healing. The physiological stress of surgery changes the insulin requirement. Careful monitoring of blood sugar is needed to prevent hypoglycemia and ketosis.

Cognitive Level: Analysis
Nursing Process: Planning
Client Need: Physiological Integrity; Reduction of Risk Potential

25-3. Answer: 4

Rationale: Benzodiazepines such as Versed are given preoperatively to reduce anxiety, increase sedation, and to smooth induction of anesthesia. Beta blockers are used to reduce the risk of atrial fibrillation. Gastric acid blockers are used to decrease gastric acid production. Narcotics are used to reduce pain.

Cognitive Level: Analysis
Nursing Process: Implementation
Client Need: Physiological Integrity; Reduction of Risk Potential

25-4. Answer: 4

Rationale: For the patient with a sensory disorder, make sure that glasses, hearing aids, and dentures are available postoperatively and assess pain frequently. Documentation of skin status would be applicable for the patient with an integumentary status disorder. Ensuring adequate hydration would be appropriate for the patient with a genitourinary disorder. Encouraging mobility would be appropriate for the patient with a gastrointestinal disorder.

Cognitive Level: Analysis
Nursing Process: Planning
Client Need: Physiological Integrity; Reduction of Risk Potential

25-5. Answer: 3

Rationale: Ambulation increases heart rate and cardiac output, and stimulates circulation to all body systems. The increase in circulation helps to rid the body of the effects of anesthesia. Ambulation increases respiratory rate and minute ventilation, and it helps to mobilize respiratory secretions. Increased circulation to the intestinal tract helps to stimulate peristalsis and increased blood flow through the kidneys stimulates the production of urine. Blood flow to skin and muscles brings nutrients needed for wound healing. Ambulation stimulates calf muscles and increases venous return. Frequent ambulation, a minimum of three times per day, may help prevent some of the complications associated with immobility. Patients need to understand the importance and emphasis that is placed on walking after an operation and shown effective ways of getting out of bed postoperatively.

Cognitive Level: Application
Nursing Process: Implementation
Client Need: Physiological Integrity; Reduction of Risk Potential

25-6. Answer: 1

> **Rationale:** Patients who smoke cigarettes are instructed to stop smoking. Eight weeks prior to surgery is suggested as the optimal time frame, although research has not established if there is any benefit to a patient who quits smoking shortly before surgery: days, or even a few weeks. The nurse should instruct the patient as to why smoking cessation is important prior to the surgery.
> **Cognitive Level:** Application
> **Nursing Process:** Implementation
> **Client Need:** Physiological Integrity; Reduction of Risk Potential

Chapter 26 – Intraoperative Nursing

Key Terms Matching Exercise

1.	f	**7.**	d
2.	b	**8.**	g
3.	j	**9.**	e
4.	l	**10.**	k
5.	a	**11.**	c
6.	h	**12.**	i

Short Answer Questions

13. The perioperative nurse's primary role in the operating room (OR) is that of the circulating nurse, whose duties are performed outside the sterile field and encompass responsibilities of nursing care management within the OR. The circulating nurse observes the surgical team from a broad perspective and assists the team to create and maintain a safe, comfortable environment for surgery. The circulating nurse communicates patient care needs to each member of the surgical team, facilitating a united effort while being the patient advocate whose actions are dedicated to ensuring that the patient's rights and wishes are respected and carried out.

14. The scrub nurse works directly with the surgeon within the sterile field passing instruments, sponges, and other items needed during the surgical procedure. This role can also be performed by personnel other than an RN, in which case the person is then called a scrub technician.

15. Compared to the traditional surgical scrub, waterless hand preparation boasts a reduction in microbial counts of hands, improved skin health, and reduced use of time and resources.

16. Advantages of a laparoscopic surgery over open surgery include less scarring, quicker recovery, shorter hospitalization, faster return to normal activities (work), fewer problems with incisions, less pain, and less use of opioids, which reduces the negative secondary effects associated with opioid use. Often patients undergoing laparoscopic surgery will be discharged the same day as surgery, whereas open surgery procedures can require 3 to 5 days of hospitalization. The intraoperative cost of MIS surgery is often more, but is offset by the reduced hospital stay and quicker recovery.

17. Safety initiatives that address communication issues such as the time-out are designed to promote correct site surgery. The time-out checklist has been adopted from the aviation industry model and requires surgical team members to cease all other activities in order to actively, verbally, and mutually verify information such as the correct patient, correct surgery, correct site/side, correct patient position, and possibly additional information such as prophylactic medications being administered at the appropriate time prior to surgery.

18. Communicate with surgical team for timing of antibiotic administration. Institute measures to maintain normothermia throughout surgery and PACU. Develop policies that ensure standards are used by all members of the surgical team regarding warming procedures.

19. Hyperglycemia is known to be associated with increased sepsis, suggesting that careful monitoring of glucose levels may be a way to reduce serious postoperative infections. Infections are a major concern for all hospitalized patients, but are especially dangerous for elderly persons. General risk factors for infection in elderly patients are known to include frailty, chronic undernutrition, reduced muscle mass, and poor dentition. Other more general factors common to all age groups are diabetes, aspiration, and the presence of an indwelling urinary catheter.

20. A surgical count to prevent a foreign object from being left behind is the responsibility of the perioperative nurses. All items brought to the operating room are documented. No items are removed from the operating room until the final count is complete and verified. Sponges, swabs, and other items are counted before surgery, before wound closure begins, and before skin closure begins. The circulating nurse and scrub nurse count items in unison. The circulating nurse and scrub nurse document the count in the record. If there is a discrepancy in the count, all personnel must locate the missing item.

True or False?

21.	F	**26.**	T
22.	F	**27.**	T
23.	T	**28.**	F
24.	F	**29.**	F
25.	T	**30.**	F

NCLEX-RN® Review Questions

Question numbers correspond to Outcome-Based Learning Objectives for this chapter.

26-1. Answer: 2

> **Rationale:** Once the surgery is completed, the anesthetist and the nurse will accompany the patient to the post-anesthesia care unit (PACU) for further monitoring. Concerns will focus on safety, infection control, medication, communication, positioning, and equipment. The PACU is where the patient will recover from the anesthetic received. Medicating for a latex allergy, estimating blood loss, and validating surgical counts are all nursing activities conducted within the surgical suite.
> **Cognitive Level:** Application
> **Nursing Process:** Implementation
> **Client Need:** Physiological Integrity; Physiological Adaptation

26-2. Answer: 1

> **Rationale:** CRNAs administer anesthesia and anesthesia-related care in four general categories to include pre-anesthetic preparation and evaluation; anesthesia induction, maintenance and emergence; post-anesthesia care; and perianesthetic and clinical support functions. The CRNA works under the supervision of the anesthesiologist.
> **Cognitive Level:** Application
> **Nursing Process:** Implementation
> **Client Need:** Physiological Integrity; Physiological Adaptation

26-3. Answer: 3
> **Rationale:** The surgeon is responsible for making decisions related to the surgical procedure and heads the surgical team.
> **Cognitive Level:** Analysis
> **Nursing Process:** Planning
> **Client Need:** Physiological Integrity; Physiological Adaptation

26-4. Answer: 1
> **Rationale:** Because of the position in which the patient needed to be placed to reach the lumbar area, this patient is most likely experiencing brachial plexus nerve injury. The positions of the arms needed to be less than 90 degrees, supinated, and adequately padded and protected.
> **Cognitive Level:** Analysis
> **Nursing Process:** Assessment
> **Client Need:** Physiological Integrity; Physiological Adaptation

26-5. Answer: 3
> **Rationale:** The most important role of the perioperative nurse is that of patient advocate. The essence of the advocacy in the perioperative role is defined as protection, giving a voice, doing, comfort, and caring. The nurse should ask that all linen be examined before removing from the surgical suite in order to locate the medal attached to the hospital gown.
> **Cognitive Level:** Analysis
> **Nursing Process:** Implementation
> **Client Need:** Safe, Effective Care Environment; Management of Care

26-6. Answer: 4
> **Rationale:** Spinal headache or post-dural puncture headache is a common postoperative complaint. It is caused by the leaking of cerebral spinal fluid through the hole in the dura. Because it develops or worsens when the patient moves to an upright position, patients may be restricted to bedrest for the first 8 to 24 hours postoperatively to reduce the incidence of spinal headache. When headache develops it is located in the occipital area and resolves in 1 to 3 days. Patients who develop a headache are treated with hydration and analgesics. The patient is placed on bedrest with the head of the bed maintained at less than 30 degrees to reduce CSF leak.
> **Cognitive Level:** Application
> **Nursing Process:** Implementation
> **Client Need:** Physiological Integrity; Physiological Adaptation

26-7. Answer: 1
> **Rationale:** The anesthesiologist heads the anesthesia team and might be assisted by a respiratory therapist, anesthesia resident, or fellow in university teaching hospital or by a Certified Registered Nurse Anesthetist. CRNAs administer anesthesia and anesthesia-related care in four general categories: pre-anesthetic preparation and evaluation; anesthesia induction, maintenance and emergence; post-anesthesia care; and perianesthetic and clinical support functions. The CRNA works under the supervision of the anesthesiologist. The perioperative nurse would not provide pre-anesthesia medications. The respiratory therapist would not be administering medication. And the RN First Assistant would be assisting the surgeon.
> **Cognitive Level:** Application

> **Nursing Process:** Implementation
> **Client Need:** Physiological Integrity; Physiological Adaptation

Chapter 27 – Postoperative Nursing

Key Terms Matching Exercise

1.	i	**7.**	d
2.	k	**8.**	a
3.	h	**9.**	c
4.	e	**10.**	b
5.	g	**11.**	i
6.	f		

Short Answer Questions

12. Care in the PACU is organized around postanesthesia phases I and II. Phase I begins with the arrival of the patient and focuses on the recovery of physiological homeostasis and protective mechanisms. During this phase, the patient requires intensive nursing observation and care. Phase II begins when the patient becomes more alert and functional. The patient requires less intensive nursing and the focus of interventions is on preparing the patient and significant others for the patient's discharge home. As such, phase II refers most specifically to ambulatory surgery.

13. In some cultures, patients may be reluctant to talk about pain and to take pain medication for fear of addition, dependence, or sedation.

14. The nurse assesses the following upon the patient's arrival in the PACU:
- Level of consciousness (LOC)
- Cardiovascular
- Respiratory
- Pain management
- Gastrointestinal
- Genitourinary
- Skin integrity
- Temperature
- Incision
- Activity/movement
- Psychosocial
- Intravenous fluids
- Drains and other tubes
- Other medical devices

15. Initially, patients are placed in a lateral position. As they become more awake, they are placed with the head of the bed elevated if not contraindicated by the surgery. Patients are repositioned every 1 to 2 hours or as needed. A patient who is experiencing nausea and vomiting may remain in a lateral position to prevent aspiration.

16. Common nursing diagnoses in the PACU are:
- Risk for Impaired Gas Exchange (airway obstruction, laryngospasm, hypoxia).
- Risk for Imbalanced Fluid Volume (bleeding, hypovolemia, fluid overload).
- Risk for Decreased Cardiac Output: (dysrhythmia, hypotension, hypertension).
- Risk for Imbalanced Body Temperature: Hypothermia
- Readiness for Enhanced Comfort: Nausea and Vomiting
- Readiness for Enhanced Comfort: Pain
- Anxiety

17. Research found that regularly scheduled rounds significantly decreased patients' use of call lights while increasing patient satisfaction. The nursing units that conducted hourly rounds also reported significant reductions in patient falls. Also, nurse satisfaction increased due to their contact with patients in more productive ways.

18. Ambulation increases respiratory rate, minute ventilation, tidal volume, and inspiratory flow rates. Patients who walk more and who walk longer distances tend to recover quicker and are discharged sooner than patients who are less mobile.

19. Surgical trauma, physiological stress, and the inflammatory process stimulate the release of catecholamines, neurotransmitters, and hormones that slow gastrointestinal motility, contributing to ileus, or hypoactive bowel with delayed peristalsis. The inhibitory effects of anesthesia and opioids further reduce peristalsis.

20. For superficial incisions, the patient must have at least one of the following within 30 days of the surgery:
    • Purulent drainage from the site.
    • Organisms isolated from a culture of fluid or tissue from the site.
    • One sign and symptom of infection: pain, tenderness, redness, localized swelling and heat.

For deep incisions, the patient must have at least one of the following within 30 days of the surgery or within 1 year if an implant was involved:
    • Purulent drainage from the deep incision but not from an organ or body cavity.
    • A deep incision dehisces, or is deliberately opened by the surgeon when the patient presents with at least one of the symptoms of infection: fever, localized pain, or tenderness.
    • Abscess or other evidence of infection involving the deep incision.

True or False?

21.	T	26.	F
22.	T	27.	T
23.	F	28.	F
24.	F	29.	T
25.	T	30.	T

NCLEX-RN® Review Questions

Question numbers correspond to Outcome-Based Learning Objectives for this chapter.

27-1. Answer: 3
Rationale: A situation requiring consultation is the report of increased pain when the pain was previously well controlled. This finding suggests the possibility of surgical complications such as infection or hematoma formation, and requires a prompt evaluation.
Cognitive Level: Application
Nursing Process: Assessment
Client Need: Physiological Integrity; Physiological Adaptation

27-2. Answer: 1
Rationale: The Aldrete Post Anesthesia Recovery Score (PARS) is a scoring system in which the patient receives a score of 0–2 for respirations, oxygen saturation, consciousness, circulation, and activity. Total scores range from 0 to 10 with higher scores indicating a higher level of functioning. A patient receives a score on admission and every 30 minutes until a score of 8 or higher is achieved. The PARS score is the criterion by which patients are progressed from Phase I PACU recovery to Phase II PACU recovery.
Cognitive Level: Application
Nursing Process: Planning
Client Need: Physiological Integrity; Reduction of Risk Potential

27-3. Answer: 4
Rationale: A Class IV wound has a 40% chance of developing an infection. A Class III wound has a 10% chance of developing an infection. Traditionally, the surgeon performs the first dressing change. The CDC clinical guidelines recommend protecting the surgical wound with a sterile dressing for 24 to 48 hours postoperatively. They also recommend using sterile technique for dressing changes.
Cognitive Level: Application
Nursing Process: Planning
Client Need: Physiological Integrity; Physiological Adaptation

27-4. Answer: 1
Rationale: Discharge teaching includes a discussion of medications including purpose, how to take the medication, and key side effects. Most postoperative patients will be discharged with an oral narcotic for pain control and some will have antibiotics prescribed. A patient should be instructed to take the full prescription of antibiotics. For most surgeries, the patient is discouraged from lifting anything heavier than 10 to 15 pounds until the incision has healed in 4 to 6 weeks. Walking at a reasonable pace is encouraged and limited only by pain and fatigue, but heavier aerobic-type workouts are restricted until approved by the surgeon.
Cognitive Level: Application
Nursing Process: Implementation
Client Need: Physiological Integrity; Reduction of Risk Potential

27-5. Answer: 4
Rationale: Effectiveness of alternative interventions in reducing postoperative pulmonary complications would provide evidence to support rationales for common nursing interventions performed after surgery. Factors influencing nurses' decisions in weaning patients off oxygen postoperatively and factors that influence the use of "alternative" nursing interventions in the prevention of postoperative complications are examples of studies to understand how nurses develop clinical judgment. Effectiveness of nonpharmacological interventions in reducing postoperative pain is an example of a study to increase postoperative patient comfort.
Cognitive Level: Analysis
Nursing Process: Planning
Client Need: Physiological Integrity; Reduction of Risk Potential

Chapter 28 – Nursing Assessment of Patients with Neurological Disorders

Key Terms Matching Exercise

1.	b	**6.**	c
2.	h	**7.**	d
3.	i	**8.**	g
4.	f	**9.**	e
5.	a	**10.**	j

Key Term Crossword Puzzle

Labeling Exercise 1: Two Neurons with a Synapse Between

a. Dendrites
b. Cell body
c. Synaptic cleft
d. Receiving dendrite
e. Receptor
f. Direction of impulse
g. Myelin sheath
h. Nucleus
i. Nerve impulse
j. Neurotransmitter
k. Vesicle
l. Axon

Labeling Exercise 2: Brain and Spinal Cord

a. Cerebrum
b. Corpus callosum
c. Cerebellum
d. Brain stem
e. Spinal cord
f. Vertebral column
g. Cauda equina
h. Dura mater
i. Pons varolii
j. Pituitary gland
k. Body of fornix

Labeling Exercise 3: Dorsal Aspect of Brain with Cranial Nerves

I. Olfactory
II. Optic
III. Oculomotor
IV. Trigeminal
V. Trochlear
VI. Abducens
VII. Facial
VIII. Vestibuocochlear
IX. Glossopharyngeal
X. Vagus
XI. Accessory
XII. Hypoglossal

NCLEX-RN® Review Questions

Question numbers correspond to Outcome-Based Learning Objectives for this chapter.

28-1. Answer: 4
Rationale: The spinal cord is shorter than the vertebral column so the spinal roots extend downward. The spinal cord ends at vertebral level L2 but nerves L2–S5 continue downward as the "cauda equina" or horse's tail.
Cognitive Level: Analysis
Nursing Process: Planning
Client Need: Physiological Adaptation; Reduction of Risk Potential

28-2. Answer: 2
Rationale: Determining if any family members have neurological disorders is an element of the Family History. Assessing the use of herbal remedies is a part of the Medication History. Listing illnesses is a part of the assessment section Major Illnesses. The social history includes highest education level, employment history, marital status, sexual orientation, and drug, alcohol, and tobacco use. The nurse is attempting to establish if there are high-risk factors present such as drinking and driving, or recreational drugs and driving, or if the patient was engaging in a high-risk endeavor without appropriate safety equipment, such as a helmet.
Cognitive Level: Application
Nursing Process: Assessment
Client Need: Physiological Adaptation; Reduction of Risk Potential

28-3. Answer: 4
Rationale: The cranial nerves III, IV, and VI are usually tested together as they supply the various muscles that move the eye, and have motor function only. These three nerves supply the extraocular muscles, pupils, and eyelids. **Ptosis** is the term for a drooping upper eyelid. Assessing the optic nerve involves inspecting the globe for cataracts, foreign bodies or other obvious abnormalities; testing visual acuity, testing visual fields, and the fundiscopic examination. The trigeminal nerve has both a sensory and motor component. Assessing for a corneal reflex would be done to determine the integrity of this nerve. The vestibulocochlear nerve supports hearing.
Cognitive Level: Analysis
Nursing Process: Assessment
Client Need: Physiological Integrity; Reduction of Risk Potential

28-4. Answer: 3
Rationale: The patient is assessed for orientation to time, place, and person. Time orientation is assessed by evaluating awareness of the year, season, month, day of the week, and date. Place orientation is assessed via awareness of the state the patient is in, followed by city, county, and name of the current location. Time orientation often is impaired early and many times may be the first sign of neurological change.
Cognitive Level: Application
Nursing Process: Assessment
Client Need: Physiological Adaptation; Reduction of Risk Potential

28-5. Answer: 3
Rationale: The biceps reflex assesses functioning at the cervical 5–6 region. The triceps reflex assesses functioning at the cervical 6–7 region. The patellar reflex assesses functioning at the lumbar 4 region. And the Achilles reflex assesses functioning at the sacral 1 region.
Cognitive Level: Application
Nursing Process: Planning
Client Need: Physiological Integrity; Reduction of Risk Potential

28-6. Answer: 4
Rationale: Pathological reflexes are graded as being either present or absent. Documentation is either present (+) for abnormal, or absent (−) for normal.
Cognitive Level: Application
Nursing Process: Assessment
Client Need: Physiological Adaptation; Reduction of Risk Potential

28-7. Answer: 2
Rationale: Muscle stretch reflexes are generally preserved in the elderly, and absence or asymmetry generally indicates disease. Decreased or absence ankle jerks are common but thought to be due to Achilles tendon inelasticity versus true neurological changes.
Cognitive Level: Analysis
Nursing Process: Assessment
Client Need: Physiological Adaptation; Reduction of Risk Potential

Chapter 29 – Acute Brain Disorders

Key Terms Matching Exercise 1

1. h		**6.** a
2. b		**7.** d
3. j		**8.** c
4. e		**9.** i
5. f		**10.** g

Key Terms Matching Exercise 2

11. d		**16.** e
12. c		**17.** h
13. i		**18.** f
14. g		**19.** a
15. j		**20.** b

Word Search

21. primary tumors
22. autoregulation
23. brain abscess
24. bacterial meningitis
25. concussion
26. contusion
27. encephalitis
28. herniation
29. gene mutations
30. schwannomas

31. secondary injury
32. primary injury
33. epidural hematoma (EDH)
34. meningismus
35. ependymomas
36. cytotoxic edema
37. ischemia cascade
38. cerebral blood flow (CBF)
39. viral meningitis
40. Cushing's triad

A	E	P	I	D	U	R	A	L	H	E	M	A	T	O	M	A	D	E	R
B	A	C	T	E	R	I	A	L	M	E	N	I	N	G	I	T	I	S	U
P	R	I	M	A	R	Y	T	U	M	O	R	S	B	N	A	T	L	U	E
E	Y	A	O	D	U	R	E	T	B	P	O	N	G	I	E	R	P	M	B
A	R	M	I	E	A	T	D	U	L	R	Y	Z	I	O	E	A	N	S	T
R	U	E	U	N	P	I	O	A	W	I	C	R	E	A	X	O	D	I	O
O	J	D	N	C	A	E	R	R	E	X	L	F	K	E	T	I	N	G	S
C	N	E	A	E	J	B	N	T	E	O	N	P	W	O	D	I	W	N	A
S	I	C	R	P	T	G	S	D	S	G	Q	O	L	O	A	T	O	I	M
A	Y	I	E	H	F	W	C	E	Y	G	U	A	I	R	G	I	S	N	O
E	R	X	L	A	Z	A	F	Z	S	M	N	L	D	S	Z	R	X	E	N
M	A	O	P	L	T	R	E	X	D	S	O	I	A	K	U	M	A	M	N
P	D	T	U	I	S	I	Q	Y	W	G	Y	M	H	T	P	T	E	B	A
S	N	O	I	T	A	T	U	M	E	N	E	G	A	S	I	M	N	U	W
B	O	T	A	I	O	N	K	A	D	I	L	C	A	S	U	O	A	O	H
A	C	Y	T	S	R	U	E	E	O	N	O	I	S	S	U	C	N	O	C
P	E	C	C	H	M	Y	R	U	J	N	I	Y	R	A	M	I	R	P	S
I	S	C	H	E	M	I	A	C	A	S	C	A	D	E	A	T	S	S	A
W	P	E	W	O	L	F	D	O	O	L	B	L	A	R	B	E	R	E	C
V	I	R	A	L	M	E	N	I	N	G	I	T	I	S	R	A	C	H	K

True or False?

41.	T	**46.**	F
42.	F	**47.**	T
43.	F	**48.**	F
44.	T	**49.**	F
45.	T	**50.**	T

NCLEX-RN® Review Questions

Question numbers correspond to Outcome-Based Learning Objectives for this chapter.

29-1. Answer: 4

Rationale: Increased CSF absorption is one mechanism to maintain a constant relationship between the 3 brain components. Brain tissue does not expand, it is compressed. Auto-regulation ensures that the brain receives required sufficient oxygen and glucose to meet metabolic needs; this may be inhibited, but it is not blocked as a normal compensatory mechanism.
Cognitive Level: Application
Nursing Process: Assessment
Client Need: Physiological Integrity; Physiological Adaptation

29-2. Answer: 3

Rationale: Complaints of a "different" headache and projectile vomiting may be an early indication of increasing ICP. Changes in cranial nerve III, the oculomotor nerve, results in changes in papillary response and are early signs of ICP. Decorticate movements are a late sign. Cushing's triad is a late sign of ICP.
Cognitive Level: Application
Nursing Process: Assessment
Client Need: Physiological Integrity; Physiological Adaptation

29-3. Answer: 2, 3, and 4

Rationale: Normocapnia levels (PaCO$_2$ levels of 35–40 mm Hg) are best for the brain; euglycemic levels of 80–120 mg/dL as the brain is adversely impacted by both hypo and hyperglycemia; and normothermia and interventions for body temperatures >99.5°F rectally. Pulse oximetry and supplemental oxygen should be used to maintain saturations of 95% or greater.
Cognitive Level: Application
Nursing Process: Assessment
Client Need: Physiological Integrity; Physiological Adaptation

29-4. Answer: 2

Rationale: A CAT scan of the head to rule out skull fracture must be performed before wound closure is undertaken. A complete neurological assessment may indicate symptoms suggestive of a cerebral contusion but a CAT scan is the diagnostic tool. A cerebral arteriogram is not appropriate in this case as the vessel is outside of the skull. A skull series is to identify bone placement and continuity and, if a hematoma was suspected, a CAT scan would be the appropriate diagnostic test.
Cognitive Level: Application
Nursing Process: Planning
Client Need: Physiological Integrity; Physiological Adaptation

29-5. Answer: 1

Rationale: With bacterial meningitis, the spinal fluid and protein levels will be high and glucose levels will be low. The spinal fluid will be clear in viral meningitis. Option #3

is false. The spinal fluid will be bloody if there has been a bleed within the cranium. If there was bleeding as a result of the puncture, the fluid would clear.
Cognitive Level: Application
Nursing Process: Assessment
Client Need: Physiological Integrity; Physiological Adaptation

29-6. Answer: 3

Rationale: Benign tumors may be surgically difficult to remove and may compress vital structure. If the tumor is deep within the brain structure, it may be extremely difficult or impossible to remove surgically. Tumors may not invade surrounding tissue but their growth will compress them and may interfere with their function. Benign tumors can progress into malignant tumors.
Cognitive Level: Application
Nursing Process: Assessment
Client Need: Physiological Integrity; Physiological Adaptation

29-7. Answer: 4

Rationale: A flexible approach due to the changing resistance patterns to specific drugs. Brain tissue has no lymph drainage and this can interfere with clearing drugs and debris. Many chemotherapeutic agents cannot cross the blood–brain barrier. Malignant cells are heterogeneous and their sensitivity to the drugs is variable.
Cognitive Level: Application
Nursing Process: Implementation
Client Need: Physiological Integrity; Physiological Adaptation

29-8. Answer: 3

Rationale: Providing answers to questions honestly as they arise, educating them about the treatment plan, and involving them in discussions of the rehabilitation process is important in keeping families informed and involved, and provides as much control as possible and appropriate. The role of the nurse extends beyond teaching about the early detection of cognitive impairment as this would severely limit the family's knowledge and support. The early implementation of rehabilitative therapies does not alter the importance of family teaching. Family teaching should offer encouragement and realistic hope.
Cognitive Level: Application
Nursing Process: Planning
Client Need: Physiological Integrity; Physiological Adaptation

Chapter 30 – Caring for the Patient with Cerebral Vascular Disorders

Key Terms Matching Exercise 1

1.	f	**5.**	d
2.	c	**6.**	g
3.	e	**7.**	b
4.	a		

Key Terms Matching Exercise 2

8.	c	**12.**	a
9.	e	**13.**	d
10.	b	**14.**	f
11.	g		

Key Term Crossword Puzzle

Crossword answers:
- 15 (across): ATHEROGENESIS
- 17 (across): ANTIPLATELET THERAPY
- 16 (across): VASOSPASM
- 1 (across): REPERFUSION INJURY
- 6 (across): INFARCTION
- 13 (across): EMBOLIZATION
- 18 (across): TRIPLEHTHERAPY
- 8 (across): STROKE

Down clues (partial letters shown): CEREBRAL, NEUROPROTECTION, LIPOPHYLINIS, ATHEROSCLEROSIS, ISCHEMIC CASCADE, BERRY ANEURYSM, LACUNAR STROKE, CLOTTING, NEURO, etc.

Short Answer Questions

15. The risk factors for stroke are hypertension, family history, atrial fibrillation, hyperlipidemia, diabetes mellitus, stress, excessive alcohol use, sedentary lifestyle, obesity, smoking, valvular disease, and coronary artery disease.

16. The risk factors for aneurysm are smoking, hypertension, previous aneurysms, family history of aneurysms, connective tissue disorder, age greater than 40 years, female, and blood vessel injury or dissection.

17. The complications of aneurysmal SAH are varied and potentially life threatening. The major risks are rebleeding, vasospasm, hyponatremia, seizures, and hydrocephalus.

18. Nursing implications for stroke treatment include considerations for blood pressure, fever, blood glucose, immobility, respiratory compromise, cardiac arrhythmias, seizures, ICP management, and identification and modification of risk factors.

19. To reduce patients' risk of stroke, the nurse can advise them to:
    1. Know their blood pressure.
    2. Find out if they have atrial fibrillation.
    3. If they smoke, STOP.
    4. If they drink, do so in moderation.
    5. Know their cholesterol levels.
    6. If they have diabetes, control it.
    7. Exercise.
    8. Reduce salt and fat in the diet.
    9. Develop awareness of circulation problems.
    10. Know the symptoms.

Labeling Exercise: The Circle of Willis

a. Anterior communicating artery
b. Anterior cerebral artery
c. Posterior communicating artery
d. Posterior cerebral artery
e. Basilar artery
f. Vertebral artery
g. Cerebellum
h. Occipital lobe
i. Pons
j. Temporal lobe
k. Pituitary gland
l. Internal carotid artery
m. Middle cerebral artery

n. Optic chiasma
o. Frontal lobe
p. The Circle of Willis

NCLEX-RN® Review Questions

Question numbers correspond to Outcome-Based Learning Objectives for this chapter.

30-1. Answer: 3
Rationale: Eighty percent of all strokes are ischemic in nature and most are caused by atherosclerosis. Hemorrhagic strokes are commonly associated with hypertension. Clients experiencing ischemic strokes are generally older than those suffering from hemorrhagic stroke.
Cognitive Level: Analysis
Nursing Process: Assessment
Client Need: Physiological Integrity; Physiological Adaptation

30-2. Answer: 2
Rationale: The fragmentation of a clot in the venous system of the leg cannot enter the arterial circulation of the brain unless there is a defect in the heart. Plaque formation that alters the internal diameter in a cerebral artery is a common cause of ischemic stroke. The plaque disrupts the integrity of the arterial lining, causing blood to enter the clot and ultimately form a thrombus. Lipohyalinosis is a process that results in a vascular abnormality in small vessels and is normally associated with hypertension.
Cognitive Level: Application
Nursing Process: Planning
Client Need: Physiological Integrity; Physiological Adaptation

30-3. Answer: 2
Rationale: The ischemic cascade further propagates cerebral edema, cerebral ischemia, and cerebral infarction, and cell death. Tissues surrounding the necrotic area have undergone tissue hypoxia and may be viable if perfusion is restored before anoxia occurs. The functional ability of the tissue has not been permanently impaired until cell death occurs. The penumbra is the area surrounding the necrotic core.
Cognitive Level: Application
Nursing Process: Planning
Client Need: Physiological Integrity; Reduction of Risk Potential

30-4. Answer: 2
Rationale: With hypervolemic therapy, plasma expanders may cause pulmonary compromise or congestive heart failure. Cerebral salt wasting is a complication of subarachnoid hemorrhage not associated with vasospasm. The nidus is a concentration of abnormal vessels located at the center of an arteriovenous malformation. Seizures may be generalized or focal depending upon the area of the brain involved.
Cognitive Level: Application
Nursing Process: Assessment
Client Need: Physiological Integrity; Reduction of Risk Potential

30-5. Answer: 3
Rationale: Endovascular coiling is associated with the client being able to return to activities of normal living and work earlier than treatment options. Endovascular coiling is associated with a shorter, not longer length of hospital stay. Endovascular coiling, not neurosurgical clipping is associated with a higher survival and lower morbidity rates one year after procedure. While the availability of an interventional neuroradiologist is important, if the client is a candidate for the endovascular coiling, this is the option of choice.
Cognitive Level: Application
Nursing Process: Implementation
Client Need: Physiological Integrity; Reduction of Risk Potential

Chapter 31 – Caring for the Patient with Chronic Neurological Disorders

Key Terms Matching Exercise

1. d
2. f
3. j
4. e
5. b
6. k
7. a
8. c
9. h
10. g
11. i

Key Term Crossword

Short Answer Questions

12. The causes of dementia are:
Alzheimer's disease
Vascular dementia
Diffuse Lewy body dementia
Frontotemporal atrophy/Pick's disease
Parkinson's disease
Huntington's disease
Postcortical or post-thalamic stroke
Postanoxic encephalopathy
Hydrocephalus
Brain tumors
Infectious disorders: meningitis, Creutzfeldt–Jakob disease, HIV, neurosyphilis
Toxins: drugs, alcohol, heavy metals
Delirium
Depression
Vitamin B_{12} deficiency
Polypharmacy

13. Risk factors associated with Alzheimer's disease are:
- Growing old is the most significant risk factor for developing AD. Late-onset AD occurs in those over the age of 65. Statistics show that, after 65, the prevalence of AD cases doubles every 5 years.

- Other risk factors that have been linked to AD include:
Genetics/family history
Atherosclerosis
High cholesterol
Elevated plasma homocysteine
Diabetes
Down syndrome
Mild cognitive impairment (MCI)

14. Without a known cause of idiopathic PD, definitive risk factors are not clear. However, certain factors have been linked with PD, including the following:
Family history
Pesticide exposure
Rural living
Farming as an occupation
Drinking well water

15. Multiple sclerosis is a neuroimmunologic disease that attacks **myelin,** the protective sheath surrounding nerve fibers. The demyelination in the white matter of the brain and spinal cord leaves sclerotic areas, also known as plaques, and subsequent scarring leading to a variety of neurological symptoms including weakness, spasticity, visual difficulties, and paresthesias.

16. Research has shown that people who spend their first 15 years of life in temperate climates, at a distance from the equator, are more at risk than those who spend the same time in tropical regions closer to the equator (Schapiro, 2003). There is evidence that a genetic link may influence susceptibility to MS. Generally, a person's chance of developing MS is about one-tenth of 1%; however, if there is a first-degree relative with MS, the risk jumps up to 3%. In identical twins, the chance that the second twin will develop MS if the first twin does is 30%; in fraternal twins, the risk is decreased to 4%. Many researchers hypothesize that MS is not caused by a single gene, virus, or environmental factor, but is the result of a combination of factors (NINDS, 2002).

17. The cause of amyotrophic lateral sclerosis is unknown.

18. In ALS, degenerative changes occur in the anterior horn cells of the spinal cord, the motor nuclei of the brainstem, and the corticospinal tracts. Upper motor neuron degeneration leads to spasticity and reduced muscle strength, while lower motor neuron degeneration causes flaccid muscles, paralysis, and atrophy. The disease lasts 3 to 4 years on average, resulting in death.

19. In myasthenia gravis, antibodies generated by an autoimmune response bind to acetylcholine receptors, blocking the transmission of nerve impulses. This inefficient neuromuscular transmission together with the normally present presynaptic rundown phenomenon results in a decremental amount of nerve fibers being activated by successive nerve fiber impulses.

20. Although further research needs to be conducted regarding specific interventions to increase knowledge, skills, and self-care for caregivers, nurses should be cognizant that there may be common family caregiver needs and challenges across the span of neurodegenerative disorders. Specifically, family caregivers for individuals with AD and PD identified high needs for information about the illness as well as the need for practical training on how to provide care. When providing education and support to individuals with these conditions, nurses need to identify and include the family caregiver. Furthermore, caregivers need information about self-care for their own health promotion, and encouragement to pursue activities to support their own health and well-being.

True or False?

21.	F	26.	F
22.	F	27.	T
23.	F	28.	T
24.	T	29.	T
25.	T	30.	F

NCLEX-RN® Review Questions

Question numbers correspond to Outcome-Based Learning Objectives for this chapter.

31-1. Answer: 4
Rationale: Myasthenia gravis is diagnosed through a detailed history and physical assessment, including a neurological examination. The Tensilon test may be given, in which 2 mg of edrophonium chloride (Tensilon), a cholinesterase inhibitor with rapid onset and short duration of action, is administered intravenously at 30–60 second intervals up to a total of 10 mg. Patients with myasthenia gravis will demonstrate a distinct increase in muscle strength within 30 to 60 seconds. The Tensilon test is not used in multiple sclerosis, Parkinson's disease, or Alzheimer's disease.
Cognitive Level: Analysis
Nursing Process: Implementation
Client Need: Physiological Integrity; Reduction of Risk Potential

31-2. Answer: 1
Rationale: In ALS, degenerative changes occur in the anterior horn cells of the spinal cord, the motor nuclei of the brainstem, and the corticospinal tracts. Upper motor neuron degeneration leads to spasticity and reduced muscle strength, while lower motor neuron degeneration causes flaccid muscles, paralysis, and atrophy. Cognition, sensory function, vision, and hearing are spared. Multiple sclerosis is a progressive demyelinating process that produces symptoms related to the location of damage. Parkinson's disease is a disease of poor dopamine production which leads to difficulties with movement, tremor, rigidity, and posture maintenance. Myasthenia gravis is a disease of muscle weakness as a result of blocked nerve impulses and the neuromuscular junction.
Cognitive Level: Analysis
Nursing Process: Assessment
Client Need: Physiological Integrity; Reduction of Risk Potential

31-3. Answer: 3
Rationale: The overall goals of nursing care for the patient with MG are to minimize symptoms and to detect early signs of myasthenic or cholinergic crisis. Symptoms of cholinergic crisis range from muscle weakness to cramps, difficulty talking, difficulty swallowing, bradycardia, bronchospasm, excessive salivation, vomiting, diarrhea, and excessive sweating. Keeping the patient NPO, providing anti-emetic medication, and providing oxygen for shortness of breath would not support the goals of care for this patient.
Cognitive Level: Analysis
Nursing Process: Planning
Client Need: Physiological Integrity; Reduction of Risk Potential

31-4. Answer: 1
Rationale: Respiratory care for a patient with ALS includes not lying down after eating, avoiding eating large meals, and sleeping with head elevated 15 to 30 degrees. The use of a blink instead of vocalization would be helpful for a communication issue. Eating foods slowly and in small bites helps support the nutritional status. Balancing activity with rest periods helps support activity status.
Cognitive Level: Application
Nursing Process: Implementation
Client Need: Physiological Integrity; Reduction of Risk Potential

31-5. Answer: 4
Rationale: Spiritual and psychological counseling would be more appropriate for a patient with ALS. Family member stress management and coping strategy teaching sessions would be appropriate for a patient with Alzheimer's disease. A regular exercise program and healthy eating habits would be beneficial for a patient with multiple sclerosis. Explaining how some Parkinson's disease patients choose to participate in clinical research studies as a way of advancing science while managing their condition with the latest, most promising treatments is the correct response for the nurse to make to this patient.
Cognitive Level: Analysis
Nursing Process: Implementation
Client Need: Physiological Integrity; Reduction of Risk Potential

31-6. Answer: 3
Rationale: People can live with Parkinson's disease for many years. The chronic and progressive nature of the disease can significantly impact older, spousal caregivers, who may not have the physical strength to handle the weight of a patient with limited mobility. Caregiver stress

and burden have been shown to increase as the disease progresses. The nurse should encourage the patient to talk about things that can help both the patient and the husband. Minimizing the patient's concerns would not be an appropriate response. Suggesting the patient discuss the concern with her physician is also not an appropriate response.
Cognitive Level: Application
Nursing Process: Implementation
Client Need: Physiological Integrity; Reduction of Risk Potential

31-7. Answer: 2
Rationale: The use of the Internet is one of many areas within the patient/family education research topic category. Areas under complementary alternative approaches would include the impact of meditation and prayer on disease management and experience. Areas under caregivers would include skill-building educational interventions and anticipatory grief. Areas under emotional and psychological would include impact of role change and successful coping.
Cognitive Level: Application
Nursing Process: Planning
Client Need: Physiological Integrity; Basic Care and Comfort

Chapter 32 – Caring for the Patient with Spinal Cord Injuries

Key Terms Matching Exercise 1

1.	i	7.	b
2.	d	8.	f
3.	g	9.	c
4.	k	10.	j
5.	e	11.	h
6.	l	12.	a

Key Terms Matching Exercise 2

13.	c	19.	a
14.	g	20.	k
15.	b	21.	j
16.	f	22.	h
17.	d	23.	e
18.	i		

Nursing Diagnoses Related to Spinal Cord Injury

24. Neurological Status: Risk for constipation related to spinal cord injury; disturbed sensory perception related to spinal cord injury; risk for injury due to spinal instability

25. Pulmonary Function: Ineffective breathing pattern related to pulmonary complications of spinal cord injury; ineffective airway clearance related to the loss of spinal innervation of the respiratory muscles

26. Cardiovascular Status: Risk for ineffective tissue perfusion related to cardiovascular effects of neurogenic shock

27. Peripheral Tissue Perfusion: Risk of ineffective peripheral tissue perfusion related to DVT

28. Gastrointestinal Function: Risk for constipation related to impaired gastric motility due to spinal cord injury; potential for gastric ulceration related to stress of critical injury; readiness for enhanced nutrition related to increased metabolic need and inadequate caloric intake

29. Urinary Elimination: Impaired urinary elimination due to neurogenic bladder; risk for autonomic dysreflexia related to autonomic dysfunction as a result of spinal cord injury

30. Pain: Readiness for enhanced comfort due to injury and/or surgical procedure

31. Psychosocial State: Ineffective coping related to loss of control over environment and uncertainty of the future

32. Adaptation: Self-care deficit related to spinal cord injury; deficient knowledge regarding adaptation strategies and resources

Labeling Exercise 1: Ventral and Dorsal Nerve Roots

a. Posterior horn
b. Anterior horn
c. Ventral root
d. Spinal nerve
e. Dorsal root ganglion
f. Dorsal root

Labeling Exercise 2: Spinal Column

a. Base of skull
b. Cervical enlargement
c. Lumbar enlargement
d. Internal terminal filum (pial part)
e. External terminal filum (dural part)
f. Coccyx
g. Termination of dural sac
h. Sacrum
i. Cauda equina
j. Conus medullaris (termination of spinal cord)

NCLEX-RN® Review Questions

Question numbers correspond to Outcome-Based Learning Objectives for this chapter.

32-1. Answer: 1
Rationale: Spinal cord injuries in persons younger than 65 years can usually be attributed to motor vehicle collisions, whereas spinal cord injury in people older than 65 years is usually the result of a fall. Persons under 30 years are more likely to have a sports-related spinal cord injury, and nontraumatic spinal cord injuries most often occur in persons over 40 years.
Cognitive Level: Analysis
Nursing Process: Evaluation
Client Need: Health Promotion and Maintenance; Prevention and/or Early Detection of Health Problems

32-2. Answers: 2, 5, and 7
Rationale: Tetraplegia and loss of motor function are associated with injuries above the first thoracic vertebra. Loss of biceps reflex occurs with injuries in the fifth or sixth cervical vertebrae. Sensation below the waist does not occur in injuries above the twelfth vertebra. Bladder function is only spared in injuries lower than the second sacral vertebra, possibly as high as the fourth lumbar vertebra. Sensation to the shoulders is preserved in any injury below the fifth cervical vertebra. Injuries above the second, third, or fourth lumbar vertebrae result in loss of knee jerk reflex.

Cognitive Level: Application
Nursing Process: Assessment
Client Need: Physiological Integrity; Physiological Adaptation

32-3. Answer: 2
Rationale: A nasogastric or oral gastric tube is inserted during the acute phase of spinal cord injury care to decompress the stomach, thus minimizing abdominal distension and the risks of vomiting and aspiration. Incentive spirometry and chest physiotherapy help improve pulmonary function and promote airway clearance, which can aid in the prevention of atelectasis and pneumonia. Pulmonary embolism can be prevented by methods that reduce the formation of deep vein thrombosis, such as antiembolic hose or anticoagulant therapy. Good nutrition is important in aiding against pressure ulcer formation, and increased caloric, protein, and micronutrient intake are used to aid in wound healing and the promotion of good skin integrity. Increased fiber and fluid intake would help promote bowel evacuation and prevent constipation. The use of clean intermittent catheterization and post void residual measurements does help ensure adequate bladder emptying, which can, in turn, also help prevent many genitourinary complications like urinary tract infections and renal calculi. It does not prevent or treat neurogenic shock.
Cognitive Level: Analysis
Nursing Process: Intervention
Client Need: Physiological Integrity; Physiological Adaptation

32-4. Answer: 3
Rationale: The identification of supportive resources for physical and psychological changes after a spinal cord injury is imperative for the patient and his or her family at discharge. Spinal cord injuries can be very stressful for patients and their families, and patients can feel any number of negative emotions such as denial, anger, grief, hopelessness, and depression. These patients are often under tremendous strain from loss of body image and independence, lifestyle changes, and loss of control over the immediate environment. The nurse should carefully monitor the patient for signs of inadequate coping such as withdrawing from social interactions, avoiding eye contact, and refusing to participate in activities. Maintaining good eye contact and participating in social situations would be signs of effective coping.
Cognitive Level: Analysis
Nursing Process: Evaluation
Client Need: Psychosocial Integrity; Coping and Adaptation

32-5. Answer: 2
Rationale: Safety is a big concern for patients after spinal cord injury, and the proper use of adaptive equipment and transfer strategies can prevent patient injury. A multidisciplinary rehabilitative approach is used to help patients with spinal cord injury become as independent as possible and aid in their reintegration back into their home and community. Proper skin care such as regular baths and frequent position changes are the best ways to prevent pressure ulcer formation. Using clean intermittent catheterization promotes a means of regular urinary management and helps avoid urinary tract infection. This can reduce the risk of developing autonomic hyperreflexia, but it will not affect constipation. A good bowel management regimen is the best way to preclude constipation and bowel impaction.
Cognitive Level: Application
Nursing Process: Evaluation
Client Need: Physiological Integrity; Reduction of Risk Potential

32-6. Answer: 4
Rationale: By auscultating the bowel sounds, the nurse is evaluating gastrointestinal function, and a dietary consult will help determine the patient's nutritional needs. Using antiembolic hose and prophylactic anticoagulant medications limits blood pooling in the lower extremities and prevents the formation of clots, respectively. Administration of oxygen aids the patient's oxygenation status, and close monitoring of hemodynamics allows for early recognition and treatment of changes. These things are important for the patient's breathing and circulation. However, airway (with cervical spine immobilization in trauma situations) is always the first priority for any patient. Therefore, if the patient has a known injury to the sixth cervical vertebra great care should be exercised to maintain spinal alignment and avoid mechanical injury to the spine. Also, institution of a thorough pulmonary toilet helps maintain effective airway clearance and gas exchange.
Cognitive Level: Application
Nursing Process: Implementation
Client Need: Physiological Integrity; Physiological Adaptation

Chapter 33 – Nursing Assessment of Patients with Respiratory Disorders

Key Terms Matching Exercise 1

1.	e	**6.**	b
2.	f	**7.**	j
3.	g	**8.**	a
4.	d	**9.**	h
5.	c	**10.**	i

Key Terms Matching Exercise 2

11.	b	**16.**	i
12.	f	**17.**	d
13.	c	**18.**	a
14.	g	**19.**	h
15.	e		

True or False?

20.	T	**27.**	T
21.	T	**28.**	F
22.	F	**29.**	T
23.	T		
24.	F		
25.	F		
26.	T		

Labeling Exercise 1: Ribs and Interspaces in Respiratory Assessment

a. Suprasternal notch
b. Sternal angle
c. 2nd rib
d. 2nd interspace
e. 2nd costal cartilage
f. Costochondral junctions

g. Costal angle
h. Costal margin
i. Xiphoid process
j. Body of sternum
k. Manubrium of sternum

Labeling Exercise 2: Lobes of the Lung (Anterior)

a. Left oblique fissure
b. 6th rib midclavicular line
c. Right oblique fissure
d. 5th rib midaxillary line
e. Horizontal fissure
f. 4th rib

Labeling Exercise 3: Lobes of the Lungs (Posterior)

a. T3
b. T10
c. T12
d. Oblique fissure

NCLEX-RN® Review Questions

Question numbers correspond to Outcome-Based Learning Objectives for this chapter.

33-1. Answer: 4

Rationale: Pleural friction rubs are low-pitched, creaking, or squeaking sounds that occur when inflamed pleural surfaces rub together during respiration. They are most easily heard on inspiration. The pitch of the sound usually increases with chest expansion. To determine if the sound is due to pleural or pericardial friction, have the patient hold his breath. The pericardial friction rub will continue with each heart beat, whereas the pleural friction rub will not occur when the patient is not actively breathing. Crackles are sounds caused by fluid in the airways. They are described as intermittent or discontinuous, nonmusical, or popping sounds. They are caused by fluid, inflammation, infection, or secretions. Wheezes are high pitched musical sounds caused by air flowing across strands of mucous, swollen pulmonary tissue, which narrows the airway, or from bronchospasm. Bronchovesicular breath sounds are normal breath sounds.
Cognitive Level: Application
Nursing Process: Assessment
Client Need: Health Promotion and Maintenance; Prevention and/or Early Detection of Health Problems

33-2. Answer: 4

Rationale: High altitude pulmonary edema can occur in persons who are not acclimated and travel to altitudes greater than 5000 feet. As altitude increases atmospheric pressure decreases, and oxygen available in air also decreases. Persons with preexisting illness may develop rapid onset of hypoxemia related to the decreased oxygen levels. Compensatory increases in respiratory rate to compensate for the decreased available oxygen may contribute to fatigue and further respiratory insufficiency. Compensatory mechanisms cause initial pulmonary vascular vasoconstriction. Later, inflammatory mediators cause vasodilation. The alveolar-capillary membrane becomes more permeable in response to these mediators and engorges with fluid causing pulmonary edema.
Cognitive Level: Analysis
Nursing Process: Assessment
Client Need: Health Promotion and Maintenance; Prevention and/or Early Detection of Health Problems

33-3. Answer: 1

Rationale: Occupational asthma may occur in many settings. Persons who work around animals are exposed to dander, hair, and allergens picked up from the environment. Any occupation in which workers come into contact with fumes or vapors may provoke occupational asthma. This includes cleaning solvents, which are utilized in all work environments and the home as well. Early recognition, diagnosis, and treatment of occupational asthma can prevent pulmonary complications. Although knowing the patient's occupation could aid in determining the socioeconomic status or the number of hours the patient stands while at work, this is not the purpose of the information at this time.
Cognitive Level: Analysis
Nursing Process: Assessment
Client Need: Health Promotion and Maintenance; Prevention and/or Early Detection of Health Problems

33-4. Answer: 4

Rationale: Tactile fremitus is palpated over the thorax by having the patient vocalize the words "ninety-nine." Voice vibrations from the large airways are transmitted to the surface skin of the thorax. The vibrations should be strongest over the large airways on the upper thorax and decrease in strength when assessing down the thorax. Unequal fremitus may be due to unilateral airway obstruction, pneumothroax, or pleural effusion causing a decrease in fremitus on the side with the defect. Increased fremitus is seen with consolidation or pneumonia and an increase in fremitus is felt over these areas.
Cognitive Level: Analysis
Nursing Process: Assessment
Client Need: Health Promotion and Maintenance; Prevention and/or Early Detection of Health Problems

33-5. Answer: 2

Rationale: Capnography is the measurement of exhaled carbon dioxide. Small disposable capnographers are utilized to test endotracheal tube placement utilizing treated paper that changes color in the presence of an acid such as carbon dioxide. Some machines also measure amounts of carbon dioxide in exhaled breath through spectography. Capnography waveforms and CO_2 values are useful in determining the patient's ventilatory status and readiness for extubation or pulmonary vessel perfusion in patients with pulmonary embolus. The oxygen saturation measured by pulse oximetry does not necessarily provide the same values obtained from the calculated oxygen saturation obtained from an ABG. Peak flow meters are utilized to determine trends in a patient's condition or to evaluate air movement to determine severity of asthma exacerbation. ABG studies are utilized to provide information on arterial oxygen and carbon dioxide levels.
Cognitive Level: Application
Nursing Process: Assessment
Client Need: Physiological Integrity; Reduction of Risk Potential

Chapter 34 – Caring for the Patient with Upper Airway Disorders

Key Terms Matching Exercise

1.	b	6.	c
2.	f	7.	j
3.	a	8.	e
4.	d	9.	h
5.	i	10.	g

Key Term Crossword

Short Answer Questions

11. Both allergic rhinitis and sinusitis have the symptoms of coughing, congestion, nasal discharge (runny nose), and headache. Sinusitis can also include fever, weakness, and fatigue, as well as pressure in some areas of the face, especially when leaning forward.

12. Risk factors for mucormycosis include:
- Diabetes mellitus
- Iron overload
- Burns
- Leukemia
- Lymphoma
- Transplantation
- Immunosuppression
- Prolonged neutropenia
- Chemotherapy
- High-dose steroids
- Donor leukocyte infusions
- AIDS
- Intravenous drug use

13. Treatment for sleep apnea includes:
- Weight loss
- Avoidance of alcohol, tobacco, and sleeping pills
- Sleeping in a side-lying position
- Use of a dental device that moves the tongue or mandible forward
- Continuous positive airway pressure (CPAP) while sleeping
- A surgical procedure known as uvulovelopalatopharyngoplasty (UVPPP)
- Surgically advancing the tongue and maxillary/mandibular bone complex

14. The most critical nursing intervention for the patient with paralysis of the vocal cords is preventing aspiration. To do this, the nurse can have the patient sit upright in a chair to eat and stay with the patient to observe for coughing or frequent throat clearing after swallowing. If the patient appears to be having significant problems with fluids or foods, the tray should be taken away and the patient's response to eating should be reported to the health care provider and documented.

15. Risk factors for head and neck cancer include:
- Alcohol consumption
- Ultraviolet light exposure
- Tobacco use
- Irritation to the lining of the mouth
- Poor nutrition
- Human papillomavirus (HPV) infection
- Immune system suppression
- Male gender

Labeling Exercise 1: Anatomical Relationship Between Nasal Bones, Cartilage, and Septum

a. Nasal bone
b. Frontal process of maxilla

    c. Upper lateral cartilage
    d. Fibroareolar tissue
    e. Medial and lateral crusa of lower lateral cartilage
    f. Medial crus
    g. Lateral crus
    h. Septal cartilage

Labeling Exercise 2: Sites of Sinusitis

    a. Frontal sinus
    b. Ethmoid sinus
    c. Maxillary sinus
    d. Sinusitis

NCLEX-RN® Review Questions

Question numbers correspond to Outcome-Based Learning Objectives for this chapter.

34-1. Answer: 1

Rationale: Management of temporal bone fractures usually is conservative. The nurse must continually assess for nerve damage and hearing loss. It is essential to test for any otorrhea significant for a CSF leak. In the interim the nurse should institute CSF leak precautions. With mandibular fractures, care is focused on nutrition and dental hygiene. Care of the patient with a transverse fracture includes hearing assessment, facial nerve integrity, and eye protection. Care of the patient with a frontal facial fracture includes an assessment of the entire body and implementing established protocols for treating major facial injuries. The nurse must be alert to patency of airway, bleeding, swelling, pain, and possible other injuries.
Cognitive Level: Analysis
Nursing Process: Implementation
Client Need: Physiological Integrity; Reduction of Risk Potential

34-2. Answer: 4

Rationale: Postoperative care is important if the patient is experiencing acute sinusitis requiring surgical intervention. This includes educating the patient as to signs and symptoms of potential complications contingent on the type of surgery that was performed. Nursing interventions and evaluation include patient education relative to the cause of the sinusitis and how to avoid the triggers: air pollution, diving, underwater swimming, and known allergens and irritants. The teaching plan should focus on the causes of the sinusitis and events that brought the patient in for care.
Cognitive Level: Application
Nursing Process: Planning
Client Need: Physiological Integrity; Reduction of Risk Potential

34-3. Answer: 3

Rationale: Nursing management of patients with rhinitis is very similar to medical management. One can often take over-the-counter (non-prescription) medications, which relieve mild to moderate symptoms but tend to cause drowsiness. Longer acting antihistamines that require prescriptions, and nasal corticosteroid sprays and decongestants are useful in relieving symptoms. A patient with allergic rhinitis should be instructed to wash bed linens, avoid animal dander, and avoid excessive humidity and standing water.
Cognitive Level: Application
Nursing Process: Implementation
Client Need: Health Promotion and Maintenance; Prevention/Early Detection of Health Problems

34-4. Answer: 3

Rationale: The mainstay of treatment for mucormycosis is early aggressive surgical intervention to remove all dead and infected tissue. Surgery is disfiguring because it may involve the removal of the palate, nasal, and orbital structures. Reconstructive surgery is inevitable. During postoperative care of the patient, the nurse should be particularly sensitive to the fear and anxiety related to possible/potential disfigurement.
Cognitive Level: Application
Nursing Process: Implementation
Client Need: Psychosocial Integrity; Coping and Adaptation

34-5. Answer: 4

Rationale: This patient could be experiencing edema of the larynx. The priority for nursing management is to summon medical assistance and support the patient's airway until expert assistance arrives. The nurse should place a tracheostomy insertion tray at the bedside, elevate the head of the bed, monitor oxygen saturations, and provide supplemental oxygen. If the obstruction is severe and the patient does not respond rapidly enough to medications, a tracheotomy can establish an airway until the edema resolves.
Cognitive Level: Application
Nursing Process: Implementation
Client Need: Physiological Integrity; Physiological Adaptation

34-6. Answer: 3

Rationale: Alcohol intake and use of tobacco products increases the risk of developing head and neck cancer. There is no evidence to suggest that genetic testing can predict the onset of this type of cancer. The nurse should not tell the patient that nothing can be done to reduce the risk of developing this type of cancer. Poor nutrition is a risk factor for the development of this disease and is linked to low intake of fruit and vegetables.
Cognitive Level: Application
Nursing Process: Implementation
Client Need: Health Promotion and Maintenance; Prevention/Early Detection of Health Problems

34-7. Answer: 1

Rationale: Following cancer resection or during radiation therapy, nutrition consults are very helpful in targeting goals of maintenance and replenishment. In a patient with an artificial airway, water loss is about 500–600 mL insensible volume with an additional 600–700 mL per day with suctioning. Replacement requirements need to be carefully calculated in order to ensure proper hydration. The choice of feeding method, whether oral or enteral, is dependent on the patient's level of consciousness and ability to swallow. Nutrition replacement must begin early and be continuous throughout the therapy for cancer. Most feeding can begin on postoperative day 1 and be advanced to goal as quickly as tolerated. Swallowing is difficult because of tumor burden, invasion of the aerodigestive tract, and pain. Aspiration is a significant concern when a patient is unable to maintain airway protection. Enteral feeding routes are used as most head and neck cancer patients have intact and functioning gastrointestinal systems. Once the patient is able to take oral food the process needs to begin slowly with careful monitoring of tolerance and risk for aspiration.
Cognitive Level: Application
Nursing Process: Planning
Client Need: Physiological Integrity; Basic Care and Comfort

Chapter 35 – Caring for the Patient with Lower Airway Disorders

Key Terms Matching Exercise 1

1.	c	**8.**	a
2.	e	**9.**	g
3.	b	**10.**	l
4.	h	**11.**	d
5.	j	**12.**	k
6.	m	**13.**	i
7.	f		

Key Terms Matching Exercise 2

14.	g	**21.**	i
15.	a	**22.**	d
16.	c	**23.**	m
17.	f	**24.**	k
18.	b	**25.**	h
19.	j	**26.**	e
20.	l		

Short Answer Questions

27. Acute bronchitis can be triggered by viruses (e.g., adenovirus, rhinovirus, and influenza types A and B), bacterias (e.g., *Streptococcus pneumoniae, Haemophilus influenzae*), yeast and fungi (e.g., *Candida albicans*), and pollutants (e.g., asthma, air pollutants, ammonia, and tobacco).

28. Symptoms of pneumonia include fever, chills, increased respiratory rates, rusty, bloody sputum, crackles, and x-ray abnormalities. Symptoms of intrinsic diseases include progressive exertional dyspnea, which is the predominant symptom; a dry cough (a productive cough is an unusual sign in most patients); and hemoptysis or grossly bloody sputum, which occurs in patients with diffuse alveolar hemorrhage syndromes and vasculitis. Wheezing is an uncommon manifestation and chest pain also is uncommon, but pleuritic chest pain may occur in patients with rheumatoid arthritis, systemic lupus erythematosus, and some drug-induced disorders.

29. Risk factors for idiopathic pulmonary fibrosis include:
- Cigarette smoking
- Exposure to commonly prescribed drugs, such as antidepressants
- Chronic aspiration
- Environmental factors, such as metal dust and wood dust, solvents
- Infectious agents, such as Epstein–Barr virus, influenza, cytomegalovirus, hepatitis C, and HIV
- Genetic predisposition, based on familial cases of IPF

30. Usually chronic bronchitis and emphysema, two specific disorders, are not seen as distinct clinical entities. Instead, they coexist in many patients, although one disease may be predominant. Unifying symptoms of these two entities are dyspnea, wheezing, and use of accessory muscles. Chronic bronchitis is defined clinically as the presence of a chronic productive cough for 3 months during each of 2 consecutive years (other causes of cough being excluded). Emphysema is defined as an abnormal, permanent enlargement of the air spaces distal to the terminal bronchioles, accompanied by destruction of their walls and without obvious fibrosis. Chronic bronchitis is defined in clinical terms and emphysema in terms of anatomic pathology. Both conditions are characterized by obstruction of airflow through the airways and out of the lungs. The obstruction generally is permanent and progressive over time.

31. Diagnostic tests for asthma are the sputum gram stain and culture; FEV_1 (volume of air that the patient can forcibly exhale in 1 second) to FVC (forced vital capacity), a CBC, and ABG study.

32. The most common risk factors for PE are a prior history of DVT or PE, recent surgery or pregnancy, prolonged immobilization, or underlying malignancy. Risks for PE include situations in which there is venous stasis or in which there is increased hypercoagulability or a clotting tendency of the blood. Aside from prolonged bed rest, inactivity may include long trips in planes, cars, and trains. Other causes are oral contraceptive use, surgery especially involving the pelvic area, massive trauma, burns, cancer, stroke, myocardial infarction, and fractures of the hips or femur.

33. The most common presenting symptoms for pulmonary hypertension are exertional dyspnea, fatigue and lethargy, angina, syncope, Raynaud's disease, and edema.

34. The primary role of the nurse is managing dyspnea by administration of oxygen and medications to treat right ventricular hypertrophy and pulmonary hypertension. This includes medications that treat the underlying disease. Patient education is another major role of the nurse. The nurse teaches the patient and caregiver to be comfortable managing oxygen equipment and medications.

35. The most common carcinogens for lung cancer are tobacco smoke, radon, and asbestos. Smoking accounts for 87% of all lung cancer deaths (ACS, 2006); approximately 3,000 of these cases are due to environmental tobacco smoke (ETS), commonly referred to as "secondhand smoke." Exposure to radon, a colorless, odorless, radioactive gas, occurs in places where there is reduced air turnover and ventilation, as in underground mines. Asbestos can still be found in products such as gaskets and roofing and friction items.

36. There is no medical treatment for occupational lung diseases.

True or False?

37.	F	**42.**	F
38.	T	**43.**	T
39.	F	**44.**	F
40.	T	**45.**	F
41.	T	**46.**	T

Labeling Exercise 1: Pleural Effusion

- **a.** Trachea
- **b.** Hilum
- **c.** Lung
- **d.** Diaphragm
- **e.** Pleural effusion
- **f.** Visceral pleura
- **g.** Parietal pleura
- **h.** Rib
- **i.** Visceral pleura
- **j.** Pleural space
- **k.** Parietal pleura

NCLEX-RN® Review Questions

Question numbers correspond to Outcome-Based Learning Objectives for this chapter.

35-1. Answer: 4

> **Rationale:** Chronic bronchitis is defined as hypersecretion of mucus and chronic productive cough that continues at least 3 months of the year for at least 2 consecutive years. Symptoms are usually in the winter months. In chronic bronchitis infection, bronchial irritants contribute to increased secretions, edema, bronchospasm, and impaired mucociliary clearance. The mucus secretions are thicker and more tenacious than normal.
> **Cognitive Level:** Analysis
> **Nursing Process:** Assessment
> **Client Need:** Physiological Integrity; Physiological Adaptation

35-2. Answer: 1

> **Rationale:** The signs and symptoms of pulmonary tuberculosis are insidious and many patients do not become aware of symptoms until the disease is well advanced. Typically, the patient presents with lethargy, exhaustive fatigue, activity intolerance, nausea, irregular menses, and low-grade fever, which may have occurred for weeks or months. Fever also may be accompanied by night sweats. The patient finally notices a cough and the production of mucoid and mucopurulent sputum, which is occasionally streaked with blood. Nursing care for the TB patient focuses on preventing the spread of the infection, assisting the patient and family to manage the environment, and prescribed chemotherapy.
> **Cognitive Level:** Application
> **Nursing Process:** Implementation
> **Client Need:** Physiological Integrity; Physiological Adaptation

35-3. Answer: 2

> **Rationale:** It is vital that the patients employ strategies to clear pulmonary secretions to prevent complications arising from airway plugging by viscous secretions. Chest physical therapy includes percussion and postural drainage performed regularly. Patients with cystic fibrosis should maintain a twice-daily routine of chest physical therapy. During periods of an exacerbation, the regimen should be performed more frequently. Fatigue and weakness related to an exacerbation of cystic fibrosis may render a young adult incapable of performing the treatment regime independently. The family should be included in all patient education and discharge planning. This includes instruction regarding the chest physical therapy regime, oral or intravenous medications, aerosols, and breathing treatments.
> **Cognitive Level:** Application
> **Nursing Process:** Planning
> **Client Need:** Physiological Integrity; Physiological Adaptation

35-4. Answer: 2

> **Rationale:** With a hemothorax, the nurse assesses vital signs regularly in order to establish blood loss and replenish blood and fluids. If a chest tube is placed, the nurse assesses for an excessive amount of bloody drainage in a short period and a repeat chest x-ray should be done in a few hours. It is likely that the hemothorax associated with a blunt trauma or injury might be treated in the emergency room setting. The chest tube is placed by the physician and the nurse assists with the procedure, continually assessing vital signs and patient status.
> **Cognitive Level:** Application
> **Nursing Process:** Implementation
> **Client Need:** Physiological Integrity; Physiological Adaptation

35-5. Answer: 2

> **Rationale:** Infection postoperatively is the leading cause of morbidity and mortality. Viral infection with cytomegalovirus and herpes simplex occur frequently. Patients are treated with antibiotics empirically to prevent infection. The use of bronchodilator drugs and respiratory therapies to provide clearance of secretions are continued as a component of the patient routine. Acute rejection may occur as soon as 5 to 7 days after the transplant. Symptoms of rejection include fever, chills, flu-like aches, shortness of breath, decreased urine output, and pain over the transplanted lung.
> **Cognitive Level:** Analysis
> **Nursing Process:** Planning
> **Client Need:** Physiological Integrity; Physiological Adaptation

35-6. Answer: 2

> **Rationale:** Physical conditioning and breathing exercises are helpful. Oxygen provides relief from dyspnea. Fluids should be taken liberally to allow for liquefication of sputum. The nurse should help the patient address emotional issues such as depression, anxiety, and anger.
> **Cognitive Level:** Application
> **Nursing Process:** Implementation
> **Client Need:** Physiological Integrity; Physiological Adaptation

Chapter 36 – Caring for the Patient with Complex Respiratory Disorders

Key Terms Matching Exercise 1

1.	h	**6.**	a
2.	d	**7.**	f
3.	j	**8.**	c
4.	i	**9.**	g
5.	e	**10.**	b

Key Terms Matching Exercise 2

11.	e	**16.**	h
12.	i	**17.**	j
13.	c	**18.**	b
14.	a	**19.**	g
15.	f	**20.**	d

Key Terms Matching Exercise 3

21.	f	**25.**	b
22.	d	**26.**	g
23.	a	**27.**	e
24.	h	**28.**	c

Complete the Sentence

29. cough
30. hypoxemic, hypercapneic, central nervous system
31. endotracheal intubation
32. heart, lungs
33. injury, alveolar-capillary membrane
34. functional residual capacity

35. pneumonia
36. aspiration
37. COPD, cardiogenic pulmonary edema, immunocompromised
38. suctioning

True or False?

39.	T	**44.**	T
40.	T	**45.**	F
41.	T	**46.**	T
42.	F	**47.**	T
43.	F	**48.**	F

Labeling Exercise 1: Alveoli with Bronchioles

a. Primary bronchus
b. Secondary bronchus
c. Tertiary bronchus
d. Bronchiole
e. Terminal bronchiole
f. Alveoli

Labeling Exercise 2: Alveolar-Capillary Membrane

a. Interstitial space
b. Capillary endothelium
c. Red blood cell
d. Capillary
e. Capillary basement membrane
f. Fluid and surfactant layer
g. Alveolus
h. Epithelial basement membrane
i. Alveolar epithelium

NCLEX-RN® Review Questions

Question numbers correspond to Outcome-Based Learning Objectives for this chapter.

36-1. Answer: 2
Rationale: Hypoxemic respiratory failure is seen in pneumothorax. Hypercapneic respiratory failure is seen in oversedation, obesity, and diaphragmatic fatigue. Nervous system causes of respiratory failure are seen in cervical spinal cord injury, Guillian-Barré Syndrome, and Myasthenia gravis.
Cognitive Level: Analysis
Nursing Process: Assessment
Client Need: Physiological Integrity; Physiological Adaptation

36-2. Answer: 2
Rationale: The patient with acute pulmonary edema develops a cough and production of pink, frothy sputum, which are the classic presenting signs of pulmonary edema. Green or yellow colored sputum usually indicates an infectious process such as pneumonia. Rust brown sputum is not indicative of pulmonary edema, and most patients have clear, thin sputum, which has no defining diagnosis.
Cognitive Ability: Analysis
Nursing Process: Assessment
Client Need: Physiological Integrity; Physiological Adaptation

36-3. Answer: 1
Rationale: Non-cardiogenic pulmonary edema is a wide spectrum of diseases that is caused by either direct or indirect injury of the pulmonary capillary membrane that allows fluids to leak into the interstitial space and then into the alveoli. Another name for non-cardiogenic pulmonary edema is non-hydrostatic pulmonary edema. Many reasons cause the client to have NCPE. Agents such as chemicals can cause severe swelling of the respiratory tract, upper airways, and lungs. The subsequent pulmonary edema that develops from the injury caused by these agents produces dyspnea, shortness of breath, and death if the inhalation is severe. These agents include ammonia, bromine, chlorine, hydrogen chlorine, phosgene, phosphine, and phosphorus. They can be inhaled as a result of an accidental exposure or because of bioterrorism. All these agents produce an injury to the lung tissue and if severe enough death. Together these agents are termed pulmonary edemagens.
Cognitive Ability: Analysis
Nursing Process: Planning
Client Need: Physiological Integrity; Physiological Adaptation

36-4. Answer: 3
Rationale: The patient at the greatest risk for developing ARDS is the patient that has chest trauma with lung contusions, aspiration, and infectious causes, such as pneumonia. This is considered the direct injury category. Aspiration of gastric secretions is one of the most common causes of acute lung injury. These entities can cause direct injury to the airways and parenchyma of the lung. In the indirect category, there are many nonpulmonary etiologies that result in acute respiratory failure. These indirect causes of acute lung injury require the action of intermediary substances that cause the lung injury. These intermediary substances are host defenses that are released when tissue is injured and when inflammation occurs. The other patient's disease processes do not have a specific link with ARDS.
Cognitive Ability: Analysis
Nursing Process: Planning
Client Need: Physiological Integrity; Physiological Adaptation

36-5. Answer: 2
Rationale: The complications of treatment PEEP, that is, PEEP greater than 5 cm of H_2O, are decreased cardiac output, and at higher levels of PEEP, pneumothorax. These complications usually are not seen at PEEP set at 5 cm of H_2O. The nurse should be aware of the level of PEEP and if none is set ask the medical team for the reason. PEEP does not have anything to do with pneumonia, and PEEP should decrease hypoxia in patients by preventing pressure in the alveoli from dropping at the end of expiration.
Cognitive Ability: Implementation
Nursing Process: Assessment
Client Need: Physiological Integrity; Physiological Adaptation

36-6. Answer: 1
Rationale: Most ventilated patients should have PEEP of at least 5 cm of H_2O to prevent the pressure in the alveoli from dropping to zero at the end of expiration. The nurse can cause auto-PEEP with overaggressive rates with an air-mask-bag-unit (AMBU). The patient is removed from the ventilator for transport or for suctioning. Rapid rates are used to bag the patient instead of the rate that was set on the ventilator. The patient might become hypotensive. The patient's intake and output should be monitored, but this does not always relate to renal failure. The patient's lung sounds should be assessed, but adventitious lung sounds could indicate many disorders. The physician often orders sedation, but the patient should have spontaneous respirations when possible to prevent

complications associated with prolonged intubation such as VAP.
Cognitive Ability: Analysis
Nursing Process: Planning
Client Need: Physiological Integrity; Physiological Adaptation

36-7. Answer: 3
Rationale: Supplies needed to intubate a patient include: laryngoscope blade, flexible stylet, AMBU bag, oxygen source, swivel adapter, nonsterile gloves, Yankuer suction apparatus, suction catheter, endotracheal tube securing apparatus or tape, stethoscope, water-soluble lubricant (not oil soluble), sedative per MD orders, Magill forceps, and ventilator.
Cognitive Ability: Application
Nursing Process: Implementation
Client Need: Physiological Integrity; Physiological Adaptation

36-8. Answer: 1
Rationale: In order to perform tracheostomy suctioning, the nurse or caregiver should wear sterile gloves in order to prevent nosocomial infections. The patient should be oxygenated prior to suctioning with 100% oxygen and the patient's head should be elevated at least 30–45 degrees. The patient should always be pre-oxygenated to prevent

hypoxemia as well. The nurse/caregiver should never suction going into the tracheostomy, only while withdrawing the catheter.
Cognitive Ability: Application
Nursing Process: Evaluation
Client Need: Physiological Integrity; Physiological Adaptation

36-9. Answer: 3
Rationale: The nurse should initially see the client with the chest tube. A pleural tube is inserted in the pleural space in order to evacuate the air or blood and allow the lung to re-expand. The pleural tube recreates the negative pressure in the chest that has been violated by trauma or surgery. A pleural chest tube should not bubble in the water seal chamber.
Cognitive Ability: Application
Nursing Process: Planning
Client Need: Physiological Integrity; Physiological Adaptation

Chapter 37 – Nursing Assessment of Patients with Cardiovascular Disorders

Key Term Crossword

Short Answer Questions

1. The most common cardiovascular symptoms are chest pain, palpitations, dyspnea, orthopnea, cough, and nocturia.

2. Modifiable risk factors include cigarette smoking, hypertension (HTN), hypercholesterolemia, physical inactivity, diabetes, stress, and obesity.

3. There is a physiological significance in distinguishing between jugular venous distention (JVD) and jugular venous pressure (JVP). Anatomically, the right jugular veins drain blood from the head into the right atrium of the heart. Both veins reflect activity on the right side of the heart. The internal jugular vein lies in a straight path to the right atrium, but because it is buried beneath the sternomastoid muscle, it is difficult to visualize. The external jugular vein curves a few times before entering the right atrium, and because it is located closer to the skin it is easier to visualize.

4. The assessment of the abdominojugular reflux (sometimes called hepatojugular reflux) can also be used as a noninvasive technique to assess cardiovascular volume status.

5. Two heart sounds can be heard with each cardiac cycle. The first heart sound is referred to as S_1 and the second heart sound, S_2. S_1 is a called a systolic sound because it signals the beginning of systole. When the pressures in the pulmonary artery and the right ventricle begin to equalize, and the pressures in the aorta and the left ventricle begin to equalize, systolic ejection tapers off and the semilunar valves snap shut. This signals the beginning of diastole, which allows the AV valves to open and diastolic ventricular filling to begin. The closing of the AV valves is heard as the S_2, or second heart sound.

Labeling Exercise 1: Diagram of the Heart in Chest

a. Suprasternal notch
b. Angle of Louis
c. 3rd rib
d. Intercostal space
e. Diaphragm

Labeling Exercise 2: Layers of the Heart

a. Endocardium
b. Myocardium
c. Epicardium
d. Serous pericardium
e. Visceral
f. Parietal
g. Cavity of pericardial sac

Labeling Exercise 3: Coronary Arteries

a. Right coronary artery
b. Left main coronary artery
c. Circumflex coronary artery
d. Left anterior descending coronary artery

Labeling Exercise 4: Clinical Reference Points for Palpation

a. Right sternal border (RSB), 2nd intercostals space (ICS)
b. Left sternal border (LSB), 2nd ICS
c. LSB, 3rd ICS
d. LSB, 4th ICS
e. Midclavicular line (MCL), 5th ICS
f. Point of maximal impulse

Labeling Exercise 5: Cardiac Blood Flow Path

a. Cardiac blood flow paths
b. Pulmonary circulation
c. Left atrium
d. Left ventricle
e. Interventricular septum
f. Systemic atrial circulation
g. Systemic venous circulation
h. Right ventricle
i. Right atrium
j. Pulmonary circulation
k. Systemic venous circulation

NCLEX-RN® Review Questions

Question numbers correspond to Outcome-Based Learning Objectives for this chapter.

37-1. Answer: 2
Rationale: Criteria that are included for diagnosis of the metabolic syndrome include the blood pressure, HDL levels, triglyceride level, waist circumference, and fasting blood sugar.
Cognitive Level: Application
Nursing Process: Assessment
Client Need: Physiological Integrity; Physiological Adaptation

37-2. Answer: 3
Rationale: Having a relative less than 55 years old who has coronary heart disease, hypertension, myocardial infarction, stroke, diabetes, lipid disorders, or collagen disorders increase the risk of cardiovascular disease in close relatives. The parent who has had a stroke also reflects a risk, but it is not as great as the sibling who is 50 years old. Multiple sclerosis and peptic ulcer disease are not risk factors.
Cognitive Level: Analysis
Nursing Process: Assessment
Client Need: Health Promotion and Maintenance; Prevention and/or Early Detection of Health Problems

37-3. Answer: 1
Rationale: A systolic blood pressure of 120–139 and diastolic blood pressure of 80–88 mmHg is considered pre-hypertension and the patient should adopt lifestyle modifications such as weight loss, exercise, and dietary modifications to reduce saturated fats and sodium. The patient may not need to start on antihypertensive medication. A recheck of the blood pressure should be done after the patient has incorporated some lifestyle modifications. All salt does not have to be eliminated, but should be limited.
Cognitive Level: Application
Nursing Process: Implementation
Client Need: Health Promotion and Maintenance; Prevention and/or Early Detection of Health Problems

37-4. Answer: 3
Rationale: A pericardial friction rub is best heard with the patient leaning forward and on the left side.
Cognitive Level: Application
Nursing Process: Implementation
Client Need: Health Promotion and Maintenance; Prevention and/or Early Detection of Health Problems

Chapter 38 – Nursing Interpretation of the Electrocardiogram

Key Terms Matching Exercise 1

1.	d	**6.**	j
2.	b	**7.**	e
3.	g	**8.**	f
4.	c	**9.**	a
5.	i	**10.**	h

Key Terms Matching Exercise 2

11.	e	**16.**	i
12.	c	**17.**	g
13.	h	**18.**	f
14.	b	**19.**	d
15.	j	**20.**	a

Word Search

21. bundles	**27.** anion	**33.** excitability	**39.** asystole
22. atrial kick	**28.** sick sinus syndrome (SSS)	**34.** lead axis	**40.** AV dissociation
23. fascicles	**29.** cation	**35.** conductivity	**41.** bipolar lead
24. escape	**30.** electrode	**36.** contractility	**42.** atrial flutter
25. automaticity	**31.** J point	**37.** bigeminy	**43.** ectopic focus
26. ion	**32.** dysrhythmia	**38.** artifact	

S	A	I	I	A	T	R	I	A	L	F	L	U	T	T	E	R	Y	T	F
P	I	P	L	U	Y	T	Y	T	Y	U	I	B	L	N	E	A	A	E	R
O	B	C	E	E	A	R	S	F	S	S	T	I	W	R	U	S	A	D	R
K	C	I	K	L	A	I	R	T	A	Y	E	G	I	Y	P	T	D	D	R
T	S	E	U	S	N	D	Q	W	R	S	S	E	U	I	A	J	B	O	P
N	A	W	R	T	I	U	A	U	T	R	C	M	C	V	M	P	I	U	Y
O	S	U	Y	E	O	N	A	X	T	A	A	I	S	F	G	O	P	H	X
I	Y	A	T	D	N	R	U	P	I	T	P	N	C	A	T	I	O	N	Y
T	S	L	I	O	T	P	N	S	L	S	E	Y	P	L	O	N	L	T	T
A	T	A	L	R	M	O	A	E	S	U	L	A	R	R	E	T	A	A	I
I	O	N	I	T	R	A	I	U	A	Y	R	K	J	I	E	S	R	S	L
C	L	A	B	C	S	J	T	E	R	T	N	W	K	P	A	R	L	L	I
O	E	E	A	E	O	N	W	I	S	E	L	D	N	U	B	N	E	R	T
S	A	U	T	L	I	U	A	J	C	S	W	W	R	I	U	O	A	N	C
S	P	A	I	E	T	I	O	K	U	I	O	N	R	O	N	E	D	I	A
I	S	L	C	W	L	T	R	R	A	T	T	O	R	O	M	P	S	T	R
D	A	T	X	D	Y	S	R	H	P	C	S	Y	I	A	L	E	I	A	T
V	T	A	E	C	T	O	P	I	C	F	O	C	U	S	E	S	T	E	N
A	R	T	I	F	A	C	T	D	Y	S	R	H	Y	T	H	M	I	A	O
R	A	R	P	E	T	T	R	Y	T	I	V	I	T	C	U	D	N	O	C

Key Term Crossword

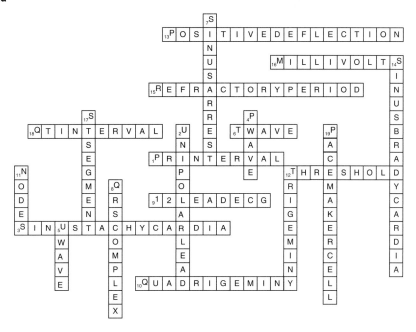

Labeling Exercise: Electrical Conduction System of the Heart

a. **sinoatrial (SA) node:** Part of the electrical conduction of the myocardium; located in the upper posterior portion of the right atrial wall near the opening of the vena cava. The SA node is commonly referred to as the primary pacemaker of the heart.

b. **atrioventricular (AV) node:** Node located on the floor of the right atrium just above the tricuspid valve. The AV node has three regions: the AV junctional tissue between the atria and the node; the nodal area between the junctional tissue and the bundle of His; and the AV junction, the region where the AV node joins the bundle of His.

c. **bundle of His:** Part of the conduction system that lies on top of the interventricular septum, between the right and left ventricles; it contains pacemaker cells. Also referred to as the *common bundle*.

d. **Purkinje network fibers:** Part of the cardiac conduction system; a network of fibers that carries impulses directly to the ventricular muscle cells. Ventricular contraction is facilitated by the rapid spread of the electrical impulse through the left and right bundle branches, the Purkinje network fibers, and the ventricular muscle.

e. **left bundle branch:** The left bundle is shorter than the right bundle and divides into pathways that spread from the left side of the interventricular septum throughout the left ventricle.

f. **right bundle branch:** The longer bundle.

Cardiac Waveform and Time Intervals Measured on ECG

P wave—The **P wave** represents contraction or depolarization of the atria. Both the right and left atria depolarize at the same time.

PR interval—The **PR interval,** sometimes referred to as the PRI or PR segment, represents the time it takes for the impulse to travel from the SA node down the intra-atrial pathways to the ventricles. In other words, it represents the beginning of the atrial contraction to the beginning of the ventricular contraction.

QRS complex—The **QRS complex** consists of the Q, R, and S waves, and represents the conduction of electrical impulses from the bundle of His near the AV junction to the Purkinje network fibers located in the ventricles, causing them to depolarize.

J point—The point at which the QRS meets the ST segment is called the J point.

ST segment—The **ST segment** is a line extending from the S wave that gradually curves upward to the T wave, represented on the ECG as an almost isoelectric line. The ST segment signifies ventricular repolarization.

T wave—The **T wave** is ventricular recovery or repolarization in the cardiac cycle. Both the absolute and the relative refractory periods are in place during the T wave.

U wave—The **U wave** is present only on some people's ECG. It follows the T wave. Its etiology is unknown, but it is frequently seen in exercise, in drug toxicity, and most frequently with low potassium levels.

Rhythm Strip Identification

a. artifact
b. normal sinus rhythm
c. sinus bradycardia
d. sinus tachycardia
e. sinus arrhythmia/dysrhythmia
f. sinus arrest (pause)
g. premature atrial contraction
h. atrial flutter
i. atrial fibrillation
j. supraventricular tachycardia
k. Wolff-Parkinson-White syndrome
l. wandering atrial pacemaker
m. sick sinus syndrome
n. junctional escape rhythm

o. accerated junctional rhythm
p. premature junctional contraction (PJC)
q. paroxysmal junctional tachycardia
r. first-degree AV block
s. Mobitz I/Wenckeback/ second-degree heart block
t. Mobitz II/second-degree heart block
u. third-degree (complete) heart block
v. bundle branch block
w. premature ventricular contractions (PVCs)
x. ventricular tachycardia
y. torsade de pointes
z. ventricular fibrillation

NCLEX-RN® Review Questions

Question numbers correspond to Outcome-Based Learning Objectives for this chapter.

38-1. Answer: 3

Rationale: The assessment of an electrocardiogram should be done as follows: Assess the P wave, ensuring that there is one P wave for every QRS complex. Assess the PR interval by measuring from the beginning of the P wave to the beginning of the QRS complex. Next assess the QRS complex by measuring from the beginning of the Q wave to the end of the S wave, remembering that not everyone has a discernable Q wave. Evaluate the QT interval by measuring from the Q wave to the end of the T wave. The heart rate is next measured by using the very top of the ECG paper, which is marked off in 3-second intervals with "tic" marks. The tic mark is a small straight line or hash mark above the tracing. Count up the number of PQRST complexes that occur in 6 seconds and multiply that number by 10. The heart rhythm is then determined by measuring the distance between two R waves and then measuring each subsequent R wave to ensure it is the same distance apart as the previous ones. With a regular rhythm the distance between the R waves is equal.
Cognitive Level: Analysis
Nursing Process: Assessment
Client Need: Physiological Integrity; Reduction of Risk Potential

38-2. Answer: 1

Rationale: This patient's heart rate is 150. The heart rate is calculated by counting the number of PQRST complexes that occur in six seconds and multiplying that number by 10. Sinus tachycardia is demonstrated by a pulse greater than 150 beats per minute with lower than normal blood pressure. The pulse rate in a wandering atrial pacemaker is between 40 to 60 beats per minute. In sick sinus syndrome, the pulse shows bradycardia alternating with tachycardia. The heart rate is irregular with premature junctional contractions.
Cognitive Level: Analysis
Nursing Process: Assessment
Client Need: Physiological Integrity; Reduction of Risk Potential

38-3. Answer: 3

Rationale: This patient is experiencing a junctional escape rhythm as evidenced by the slow heart rate, dizziness, and weakness. Treatment would include oxygen and atropine or dopamine. A pacemaker or cardioversion could also be a part of this patient's treatment. Vagal maneuvers are used to treat paroxysmal junctional tachycardia. A temporary pacemaker is used to treat third-degree atrioventricular block. Amiodarone is used to treat ventricular dysrhythmias.
Cognitive Level: Analysis
Nursing Process: Planning
Client Need: Physiological Integrity; Physiological Adaptation

38-4. Answer: 4

Rationale: The onset of Mobitz II and complete heart block are emergent situations that require immediate intervention. Mobitz II is described as a "treacherous and unpredictable" rhythm that can deteriorate to become a complete heart block. If untreated, these rhythms may progress to cardiac asystole and sudden death. At any indication of rhythm changes indicative of Mobitz II or complete heart block, the health care practitioner should be notified at once. The nurse should prepare for a temporary pacemaker insertion, which generally is indicated for these types of dysrhythmias. A permanent pacemaker may be necessary if the block persists. Observation is the treatment of choice for Mobitz Type I/Wenkebach. Magnesium is the treatment of choice for torsade de pointes. Amiodarone is indicated in the treatment of ventricular dysrhythmias.
Cognitive Level: Application
Nursing Process: Implementation
Client Need: Physiological Integrity; Physiological Adaptation

Chapter 39 – Diagnostic and Interventional Therapies for Cardiovascular Disorders

Key Terms Matching Exercise 1

1.	e	**6.**	g
2.	f	**7.**	c
3.	h	**8.**	d
4.	a	**9.**	j
5.	i	**10.**	b

Key Terms Matching Exercise 2

11.	b	**16.**	d
12.	e	**17.**	g
13.	a	**18.**	f
14.	i	**19.**	j
15.	h	**20.**	c

Key Term Crossword

13 Across: EXERCISETESTING
15 Across: CARDIOVERSION
1 Across: TOMOGRAPHY
10 Across: CAPTURE
4 Across: BRACHYTHERAPY
12 Across: STENT
14 Across: PREDICTIVEACCURACY

20 Down: MYOCARDIALPERFUSION
19 Down: CARDIACPACEMAKER
18 Down: HILTERMONITORING
7 Down: POSTTEST
9 Down: ABLATION
3 Down: DEFICIT
2 Down: POSTTESTICISION
16 Down: SPECICISION
5 Down: ECHOCARDIOGRAPHY
17 Down: REVASCULARIZATION
8 Down: MULTISLICE
6 Down: SENSITIVITY
11 Down: GRAPHITHERAPY

True or False?

21.	T	**26.**	T
22.	T	**27.**	F
23.	F	**28.**	T
24.	F	**29.**	T
25.	T	**30.**	F

Labeling Exercise: Pacemaker Components

a.	Pacemaker lead	**e.**	Anode
b.	Left atrium	**f.**	Right ventricle
c.	Left ventricle	**g.**	Right atrium
d.	Cathode	**h.**	Implantable generator

NCLEX-RN® Review Questions

Question numbers correspond to Outcome-Based Learning Objectives for this chapter.

39-1. Answer: 2

Rationale: Specificity is calculated by dividing the number of true negatives in the population by the sum of true negatives plus false positives. Thus, specificity describes the frequency with which the test is normal in subjects who are free of disease.

Cognitive Level: Application
Nursing Process: Implementation
Client Need: Health Promotion and Maintenance; Prevention and/or Early Detection of Health Problems

39-2. Answer: 1

Rationale: Coronary angiography provides only a two-dimensional image of the coronary artery lumen and provides no information regarding the arterial wall. Intravascular ultrasound (IVUS) fills that void. To obtain these images a small ultrasound catheter is threaded into a coronary artery. From it ultrasound images that provide 360-degree cross sectional images of the artery can be obtained. Important information can be gathered regarding not only the coronary lumen, but also the intima, media, and adventitia of the vessel wall. Percutaneous transluminal coronary angioplasty refers to treatment of CAD using expandable balloons to crack atherosclerotic plaque, thereby enlarging the lumen of the coronary artery. Left heart catheterization allows for the direct measurement of left heart pressures and pressures on both sides of the aortic valve, ventriculography to measure cardiac output and evaluation of both left ventricular function as well as the severity of any mitral or aortic valvular disease. Right heart catheterization allows for measurement and analysis of right heart pressures and oxygen saturations, pulmonary artery pressures including pulmonary capillary wedge pressures, screening for intracardiac shunts, and temporary ventricular pacing.

Cognitive Level: Application
Nursing Process: Planning
Client Need: Health Promotion and Maintenance; Prevention and/or Early Detection of Health Problems

39-3. Answer: 3

Rationale: There are a variety of clinical conditions that can be detected from the 12-lead ECG including effects from medications. This is the diagnostic test that should be done first to help this patient. This patient is not demonstrating any signs of valvular disease, coronary artery disease, chest pain, shortness of breath, exercise intolerance, or rhythm disturbances.

Cognitive Level: Analysis
Nursing Process: Assessment
Client Need: Health Promotion and Maintenance; Prevention and/or Early Detection of Health Problems

39-4. Answer: 1

Rationale: Technetium-99 is useful for imaging acute (emergency room) patients. Thallium-201 is not useful in evaluating chest pain in the emergency department. The TEE is not considered a cardiac nuclear study. The ECG single-photon emission computed tomography or SPECT obtains cardiac images by a rotating gamma camera that stops at preset angles to record the image.

Cognitive Level: Analysis
Nursing Process: Planning
Client Need: Physiological Integrity; Reduction of Risk Potential

39-5. Answer: 1

Rationale: Discharge instructions for a patient recovering from a cardiac catheterization include: assess the site daily; shower or bath as usual; no special dressing is needed; if the access site was in the groin, avoid bending over or straining for the first 48 hours; avoid heavy lifting for the first week; if bright red bleeding from the site occurs, lie down and have someone apply firm pressure just above the site for 20 minutes, then gently release the pressure. If the bleeding cannot be controlled, call 911.

Cognitive Level: Application
Nursing Process: Planning
Client Need: Physiological Integrity; Reduction of Risk Potential

Chapter 40 – Caring for the Patient with Coronary Artery Disease

Key Terms Matching Exercise 1

1.	i	**6.**	g
2.	e	**7.**	d
3.	c	**8.**	h
4.	j	**9.**	f
5.	b	**10.**	a

Key Terms Matching Exercise 2

11.	j	**16.**	g
12.	e	**17.**	c
13.	a	**18.**	h
14.	f	**19.**	b
15.	i	**20.**	d

Key Term Crossword

Short Answer Questions

21. Plaque pathogenesis is a response to injury to the vessel wall. Potential causes of injury include mechanical, chemical, immunologic, viral, bacterial, and subendothelial stressors. Once the endothelial lining has been injured, it undergoes a number of structural and functional changes. Vasoconstriction occurs in areas of vessel disruption. Smooth muscle extends into the inner layer of the vessel, decreasing the lumen of the artery and causing a loss of elasticity. The aggregation of platelets and coagulation factors further decreases the size of the lumen.

22. A stage I lesion has grossly visible yellow lesions, known as fatty streaks, in the intimal layer that cause little or no obstruction to coronary blood flow and therefore no symptoms. Stage II lesions are grossly white in appearance and most frequently develop where arteries bifurcate. Advanced or stage III lesions are plaque with a well-established fibrous cap and lipid core.

23. Modifiable risk factors for coronary artery disease are:
    - Elevated low density lipoprotein cholesterol (LDL-C)
    - Low high density lipoprotein cholesterol (HDL-C)
    - Triglycerides
    - Elevated total cholesterol
    - Hypertension
    - Tobacco smoke
    - Diabetes
    - Physical inactivity
    - Overweight and obesity

24. When cardiac tissue becomes ischemic, the ST segment becomes abnormal and indicates a total reduction in localized blood flow. Prolonged, persistent ST segment elevation indicates acute ischemia and injury/infarction, and is associated with elevated cardiac blood markers. With transmural injury, the ST segment begins to rise almost immediately and can remain elevated for several hours to several days, as long as the ischemia continues. As the ischemia/injury subsides, the ST segment returns to the baseline. Once the ST segment has returned to the baseline, one of the main indicators of the acute MI is lost.

25. Typical symptoms include chest pain, diaphoresis, shortness of breath, and generalized weakness. Patients describe the pain from an acute myocardial infarction (AMI) in the same terms as the pain from angina pectoris, only usually more intense and longer in duration.

26. Laboratory tests include myoglobin, cardiac enzymes (CK total, CK-MB), troponin (T or I), and possibly a C-reactive protein level. A 12-lead ECG is done to evaluate the electrical activity in the heart.

27. (1) Raise the amount of oxygenated blood delivered to the tissues with supplemental oxygen and blood transfusions; (2) relieve coronary smooth muscle vasoconstriction or spasm with vasodilators; (3) reperfuse ischemic tissue by dissolving thrombus with thrombolytic agents; (4) prevent thrombus formation with anticoagulant therapy; and (5) reestablish blood flow through invasive revascularization procedures such as coronary artery bypass graft surgery (CABG) and percutaneous coronary intervention (PCI).

28. Methods used to treat patients with ACS are activity progression, reducing autonomic stress responses, an intra-aortic balloon pump, beta- (β-) adrenergic blocking agents, angiotensin-converting enzyme inhibitors, angiotensin II receptor blockers, nitrate therapy, vasodilator therapy, thrombolytic agents, and anticoagulation therapy.

29. Post-AMI complications include recurrent chest pain from ischemia, pericarditis, heart failure, cardiogenic shock, dysrhythmias, infarct expansion, ventricular remodeling, left ventricular aneurysm and thrombus formation, mitral valve disruption, ventricular free wall rupture, and ventricular septal defect.

30. There must be substantial evidence that CABG will prolong survival.

True or False?

31. T
32. F
33. T
34. T
35. F
36. F
37. F
38. T
39. T
40. T
41. F

Increase or Decrease?

42. Increase
43. Increase
44. Decrease

45. Increase
46. Decrease
47. Decrease

Labeling Exercise 1: Normal Artery Layers

a. Internal elastic lumina
b. Tunica intima
c. Tunica media
d. Tunica adventitia

Labeling Exercise 2: Thrombosis in a Coronary Artery

a. Superior vena cava
b. Aorta
c. Pulmonary trunk
d. Left coronary artery
e. Right coronary artery
f. Coronary thrombosis
g. Right ventricle
h. Atherosclerosis w/thrombosis
i. Left ventricle
j. Fat
k. Inferior vena cava

NCLEX-RN® Review Questions

Question numbers correspond to Outcome-Based Learning Objectives for this chapter.

40-1. Answer: 2
Rationale: Smoking, hypertension, diabetes, obesity, and a high sedentary lifestyle are modifiable risk factors. Being 50 pounds overweight is a modifiable risk factor for this patient. Eating a high-fat, high-cholesterol diet has also been identified as a contributing risk factor to CAD. Being a male over 40 years of age and having a close relative with a history of CAD are nonmodifiable risk factors.
Cognitive Level: Application
Nursing Process: Planning
Client Need: Health Promotion and Maintenance; Reduction and/or Early Detection of Health Problems

40-2. Answer: 2
Rationale: Angina is frequently precipitated by activity, such as walking or climbing stairs. Pain that is fleeting, or comes and goes, and that lasts for days is usually not angina. Pain not relieved by nitroglycerin is more indicative of a myocardial infarction.
Cognitive Level: Application
Nursing Process: Assessment
Client Need: Physiological Integrity; Physiological Adaptation

40-3. Answer: 3
Rationale: Vasospastic angina is the most serious type of angina caused by vasospasm of the arteries and symptoms are often precipitated by exercise. Ingestion of a large meal can precipitate angina in general, but is not associated with vasospastic angina. Exposure to cold, not heat is known to precipitate angina. Ingestion of alcohol is not a trigger for angina.
Cognitive Level: Application
Nursing Process: Implementation
Client Need: Physiological Integrity; Physiological Adaptation

40-4. Answer: 1
Rationale: Marked T wave peaking is often present in the early stages of an acute MI. ST depression is seen with subendocardial injury. T wave inversion is present as the MI evolves and may stay inverted for weeks. A bundle branch block may occur following an MI, but is not diagnostic of having one.
Cognitive Level: Analysis
Nursing Process: Assessment
Client Need: Physiological Integrity; Reduction of Risk Potential

40-5. Answer: 3
Rationale: ST elevations occur when the ischemia transverses the entire width of the cardiac muscle, or transmural. ST elevations are not normal. ST segment depression is seen when the muscle ischemia only involves a portion of the heart wall, or subendocardial. ST elevations are not indicative of pericarditis.
Cognitive Level: Analysis
Nursing Process: Assessment
Client Need: Physiological Integrity; Physiological Adaptation

40-6. Answer: 1
Rationale: Class I recommendations for a patient with ST segment elevation MI to receive a CABG include failed angioplasty with persistent pain. Life-threatening ventricular dysrhythmias, not bradycardia, are qualifying criteria. An elevated systolic pressure and episodes of dyspnea alone are not qualifying criteria.
Cognitive Level: Application
Nursing Process: Assessment
Client Need: Physiological Integrity; Physiological Adaptation

40-7. Answer: 1
Rationale: Early and aggressive mobilization helps to prevent deep vein thrombosis and PEs. Activity should not be restricted to the patients' room. A bedside commode may provide convenience, but it will not allow for greater mobility and ambulation. Encouraging fluids is also recommended, but it is not the best option for prevention of PE.
Cognitive Level: Application
Nursing Process: Planning
Client Need: Physiological Integrity; Reduction of Risk Potential

Chapter 41 – Caring for the Patient with Cardiac Inflammatory Disorders

Key Terms Matching Exercise 1

1. b
2. f
3. h
4. j
5. g

6. d
7. a
8. c
9. i
10. e

Key Terms Matching Exercise 2

11. j
12. c
13. g
14. e
15. d

16. i
17. h
18. a
19. f
20. b

Word Search

21. mitral valve stenosis
22. annuloplasty
23. annulus
24. commissure
25. commissurotomy
26. valvuloplasty
27. mechanical valve
28. allograft valve

29. autograft valve
30. biological valve
31. homograft valve
32. cardiomyopathies (CMPs)
33. pancarditis
34. myocarditis
35. pericarditis
36. aortic valve stenosis

M	M	Y	O	C	A	R	D	I	T	I	S	A	C	E	D	F	G	B	A
A	I	E	A	U	T	O	G	R	A	F	T	V	A	L	V	E	I	C	O
E	A	T	C	E	C	F	G	A	H	I	M	B	J	L	M	V	E	P	R
V	B	C	R	H	H	O	M	O	G	R	A	F	T	V	A	L	V	E	T
L	A	D	H	A	A	I	M	J	N	O	P	N	A	L	J	A	G	R	I
A	A	L	J	N	L	N	T	M	R	U	A	T	S	A	C	V	F	I	C
V	E	I	V	N	L	V	I	Q	I	V	R	W	X	B	V	L	N	C	V
T	S	U	L	U	N	N	A	C	T	S	E	Y	A	P	L	A	W	A	A
F	A	H	C	L	L	G	D	L	A	Y	S	Z	U	Q	I	C	A	R	L
A	I	M	L	O	E	O	T	Q	V	L	C	U	W	A	S	I	G	D	V
R	O	A	N	P	M	S	P	O	Z	E	V	Z	R	S	E	G	A	I	E
G	A	F	P	L	A	M	F	L	Y	R	S	A	T	O	H	O	N	T	S
O	B	N	R	A	C	X	I	W	A	Y	A	T	L	I	T	L	A	I	T
L	O	E	J	S	U	E	H	S	O	S	C	P	E	V	E	O	D	S	E
L	A	C	M	T	D	I	Q	S	S	V	T	M	O	N	E	I	M	J	N
A	E	G	L	Y	N	A	U	L	P	U	L	Y	A	M	O	B	E	Y	O
F	A	H	A	I	R	O	S	E	G	R	R	E	B	E	C	S	F	B	S
P	A	N	C	A	R	D	I	T	I	S	I	E	G	A	D	Z	I	E	I
A	B	E	C	A	R	D	I	O	M	Y	O	P	A	T	H	I	E	S	S

Short Answer Questions

37. Clinical manifestations of rheumatic fever include:
    • Fever
    • Malaise
    • Headache
    • Erythema marginatum: red, raised, lattice-like rash, usually on the chest, back, and abdomen
    • Swollen tender joints with small bony protuberances with or without the presence of subcutaneous nodules
    • May have weakness and shortness of breath
    • Sydenham chorea: sudden, irregular, aimless involuntary movements that are self-limiting with no permanent damage
    • Elevated white blood count (WBC)

38. A pericardial friction rub is a key factor in the diagnostic assessment of a patient being evaluated for pericarditis. Friction rubs are described as a grating, scraping, squeaking, or crunching sound that is the result of friction between the roughened, inflamed layers of the pericardium.

39. The three diseases that affect the mitral valve are mitral valve stenosis, mitral valve regurgitation, and mitral valve prolapse.

40. The most sensitive diagnostic test for valve disease is the echocardiogram because it provides information about the structure and function of the heart valves and enlargement of the chambers that is often a result of malfunctioning valves. It is able to identify thickened valve leaflets, vegetative growths, thrombus, myocardial function, and chamber size. In addition, the echocardiogram is able to measure pressure gradients across valves and pulmonary artery pressures can be estimated.

41. Cardiomyopathies are classified as primary and secondary. With primary CMPs, the etiology of the disease is unknown and the only abnormality is in the heart muscle itself. Secondary CMPs are caused by other disease processes such as ischemia, viral infections, alcohol intake and drug abuse, inherited disorders, and pregnancy. There are four types of CMPs: dilated, hypertrophic, restrictive, and arrhythmogenic.

True or False?

42.	T	**47.**	T
43.	T	**48.**	F
44.	F	**49.**	T
45.	T	**50.**	F
46.	F		

Labeling Exercise 1: Layers of the Heart Wall

a. Pericardium (covering)
b. Interior of chamber
c. Endocardium (lining)
d. Myocardium (muscle)

Labeling Exercise 2: Cardiac Valves, Chordae Tendineae, and Papillary Muscle

a. Tricuspid valve
b. Pulmonic valve
c. Vessels in lungs
d. Mitral valve
e. Chordae tendineae
f. Papillary muscle
g. Aortic valve

NCLEX-RN® Review Questions

Question numbers correspond to Outcome-Based Learning Objectives for this chapter.

41-1. Answer: 1
Rationale: A pericardial friction rub is indicative of pericarditis and the patient may also exhibit chest pain and distant muffled heart sounds. Murmurs are heard secondary to mitral, tricuspid, or aortic stenosis or insufficiency. Bradycardia and atrial fibrillation are not indicative of pericarditis.
Cognitive Level: Analysis
Nursing Process: Assessment
Client Need: Physiological Integrity; Physiological Adaptation

41-2. Answer: 1
Rationale: The hallmark clinical manifestation of AVR is a diastolic murmur heard at the second right intercostal space. A widened pulse pressure, not narrow, may develop. Temperature elevation and intolerance to cold are not associated with AVR.
Cognitive Level: Application
Nursing Process: Assessment
Client Need: Physiological Integrity; Physiological Adaptation

41-3. Answer: 1
Rationale: Nitrates increase peripheral dilation of blood vessels, which decreases the amount of blood returning to the heart, or preload. They also dilate coronary arteries, bringing more blood to the myocardium. Their major effect is on preload, not afterload and they do not increase the workload on the heart. They do not affect heart rate, conduction, or rhythm.
Cognitive Level: Application
Nursing Process: Implementation
Client Need: Physiological Integrity; Pharmacological and Parenteral Therapies

41-4. Answer: 4
Rationale: The greatest danger following invasive procedures such as dental work or medical procedures is the development of endocarditis. The patient should not avoid all such procedures, but must take a prophylactic antibiotic before having the procedure. The other comments are all correct.
Cognitive Level: Application
Nursing Process: Evaluation
Client Need: Physiological Integrity; Physiological Adaptation

41-5. Answer: 2
Rationale: Activity must be spaced and strenuous activity avoided in order to prevent increasing the workload of the heart. Nitroglycerin may be part of the treatment plan to reduce preload to the heart and may be taken if the patient experiences chest pain. The patient should be taught to have a consistent fluid intake since excessive fluid restriction can lead to dehydration, which will decrease preload and cardiac output. The patient should be instructed to monitor weight daily at home.
Cognitive Level: Application
Nursing Process: Implementation
Client Need: Physiological Integrity; Physiological Adaptation

41-6. Answer: 2
Rationale: Including some sedentary activities allows for a diversion that does not place demands on the workload of the heart. All fats should not be eliminated from the diet,

although the patient should be taught to limit saturated fats. All housework does not have to be avoided; the patient should be instructed to avoid those activities that are strenuous, such as vacuuming and lifting, or anything that induces dyspnea. Telling the patient to restrict calories is too general; specific caloric restrictions, such as salt or simple sugars, should be provided if part of the patients' dietary restrictions.

Cognitive Level: Application
Nursing Process: Implementation
Client Need: Physiological Integrity; Physiological Adaptation

Chapter 42 – Caring for the Patient with Heart Failure

Key Terms Matching Exercise 1

1.	f	7.	c
2.	b	8.	j
3.	a	9.	g
4.	k	10.	d
5.	h	11.	i
6.	e		

Key Terms Matching Exercise 2

12.	c	18.	i
13.	e	19.	a
14.	g	20.	f
15.	j	21.	h
16.	k	22.	b
17.	d		

Short Answer Questions

23. Contributing to the rising prevalence of heart failure are the aging U.S. population and increased survival rates among patients with hypertension and coronary artery disease. With the rise of conditions such as diabetes, obesity, and the metabolic syndrome, increases in the risk of developing heart failure are significant.

24. Nonmodifiable risk factors for heart failure are age, positive family history of CAD, gender, and genetics.

25. Symptoms of right-sided heart failure include elevated neck veins, abdominal ascites, edema, poor appetite, nausea and vomiting, and swelling of the ankles and calves. Symptoms of left-sided failure include poor concentration/mentation, pulmonary congestion, cough, paroxysmal nocturnal dyspnea, orthopnea, crackles, and activity intolerance.

26. Clinical manifestations of heart failure include hypotension, jugular venous distention, rales, pleural effusion, wheezing, tachypnea, tachycardia, third heart sound, ascites, engorged liver, positive hepatojugular reflux, splenomegaly, cyanosis, cool extremities, cachexia, confusion, and disorientation.

27. Treatment goals for chronic heart failure include:
    - Alleviate symptoms of congestion.
    - Improve perfusion.
    - Increase activity tolerance.
    - Improve quality of life.
    - Decrease hospitalizations.
    - Reduce readmissions.
    - Slow or reverse progression of cardiac dysfunction.
    - Improve survival.
    - Minimize risk factors.

    - Provide palliative care.
    - Decrease heart failure–related costs.
    - Track outcomes.

28. PCIs include percutaneous transluminal coronary angioplasty (PTCA), atherectomy, laser angioplasty, implantation of intracoronary stents, and other catheter devices for treating CAD.

29. Surgical techniques to treat heart failure beyond CABG surgery include valve replacement or repair, cardiac transplantation, long-term mechanical assist devices, and investigational surgical therapies.

30. General health promotion strategies that the nurse should present include:
    - Smoking cessation
    - Regular physical activity and weight control
    - Limiting alcohol use and discouraging illicit drug use
    - Stress management
    - Dental care

31. Cardiovascular disease is not a "man's" disease. It is the number one killer of women and has killed more women than men, causing the death of over 500,000 women annually. Nursing care of both male and female patients should be consistent and thorough.

32. End-stage treatment options for patients with heart failure include transplant, mechanical circulatory support, and intravenous medications.

True or False?

33.	T	38.	T
34.	F	39.	T
35.	T	40.	F
36.	F	41.	F
37.	T	42.	F

NCLEX-RN® Review Questions

Question numbers correspond to Outcome-Based Learning Objectives for this chapter.

42-1. Answer: 2
   Rationale: People with a diagnosis of heart failure have a higher incidence of suffering sudden death. Having diabetes, a myocardial infarction, and hypertension are conditions that place the person at risk of developing heart failure.
   Cognitive Level: Application
   Nursing Process: Implementation
   Client Need: Physiological Integrity; Physiological Adaptation

42-2. Answer: 1
   Rationale: Systolic dysfunction occurs when the ventricle is unable to contract forcefully during systole and often hypertrophies in an effort to compensate. Diastolic dysfunction occurs when the ventricle is unable to relax and stiffening prevents the ventricle from filling with sufficient blood. Quivering describes fibrillation of the heart muscle. Inability to sense electrical impulses occurs with different types of cardiac dysrhythmias.
   Cognitive Level: Application
   Nursing Process: Implementation
   Client Need: Physiological Integrity; Physiological Adaptation

42-3. Answer: 4
   Rationale: Activation of the SNS causes an increase in heart rate and blood pressure as epinephrine and norepinephrine are released. Lung sounds should improve

as bronchodilation is also stimulated by the SNS. Gastric motility would decrease with SNS activation.
Cognitive Level: Application
Nursing Process: Assessment
Client Need: Physiological Integrity; Physiological Adaptation

42-4. Answer: 3
Rationale: Right-sided failure causes venous congestion, which is manifested in jugular venous distention. A reduction in blood flow to the brain and hypoxemia occurs with left-sided failure, causing difficulty in concentration. Fluid accumulation in the lungs also occurs with left-sided failure, leading to PND and crackles.
Cognitive Level: Application
Nursing Process: Assessment
Client Need: Physiological Integrity; Physiological Adaptation

42-5. Answer: 2
Rationale: Elevations of BNP correlate with significant heart failure symptoms and increased risk of mortality. The patient is at risk for hypertension, not hypotension, due to volume overload with heart failure. Liver failure and ventricular dysrhythmias are not associated with elevated BNP levels.
Cognitive Level: Analysis
Nursing Process: Assessment
Client Need: Physiological Integrity; Physiological Adaptation

42-6. Answer: 1
Rationale: Stage D involves end-stage heart failure and advanced interventions may be needed, including heart transplantation or insertion of mechanical circulatory devices, or hospice services may be needed. Insertion of a pacemaker or implantable defibrillator is indicated for Stage C heart failure. Frequent blood transfusions are usually not indicated for treatment of heart failure.
Cognitive Level: Application
Nursing Process: Implementation
Client Need: Physiological Integrity; Physiological Adaptation

42-7. Answer: 4
Rationale: A 2-pound weight gain in one day should be reported since it may reflect fluid retention. Weights should be done and recorded daily. A weight gain or loss of 5 pounds of goal weight should be reported. Omitting a dose of diuretics should not be recommended.
Cognitive Level: Application
Nursing Process: Implementation
Client Need: Physiological Integrity; Physiological Adaptation

42-8. Answer: 1
Rationale: Counseling patients to better understand their disease can help them to understand the treatment plan and decrease anxiety levels, which in turn empower them to be more proactive in self-management of the disease. Speaking with another person with heart failure may be helpful, but will not empower the patient as much as gaining understanding of the treatment plan. A spiritual advisor and antidepressant medications are not the best way to empower the patient.
Cognitive Level: Analysis
Nursing Process: Implementation
Client Need: Psychosocial Integrity; Coping and Adaptation

42-9. Answer: 1
Rationale: Criteria symptomatic of poor prognosis include: creatinine greater than 2mg/dL, sodium less than 134 mEq/L, heart rate greater than 100, anemia and increased dosing of ACE inhibitors and beta blocker to keep patient normotensive. The serum sodium and heart rate do not meet the criteria. The hemoglobin level does not reflect anemia.
Cognitive Level: Analysis
Nursing Process: Evaluation
Client Need: Physiological Integrity; Physiological Adaptation

Chapter 43 – Caring for the Patient with Peripheral Vascular Disorders

Key Terms Matching Exercise 1

1.	g	6.	a
2.	e	7.	d
3.	c	8.	j
4.	i	9.	b
5.	f	10.	h

Key Terms Matching Exercise 2

11.	b	17.	j
12.	e	18.	i
13.	h	19.	f
14.	a	20.	d
15.	g	21.	c
16.	k		

Complete the Sentence

22. Intermittent claudication (IC), exercise-induced leg pain
23. Raynaud's disease
24. smoking history
25. first rib, clavicle
26. stenosis
27. aortorenal bypass
28. aneurysm
29. myocardial infarction, pulmonary embolus, ruptured abdominal aortic aneurysm
30. varicose veins
31. Lymphedema

Labeling Exercise 1: The Lymphatic System

a. Cervical nodes
b. Axillary nodes
c. Inguinal nodes
d. Right lymphatic duct
e. Internal jugular vein
f. Entrance of thoracic duct into left subclavian vein
g. Thoracic duct
h. Aorta
i. Cisterna chyli
j. Lymphatic collecting vessels

Labeling Exercise 2: Major Arteries of the Body

a. External carotid artery
b. Internal carotid artery
c. Vertebral artery
d. Brachiocephalic artery
e. Axillary artery
f. Ascending aorta
g. Brachial artery
h. Abdominal aorta
i. Superior mesenteric artery
j. Gonadal artery
k. Inferior mesenteric artery
l. Common iliac artery
m. External iliac artery
n. Digital arteries
o. Femoral artery
p. Popliteal artery
q. Anterior tibial artery

r. Posterior tibial artery
s. Common carotid arteries
t. Subclavian artery
u. Aortic arch
v. Coronary artery
w. Thoracic aorta
x. Branches of celiac trunk
y. Left gastric artery
z. Common hepatic artery
aa. Splenic artery
bb. Renal artery
cc. Radial artery
dd. Ulnar artery
ee. Internal iliac artery
ff. Deep palmar arch
gg. Superficial palmar arch

Labeling Exercise 3: Major Veins of the Body

a. Dural sinuses
b. External jugular vein
c. Vertebral vein
d. Internal jugular vein
e. Superior vena cava
f. Axillary vein
g. Great cardiac vein
h. Hepatic veins
i. Hepatic portal vein
j. Superior mesenteric vein
k. Inferior vena cava
l. Ulnar vein
m. Radial vein
n. Common iliac vein
o. External iliac vein
p. Internal iliac vein
q. Digital veins
r. Femoral vein
s. Great saphenous vein
t. Popliteal vein
u. Posterior tibial vein
v. Anterior tibial vein
w. Peroneal vein
x. Subclavian vein
y. Right and left brachiocephalic veins
z. Cephilic vein
aa. Brachial vein
bb. Basilic vein
cc. Renal vein
dd. Median cubital vein
ee. Splenic vein
ff. Inferior mesenteric vein

Labeling Exercise 4: Peripheral Pulses

a. Temporal
b. Carotid
c. Apical
d. Brachial
e. Radial
f. Femoral
g. Popliteal
h. Posterior tibial
i. Dorsalis pedis

NCLEX-RN® Review Questions

Question numbers correspond to Outcome-Based Learning Objectives for this chapter.

43-1. Answer: 2
   Rationale: Ulceration can occur as a result of poor blood supply, pressure, or trauma to an ischemic limb. Arterial ulceration is most likely to occur at the distal-most point of arterial flow. The toes are a common site for arterial ulceration. In arterial ulcerations, the base is pale, gray, or yellowish in color with little drainage and regular borders. Shallow, irregularly shaped, and exudative ulcers are venous stasis ulcers.
   Cognitive Level: Application
   Nursing Process: Assessment
   Client Need: Physiological Integrity; Physiological Adaptation

43-2. Answer: 4
   Rationale: Evidence of sufficient perfusion to the extremities would include warm extremities, palpable pulses, reduction in pain, and prevention of ulceration. The patient's ability to discuss disease process, management, prevention, and verbalization of adherence to the treatment plan is evidence of an adequate knowledge level for the patient.
   Cognitive Level: Application
   Nursing Process: Evaluation
   Client Need: Physiological Integrity; Physiological Adaptation

43-3. Answer: 4
   Rationale: There are three color changes that occur with Raynaud's disease: (1) pallor in response to the vasospasms; (2) cyanosis due to the reduction of oxygenation of the blood; and (3) rubar when the vasospasms stop and the arterial blood returns. Other factors that may trigger ischemia include smoking, alcohol use, caffeine intake, cocaine, and amphetamines. The vascular changes also cause paresthesia to the affected parts. The episode ends when the arterial spasm relaxes and perfusion normalizes. Digits appear normal between attacks.
   Cognitive Level: Application
   Nursing Process: Implementation
   Client Need: Physiological Adaptation; Physiological Integrity

43-4. Answer: 2
   Rationale: Postoperative complications can be caused by bleeding, hypovolemia, and third spacing of fluid, myocardial ischemia/infarction, hypertension, and hypothermia. Vasoactive drugs may be required in the immediate postoperative phase to support and control the blood pressure and other hemodynamic parameters. Increasing intravenous fluids might not be adequate to increase the patient's blood pressure. Raising the head of the bed could cause the patient to experience more symptoms. Vasodilator medications would not assist with raising the patient's blood pressure.
   Cognitive Level: Application
   Nursing Process: Implementation
   Client Need: Physiological Integrity; Reduction of Risk Potential

43-5. Answer: 2
   Rationale: Even though the duplex ultrasound is the most commonly used diagnostic test for deep vein thrombosis, it may be difficult to perform in the obese patient. The MRI is useful for suspected iliac vein or inferior vena caval thrombosis. The CT scan is useful to aid in the diagnosis of deep vein thrombosis in the obese patient. Homan's sign, or

pain in the calf when the foot is dorsiflexed, is not a reliable indicator of deep vein thrombosis.
Cognitive Level: Analysis
Nursing Process: Planning
Client Need: Physiological Integrity; Reduction of Risk Potential

43-6. Answer: 1
Rationale: Trental interacts with some medications, one of which is insulin. This medication should be taken with food. Muscle pain is most likely associated with HMG-CoA reductase inhibitors. The avoidance of grapefruit juice is associated with anticholesterol medications.
Cognitive Level: Application
Nursing Process: Implementation
Client Need: Physiological Integrity; Pharmacological and Parenteral Therapies

43-7. Answer: 4
Rationale: Prior to discharge, the patient should be taught to avoid activities that cause venous pooling, such as sitting for long periods of time and standing in one position for long periods of time. The nurse needs to explain the proper method for applying and wearing compression stockings. The patient should be encouraged to develop a walking program and to lose weight, if needed.
Cognitive Level: Application
Nursing Process: Planning
Client Need: Physiological Integrity; Reduction of Risk Potential

43-8. Answer: 3
Rationale: Most patients with aortic dissection present with sudden, sharp, shifting chest or back pain that can mimic acute myocardial infarction, pulmonary embolus, or ruptured abdominal aortic aneurysm. The patient may describe it as "ripping" or "tearing." The pain is not affected by position changes and it may wax and wane. Because aortic dissection is a life-threatening situation, prompt and careful assessment of the clinical manifestations also is essential. Surgical intervention is indicated for type A dissections, which are those that involve the ascending aorta when the patient develops ischemic complications and/or when medical management fails.
Cognitive Level: Application
Nursing Process: Assessment
Client Need: Physiological Integrity; Physiological Adaptation

Chapter 44 – Nursing Assessment of Patients with Gastrointestinal, Renal, and Urinary Disorders

Key Terms Matching Exercise 1

1.	k	7.	e
2.	d	8.	a
3.	h	9.	i
4.	g	10.	j
5.	b	11.	f
6.	l	12.	c

Key Terms Matching Exercise 2

13.	e	19.	g
14.	h	20.	d
15.	b	21.	l
16.	i	22.	k
17.	f	23.	a
18.	j	24.	c

True or False?

25.	T	30.	F
26.	F	31.	T
27.	T	32.	T
28.	F	33.	F
29.	F	34.	T

Labeling Exercise 1: Organs of the Gastrointestinal (GI) System

a. Pharynx
b. Tongue
c. Esophagus
d. Liver
e. Gallbladder
f. Duodenum
g. Common bile duct
h. Cecum
i. Appendix
j. Rectum
k. Anus
l. Parotid
m. Sublingual
n. Submandibular
o. Stomach
p. Pancreas
q. Pancreatic duct
r. Ileum (small intestine)
s. Transverse colon
t. Ascending colon
u. Descending colon

Labeling Exercise 2: The Stomach

a. Fundus
b. Greater curvature
c. Pyloric sphincter valve
d. Duodenum
e. Rugae
f. Lesser curvature
g. Oblique layer
h. Circular layer
i. Cardia
j. Longitudinal layer
k. Esophagus

Labeling Exercise 3: The Pancreas and Gallbladder

a. Stomach
b. Gallbladder
c. Common bile duct
d. Pancreatic duct
e. Duodenum
f. Pancreas

Labeling Exercise 4: Abdominal Muscles

a. Latissimus dorsi
b. Serratus anterior
c. Rectus abdominis
d. Rectus sheath (cut edges)
e. Iliac crest
f. Inguinal ligament
g. Pectoralis major
h. Rectus abdominis covered by sheath
i. Linea alba

j. Umbilicus

k. External abdominal oblique

l. Inguinal canal

Labeling Exercise 5: The Renal System

a. Renal artery

b. Renal vein

c. Left kidney

d. Aorta

e. Ureter

f. Bladder

g. Urethra

h. Inferior vena cava

i. Right kidney

j. Adrenal gland

k. Diaphragm

NCLEX-RN® Review Questions

Question numbers correspond to Outcome-Based Learning Objectives for this chapter.

44-1. Answer: 3

Rationale: If a patient lives in an agricultural area or has well water as a source of drinking water, Giardia and Cryptosporidium infections need to be considered in the case of ongoing diarrhea and abdominal cramping. This might not be the common differential diagnosis for a person who lives in a high-rise apartment in the city.

Cognitive Level: Application

Nursing Process: Assessment

Client Need: Physiological Integrity; Reduction of Risk Potential

44-2. Answer: 2

Rationale: The correct order for examination is inspection, auscultation, percussion, and palpation. Bowel sounds should be auscultated prior to percussion to avoid changing the frequency or rate. Light palpation in all quadrants precedes deep palpation.

Cognitive Level: Application

Nursing Process: Assessment

Client Need: Health Promotion and Maintenance; Prevention and/or Early Detection of Health Problems

44-3. Answer: 2

Rationale: Painful areas should be assessed last. Pulsatile areas are commonly palpated in this area. The right kidney is easily palpated; the left is more difficult. If the patient has cirrhosis, the lower edge may extend further into the abdomen and may feel stiff and irregular.

Cognitive Level: Application

Nursing Process: Assessment

Client Need: Health Promotion and Maintenance; Prevention and/or Early Detection of Health Problems

44-4. Answer: 4

Rationale: Bowel sounds may mean very little. A person can have acute peritonitis but still have bowel sounds. A patient with a postoperative ileus may have very loud bowel sounds, but the patient is distended and the bowels are not functioning in a coordinated pattern. Complete absence of bowel sounds would be significant, but the nurse would have to listen for a minimum of 5 minutes in all four quadrants. Bowel sounds should be auscultated prior to palpation, as the deep palpation can affect the frequency of bowel sounds. The nurse should listen over all four quadrants for a period of 2 to 5 minutes. Note the frequency, pitch, and character of the bowel sounds. Ask the patient about passing flatus.

Cognitive Level: Analysis

Nursing Process: Assessment

Client Need: Physiological Integrity; Reduction of Risk Potential

44-5. Answer: 3

Rationale: The nurse must develop a system to use as a template. When obtaining a history of the chief complaint, it is preferable to allow the patient to express concerns in his or her own way. Documentation should include all data whether or not they specifically reflect a pathologic process. Notes may be taken as appropriate during the examination as long as this process does not interfere with the physical examination.

Cognitive Level: Application

Nursing Process: Assessment

Client Need: Health Promotion and Maintenance; Prevention and/or Early Detection of Health Problems

Chapter 45 – Caring for the Patient with Gastrointestinal Disorders

Key Terms Matching Exercise 1

1. d		**6.** i	
2. a		**7.** c	
3. e		**8.** h	
4. j		**9.** b	
5. g		**10.** f	

Key Terms Matching Exercise 2

11. a		**16.** i	
12. f		**17.** c	
13. e		**18.** j	
14. g		**19.** h	
15. b		**20.** d	

Key Terms Matching Exercise 3

21. j		**26.** c	
22. f		**27.** e	
23. i		**28.** b	
24. g		**29.** a	
25. d			

Key Term Crossword

10. MALDIGESTION
18. ACHALASIA
4. CELIAC DISEASE
6. GASTRIC ULCER
1. LACTASE
16. BOTOX
11. ACHLORHYDRIA
13. COLON CANCER
9. STOMATITIS

Short Answer Questions

30. Stomatitis disorders can be caused by viral, bacterial, fungal, traumatic, chemical, and even nutritional deficiencies. Some disorders, such as benign migratory glossitis, have no known cause.

31. Excision of the tumor is usually the treatment of choice for oral cancer unless the tumor is very far advanced and considered unresectable. The goal of surgery is to remove the cancerous tissue, but the surrounding tissue and lymph nodes may also be removed to ensure there is no local infiltration of cancerous cells. A radical neck dissection may be performed if the tumor is advanced.

32. The majority of individuals with hiatal hernia have no symptoms. The primary symptom is reflux and heartburn. Patients often complain of feeling full, belching, and indigestion.

33. Factors that increase the likelihood of developing GERD include obesity, pregnancy, and hiatal hernia. Some foods can increase the risk of GERD, such as alcohol, caffeine, chocolate, fatty foods, citrus fruit, onions, tomatoes, and peppermint. Beta-adrenergic blockers (Inderal), calcium channel blockers (verapamil), estrogen, progesterone, diazepam (Valium), and theophylline can also contribute to its development, as well as nicotine.

34. The development of esophageal cancer is facilitated by any process that allows food and drink to remain in the esophagus for prolonged periods, by ulceration and metaplasia usually caused from esophageal reflux, and by long-term exposure of the esophagus to irritants. The major risk factor for the development of esophageal cancer is long-term alcohol use. The risk increases as the amount of alcohol consumed increases. Tobacco use increases the risk of esophageal cancer, but pipe and cigar smokers have a higher risk.

35. Gastric carcinoma rarely has symptoms, preventing the patient from seeking medical help until the disease is far advanced. The patient may complain of anorexia, indigestion, heartburn, or early satiety, but these are vague and often the patient does not consider them serious.

36. Lactase deficiency, which causes lactose intolerance, is diagnosed using the lactose breath test. This noninvasive test measures the amount of hydrogen gas exhaled after a 50-gram dose of lactose is given to a fasting patient. A lactose tolerance test can also be done to determine the degree of lactase deficiency.

37. Persons with diverticular disease should avoid popcorn, corn, sesame seeds, poppy seeds, sunflower seeds. nuts, cucumbers, okra, berries, strawberries, raspberries, blueberries, figs, and rye bread with caraway seeds.

38. UC involves only the large intestine and usually only the sigmoid colon and rectum. Crohn's disease differs from UC in that it can occur in any portion of the gastrointestinal tract from the mouth to the anus; however, it is usually limited to the ileum or ileocecal valve.

39. Where diets are high in animal protein, fat, and calories, such as in the United States, the prevalence of colorectal cancer is higher.

True or False?

40. T
41. F
42. F
43. F
44. T
45. F
46. T
47. T
48. F
49. F

NCLEX-RN® Review Questions

Question numbers correspond to Outcome-Based Learning Objectives for this chapter.

45-1. Answer: 4

Rationale: Viscous lidocaine provides an anesthetic to the oral mucosa, which may help to reduce pain and irritation when the patient eats, thereby allowing more food to

be consumed. Antibiotics may help to treat the cause of the stomatitis if it is bacterial, but would not help to reduce the pain associated with oral ulcers. A full-strength peroxide solution may be too strong and would further irritate the mucosa; a half-strength solution should be used. A warm bicarbonate solution would be better used for oral care to cleanse the mouth; it will not help as much as the viscous lidocaine to relieve pain and allow eating.
Cognitive Level: Application
Nursing Process: Implementation
Client Need: Physiological Integrity; Physiological Adaptation

45-2. Answers: 2, 3
Rationale: *H. pylori* accounts for approximately 80% of ulcers; it produces an enzyme that catalyzes the formation of ammonia, which is toxic to gastric epithelial cells, leading to gastritis and ulcer formation. NSAIDS inhibit prostaglandin formation, which has a protective function in the gastric mucosa. Loss of the protective prostaglandins leads to ulcer formation. Heavy alcohol intake would contribute to gastritis, but not occasional use. A proton pump inhibitor would decrease stomach acid production and help to prevent peptic ulcers. A high-fat diet does not contribute to ulcer formation.
Cognitive Level: Application
Nursing Process: Assessment
Client Need: Physiological Integrity; Physiological Adaptation

45-3. Answer: 3
Rationale: Patients with celiac disease must adhere to a gluten-free diet. Gluten is found in wheat, barley, and rye grains and some sources indicate oat should also be avoided. Corn would be the only item that does not contain gluten. The sandwich and muffin contain wheat and the soup contains barley.
Cognitive Level: Application
Nursing Process: Implementation
Client Need: Physiological Integrity; Reduction of Risk Potential

45-4. Answer: 2
Rationale: This medication is contraindicated in pregnancy. An allergy to sulfa, not penicillin should be determined since the drug is a sulfa derivative. It would not be contraindicated with beta blockers and a baseline temperature is not necessary.
Cognitive Level: Application
Nursing Process: Assessment
Client Need: Physiological Integrity; Physiological Adaptation

45-5. Answer: 4
Rationale: Eating the last meal at least 2 hours before sleeping will help to reduce pressure put on the lower esophageal sphincter (LES). Eating 6 small meals rather than 3 large meals will also help to reduce pressure on the LES. Lying down after eating should be avoided as it will increase pressure against the LES. Drinking large amounts of fluid with the meal will increase gastric distention and also increase pressure on the LES.
Cognitive Level: Application
Nursing Process: Implementation
Client Need: Physiological Integrity; Reduction of Risk Potential

45-6. Answer: 4
Rationale: A colonoscopy only needs to be done every 5–10 years. A tissue biopsy does provide a definitive diagnosis of cancer but it is not indicated unless suspicious tissue is seen. A sigmoidoscopy is recommended every 5 years, but since it can only detect cancer in the sigmoid

colon and rectum, most physicians recommend a colonoscopy since it detects colon cancer with much greater accuracy.
Cognitive Level: Application
Nursing Process: Implementation
Client Need: Physiological Integrity; Physiological Adaptation

45-7. Answer: 3
Rationale: Sequestration of fluids in the bowel along with NG fluid losses put the patient at risk of developing a fluid volume deficit. Potassium and sodium are also lost with the NG drainage and in the bowel, so hypokalemia and hyponatremia would be expected. Because of the loss of hydrochloric acid from the stomach with NG drainage, the patient is at risk for metabolic alkalosis.
Cognitive Level: Analysis
Nursing Process: Assessment
Client Need: Physiological Integrity; Physiological Adaptation

45-8. Answer: 2
Rationale: In most cases dumping syndrome resolves within 6–12 months. The symptoms will disappear when the dumping syndrome resolves. Sympathizing with the patient's sweets deprivation does not offer the best explanation. The patient will indeed adjust to the symptoms, but this does not provide encouragement that they will most likely resolve.
Cognitive Level: Application
Nursing Process: Implementation
Client Need: Physiological Integrity; Physiological Adaptation

45-9. Answer: 1
Rationale: Flatulence from the stoma indicates the return of bowel function and would be a normal finding 3 days after surgery. It should not take weeks for stool to form. If peristalsis does not resume, a prokinetic drug may need to be given, but passage of gas is indicative of peristalsis. Activity should be encouraged to promote peristalsis, not restricted.
Cognitive Level: Application
Nursing Process: Implementation
Client Need: Physiological Integrity; Physiological Adaptation

Chapter 46 – Caring for the Patient with Hepatic and Biliary Disorders

Key Terms Matching Exercise 1

1. c
2. d
3. b
4. f
5. a
6. j
7. g
8. i
9. h
10. e

Key Terms Matching Exercise 2

11. g
12. e
13. i
14. c
15. j
16. d
17. a
18. f
19. b
20. h

Key Terms Matching Exercise 3

21. g
22. b
23. j
24. f
25. d
26. i
27. h
28. a
29. c
30. e

Word Search

31. alpha-amylase
32. hypoalbuminemia
33. gluconeogenesis
34. esophageal varices
35. portal hypertension
36. exocrine pancreas
37. cholangiocarcinoma
38. chymotrypsin
39. bile
40. bile canaliculi
41. hepatocellular
42. bilirubin

43. asterixis
44. cirrhosis
45. melena
46. sclerotherapy
47. paracentesis
48. pancreatitis
49. apudomas
50. lipase
51. trypsin
52. steatorrhea
53. Kupffer cells

H	S	E	X	O	C	R	I	N	E	P	A	N	C	R	E	A	S	I	P
C	Y	T	S	B	D	B	C	A	G	E	I	A	N	C	A	E	C	A	O
G	H	P	E	O	G	E	H	K	M	O	B	P	I	L	L	K	L	F	R
B	L	Y	O	A	P	I	J	A	R	W	V	T	B	F	P	U	E	O	T
D	I	U	M	A	T	H	L	N	E	S	A	Q	U	H	H	P	R	S	A
A	G	L	C	O	L	O	A	O	T	U	S	X	R	Y	A	F	O	A	L
R	E	A	E	O	T	B	R	G	Q	E	W	R	I	N	A	F	T	E	H
A	B	F	I	C	N	R	U	R	E	J	F	A	L	P	M	E	H	A	Y
L	S	C	E	A	A	E	Y	M	H	A	B	L	I	H	Y	R	E	B	P
U	I	A	G	D	I	N	O	P	I	E	L	I	B	D	L	C	R	S	E
L	S	C	H	K	M	A	A	G	S	N	A	V	A	C	A	E	A	I	R
L	E	B	J	A	N	Q	S	L	E	I	E	N	A	E	S	L	P	X	T
E	T	S	L	M	E	F	I	G	I	N	N	M	G	R	E	L	Y	I	E
C	N	A	T	R	Y	P	S	I	N	C	E	D	I	L	I	S	B	R	N
O	E	M	A	C	H	O	O	B	A	H	U	S	M	A	J	C	A	E	S
T	C	O	B	D	F	L	H	N	E	O	N	L	I	P	A	S	E	T	I
A	A	D	P	A	N	C	R	E	A	T	I	T	I	S	E	B	A	S	O
P	R	U	C	E	A	I	R	L	K	C	A	D	F	M	H	C	G	A	N
E	A	P	A	F	G	J	I	B	E	A	F	M	E	L	E	N	A	D	A
H	P	A	M	O	N	I	C	R	A	C	O	I	G	N	A	L	O	H	C

True or False?

54.	F	59.	T
55.	T	60.	F
56.	T	61.	F
57.	F	62.	T
58.	T	63.	T

Labeling Exercise 1: Liver and Biliary System

a. Spleen
b. Hepatic duct
c. Tail of the pancreas
d. Pancreatic duct
e. Head of the pancreas
f. Duodenum
g. Sphincter of Oddi
h. Ampulla of Vater
i. Common bile duct
j. Cystic duct
k. Gallbladder
l. Liver
m. Diaphragm

Labeling Exercise 2: (A) Extrahepatic Bile Passages, Gallbladder, and Pancreatic Ducts. (B) Entry of the Pancreatic and Bile Ducts into the Hepatopancreatic Ampula, then into the Duodenum

Drawing A:

a. Liver
b. Gallbladder
c. Cystic duct
d. (Common) bile duct
e. Accessory pancreatic duct
f. Main pancreatic duct
g. Hepatopancreatic ampulla
h. Duodenum
i. Right and left hepatic ducts
j. Common hepatic duct
k. Spiral valve in cystic duct
l. Pylorus

Drawing B:

m. Descending part of duodenum
n. Major duodenal papilla
o. Hepatopancreatic ampulla
p. Sphincter of pancreatic duct
q. Pancreatic duct
r. Bile duct
s. Sphincter of bile duct

Labeling Exercise 3: Portal Circulation

a. Hepatic veins
b. Coronary (gastric)
c. Short gastric
d. Left gastroepiploic
e. Splenic
f. Right gastroepiploic
g. Pancreatic
h. Inferior mesenteric
i. Superior mesenteric
j. Portal

k. Cystic
l. Pyloric
m. Inferior vena cava

NCLEX-RN® Review Questions

Question numbers correspond to Outcome-Based Learning Objectives for this chapter.

46-1. Answer: 2
Rationale: Hepatitis C is found predominantly in blood, blood products, and transplanted tissue, and it has been transmitted by percutaneous exposures, such as tattooing, body piercing, barbering, and folk medicine practices. Insertion of a central venous catheter and long-term therapy with antibiotics are not risk factors for hepatitis C. Eating unwashed fruit in Mexico poses a risk for hepatitis A.
Cognitive Level: Application
Nursing Process: Assessment
Client Need: Physiological Integrity; Physiological Adaptation

46-2. Answer: 3
Rationale: Due to the elevated bilirubin levels and jaundice accompanying the icteric phase, the skin becomes dry and itchy. Other symptoms of this phase include continued fatigue and anorexia, abdominal pain, and dark-colored urine. Urinary frequency, constipation, and headaches are not associated with the icteric phase.
Cognitive Level: Application
Nursing Process: Implementation
Client Need: Physiological Integrity; Physiological Adaptation

46-3. Answer: 3
Rationale: A bilirubin level of 2 is elevated and would contribute to dark-colored urine in the patient. Confusion and asterixis are seen in patients with elevated ammonia levels. An irregular pulse is not related to any of the abnormal laboratory values given.
Cognitive Level: Analysis
Nursing Process: Assessment
Client Need: Physiological Integrity; Physiological Adaptation

46-4. Answer: 1
Rationale: Cephulac is used to lower ammonia levels in the patient with hepatic encephalopathy and so a desired effect would be an improvement of cognitive abilities; confusion and agitation, if present, should be improved. It will not cause the patient to be drowsy or increase the appetite. Although it is also a laxative and aids in removal of the ammonia in this way, it should produce several soft, loose stools, not diarrhea. This would also not be the best way to evaluate desired effect of the medication for this patient.
Cognitive Level: Analysis
Nursing Process: Evaluation
Client Need: Physiological Integrity; Physiological Adaptation

46-5. Answers: 1, 2
Rationale: Risk factors for liver cancer include alcoholism and chronic infections with hepatitis B and C. GERD and hepatitis A are not risk factors. Although having multiple transfusions may carry a small risk for hepatitis C, they are not associated with being a risk factor for liver cancer.
Cognitive Level: Application
Nursing Process: Assessment
Client Need: Physiological Integrity; Physiological Adaptation

46-6. Answer: 1

Rationale: The rapid weight loss of restrictive diet following bariatric surgery put the patient at an increased risk to develop gallbladder disease. An MI, hepatitis infection, or colon resection are not risk factors.

Cognitive Level: Application

Nursing Process: Analysis

Client Need: Physiological Integrity; Physiological Adaptation

46-7. Answer: 4

Rationale: Following an open cholecystectomy patients often avoid deep breathing secondary to incisional pain: early ambulation promotes lung expansion and helps to prevent pneumonia. Having the patient do leg exercises, choose low-fat foods, and reposition would all be appropriate interventions, but not of the highest priority.

Cognitive Level: Application

Nursing Process: Implementation

Client Need: Physiological Integrity; Reduction of Risk Potential

46-8. Answer: 3

Rationale: The knee-chest position often takes pressure off the capsule surrounding the pancreas, helping to ease the pain. Positioning the patient on the left side alone would not be as beneficial as the knee-chest position. Placing the patient in a recumbent position stretches the pancreatic capsule and would increase the pain. A diversionary activity could be suggested if positioning is not effective.

Cognitive Level: Application

Nursing Process: Implementation

Client Need: Physiological Integrity; Physiological Adaptation

46-9. Answer: 2

Rationale: Risk factors for pancreatic cancer include obesity, chronic pancreatitis, a family history of pancreatic cancer, cigarette smoking, and a history of abdominal radiation. A vegetarian diet and diabetes insipidus are not risk factors. A BMI of 22 reflects a healthy weight.

Cognitive Level: Application

Nursing Process: Assessment

Client Need: Physiological Integrity; Physiological Adaptation

46-10. Answer: 4

Rationale: Medications such as proton pump inhibitors may be prescribed to prevent gastritis in the patient with chronic pancreatitis. The patient should be instructed to abstain from all alcohol, not to restrict it. Activity does not have to be restricted. A low-fat, high-protein diet is indicated.

Cognitive Level: Application

Nursing Process: Implementation

Client Need: Physiological Integrity; Reduction of Risk Potential

Chapter 47 – Caring for the Patient with Renal and Urinary Disorders

Key Terms Matching Exercise 1

1.	h	**5.**	d
2.	b	**6.**	g
3.	f	**7.**	e
4.	a	**8.**	c

Key Terms Matching Exercise 2

9.	b	**13.**	h
10.	g	**14.**	e
11.	c	**15.**	d
12.	f	**16.**	a

Short Answer Questions

17. Polycystic kidney disease is diagnosed from family history and examination revealing grossly enlarged and palpable kidneys. Diagnostic tests include ultrasonography, tomography, and radioisotope scans; retrograde ureteropyelography; urinalysis; serum creatinine; and blood urea nitrogen.

18. Risk factors for renal carcinoma include cigarette smoking, occupational exposure to toxic compounds, obesity, and acquired cystic disease of the kidney.

19. Continuous renal replacement therapy is a way to remove solute and fluids slowly and continuously in a patient that may be hemodynamically unstable.

20. Being African American, having close relatives with end-stage renal disease (ESRD), or having polycystic kidney disease predispose one to renal failure.

True or False?

21.	T	**26.**	T
22.	T	**27.**	F
23.	F	**28.**	F
24.	F	**29.**	T
25.	T	**30.**	T

Complete the Sentence

31. diuretics, antihypertensives
32. infection
33. scar tissue
34. prostate gland, urethral strictures, renal calculi
35. fatal uremia
36. renal artery
37. pain management
38. Acute tubular necrosis
39. infection, volume depletion, volume depletion, nephrotoxic medications
40. renal pelvis, calyces, kidney stones

Labeling Exercise 1: The Kidney and Nephron

a.	Ureter	**j.**	Loop of Henle
b.	Renal vein	**k.**	Vein
c.	Renal artery	**l.**	Glomerulus
d.	Hilum of kidney	**m.**	Afferent arteriole
e.	Pyramid in renal medulla	**n.**	Efferent arteriole
f.	Renal capsule	**o.**	Bowman's capsule
g.	Renal cortex	**p.**	Proximal tubule
h.	Renal pelvis	**q.**	Distal tubule
i.	Calyx	**r.**	Collecting tubule

NCLEX-RN® Review Questions

Question numbers correspond to Outcome-Based Learning Objectives for this chapter.

47-1. Answer: 2

Rationale: In chronic renal failure most electrolytes are elevated due to impaired kidney ability to excrete excess amounts. The exception is calcium, which is low secondary to the impaired ability of the kidney to convert vitamin D to its active form and in response to the elevated phosphorus level. A phosphorus level of 4.9 is elevated. A potassium level of 4.2 is decreased. A chloride level of 98 is normal and a calcium level of 9.2 is normal.

Cognitive Level: Analysis

Nursing Process: Assessment

Client Need: Physiological Integrity; Physiological Adaptation

47-2. Answer: 2

Rationale: Due to the increased permeability of the glomeruli, protein, red blood cells, white blood cells, and mixed cell casts are found in the urine. Presence of glucose in the urine is indicative of diabetes. Presence of *E. coli* is often associated with pylonephritis; group A beta-hemolytic streptococci are often seen with glomeruloneprhritis. Creatinine clearance would be expected to be decreased.

Cognitive Level: Application

Nursing Process: Assessment

Client Need: Physiological Integrity; Physiological Adaptation

47-3. Answer: 2

Rationale: Complaints of lumbar pain would be most specific to this disorder. The enlarging kidneys contribute to abdominal and lumbar pain, and a swollen and tender abdomen. Ankle edema could occur as the disease progresses and the kidneys go into failure, but this symptom occurs with many other conditions, such as congestive heart failure, renal failure, and cirrhosis. Frequent urinary tract infections are also symptomatic of polycystic kidney disease but occur with many other renal and urinary conditions, such as pyelonephritis and glomerulonephritis. Urgency with voiding is also very nonspecific and is often associated with urinary tract infections and benign prostatic hypertrophy.

Cognitive Level: Application

Nursing Process: Assessment

Client Need: Physiological Integrity; Physiological Adaptation

47-4. Answer: 2

Rationale: The pericariditis associated with CRF is secondary to uremic toxins and is metabolic pericarditis; injury to the epicardium is unusual. Dialysis is usually instituted when it develops and most patients have a resolution of chest pain and a decrease in the size of the effusion. Complete bed rest is not necessary. A pericardial window and antibiotics are also not indicated.

Cognitive Level: Application

Nursing Process: Assessment

Client Need: Physiological Integrity; Physiological Adaptation

47-5. Answer: 4

Rationale: Foods high in oxalate should be avoided. These include: beets, chocolate, coffee, cola, nuts, rhubarb, spinach, strawberries, tea, and wheat bran.

Cognitive Level: Application

Nursing Process: Implementation

Client Need: Physiological Integrity; Physiological Adaptation

47-6. Answer: 2

Rationale: When the fluid is removed, it is important to assess its appearance. The outflow fluid should be straw colored and not be cloudy or blood tinged, which might indicate peritonitis. If the patient will be doing CAPD or CCPD, the nursing focus is on teaching the patient/family how to perform the dialysis. Use of aseptic technique and signs and symptoms of infection are particularly important aspects to be taught.

Cognitive Level: Analysis

Nursing Process: Assessment

Client Need: Physiological Integrity; Physiological Adaptation

Chapter 48 – Nursing Assessment of Patients with Reproductive Disorders

Key Terms Matching Exercise 1

1.	b	**6.**	f
2.	a	**7.**	h
3.	g	**8.**	e
4.	d	**9.**	c
5.	i		

Key Terms Matching Exercise 2

10.	c	**14.**	e
11.	a	**15.**	h
12.	d	**16.**	f
13.	b	**17.**	g

Short Answer Questions

18. The 5 areas of concern are partners, prevention of pregnancy, protection from STIs, practices, and past history of STIs.

19. Before proceeding with a male genital examination with the wife present, ask the wife whether she would prefer to leave. In certain cultures, the wife's presence during a genital examination of her husband would be considered taboo or against cultural mores.

20. Changes in mobility brought on by aging may necessitate a change in positioning. For women who find the lithotomy position difficult, a side-lying position with the top leg drawn up will allow for small speculum examination of the vagina and cervix. Males who find it difficult to stand for long periods of time should lie on the left side, bending at the hips, and drawing the right leg up so that the anal area is accessible to the examiner.

Labeling Exercise 1: The Female Breast

a. Thoracic branch of axillary artery

b. Adipose tissue (lobules of fat)

c. Cooper's ligaments (suspensory)

d. Glandular tissues (alveolar glands)

e. Lactiferous ducts

f. Areola

g. Nipple

h. Ampulla

i. Alveolar duct

j. Branches of intercostal and internal thoracic artery

k. Subcutaneous fat of the breast

l. Cooper's ligaments

m. Inframammary fold

Labeling Exercise 2: Female Internal Genitalia

a. Uterus
b. Rectouterine cul-de-sac
c. Cervix
d. Rectum
e. Vagina
f. Urethra
g. Bladder
h. Round ligaments
i. Ovaries
j. Oviducts
k. Infundibulo-pelvic ligament

Labeling Exercise 3: Male Genitalia

a. Seminal vesicle
b. Urinary bladder
c. Vas deferens
d. Pubic bone
e. Penis
f. Epididymis
g. Glans penis
h. Scrotum
i. Testicle
j. Prostate

NCLEX-RN® Review Questions

Question numbers correspond to Outcome-Based Learning Objectives for this chapter.

48-1. Answer: 3

Rationale: Sperm pass through the vas deferens to the seminal vesicles that produce 60% of semen and into the prostate to be mixed with prostate fluid before ejaculation during intercourse. The prostate is about 2.5 centimeters long with a median sulcus between two lateral lobes. A third, anterior lobe is not palpable. The prostate is fibrous and firm to touch.
Cognitive Level: Application
Nursing Process: Implementation
Client Need: Health Promotion and Maintenance; Growth and Development Through the Lifespan

48-2. Answer: 4

Rationale: If the patient answers questions about alcohol intake in such a way that the examiner is suspicious of problem drinking, then screening questions such as the CAGE questionnaire can be used to help identify alcohol abuse. CAGE stands for "cutting down, annoyance if criticized, guilty feelings, eye-openers" and includes the following questions: (1) Have you ever felt the need to **C**ut down on drinking? (2) Have you ever felt **A**nnoyed by criticism of your drinking? (3) Have you ever felt **G**uilty about drinking? and (4) Have you ever taken a drink first thing in the morning (**E**ye-opener) to steady your nerves or get rid of a hangover?
Cognitive Level: Application
Nursing Process: Assessment
Client Need: Health Promotion and Maintenance; Prevention and/or Early Detection of Health Problems

48-3. Answer: 3

Rationale: Alcohol and illicit drug use have been shown to increase the incidence of sexually transmitted disease and HIV. The nurse should assess this patient's sexual partner history. Although important, assessment of blood pressure and nutritional status would not be indicated for this current health issue. Cigarette smoking and second-hand smoke increase the

risks for cancer and should be assessed, but this is not directly relevant to the patient's illicit drug and alcohol use.
Cognitive Level: Application
Nursing Process: Assessment
Client Need: Health Promotion and Maintenance; Prevention and/or Early Detection of Health Problems

48-4. Answer: 4

Rationale: While assessing a female patient's genitalia, the nurse should look for lesions, warts, vesicles, changes in pigmentation, signs of abuse such as bruises or lacerations, swollen Bartholin glands, or vaginal discharge or blood at the introitus. Ask the patient to bear down as if to move her bowels and observe for any bulges of cystocele or a relaxation of the anterior vagina wall under the urinary bladder, or rectocele, which is a relaxation of the posterior vaginal wall over the rectum.
Cognitive Level: Analysis
Nursing Process: Assessment
Client Need: Health Promotion and Maintenance; Prevention and/or Early Detection of Health Problems

48-5. Answer: 1

Rationale: Men experience andropause or a decrease in testosterone beginning gradually in about the third decade. This causes decreased spermatogenesis, a shortening of the penis, the penis is slower to erection, and the scrotum hangs lower. There is no evidence to suggest that a woman's vagina will get longer with aging. There's no evidence to suggest that exercise or a diet high in calcium will affect the length of a male penis.
Cognitive Level: Application
Nursing Process: Implementation
Client Need: Health Promotion and Maintenance; Growth and Development Through the Lifespan

48-6. Answer: 4

Rationale: Early detection of disease through screening examinations is a tactic for health promotion. For women, cervical and breast cancer screening are recommended. The United States Preventive Services Task Force recommends that sexually active women have annual Pap smears until age 65. At this point, the benefit of screening seems to diminish. The nurse should guide the patient to discuss her feelings with her physician.
Cognitive Level: Application
Nursing Process: Implementation
Client Need: Health Promotion and Maintenance; Prevention and/or Early Detection of Health Problems

Chapter 49 – Caring for the Patient with Female Reproductive Disorders

Key Terms Matching Exercise 1

1.	b	**6.**	a
2.	e	**7.**	h
3.	g	**8.**	d
4.	j	**9.**	i
5.	f	**10.**	c

Key Terms Matching Exercise 2

11.	c	**16.**	d
12.	f	**17.**	i
13.	e	**18.**	a
14.	h	**19.**	g
15.	j	**20.**	b

Key Term Crossword

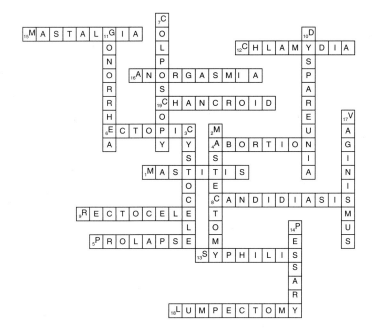

Short Answer Questions

21. Cervical discharge can be cultured to confirm the presence of infectious bacteria, when present.

22. Women at risk for PID are those who are adolescent and young; are nonwhite; have had multiple sex partners; have a history of sexually transmitted infection; have had intercourse with a partner who has untreated urethritis; have had a recent intrauterine device insertion; and who have not had children.

23. Syphilis, herpes simplex virus (HSV), and human papillomavirus (HPV) cause ulcers in the genital area.

24. Three infections are associated with vaginitis conditions: trichomoniasis, bacterial vaginosis, and candidiasis.

25. Risk factors for breast cancer include the following:
- Long menstrual histories
- Use of birth control pills
- Hormone replacement therapy
- Early menarche (<12 years)
- Late menopause (> 55 years)
- Age at first full-term pregnancy (after 30 years)
- Women with a family history of breast cancer
- Lack of regular exercise
- Postmenopausal obesity
- Increased use of alcohol
- Night shift workers
- Age (65 years +)
- Caucasian women after age 40
- High breast tissue density
- No full-term pregnancies
- Never breast-fed
- Higher socioeconomic status
- Tall
- Jewish heritage
- Two or more first-degree relatives with breast cancer at an early age

26. Risk factors for uterine fibroid tumors are 40 years of age or older, nulliparity, obesity, family history, African American, and hypertension.

27. Nursing diagnoses for endometriosis include:
- Potential for *Tissue Perfusion, Ineffective,* from prolonged and heavy periods
- *Fatigue* related to anemia
- *Chronic Pain* and *Acute Pain* related to pelvic lesions
- *Deficient Knowledge* related to management of symptoms and treatment options
- *Ineffective Sexuality Pattern* related to dyspareunia
- *Anxiety* and *Grieving* related to decreased fertility

28. Causes of ectopic pregnancy are varied but often include problems that may leave scar tissue or prevent movement of the fertilized ovum appropriately down the fallopian tube and into the uterine cavity. These problems include pelvic inflammatory disease (PID), previous ectopic pregnancy, endometriosis, tubal surgery, and use of an intrauterine device (IUD) for birth control. Also contributing to the risk of ectopic pregnancy are procedures used in infertility treatments, including *in vitro* fertilization and embryo transfer. Any condition that leaves residual scar tissue can cause partial or complete blockage of the fallopian tubes.

29. Women with PCOS have a 4 to 7 times' higher risk of coronary artery disease and myocardial infarction than do women of the same age without PCOS. Additionally, PCOS patients are at greater risk of having high blood pressure. The increased risk for the development of endometrial cancer is another concern for women with PCOS.

30. Diagnosis of TSS is based on fever, low blood pressure, rash that peels after 1 to 2 weeks, and at least 3 organs with signs of dysfunction. In some cases, blood cultures may be positive for growth of *S. aureus*).

True or False?

31. T	**36.** F
32. T	**37.** T
33. F	**38.** T
34. F	**39.** F
35. T	**40.** T

NCLEX-RN® Review Questions

Question numbers correspond to Outcome-Based Learning Objectives for this chapter.

49-1. Answer: 2

Rationale: The patient's complaints are seen in candidiasis or a yeast infection. Causes of this type of infection include pregnancy, diabetes mellitus, use of antibiotics/corticosteroids, tight-fitting undergarments, and frequent douching. The other choices are not typical causes of candidiasis.

Cognitive Level: Application

Nursing Process: Assessment

Client Need: Physiological Integrity; Reduction of Risk Potential

49-2. Answer: 3

Rationale: A woman who chooses a lumpectomy and radiation will have the same expected long-term survival as if she had chosen a more invasive surgery such as a mastectomy. Breast reconstructive surgery occurs after a mastectomy for breast cancer. Chemotherapy is used to destroy cancer cells that may have migrated to other body tissues or to decrease the size of a tumor to allow a more conservative approach to surgery.

Cognitive Level: Analysis

Nursing Process: Planning

Client Need: Physiological Integrity; Physiological Adaptation

49-3. Answer: 1

Rationale: The nurse should instruct the patient to establish a regular schedule. The breasts should be examined standing (in front of a mirror and in the shower) and lying down on a flat surface. Nipple discharge should be reported to a health care practitioner. Breast dimpling should be reported to a health care practitioner.

Cognitive Level: Application

Nursing Process: Implementation

Client Need: Health Promotion and Maintenance; Prevention and/or Early Detection of Health Problems

49-4. Answer: 3

Rationale: Uterine muscle growths lead to fibroids. Weak posterior vaginal walls cause a rectocele. Bladder protrusion into the vagina is the cause of a cystocele. Endometriosis is a condition in which endometrial-like cells that are normally found only in the uterus are found outside the uterus. These cells attach to ovaries, fallopian tubes, the bowels, or abdominal organs. During the menstrual cycle, these cells respond to hormone production and may swell and bleed. In response, the body will surround these lesions with scar tissue, which can form adhesions on the area of attachment. These adhesions respond to the hormones that stimulate the monthly period with the proliferation of blood and tissue. Tissue and blood that are shed into the body cause inflammation, scar tissue, and subsequently pain.

Cognitive Level: Application

Nursing Process: Implementation

Client Need: Physiological Integrity; Reduction of Risk Potential

49-5. Answer: 3

Rationale: Dyspareunia, painful intercourse, can be a result of several factors including both physiological and psychological ones. Menopause is a physiological cause, resulting from a decrease in hormone production, which in turn decreases the normal lubricating mechanism of the vagina. In addition, the vagina may become somewhat smaller during menopause, causing a more difficult penetration. Hormone replacement therapy and lubricating gel can assist in the treatment of dyspareunia related to menopause.

Cognitive Level: Application

Nursing Process: Implementation

Client Need: Health Promotion and Maintenance; Growth and Development Through the Life Span

49-6. Answer: 4

Rationale: Intracytoplasmic sperm injection or ICSI is indicated for severe male infertility. Zygote intrafallopian transfer (ZIFT) and gamete intrafallopian transfer (GIFT) are indicated after in vitro fertilization has failed or in the event of blocked fallopian tubes and severe male infertility. In vitro fertilization and embryo transfer are indicated when the cervix has an unfavorable environment due to acidic secretions.

Cognitive Level: Analysis

Nursing Process: Planning

Client Need: Health Promotion and Maintenance; Growth and Development Through the Life Span

49-7. Answer: 1

Rationale: A colposcopy is a test to evaluate the cells of the cervix. The procedure can be done in an office setting. The patient is encouraged to take ibuprofen or extra-strength Tylenol shortly before the procedure to help control the pain of the procedure. It is important to remind the patient not to insert anything into the vagina, including not having intercourse, for 24 to 48 hours before the procedure. Spermicides, tampons, and semen can interfere with test results.

Cognitive Level: Application

Nursing Process: Implementation

Client Need: Physiological Integrity; Reduction of Risk Potential

49-8. Answer: 3

Rationale: Victims of sexual assault should never be allowed to leave the hospital alone after treatment. Rape advocates should be available to ensure the patient's safety once released from the hospital. A safe house, family member's home, or women's shelter may be possible options for the patient. Providing the number of the police department is not as helpful to the patient as ensuring she be accompanied upon leaving the hospital. Nurses can help prevent sexual assaults by educating young women about self-defense and avoiding risky situations, but this is not most helpful immediately after a rape has occurred.

Cognitive Level: Application

Nursing Process: Implementation

Client Need: Psychosocial Integrity; Psychosocial Adaptation

Chapter 50 – Caring for the Patient with Male Reproductive Disorders

Key Terms Matching Exercise 1

1.	e	**6.**	i
2.	h	**7.**	b
3.	a	**8.**	c
4.	d	**9.**	g
5.	f		

Key Terms Matching Exercise 2

10.	d	**14.**	b
11.	c	**15.**	f
12.	g	**16.**	e
13.	h	**17.**	a

Key Terms Matching Exercise 3

18.	b	**22.**	f
19.	a	**23.**	d
20.	e	**24.**	g
21.	h	**25.**	c

Complete the Sentence

26. immediate surgery
27. testicular
28. 65, African American, high-fat, meat, smoking
29. prostate-specific antigen (PSA)
30. retention, hydroephrosis
31. squamous cell carcinomas
32. diabetes, stroke, atherosclerosis, prostate surgery
33. surgery, bowel resection
34. human papillomavirus
35. Genital ulcers

Labeling Exercise: Extrascrotal Testicular Sites

a. Abdominal
b. Suprapubic
c. Intracanalicular
d. Superficial inguinal
e. High scrotal
f. Femoral
g. Perineal
h. Normal

NCLEX-RN® Review Questions

Question numbers correspond to Outcome-Based Learning Objectives for this chapter.

50-1. Answer: 2
Rationale: In older males, hydrocele may develop after infection in the scrotum, injury, radiation, or testicular cancer. Testicular torsion occurs when a mobile testicle causes a twisting of the spermatic cord, essentially closing off the blood supply to the testicle. Annually, 1 in 4,000 males under the age of 25 experience testicular torsion. Orchitis is an inflammation or infection of one or both testes. Epididymitis is an infection or inflammation of the ductus epididymidis.
Cognitive Level: Analysis
Nursing Process: Assessment
Client Need: Physiological Integrity; Reduction of Risk Potential

50-2. Answer: 4
Rationale: Symptoms of acute prostatitis include flu-like symptoms, pain in genitalia, pelvis, or low back, dysuria, nocturia, urgency, frequency, hematuria, and painful ejaculation. Hypotension, tachycardia, and dyspnea are not symptoms of acute prostatitis.
Cognitive Level: Analysis
Nursing Process: Assessment
Client Need: Physiological Integrity; Physiological Adaptation

50-3. Answer: 2
Rationale: An elevated white blood cell count in the diagnosis of epididymitis is due to an inflammatory and/or infectious process. While systemic disease, upper respiratory infections, and urinary tract infections may result in

elevating the white blood cell count, it is the inflammatory process that is directly responsible for its elevation in acute prostatitis.
Cognitive Level: Analysis
Nursing Process: Assessment
Client Need: Physiological Integrity; Reduction of Risk Potential

50-4. Answer: 1
Rationale: Instructions for this patient should include: continue antibiotics as prescribed; report continuation or worsening of symptoms to health care provider; regular voiding and complete emptying of bladder; increase fluids, such as water, to 64 to 128 ounces per day to flush the bladder; and avoid beverages and food that are irritating to the bladder such as alcohol, caffeine, citrus juices, and hot/spicy foods.
Cognitive Level: Application
Nursing Process: Planning
Client Need: Physiological Integrity; Physiological Adaptation

50-5. Answer: 2
Rationale: Home care needs include verbal and written instructions for a variety of aspects of daily life. The patient may go home with catheter in place and will need education about maintaining patency of the tubing and cleansing the urinary meatus. The patient may experience urinary incontinence after removal of the catheter but it will improve. The patient should be encouraged to rest, and avoid lifting heavy objects, sitting for long periods, or straining at stool. Additionally, the patient should be instructed to maintain increased oral intake at about 2–3 quarts a day, unless medically contraindicated. The patient should also practice pelvic exercises, stopping urinary stream, and contracting and relaxing pelvic muscles. The patient should follow up with the health care provider in 1 to 3 weeks.
Cognitive Level: Application
Nursing Process: Planning
Client Need: Physiological Integrity; Physiological Adaptation

50-6. Answer: 4
Rationale: In the United States, it is estimated based on imprecise data that 10 to 20 million men over age 18 have had at least a few instances of erectile dysfunction. The prevalence increases to 50% of men aged 40 to 70. The major organic causes include diabetes, stroke, atherosclerosis, spinal cord injuries, and complications of prostate surgery. Hormones, significant smoking, alcohol, drugs, and structural problems may also contribute to erectile dysfunction.
Cognitive Level: Application
Nursing Process: Implementation
Client Need: Health Promotion and Maintenance; Prevention and/or Early Detection of Health Problems

Chapter 51 – Nursing Assessment of Patients with Endocrine Disorders

Key Terms Matching Exercise

1.	d	**5.**	a
2.	f	**6.**	g
3.	c	**7.**	b
4.	h	**8.**	e

Short Answer Questions

9. The glands of the endocrine system include
   - Hypothalamus
   - Pituitary gland
   - Adrenal glands
   - Thyroid gland
   - Parathyroid glands
   - Islet cells of the pancreas
   - Gonads

10. Abnormalities of endocrine function are produced by five indistinct mechanisms: difficulty with the appropriate transport of a hormone, production of hormones by hypersecretion (excessive production) or hyposecretion (decreased production), inability of target tissues to respond to a secreted hormone, and inappropriate stimulation of target tissue.

11. Symptoms of disorders associated with abnormal levels of growth hormone include gigantism in children, acromegaly in adults, and dwarfism in children.

12. Symptoms of disorders associated with abnormal levels of antidiuretic hormone include SIADH, weight gain, hyponatremia, diabetes insipidus, psychogenic polydipsia, enuresis, and nephrotic syndrome.

13. The gonads are the body's primary source of sexual hormones. Gonads are important for the progression into puberty, and they control other physical traits that differentiate men from women. The principal hormone produced by the testes is testosterone.

14. The first adrenal cortex disorder is Cushing's disease, caused by an excess of cortisol. Cortisol causes breakdown of fat and muscle from the extremities for conversion to glucose (gluconeogenesis), which is subsequently deposited as fat in the abdomen and face and back. Symptoms of Cushing's disease include truncal obesity, thin arms and legs, moon face, buffalo hump, severe fatigue and muscle weakness, hyperglycemia, easy bruising, gastrointestinal bleeding, depression, and osteoporosis. The second cortex disorder is Addison's disease, caused by an autoimmune response that destroys the adrenal cortex. It is characterized by lack of aldosterone, a mineralocorticoid responsible for sodium and water reabsorption from the kidney tubules.

15. Symptoms of hypothyroidism include fatigue, weight gain, elevated cholesterol levels, heavy menstrual periods, constipation, and decreased deep tendon reflexes. Hair is thinned and dry and loses its shine, and the skin is dry. Patients with hypothyroidism may complain of cold intolerance and have bradycardia. Because hypothyroidism causes slow mentation, cognitive disorders, and decreased orientation, a mental status exam should be completed. Hypothyroidism is sometimes associated with nodular goiters and the swallowing process may be involved and needs to be assessed.

16. The islet cells within the pancreas regulate glucose levels through secretion and inhibition of insulin and glucagons. One type of islet cell, the alpha cell, is responsible for the production of glucagon. This hormone decreases the oxidation of glucose and promotes an increase in the serum glucose level by signaling the liver to release glucose from the glycogen stores. Beta cells, another type of islet cell, are responsible for the production of insulin. Insulin facilitates the uptake and use of glucose by the cells and prevents excessive breakdown of glycogen in the liver and muscle. Together, insulin and glucagon control blood sugar levels by a simple feedback loop. Diabetes mellitus is a disorder characterized by either lack of insulin (type 1) or impaired use of insulin (type 2).

17. DM is diagnosed in the presence of any random blood sugar higher than 200 mg/dL and/or a fasting blood sugar of >125 mg/dL. Prediabetes is diagnosed with a fasting blood sugar of between 110 and 125 mg/dL.

18. With endocrine disorders, the history is the most essential piece of data collection. Many times, patients will have a constellation of symptoms that do not clearly fit into one hormone imbalance. The nurse is in a unique position to analyze the data to determine the relevance of each symptom to the underlying disorder.

Labeling Exercise: General Feedback Loop

a. External and internal stimuli
b. Central nervous system
c. Hypothalamus neurosecretory cells
d. Stimulating hormones
e. Short feedback loop
f. Short feedback loop
g. Long feedback loop
h. Target hormone
i. Effector cells or physiologic effects
j. Target gland
k. General circulation
l. Pituitary
m. Hypothalamic portal veins
n. Releasing factor

NCLEX-RN® Review Questions

Question numbers correspond to Outcome-Based Learning Objectives for this chapter.

51-1. Answer: 2
   Rationale: The endocrine system's functioning is intimately connected to that of the nervous system. Together, they provide a mechanism for communication between cells and organs. This connection is referred to as neuroendocrine regulation. They work synergistically to regulate overall physiologic functioning by regulating responses to the internal and external environment. Through their combined efforts, growth and development, maintenance of homeostasis, the ability to adapt to changes in the external environment, and reproduction can occur. Hearing deficit, low blood pressure, and renal calculi do not directly impact endocrine functioning.
   Cognitive Level: Analysis
   Nursing Process: Assessment
   Client Need: Physiological Integrity; Physiological Adaptation

51-2. Answer: 1
   Rationale: Hormones travel through the bloodstream to reach target tissues or receptors. They exist as proteins, peptides, lipids, or amino acid analogues. As they circulate in the bloodstream they may be free or bound. The majority of hormones are secreted in their active form. Others must undergo metabolic conversion to their active form in peripheral tissue. A feedback system is a regulatory system that keeps certain activities of body function within a prescribed range to sustain homeostasis. Hormones that affect cells within the vicinity of their release are considered paracine functioning.
   Cognitive Level: Analysis
   Nursing Process: Assessment
   Client Need: Physiological Integrity; Pharmacological and Parenteral Therapies

51-3. Answer: 1
   Rationale: The islet cells within the pancreas provide endocrine functioning. There are four types of islet cells:

alpha, beta, delta, and F cells. Alpha cells are responsible for the production of glucagon. Beta cells are responsible for the production of insulin. Delta cells produce somatostatin, which inhibits GH, TSH, and gastrointestinal hormones. F cells produce pancreatic polypeptide, or digestive enzymes, which are responsible for the exocrine activity of the pancreas.
Cognitive Level: Analysis
Nursing Process: Assessment
Client Need: Physiological Integrity; Physiological Adaptation

51-4. Answer: 1
Rationale: Assessment of the head and neck involves both internal and external examination. The swallowing process is observed along with the character and quality of voice. When clients experience thyroid enlargement they will have palpable or visible enlargement of the thyroid, which can displace the trachea, affecting breathing and swallowing. Visual changes can be associated with hyperglycemia seen in diabetes and with thyroid disorders. Hyperglycemia causes osmotic fluid shifts in the vitrous fluid resulting in blurred vision. Increased pigmentation of the oral mucosa may indicate Addison's disease. Hypertrophy of the tongue and enlarged jaw, ears, and hands can be seen in clients with acromegaly. Tumors of the pituitary may erode into the oral mucosa. Loss of the outer potion of the eyebrows is associated with endocrine dysfunction.
Cognitive Level: Analysis
Nursing Process: Assessment
Client Need: Physiological Integrity; Physiological Adaptation

51-5. Answer: 2
Rationale: An oral glucose tolerance test of >200 mg/dL is diagnostic for diabetes mellitus. An elevated fasting blood glucose is seen in physiological stress. A decrease in fasting blood glucose and an oral glucose tolerance test of <140 mg/dl is seen in insulinomas. A decrease in fasting blood glucose and a low hemoglobin A1c level of <4% is seen in Addison's disease.
Cognitive Level: Analysis
Nursing Process: Assessment
Client Need: Physiological Integrity; Physiological Adaptation

Chapter 52 – Caring for the Patient with Glandular and Hormonal Disorders

Key Terms Matching Exercise 1

1.	c	**6.**	d
2.	f	**7.**	h
3.	i	**8.**	b
4.	a	**9.**	e
5.	j	**10.**	g

Key Terms Matching Exercise 2

11.	b	**16.**	d
12.	g	**17.**	e
13.	j	**18.**	c
14.	i	**19.**	a
15.	h	**20.**	f

Key Term Crossword

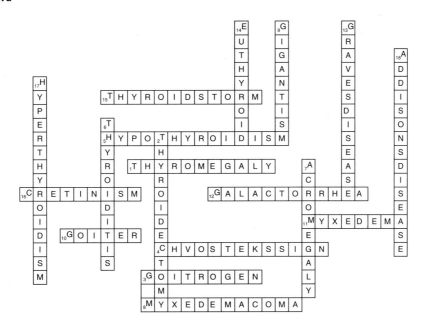

Short Answer Questions

21. The primary function of the thyroid gland is to produce thyroid hormone, which regulates body metabolism.

22. Risk factors for hypothyroidism include familial history of thyroid disease, a history of autoimmune disease, pernicious anemia, aging, an inadequate supply of dietary iodine, and previous treatment for hyperthyroidism. Hypothyroidism can occur at any age but is particularly common in older adults, affecting 17% of women and 9% of men over age 60. An iodine-deficient diet also is a risk factor in the development of hypothyroidism.

23. **Cardiopulmonary symptoms**: slowed heartbeat/pulse, high blood pressure, high cholesterol levels, cardiac enlargement, congestive heart failure, ascites

    Neuromuscular symptoms: drowsiness, fatigue, mental lethargy, forgetfulness, depression, muscular weakness, emotional lability, paranoia

    Gastrointestinal symptoms: enlarged tongue, constipation, reduced bowel sounds

    Skin/hair symptoms: dry patchy skin, coarse and thinning hair (alopecia), fluid retention in skin, cold intolerance, decreased perspiration, edema of face and eyelids

    Other symptoms: weight gain, fatigue, heavy and irregular menstrual periods, lowered body temperature

24. **Cardiopulmonary symptoms**: rapid heartbeat/pulse, palpitations, angina, irregular heart rhythm, heat intolerance, and hot flashes

    Neuromuscular symptoms: insomnia, jitteriness, shaking, nervousness, irritability, hand tremors, muscle weakness, myalgia, and muscle cramps

    Gastrointestinal symptoms: difficulty swallowing, more frequent bowel movements, diarrhea

    Skin/hair symptoms: thinning hair or alopecia, warm, moist skin (sweating), heat intolerance

    Other symptoms: unexplained weight loss, change in or lighter menstrual cycles, bulging eyes (exophthalmos), goiter (thyroid enlargement), accelerated loss of calcium from bones

25. The leading cause of Addison's disease is autoimmune disease in which the body's immune system makes antibodies that gradually destroy the cells of the adrenal cortex.

True or False?

26.	T	**31.**	T
27.	F	**32.**	T
28.	T	**33.**	F
29.	T	**34.**	T
30.	F	**35.**	F

Complete the Sentence

36. endocrine, exocrine
37. Graves' disease
38. muscles, nerves
39. pituitary tumors
40. chemical balance, metabolism, glands

Labeling Exercise: Location of the Endocrine Glands in the Male and Female Bodies

a. Pituitary gland
b. Thyroid and parathyroid glands
c. Adrenal glands
d. Pancreas
e. Ovaries (female)
f. Testes (male)

NCLEX-RN® Review Questions

Question numbers correspond to Outcome-Based Learning Objectives for this chapter.

52-1. Answer: 4
Rationale: Melatonin influences the circadian rhythm. Thymosin aids in the development of the body's immune system. Insulin lowers blood sugar and controls utilization and storage of carbohydrates. Testosterone stimulates male sex characteristics and promotes enlargement of muscle mass.
Cognitive Level: Analysis
Nursing Process: Assessment
Client Need: Physiological Integrity; Reduction of Risk Potential

52-2. Answer: 3
Rationale: An overproduction of the hormones from the posterior pituitary gland can lead to diabetes insipidus. Adrenal gland disorders can be either adrenal insufficiency or Cushing's syndrome. A disorder in the adrenal medulla can lead to pheochromocytoma. Disorders caused by the thyroid include cretinism and Graves' disease.
Cognitive Level: Analysis
Nursing Process: Assessment
Client Need: Physiological Integrity; Physiological Adaptation

52-3. Answer: 2
Rationale: Patients with Addison's disease feel light-headed because their blood pressure is low, and they may experience orthostatic hypotension. Hyperpigmentation of skin is common, with scars, skinfolds, and pressure points such as elbows, knees, and knuckles becoming characteristically dark. Patients with Cushing's syndrome will present with a particular pattern of fat deposition on their face and bodies. The face will be round and typically referred to as "moon face" and the trunk will appear large. The patient will be obese with slender arms and legs. In hyperaldosteronism, patients present with hypertension, headache, orthostatic hypotension, muscle weakness and cramps, fatigue, temporary paralysis, constipation, numbness, pricking, tingling sensations, excessive thirst and urination. Pheochromocytoma causes hypertension by producing an excess of epinephrine (adrenalin) and norepinephrine.
Cognitive Level: Analysis
Nursing Process: Assessment
Client Need: Physiological Integrity; Physiological Adaptation

52-4. Answer: 4
Rationale: In hypoparathyroidism, patients complain about weakness; muscle cramps, particularly of wrists and feet; abnormal paresthesias with tingling, numbness, and burning of hands; excessive nervousness; loss of memory; and headaches. Nerve excitability, triggered by low blood calcium, causes continuous nerve impulses, which stimulate nerve contraction. Other symptoms may include malformations of the teeth and fingernails, spasms of facial muscles or Chvostek's sign, and contraction of carpal muscles with mild compression of the nerves or Trousseau's sign. Chvostek's sign can be induced by tapping on the inferior margin of the zygoma, which will cause facial spasms, and Trousseau's sign can be elicited by inflating the blood pressure cuff and maintaining the cuff pressure above systolic, which will produce carpal spasms if the serum calcium level is low. A low calcium level is not a symptom of difficulty with ambulation, muscle strength, or hand grasps.
Cognitive Level: Application
Nursing Process: Assessment
Client Need: Health Promotion and Maintenance; Prevention and/or Early Detection of Health Problems

52-5. Answer: 3

Rationale: Preparation of patients for discharge with adrenal insufficiency must include instruction regarding the need to take hormone replacement therapy for life. Of particular importance is for patients to understand that stress or illness is likely to increase their need for hydrocortisone. In such situations, they should increase the dosage of hormone as advised by their health care provider. Persistence of vomiting or diarrhea indicates a need for urgent care, which may include intravenous saline and intramuscular hydrocortisone. Flu-like symptoms should never be ignored because they may be the initial indicators of adrenal crisis.
Cognitive Level: Application
Nursing Process: Planning
Client Need: Physiological Integrity; Physiological Adaptation

52-6. Answer: 1

Rationale: Older patients may be overwhelmed when trying to understand the nature of hyperpituitarism. Older patients may need simple but clear instructions on medications and potential side effects. Resolution of symptoms may take some time leading to discouragement, and lack of change in physical appearance may be particularly disheartening and lead to depression. Patients may experience improvement in their field of vision with tumor excision, but failure to remove the tumor, even if other symptoms are controlled, may lead to diminished quality of life for patients who are unable to drive.
Cognitive Level: Application
Nursing Process: Planning
Client Need: Physiological Integrity; Physiological Adaptation

52-7. Answer: 2

Rationale: Increasing the genetic screening of infants at birth for potentially treatable endocrine diseases such as congenital adrenal hyperplasia would save lives. Studies on the genetic etiology of endocrine disease and potential gene therapy also offer significant potential benefits in terms of disease prevention. Saying that nothing can be done is inaccurate. Saying that it is really unlikely is not helpful to the patient. Telling the patient not to worry about it is insensitive.
Cognitive Level: Application
Nursing Process: Implementation
Client Need: Health Promotion and Maintenance; Prevention and/or Early Detection of Health Problems

Chapter 53 – Caring for the Patient with Diabetes

Key Terms Matching Exercise 1

1.	i	**6.**	f
2.	c	**7.**	h
3.	b	**8.**	e
4.	g	**9.**	a
5.	d		

Key Terms Matching Exercise 2

10.	a	**15.**	h
11.	d	**16.**	c
12.	e	**17.**	b
13.	g	**18.**	i
14.	f		

Key Terms Matching Exercise 3

19.	c	**24.**	h
20.	f	**25.**	e
21.	d	**26.**	g
22.	i	**27.**	b
23.	a		

Key Term Crossword

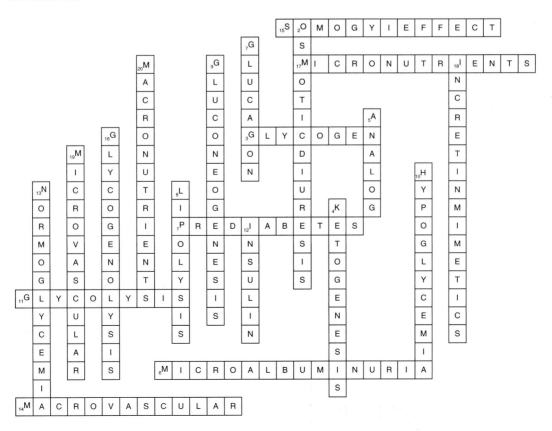

Short Answer Questions

28. Changes in the eyes, nerves, kidneys, heart, veins, and arteries can result in retinopathy (eye disease), neuropathy (nerve disease), nephropathy (kidney disease), and accelerated development of coronary heart disease (CHD), cerebrovascular disease, and peripheral vascular disease (PVD).

29. Type 1 diabetes appears to result from an interaction among genetics, environment, and autoimmunity.

30. Risk factors for type 2 diabetes include a strong genetic linkage, ethnicity, racial admixture, family history, diet, obesity, physical inactivity, urbanization, socioeconomic status and education, and intrauterine environment.

31. Most diabetic lower extremity amputations originate from diabetic foot ulcers, peripheral arterial disease (PAD), peripheral vascular disease (PVD), peripheral neuropathy, minor trauma, deformity, increased plantar pressures, and infection contributing to the development and progression of these ulcers.

32. In hospital settings, insulin drips have been used for DKA and HHS for many years. Currently, insulin drips are being used to maintain normal blood glucose levels in non-DKA or non-HHS patients to maintain normal blood glucose levels. As a result, nurses must assess patients on insulin drips frequently for signs and symptoms of hypoglycemia and assess blood glucose levels on a planned basis (more intense insulin regimens require more frequent monitoring) and any time hypoglycemia is suspected.

True or False?

33.	T	38.	F
34.	T	39.	T
35.	T	40.	F
36.	T	41.	T
37.	F	42.	F

Complete the Sentence

43. counterregulatory hormones, insulin
44. deficiency, increase
45. hyperglycemia, ketosis, hyperglycemia
46. continuous blood glucose monitoring
47. cerebral edema

NCLEX-RN® Review Questions

Question numbers correspond to Outcome-Based Learning Objectives for this chapter.

53-1. Answer: 2
  Rationale: The lifetime probability of developing diabetes is greater in females than males in the United States. The epidemic is not limited to the United States but rather is global in nature. The incidence in Mexican Americans and children is increasing.
  Cognitive Level: Analysis
  Nursing Process: Assessment
  Client Need: Health Promotion and Maintenance; Prevention and/or Early Detection of Health Problems

53-2. Answer: 2
  Rationale: Individuals with type 2 diabetes are not dependent on exogenous insulin; it is controlled with diet, exercise and sometimes oral hypoglycemic medications. However, insulin therapy may be needed to control hyperglycemia, especially when under added stress or an infectious process is present. Individuals with type 1 diabetes

require an exogenous source of insulin daily to maintain blood sugar levels. Latent autoimmune diabetes is an adult form of autoimmune type I diabetes in which the patient would be dependent on exogenous insulin. Hyperosmolar hyperglycemic syndrome occurs in type 2 diabetes and is characterized by excessive hyperglycemia and dehydration.
  Cognitive Level: Analysis
  Nursing Process: Assessment
  Client Need: Physiological Integrity; Physiological Adaptation

53-3. Answer: 1
  Rationale: Gestational diabetes does pose an increased risk for later development of type 2 diabetes, with as many as 50% of women developing it later in life. But it is not an absolute certainty. Since it does increases the risk, the nurse should encourage the patient to make healthy lifestyle changes that will keep the blood sugar within normal levels.
  Cognitive Level: Application
  Nursing Process: Implementation
  Client Need: Physiological Integrity; Physiological Adaptation

53-4. Answer: 2
  Rationale: It is recommended to test for microalbuminuria yearly, since this can detect early diabetic nephropathy and steps can be taken to prevent further damage. Potassium and fluids do not need to be restricted unless renal impairment has been diagnosed. A diet low in fat is recommended if cardiovascular disease is present and fiber restriction is recommended if the patient is experiencing diabetic gastroparesis.
  Cognitive Level: Application
  Nursing Process: Implementation
  Client Need: Physiological Integrity; Reduction of Risk Potential

53-5. Answer: 2
  Rationale: In the second stage of type 2 diabetes, insulin resistance increases and compensatory hyperinsulinemia is insufficient to maintain normal glucose levels. At this stage fasting glucose levels remain normal, but the postprandial glucose levels rise. A postprandial level of 190 mg/dL is elevated. The fasting level of 130 mg/dL is elevated and should be normal (80–110) in the second stage. Weight loss and muscle cramps are not associated with the second stage.
  Cognitive Level: Analysis
  Nursing Process: Assessment
  Client Need: Physiological Integrity; Physiological Adaptation

53-6. Answer: 3
  Rationale: The patient is at risk for hypoglycemia, a side effect of meglitinides. Tachycardia, tremors, palpitations, irritability, headache, and moist skin are common signs of hypoglycemia. A drop in blood pressure and bradycardia are not associated with hypoglycemia. Hot, flushed skin is a sign of hyperglycemia.
  Cognitive Level: Application
  Nursing Process: Planning
  Client Need: Physiological Integrity; Reduction of Risk Potential

53-7. Answer: 2
  Rationale: When patients have decreased or absent lower extremity sensation, the patient should avoid weight-bearing activities. Non-weight-bearing activities such as swimming and bicycling also provide an aerobic exercise that is beneficial. Walking, rowing, and weight lifting are all types of weight-bearing activities.
  Cognitive Level: Application
  Nursing Process: Implementation
  Client Need: Physiological Integrity; Reduction of Risk Potential

53-8. Answer: 2

Rationale: Meglitinides cause a rapid secretion of insulin from the pancreas which reduces the chances of postprandial hyperglycemia, but this may cause hypoglycemia. Tremors, shakiness, and palpitations are signs of hypoglycemia. The speed at which the meal is consumed should not affect the reaction; patients should eat within 20 minutes of taking the medication. An excessively high dose may cause hypoglycemia, not an insufficient dose. The drug should be given before meals.

Cognitive Level: Analysis

Nursing Process: Assessment

Client Need: Physiological Integrity; Pharmacological and Parenteral Therapies

53-9. Answer: 2

Rationale: Insulin requires potassium for transport into the cell; in DKA large amounts of insulin are given, which drives potassium into the cell, leading to a drop in extracellular levels. The creatinine level may be elevated if the patient is dehydrated or has renal impairment. Sodium levels may be increased in DKA, dependent on fluid shifts and losses, but this is not related to the insulin therapy. Phosphorus levels are also not related to the insulin therapy.

Cognitive Level: Application

Nursing Process: Assessment

Client Need: Physiological Integrity; Physiological Adaptation

53-10. Answer: 4

Rationale: Trimming the nails straight across helps to prevent ingrown nails and filing them smooth helps to prevent ragged edges that may cut the skin. The feet should be washed daily with sudsy water and rinsed well, but soaking the feet should be avoided. Lotion can be applied daily to keep the skin from drying and cracking, but the area between the toes should be avoided; the area can become moist and harbor bacteria and cause skin breakdown. The patient should never walk barefoot; shoes should be worn at all times.

Cognitive Level: Application

Nursing Process: Implementation

Client Need: Physiological Integrity; Reduction of Risk Potential

Chapter 54 – Nursing Assessment of Patients with Musculoskeletal Disorders

Key Terms Matching Exercise

1.	b	**6.**	f
2.	a	**7.**	c
3.	d	**8.**	j
4.	g	**9.**	e
5.	i	**10.**	h

Key Term Crossword

Complete the Sentence

11. long, flat, short, irregular
12. age, gender, culture, educational background
13. flexibility, mobility, range of motion
14. resistance, 0, 5
15. temperature, redness, tenderness
16. crepitus, pain
17. thumb abduction, Tinel's sign, Phalen's test
18. ligament, meniscus, cruciate ligaments, collateral ligaments
19. pain
20. Flexibility, strength, muscle mass

Labeling Exercise 1: Ligaments of the Knee Joint

a. Femur
b. Inner side of the knee
c. Articular cartilage
d. Anterior cruciate ligament (ACL)
e. Medial collateral ligament (MCL)
f. Medial meniscus
g. Tibia
h. Lateral meniscus
i. Lateral collateral ligament (LCL)
j. Posterior cruciate ligament (PCL)
k. Outer side of the knee

Labeling Exercise 2: Knee Joint

a. Quadricep muscle
b. Tendon
c. Femur
d. Patella
e. Cartilage
f. Patellar ligament
g. Tibia

NCLEX Review Questions

54-1. Answer: 4
Rationale: Ligaments play a crucial role in the function of the skeletal joints in that they bind the ends of different bones together, preventing dislocations or displacement of a bone from its normal position. Tendons connect muscle to bone. A joint is where two or more bones meet or come together. Cartilage is an elastic, flexible connective tissue. The main function of cartilage is as a cushioner.
Cognitive Level: Analysis
Nursing Process: Assessment
Client Need: Physiological Integrity; Reduction of Risk Potential

54-2. Answer: 1
Rationale: Demographic data may be helpful in determining causes of injury. For instance, if the patient's job requires sitting and typing on a computer all day, he or she may complain of back and neck pain from sitting in a chair that does not support the back, or pain in the joints of the hand, wrist, or arm from the repetitive motion during typing or improper height of the desk placing strain on the joints. Biographical data should include age, gender, culture, and educational background. A social history provides additional information about the patient's lifestyle that may affect the potential disorder or complaint. Characteristics, lengths, exacerbation, or diminishment of symptoms, and what is wrong or feared by the patient, defines the chief complaint.
Cognitive Level: Application
Nursing Process: Assessment

Client Need: Physiological Integrity; Reduction of Risk Potential

54-3. Answer: 4
Rationale: Muscle strength is measured by placing the hand firmly against the body part in question and asking the patient to push hard against the hand. Perform the test on both sides and compare findings. The strength of the patient's ability to push is described by a number ranging from 0 or complete paralysis to the number 5 or normal. Range of motion is used to determine the functionality of joints. Palpation is used to determine skin temperature, the presence of any nodules, or muscle or joint tenderness and swelling. Inspection is used to compare corresponding paired joints for symmetry. The nurse should observe for skin color, scars, and shape of the site, deformities, muscle atrophy, masses, or swelling.
Cognitive Level: Application
Nursing Process: Assessment
Client Need: Health Promotion and Maintenance; Prevention and/or Early Detection of Health Problems

54-4. Answer: 1
Rationale: The bulge sign is used to detect fluid in the knee and is performed by placing the hand on the medial aspect of the patient's knee and pushing upward two to four times to displace the fluid. Then place the hand on the lateral side of the knee and look for a bulge of fluid in the hollow area medial to the patella. The bulge sign is not used to assess the hip, ankle, or elbow.
Cognitive Level: Analysis
Nursing Process: Assessment
Client Need: Health Promotion and Maintenance; Prevention and/or Early Detection of Health Problems

54-5. Answer: 2
Rationale: The abnormal finding of unequal leg length could indicate scoliosis. Leg shortening could mean muscle deformities or hip fracture. Difficulty in ambulation with irregular gait could indicate a dislocation or fracture of the hip, degenerative joint disease, or muscle weakness.
Cognitive Level: Analysis
Nursing Process: Assessment
Client Need: Health Promotion and Maintenance; Prevention and/or Early Detection of Health Problems

54-6. Answer: 1
Rationale: The nurse is assessing the patient's wrists for carpal tunnel syndrome. Carpal tunnel syndrome occurs when the median nerve is compressed as it travels with the flexor tendons through a canal made by the carpal bones and the transverse carpal ligament. To assess for carpal tunnel syndrome, the patient is asked to perform three tests: thumb abduction; Tinel's sign; and the Phalen's test, which is done by asking the patient to place the backs of the hands against each other while flexing the wrists 90 degrees for 60 seconds.
Cognitive Level: Analysis
Nursing Process: Assessment
Client Need: Health Promotion and Maintenance; Prevention and/or Early Detection of Health Problems

Chapter 55 – Caring for the Patient with Musculoskeletal Disorders

Key Terms Matching Exercise 1

1. c
2. l
3. e
4. b
5. h
6. i
7. a
8. d
9. k
10. g
11. j
12. f

Key Terms Matching Exercise 2

13. k	19. i
14. d	20. a
15. c	21. e
16. h	22. g
17. f	23. b
18. j	

Short Answer Questions

24. The anterior pituitary, thyroid, parathyroid, and adrenal glands influence bone growth.

25. Loss of bone mass is a universal characteristic of humans; however, research findings suggest that genetic factors, body weight, smoking, alcohol, physical activity, and diet provide direct and indirect influences on the amount of bone mineral density loss.

26. Menopause is associated with the reduction of estrogen that is needed for the bone formation process, causing a decline in bone mineral density and strength that results in thin, fragile bones. Bone loss generally stabilizes about 10 years after menopause.

27. Acute osteomyelitis falls into two categories: hematogenous and direct contact. Hematogenous osteomyelitis is an infection caused by bacterial infection from a distant site migrating by way of the bloodstream to the bone. The other category of acute osteomyelitis, direct contact, results from direct trauma or surgery. It is the direct contact of bacteria or the implanting of bacteria from the outside environment that can cause infection.

28. Osteitis deformans rarely causes symptoms. When symptoms do occur they usually include bone pain at the site. The pain can become disabling because it is constant and worse at night. Patients may experience edema or deformity at the affected site. If the ossicles of the ear are involved, hearing loss or deafness will occur.

29. The primary focus of nursing care for the patient with bone cancer is relief of pain, prevention of pathologic fractures, and provision of a supportive environment.

30. The most serious complications are cardiomyopathy and respiratory distress. Other complications include muscle atrophy and contractures, cognitive effects, spinal abnormalities, and osteoporosis.

31. Safety in the home, proper nutrition, self-care activities, maintenance of mobility, and preventing constipation are teaching and discharge priorities for patients with MD and their families.

32. Some of the causes of rhabdomyolysis include trauma with muscle compression, surgical procedures in which there is a long period of muscle compression, immobilization due to a comatose or postictal state (usually occurring after seizure activity when the patient has been unconscious and unresponsive to stimuli) in which the patient is lying in one position for long periods of time, extreme physical exertion, snakebite, toxins, and viral, bacterial, or fungal infection.

33. Idiopathic muscle cramps are muscle cramps that occur with no particular etiology. The cramps are usually without accompanying weakness. Idiopathic muscle cramps generally affect healthy, middle-aged or older adults and generally occur during the nighttime or when the person is sleeping. The most common muscles affected are the calf or foot muscles, causing plantar flexion to the afflicted foot.

True or False?

34. T	39. F
35. F	40. T
36. T	41. F
37. T	42. T
38. F	43. T

Labeling Exercise 1: Bone Tissues

a. Subchondral tissue
b. Cancellous tissue
c. Marrow
d. Compact tissue
e. Subchondral tissue

Labeling Exercise 2: Cortical and Cancellous Bone

a. Periosteum
b. Compact bone (cortical)
c. Marrow
d. Spongy bone (cancellous)

Labeling Exercise 3: Compact and Cancellous Bone with Haversian Canal

a. Lamellae
b. Canaliculi
c. Osteon
d. Volkmann's canal
e. Lacunae containing osteocytes
f. Osteon of compact bone
g. Haversian canal
h. Trabeculae of spongy bone
i. Periosteum

NCLEX-RN® Review Questions

Question numbers correspond to Outcome-Based Learning Objectives for this chapter.

55-1. Answer: 1, 2, 3, 4
Rationale: Several endocrine glands influence bone modeling and remodeling processes. Endocrine glands that produce hormones that influence bone growth include the pituitary, parathyroid, thyroid, and adrenal glands. The thymus and parotid glands are not associated with bone growth.
Cognitive Level: Analysis
Nursing Process: Assessment
Client Need: Health Promotion and Maintenance; Prevention and/or Early Detection of Health Problems

55-2. Answer: 1
Rationale: Testing for osteoporosis, especially in females, should start at age 50 and men aged 70 and older, which involves bone mineral density measurement (vs. a serum analysis). In 1998, the Bone Mass Measurement Act required Medicare to reimburse for bone mineral density tests.
Cognitive Level: Application
Nursing Process: Implementation
Client Need: Health Promotion and Maintenance; Prevention and/or Early Detection of Health Problems

55-3. Answer: 2
Rationale: Twenty percent of older people who sustain a hip fracture die within a year. Two years after the fracture, survivors are more than 4 times more likely to have limited mobility than people of similar age without a fracture, and more than twice as likely to be functionally dependent. Evidence shows that women are at greater risk of hip fracture than men, and this risk increases steadily and substantially with age.
Cognitive Level: Application
Nursing Process: Assessment
Client Need: Health Promotion and Maintenance; Prevention and/or Early Detection of Health Problems

55-4. Answer: 4

Rationale: Scoliosis is a lateral curvature of the spine. Lordosis, or swayback, is noticed mostly in those young men who are still able to ambulate. Kyphosis is hunchback. Scoliosis that is severe can lead to respiratory problems, sleeping problems, and the inability to sit straight or remain seated for prolonged periods of time.

Cognitive Level: Analysis

Nursing Process: Assessment

Client Need: Health Promotion and Maintenance; Prevention and/or Early Detection of Health Problems

55-5. Answer: 3

Rationale: As with all patients with muscle diseases, safety concerns are a priority. The older a person becomes, the more brittle the bones become. Muscle mass and tone decrease and combined with the effects of aging, the added muscle weakness associated with myopathy puts the patient at risk for falls and other injuries. In creating a plan of care for a patient diagnosed with a myopathy, safety must be a priority. Fatigue, economic status, and emotional welfare are secondary concerns to safety.

Cognitive Level: Application

Nursing Process: Planning

Client Need: Safe, Effective Care Environment; Safety and Infection Control

55-6. Answer: 3

Rationale: The Federal Food and Drug Administration (FDA) has approved the use of pregabalin (Lyrica) for patients with fibromyalgia. Two double-blinded studies showed that the use of the medication provided rapid and sustained pain reduction and improved sleep patterns for six months. Mood, appetite, and energy are not directly approved by the drug.

Cognitive Level: Application

Nursing Process: Implementation

Client Need: Physiological Integrity; Pharmacological and Parenteral Therapies

Chapter 56 – Caring for the Patient with Musculoskeletal Trauma

Key Terms Matching Exercise 1

1.	f	**7.**	d
2.	l	**8.**	b
3.	c	**9.**	i
4.	e	**10.**	a
5.	h	**11.**	g
6.	k	**12.**	j

Key Terms Matching Exercise 2

13.	b	**19.**	j
14.	f	**20.**	e
15.	a	**21.**	c
16.	h	**22.**	k
17.	g	**23.**	i
18.	l	**24.**	d

Complete the Sentence

25. Sprains, ligaments

26. transverse, oblique, spiral, comminuted, segmental, butterfly, and impacted

27. deformities, breaks, vascular

28. bladder, urethra, vagina, prostate, gastrointestinal

29. hemodynamic, pelvic ring

30. mobility, assistive devices

31. nutritional

32. pain, pallor, poor capillary, paresthesia, pulselessness

33. bowel, ischemia, necrosis

34. Hip, wrist

Labeling Exercise 1: Ankle Ligaments and Inversion Injury

a. Inversion injury

b. Tibiofibular ligaments

c. Posterior talofibular ligament

d. Anterior talofibular ligament

e. Calcaneofibular ligament

Labeling Exercise 2: Long Bone

a. Proximal epiphysis

b. Metaphysis

c. Diaphysis

d. Metaphysis

e. Distal epiphysis

f. Articular cartilage

g. Spongy bone (contains red bone marrow)

h. Epiphyseal line

i. Compact bone

j. Medullary cavity (contains yellow bone marrow in adult)

k. Endosteum

l. Periosteum

m. Perforating fibers

n. Nutrient artery through nutrient foramen

o. Articular cartilage

Labeling Exercise 3: Vascular Anatomy of the Pelvis

a. Aorta

b. Middle sacral artery

c. Lateral sacral artery

d. Pudendal artery

e. Obturator artery

f. Inferior epigastric artery

g. Common femoral artery

h. Sciatic artery

i. Vesicular arteries

j. Deep iliac circumflex artery

k. Inferior gluteal artery

l. Superior gluteal artery

m. Internal iliac artery

n. External iliac artery

o. Iliolumbar artery

p. Common iliac artery

Labeling Exercise 4: Ligaments of the Pelvis

a. Iliolumbar ligament

b. Sacrotuberous ligament

c. Sacrospinous ligament

d. Sacroiliac ligament

Labeling Exercise 5: Neuroanatomy of the Pelvis

a. Lumbosacral plexus

b. Sciatic nerve

c. Obturator nerve

d. Femoral nerve

e. Lateral femoral cutaneous nerve

f. Ilioinguinal nerve

NCLEX-RN® Review Questions

Question numbers correspond to Outcome-Based Learning Objectives for this chapter.

56-1. Answer: 4

Rationale: Prevention of trauma related to motor vehicle crashes is a major health care issue. Health education that stresses prevention of the problems associated with alcohol consumption and driving is a common goal of public health and other groups such as Mothers Against Drunk Driving and Students Against Destructive Decisions, founded as Students Against Driving Drunk. To fight the high incidence of teen crashes nationwide, the Recording Artists, Actors and Athletes Against Drunk Driving Coalition and the National Highway Traffic Safety Administration, both members of the National Organizations for Youth Safety, have joined forces with others to develop programs to educate teens regarding this issue. Musculoskeletal injuries are not directly caused poor nutrition, lack of sleep, or the hour that homework is completed.

Cognitive Level: Application

Nursing Process: Planning

Client Need: Health Promotion and Maintenance; Prevention and/or Early Detection of Health Problems

56-2. Answer: 4

Rationale: With long bones, displaced fractures, and fractures with less surface area, strength and function usually return within 6 months after bone union is complete. Small nondisplaced fractures require less time to heal and the patient will usually have full function within 2–4 weeks.

Cognitive Level: Application

Nursing Process: Implementation

Client Need: Physiological Integrity; Physiological Adaptation

56-3. Answer: 1

Rationale: Long bone fractures may be described by their appearance, using descriptors such as transverse, oblique, spiral, comminuted, butterfly, segmental, and impacted. Fracture apposition speaks to the relation of the bone ends to each other, for example, if half of each bone end is touching the other, it is considered 50% opposed. Fracture angulation describes the angle at the apex of the fracture in relation to the proximal fragment of bone. Some spine fractures are described by the mechanism of injury, such as a burst fracture, but describing a fracture as comminuted is a description of appearance, not a description of mechanism of injury.

Cognitive Level: Analysis

Nursing Process: Assessment

Client Need: Physiological Integrity; Physiological Adaptation

56-4. Answer: 1

Rationale: Constriction of circulation decreases venous return and increases pressure within vessels. Fluid then shifts into the interstitial space causing edema, in this case the swelling of the toes. Drainage, increased temperature, and foul odor would indicate potential infection.

Cognitive Level: Analysis

Nursing Process: Assessment

Client Need: Physiological Integrity; Physiological Adaptation

56-5. Answer: 4

Rationale: The signs and symptoms of compartment syndrome are referred to as the "five Ps," and include pain out of proportion to the injury or pain with passive stretch of the muscle within that compartment, pallor, poor capillary refill, paresthesia, and pulselessness in the affected extremity. Pain that seems out of proportion to the injury or is not relieved by analgesia is the earliest of the symptoms. The patient's complaint should not be interpreted by the nurse as an indication that the patient is dependent on narcotics. For the nurse to interpret the complaint as an indication of fear or anxiety would be inappropriate.

Cognitive Level: Analysis

Nursing Process: Assessment

Client Need: Physiological Integrity; Physiological Adaptation

56-6. Answer: 4

Rationale: Wishful thinking as a coping mechanism was distinctive in predicting those who were at risk for post-traumatic stress disorder in one study. Substance abuse and unemployment may be the results of post-traumatic stress disorder, not a reliable way to predict it. The individual's age at the time of injury has not been associated with the risk of developing post-traumatic stress disorder.

Cognitive Level: Analysis

Nursing Process: Assessment

Client Need: Psychosocial Integrity; Coping and Adaptation

Chapter 57 – Caring for the Patient During Musculoskeletal Surgical Procedures

Key Terms Matching Exercise

1.	f	**7.**	a
2.	e	**8.**	h
3.	i	**9.**	l
4.	g	**10.**	b
5.	c	**11.**	j
6.	k	**12.**	d

Short Answer Questions

13. Clinical manifestations include:
    - Atrophy or thinning of the muscles about the shoulder
    - Pain in the front of the shoulder that radiates down the arm when lifting the arm or when lowering the arm from a fully raised position
    - Weakness when lifting or rotating the arm
    - Crepitus or crackling sensation when moving the shoulder in certain positions

    When the tear occurs with an injury, there may be sudden acute pain, a snapping sensation, and an immediate weakness of the arm.

14. The causes of carpal tunnel syndrome include:
    - Heredity
    - Repetitive motions of the hands or wrist over a very long period of time
    - Hormonal changes related to pregnancy and menopause
    - Diabetes, rheumatoid arthritis, and thyroid gland imbalance
    - In some cases idiopathic

15. Patients should use an abduction pillow, a walker, and a raised toilet seat. Instruct the patient on hip precautions and transfer techniques. Discuss with the patient the advantages of a skilled nursing facility as opposed to going directly home. Instruct the patient or family on LMWH injection and wound care if the patient is discharged to home.

16. Changing direction rapidly, slowing down when running, and landing from a jump may cause tears in the ACL. Athletes who participate in skiing and basketball, and those who wear cleats, such as football players, are susceptible to ACL injuries.

17. Bunions can be caused by polio or arthritis, but most commonly are caused by ill-fitting shoes and heels that squeeze the toes into an unnatural position. Bunions are nine times more common in women than in men, most likely because women's shoes are not designed for foot health and because many women wear shoes that are too small.

18. Nurses can provide information on home safety to prevent injury, such as bathroom safety bars. Nurses can also review medications at each visit to prevent falls from polypharmacy errors. They can also teach about exercise, calcium supplementation, or oral bisphosphonates. Nurses also instruct patients postoperatively on how to prevent the recurrence of their injury.

Complete the Sentence

19. Pain, loss of function, deformity
20. resection arthroplasty
21. slings, immobilizing dressings, splints, binders
22. stable fractures
23. herniated disk, lower back

Labeling Exercise 1: Shoulder Anatomy

a. Clavicle
b. Acromion
c. Socket
d. Scapula
e. Humerus
f. Bursa
g. Rotator cuff

Labeling Exercise 2: Knee Anatomy

a. Femur
b. Tibia
c. Articular cartilage
d. Lateral collateral ligament (LCL)
e. Medial collateral ligament (MCL)
f. Posterior cruciate ligament (PCL)
g. Anterior cruciate ligament (ACL)
h. Medial meniscus
i. Lateral meniscus

NCLEX-RN® Review Questions

Question numbers correspond to Outcome-Based Learning Objectives for this chapter.

57-1. Answer: 3
   Rationale: Although it may cause pain, the neurovascular assessment should be performed bilaterally so that the affected extremity can be compared to the unaffected extremity. The nurse should anticipate performing the neurovascular assessment in conjunction with vital signs. The neurovascular assessment includes assessment of the five "P's": pain, pulse, parathesia, paralysis, and pallor. A complete assessment of circulation, motor, and sensory function must be performed.
   Cognitive Level: Application
   Nursing Process: Implementation
   Client Need: Physiological Integrity; Reduction of Risk Potential

57-2. Answer: 1
   Rationale: Discharge teaching should include precautions to avoid adduction, flexion, or any movement that may dislocate the hip prosthesis. Sitting in a low chair, such as riding in a "little sports car," could be harmful. Other precautions include: use of an elevated toilet seat, hip abductor pillow while in bed, do not bend hip greater than 90 degrees, do not twist or turn the body toward the operative side, do not turn leg and foot inward, and keep operative leg straight when getting up, using arms to push.
   Cognitive Level: Application
   Nursing Process: Planning
   Client Need: Physiological Integrity; Reduction of Risk Potential

57-3. Answer: 3
   Rationale: If the nurse suspects compartment syndrome, the surgeon should be notified immediately to prevent permanent disability or loss of limb. Treatment requires release of the constriction to accommodate swelling. The extremity should be maintained at the level of the heart to improve perfusion. As edema and engorgement increase, pain increases and is unrelieved by narcotic pain medication administration. The patient likely cannot feel warmth or coolness under the cast; the priority is to notify the surgeon.
   Cognitive Level: Application
   Nursing Process: Implementation
   Client Need: Physiological Integrity; Reduction of Risk Potential

57-4. Answer: 2, 3, 4
   Rationale: A raised toilet seat, shower bench, and sock aid or shoe horn are necessary items to avoid bending over, adduction, or excess flexion of the hip to promote placement and healing. A recliner chair is contraindicated as the knees should be lower than the hips. The wheelchair would encourage long periods of sitting versus being up and mobile with a cane or walker.
   Cognitive Level: Application
   Nursing Process: Planning
   Client Need: Physiological Integrity; Reduction of Risk Potential

57-5. Answer: 3
   Rationale: Surgical pain is concentrated at the surgical site and is generally described as sharp and nonradiating. Pain assessment should be based on a consistent scale. Many scales are available that use a numeric scale or pictures to help the patient describe the pain level. Each patient has a particular comfort level or pain tolerance level.
   Cognitive Level: Application
   Nursing Process: Assessment
   Client Need: Physiological Integrity; Basic Care and Comfort

Chapter 58 – Caring for the Patient with Arthritis and Connective Tissue Disorders

Key Terms Matching Exercise 1

1. a
2. h
3. b
4. e
5. g
6. d
7. f
8. c

Key Terms Matching Exercise 2

9. d
10. a
11. h
12. e
13. g
14. b
15. f
16. c

Short Answer Questions

17. Osteoarthritis results from a complex interplay of multiple factors, including joint integrity, genetic predisposition, local inflammation, mechanical forces, and cellular and biochemical processes.

18. The desired outcomes for patients with RA include control of pain and stiffness, maintenance of patient's quality of life, and ability to perform self-care activities.

19. Reactive arthritis is caused by a reaction to an infection somewhere else in the body. It usually begins between 1 and 3 weeks after becoming infected. One organism, *Chlamydia trachomatis*, is spread through sexual contact and without treatment can cause reactive arthritis and respiratory infection, called *Chlamydia pneumonia*. Gastrointestinal infections, such as *Salmonella*, *Shigella*, *Yersinia*, and *Campylobacter*, also can cause reactive arthritis.

20. Rest is just as important as having physical activity. The patient needs to plan rest periods. The patient needs to sleep an ample amount of time during the night as well.

21. Patients at risk for septic arthritis are those who are older, diabetic, have RA, or have preexisting joint disease or joint replacement. Elderly patients and those taking immunosuppressive or steroid medications may not exhibit as dramatic a reaction to the infection.

True or False?

22.	T	27.	F
23.	F	28.	T
24.	T	29.	T
25.	T	30.	T
26.	F	31.	F

Complete the Sentence

32. plain radiographs, computed tomography (CT), magnetic resonance imaging (MRI)
33. autoimmune, genetic
34. bacterial, viral, trauma
35. psoriasis
36. gouty arthritis
37. physical activity, stiffness, flexibility
38. systemic lupus erythematosus
39. symptom, quality of life
40. Lyme disease
41. creatine kinase

NCLEX-RN® Review Questions

Question numbers correspond to Outcome-Based Learning Objectives for this chapter.

58-1. Answer: 2
   Rationale: Common connective tissue disorders include lupus erythematosus, gout, and Lyme disease. A term used to describe rheumatic disease is arthritis. A chronic inflammatory process that affects joints is rheumatoid arthritis. An inflammation associated with psoriasis is psoriatic arthritis.
   Cognitive Level: Application
   Nursing Process: Assessment
   Client Need: Physiological Integrity; Physiological Adaptation

58-2. Answer: 3
   Rationale: When planning care for a patient with ankylosing spondylitis, physical and occupational therapy can assist the patient in remaining functional. Encourage the patient to remain as independent as possible with therapeutic and nontherapeutic measures. Exercise programs can maintain posture and joint flexibility. It is important for the patient to maintain a program of continued care.
   Cognitive Level: Application
   Nursing Process: Planning
   Client Need: Physiological Integrity; Physiological Adaptation

58-3. Answer: 4
   Rationale: Septic arthritis is the most destructive form of acute arthritis and can result from the spread of an infection from another part of the body. Predisposing factors include being over the age of 80. Patients with septic arthritis present with a single swollen and painful joint. Common joints affected are the knee, wrist, ankles, and hips. There may also be evidence of an associated skin, urinary, or respiratory infection. Reactive arthritis, gout, and osteoarthritis present with different symptoms than those described.
   Cognitive Level: Analysis
   Nursing Process: Assessment
   Client Need: Physiological Integrity; Physiological Adaptation

58-4. Answer: 1
   Rationale: For the patient with rheumatoid arthritis, priority nursing diagnoses include: *Pain, Chronic; Mobility: Impaired; Physical; Falls, Risk for; Body Image, Disturbed; Activity Intolerance* related to fatigue; *Self-Care, Readiness for Enhanced; Nutrition: Imbalanced, Less than Body Requirements*; and *Powerlessness.*
   Cognitive Level: Application
   Nursing Process: Planning
   Client Need: Physiological Integrity; Physiological Adaptation

58-5. Answer: 2
   Rationale: Nursing interventions appropriate to reduce the pain associated with gout include assess pain, monitor uric acid levels, provide alternative pain interventions to include posturing, elevation, ice, and distraction, and medicate as prescribed. Monitoring blood count, applying heat, and massaging the affected limb are not indicated for gout.
   Cognitive Level: Application
   Nursing Process: Planning
   Client Need: Physiological Integrity; Physiological Adaptation

58-6. Answer: 2
   Rationale: Juvenile myositis is a combination of the three other kinds of myositis: polymyositis, dermatomyositis, and inclusion body myositis.
   Cognitive Level: Analysis
   Nursing Process: Assessment
   Client Need: Physiological Integrity; Physiological Adaptation

Chapter 59 – Nursing Assessment of Patients with Immunologic and Inflammatory Disorders

Key Terms Matching Exercise 1

1.	b	6.	i
2.	a	7.	g
3.	f	8.	d
4.	e	9.	j
5.	c	10.	h

Key Terms Matching Exercise 2

11.	c	16.	h
12.	f	17.	d
13.	b	18.	a
14.	j	19.	e
15.	g	20.	i

Word Search

21. antigen
22. immunity
23. chyle
24. nongranulocyte
25. lymph nodes
26. apoptosis
27. B cells
28. non-self antigen
29. self antigen
30. T cells
31. T lymphocyte
32. chemotaxis
33. cytokines
34. interferon

35. interleukin
36. lymphokines
37. opsonization
38. antibody
39. complement
40. agglutination
41. immune complex
42. neutralization
43. plasma cells
44. precipitation
45. immunization
46. vaccine
47. anergy

T	L	Y	M	P	H	O	C	Y	T	E	A	Y	D	O	B	I	T	N	A
N	A	N	O	P	S	O	N	I	Z	A	T	I	O	N	E	F	C	A	B
E	O	O	C	R	D	E	G	H	O	C	P	L	J	I	A	D	H	N	G
U	L	N	E	T	N	E	M	E	L	P	M	O	C	S	P	E	K	E	A
T	B	S	G	I	A	R	E	S	O	K	A	B	P	E	Q	T	L	R	V
R	D	E	I	R	G	T	N	O	I	T	A	N	I	T	U	L	G	G	A
A	S	L	C	M	A	R	S	L	L	E	C	B	G	R	O	U	F	Y	C
L	L	F	A	I	M	N	L	Y	M	P	H	N	O	D	E	S	H	E	C
I	L	A	E	B	N	U	U	Y	A	E	Y	D	J	C	B	E	I	S	I
Z	E	N	N	H	F	T	N	L	M	I	L	H	T	C	E	L	L	S	N
A	C	T	E	T	L	C	E	E	O	P	E	B	A	G	Q	F	C	A	E
T	A	I	D	G	I	B	E	R	C	C	H	E	M	O	T	A	X	I	S
I	M	G	M	F	H	G	O	S	F	O	Y	O	U	D	O	N	E	T	F
O	S	E	C	M	K	A	E	P	C	E	M	T	K	H	A	T	C	G	A
N	A	N	I	J	U	G	I	N	R	T	R	P	E	I	L	I	K	V	D
A	L	B	S	D	A	N	E	H	C	F	A	O	L	P	N	G	A	O	B
D	P	R	E	C	I	P	I	T	A	T	I	O	N	E	S	E	C	E	E
I	M	M	U	N	I	Z	A	T	I	O	N	L	J	O	X	N	S	R	A
C	A	E	G	P	H	E	I	C	Y	T	O	K	I	N	E	S	O	G	I
A	F	D	E	B	A	I	N	T	E	R	L	E	U	K	I	N	D	A	C

Short Answer Questions

48. Stem cells have the capacity to produce any type of cell that they are chemically directed to make. For example, stem cells differentiate into white blood cells such as granulocytes, lymphocytes, and monocytes. Granulocytes become neutrophils, eosinophils, and basophils. Lymphocyte precursors in bone marrow become B- and T-cell lines. Monocytes differentiate from white blood cell precursors. Monocytes circulate in the blood and mature into macrophages. Bone marrow stem cells also differentiate into red blood cells.

49. Bacteria are always present on the surface of the skin in varying quantities. The small amount of moisture and pH of the skin protect it from bacterial growth. Therefore, intact skin is critical to the survival of the organism. Even small breaks in the integrity of skin can lead to large wounds or infections locally or systemically because organisms are able to enter the body.

50. Immune tolerance begins during embryonic development of the immune system. Lymphocytes that react with self antigens are selectively eliminated as the immune system develops. This leaves the newborn with B-cell and T-cell lines that do not attack self antigens. Self antigens include HLAs and MHC, as well as several other antigenic particles that are often cell receptors. When the body reacts to self receptors or other cell parts as an antigen, autoimmune disease may result.

51. The number and percentage of T cells and the ability of lymphocytes to produce interleukins decrease with age. The slower response of T cells and B cells can result in severe infections. When allergy testing is done in older adults, there may be a depressed ability to mount an inflammatory response to the antigen injected. This is referred to as anergy, and results from the diminished ability of the T-cell line to produce chemical mediators of inflammation. Individuals who show evidence of anergy are at greater risk of developing cancer and have higher rates of mortality in general. Aging also results in a decreased ability on the part of immune cells to identify self antigens, while at the same time there is an increase in the number of auto-antibodies produced. This results in higher incidences of autoimmune disease with aging.

52. Erythrocyte sedimentation rate (also known as a "sedimentation rate" or "sed rate"), C-reactive protein, antinuclear antibody tests, anti-IgG, IgG levels, IgM levels, enzyme-linked immunosorbent assay, and Western blot are all examples of serum tests designed to look at one specific chemical or antigen and the body's response to it.

True or False?

53.	T	**58.**	T
54.	T	**59.**	F
55.	T	**60.**	T
56.	F	**61.**	F
57.	F	**62.**	T

Labeling Exercise: Lymphatic System with Lymph Nodes

a. Adenoid
b. Lymph node
c. Thoracic duct
d. Large intestine
e. Appendix
f. Bone marrow
g. Tonsil
h. Thymus
i. Heart
j. Spleen
k. Peyer's patch in small intestine
l. Lymphatics

NCLEX-RN® Review Questions

Question numbers correspond to Outcome-Based Learning Objectives for this chapter.

59-1. Answer: 2
Rationale: T lymphocytes, also known as CD4 cells, are responsible for regulating and initiating the immune response. The primary function of B cells is the production of antibodies such as immunoglobulins. Lymph nodes and lymph tissue filter debris from the breakdown of cells, bacteria, virus, and fungal antigens. The spleen plays a significant role in immune function as part of the lymphatic system. It is comprised of white and red pulp and is involved in hematologic filtration, sequestering of red and white cells, and immune response.
Cognitive Level: Analysis
Nursing Process: Assessment
Client Need: Physiological Integrity; Physiological Adaptation

59-2. Answer: 4
Rationale: When the immune system can differentiate self cells from non-self, the process is referred to as immune tolerance. An antigen is a foreign substance perceived by the immune system as a threat. Antibodies are proteins that are capable of attaching to antigens and stimulating immune responses.
Cognitive Level: Analysis
Nursing Process: Assessment
Client Need: Physiological Integrity; Physiological Adaptation

59-3. Answer: 3
Rationale: T-helper 2 cells stimulate B cells to make antibodies to specific antigens. This is accomplished through the release of chemicals such as interleukins and the antigen presentation process (DeFranco et al., 2007). Memory T cells function to retain a "chemical memory" of virus particles encountered by the memory cells. The next exposure to the "remembered" virus results in a quick immune response to the virus. T-helper 1 cells help upregulate immune activity and produce chemicals called cytokines that stimulate cytotoxic cells to destroy mutant and cancer cells. Suppressor T cells, also called CD8 cells, slow or stop the immune response. Natural killer cells, also referred to as "null cells," are types of T cells that lack CD4 or CD8 external receptors, but are able to directly kill cells or send cytokine messages to start the process of programmed cell death.
Cognitive Level: Analysis
Nursing Process: Assessment
Client Need: Physiological Integrity; Physiological Adaptation

59-4. Answer: 4
Rationale: Interferons are proteins made and released by T cells when the invading organism is a virus. This group of lymphokines functions to protect other cells from viral attack. They inhibit the production of the virus within infected cells, prevent the spread of the virus to other cells, and enhance the activity of macrophages, natural killer cells, and cytotoxic T cells. Complement is a group of small proteins made in the liver and present in blood that can interact with cells and each other for a variety of functions. Complement proteins are important in the inflammatory and immune responses. Tumor necrosis factor (TNF) is a small

peptide that is produced by a variety of cells, including granulocytes and lymphocytes. Interferons are proteins made and released by T cells when the invading organism is a virus. Interleukins are lymphokines, chemical mediators released by lymphocytes, that enable the cells of the immune system to communicate and coordinate the immune response.
Cognitive Level: Analysis
Nursing Process: Assessment
Client Need: Physiological Integrity; Physiological Adaptation

59-5. Answer: 1
Rationale: The CDC encourages annual immunization of the general population with the influenza vaccine, and strongly recommends it for adults 50 years and older, residents of long-term care facilities, individuals with chronic illnesses, immunosuppressed individuals, health care workers, and any other individuals coming in close contact with people at risk of contracting influenza. Inactive influenza vaccine has been used in the United States for many years and is given annually because the flu virus mutates annually. Immune protection develops approximately 2 weeks after the immunization and lasts up to a year. Some immunized individuals will still get the flu; however, they will usually get a milder case than those who did not get the shot.
Cognitive Level: Application
Nursing Process: Implementation
Client Need: Health Promotion and Maintenance; Prevention and/or Early Detection of Health Problems

59-6. Answer: 3
Rationale: The first exposure to a specific antigen is known as a primary immune response. A primary immune response results in evidence of immunoglobulin production in 4 to 8 days after the initial exposure to an antigen. During this period some B cells differentiate into memory B cells that retain the ability to quickly recognize and produce antibodies to the antigen. The second time the host encounters the same antigen it produces antibodies in greater numbers, and more quickly than during the primary exposure. This stronger immune response is referred to as the secondary immune response and occurs in 1 to 3 days. Immunization is a term often used interchangeably with vaccination or inoculation and involves the process of stimulating the immune system to create active immunity for protection against a disease.
Cognitive Level: Analysis
Nursing Process: Assessment
Client Need: Physiological Integrity; Physiological Adaptation

59-7. Answer: 3
Rationale: The effects of aging on the immune system include: decreased percentage of suppressor T cells, which means the body cannot downregulate the immune system as quickly; decreased primary and secondary production of antibodies, which means the body has a reduced response to infectious organisms, leading to more severe infection; increased auto-antibody production, which means the body shows evidence of more exacerbations of autoimmune disease; and delayed hypersensitivity response, which means the body has a decreased allergic response.
Cognitive Level: Application
Nursing Process: Assessment
Client Need: Physiological Integrity; Physiological Adaptation

59-8. Answer: 4
Rationale: Many autoimmune diseases have a neurological component. Physical examination of immune function in the neurological system includes assessment of the symmetry of the face. Examine the face for presence of facial droop or a facial expression that is frozen or not responsive to emotion. Disorders of the immune system that affect the neurological system include Guillain-Barré, myasthenia gravis, and cerebral vascular accident. Additionally, Bell's palsy also can present with an asymmetrical facial expression.
Cognitive Level: Application
Nursing Process: Assessment
Client Need: Physiological Integrity; Reduction of Risk Potential

59-9. Answer: 3
Rationale: The CD4 count is used to determine the total number of T helper lymphocytes. A low number may indicated HIV or other immunodeficiency. Antinuclear antibodies measure the number of antibodies made to parts of the patient's cells' nuclei, which indicate autoimmune disease. Erythrocyte sedimentation rate measures the time it takes red cells to precipitate out of serum. An increased rate implies inflammation, a common problem in many immune diseases. C-reactive protein measures acute inflammation 6–10 hours postinjury and tissue destruction. It is a nonspecific test for inflammation that rises early.
Cognitive Level: Analysis
Nursing Process: Assessment
Client Need: Physiological Integrity; Reduction of Risk Potential

Chapter 60 – Caring for the Patient with Immune Response Disorders

Key Terms Matching Exercise 1

1.	e	**7.**	i
2.	b	**8.**	f
3.	j	**9.**	c
4.	h	**10.**	g
5.	k	**11.**	a
6.	d		

Key Terms Matching Exercise 2

12.	d	**18.**	j
13.	a	**19.**	i
14.	g	**20.**	f
15.	k	**21.**	h
16.	b	**22.**	c
17.	e		

Key Terms Matching Exercise 3

23.	c	**29.**	a
24.	k	**30.**	i
25.	h	**31.**	d
26.	b	**32.**	l
27.	j	**33.**	g
28.	f	**34.**	e

Key Term Crossword

DESENSITIZATION

PLASMAPHERESIS

ALLERGEN

NEOANTIGENS

ANAPHYLAXIS

WINDOW PERIOD

FLARE

VIRAL LOAD

WESTERN BLOT

IMMUNE DEFICIENCIES

Short Answer Questions

35. Type I: allergy, anaphylaxis
Type II: blood transfusion reaction, Goodpasture's syndrome
Type III: serum sickness, SLE
Type IV: latex allergies, PPD reactions

36. Risk factors for respiratory allergies include
- Genetic predisposition
- Frequency of viral infections
- Increased use of antimicrobial cleansing products in the home
- Early childhood exposure to allergens
- Dietary factors
- Air pollution
- Immunizations

37. What causes a loss of immune tolerance is unknown, but research centers on theories that it is due to (1) exposure to a previously sequestered antigen, (2) development of a neoantigen, (3) complications of an infectious disease, (4) emergence of a forbidden clone, and (5) alteration of a suppressor T cell.

38. Symptoms often seen early in SLE include swollen joints, fatigue, unexplained fever, red rash (commonly a "butterfly" shape over the cheeks), arthritis, arthralgias, unexplained hair loss, photosensitivity, swollen lymph nodes, and edema in the legs or around the eyes. As the disease progresses, SLE can affect several organ systems.

39. Matching the antigens between the donor and recipient of transplanted cells and suppressing the immune response are the key concepts in preventing organ and tissue transplant rejection.

40. Causes of secondary immunodeficiency include:
- Drug-induced immunodeficiency: chemotherapy drugs, corticosteroids
- Age: infants and older adults
- Malnutrition: dietary deficiency, cirrhosis, cachexia
- Stress
- Medical treatments: surgery, anesthesia, radiation
- Injury: trauma, burns
- Diseases: AIDS, diabetes mellitus, chronic renal disease, malignancies, alcoholic cirrhosis, SLE

41. Treatment for HIV involves combinations of various antiretroviral drugs that interfere with different aspects of the HIV replication cycle, and the treatment is referred to as highly active antiretroviral drug therapy (HAART). Combination therapy has the greatest effect in controlling HIV proliferation and minimizing the development of drug resistance.

42. Kaposi's sarcoma, B-cell lymphoma (non-Hodgkin's), primary lymphoma of the brain, and invasive cervical carcinoma are the secondary cancers included in the CDC's classification of AIDS diseases.

43. During the period of primary infection (1 to 3 weeks) the individual may by asymptomatic or display symptoms of acute retroviral syndrome, which is characterized by vague, flulike symptoms, making early diagnosis of HIV infection difficult. Additionally, the first months after infection encompass the "window period" in which the infected individual has not produced sufficient HIV antibodies that can be measured by an HIV antibody test. The window period usually lasts up to 3 months, but can extend to 6 months in some individuals. During the window period HIV antibody tests are negative, even in the presence of HIV infection.

44. HIV infection can be transmitted any time that infected body fluids have lymphocytes that can harbor HIV. In addition to sexual transmission, this can occur through contaminated needles, contaminated blood products, and perinatal transmission. An infant breastfed by an infected mother can also be infected. Health care workers, especially lab technicians and nurses, risk exposure through needlestick injuries and exposure to mucous membranes of infected patients.

True or False?

45.	T	**50.**	T
46.	F	**51.**	T
47.	T	**52.**	F
48.	T	**53.**	T
49.	F	**54.**	T

Labeling Exercise: HIV Infecting CD4+ T Cell

a. CD4 receptor T4 molecule
b. gp120
c. HIV
d. Reverse transcriptase
e. Genomic RNA
f. cDNA
g. Doublestranded DNA
h. Unintegrated DNA
i. Postviral DNA
j. Host chromosome
k. Viral mRNA
l. Doublestranded circularized DNA
m. Protein synthesis and processing
n. Budding particle
o. Mature virion

NCLEX-RN® Review Questions

Question numbers correspond to Outcome-Based Learning Objectives for this chapter.

60-1. Answer: 2
> **Rationale:** Hypersensitive reactions are determined by the type of antigen, the time sequence of the reaction, and the immunological response. When the immune system loses self-tolerance, immune hypersensitivity reactions result. The primary mechanism of an immune deficiency is a genetic disorder that occurred during the embryonic development of the immune system. Immune deficiency is associated with opportunistic infections.
> **Cognitive Level:** Analysis
> **Nursing Process:** Assessment
> **Client Need:** Physiological Integrity; Physiological Adaptation

60-2. Answer: 3
> **Rationale:** The trigger for an autoimmune response is a self-antigen. The primary trigger for a hypersensitive reaction is an environmental antigen. An alloimmune reaction is triggered by antigens from another individual. The symptoms of different categories of hypersensitive responses vary according to the origin of the antigen.
> **Cognitive Level:** Analysis
> **Nursing Process:** Assessment
> **Client Need:** Physiological Integrity; Physiological Adaptation

60-3. Answer: 2
> **Rationale:** A syndrome of opportunistic infections, AIDS occurs as a final stage in clients infected with HIV. Transmission of HIV is limited to contact with infected body fluids that have lymphocytes that can harbor HIV. AIDS is the end disease manifestation of HIV. HIV transmission occurs upon contact with infected body fluids. HIV precedes AIDS and is associated with the virus' entry into the host's lymphocytes.
> **Cognitive Level:** Analysis
> **Nursing Process:** Assessment
> **Client Need:** Physiological Integrity; Physiological Adaptation

60-4. Answer: 2
> **Rationale:** Obtain cultures prior to starting antibiotics to ensure the appropriate therapy is initiated in a timely manner. Subjective assessment promotes the early detection of infection. Health care providers and family members wash hands before and after patient contact to reduce the risk of opportunistic infection cross contamination. Encourage hydration and maintenance of weight to support the immune system.
> **Cognitive Level:** Application
> **Nursing Process:** Assessment
> **Client Need:** Physiological Integrity; Physiological Adaptation

Chapter 61 – Caring for the Patient with Inflammatory Response, Shock, and Severe Sepsis

Key Terms Matching Exercise

1.	c	**6.**	f
2.	e	**7.**	b
3.	j	**8.**	d
4.	g	**9.**	i
5.	a	**10.**	h

Short Answer Questions

11. Cardiogenic shock can be caused by myocardial infarction, myocardial contusion, ruptured ventricles, ruptured papillary muscles, and cardiomyopathy.

12. The primary goal of shock management is to identify the cause and intervene to prevent the pathophysiology that results from ischemic and anoxic cell injury. The care of the patient will be directed at identifying and correcting the cause of the shock, maintaining oxygen perfusion, controlling active bleeding, supporting the patient's circulatory status, maintaining the patient's body temperature, managing pain, and providing emotional support.

13. Nursing diagnoses for shock include:
    - *Tissue Perfusion, Ineffective* related to alterations in circulating volume

- *Fluid Volume Deficient* related to alterations in circulating volume
- *Cardiac Output, Decreased* related to alterations in circulating volume and cardiac pump function
- *Airway Clearance, Ineffective* related to altered level of consciousness, obstruction by secretions, and aspiration of foreign matter
- *Imbalanced Nutrition Risk, Less than Body Requirements* related to decreased appetite secondary to treatments, fatigue, environment, and increased protein and vitamin requirements for healing
- *Coping, Readiness for Enhanced Grieving*

14. Septic shock in pediatric patients is manifested by tachycardia with signs of decreased perfusion including altered peripheral pulses, altered mental status, and capillary refill greater than 2 seconds.

15. Nurses are responsible for the continuous monitoring and administration of medications and fluids as well as the emotional and spiritual support of the patient and family.

True or False?

16. T	**21.** F
17. F	**22.** T
18. T	**23.** T
19. T	**24.** F
20. F	**25.** T

Complete the Sentence

26. hypovolemic
27. Septic
28. airway management
29. pneumatic antishock garments
30. domain, predisposition, insult (infection), response, organ dysfunction
31. inflammation, coagulation, fibrinolysis
32. hypoperfusion, hypoxia, cause
33. hand hygiene
34. prevent it from occurring
35. oxygen consumption

NCLEX-RN® Review Questions

Question numbers correspond to Outcome-Based Learning Objectives for this chapter.

61-1. Answer: 4
Rationale: Hypovolemic shock results from significant fluid loss that alters the amount of circulating volume in the body. It can be caused by traumatic injury to the abdomen, chest, or musculoskeletal system; gastrointestinal bleeding; vomiting and diarrhea; osmotic diuresis; diabetic ketoacidosis; and thermal injuries. Anaphylactic shock can be caused by insect bites, medication allergies, food allergies, latex allergies, and idiopathic reactions. Cardiogenic shock can be caused by myocardial infarction/contusion, ruptured ventricles or papillary muscles, and cardiomyopathy. Neurogenic shock can be caused by spinal cord or medulla trauma, anesthetic agents, severe emotional stress, or severe pain.
Cognitive Level: Analysis
Nursing Process: Assessment
Client Need: Physiological Integrity; Physiological Adaptation

61-2. Answer: 3
Rationale: When the patient has suffered an injury or illness that has caused an alteration in the blood flow for any reason, an oxygen debt will occur. Sodium moves from outside the cell to increase water into the cell. Bleeding, metabolic alkalosis, and prerenal failure are not symptoms of hypovolemic shock.
Cognitive Level: Analysis
Nursing Process: Assessment
Client Need: Physiological Integrity; Physiological Adaptation

61-3. Answer: 4
Rationale: Urinary output is decreased because of the shift of sodium, which pulls water into the cells for conservation of fluid. Decreased blood flow to the kidneys impairs their ability to detoxify the toxic substances that result from anaerobic metabolism. Inadequate blood flow to the gastrointestinal tract causes the activation of circulating neutrophils that provoke multiple organ failure.
Cognitive Level: Analysis
Nursing Process: Assessment
Client Need: Physiological Integrity; Physiological Adaptation

61-4. Answer: 4
Rationale: Patient risk factors such as significant injuries, catastrophic illness, age, and allergies must be quickly acknowledged. It is interesting that both the very young and aged share similar risk factors for developing shock, including compromised immune systems due to age; fluid shifts; and an integumentary system that may not afford needed protection.
Cognitive Level: Application
Nursing Process: Assessment
Client Need: Physiological Integrity; Physiological Adaptation

61-5. Answer: 3
Rationale: When appropriate fluid challenge fails and there is a need to restore end-organ perfusion, therapy with vasopressors may be started. Steroids are recommended only in patient with adequate volume replacement and who require vasopressors to maintain an adequate blood pressure. Recombinant human activated protein C is recommended for patients who are at high risk of death and with no absolute contraindication related to bleeding risk or a relative contraindication that outweighs the risk of the treatment.
Cognitive Level: Analysis
Nursing Process: Planning
Client Need: Physiological Integrity; Physiological Adaptation

61-6. Answer: 4
Rationale: Interventions to improve nutritional intake include determining the patient's food preferences and arrange to have those foods provided. Staying with the patient during meals, inserting a feeding tube, and using an intravenous access device are not among the recommended interventions.
Cognitive Level: Application
Nursing Process: Planning
Client Need: Physiological Integrity; Basic Care and Comfort

61-7. Answer: 3
Rationale: Severe sepsis is defined as sepsis or the presence of a confirmed infection and a systemic inflammatory response, and single or multiple organ failure. Sepsis is a clinical syndrome defined as the presence of SIRS associated with a confirmed infectious process. Systemic

inflammatory response syndrome is an organized immune response that can be triggered by infectious or noninfectious clinical insults including burns, pancreatitis, acute respiratory distress syndrome, surgery, and trauma. Septic shock is a state of acute circulatory failure characterized by persistent hypotension unexplained by other causes, for example, despite the fact that adequate fluids have been administered.
Cognitive Level: Analysis
Nursing Process: Assessment
Client Need: Physiological Integrity; Physiological Adaptation

61-8. Answer: 2
Rationale: Before infection can be diagnosed, blood cultures must be obtained. To control the source, abscesses should be drained, necrotic tissue should be debrided, and infected devices should be removed. Antibiotic therapy should be started within one hour of recognizing the offending organism after appropriate cultures are obtained.
Cognitive Level: Application
Nursing Process: Implementation
Client Need: Physiological Integrity; Physiological Adaptation

61-9. Answer: 3
Rationale: Clinical manifestations of MODS include paralytic ileus, hyperglycemia, increased heart rate, and increased right arterial pressure, among others.
Cognitive Level: Analysis
Nursing Process: Assessment
Client Need: Physiological Integrity; Physiological Adaptation

61-10. Answer: 2
Rationale: Nursing care for the patient with MODS includes early recognition of the risk factors for the development of MODS, and close monitoring of interventions initiated to treat the patients such as invasive lines and catheters. Meticulous skin care and aseptic technique must be used to insert and change any lines. The nurse should ensure that all who come in contact with the patient use meticulous hand hygiene and aseptic technique to prevent the risk of infection. There is no evidence to suggest a flu inoculation or pneumonia vaccine will reduce the risk of developing MODS.
Cognitive Level: Application
Nursing Process: Planning
Client Need: Physiological Integrity; Physiological Adaptation

Chapter 62 – Nursing Assessment of Patients with Hematologic Disorders

Key Terms Matching Exercise

1.	j	**6.**	h
2.	d	**7.**	a
3.	g	**8.**	f
4.	e	**9.**	i
5.	b	**10.**	c

Key Term Crossword

Short Answer Questions

11. The components of the hematologic system include the blood, the lymphatic system, the spleen (a lymphatic organ), the liver, and the reticuloendothelial/mononuclear phagocyte system.

12. Leukocytes are categorized as granulocytes and agranulocytes. Granulocytes are composed of neutrophils, basophils, and eosinophils. Agranulocytes are made up of monocytes and lymphocytes.

13. The purpose of lymphocytes is to recognize and respond to foreign antigens by producing antibodies that include the T cells, B cells, and natural killer cells.

14. Primary hemostasis begins immediately after endothelial disruption and is characterized by vascular contraction, platelet adhesion, and formation of a soft aggregate plug. After the injury occurs there is an initial, temporary response of vasoconstriction, which stops or minimizes blood loss, enhancing platelet adhesion and activation. This vasoconstriction promotes the ability of platelets to gather at the site of injury. Secondary hemostasis is responsible for stabilizing the soft clot and maintaining vasoconstriction. This phase is initiated when the cascade system of coagulation is activated by substances released at the time of injury.

15. A decreased erythrocyte count (RBC) can be caused by:
    • Abnormal loss of erythrocytes (bleeding)
    • Abnormal destruction of erythrocytes
    • Lack of needed hormones and elements for production of erythrocytes
    • Bone marrow suppression

True or False?

16.	T	21.	T
17.	F	22.	T
18.	F	23.	T
19.	F	24.	F
20.	T	25.	T

NCLEX-RN® Review Questions

Question numbers correspond to Outcome-Based Learning Objectives for this chapter.

62-1. Answer: 1

Rationale: The hematologic system has two primary functions. The first is to transport oxygen, nutrition, secretory products, and waste products, and the second is to house and transport the immunological products that are critical to the body's defense against infections. By performing these two functions the hematologic system helps maintain body temperature, control pH, remove toxic materials from the body, and regulate body fluid electrolytes. The lymphatic system collects and returns interstitial fluid to the blood, maintaining fluid balance. It also defends against infection by producing lymphocytes and absorbs and transports lipids from the intestines to the blood. The presence of lymph vessels also maintains blood volume in all the organs.
Cognitive Level: Analysis
Nursing Process: Assessment
Client Need: Physiological Integrity; Reduction of Risk Potential

62-2. Answers: 1, 4, 6

Rationale: The erythrocytes do contain one-third oxygen-carrying hemoglobin by volume. They are also terminally differentiated, meaning they never divide. They are broken down by the spleen into bilirubin and iron and by the liver into bile pigments. Immature red cells have a nucleus, but mature cells do not. The lifespan of the erythrocyte is about 120 days, but the longevity of the thrombocyte is only 5 to 9 days. There are approximately 4.5 to 5.8 million erythrocytes per microliter of healthy blood. There are approximately 5,000 to 10,000 leukocytes per microliter of blood. The reticuloendothelial system is responsible for removing senescent cells from circulation. The bursa of Fabricius is the gland in birds where cells mature and the first such tissue discovered in vertebrates. From this the name "B" lymphocyte originated.
Cognitive Level: Analysis
Nursing Process: Assessment
Client Need: Physiological Integrity; Reduction of Risk Potential

62-3. Answer: 2

Rationale: For either a male or female patient RBC 5.2×10^6 cells/mm³, MCV 90 microliters per mm³, and HGB 16 g/dL are normal laboratory values. However, a PLT 620,000/μL is abnormally high for any patient, and an unexplained excessive peripheral blood cell count is an indication for a bone marrow examination.
Cognitive Level: Analysis
Nursing Process: Planning
Client Need: Physiological Integrity; Reduction of Risk Potential

62-4. Answer: 3

Rationale: The patient's white blood cell count is dangerously low, placing the patient at risk for infection. This patient should immediately be placed on neutropenic precautions and the physician should be notified of the lab result. Obtaining a set of vital signs, especially temperature, is important, considering the patient's risk of infection, but it is more important to put the reverse isolation into effect and call the physician. The physician may want to perform a bone marrow examination, administer prophylactic antibiotics, obtain blood cultures, give the patient a bath with special soap, or administer steroid medications, but the cause of the neutropenia will be determined and treated accordingly by the physician once he or she is notified. Until that time, the nurse should continue with the neutropenic precautions.
Cognitive Level: Application
Nursing Process: Implementation
Client Need: Physiological Integrity; Reduction of Risk Potential

62-5. Answer: 4

Rationale: The first step in primary hemostasis is vascular contraction, followed by platelet adhesion and formation of a soft aggregate plug, respectively. The initial platelets that respond to the site of insult release intrinsic adenosine diaphosphate, which causes more platelets to aggregate together. Once the short-lived primary hemostasis has occurred, secondary hemostasis begins through either the intrinsic or extrinsic pathway. During these mechanisms factor XII activates factor XI, active factor VII and active factor XI start a cascade of events that eventually activates factor X, and active factor X, along with factor III, factor V, Ca⁺, and platelet thromboplastic factor activate prothrombin activator. Also, prothrombin activator converts prothrombin into thrombin, and thrombin converts fibrinogen into fibrin. Fibrin and factor XIII eventually create a fibrous mesh that traps platelets and erythrocytes, forming a blood clot.
Cognitive Level: Analysis
Nursing Process: Assessment
Client Need: Physiological Integrity; Reduction of Risk Potential

62-6.   Answer: 3

  Rationale: The gastrointestinal tract is the primary source of necessary nutrients for blood cell development. Therefore, any disease or surgical manipulation of the stomach or intestine may impact blood cell production. Surgical excision of the appendix 3 years earlier would not cause problems with the hematologic system. Kidney disease does affect the production of erythropoietin, and thus the production of red blood cells. However, urinary tract infection should not cause hematologic problems. A widened pulse pressure or tachycardia may indicate compensatory mechanisms during states of hypoxia, such as with anemia, but hypertension is not known to cause or be caused by a primary hematologic issue.

  Cognitive Level: Analysis

  Nursing Process: Assessment

  Client Need: Physiological Integrity; Reduction of Risk Potential

62-7.   Answer: 2

  Rationale: A shift to the left indicates that the total white blood cell count has increased because of the proliferation of juvenile band and immature blast cells. This phenomenon is the result of bone marrow stimulation to release large amounts of leukocytes, usually in response to severe infection. A shift to the left might often be an early sign of infection in the otherwise healthy patient, or it could indicate insufficient host defenses if it occurs, but the total white blood cell count remains normal or below normal. The mean corpuscular hemoglobin (MCH) and mean corpuscular hemoglobin concentration (MCHC) measure the hemoglobin part in an erythrocyte, indicating the efficacy of interaction between the hemoglobin molecule and the red cell.

  Cognitive Level: Analysis

  Nursing Process: Evaluation

  Client Need: Physiological Integrity; Reduction of Risk Potential

Chapter 63 – Caring for the Patient with Blood Disorders

Key Terms Matching Exercise 1

1.	e	**7.**	i
2.	g	**8.**	d
3.	k	**9.**	b
4.	j	**10.**	l
5.	a	**11.**	h
6.	f	**12.**	c

Key Terms Matching Exercise 2

13.	b	**19.**	j
14.	a	**20.**	e
15.	g	**21.**	i
16.	d	**22.**	f
17.	h	**23.**	l
18.	k	**24.**	c

Word Search

25. hematology
26. hematopoiesis
27. differentiation
28. anemia
29. hypoxia
30. hemoglobin
31. hypoxic hypoxia
32. progenitor cells
33. erythropoiesis
34. erythropoietin
35. anemic hypoxia
36. melena
37. desquamation
38. hemosiderin

39. hypochromic
40. microcytic
41. transferrin
42. hepcidin
43. bioavailable
44. heme iron
45. nonheme iron
46. elemental iron
47. folate
48. megaloblast
49. intrinsic factor
50. pernicious anemia
51. thrombopoietin

C	E	R	Y	T	H	R	O	P	O	I	E	T	I	N	A	B	D	H	N
I	P	R	O	G	E	N	I	T	O	R	C	E	L	L	S	C	A	E	O
T	E	A	Y	T	H	R	O	M	B	O	P	O	I	E	T	I	N	P	R
Y	R	E	E	T	A	L	O	F	G	H	E	M	E	I	R	O	N	C	I
C	N	A	R	D	H	E	M	O	G	L	O	B	I	N	B	C	A	I	E
O	I	G	N	I	R	R	E	F	S	N	A	R	T	G	D	E	A	D	M
R	C	E	A	B	H	I	O	H	E	M	A	T	O	L	O	G	Y	I	E
C	I	J	K	A	I	X	O	P	Y	H	C	I	X	O	P	Y	H	N	H
I	O	A	H	D	M	H	L	F	O	P	N	I	T	I	R	R	E	F	N
M	U	K	N	O	E	I	Y	R	D	I	O	A	C	H	B	A	M	E	O
I	S	E	P	G	W	S	U	P	V	E	E	C	N	O	D	N	A	U	N
B	A	I	M	E	N	A	X	Q	O	S	G	S	H	M	I	E	T	L	A
A	N	E	M	I	C	H	Y	P	O	X	I	A	I	R	P	L	O	E	G
H	E	M	O	S	I	D	E	R	I	N	I	N	A	S	O	E	P	H	D
A	M	H	C	B	I	O	A	V	A	I	L	A	B	L	E	M	O	F	B
F	I	E	R	O	T	C	A	F	C	I	S	N	I	R	T	N	I	J	A
O	A	D	L	R	N	O	R	I	L	A	T	N	E	M	E	L	E	C	E
J	B	P	A	M	T	G	K	N	O	I	T	A	M	A	U	Q	S	E	D
A	E	N	I	N	O	I	T	A	I	T	N	E	R	E	F	F	I	D	C
G	H	C	L	R	D	E	A	M	E	G	A	L	O	B	L	A	S	T	A

True or False?

52.	T	60.	F
53.	T	61.	F
54.	F	62.	T
55.	T	63.	F
56.	F	64.	T
57.	T	65.	F
58.	T	66.	T
59.	T		

Complete the Sentence

67. blood volume, erythrocytes, red blood cells
68. vitamin B_{12}, folate, iron
69. cardiovascular, respiratory, neurological
70. prevention, assessment
71. compensatory mechanisms, shock
72. cardiovascular collapse, hypoxia
73. adequate hydration, oxygenation, hypercoagulability
74. Factors, coagulation cascade
75. aspirin, antiplatelet
76. environmental risk, replacement factors

Labeling Exercise: Erythropoiesis

a. Ribosome synthesis
b. Hemoglobin accumulation
c. Ejection of nucleus
d. Hemocytoblast
e. Proerythroblast
f. Early erythroblast
g. Late erythroblast
h. Normoblast
i. Reticulocyte
j. Erythrocyte

NCLEX-RN® Review Questions

Question numbers correspond to Outcome-Based Learning Objectives for this chapter.

63-1. Answer: 2

Rationale: When injury to a vessel occurs, injured blood vessels interact with circulating platelets ultimately leading to the formation of a clump of platelets, called the soft platelet plug, a process known as the primary hemostasis. The catalyst for primary hemostasis is the release of substances from the exposed subendothelial layer that interact with protein receptors on platelet surfaces, inducing chemical and configurational changes, a process termed activation. Once activated individual platelets undergo geometric and chemical changes that allow them to form a soft platelet plug. Formation of the platelet plug occurs rapidly and results in four distinct actions: adhesion, aggregation, secretion, and initiation of the clotting cascade.
Cognitive Level: Analysis
Nursing Process: Assessment
Client Need: Physiological Integrity; Physiological Adaptation

63-2. Answer: 3

Rationale: The major patient care issue associated with thrombocytopenia is increased tendency for bleeding. Thrombocytopenia is defined as a decrease in the number of circulating platelets from the normal value of 150,000/microliter. Although significant, spontaneous bleeding usually is not observed until levels reach below 50,000/microliter. Diseases such as leukemia, lymphoma, multiple myeloma, metastatic cancers, and aplastic anemia all are associated with global suppression of hematopoeisis, which will thus include suppressed platelet production. Additionally, most of the treatment approaches such as chemotherapy and radiation used in cancer and other bone marrow diseases independently suppress thrombopoeisis. Fluid volume deficit/overload and sensory perception disorder are not risks of radiation.
Cognitive Level: Analysis
Nursing Process: Planning
Client Need: Physiological Integrity; Physiological Adaptation

63-3. Answer: 3

Rationale: In the absence of sufficient folate and vitamin B_{12} the patient can manifest gastrointestinal and integumentary signs and symptoms. Neurological symptoms occurring with vitamin B_{12} deficiencies include peripheral neuropathy, unsteadiness, lack of coordination, ataxia, confusion, and memory loss. The symptoms described are not found in iron deficiency anemia, anemia from blood loss, or anemia of chronic disease.
Cognitive Level: Analysis
Nursing Process: Assessment
Client Need: Health Promotion and Maintenance; Prevention and/or Early Detection of Health Problems

63-4. Answer: 1

Rationale: An increase in lactate dehydrogenase (LDH) supports a diagnosis of hemolytic anemia. An increase in serum AST and an elevated reticulocyte count are also seen in the early stages of hemolytic anemia. Plasma haptoglobin levels may be decreased, not increased.
Cognitive Level: Analysis
Nursing Process: Assessment
Client Need: Physiological Integrity; Physiological Adaptation

63-5. Answer: 1

Rationale: Nursing care should be focused on the prevention of bleeding. to include: avoid intramuscular and subcutaneous injections; hold firm pressure to venipuncture sites for a minimum of 5 minutes; minimize venipunctures and invasive procedures; provide a soft toothbrush or tooth sponges for mouth care; avoid rectal suppositories, thermometers, enemas and other rectal/vaginal manipulation; prevent constipation and straining with stools; use electric razor only; maintain a safe environment to avoid injury; assist with activities of daily living and ambulation as necessary to avoid injury; and avoid medications with antiplatelet activity such as aspirin and aspirin-containing products, and nonsteroid anti-inflammatory drugs.
Cognitive Level: Application
Nursing Process: Planning
Client Need: Physiological Integrity; Physiological Adaptation

63-6. Answer: 2

Rationale: The primary physical manifestations of thrombocytopenia are the appearance of mucosal and cutaneous bleeding, and prolonged bleeding after invasive procedures. Mucosal bleeding can be observed in the gums especially following aggressive brushing or flossing, in the urinary tract, or from the nares. No evidence has been given to support the risk for prolonged postoperative bleeding, cranial bleeding, or pericardial space bleeding.
Cognitive Level: Analysis
Nursing Process: Assessment
Client Need: Physiological Integrity; Physiological Adaptation

Chapter 64 – Caring for the Patient with Cancer

Key Terms Matching Exercise 1

1. h
2. b
3. f
4. d
5. g
6. e
7. a
8. c

Key Terms Matching Exercise 2

9. d
10. a
11. g
12. h
13. f
14. e
15. b
16. c

Key Terms Matching Exercise 3

17. e
18. b
19. h
20. a
21. j
22. i
23. g
24. c
25. f
26. d

Matching: TNM System of Tumor Classification and Staging

27. b
28. e
29. j
30. h
31. k
32. d
33. a
34. f
35. i
36. c
37. g

Short Answer Questions

38. A grade 1 tumor is small in size, more differentiated, and the least malignant. Grade 4 tumors are those with cells that appear more abnormal, are usually very aggressive in nature, and are considered to have a high degree of malignancy.

39. Exogenous risk factors for cancer are:
    - Drugs and chemicals: Environmental and occupational factors influence the number of chemicals and drugs proven to be carcinogenic.
    - Lifestyle behaviors: Tobacco is the most deadly carcinogen.
    - Nutrition: Diets low in fiber and high in fat.
    - Sexual activity: Women who engage in sex with multiple partners and begin relations early in life have increased risk of cancer.
    - Alcohol: Large consumptions of ethyl alcohol are linked to certain cancers of the head and neck.
    - Radiation: Ionizing and ultraviolet radiation can cause cancer; the effects of EMFs, if any, are unknown.
    - Viruses: Several different cancers have been linked to viruses.
    - Psychosocial: Stress and the relationship to neoplasms are still being investigated.

40. The seven warning signs of cancer are:
    - C: hange in bowel or bladder habits
    - A: sore that does not heal
    - U: nusual bleeding or discharge from any body orifice
    - T: hickening or a lump in the breast or elsewhere
    - I: ndigestion or difficulty swallowing
    - O: bvious change in a wart or mole
    - N: agging cough or hoarseness

41. Primary treatment for cancer involves the removal of a malignancy and a margin of surrounding normal tissue. Reducing the amount of total body tumor burden and improving the survival rate is the goal of this surgical approach.

42. Radiation therapy in the treatment of cancer serves several purposes: to make a curative attempt to eradicate the disease; to control metastatic activity, allowing the patient relief of symptoms; to prevent microscopic disease associated with specific primary tumors; and to improve a patient's quality of life by relieving or reducing symptoms seen with advanced cancer.

43. The primary reasons for prescribing chemotherapy are to prevent tumor cells from multiplying, spreading to adjacent tissues, or developing metastasis. Therapy aims to provide a cure by preventing tumor cells from multiplying, control spread of the disease to adjacent tissues, prevent the development of metastasis, or palliate signs of suffering.

44. The gastrointestinal system, genitourinary system, cardiopulmonary system, hematopoietic system, reproductive system, and neurological system sustain side effects from chemotherapy.

45. Immobility, malnutrition, stress, lack of sleep, anemia, hypoxia, infection or febrile states, pain, and multiple cancer therapies can cause fatigue.

46. Artificial nutrition and hydration toward the end of life are controversial therapies and have not been proven to be beneficial to the patient. In fact, administration of these therapies has been associated with complications and suffering.

47. An increased number of older people in the population along with an increased number of older people with cancer has caused more attention to this topic. The aging of the baby boomers (those born between 1946 and 1964) is the major cause of the increasing number of aging adults. Americans who are over the age of 65 have an 11 times more likely chance of developing cancer than people under the age of 65 years of age.

True or False?

48. F
49. T
50. F
51. F
52. F
53. T
54. T
55. F
56. T
57. T

Complete the Sentence

58. initiation, promotion, progression
59. Cigarettes
60. malignant cell kill, damage
61. noncycling cells, drug resistance
62. nausea, vomiting
63. relaxation techniques, guided imagery, diet
64. life, interpersonal relationships, spirituality, lifestyles
65. side effects, toxicities, in-home treatments, coping

NCLEX-RN® Review Questions

64-1. Answer: 4

Rationale: Incidence is the number of newly diagnosed cases of cancer in a specific time period in a defined population. It will be expressed as a rate per 100,000 persons, allowing for comparison between different populations. Prevalence is the measurement of all cancer cases at a designated point in time. The number is divided by the total

population living at the time. Mortality is the number of deaths from cancer in a specific period of time and within an identified population. The total number of persons dying of cancer is divided by the total population living at that time. Survival is the observation of persons with cancer over time and the likelihood of their dying over several time periods. This information is the link between incidence and mortality data, providing useful measures of the end result of treatment.
Cognitive Level: Analysis
Nursing Process: Evaluation
Client Need: Health Promotion and Maintenance; Reduction of Risk Potential

64-2. Answer: 1
Rationale: Growth factors contribute substantially to the metastatic process. Angiogenesis is potentiated or impeded by growth factors. In addition, tumor proliferation produces a decreased reliance on exogenous growth factors. The existence of growth factors at the metastatic site is imperative for continued growth of cancerous cells. Epidermal growth factor supports the proliferation of prostate and anal cancer. Platelet-derived growth factor supports the development of melanoma. Transforming growth factor supports the development of colorectal cancer. Epidermal growth factor, transforming growth factor, platelet-derived growth factor, amphiregulin, insulin-like growth factor, and fibroblast growth factor all contribute to the development of breast cancer.
Cognitive Level: Analysis
Nursing Process: Assessment
Client Need: Physiological Integrity; Physiological Adaptation

64-3. Answer: 4
Rationale: Early signs of brain or spinal cord cancer include headache, seizures, nausea, and vomiting. Late signs include impaired cognitive skills, short-term memory loss, difficulty with speech, sensory and motor defects, visual changes, personality changes, and loss of sphincter control. Changes in vision and mental function are not symptoms of colon cancer, prostate cancer, and melanoma.
Cognitive Level: Analysis
Nursing Process: Assessment
Client Need: Physiological Integrity; Physiological Adaptation

64-4. Answer: 1
Rationale: To reduce the patient's risk of bleeding, pressure should be applied to all venipuncture sites for at least 5 minutes. Rectal procedures such as temperature measuring and enemas should be avoided. The patient should be instructed to avoid the use of commercial mouth washes and to use a soft tooth brush or toothette. Straight edge razors should also be avoided.
Cognitive Level: Application
Nursing Process: Planning
Client Need: Physiological Integrity; Reduction of Risk Potential

64-5. Answer: 2
Rationale: The nurse should administer antiemetics and appetite stimulants per orders. Small frequent meals that are high in calories and protein should be provided. Fluids should be limited during mealtime to prevent satiety.
Cognitive Level: Application
Nursing Process: Implementation
Client Need: Physiological Integrity; Basic Care and Comfort

64-6. Answer: 4
Rationale: Bone marrow transplantation offers patients the ability to receive intensive chemotherapy or radiation therapy when resistance to or failure of standard treatment occurs. Bone marrow transplantation is the transfer of hematopoietic cells from the bone marrow of one person into another person and has been used to treat a variety of diseases. It does not necessarily prevent the need for further surgery, reduce the amount of chemotherapy needed, or eliminate the need for radiation treatment.
Cognitive Level: Analysis
Nursing Process: Evaluation
Client Need: Physiological Integrity; Physiological Adaptation

Chapter 65 – Nursing Assessment of Patients with Integumentary Disorders

Key Terms Matching Exercise

1.	h	8.	g
2.	m	9.	l
3.	c	10.	k
4.	f	11.	b
5.	i	12.	e
6.	d	13.	a
7.	j		

True or False?

14.	F	19.	T
15.	T	20.	T
16.	T	21.	F
17.	F	22.	T
18.	F	23.	T

Labeling Exercise: Skin Layers

a. Epidermis
b. Dermis
c. Hypodermis

NCLEX-RN® Review Questions

Question numbers correspond to Outcome-Based Learning Objectives for this chapter.

65-1. Answer: 1
Rationale: The epidermis is the thin, avascular outer layer that is nourished by the blood vessels from the dermis. Four distinct cell types are contained in the epidermis: keratinocytes, melanocytes, Merkel's cells, and Langerhans' cells. Melanocytes are the pigment-producing cells that protect the skin from ultraviolet rays. The dermis, subcutaneous tissue, and subaceous glands do not produce melanocytes.
Cognitive Level: Analysis
Nursing Process: Assessment
Client Need: Health Promotion and Maintenance; Prevention and/or Early Detection of Health Problems

65-2. Answer: 2
Rationale: Drugs may produce skin eruptions, decrease or increase sunlight sensitivity, and cause hyperpigmentation. The symptoms described would not be appropriately recorded under childhood illnesses, immunizations, or allergies.
Cognitive Level: Analysis
Nursing Process: Assessment
Client Need: Physiological Integrity; Pharmacological and Parenteral Therapies

65-3. Answer: 1

Rationale: The nurse should inquire about the patient's exercise habits. There may be a risk for contracting fungal infections or community acquired methicillin-resistant *Staphylococcus aureus* (MRSA) from exercise equipment or locker room showers. Caution the patient not to share towels and to cover and protect any open areas on the skin. A diagnosis of MRSA is not as immediately associated with habits, nutritions, or culture as it is with exercise.

Cognitive Level: Application

Nursing Process: Assessment

Client Need: Physiological Integrity; Physiological Adaptation

65-4. Answer: 2

Rationale: Using the dorsal surface of the hand, which is most sensitive to temperature, the nurse first palpates the forehead and proceeds in a systematic fashion downward, being certain to include the hands and feet. The nurse should always make side-to-side comparisons. Assess for bilateral symmetry by palpating similar areas simultaneously, using both the right and left hand. Wearing sterile gloves in not appropriate for assessing skin temperature.

Cognitive Level: Application

Nursing Process: Assessment

Client Need: Health Promotion and Maintenance; Prevention and/or Early Detection of Health Problems

65-5. Answer: 1

Rationale: The hair should be evenly distributed on the head. Alopecia, loss of hair, can be a result of familial patterns of baldness, disease, medications, or a pathologic condition. Diffuse hair loss may be caused by hormonal changes, systemic infections, and reaction to chemicals or medications. Patchy hair loss can be caused by scalp infections such as ringworm, burn injuries, and trauma, and from permanent waving or other harsh chemical treatments. Cigarette smoking is not implicated with hair loss.

Cognitive Level: Analysis

Nursing Process: Assessment

Client Need: Physiological Integrity; Reduction of Risk Potential

65-6. Answer: 2

Rationale: A cyst is a palpable fluid-filled or solid subcutaneous sac. A bulla is a vesicle or blister, usually about 1 centimeter in diameter. A nodule is a well-circumscribed, firm, palpable lesion found deeper within the dermis than a papule. A tumor is a solid mass generally larger than 1 centimeter.

Cognitive Level: Analysis

Nursing Process: Assessment

Client Need: Physiological Integrity; Reduction of Risk Potential

65-7. Answer: 1

Rationale: Carotenemia is a yellowish discoloration of skin that differs from jaundice because it does not involve the sclera or mucous membranes. Cyanosis is a bluish-gray discoloration of the skin that is often caused by decreased perfusion of the tissues with oxygenated blood. Ecchymosis are purplish, blue, and black marks that are usually caused by trauma. Erythema is a reddish discoloration of the skin that is caused by dilation of the capillaries.

Cognitive Level: Analysis

Nursing Process: Assessment

Client Need: Physiological Integrity; Reduction of Risk Potential

Chapter 66 – Caring for the Patient with Skin Disorders

Key Terms Matching Exercise 1

1.	k	**7.**	g
2.	c	**8.**	i
3.	a	**9.**	e
4.	f	**10.**	h
5.	b	**11.**	d
6.	j		

Key Terms Matching Exercise 2

12.	d	**18.**	g
13.	e	**19.**	k
14.	a	**20.**	i
15.	c	**21.**	f
16.	j	**22.**	h
17.	b		

Key Term Crossword

Down 9: ERYSIPELAS
Across 17: URTICARIA
Down 13: FISSURES
Across 16: FOLLICULITIS
Across 15: CELLULITIS
Down 14: FURUNCLE
Down 18: CANDIDIASIS
Down 7: HIRSUTISM
Across 11: PARONYCHIA
Across 8: LIPOMA
Down 6: CARBUNCLE
Across 4: SCABIES
Across 10: NEVI
Down: SHINGLES
Across 12: NITS
Across 1: VERRUCAE
Across 3: IMPETIGO
Across 5: PEDICULOSIS
Across 2: PSORIASIS

Short Answer Questions

23. The United Kingdom has begun a campaign to reduce exposure to sunlight and prevent sunburn. Part of that effort is the Sun-Smart program. The SMART acronym was developed as a part of that program and stands for these reminders:
    - Stay in the shade 11 A.M.–3 P.M.
    - Make sure you never burn.
    - Always cover up.
    - Remember to take extra care with children.
    - Then use factor 15+ sunscreen.

24. Urticaria can occur as an allergic reaction to medications, foods, or insect bites. They also can be related to infections such as viral hepatitis, sinusitis, gingivitis, or cystitis. Aggravating factors include chemical irritants, fever, alcohol, exercise, and emotional stress.

25. Skin tags, keratosis, lentigines, and vascular lesions all occur as a part of the aging process.

26. The exact cause of psoriasis is unknown, but there is a genetic tendency and evidence of an immune response that involves T-cell activation by an antigen stimulating the inflammatory process. Certain trigger factors cause an exacerbation, and these include stress, infection, medications such as beta-adrenergic blockers, smoking, and high alcohol consumption.

27. Herpes zoster occurs because of the reactivation of latent varicella-zoster virus, or the virus that causes chickenpox. After having the chickenpox, this virus remains dormant in the dorsal root and cranial nerve ganglia, and becomes activated usually when a person is immunocompromised due to age or some other disease process such as AIDS, Hodgkin's disease, and some cancers.

28. It commonly occurs in immunocompromised individuals but has other predisposing factors such as crowded conditions, poor hygiene, or wearing tight clothing.

29. Necrotizing fasciitis (NF) should be suspected if the following symptoms are present:
    - Tissue ischemia
    - Superficial nerve damage
    - Vascular thrombosis and occlusion
    - Tissue liquification necrosis
    - Septicemia when systemic toxicity occurs

30. Possible nursing diagnoses for NF are:
    - *Impaired Skin Integrity* related to skin lesions
    - *Risk for Imbalanced Fluid Volume* related to fluid loss
    - *Impaired Physical Mobility* related to discomfort
    - *Acute Pain* related to exposed nerve endings
    - *Disturbed Body Image* related to illness
    - *Readiness for Enhanced Sleep* related to pain and anxiety
    - *Ineffective Protection* related to interrupted skin integrity
    - *Imbalanced Nutrition: Less than Body Requirements*
    - *Social Isolation* due to prolonged illness

31. SJS generally begins with flu-like symptoms such as headache, rhinorrhea, cough, and body aches. Target skin lesions are present and are described as having a bright-pink or red inner ring, a ring of lighter pink, and then a ring of dark pink. These lesions are concentric macular exanthemas that focus on the face, neck, and extremities, which then become blisters that grow together and break open such as might be seen in burns. The lesions are found on less than 20% of body surface area in the first 48 hours and result in skin detachment.

32. It is important to understand that the ethnic characteristics of the facial features need to be maintained. The noses of many African American, Hispanic, and Asian patients may look different from the noses of other nationalities and will require individualized approaches and goals for surgery. Darker skin types are more prone to changes in pigmentation of the skin and scarring.

True or False?

33.	T	**38.**	F
34.	T	**39.**	T
35.	F	**40.**	T
36.	T	**41.**	F
37.	F	**42.**	T

Complete the Sentence

43. A = Asymmetry, B = Border irregularity, C = Color variation, D = Diameter greater than the size of a pencil eraser
44. heels, sacrococcygeal
45. Burrow's, acetic acid, silver nitrate
46. medication, infection
47. neck, migraine headaches, hyperhidrosis, mastectomy

NCLEX-RN® Review Questions

Question numbers correspond to Outcome-Based Learning Objectives for this chapter.

66-1. Answer: 3
Rationale: Impetigo is a common skin infection caused by *Staphylococcus aureus* and/or group A beta-hemolytic streptococcus. It is a contagious, rapidly spreading infection that may occur after a minor skin injury such as an insect bite. It is usually transferred from individual to individual by direct contact and is more common in children and infants. Treatment involves removal of crusts by soaking in warm tap water and washing with gentle antibacterial soap such as Dial or Hibiclens. Topical antibiotics such as Bactroban may be helpful, but if the infection is widespread, an oral antibiotic may be indicated. The patient should avoid contact with others and sharing towels or sheets.
Cognitive Level: Application
Nursing Process: Planning
Client Need: Physiological Integrity; Physiological Adaptation

66-2. Answer: 3
Rationale: The nurse should instruct this patient to avoid things that are irritating or intensify itching such as excessive bathing. Other instructions should include applying cold or emollient lotion to rehydrate the skin, taking baths with cornstarch or oatmeal, applying and using prescribed medications, and wearing nonrestrictive, light clothing.
Cognitive Level: Application
Nursing Process: Planning
Client Need: Physiological Integrity; Reduction of Risk Potential

66-3. Answer: 2
Rationale: The nurse should use the pneumonic SMART: **S**tay in the shade 11 A.M.–3 P.M; **M**ake sure you never burn; **A**lways cover up; **R**emember to take extra care with children; and **T**hen use factor 15+ sunscreen. There is no mneumic used with COLD. It would be excessive to use the contents of a bottle of sunscreen, though sunscreen application is important. While knowing the statistics surrounding skin cancer and sun exposure may be helpful, they are not as directive or easy to recall as the SMART pneumonic.

Cognitive Level: Application
Nursing Process: Planning
Client Need: Health Promotion and Maintenance; Prevention and/or Early Detection of Health Problems

66-4. Answer: 2
Rationale: Symptoms of the advanced stage of necrotizing fasciitis include swollen and tight skin with erythema; dusky blue in color; blisters or bullae filled with purplish, foul-smelling, thin, watery fluid; skin has paper-like appearance; palpable crepitation due to the presence of gas; spread of the infection—increasing wound size; increased leukocytes; and decreased sodium. Flu-like symptoms are seen in the first stage of necrotizing fasciitis. Gangrene and fever are seen in the critical stage of necrotizing fasciitis.
Cognitive Level: Application
Nursing Process: Assessment
Client Need: Physiological Integrity; Physiological Adaptation

66-5. Answer: 3
Rationale: Nutrition is essential for wound healing to occur. The nurse must assess the amount and type of food intake and intervene if lack of appetite persists. Hydration is also important for wound healing. Therefore, assessing fluid intake is essential, encouraging the patient to take in an adequate amount of fluid, and if necessary obtaining a health care provider's order for intravenous fluids.
Cognitive Level: Application
Nursing Process: Implementation
Client Need: Physiological Integrity; Reduction of Risk Potential

66-6. Answer: 2
Rationale: Stevens–Johnson syndrome is a severe, acute, self-limiting skin reaction to infection or certain medications. It affects the epidermal layer of the skin and mucous membranes and usually begins with flu-like symptoms or symptoms of an upper respiratory infection and progresses to mucosal erosions and erythematous skin macules that blister and cause denudation or skin detachment. The cause is most commonly an adverse reaction to medication or an infection. Hives are raised, erythematous, intensely pruritic plaques or wheals that are surrounded by a white halo. The lesions of psoriasis are erythematous papules and plaques with silver-white scales that are sharply demarcated. In the early stage of necrotizing fasciitis the wound site looks essentially normal with wound margins not obvious, but the patient experiences flu-like symptoms, localized pain, erythema, and swelling.
Cognitive Level: Analysis
Nursing Process: Assessment
Client Need: Physiological Integrity; Physiological Adaptation

66-7. Answer: 1
Rationale: Many anatomic changes occur during the aging process: skin loses elasticity and water content; the texture and turgor of the skin change; the retaining ligaments of the soft tissue of the face weaken; face loses volume from decreased subcutaneous adipose stores and muscle mass; facial bones undergo resorption; the eye orbit changes shape, allowing for positional changes of the eye globe; face becomes elongated and flattened; and smoking, genetics, and sun exposure contribute to the loss of skin elasticity and wrinkle formation. While poor diet, over-bathing, and vitamin deficiencies can adversely affect the health of the skin, the effects on the skin from smoking, genetics, and sun exposure is much greater.
Cognitive Level: Application
Nursing Process: Implementation
Client Need: Health Promotion and Maintenance; Growth and Development Through the Life Span

Chapter 67 – Caring for the Patient with Wounds

Key Terms Matching Exercise 1

1. c
2. f
3. e
4. a
5. h

6. b
7. j
8. g
9. i
10. d

Key Terms Matching Exercise 2

11. e
12. f
13. d
14. j
15. h

16. b
17. g
18. i
19. a
20. c

Word Search

21. homeostasis
22. angiogenesis
23. fibroblasts
24. growth factors

25. phagocytes
26. phagocytosis
27. prostaglandin
28. remodeling

29. rete pegs
30. senile purpura
31. xerosis
32. acute wounds

33. chronic wounds
34. pressure ulcer
35. hematoma
36. seroma

S	T	S	A	L	B	O	R	B	I	F	D	A	E	A	C	I	B	J	B
C	H	R	G	N	F	R	E	C	L	U	E	R	U	S	S	E	R	P	A
E	D	O	E	H	G	L	K	E	M	R	E	T	E	P	E	G	S	H	C
P	E	T	M	M	L	I	N	A	P	L	N	F	O	H	N	J	A	E	I
R	H	C	G	E	O	E	O	G	B	Q	M	P	I	A	I	B	G	R	C
O	B	A	M	A	O	D	O	G	E	P	A	D	R	G	L	O	Q	H	E
S	D	F	G	M	J	S	E	F	E	L	E	S	W	O	E	T	E	Z	N
T	I	H	A	O	P	C	T	L	H	N	N	K	U	C	P	W	V	S	D
A	C	T	E	T	C	B	T	A	I	D	E	Z	M	Y	U	G	E	O	E
G	A	W	K	A	G	Y	N	W	S	N	O	S	L	T	R	X	A	C	T
L	H	O	B	M	F	H	T	I	B	I	G	P	I	E	P	C	W	I	D
A	O	R	Q	E	A	O	D	O	M	S	S	A	J	S	U	A	B	S	K
N	I	G	P	H	U	V	E	C	S	Y	E	Y	X	T	R	Q	C	L	E
D	M	L	E	S	G	O	F	X	L	I	F	M	E	Z	A	P	U	A	N
I	H	B	I	U	X	E	R	O	S	I	S	W	B	E	Y	R	E	F	I
N	O	R	C	S	D	R	T	W	L	Z	O	S	V	J	K	G	W	P	M
D	E	A	F	K	N	B	G	N	T	U	Q	A	C	M	T	A	H	O	B
J	L	D	M	Q	E	T	P	U	N	F	H	Y	J	R	I	D	V	E	N
A	F	G	I	A	N	O	S	D	N	U	O	W	C	I	N	O	R	H	C
C	B	A	M	O	R	E	S	I	J	E	H	K	A	L	C	F	B	A	D

Short Answer Questions

37. The three phases are:

Phase 1: Inflammatory phase—vasoconstriction, platelet aggregation, thrombin

Phase 2: Proliferative phase—vasodilation, macrophages, leukocytes, phagocytosis, collagen matrix

Phase 3: Remodeling phase—collagen matrix, epithelialization, increase tensile strength, may last up to 2 years

38. Stress causes a release of hormones, including glucocorticoids, which reduces the production of cytokines, an essential component of the inflammatory process. The glucocorticoids also alter leukocyte movement. Reduction in these two factors causes immunosuppression. Previous research has demonstrated that stress was associated with a 25% to 40% delay in wound closure across the models tested.

39. The mitigating factors that promote development of a wound in a patient with diabetes are neuropathy, macro/microvascular changes, and a slow, decreased immune response. Neuropathy is decreased or absent sensation in an area due to elevated blood glucose levels that over time affect the myelin sheath surrounding the nerves and degrade the sheath, exposing the nerves. The nerves then die over time without the myelin sheath to protect them from the body's own immune response. Without sensation in the feet, the patient may not be aware of the severity of the wound.

40. Compression therapy increases pressure to the lower extremity to promote venous return and decrease venous congestion, allowing the capillary beds at the level of the wound to open and the healing process to occur. Compression can be achieved by the use of compression stockings, wraps, or a compression pump.

41. Partial thickness wounds involve only the skin layers of the epidermis- and/or part of the dermis. These wounds are shallow and appear bright pink to red. Full-thickness wounds involve both the epidermis and the dermis and may extend into the subcutaneous tissue, fascia, muscle, and bone.

42. The scale consists of six categories with subscales: sensory perception, moisture, activity, mobility, nutrition, and friction and shear. Each category is assigned a score of 1 to 4 with the exception of friction and shear. The scores are assigned and added up. Lower scores indicate higher risk of pressure ulcer development. The highest score is 23 and the lowest is 6. A score of 18 or lower indicates a risk for pressure ulcer development.

43. Sharp débridement is done with scalpel, scissors, or nippers. Mechanical débridement is the dislodging of necrotic tissue, which is accomplished in several ways, including wet-to-dry dressings, whirlpool method, and pulse lavage. Enzymatic débridement is chemically induced by prescriptive ointments that contain papain urea or collegenase, which penetrates the slough and eschar causing them to soften and "melt down." Autolytic débridement is allowing the body to utilize the phagocytes to destroy the necrotic tissue.

44. Benefits of moist wound healing are faster epidermal resurfacing and fewer infections.

45. The factors in making a decision on a particular product are protection, degree of drainage or lack thereof, antimicrobial activity, biochemical needs, collagen requirements, and pain relief.

46. Patients who are obese or on steroids are at a higher risk for the development of dehiscence.

47. The following nursing diagnoses are related to wound healing:
- *Risk for Infection*
- *Impaired Tissue Integrity*
- *Ineffective Tissue Perfusion, Peripheral*
- *Disturbed Body Image*

True or False?

48.	F	**53.**	F
49.	T	**54.**	F
50.	T	**55.**	T
51.	F	**56.**	F
52.	T	**57.**	F

NCLEX-RN® Review Questions

67-1. Answer: 2

Rationale: Suppression of the inflammatory phase can contribute to a delay in wound healing. Radiation therapy can suppress the inflammatory phase by causing depletion of the neutrophils and macrophages, which release the growth factors. Malnutrition, dehydration, and chronic steroid use also can suppress the inflammatory phase. Chronic use of steroids specifically results in decreased production of histamines, suppressing the inflammatory response.

Cognitive Level: Analysis

Nursing Process: Assessment

Client Need: Health Promotion and Maintenance; Prevention and/or Early Detection of Health Problems

67-2. Answer: 1

Rationale: Serous drainage (plasma only) may occur when edema has forced fluid to move from the intravascular department into the tissue and then leak through the wound bed. Serosanguineous drainage (bloody with plasma fluid) is more related to overall edema leading to capillary weakness and leakage. Sanguineous drainage (bloody) occurs when there is acute trauma to the vascular bed. Purulent drainage (infected) is a sign of infection.

Cognitive Level: Application

Nursing Process: Assessment

Client Need: Physiological Integrity; Physiological Adaptation

67-3. Answer: 4

Rationale: Friction during bathing and massage over bony prominences should be avoided because they have been shown to cause additional tissue damage. Baths should be given only when needed to avoid drying out the skin. When bathing, use gentle cleansers with warm, not hot, water. The skin should be kept well hydrated with nonalcohol moisturizers used for dry skin.

Cognitive Level: Application

Nursing Process: Planning

Client Need: Physiological Integrity; Reduction of Risk Potential

67-4. Answer: 2

Rationale: The treatment for the patient is to get rid of the edema by compression. Compression therapy will allow pressure to be increased to the lower extremity to promote venous return and decrease venous congestion, allowing the capillary beds at the level of the wound to open and the healing process to occur. Venous return now under control allows the wound to heal. Surgery would be indicated for an arterial wound. Debridement would be appropriate for wounds with dead tissue. Moist dressing wound be appropriate for a pressure ulcer or skin tear.

Cognitive Level: Analysis

Nursing Process: Planning

Client Need: Physiological Integrity; Physiological Adaptation

67-5. Answer: 4

Rationale: It is very important to understand that despite algorithms and protocols, what drives choices for dressings is a skilled assessment of the wound on which to base decisions about dressings. The wound is viable and changing; flexibility regarding the type of dressings used is necessary to continue to show improvement in the wound. Basic, good wound care is pretty simple: If a wound is dry, add moisture; if a wound is wet, use an absorbent dressing; and always protect the periwound skin.

Cognitive Level: Analysis
Nursing Process: Assessment
Client Need: Physiological Integrity; Reduction in Risk Potential

67-6. Answer: 4

Rationale: Pressure ulcers, for the most part, are preventable. Prevention requires a plan of action that is individualized and vigilant. Pain medication will alleviate pain but will not prevent the formation of a pressure ulcer or halt its progression. Sitting on the side of the bed and dangling his legs will not prevent the formation of a pressure ulcer or halt its progression. Discussing discharge planning needs will not address the issues the patient has mentioned.

Cognitive Level: Application
Nursing Process: Implementation
Client Need: Physiological Integrity; Reduction of Risk Potential

67-7. Answer: 3

Rationale: Wound cleansers and dressings will impact infection rates. Hyperbaric oxygen treatment and nutrition will impact wound healing rates. Pain management will impact patient comfort and wound pain. Mechanisms to prevent scar formation will impact wound appearance.

Cognitive Level: Analysis
Nursing Process: Evaluation
Client Need: Physiological Integrity; Physiological Adaptation

Chapter 68 – Caring for the Patient with Burn Injuries

Key Terms Matching Exercise 1

1. i
2. c
3. e
4. h
5. d
6. f
7. g
8. a
9. b

Key Terms Matching Exercise 2

10. f
11. d
12. c
13. g
14. a
15. i
16. b
17. h
18. e

Key Terms Matching Exercise 3

19. c
20. f
21. d
22. h
23. g
24. a
25. e
26. b

Short Answer Questions

27. Burn shock is the pathophysiological mechanism that underlies most of the systemic effects of a burn injury on the tissues and organs of the body. Burn shock occurs because of a loss of intravascular fluid and, thus, circulating blood volume. Fluid is lost to the environment through the wound (insensible loss), and fluid is lost due to movement from the intravascular space into the interstitial space. At the time of the injury there is a release of an excessive amount of the Hageman factor (factor XII), which initiates and activates the inflammatory cascade. The development of shock is due to loss of the circulating blood volume, causing an intravascular hypovolemic state. The end result is decreased oxygen and nutrients to the tissues.

28. This assessment includes: A = airway, B = breathing, C = circulation, D = disability, neurological deficit, E = exposure and evaluation, and F = fluid resuscitation.

29. Assessing normal organ function provides a means of monitoring fluid replacement. Fluid resuscitation end points include mentation, skin color and temperature, heart rate, blood pressure, urine output, specific gravity, central venous pressure, hemoconcentration factors, and gastrointestinal function.

30. Biologic, biosynthetic, synthetic, and composite dressings are useful as temporary coverings for burn wounds. The agent selected for use is determined by the condition of the wound, the inherent properties of each agent, and the goals of treatment.

31. Inadequate nutrition has a negative impact on the immune response, wound healing, metabolic function, and survival. The key cause of ineffective wound healing is malnutrition. After a burn injury, the resting energy expenditure (REE) increases by as much as 50% to 150% higher than that of the average trauma patient. This hypermetabolic response and the mobilization of glucose are necessary for wound healing. The hypermetabolic state tends to decrease in the weeks following the injury, but the metabolic rate does not return to normal until the wound is completely healed.

True or False?

32.	T	37.	T
33.	F	38.	F
34.	T	39.	T
35.	T	40.	T
36.	F	41.	T

Complete the Sentence

42. fire, electricity, radiation, chemicals, scalds
43. coagulation, stasis, hyperemia
44. catecholamines, angiotension II
45. skin integrity, oxygen, metabolic
46. rule of nines, Lund-Browder

Labeling Exercise: Skin Layers of Partial-Thickness Versus Full-Thickness Injury

a. Epidermis
b. Dermis
c. Subcutaneous tissue
d. Muscle
e. Bone
f. Partial
g. Full

NCLEX-RN® Review Questions

Question numbers correspond to Outcome-Based Learning Objectives for this chapter.

68-1. Answer: 3

Rationale: The 40-year-old patient does have some chronic conditions, but the burns are only 20% TBSA partial thickness burns to the chest and upper extremities. Therefore, this injury would be moderate. The 94-year-old patient's extreme age, chronic illnesses, and facial burns make the injuries major. The 20-year-old patient also has severe chronic medical conditions that would make the burns major ones. The 67-year-old patient has asthma, which may make treatment and healing more difficult, but more importantly, the patient has perineal burns, which are major.

Cognitive Level: Analysis
Nursing Process: Assessment
Client Need: Physiological Integrity; Physiological Adaptation

68-2. Answer: 4

Rationale: Locking chemicals up high, out of reach of children and in their original container, are good ways to help avoid chemical burns. Avoiding cigarette smoking in bed decreases one's risk of setting a fire, not an electrical fire, and sustaining thermal and inhalation injuries. Plastic outlet covers should be used in all plugs within the reach of a child to help avoid electrical burn injuries, not thermal burns. Tanning beds and booths and sunlamps are sources of UV radiation, like the sun. Overexposure to any of these sources will result in radiation burns. Therefore, these artificial sources of UV light are not a safe alternative to sun exposure.

Cognitive Level: Analysis
Nursing Process: Evaluation
Client Need: Safe, Effective Care Environment; Safety and Infection Control

68-3. Answers: 1, 3, 6

Rationale: Release of mediators such as serotonin causes increased pulmonary vascular resistance. Release of catecholamines and some negative inotropic factors may cause congestive heart failure. The increased capillary permeability causes severe third spacing and loss of intravascular fluid volume. Cell damage that occurs during burns causes release of intracellular potassium into the vasculature, resulting in serum hyperkalemia. After a burn injury peripheral vasoconstriction occurs because of catecholamine release, whereas local vasodilation occurs because of increased capillary permeability and inflammatory response at the site. The burn injury causes an increased release of Hageman factor, and T-cell production is decreased because of protein loss.

Cognitive Level: Analysis
Nursing Process: Assessment
Client Need: Physiological Integrity; Physiological Adaptation

68-4. Answer: 2

Rationale: Once the patient is physically stable and cognizant of the injury and its ramifications, psychological and physical restorative therapies are often needed. However, this is during the rehabilitative phase of burn care. Application of cool soaks for burn treatment can lead to hypothermia and further skin injury if not used properly, but this is describing treatment during the emergency phase of burn care. Younger patients have an increased risk of complications because they have a greater surface area to

body mass ratio causing a higher risk for hypovolemic shock. Older patients may have exacerbations of their previous medical conditions and higher risk of shock and organ failure because of decreased physiologic stores and stress responses. The acute care phase of burn care includes strict wound care regimens with medical asepsis and debridement to promote wound healing and prevent infection.

Cognitive Level: Analysis
Nursing Process: Planning
Client Need: Physiological Integrity; Physiological Adaptation

68-5. Answers: 1, 2, 5, 8

Rationale: When calculating burn injury severity, the health care team uses five factors: size of the burn, depth of the burn, the patient's age, past medical history, and anatomical location of the burn. The "Rule of Nines" is one way of determining the size of the burn injury. The patient's blood glucose is important, but it does not help determine burn severity. The Parkland formula is used by some institutions for calculating the fluid resuscitation needs of the burned patient. The time the burn occurred is needed for making the calculation. Urine output is a useful indicator of fluid status.

Cognitive Level: Analysis
Nursing Process: Assessment
Client Need: Physiological Integrity; Physiological Adaptation

68-6. Answer: 2

Rationale: All the choices might be seen on the orders for a patient with this type of burn injury, but the priority on admission would be to infuse the lactated ringers solution. Fluid resuscitation is crucial to the burned patient during the emergency phase. This phase usually continues even into the burn unit for 48–72 hours. Glutamine administration is used in some burn units to aid in the prevention of gut atrophy and its associated problems. Silver sulfadiazine is also used in most burn centers as an antimicrobial agent to help prevent open wound infections. Also, pain management is a vital part of caring for the burned patient. It causes both physical and psychological complications when not treated properly, but the physiologic need for fluid stabilization should still be addressed prior to comfort needs.

Cognitive Level: Application
Nursing Process: Implementation
Client Need: Physiological Integrity; Physiological Adaptation

68-7. Answer: 1

Rationale: Excessive weight gain should be avoided by tapering calorie intake once pre-injury or ideal body weight has been achieved. The patient may need vocational counseling after discharge, so he or she should contact the local office of the State Labor and Industry Board. Rubbing or massaging healed burn areas can actually be beneficial and is recommended. However, scratching the areas may cause breakdown and should be prevented. If a pressure garment causes an area to become numb or tingling, it should be removed and replaced with a new garment that is not too tight.

Cognitive Level: Application
Nursing Process: Planning
Client Need: Health Promotion and Maintenance; Prevention and/or Early Detection of Health Problems

68-8. Answers: 2, 6, 7

Rationale: Hypovolemic shock, congestive heart failure, grief with denial, and immunosuppression are complications usually associated with the emergency period of burn injuries. Wound infections are seen in the acute care period,

and contractures, scars, and loss of function are found
during the rehabilitative period. Interestingly, psychological
problems are found in all three phases.
Cognitive Level: Application
Nursing Process: Assessment
Client Need: Physiological Integrity; Physiological
Adaptation; Psychosocial Integrity; Coping and Adaptation

Chapter 69 – Nursing Assessment of the Patient with Sensory Disorders

Key Terms Matching Exercise 1

1.	c	**7.**	k
2.	e	**8.**	d
3.	a	**9.**	j
4.	f	**10.**	h
5.	i	**11.**	b
6.	g		

Key Terms Matching Exercise 2

12.	d	**17.**	h
13.	g	**18.**	i
14.	e	**19.**	a
15.	b	**20.**	f
16.	j	**21.**	c

True or False?

22.	T	**27.**	F
23.	F	**28.**	T
24.	T	**29.**	T
25.	T	**30.**	T
26.	F	**31.**	F

Labeling Exercise 1: Outer, Middle, and Inner Ear

a. Outer ear
b. Middle ear
c. Inner ear (labyrinth)
d. Vestibular nerve
e. Cochlea
f. Cochlear nerve
g. Vestibule
h. Oval window
i. Round window
j. Auditory (eustachian) tube
k. Mallous
l. Incus
m. Stapes
n. Ossicles
o. Lobe
p. Helix
q. External auditory canal
r. Tympanic membrane (eardrum)
s. Auricle

Labeling Exercise 2: The Nose

a. Cribriform plate of ethmoid bone
b. Sella turcica
c. Sphenoid sinus
d. Pharyngeal tonsil
e. Posterior naris

f. Opening of auditory (eustachian) tube
g. Uvula
h. Soft palate
i. Hard palate
j. Anterior naris
k. Vestibule
l. Inferior turbinate
m. Middle turbinate
n. Superior turbinate
o. Frontal sinus

Labeling Exercise 3: Structures of the Mouth

a. Hard palate
b. Uvula
c. Palatine tonsil
d. Dorsum of tongue
e. Vestibule of mouth
f. Frenulum of lower lip
g. Gingiva
h. Buccinator muscle
i. Posterior wall of oropharynx
j. Soft palate
k. Frenulum of upper lip

Labeling Exercise 4: The Neck

a. Thyroid cartilage
b. Cricothyroid ligament
c. Cricothyroid muscle
d. Thyroid gland
e. Cupula (dome) of pleura
f. Cricoid cartilage
g. Medial margin of sternocleidomastoid muscle
h. Common carotid artery

NCLEX-RN® Review Questions

Question numbers correspond to Outcome-Based Learning Objectives
for this chapter.

69-1. Answer: 3
> **Rationale:** Under normal circumstances, the sense of smell
> diminishes slightly with age. The sense of smell can be
> partially or completely impaired due to obstruction from
> trauma, polyps, sinus infections, hormonal disorders, and
> dental problems. However, no evidence was provided to
> support those causes.
> **Cognitive Level:** Analysis
> **Nursing Process:** Assessment
> **Client Need:** Health Promotion and Maintenance;
> Prevention and/or Early Detection of Health Problems

69-2. Answer: 3
> **Rationale:** Many medications, including antibiotics, are
> ototoxic and cause permanent bilateral hearing loss with
> eighth cranial nerve damage and some cause tinnitus. In
> particular, patients with compromised renal function are at
> risk for developing deafness and tinnitus from medications.
> The use of herbal and home remedies may cause ENT
> problems, but no evidence was provided to support that as a
> cause. Age impacts hearing ability, but no evidence
> was provided about the patient's age. The use of over-the-
> counter preparations may cause hearing loss, but no
> evidence was provided to support that as a cause.
> **Cognitive Level:** Analysis
> **Nursing Process:** Assessment
> **Client Need:** Health Promotion and Maintenance;
> Prevention and/or Early Detection of Health Problems

69-3. Answer: 1
  Rationale: Lesions can reveal a generalized inflammatory disorder. Any local lesion on the lip needs to be evaluated for the possibility of basal cell or squamous cell cancer, infections, or nutritional deficiencies. Cheilosis, manifested by increased moisture in the corners of the mouth, reflects a riboflavin deficiency, poorly fitting dentures, or immune deficiencies. Merkel cell carcinoma generally affects the eye area, not the mouth. Bleeding from the lips can occur as a result of certain drugs that cause a deficiency in clotting mechanisms or from some congenitally acquired conditions that manifest as generalized bleeding disorders, but no evidence of bleeding was provided to suppor these causes.
  Cognitive Level: Analysis
  Nursing Process: Assessment
  Client Need: Health Promotion and Maintenance; Prevention and/or Early Detection of Health Problems

69-4. Answer: 2
  Rationale: Many elderly people wear dentures, which can interfere with swallowing when not properly fitted. Assessing for difficulty swallowing would be the initial course of action. A patient who has trouble swallowing because of limited tongue movement needs to be referred to a speech and swallowing therapist to learn techniques to swallow without choking or pocketing food. The patient's cognitive status is unlikely the cause of the weight loss. Assessment of nutritional status would reinforce the daughter's finding. Medication may interfere with the patient's appetitie, but difficulty swallowing is more likely the cause.
  Cognitive Level: Analysis
  Nursing Process: Assessment
  Client Need: Psychosocial Integrity; Coping and Adaptation

69-5. Answer: 4
  Rationale: Swallow and gag reflexes are tested with a tongue blade touching the back of the mouth, which causes gagging to occur. To test the glossopharyngeal nerve (CN IX) and vagus nerve (CN X), use a tongue depressor to press down on the tongue when the patient says "aaah." Note the rise and fall of the uvula and check for symmetry, edema, or discharge. A diminished sense of taste is called hypogeusia. A complete loss of a sense of taste is called ageusia.
  Cognitive Level: Analysis
  Nursing Process: Assessment
  Client Need: Health Promotion and Maintenance; Prevention and/or Early Detection of Health Problems

Chapter 70 – Caring for the Patient with Hearing and Balance Disorders

Key Terms Matching Exercise 1

1.	d	**6.**	h
2.	i	**7.**	c
3.	g	**8.**	f
4.	e	**9.**	b
5.	a		

Key Terms Matching Exercise 2

10.	a	**15.**	e
11.	f	**16.**	h
12.	i	**17.**	d
13.	g	**18.**	c
14.	b		

Key Terms Matching Exercise 3

19.	e	**24.**	d
20.	b	**25.**	g
21.	a	**26.**	f
22.	i	**27.**	c
23.	h		

Short Answer Questions

28. The causes of hearing impairment or loss are mechanical, inflammatory, or obstructive. Causes of mechanical hearing loss include external otitis, exostosis, foreign bodies, trauma, and otosclerosis. Hearing loss due to an inflammatory process is seen in conditions that cause the accumulation of drainage in the ear canal (otitis external, acute/chronic otitis media), and chronic mastoiditis. Examples of obstructions that cause changes in hearing include a malignancy within any of the ear structures or a benign acoustic neuroma.

29. The symptoms of BPPV include dizziness or vertigo, lightheadedness, imbalance, and nausea. Activities that bring on the symptoms of BPPV vary among individuals, although a change in position most commonly precipitates them.

30. The first step is to stop medications to determine if they are causing the tinnitus. If no cause is found, then masking the sound with noise or music is recommended. Ear molds and hearing aids can amplify sound to drown out tinnitus.

31. Electrodes are placed in the cochlea and attached to a microphone and signal processor, which are surgically placed under the skin behind the ear. The microphone and signal processor transmit electrical stimuli to the 22 implanted electrodes. The electrical signals stimulate the auditory nerve fibers and then the brain, where the sounds are interpreted. Once the cochlear implants are in place, the patient undergoes extensive cochlear rehabilitation to learn to interpret the sounds.

32. The causes of hearing loss and balance disorders in the elderly can be from a metabolic disorder, such as type II diabetes mellitus, or from the aging process. In diabetes, the disorder can go undetected for many years. The impact of unstable blood glucose levels can also lead to a balance disorder.

Complete the Sentence

33. otitis media
34. 85, 90, 90
35. motion sickness
36. frequency, pitch, intensity
37. mineral oil

Labeling Exercise 1: Anatomical Structures of the Ear

a.	Tympanic membrane (eardrum)	**f.**	Cochlear nerve
b.	Semicircular canals	**g.**	Saccule
c.	Utricle	**h.**	Stapes
d.	Vestibular nerve	**i.**	Incus
e.	Cochlea	**j.**	Malleus

Labeling Exercise 2: Anatomical Structures of Balance

a.	Superior canal	**e.**	Vestibule
b.	Utricle	**f.**	Horizontal canal
c.	Cochlea	**g.**	Posterior canal
d.	Saccule		

NCLEX-RN® Review Questions

Question numbers correspond to Outcome-Based Learning Objectives for this chapter.

70-1.   Answer: 4

Rationale: The middle ear begins from the inner side of the tympanic membrane and extends to the eustachian tube. Within this portion of the ear sit the three auditory bones: the malleus, the incus, and the stapes. The malleus is attached to the inner portion of the tympanic member. When the tympanic membrane vibrates with sound, so does the malleus. This is most likely the bone that was broken in conjunction with the ruptured eardrums. The incus is attached to the malleus and also vibrates in response to sound but is not as close to the eardrum as the malleus. The stapes is the structure that separates the middle from the inner ear. The base of the stapes, the footplate, fills the oval window, which leads to the inner ear. The footplate of the stapes fits tightly into a tiny oval window of the bony cochlea that opens into the inner ear.

Cognitive Level: Analysis

Nursing Process: Assessment

Client Need: Health Promotion and Maintenance; Prevention and/or Early Detection of Health Problems

70-2.   Answer: 1

Rationale: There are actually two mechanisms involved with hearing: bone conduction and air conduction. Bone conduction is the conduction of sound to the inner ear through the bones of the skull. Air conduction begins the process when noise enters the external ear and travels to the middle ear. Once inside the middle ear, the sound is transmitted through the three auditory bones, the malleus, incus, and stapes. Once the sound or noise reaches the stapes, it is then transmitted to the inner ear where it reaches the acoustic nerve and is transmitted to the brain for interpretation. Hearing disorders can be caused by an alteration anywhere within the auditory structures.

Cognitive Level: Analysis

Nursing Process: Assessment

Client Need: Health Promotion and Maintenance; Prevention and/or Early Detection of Health Problems

70-3.   Answer: 1

Rationale: With sensorineural hearing loss, the cause is damage to the auditory nerve or possibly damage to the small hair cells within the inner ear. Ototoxic drugs such as antibiotics can cause sensorineural hearing loss. Conductive hearing loss is not caused by ototoxic drugs but by the inability of sound waves to reach the inner ear for processing and interpretation. Mixed hearing loss refers to both conductive and sensorineural hearing loss caused by a dysfunction of both air and bone conduction processes. Interpretive is not a type of hearing loss.

Cognitive Level: Analysis

Nursing Process: Assessment

Client Need: Health Promotion and Maintenance; Prevention and/or Early Detection of Health Problems

70-4.   Answer: 4

Rationale: Otitis media, an inflammation of the middle ear, is the most frequently diagnosed disease in infants and children. The eustachian tube is smaller and more nearly horizontal in children than adults and is more easily blocked by conditions such as large adenoids and infections. Until this tube changes in size and angle as the child grows, children are more susceptible to otitis media. Repeated episodes of otitis media, however, may lead to permanent sensorineural hearing loss. While completing a course of

antibiotics is advised, there is no evidence to suggest the patient has not been doing this. While keeping appointments for annual hearing evaluation is recommended, there is not evidence to suggest the patient has not done so.

Cognitive Level: Analysis

Nursing Process: Assessment

Client Need: Health Promotion and Maintenance; Prevention and/or Early Detection of Health Problems

70-5.   Answer: 2

Rationale: Hearing loss due to an inflammatory process is seen in conditions that cause the accumulation of drainage in the ear canal such as otitis externa, acute/chronic otitis media, and chronic mastoiditis. Depending on the cause, treatment could be with local or systemic antibiotics and instruction to protect the ears. Should the offending organism be isolated to the middle ear area and if the infections reoccur frequently, further treatment may include tube placement or other surgical interventions. The insertion of tubes in the ears, or a myringotomy, can be done on an outpatient basis. Mechanical, obstructive, or mixed hearing loss are not usually treated with a myringotomy.

Cognitive Level: Analysis

Nursing Process: Assessment

Client Need: Physiological Integrity; Physiological Adaptation

70-6.   Answer: 4

Rationale: When planning for discharge from an acute care facility for treatment of a hearing or balance disorder, the nurse is in the best position to help the patient and family with physical, psychological, and future occupational needs. Helping the patient and family deal with the cause of the hearing or balance deficit and identify choices to avoid future problems associated with hearing and balance are the approaches of choice. While nutritional needs are important, they are not a primary element of a discharge plan for this patient. Resumption of normal activities of daily living is secondary to counseling on future occupational needs and choices. A return-to-work plan is secondary to counseling on future occupational needs and choices.

Cognitive Level: Application

Nursing Process: Planning

Client Need: Psychosocial Integrity; Coping and Adaptation

70-7.   Answer: 3

Rationale: The elderly patient experiencing a change in hearing might be embarrassed to admit the change. Oftentimes, elderly patients might not have adequate finances to purchase a hearing aid or they might feel that needing such a device is a sign of weakness or aging. The nurse must be knowledgeable and sensitive to the needs of people with hearing impairments to ensure safety and decrease anxiety.

Cognitive Level: Application

Nursing Process: Implementation

Client Need: Psychosocial Integrity; Coping and Adaptation

70-8.   Answer: 4

Rationale: The nurse should attempt to reduce the patient's anxiety and stress related to the change or loss in hearing. This would include teaching about the disease process. The nurse should also speak clearly and slowly in a normal to deep voice, face the patient when speaking, and use touch to gain the patient's attention. The nurse should provide emotional support to the patient having difficulty coping with the new sensory deficit.

Cognitive Level: Application

Nursing Process: Implementation

Client Need: Psychosocial Integrity; Coping and Adaptation

Chapter 71 – Caring for the Patient with Visual Disorders

Key Terms Matching Exercise 1

1.	h	**6.**	j
2.	c	**7.**	a
3.	b	**8.**	f
4.	d	**9.**	i
5.	e	**10.**	g

Key Terms Matching Exercise 2

11.	i	**16.**	f
12.	e	**17.**	a
13.	g	**18.**	d
14.	h	**19.**	b
15.	c	**20.**	j

Key Term Crossword

Short Answer Questions

21. Potential contraindications that negate refractive surgery may be unrealistic expectations, too high of a refractive or astigmatic error, cornea that is too thin (< 560 micrograms), pupil natural dilation that is too large (> 6.5 to 9 millimeters), severely dry corneas, previous eye surgery, and lack of understanding of the procedure and its risks and benefits.

22. As one ages, the nucleus fibers become compressed with additive cortical fibers, resulting in decreasing accommodation or a more rigid lens. It generally is during the fourth decade of life that one experiences the loss of elasticity of the natural crystalline lens, which causes the loss of the ability to focus up close, resulting in presbyopia.

23. The more common risk factors associated with macular degeneration include aging, hypertension, atherosclerosis and cardiovascular disease, smoking, lung conditions, diabetes, hyperlipidemia, hyperopia, lightcolored iris, ultraviolet light exposure, and heredity.

24. Glaucoma is diagnosed by measuring central corneal thickness and intraocular pressure. If the cornea is too thick, the intraocular pressure reading can be falsely read as too high; or if the cornea is too thin, the intraocular pressure reading can be falsely read as too low.

25. Usually cataracts are a painless, progressive loss of vision with aging. Patients start to notice that headlights from automobiles look like starbursts. They are bothered with glare, have difficulty reading street signs at night, and experience progressive reading difficulty even with glasses or bifocals. The refractive index changes and the power increases possibly may make patients more nearsighted. This is called a myopic shift and temporarily provides better vision without glasses for the hyperopic or farsighted person.

26. The three most common types of conjunctivitis are viral, allergic, and bacterial. Viral conjunctivitis has a clear, sticky discharge, minimal eyelid edema, and usually no lymph node involvement. Allergic conjunctivitis has a clear runny discharge, moderate to severe eyelid edema, no lymph node involvement, and intense pruritus. Bacterial conjunctivitis has purulent discharge, moderate eyelid edema, no lymph node involvement, and no pruritus.

27. The most common causative organisms in adults for orbital cellulitis are staphylococci and streptococci from bacterial sinusitis.

28. Causes of endophthalmitis can be bacterial (more frequent) or fungal infection. *Staphylococcus epidermidis* is the most widespread exogenous infecting organism of the eye. Fungal endophthalmitis can be the result of *Candida* species and *Aspergillus* species organisms.

29. Clinical manifestations of retinal detachment include blurry visions, a shower of floaters, flashes of light, a curtain- or veil-like shape, or no symptoms or pain at all.

30. Vision change; strabismus; changed moles, freckles, or wartlike lesions; periorbital ecchymosis; proptosis; ptosis; or a subcutaneous mass are signs of ocular tumors.

True or False?

31.	F	36.	F
32.	T	37.	T
33.	T	38.	T
34.	T	39.	F
35.	T	40.	T

Labeling Exercise: The Human Eye

a.	Eyelid	i.	Inferior rectus muscle
b.	Sclera	j.	Inferior oblique muscle
c.	Pupil	k.	Sclera
d.	Iris	l.	Conjunctiva
e.	Superior rectus muscle	m.	Iris
f.	Optic nerve	n.	Lens
g.	Macula	o.	Cornea
h.	Medial rectus muscle	p.	Retina

NCLEX-RN® Review Questions

Question numbers correspond to Outcome-Based Learning Objectives for this chapter.

71-1. Answer: 4
    Rationale: Two of the major retina layers are the photoreceptor layer and the retinal pigment epithelium. The photoreceptor layer is composed of cones and rods for photopic (day) and scotopic (night) vision. The two main functions of the retinal pigment epithelium are the metabolism of vitamin A and the absorption of light, which aid in visual acuity by providing nutrients to the photoreceptors. The optic disc is an extension of the central nervous system that forms a visual pathway behind the eye.

The vitreous body is the largest chamber (roughly two-thirds) of the eye that maintains the shape of the eyeball.
    Cognitive Level: Analysis
    Nursing Process: Assessment
    Client Need: Health Promotion and Maintenance; Prevention and/or Early Detection of Health Problems

71-2. Answer: 1
    Rationale: If the just uncovered eye moves inward, then it was fixed outward, so it is exo; and if the just uncovered eye moves outward, then it was fixed inward, so it is eso. If the just uncovered eye does not move and has steady fixation, no strabismus exist. The eye would move up and down to indicate vertical phoria.
    Cognitive Level: Analysis
    Nursing Process: Assessment
    Client Need: Health Promotion and Maintenance; Prevention and/or Early Detection of Health Problems

71-3. Answer: 3
    Rationale: Laser photocoagulation provides the major direct treatment modality for diabetic retinopathy. Blood sugar levels are not associated with cataracts, glaucoma, or retinal detachment.
    Cognitive Level: Analysis
    Nursing Process: Assessment
    Client Need: Physiological Integrity; Physiological Adaptation

71-4. Answer: 1
    Rationale: Postoperative instructions for cataract surgery are to take it easy for a few days and to use topical ophthalmic antibiotic/anti-inflammatory drops as prescribed, for approximately 4 weeks. Examination for corrective lenses is not recommended for 6 to 12 weeks postoperatively. The eye patch can be removed 1 day postoperatively.
    Cognitive Level: Application
    Nursing Process: Planning
    Client Need: Physiological Integrity; Physiological Adaptation

71-5. Answer: 1
    Rationale: To prevent damage of the macula, the nurse should instruct the daughter to wear protective eyewear to block ultraviolet light, such as wearing sunglasses and hats to prevent long periods of sunlight exposure to central vision. While initial research suggests that taking antioxidant vitamins, aspirin, or statins may be helpful in preventing prevent macular damage, shielding the eye from ultraviolet light is much more beneficial.
    Cognitive Level: Application
    Nursing Process: Implementation
    Client Need: Health Promotion and Maintenance; Prevention and/or Early Detection of Health Problems

Chapter 72 – Disaster and Bioterrorism Nursing

Key Terms Matching Exercise

1.	f	8.	l
2.	b	9.	k
3.	j	10.	i
4.	d	11.	c
5.	h	12.	m
6.	a	13.	e
7.	g		

Key Term Crossword

Crossword solution (key terms): ICS, PPE, IRRITANTS, TERRORISM, CISD, INCMCE, DECONTAMINATION, PERSISTENT, SNS, RD, SARS, CYANIDE, WMD, ASPHYXIATES, BUB, and related terms.

Short Answer Questions

14. Identification of an incident can be difficult, especially if the agent is one in which the symptoms have a delayed onset from the time of exposure. Patients will self-present to a variety of health care facilities, so there often is a delay before the event is recognized. In biologic agents, it is harder to discern initially without a direct clue such as a threatening note or direct identification of munitions or tampering.

15. There are many problems with PPE for the user, including hyperthermia, dehydration, and claustrophobia. In addition, there are limited vision, limited dexterity, limited movement, and communication problems. The user must don and use the equipment properly and be alert for breach of protection. Also, the level of protection must be appropriate for the situation.

16. Most dissemination of chemical agents is by aerosol. Chemical agents can be ingested, inhaled, or injected. They can also enter the body through dermal exposure.

17. The signs and symptoms are remembered by the mnemonic SLUDGEM: salivation, lacrimation, urination, defecation, gastric upset, emesis, and miosis. Often there is a complaint of dim vision. The nerve agents also cause cardiac dysrhythmias, confusion, fasciculations, and convulsions, along with unconsciousness. Almost all people affected by a nerve agent will have miosis, and most will have a runny nose and shortness of breath. The combination of pinpoint pupils and muscle fasciculations is the most reliable sign of nerve poisoning.

18. Because the period of illness is longer than with chemical agents, the impact on health care is much longer and larger than with chemicals. If such an agent were dispersed, there would be waves of patients depending on the incubation and population affected, as opposed to a single influx.

19. Gas-filled structures are the most susceptible to injury: lungs, gastrointestinal (GI) tract, and middle ear.

20. The media can be used to decrease the mass hysteria and get vital information to the public.

True or False?

21.	F	26.	F
22.	T	27.	T
23.	F	28.	T
24.	T	29.	F
25.	T	30.	T

NCLEX-RN® Review Questions

Question numbers correspond to Outcome-Based Learning Objectives for this chapter.

72-1. Answer: 4

Rationale: While controversial businesses, like abortion clinics, and large gatherings of people, like soccer games, are possible targets for terrorist activities, protests and riots are not considered acts of terrorism. A suicide bomber in an Israeli market would be an act of "international" terrorism, but an American soldier bombing the Pentagon would definitely be considered an act of "domestic" terrorism.

Cognitive Level: Analysis
Nursing Process: Assessment
Client Need: Safe, Effective Care Environment; Safety and Infection Control

72-2. Answer: 2
Rationale: During the Vietnam War the Viet Cong placed pungi sticks in the rice paddies. Because they were contaminated with human waste, these sticks would cause severely infected wounds. The Bulgarian defector, Georgi Markov, was shot with a pellet containing the toxin ricin. The subsequent physical problems he developed from the ricin led to his death. The Japanese used many different biologic agents to conduct experiments during World War II. However, chlorine gas and sulfur mustard are both chemical agents used during this same time by the Germans. The Chernobyl Nuclear Reactor Unit in Ukraine accidentally released a large cloud of radioactivity in 1986. Polonium-210, however, is the alpha ionizing radiation used during the assassination of Russian spy Alexander Litvinenko.
Cognitive Level: Analysis
Nursing Process: Evaluation
Client Need: Safe, Effective Care Environment; Safety and Infection Control

72-3. Answers: 1, 2, 5
Rationale: Upon exposure to smallpox, the patient should be placed on droplet isolation. The patient and his or her close contacts should also be vaccinated against the virus and placed under surveillance. The vaccine can prevent or decrease the symptoms if given up to 4 days postexposure. Doxycycline and Rifampin are both antibiotics and, therefore, are not useful in treating the smallpox virus. Venezuelan equine encephalitis is a viral mosquito-borne illness, and patients with this illness must be treated in a screened-in area because the patient is a reservoir for mosquitoes for several days after symptom onset. The toxins Botulinum and Ricin are treated in part with antitoxin and vigorous gastric lavage, respectively.
Cognitive Level: Application
Nursing Process: Implementation
Client Need: Physiological Integrity; Reduction of Risk Potential

72-4. Answer: 2
Rationale: While all the choices are chemical agents, only mustard is a vesicant. Vesicants can cause all the signs and symptoms listed, but the key is the hematemesis and dermal changes. These signs are seen exclusively with vesicants, as these agents cause mucosal sloughing and erythema, pruritis, and blisters on the skin. Cyanide is a blood agent that can cause neurological changes, respiratory depression, metabolic acidosis, and death. V agent, or VX, is a nerve agent that causes signs and symptoms consistent with increased acetylcholine activity, such as muscle fasciculations, miosis, salivation, gastrointestinal upset, and death. Phosgene is a choking agent. These agents are also called asphyxiates because of the severe respiratory complications they cause.
Cognitive Level: Application
Nursing Process: Assessment
Client Need: Physiological Integrity; Reduction of Risk Potential

72-5. Answer: 1
Rationale: Radiation does generate free radicals that cause damage to the protein, mRNA, and DNA of a cell. It is because of this that body tissues with high cell proliferation rates have an increased susceptibility to the effects of radiation. Therefore, the central nervous system is one of the most radiation-resistant tissues in the human body, but the hematopoietic system is one of the most susceptible. With higher dose radiation exposures the severity of symptoms increases but the duration of each phase of ARS decreases.
Cognitive Level: Analysis
Nursing Process: Assessment
Client Need: Physiological Integrity; Reduction of Risk Potential

72-6. Answer: 3
Rationale: This patient is stable at this time based on the information given. The patient is not ambulatory with an open tibial fracture, so he or she would not be Green. Respirations are between 8 and 30, capillary refill time is brisk, and the patient is awake, alert, and oriented. Therefore, the patient does not meet the criteria for Red or Black. Yellow identifies patients for whom care may be delayed for a limited time or whose injuries may be controlled or treated in the field for a time.
Cognitive Level: Application
Nursing Process: Assessment
Client Need: Physiological Integrity; Physiological Adaptation

72-7. Answer: 4
Rationale: The receiving site is responsible for providing many of its own supplies, including gloves, Bandaids, and sharps containers. The SNS became part of the Department of Homeland Security in March 2003. The affected state's governor requests SNS assistance from the CDC. The CDC then processes the request and releases the supplies if deemed necessary. Vaccines and antitoxins are kept in the Vendor Managed Inventory.
Cognitive Level: Analysis
Nursing Process: Evaluation
Client Need: Safe, Effective Care Environment; Safety and Infection Control

72-8. Answers: 1, 3, 4, 5, 6
Rationale: Stress can be expressed in emotional, behavioral, cognitive, and physical ways. Episodes of near syncope and excessive sweating and periods of hopelessness, memory problems, and withdrawal might be expected in the patient who has experienced a stressful event. Also, there may be an increased heart rate and confusion in thinking.
Cognitive Level: Application
Nursing Process: Assessment
Client Need: Psychosocial Integrity; Coping and Adaptation

Chapter 73 – Caring for the Patient in the Emergency Department

Key Terms Matching Exercise

1. d   **4.** c
2. a   **5.** b
3. e

Short Answer Questions

6. A *general (blanket) consent* is usually obtained at registration and allows for evaluation and treatment, such as radiographs, laboratory tests, and medications. *Informed consent* involves the patient stating by signing that he has a full understanding of the procedure, including its risks, and is competent to give consent. Finally, *implied consent* allows treatment in an emergency situation based on the presumption that if the patient were able to, she would give permission for treatment.

7. Emergency situations available to nurses include urgent care center nursing, prehospital nursing, transport nursing, military nursing, industrial and occupational health nursing, and correctional nursing.

8. Triage begins with an evaluation of what the nurse sees, smells, or sometimes even feels when first evaluating the patient. For example:
   - Is the patient's airway open or is he drooling?
   - Is the patient breathing and, if so, is the breathing effective?
   - What is the patient's skin color: normal, pale, flushed?
   - Are there any obvious signs of illness or injury?
9. Even when patients have been assigned a triage category, their condition may change, so patients who must wait for care must be reassessed at specific intervals. Triage policies and procedures should reflect when this must be done and documented. Unfortunately, patients have suffered significant harm and even death while waiting to be seen!
10. Both triage urgency scales include categories for resuscitation, emergent, urgent, and nonurgent patients, but the five-level scale includes a level between urgent and nonurgent called semiurgent.

True or False?

11.	T	**16.**	T
12.	F	**17.**	F
13.	F	**18.**	T
14.	T	**19.**	F
15.	T	**20.**	T

NCLEX-RN® Review Questions

73-1. Answer: 1

Rationale: One unique facet of emergency nursing is its requirement to apply the nursing process to patients of all ages who require immediate stabilization or resuscitation. Florence Nightingale is often associated with the origins of emergency nursing from her role of caring for wounded soldiers in the field. However, emergency nursing and emergency medicine have developed into their respective specialties over the past 50 years, when rapid triage and care during the Korean and Vietnam Wars demonstrated differences in patient outcomes. The unique demands presented with an increasingly diverse patient population make the field of emergency nursing more challenging each day. Emergency nursing does have a certification exam called the CEN (Certified Emergency Nurse). The EMTALA (Emergency Medical Transport and Labor Act) states that emergency departments must provide a medical screening examination with any necessary stabilization upon presentation for care.
Cognitive Level: Analysis
Nursing Process: Evaluation
Client Need: Safe, Effective Care Environment; Management of Care

73-2. Answer: 3

Rationale: The CIAMPEDS mnemonic is useful when evaluating pediatric patients. The letters represent chief complaint, immunizations and isolation, allergies, medications, parental impressions, events surrounding the complaint, diet and diapers (output), and symptoms. The EMTALA (Emergency Medical Transport and Labor Act) states that emergency departments must provide a medical screening examination with any necessary stabilization upon presentation for care. The ACEP (American College of Emergency Physicians) is the organization representing emergency physicians and the field of emergency medicine. The MVIT mnemonic may be useful in collecting data about the patient with trauma. The letters stand for mechanism of injury, vital signs, injury, and treatment.
Cognitive Level: Application

Nursing Process: Assessment
Client Need: Health Promotion and Maintenance; Prevention and/or Early Detection of Health Problems

73-3. Answer: 3

Rationale: The patient's complaint is acute in nature, with a history and presentation strongly suggestive of a right ankle sprain or possible fracture. Because the patient's condition does not require immediate resuscitative efforts nor does the injury indicate neurovascular compromise, categorizing the patient as a Level I or Level II, respectively, would be inappropriate. The Level V category, nonurgent, would also be incorrect in this case, as the patient's condition is urgent and warrants timely intervention. Thus, Level III, urgent, is the best choice for this patient in the five-level Emergency Severity Index triage system.
Cognitive Level: Application
Nursing Process: Assessment
Client Need: Health Promotion and Maintenance; Prevention and/or Early Detection of Health Problems

73-4. Answer: 2

Rationale: Photographs should be taken prior to providing wound care, if this is possible and if this does not adversely affect the patient. Gloves should be changed frequently during evidence collection so as not to cause cross contamination. Once evidence has been collected it should be locked in a secure area until it is released to the proper authorities. Evidence should always be placed in a paper bag, regardless if it is bloody. Wet evidence may be allowed to dry, but it must still be placed in paper.
Cognitive Level: Analysis
Nursing Process: Evaluation
Client Need: Safe, Effective Care Environment; Management of Care

73-5. Answer: 4

Rationale: The field of emergency nursing is very demanding, especially for those nurses who are unfamiliar with its practices. Preparation for this field should include familiarity with diverse patient populations, as well as the ability to perform a limited and focused patient assessment. Emergency nurses are often the ones initiating diagnostics and treatments, such as venipuncture and intravenous line insertion. Therefore, proficiency in these areas is crucial. Also, patients vary in age from birth to geriatric, and the emergency nurse should be prepared to care for them all.
Cognitive Level: Analysis
Nursing Process: Assessment
Client Need: Safe, Effective Care Environment; Management of Care

Chapter 74 – Caring for the Patient with Multisystem Trauma

Key Terms Matching Exercise 1

1.	b	**5.**	f
2.	a	**6.**	c
3.	e	**7.**	d
4.	g		

Key Terms Matching Exercise 2

8.	e	**12.**	b
9.	d	**13.**	g
10.	f	**14.**	a
11.	c		

Short Answer Questions

15. Motorcycles do not have the surface area to absorb energy from impacts. Therefore, energy is directly absorbed by the rider and injuries are substantially more severe than in vehicle crashes.

16. Patterns of injury from falls include calcaneus fractures, compression fractures to T12–L1, bilateral wrist fractures (as the body falls forward after the first impact), and traumatic brain injury.

17. The three phases of blast injury are: (1) The concussive effects of the pressure wave can cause central nervous system (CNS) injury, rupture of air-containing organs, and tearing of membranes and small vessels. (2) Fragments of glass, rock, and metal debris become high-velocity projectiles that can cause penetrating injury. (3) The victim may be thrown through the air and sustain injury similar to that sustained when ejected from a vehicle or when a person has fallen from a height.

18. The primary survey follows a specific sequence:

    A Airway maintenance with cervical spine immobilization
    B Breathing and ventilation
    C Circulation and hemorrhage control
    D Disability (neurological status)
    E Exposure/environmental control (e.g., remove all clothing but prevent hypothermia by placing warm blankets on the patient or using ambient warmers)

19. The secondary survey consists of a detailed head-to-toe evaluation of the patient with reassessment of all vital signs and should ideally be performed in 5 to 10 minutes. As with the primary survey, the secondary survey is done in a systematic fashion to reveal all injuries the patient has sustained.

20. Covering the patient with a sheet and warm blankets and administering warm and room temperature intravenous fluids have been proven to decrease the risk of coagulopathy in trauma patients.

True or False?

21.	T	26.	T
22.	T	27.	T
23.	F	28.	F
24.	T	29.	F
25.	F	30.	T

NCLEX-RN® Review Questions

Question numbers correspond to Outcome-Based Learning Objectives for this chapter.

74-1. Answer: 4

Rationale: Liver laceration is the most likely injury, based on the understanding of kinematics and since the impact was on the right. Left-sided impacts would likely cause injury to the spleen. Lateral impacts are associated with contralateral neck sprain, so the client may have a left neck sprain. Calcaneus fracture is usually seen in clients that fall and land feet first.
Cognitive Level: Analysis
Nursing Process: Assessment
Client Need: Physiological Integrity; Physiological Adaptation

74-2. Answer: 1

Rationale: The correct order for the primary trauma survey is—airway with simultaneous cervical spine immobilization, breathing and ventilation, circulation and hemorrhage control, disability, and exposure and environment—followed by secondary and tertiary surveys, respectively. All of the choices included interventions that would be appropriate in a client with trauma, but the first choice was the only one to include interventions that are in the correct sequence. Oxygen administration would address breathing and ventilation, while obtaining IV access addresses circulation. Nasogastric tube insertion and log rolling the client are part of the secondary survey. The second choice addresses pupil assessment before controlling external bleeding, which is incorrect. The third choice places chin lift, which is a form of airway maintenance, at the end of the list, and again this is incorrect sequencing. The last choice has warming lights at the end of the list. This is wrong because it intervenes with exposure and environmental concerns, and these should be dealt with before emotional support and obtaining a past medical history.
Cognitive Level: Application
Nursing Process: Implementation
Client Need: Health Promotion and Maintenance; Prevention and/or Early Detection of Health Problems

74-3. Answer: 2

Rationale: A study at Harberview Medical Center, University of Washington, Seattle, found that the TTS could identify patterns of errors that contributed to inpatient trauma deaths. Of the error patterns it found, excessive fluid resuscitation, unsuccessful intubation, inadequate gastrointestinal prophylaxis, and delayed angiographic control for acute abdominal or pelvic hemorrhage were among them. Recognition of hyphema, describing cardiac tamponade, and performing a chest x-ray are all appropriate interventions or assessment findings in the client with trauma. "Halo effect" is only one means of determining if cerebrospinal fluid is present in the nasal or otic drainage in the trauma client.
Cognitive Level: Analysis
Nursing Process: Assessment
Client Need: Health Promotion and Maintenance; Prevention and/or Early Detection of Health Problems

74-4. Answer: 4

Rationale: Traditionally, the treatment for hemorrhagic shock has been immediate, aggressive infusion of normal saline or Ringer's lactate solution. Current data suggest, however, that although aggressive fluid resuscitation may be useful for patients with isolated extremity, thermal, or head injury, fluid resuscitation should be limited in patients with potentially uncontrollable internal hemorrhage, especially in patients with penetrating truncal injury that will be treated at a trauma center. Aggressive fluid resuscitation may be harmful because increasing the mean arterial pressure in a patient who is actively bleeding will lead to increased blood loss. The hemostatic mechanisms of the body are overcome by the artificially elevated blood pressure and formed clots are dislodged. Due to the increased bleeding, more fluids and blood are required and the proinflammatory effects of the products develop. Aggressive infusion of crystalloid in the presence of uncontrolled hemorrhage promotes continued bleeding and increases mortality. The amount of initial fluid resuscitation will be determined by the patient's response to fluids. The response should be continually assessed to determine if perfusion is adequate. The nurse must also be aware that many factors including age, comorbidities, and medications can affect a patient's response to fluid resuscitation. The goal is to control the bleeding and promote oxygenation at the cellular level.
Cognitive Level: Application
Nursing Process: Implementation
Client Need: Physiological Integrity; Physiological Adaptation